CHILDREN AND THEIR FAMILIES.
CONTACT, RIGHTS AND WELFARE

GST NOTED 20/5/16

Children and their Families: Contact, Rights and Welfare

Edited by
ANDREW BAINHAM
BRIDGET LINDLEY
MARTIN RICHARDS
LIZ TRINDER

For the Cambridge Socio-Legal Group

·HART·
PUBLISHING
OXFORD – PORTLAND OREGON
2003

Hart Publishing
Oxford and Portland, Oregon

Published in North America (US and Canada) by
Hart Publishing c/o
International Specialized Book Services
5804 NE Hassalo Street
Portland, Oregon
97213-3644
USA

Hart Publishing is a specialist legal publisher based in Oxford, England.
To order further copies of this book or to request a list of other
publications please write to:

Hart Publishing, Salter's Boatyard, Folly Bridge,
Abingdon Road, Oxford OX1 4LB
Telephone: +44 (0)1865 245533 or Fax: +44 (0)1865 794882
e-mail: mail@hartpub.co.uk
WEBSITE: http//www.hartpub.co.uk

British Library Cataloguing in Publication Data
Data Available
1–84113–253–5 (paperback)

Typeset by Hope Services (Abingdon) Ltd.
Printed and bound in Great Britain on acid-free paper by
Biddles Ltd, www.biddles.co.uk

Preface

This collection of essays is the product of the third seminar series held by the Cambridge Socio-Legal Group in 2002. As with our earlier books, each chapter was originally presented as a paper for discussion by the Group before it was edited for the book.

The Editors are very grateful to Jill Brown, Administrative Secretary of the Centre for Family Research for all her efficient work which has ensured the smooth running of the seminars and for her invaluable assistance with the editorial work for this volume. We would also like to thank Frances Murton for her sub-editing and Sally Roberts for her very helpful technical assistance.

The Editors
Cambridge, January 2003

Contents

Notes on Contributors

Andrew Bainham is Reader in Family Law and Policy at the University of Cambridge and a Fellow of Christ's College. He is editor of the *International Survey of Family Law* and author of a leading text on children and the law. Since June 2002 he has been acting as Special Adviser to Baroness Nicholson of Winterbourne MEP in her role as rapporteur for Romania in the European Parliament.

Belinda Brooks-Gordon is a University Lecturer at Birkbeck College, University of London. Her research addresses questions on human sexuality, sexual offences and also prostitution. Her research activity on sex work and the sex industry includes the psychological, policy, methodological and human rights issues surrounding prostitution, the clients who pay for it and the officers who police it. She is currently carrying out a systematic review for the Department of Health on psychological interventions for people convicted of sexual offences. Belinda convenes the MSc in Family and Systemic Therapy—a course run jointly by Birkbeck and the Institute of Family Therapy.

Ann Buchanan is the Director of the Centre for Research into Parenting and Children and University Reader in Applied Social Studies at the University of Oxford. She has published widely on issues relating to children and their well-being. In 2001, together with Joan Hunt and Harriet Bretherton, she published *Families in Conflict* (Policy Press, 2001), a study of parents' and children's perspectives of the Family Court Welfare Service, the service which is now known as CAFCASS.

Shelley Day Sclater is a Reader in Psychosocial Studies, Co-Director of the Centre for Narrative Research, University of East London and an associate member of the Centre for Family Research, Cambridge. She has published widely in the area of socio-legal studies and her most recent book is *Surrogate Motherhood: International Perspectives* (edited with Rachel Cook and Felicity Kaganas, Hart, 2003).

Judy Dunn is a Developmental Psychologist, currently MRC Research Professor at the Institute of Psychiatry, King's College, London. She has published extensively on children's social development, on the development of social understanding, and on stepfamilies and children's outcome following parental separation, based on her longitudinal research in the UK and the USA.

John Eekelaar is a Fellow of Pembroke College, Oxford, Reader in Law at Oxford University and a Fellow of the British Academy. He is co-editor of the *International Journal of Law, Policy and the Family* and has conducted socio-legal research into and written on family law for many years. Most recently, he co-edited with Sanford N Katz and Mavis Maclean *Cross Currents: Family Law and Policy in the US and England*(Oxford University Press, 2000).

Bob Geldof is a musician. He has made many albums, the latest 'Sex, Age and Death' being released last year. He is also a businessman, producing TV and radio programmes and events. Combining both these skills, he produced the Band Aid record and Live Aid Concerts in 1984–5 in aid of African famine relief. He is still extremely active in third world politics. He has written his autobiography 'Is that it?', and has received many national and international awards in the academic, political and artistic arena, including three nominations for the Nobel Peace Prize and a knighthood from the Queen in 1986. The intervention of the legal system, following the separation from his late wife and its impact upon his family, have prompted him to contribute to this book by writing about these experiences and how the system should be changed.

Jonathan Herring is a fellow of Exeter College and University Lecturer in Law at Oxford University. He is the author of *Family Law* (Longman, 2001) and *Criminal Law* (Macmillan, 2002); and edited *Family Law: Issues, Debates, Policy* (Willan, 2001). He is also an advisory editor for the *Family Court Reports*.

Claire Hughes is a Fellow of Newnham College and a Lecturer in Developmental Psychology in the Faculty of Social & Political Sciences and a member of the Centre for Family Research, University of Cambridge. She is an editor of *Infant and Child Development* and her research interests include developmental psychopathology (including disruptive behaviour and autism) and individual differences in early social and cognitive development. Her current research includes a new longitudinal study (funded by the PPP Foundation, and in collaboration with Professor Judy Dunn) of social and cognitive development in toddlers from young mother, lone parent or low-income families.

Joan Hunt is Senior Research Fellow in the Oxford University Centre for Family Law and Policy, recently established within the Department for Social Policy and Social Work. She has researched and published extensively in the area of children's law, both public and private, focusing on the operation of the family justice system and its interface with families and social welfare agencies.

Adrian James is Professor of Applied Social Sciences at the University of Bradford. He is a member of the Editorial Advisory Boards for the *Journal of Social Welfare and Family Law* and *Representing Children*. He has researched and published widely in the field of socio-legal studies, with particular reference to issues concerning the welfare of children in divorce.

Julie Jessop is a Research Associate at the Centre for Family Research, University of Cambridge. She has worked on various research projects connected with divorce and post-divorce parenting and is currently involved with a project predicting problem behaviour in young children. She has co-edited a book on *Ethics in Qualitative Research* (Sage, 2002).

Felicity Kaganas is a Senior Lecturer in Law at Brunel University and a Co-Director of the Centre for the Study of Law, the Child and the Family there. Her writing has focused on feminist issues and on child and family law. She has published both in the UK and in South Africa, where she was previously a lecturer at the University of the Witwatersrand. Her publications include *Family Law, Gender and the State* (with Alison Diduck, Hart, 1999), *Contact, Conflict and Risk* in Day Sclater and Piper (eds),*Undercurrents of Divorce* (Ashgate, 1999) and *Domestic Homicide, Gender and the Expert* in Bainham, Day Sclater and Richards (eds), *Body Lore and Laws* (Hart, 2002).

Bridget Lindley is a solicitor who has specialised in family law for 20 years. She has a particular interest in public law children's cases. She is a socio-legal researcher at the Centre for Family Research, University of Cambridge, where she has recently completed a research project on Advice and Advocacy for Parents in Child Protection Cases. In addition to publishing the research findings from this study, she has also produced a protocol, funded by the Department of Health, to promote best practice in this area. She is also Legal Adviser at the Family Rights Group, London, and has been centrally involved in the work of the Adoption Law Reform Group which coordinated the lobbying of stakeholder organisations on the Adoption and Children Act 2002. Finally, she is also a family mediator at the Cambridge Family Mediation Service.

Mavis Maclean has carried out socio-legal research in Oxford since 1974, and is now joint Director of the Oxford Centre for Family Law and Policy. She has acted as the Academic Adviser to the Lord Chancellor's Department since 1997, and served as a panel member on the Bristol Royal Infirmary Inquiry between 1998 and 2001, a major public inquiry into the National Health Service. Her research interests are Family Law and Family Policy, particularly from a comparative perspective. Recent Books include *Family Lawyers*, with John Eekelaar, and Sarah Beinart (Hart, 2000), *Making Law for Families* (ed), (Hart, 2000), *Cross Currents* (ed), with John Eekelaar and Sanford Katz (Oxford University Press, 2000), *The Parental Obligation* with John Eekelaar (Hart, Oxford 1997), *Family Law and Family Policy in the New Europe* (eds), with Jacek Kurczeswki (Ashgate, 1997).

Joanna Miles is a Fellow of Trinity College and a Norton Rose Lecturer at the University of Cambridge. She has written on various aspects of family law, with a particular interest in state intervention and human rights in the family.

Katrin Mueller-Johnson received a Diploma in Psychology from the Free University of Berlin, Germany, and holds a Masters in Legal Research from the

Centre for Socio-Legal Studies at Oxford University. She is currently a PhD student at the Department of Human Development at Cornell University and an international associate of the Oxford Centre for Family Law and Policy. Her current research focuses on two distinct areas: the facilitation of post-divorce parental contact through child contact centres, and the suggestibility of vulnerable witnesses, such as children and the elderly.

Elsbeth Neil is a Faculty member of the School of Social Work and Psychosocial Studies at the University of East Anglia. She has been researching the area of contact after adoption since 1996, is currently heading up a Nuffield Foundation funded longitudinal study on this topic, and has a number of publications in this field.

Jan Pryor is a Senior Lecturer in the School of Psychology at Victoria University of Wellington, New Zealand. She teaches family and developmental psychology, and recently co-authored with Bryan Rodgers from the Australian National University a book entitled *Children in Changing Families. Life after Parental Separation* (Blackwell, 2001).

Martin Richards is Director of the Centre for Family Research and Professor of Family Research at the University of Cambridge. His research interests include marriage, divorce and family life and psychosocial aspects of new genetic and reproductive technologies. He is a member of the Human Genetics Commission and is currently working on a book on the history of reproductive technologies. Books include *Sexual Arrangements: Marriage and Affairs* (with Janet Reibstein, Heinemann/Charles Scribners Sons, 1992), *What is a Parent? A Socio-Legal Analysis* and *Body Lore and Laws* (both edited with Andrew Bainham and Shelley Day Sclater. Hart 2001 and 2002).

Bob Simpson is a Senior Lecturer in Anthropology at the University of Durham. He was formerly a researcher with the Centre for Family Studies at the University of Newcastle and has carried out research in the fields of divorce, separation, conflict resolution, mediation, and fatherhood. He is the author of *Changing Families: An Ethnographic Approach to Divorce and Separation* (Berg,1998).

Donna Smith is a PhD student at the University of Cambridge Faculty of Law. She is currently writing her doctoral thesis following 3 years research into the law and practice relating to international parental child abduction. She has attended several world conferences on international child abduction and the Fourth Special Commission to Review the Operation of the Hague Convention of 25 October 1980 on the Civil Aspects of International Child Abduction, held in the Hague in March 2001. She is a member of the Family Law Bar Association and Children Law UK, and has worked very closely with the Reunite International Child Abduction Centre throughout her research.

Liz Trinder is a Senior Lecturer in the School of Social Work and Psychosocial Studies at the University of East Anglia. She has a longstanding interest in post-divorce family relationships. She has recently completed a study on contact after divorce for the Joseph Rowntree Foundation and is currently undertaking a study on the process and outcomes of in-court conciliation for the Lord Chancellor's Department.

1

Introduction

LIZ TRINDER[1]

INTRODUCTION

AN EARLIER VOLUME in this series posed the question 'What is a Parent?' (Bainham *et al*, 1999). In a series of papers the contributors to that volume highlighted the complex and contested nature of contemporary parenthood and childhood. In this volume we extend this analysis further to explore the meaning and significance of parent-child relationships after divorce or other forms of family separations including reception into care and adoption. Put simply, to what extent, and how, should children's relationships with non-resident or non-caretaking parents be preserved?

At the start of the twenty-first century we can no longer take for granted that children will spend their childhood living continuously with both biological parents. As Lewis and Kiernan (1996) have noted, since the nineteen sixties the formerly co-terminous 'family practices' of sex, marriage and parenthood have become increasingly separated with the significant rise in cohabitation, divorce and lone parenting. One logical consequence of this increased separation of sex, marriage and parenthood is that a significant proportion of children will spend some of their childhood physically separated from, or living apart from, at least one parent.[2] Divorce or cohabitation breakdown are not the only reasons why children might be separated from one or even both parents. There are other groups of children who may live apart from a biological parent, including children who are in care or who are being 'looked after', children who have been adopted, children with an incarcerated parent or children born as a result of conception via new reproductive technologies such as artificial insemination by donor.

Of course, in historical terms it is not unusual for a significant number of children to be living away from home on a day-to-day basis. Until the relatively recent past many children left home to be apprenticed or to enter service. Many still leave home for regular periods to attend boarding school. What is new about

---

[1] I would like to express my gratitude to my co-editors for their helpful comments on earlier versions of this chapter.

[2] On current predictions 28% of children are likely to experience the divorce of their parents (Haskey 1997).

the present situation is the profound importance that is now placed on ensuring, where possible, that children retain their relationships with both biological parents and other kin in both short-term and long-term or permanent separations. Over the last two decades the response of family law, policy and practice has shifted dramatically. In the nineteen seventies law and practice were largely concerned with sustaining and strengthening the child's relationship with his (usually) custodial mother after divorce based on the concept of the 'single psychological parent' (Goldstein *et al*, 1979). Since then, however, the pendulum has swung firmly in the direction of emphasising the profound and enduring importance of children's relationships with both parents and a strong legal presumption of contact with the non-residential parent[3] after divorce or separation.

Whilst children of divorce are numerically the largest group of children separated from one parent, they are by no means the only group. As the contributors to this volume describe, the contact presumption—that continuing relationships with parents and parent figures are in a child's best interest save where there is specific evidence to the contrary—has also surfaced in a wide range of associated areas of family life as diverse as adoption, children in care or being 'looked after' and where parents are imprisoned. At least at first reading, similar principles and assumptions about children's psychosocial needs and interests and ideas about openness and inclusivity, underpin policy and practice in each of these fields.

The apparent wholesale adoption of a commitment to promoting ongoing parent-child relationships across such diverse fields of family law and practice, does raise a whole series of questions. The primary questions we endeavour to explore in this book are:

1. Why has the presumption in favour of enduring parent-child relationships after family separations emerged? What is the value and purpose of supporting children's relationships with non-resident or non-caretaking parents and other relatives?
2. How are family relationships sustained? What makes ongoing contact work or not work?
3. What is the role of law and other forms of external intervention in asserting, regulating or facilitating family relationships? What is the value and purpose of court-ordered contact and contact orders?
4. What is, and should be, the relative weight to be attached to the relationship or contact 'rights' and 'needs' of adults and children, mothers and fathers, resident and non-resident parents, biological and social parents and parents and other kin?

---

[3] We use the term 'non-resident parent' here to refer to the parent with whom the child lives for less than 50% of the time. An alternative term is 'contact parent'. The terms resident/non-resident and contact parent have been criticised on the grounds that they assume an asymmetrical division of roles and involvement between a 'primary caretaker' parent and consequently a 'secondary' contact parent. Some post-divorce arrangements are, however, based on presumptions of shared or equal care with roughly equal involvement of both parents. For an analysis of children's experience of co-parenting see Smart *et al*, 2001.

In selecting contributions for this book we had a number of aims in mind. We sought to include studies of current research, law and theorising to examine issues of contact from across the full spectrum of family law and practice rather than simply divorce or public law. By bringing together contributions from such divergent areas we also aimed to explore similarities and differences in the way in which parental relationships, and familial relationships more generally, are conceptualised, analysed and regulated by the legal system. The book is also deliberately multidisciplinary in character. This is a contested area, as is perhaps most evident in the dialogue and debate in these pages between social scientists and legal scholars. We have not sought to reach a consensus; instead the remainder of this chapter provides an introduction to some of the key debates that the book addresses.

To this point we have been using the terms 'contact' and 'family relationships' almost interchangeably. Before continuing any further we should attempt to define what is meant by 'contact' and 'family relationships' in this context.

The word 'contact' entered socio-legal discussions with the Children Act 1989. This replaced the traditionally named 'access orders' with 'contact orders'—orders which typically define the frequency and duration of visits by a child to a non-resident parent. The first possible meaning of 'contact' therefore is as a legal mechanism, a court order, specifying when, where and possibly how a child will see a named person (most commonly a non-resident father after divorce or separation).

A second, and somewhat broader, definition is of contact as the physical mechanism or process by which a relationship can be conducted. This is the meaning of contact as set out by Lord Justice Thorpe[4] where contact is understood not as the relationship itself, and instead simply as the means by which a relationship is maintained and developed. Contact therefore refers to face-to-face 'meetings' or visits between a child and another person with whom the child is not currently living. It also includes other forms of indirect communication, including letters, cards, presents, phone calls, text and email. This definition includes both court-defined contact orders as well as non-court arrangements established informally by the participants.

However, in practice the distinction between contact as the mechanism and the relationship may be less clear cut. It is hard to envisage a relationship without some form of direct or indirect contact. Relationships are, at least in part, about the process of relating by some form of face-to-face or indirect communication. Perhaps therefore a third definition of contact is as one component or dimension of a relationship, rather than simply an instrument. Here contact is an essential part, but nonetheless still a sub-set, of the larger concept. Put more simply being able to see or talk with someone is part of relating to them; it is not just a means to an end it is also an end in itself. One of the problems with conceptualising contact as simply visits and phone calls is that it can indeed seem

---

[4] *Re L, V, M, H (Contact: Domestic Violence)* [2000] 2 FLR 334. See Herring (this volume).

mechanistic, failing to capture the sense in which these are interactions in their own right. That is not to say that seeing or communicating with someone is the entirety of a relationship. It quite clearly is not. Relationships consist of a range of different dimensions, including the quality of interaction. A court, for example, may define the duration and frequency of visits a child may have with an adult, but this neither describes the quality of the relationship between the two nor ensures a good-enough relationship between them. Indeed researchers have found that the quality of relationships is more clearly associated with children's well-being than the quantity of contact (Amato & Gilbreth, 1999; Pryor and Rogers, 2001, Hawthorne, *et al*, 2003), although Dunn's recent research (this volume) also found the quantity of contact to be associated with both relationship quality and children's adjustment.

We have then three different definitions of contact. Contact as contact orders/court-regulated contact, contact as the mechanism supporting relationships and contact as an integral component of, but not a synonym for, a relationship. What these three definitions have in common is that they all presume some form of interaction between two or more participants. In takes two, in other words, to have contact. There is however a fourth possible definition of contact, one that establishes a one-way 'connection' without leading to a bi-directional relationship. Access to birth records, information for adopted people and people born as a result of donor insemination would fall within this definition as indeed might some restricted forms of post-adoption letterbox contact (see chapters by Richards and Neil, this volume). Most people would probably disagree that simply knowing of, but not knowing, a family member should be called contact. It does not constitute a relationship in itself, although having access to birth records, for example, may well be an essential first stage in attempting to establish a relationship.

Finally, before we consider the substantive issues addressed by contributors, we should set out which parent-child relationships are of central concern in this volume. There are three main issues or parent-child relationships that could concern us here:

1. The preservation of child-parent (or other relative) relationships in 'disrupted' families. This includes situations where parents have separated, typically resulting in the separation of one parent from any children, or families where state intervention has resulted in the separation of a child from one or both parents.
2. The creation, or encouragement, of potential child-parent (or other relative) relationships. Examples could include children born as a result of AID or adopted children who have never known a birth parent.
3. The preservation of child-parent (or other relative) relationships in 'intact' families. Here we have in mind everyday contact between children and their non-residential kin, including seeing extended family members such as grandparents or cousins. It could extend to other situations where children

live apart from their families for significant periods, for example children away at boarding school.

In practice most socio-legal attention has been addressed primarily to the first type of relationship, that of parent-child relationships in disrupted families. This indeed is the primary focus of this volume.

WHY CONTACT?

So what has driven the increased emphasis on contact across all the different areas of family law? Why are parental and familial relationships deemed to be important? Three elements underpinning this shift can be identified[5]—social science research, campaigns by interest groups and human rights frameworks, each represented to some degree in this volume.

One of the primary forces driving or fuelling the contact presumption has been the ever-expanding body of social science research on the relationship between parental and familial relationships and children's well-being. Some of this research is represented in Section 1 of this volume. Judy Dunn's chapter presents the findings from a large-scale community sample on children's psycho-social adjustment within different family structures, with a clear conclusion that continuing relationships are helpful for children. In her chapter, Hughes reviews the theoretical and empirical research on the importance of relationships for children's cognitive and socio-emotional development, and especially theory of mind skills. Pryor then reviews the empirical research on the importance of relationships with family members other than parents.

The second source of influence on the development of the contact presumption has been the powerful articulation of personal experience, by individuals or campaign groups (see especially Geldof, this volume). The influence of campaigning groups is particularly evident in the field of post-divorce parenting with groups like Families Need Fathers, but organisations like the Family Rights Group and NORCAP have also been influential in the public law field and adopted people's rights to information.

The final, and most recent, influence on the presumption of contact is the conceptualisation of parental relationships as a human right, most notably in the United Nations Convention on the Rights of the Child, the European Convention on Human Rights (ECHR) and the Human Rights Act 1998 (see especially the chapters by Bainham, Herring, Miles and Lindley).

These three different sources of influence on parental relationships do pose some interesting questions and dilemmas, not least because they are founded upon different types of knowledge, sourced from different constituencies. The bulk of social science research is based on large samples with conclusions drawn

[5] For a fuller account in relation to public law see Fox Harding (1997).

at the group rather than individual child level. As Neil argues, the empirical research can provide a clear, but never a definitive, guide as to what is likely to be the right course of action in the individual case. In contrast, knowledge put forward by campaigning groups draws upon personal experience, often based on hard cases, and though compelling may well reflect only the needs and rights of certain parties within the contact framework (eg non-resident parents or adopted people). The third approach is to identify and support rights claims for individuals, established not on the basis of personal experience or empirical evidence but as universal entitlements for all with the rights of mothers, fathers and children weighted equally.

These different sources of knowledge, gathered from potentially distinctive constituencies may well lead to different prescriptions, and may pose problems when applied to individual cases. These tensions are reflected in the contributions to this volume, with different responses to the relative weight to be given to the question of rights versus relationships, the role of law in regulating relationships and which relationships (or rights) are important. That is not to assume that rights and relationships are inherently antithetical, but as we shall see in the next section, achieving a balance can be problematic in many situations.

WHAT MAKES CONTACT WORK, OR NOT WORK?

One of the consistent messages emerging from the social science contributions to this book is that well-being depends as much on the quality of relationships as on the quantity of contact. Although the social science literature suggests that continuing relationships are beneficial, the contributors to this volume also identify the major challenges in making imposed contact work, whether in the field of public law (Section 4) or the private law field (Section 5).

A number of chapters address the problem of conflict between parents over continuing contact, including Buchanan and Hunt's analysis of the experiences of parents and children of the court welfare process and Day Sclater and Kaganas' analysis of the perspectives of mothers in protracted contact disputes. Other chapters explore the risk posed to children or adults by the exercise of contact orders. Smith's chapter examines how the law can both promote continuing relationships whilst minimising the threat of international abduction. Brooks-Gordon looks at the balance between the potential threat to children of contact with some imprisoned parents and the benefits otherwise to be derived, and Buchanan and Hunt identify high levels of concern about abusive parents in their court welfare sample.

Not all contact problems concern conflict and/or risk. An often neglected area within policy debates is the large numbers of children who lose contact due to an apparently weak commitment on the part of non-resident or non-caretaking parents. The reasons for this are complex, but several contributors make the point that the amount of contact may not necessarily reflect a lack of commitment or care. Geldof and Simpson, Jessop and McCarthy highlight the painful everyday reality of being a 'visiting' parent. Similarly the chapters by Neil and Miles and Lindley highlight the logistical as well as emotional barriers for parents and other birth relatives visiting children in someone else's home. Although the quality of relationships underpinning contact is a central theme in this book, the additional importance of structural constraints, of distance, cost and suitable accommodation should not be overlooked, as Simpson, Jessop and McCarthy and Brooks-Gordon also point out.

In terms of what makes contact work, most of the contributors to this volume would concur with Dunn's identification of continuing parental relationships as being governed by and located within a network of other relationships each influencing the other, rather than viewing contact as isolated and distinctive dyadic relationships between contact parent and child or contact and resident parent. Making this network of relationships function, however, is a challenge, although several contributors begin to identify the necessary pieces of the jigsaw. Dunn's analysis clearly highlights the importance of positive relationships between resident and non-resident parents. The chapters by Simpson, Jessop and McCarthy, Neil and Trinder also emphasise how important it is that resident or adoptive parents actively facilitate contact rather than just not hinder it. At the same time these authors also argue that for these contact relationships to work then non-resident or birth parents must accept and adjust to their new status, a conclusion that will not sit easily with all.

WHAT IS THE ROLE OF LAW?

It is possible for contact to be a non-zero sum game with benefits for all parties. Not all contact will work, however, or continue to work. One of the central and most contentious questions running throughout this book is what should be done when contact is not straightforward or not working. This is the central question addressed by the contributors in Section 2, but is such an important issue that most chapters address it at least in part. Put simply, the key question is what can, or should, be done to enable contact to work, and what is the role and appropriate extent of legal and other forms of external intervention in promoting, regulating or facilitating relationships?

A number of contributors could be described as legal sceptics, emphasising the limited potential of the law for changing parental attitudes and behaviour. In their chapter Day Sclater and Kaganas, citing the work of Michael King, argue that law has only a marginal impact on parental behaviour. They note that, despite the best intentions of the architects of the Children Act 1989, parents have not fallen in with the agenda of shared parenting and the Act has not eradicated disputes about contact post-divorce. Similarly, the chapters by Simpson, Jessop and McCarthy and by Trinder highlight the inability of the law to ensure the commitment and involvement of non-resident parents after divorce. In the public law field too, contributors question the capacity of the law to change attitudes, whether in relation to looked-after children (Miles and Lindley) or in adoption (Eekelaar). Miles and Lindley, amongst others, also highlight the restricted capacity of the law to ensure or to enhance the quality of relationships.

Several commentators point out that whilst the law offers a framework for contact, the actual implementation or delivery of contact remains in the hands of individuals (eg divorced or adoptive parents, social workers) who may, as Day Sclater and Kaganas observe, have very different ideas about what is appropriate in their particular case. Equally, it is apparent that contact in real life is characterised by a whole series of ongoing daily decision-making at odds with the formal and inherently static form of contact decisions delivered in court (see for example, Geldof, Simpson, Jessop and McCarthy, Miles and Lindley, Neil and Trinder). In this sense then the practical utility of the law may well be restricted.

For some commentators the principal problem goes beyond practical issues to the larger question of the relevance of law as a mechanism, blunt or otherwise, for dealing with the complexities of human relationships and human emotions. Most, if not all, authors in this volume would concur with the conceptualisation of contact by Lord Justice Thorpe as merely the mechanism for the maintenance and development of relationships.[6] In other words, contact is much more than a phone call or a visit, it is the means by which a relationship is expressed. However, as John Eekelaar (2001 and this volume) has argued strongly, some things, notably enhancing the quality of human relationships, are quite simply beyond the power of law to achieve. Similarly Adrian James argues strongly that attempts to enforce contact orders in private law disputes are doomed to fail in that the legal language of co-operation is at odds with social practices based on ideas of fault and 'ownership' of children.

Somewhat surprisingly even amongst lawyers there are doubts about the potential effectiveness of courts as a means of dispute resolution in cases of conflict between parents (see for example the chapters by Herring and Bainham). However that is not to say that there is a general acceptance that the law is redundant, inappropriate or that its reach should be restricted. In some areas there is a call for more rather than less legal involvement. Miles and Lindley, for example, argue for more legal rights for parents in public law cases, specifically seeking rights to independent representation. Herring and Bainham take a quite different tack, both proposing more creative use of law in the private law context, beyond or outside of what might be seen as its central role of dispute resolution and contact orders. Herring's chapter explores other potential means by which the law can influence relationships, arguing for better and swifter responses to domestic violence in contact cases and more vigorous enforcement of child support to increase the frequency of contact.

---

[6] See n 4 above.

Andrew Bainham acknowledges that the law is limited, but not impotent. He argues that contact orders and their enforcement are a secondary function of the law. The primary function, he argues, should be an educative or hortatory role, reflecting social norms. Bainham outlines what he terms a 'mutuality principle' where contact is the right of both parent and child, but, importantly, where rights to contact are accompanied by a responsibility or duty for both adults and children to exercise contact. In Bainham's framework rights to contact can be lost, eg through violence. However Bainham does not intend the duty to remain in contact necessarily to be enforceable; what is intended is that the law performs a symbolic function.

Whatever the merits of Bainham's suggestions, he highlights a key issue about the extent to which the state/the law can impose or enforce obligations or duties on individuals in the context of family relationships. Traditionally family policy in the UK has been based on an approach which Finch (1989:7) terms 'reluctant but necessary intervention' where the principle of family autonomy is dominant, circumscribed only to the extent that the state ensures that obligations are fulfilled to other family members, especially children. Nevertheless the boundaries between state intervention and family privacy or autonomy have constantly shifted. In the light of the ECHR Bainham argues that the state has a clear duty to foster contact in public law cases, and now also in private law cases. This raises interesting questions as to how far this might extend, and whether the state can or should impose negative obligations not to interfere with another's right to contact (as is evident in enforcement cases), or go even further in terms of positive obligations to promote or foster contact. Bainham's suggestion for a duty to exercise contact is just such an example of a positive obligation. No such positive obligation exists currently in English law.

BALANCING WHOSE RIGHTS AND NEEDS, AND HOW?

Whatever the individual positions taken on the appropriate role and limits of the law, decisions still have to be made on which contact rights and relationships are to be supported or discouraged. One recurrent theme throughout the book is the need to have a broader conceptualisation of contact beyond the creation of space for the relationship of child and absent parent or family member. These relationships always take place in the context of a triad, at a minimum of child, caretaking (or 'sending') parent(s) and non-caretaking (or 'receiving') parent(s). There may well be other relationships too that impact upon or are influenced by the contact relationship, including those involving other children and other family members or carers. Once we begin to think about contact beyond the pairing of child and absent parent we immediately run into the question of how the rights and responsibilities of each can be balanced and/or accommodated.

Where contact arrangements are made privately, in divorce or open adoption for example, the balances between the rights and interests of the various parties can be struck in numerous different ways by the parties (see chapters by Neil and Trinder, this volume). But where decisions about contact are made by courts or professionals, how and on what basis is the balance to be struck between the needs and rights of adults and children, men and women, caretaking and non-caretaking parents, social and biological parents and parents and other kin and is this balance struck consistently in each sphere and across the fields of public and private law?

One solution to the multiple rights problem is to restrict the number of rights to be balanced. This is exactly the approach found in the Children Act 1989 where contact was quite deliberately established only as the right of the child, with 'parental rights' reconstructed as parental responsibilities. However the ECHR has presented a fundamental challenge to that formulation (see chapters by Miles and Lindley, Bainham). Instead of contact simply as the right of the child, the ECHR embraces the notion of adult rights to contact alongside the rights of children. Perhaps of even greater significance is that the paramountcy of children's welfare of the Children Act 1989 is arguably diluted by the ECHR, under which, as Bainham points out, the scales start even for all parties, both adults and children.

Whether or not the scales should start even is one of the more interesting issues explored in different chapters. In terms of the balance between the needs/rights of 'caretaking' and 'non-caretaking' parents, Dunn's research emphasises that whilst the relationship with the non-caretaking parent is important for children's adjustment, it is the relationship with the primary carer (usually the mother) that is the most important predictor or influence on children's adjustment. The difficulty then, as Maclean and Mueller note, is how to ensure or safeguard the relationship with the primary caretaker whilst facilitating the relationship with the other parent. This issue is particularly pertinent as some contributors argue that what does make contact work in practice after divorce or in open adoption is an asymmetrical involvement in parenting, based on acceptance of the primary role of the caretaker parent(s) coupled with facilitation of contact with the other parent (see chapters by Neil and Trinder). Inclusivity in contact does not necessarily ensure or relate to equality of involvement.

The unequal division of roles and responsibilities may well be unpalatable or unacceptable to 'non-caretaker' parents with higher aspirations of shared residence or equal involvement. Simpson, Jessop and McCarthy, in their chapter on non-resident fathers after divorce, illustrate just how hard it is to accept a secondary status and to lose daily interaction with their children. How the balance is struck between resident and contact parents is obviously contentious. In contrast to the 'asymmetrical' view which some would see inherent in the Children Act 1989 menu of residence and contact orders, Bob Geldof argues strongly for a quite different balance, based on equality between parents or shared care. In his view, inclusivity has to be founded upon equality.

Underpinning the discussion of the respective rights of resident and non-resident parents are, of course, sets of ideas about the respective rights of mothers and fathers, despite the gender-neutral use of 'parent'. How the state balances or promotes the respective rights of mothers and fathers and the gendered nature of family law in practice is a central theme in several chapters and is the primary issue in Section 3. For some contributors, most notably Geldof, the argument is that fathers' rights and claims are downgraded; in contrast the mothers reported in the chapter by Day Sclater and Kaganas argue that the law favours fathers' rights. Buchanan & Hunt observe from their study of court welfare reporting that many mothers and fathers thought that the system favoured the other gender.

Whatever position one takes on the fairness and appropriateness of the balance of rights between men and women, it is apparent that contact rights are heavily gendered, albeit with the balance being struck differently, or perhaps more overtly, in different spheres of family law. Brooks-Gordon's chapter makes clear that in the case of imprisoned parents there is far greater institutional and legal support for biological mothers than biological fathers. In his chapter on assisted reproduction, Richards highlights the discrepancy between the position of surrogate mothers who retain parental rights until children are signed over to commissioning parents, and that of donor fathers who have no legal rights or duties in the UK. Similarly, Bainham notes that the approach of the ECHR of conferring rights if 'family life' is established disadvantages certain biological fathers who have not had the opportunity to establish family life, for example donor fathers, parents who have never lived together or fathers whose children are being placed for adoption.

Bainham's point raises another critical issue, about the relative support extended to contact rights based on existing parent-child relationships as against the mere prospect of a relationship based on a biological tie. In other words, are rights of contact conferred only in order to retain, expand or re-establish an existing or lapsed relationship or should rights be extended to create or build a non-existent relationship? At present the requirement that family life be established in order to trigger Article 8 rights would suggest the former, that contact rights are restricted to existing relationships. In his chapter, John Eekelaar appears to endorse this view, suggesting that contact after adoption should be about supporting existing relationships, rather than building up non-existent ones.

However some commentators do make a case for the extension of rights to situations where there is a biological but not a pre-existing social relationship. Richards' chapter on assisted reproduction considers the arguments for and against extending rights to identifying information of children born as a result of donor insemination, concluding that, on balance, such a right should be conferred. Neil's chapter on open adoption suggests that contact may in fact be more straightforward for children who have no memories of their birth parents simply because no attachment has been established. The recent Adoption and Children Act 2002 includes a new provision for intermediary services for birth relatives of adult adopted children suggesting that the move towards openness and inclusivity is being further extended, albeit for adult children.

The final issue to be considered is the relative balance of rights of parents and other family members, including siblings, grandparents and aunts and uncles. The chapters by Pryor, Dunn and Hughes in Section 1 all highlight the potential importance of these relationships to children's development and adjustment. However although these relationships might be highly salient for children, as Pryor and Dunn indicate, the institutional recognition and support for them is far less pronounced. Bainham notes in his chapter that grandparent rights to contact are contingent upon the quality of the relationship rather than automatic. Neil highlights the importance of sibling contact in open adoption, although as Miles and Lindley point out, sibling contact is not habitually included in contact planning.

It is clear that contact, in that it facilitates continuing relationships, is of potential benefit to children, and to adults as well. Few, if any, contributors to this volume would suggest that contact can always work or be helpful. The move towards contact, based on principles of openness and inclusivity, does encapsulate a range of children and adults with potentially competing rights and interests. As the contributors to this book identify, precisely how these rights and interests are balanced is not necessarily consistent across the spectrum of family structures and processes, nor indeed is there consensus about where the appropriate balance should be drawn, or by whom.

REFERENCES

AMATO, P and GILBRETH, J, 'Nonresident Fathers and Children's Well-being: a Meta-Analysis' (1999) 61 *Journal of Marriage & The Family* 557.

BAINHAM, A, DAY SCLATER, S and RICHARDS, M (eds), *What is a Parent? A Socio-Legal Analysis* (Oxford, Hart, 1999).

EEKELAAR, J, 'Contact—Over the Limit' (2002) 32 *Family Law* 271.

FINCH, J, *Family Obligations and Social Change* (Cambridge, Polity Press, 1989).

FOX HARDING, L, *Perspectives in Child Care Policy* (2nd edn, Harlow, Longman, 1997).

GOLDSTEIN, J, FREUD, A and SOLNIT, A, *Beyond the Best Interests of the Child* (New York, Free Press, 1979).

HASKEY, J, 'Children who Experience Divorce in their Family' (1997) 87 *Population Trends* 5.

HAWTHORNE, J, JESSOP, J, PRYOR, J and RICHARDS, M, *Supporting Children through Family Change* (York, Joseph Rowntree Foundation/YPS, 2003).

LEWIS, J and KIERNAN, K, 'The Boundaries between Marriage, Non Marriage, and Parenthood: Changes in Behavior and Policy in Postwar Britain' (1996) 21 *Journal of Family History* 372.

PRYOR, J and RODGERS, B, *Children in Changing Families. Life after Parental Separation* (Blackwell: Oxford, 2001).

SMART, C, NEALE, B and WADE, A, *The Changing Experience of Childhood: Families and Divorce* (Cambridge, Polity Press, 2001).

Section 1:
Children and Families

2

Contact and Children's Perspectives on Parental Relationships

JUDY DUNN

THE FOCUS OF this chapter is on children's perspectives on the quality of their relationships with both resident and non-resident parents, following parental separation and repartnering, and on links between these relationships and patterns of contact with non-resident parents. The question of how contact patterns are linked to children's adjustment is considered. Although it is clear that problems arise for many children during and following family transitions, the emphasis in past research has been chiefly upon *adults'* accounts of children's difficulties and the quality of their relationships. The importance of understanding the perspectives of children on their family situations is increasingly stressed by researchers (eg Fine *et al*, 1999), policy makers, those concerned with care and custody arrangements and the rights of the child (Bainham, this volume), and clinicians (eg Dowling and Gorrell Barnes, 2000).

Yet we remain relatively ignorant of children's views, especially the perspectives of those in early and middle childhood (Pryor and Rodgers, 2001; for exceptions see Morrow, 1998; Smart, Wade and Neale, 1999). We consider here how their accounts of their relationships with *all* their parents—both resident and non-resident, and their adjustment and well-being relate to the issue of contact between children and their non-resident parents. What are the links between the children's experiences and relationships with their mothers and stepfathers, and their relationships with their non-resident fathers? How does the extent of their contact and the quality of their relationships with their *non-resident* fathers relate to their adjustment as they grow up?

The research literature on non-resident fathers has, until relatively recently, focused chiefly on the extent of contact between children and their non-resident fathers and the payment of support, and much less on the emotional closeness and psychological significance of their relationships. The findings on the issue of contact have been mixed: In a recent meta-analysis of 63 studies dealing with non-resident fathers and children's well-being, Amato and Gilbreth (1999) reported that frequency of contact was not consistently related to child outcomes, but they comment that support for the hypothesis that non-resident paternal contact may be linked to children's well-being has become stronger in the more recent studies. They also report evidence that studies focusing on the emotional closeness of father and child, and on authoritative parenting find these aspects of father-child relationships are associated with children's academic achievement and adjustment (with authoritative parenting of particular significance, see Marsiglio, Amato, Day, *et al*, 2000). They emphasise the importance of including measures of relationship quality as well as contact frequency in studies of non-resident fathers and children.

Levels of contact between children and their non-residential fathers vary widely, but have been reported to be low for many children, especially in the earlier studies. In the US, a number of studies reported that over half the children whose parents separated lost contact with their fathers completely 10 years after separation (Furstenberg and Nord, 1985; Seltzer, 1991). Other research reports that one in five children see their non-resident fathers weekly (Thompson, 1986). Both Amato and Gilbreth (1999) and Pryor and Rodgers (2001) in their overviews of research on families in transition comment that there is some indication that children and their non-resident fathers may be seeing each other more frequently in recent years; thus in the UK, Maclean and Eekelaar (1997) reported that only 5 per cent of non-resident parents did not have contact with their children. A recent representative community study of stepfamilies in the London area reports that around half the children were in frequent and regular contact with their non-resident fathers (Smith *et al*, 2002) and that it was the nature of the relationship rather than frequency of contact that was important in relation to the children's outcome, supporting Amato and Gilbreth's (1999) argument for a focus on the quality of child-father relationships, rather than solely on contact patterns.

In this chapter we take the opportunity of findings from a longitudinal study of children in the UK growing up in different family settings (Dunn *et al*, 1998) to consider the question of how children's perspectives on relationships with their non-resident fathers, and the contact between children and their fathers, were associated with their relationships with their mothers and stepfathers and with their adjustment outcome. We discuss here five general questions. The first concerns the quality of children's relationships with their non-resident fathers and its relation to contact, and time since parental separation; the second concerns links between the children's relationships with resident and non-resident parents; the third concerns the associations between children's adjustment and their contact and relations with their non-resident fathers, the fourth the question of how much non-resident fathers know about and influence their children's smoking, drinking and drug use. The final issue discussed concerns children's views on family boundaries, and patterns of contact with non-resident fathers.

1. THE STUDY

The study from which the findings on contact and relationships come is very briefly summarised here (for details see Dunn *et al*, 1998; Dunn *et al*, 1999). The Avon Brothers and Sisters Study (ABSS) is a subsample of families drawn from the Avon Longitudinal Study of Parents and Children (ALSPAC), a study of around 10,000 families. The design of ALSPAC included all the women in the Avon Health District who gave birth between April 1991 and December 1992 (Golding, 1996). It was estimated that 85–90 per cent of the eligible population took part. The families in the ALSPAC study represent those in Britain as a whole, with the possible exception of ethnic minority representation: at 3 per cent this is lower than the 7.6 per cent for Britain as a whole, but similar to the 4 per cent rate for the geographical area from which the sample is drawn (Baker, Morris and Taylor, 1997). The level of retention over the first five years of the study was 75 per cent, an attrition rate within the range reported for large-scale surveys (eg, Booth and Amato, 1991). The rates of stepfamilies, single-parent and non-step families resembles that of the UK population (O'Connor, Hawkins, Dunn, *et al*, 1998).

For the ABSS subsample, approximately 50 families with two or more children were randomly selected from each of four household types: (a) non-stepfamilies in which both parents were biologically related to all children in the family, (b) stepfather families in which at least one child was not biologically related to the resident father, (c) 'complex' stepfamilies in which both parents had brought children from previous relationships or there was a stepmother, (d) single-mother families. 192 families were initially recruited: 50 non-stepfamilies, 49 stepfather families, 45 complex stepfamilies and 48 single-mother families. The representativeness of the families in each household type group in ABSS was assessed by comparing them with families in these household type groups within the large representative ALSPAC sample, in terms of maternal education, paternal education, family income, children's adjustment: Externalising and Internalising scores on the Child Behavior Checklist (Achenbach, 1991) and Total Deviance and Prosocial scores on the Strengths and Difficulties Questionnaire (Goodman, 1997). There were no significant differences between the ABSS and the ALSPAC families in each of the household type groups on these measures.

The findings we discuss here come from the first and second data collection points in this longitudinal research; by the second time point, 170 families provided data, a response rate of 90.6 per cent. Children older than seven years were interviewed; of these 162 had non-resident fathers, and formed the sample for this study. There were 83 (51.2 per cent) boys (mean age = 10.52 years, SD = 3.30), and 79 girls (mean age 10.61, SD = 3.02). Mothers of all 162 children were interviewed, and completed questionnaires. Children's accounts of their relationships with their non-resident fathers, stepfathers, and mothers, and mothers' reports of children's contact with their fathers, their adjustment, and of their own contact with non-resident fathers (their ex-partners) were employed, to avoid the problem of single reporters. For details on the measures included in the study see Dunn, Cheng and O'Connor (submitted).

Contact and Relationship Quality

Alternative proposals have been made about the links between contact frequency and children's relationships with their non-resident parents. We investigated both of these alternatives: (a) that contact frequency was unrelated to children's accounts of the closeness or negativity in their relationships with their non-resident fathers (see Furstenberg and Cherlin, 1991; Munsch, Woodward and Darling, 1995), or (b) that contact was associated with a positive relationship between child and non-resident parent. We also investigated the possibility that there would be a decrease over time in contact and in both positivity and negativity in the relationship between child and non-resident father. Changes in the contact and quality of children's relationships with their non-resident fathers over time, were examined with data collected on the participating children from two time points two years apart. The significance of the time since the father left the mother's household for the quality of the relationship between child and father was also investigated.

Of the 162 children who had non-resident fathers, 133 had some contact with them and 29 had no contact, according to mothers' reports. For those who had contact, the extent of contact ranged from 'less than once per month' (10 per cent) to 'once per week or more' (33 per cent). Among the children who had contact with their non-resident fathers, 72 per cent had non-resident fathers who lived within the same town or city, 14 per cent had non-resident fathers who lived within 25 miles, and 13 per cent had non-resident fathers who lived more than 50 miles away. The age of the children when their fathers had left ranged from $-.3$ years (that is, the father had left during the mother's pregnancy) to 8.3 years, with a mean of 2.8 (SD = 2.4) years. The duration of time since the father had left also varied widely, from 0.3 years to 16.1 years, with a mean of 7.5 (SD = 3.1) years.

The quality of the children's relationships with their non-resident fathers showed wide individual differences (see Dunn *et al*, submitted). Comparison of the children's accounts of their relationships with their fathers, mothers and stepfathers showed they reported on average significantly higher levels of warmth, confiding, support and companionship (the positivity dimension) and also higher levels of negativity with their mothers than with either their non-resident fathers or their stepfathers. The children also described significantly higher levels of positivity with their non-resident fathers than with their resident stepfathers.

Children's frequency of contact with non-resident fathers was positively associated both with more positive and more negative/conflicted relationships with their non-resident fathers. Child gender, child age at the time of interview, the time since the father left the household, and the children's age when their fathers left were unrelated to the variation in the quality of their relationships with non-resident fathers. However the older children reported less negativity in their relationships with their non-resident fathers than the younger; also, as time since the father had left increased, the amount of negativity in the relationship decreased.

We also examined changes in contact and relationship quality over the two years for which the children had participated in the study. There was no significant change in the overall measure of children's contact with their non-resident parent, nor in the quality of their relationships. Frequency of children's talking on the phone with their non-resident fathers actually increased over the two years they were studied. Mothers reported that they themselves saw and talked on the phone with their ex-partners significantly more frequently over the two years.

Individual differences in children's contact were very stable over this period, while the quality of their relationships with their non-resident fathers was also moderately stable over this period. Contact between mother and ex-partner was stable too. There was no evidence that the extent of contact at the first time point affected the quality of child-non-resident father relationships at the second time point, nor vice versa. No significant differences in the quality of children's relationships with their non-resident father in children from single-parent or stepfamilies were found.

Summary

Earlier studies have reported some inconsistent findings on the significance of the extent of contact for the quality of children's relationships with their non-resident fathers. Our results were unequivocal: more contact was associated with closer relationships with non-resident fathers (both more positive and more negative), and fewer adjustment problems in the children. In this relatively stable community, the majority of the children saw their non-resident fathers quite frequently, and most fathers did not live very far away. While we should be cautious about generalising from this study to samples in which separated parents live far apart, it is worth noting that recent reviews of the literature world-wide have argued that there is a general trend for more extensive and regular contact between non-resident fathers and their children (Amato and Gilbreth, 1999; Pryor and Rodgers, 2001).

The direction of effects in these patterns of association between contact and relationship quality remains unclear. On the one hand, it could be that non-resident fathers enjoyed and encouraged more frequent contact because of their closer relationships with their children. On the other hand, it could be that the contact in itself contributed to the close child-father relationships, or that both processes were important. However in terms of practical implications, it is important that there was no evidence here for *discouraging* frequent contact between child and father. Rather, the findings suggest encouragement of frequent contact can be helpful in terms of two key issues (Bainham, this volume), namely the maintenance of the child-father relationship, and as we see below, the welfare and well-being of the child; both of these depended on the quality of the relationship between the mother and her ex-partner, the issue considered next.

2. CONTACT AND RELATIONS AMONG RELATIONSHIPS

The second set of questions considered here concerns links between children's relationships with their parents and stepparents. Various alternative and contrasting proposals have been made concerning the links between children's relationships within their immediate household and with their non-resident fathers. For instance, it has been proposed that there would be no association between child-stepfather and child-non-resident father relationships (White and Gilbreth, 2001); in contrast it has also been argued that there would be negative associations (Wallerstein and Kelly, 1980)—it is possible that children may resent the entrance of a stepfather and resist viewing him as a replacement for their non-resident father; it has also been suggested that there would be positive associations between these relationships—with a positive mother-child relationship being associated with positive relations between child and non-resident father. Such positive associations would be expected in terms of attachment theory, social learning theory, or on the grounds of child characteristics playing a significant role in contributing to relationship quality.

The findings here showed how important it is to view the pattern of children's relationships with non-resident fathers within the framework of other family relationships. In our sample, the affection, companionship and support children reported within their relationship with their non-resident fathers was closely linked to the positivity in children's relationships with their mothers, as would be predicted in terms of attachment theory or social learning theory, or on the grounds that children's characteristics play a role in the quality of their various relationships. In contrast, the positivity in the child-non-resident father relationships showed no relation to the positivity in their relationship with their stepfathers; here the findings parallel those of White and Gilbreth (2001). In this respect the children's relationships with father and stepfather were independent of one another.

Negativity in children's relationships with their non-resident fathers, in contrast, was significantly correlated with negativity in both child-mother and child-stepfather relationships. While the direction of effects in these associations remains uncertain, the idea that the characteristics of difficult children contribute to negative relationships with all three parents by eliciting similar responses from different people (Caspi and Elder, 1988), is a plausible one. And as noted, these associations also fit with the predictions of attachment and social learning theories.

The significance of the family situation in which the children lived—in a single-parent family or a stepfamily—was examined. The hypothesis we investigated was that children's relationships with their non-resident fathers would differ in quality if they were in single parent families and in stepfather families: the possibility that children in single parent families who had no other father-figure within the family household would have more positive relationships with their non-resident fathers than those who had stepfathers was examined. In fact, the quality of child-father relationships did not differ significantly across these family settings.

We examined these questions within a broad framework, including the mothers' current relationships with their ex-partners, and their own earlier life-course experiences. One hypothesis was that mothers' contact and current relations with the non-resident father would be significantly related to the children's relationships with their fathers: that children's relationships with their non-resident fathers would be more positive if mothers had more frequent contact with their ex-partner and described their relationship as supportive.

A further issue concerned the mothers' life-course experiences. We were interested in the possibility that children's relationships with their non-resident fathers were less positive, and more negative, if their mothers had experienced more adverse life course experiences. There is accumulating evidence that women's experience of teenage pregnancy, and the number of their adult relationship transitions are importantly linked to the current quality of their relationships with their children (Dunn, Davies, O'Connor, *et al*, 2000) and to the outcome for their children (Hardy, Astone, Brooks-Gunn, *et al*, 1998; Jaffe, in press; Jaffe, Caspi, Moffitt, *et al*, 2001). Here we examined the possibility that these children were also 'at risk' for less supportive and affectionate relationships with their non-resident fathers.

The findings showed again how important it is to view the pattern of children's relationships with their non-resident fathers within the framework of other family relationships. Children's contact with their non-resident fathers was strongly correlated with mothers' contact with non-resident fathers, and with mothers' accounts of the support they received from non-resident fathers. Whether mothers had been pregnant as teenagers, and their current mental well-being were also important. Children tended to have less contact with their non-resident fathers if their mothers had been pregnant as teenagers, and if their mothers were high in depressive symptomatology. Mothers who had been pregnant as teenagers tended to have more relationship conflict with their current partners, less frequent contact with ex-partners, and less support from non-resident fathers than mothers whose first pregnancy was when they were over 19 years old. Note that the quality of children's relationships with their non-resident parents was not however significantly different for the two groups of families (those in which mothers had been pregnant as teenagers versus those in which mothers had not been not pregnant as teenagers).

Summary

We found that the children's contact with their non-resident fathers, and the positivity of the child-non-resident father relationship were related to their mothers' contact with their ex-partner, and the support over parenting issues that the mothers described in this relationship. Evidence that supportive co-parenting between mother and ex-partner is a key factor influencing father-child contact, the involvement of non-resident fathers with their children, and better parent-child relationships has been consistently found from the initial studies of Hetherington, Cox and Cox (1982) to the recent research (eg Funder, 1996; see meta-analysis of Whiteside and Becker, 2000). Again, the practical implications for those concerned with advising and counselling parents over these 'divided family' issues indicate that encouraging both parents to support each other is appropriate.

3. CONTACT, RELATIONSHIPS AND ADJUSTMENT

The third set of questions we examined concerned the possible association between the quality of children's relationships with their non-resident fathers, the extent of their contact with them, and their adjustment outcome. We examined the possibility (a) that high levels of negativity and low positivity in child-non-resident father relationships would be associated with high internalising and externalising scores on standard assessments of adjustment (the Child Behavior Checklist, Achenbach, 1991); (b) that these associations were independent of the children's relationships with their mothers and stepfathers; (c) that frequency of contact between child and non-resident father was key to individual differences in children's adjustment.

Contact was indeed significantly related to the children's adjustment: the children who had more frequent contact with their non-resident fathers were less likely to show externalising behaviour (such as disruptive, aggressive, or bullying behaviour, or conduct disorder) or internalising problems (depressive, anxious, withdrawn behaviour). We had hypothesised that difficult or unaffectionate relationships with non-resident fathers would be associated with high levels of externalising and internalising problems. Support for this was found in the evidence that low levels of positivity in the children's accounts of their relationships with their non-resident fathers were correlated with more frequent/extensive externalising problems.

Was this pattern of links between low child-father positivity and children's externalising problems in fact explained by the quality of the children's relationships with their mothers? We have seen that there were links in the quality of these relationships, and the key importance of the quality of child-mother relationships in children's adjustment had already been established in many other studies as well as in this particular study (Dunn *et al*, 1998). We used regression approaches to investigate whether children's contact with their fathers and positive relationships with their mothers actually explained the association between child-father relationships and adjustment. These regression analyses showed first, that contact with non-resident fathers made a key independent contribution to the children's adjustment (internalising problems), and second, that the positivity in the children's relationships with their *mothers* was the key relationship variable contributing to adjustment. The quality of the relationship between child and non-resident father did not make an *independent* contribution to the variance in externalising problems, but was closely linked to the quality of the mother-child relationship.

The results here again underline how important it is to consider the links between children's adjustment and their relationships with their non-resident fathers within the framework of the larger family system. We also examined the possibility that the significance of the quality of the relationship with the non-resident father for children's adjustment would be greater for those children who did not have a 'second' father—that is, the children who were growing up in a single parent family rather than a stepfamily. Specifically the hypothesis that a poor or conflicted relationship with a non-resident father would be more closely linked to adjustment problems for children from single-parent families than for children in stepfamilies, who had a stepfather, was examined. We also tested the hypothesis that a poor relationship with the non-resident father would be particularly closely linked to adjustment for those children who were 'at risk' in terms of their mothers' earlier life course experiences. That is, the possibility was examined that within the single parent families, the adjustment of those children whose mothers had experienced adverse earlier experiences (had been pregnant as teenagers, for instance) would be more closely linked to the quality of their relationship with their non-resident fathers than the adjustment of children whose mothers' life course experiences had not included such risks. This hypothesis was grounded in the accumulating evidence (noted above) that children whose parents had suffered adverse life course experiences were at greater risk for adjustment problems (Hardy *et al*, 1998). The implication of the findings of Hardy and colleagues is that the risks associated with teenage parenting are derived from characteristics of the mothers rather than (or in addition to) the actual experience of having a teenager as a parent.

Evidence supporting both these hypotheses was found. For children in single-mother families, the quality of the relationship with their non-resident father was more important in relation to their adjustment than for children who had two fathers. The associations between the quality of children's relationships with their fathers and their adjustment were particularly close if the children were in single-mother families—that is, if they had only one father figure, and no stepfather (Dunn *et al*, submitted)—or if they came from 'high risk' families in which their mothers had been pregnant as teenagers. The findings add to a growing literature showing that adversities in women's early lives cast a long shadow—not only in women's own lives but in those of their children (Dunn *et al*, 2000; Jaffe *et al*, 2001).

4. WHAT DO NON-RESIDENT PARENTS KNOW ABOUT THEIR CHILDREN'S LIVES AND HOW FAR DO THEY INFLUENCE CHILDREN?

The fourth issue we considered is how much—according to the children—the non-resident fathers in our study knew about their children's lives and problems, and how much influence the children felt that their non-resident father had upon their activities, including their smoking, use of drugs and alcohol and their problems with peers. The older children in the sample, the 75 who were 10 years and over, completed self-report questionnaires on these issues, scales from the large scale study of adolescents by Hetherington and colleagues (Hetherington *et al*, 1999). The key findings of relevance for the issues addressed in this volume were as follows.

First, the children's accounts of both what their non-resident fathers knew about their lives and how far their fathers influenced their activities were correlated with the positive quality of their relationships with their fathers. Children who reported more warm, affectionate and supportive relationships described their non-resident fathers as knowing more about their lives and difficulties at school, their friends, as well as their use of drugs, alcohol and tobacco, and also reported that their fathers influenced their behaviour in these areas of their lives. Interestingly, the extent of negativity in the child-non-resident father relationships was not a key factor here, but was unrelated to the pattern of fathers' knowledge and influence. And contact per se was not significantly linked to fathers' knowledge and influence.

Second, the children's evidence highlighted the significance of shared family activities (eating meals together, going out together as a 'family', doing things together; the measure developed by Sweeting, West and Richards, 1998) in the time that they spent with their non-resident father. This aspect of their lives was correlated not only with the positive quality of their relationship, but with their fathers' knowledge of their activities, and influence on these activities, and with their own adjustment.

5. FAMILY BOUNDARIES: CHILDREN'S VIEWS ON DIFFICULTIES IN PATTERNS OF CONTACT

What are children's views on the divisions between their two families, and the patterns of contact they have with their non-resident parents? The final issue discussed here is how children see their divided lives with separated parents—what they find difficult or troubling, how they view the relations between their parents, and what particular features of their lives in two households raise problems for them. What did children see as difficulties or advantages in the divided lives they led, with separated parents, and arrangements about contact? In this section some of the key issues highlighted by the children in their accounts are briefly summarised. Detailed accounts of the findings are given in Dunn *et al*, submitted; Dunn and Deater Deckard, 2001.

First, a general point: Over half the children looked on living in two households with some positive feelings (some pleased to get away from their stepsiblings or half siblings), or without strong negative feelings. Children who had been given an active role in decisions about arrangements for contact with their non-resident fathers were more likely to have positive feelings about their divided lives.

Second, we talked to the children about a range of potentially difficult issues raised by the patterns of contact with their non-resident fathers. A source of particular distress to children was the cancellation, by the non-resident father, of plans to see his child. Children whose fathers cancelled plans relatively frequently were more likely to describe their relationships with their fathers as relatively high in negativity, and to show problems of adjustment—both internalising and externalising (the problem of making inferences about direction of effects of course applies here). Other problems the children described included the non-resident father criticising the resident stepfather, parents who made children take sides in disagreements between parents, the difficulty the children experienced when non-resident parents came to school occasions or other events when the resident parents were present, and their experience of feeling torn loyalties between parents. Being made to act as a go-between between resident and non-resident parents was another problem described by some children. However the majority of children did not see these as frequent problems.

Third, most children expressed how much they missed the non-resident parent, and would like to see more of them. Many children had practical suggestions about how changes in the patterns of contact and visits would improve the situation (changing from weekday visits to weekends, or vice versa). Some also made useful suggestions about what would improve their relationship with their non-resident father: for example some commented that they wanted to *do* things with their non-resident parents when they saw them—not just to sit and watch TV. The findings on shared family activities (see above) confirmed the importance of such joint activities. The evidence from the research of Simpson, Jessop and McCarthy (this volume) shows us vividly how difficult it is for some fathers, because of financial problems and unemployment, to provide such family activities. But the children's accounts indicate that the effort and commitment of non-resident fathers to making a family life for their children are of real importance to children's welfare.

Fourth, many children were aware that their parents did not like them talking about the absent parent; one 9-year-old commented 'Every time I mention Dad, she goes off crying and all that stuff, so I can't mention Dad any more'. Here the issue of parental gatekeeping is raised. The sensitivity of the children to tension between their parents, and to parental distress generated by interaction with the other parent was evident; such sensitivity fits with what has been learned by developmental psychologists about the development of children's emotional understanding and their response to conflict between parents (Denham *et al*, 2002). The close associations between mothers' relationships with their ex-partners and the children's contact and relationships with their fathers are of course relevant here. However there was not direct evidence in the children's accounts of explicit 'gatekeeping' in the sense of one parent keeping the child away from the other. The children did not discuss contact in such terms. The instances of children *not wanting to see* their non-resident parents were infrequent, and we do not know the origins of this refusal or reluctance. The more general point is that very little reliable systematic evidence is available on why young children do not want contact with a non-resident parent. Further, it is very difficult to access the sources of *very young* children's reluctance about contact; in contrast, once the children are adolescent, they may reflect on and articulate their own perspective clearly. But for children who are pre-schoolers or in their early school years, it is much more problematic. For the accounts that the children in our study gave, the notion of parent alienation syndrome (PAS) originally coined by Gardner, as summarised by Hobbs (2002a, 2000b) does not appear appropriate or useful. Hobbs reports that the 'symptomatic behaviours that combine to form this syndrome' include evidence that 'the child is aligned with the alienating parent in a campaign of denigration . . .'; 'rationalisations for denigrating the target parent are weak, frivolous or absurd'; 'animosity towards the rejected parent lacks the ambivalence of normal relationships'. While some alienating processes may well be common among angry, divorcing parents, the elevation of alienation to an illness, and to a 'syndrome' of this nature is not generally recognised by psychiatrists here or in the US. It is worth noting the point made by Freely (2002), that PAS as Gardner defines it is not caused by alienating parents in isolation. As she notes 'the biggest alienators of all are the adversarial mechanisms of the courts' (Freely, 2002, p 17).

The issue of children's opportunities to communicate about troublesome issues with both sets of parents remains important, however. A general finding in our study was that children who felt that they could talk with a parent about problems in the 'other' household were more likely to feel positive about dividing their lives between the two households.

Some other issues that have been given prominence in legal discussions of post-parental separation appeared relatively unimportant to the children in our study. Thus, the distinction between whether a separated parent was *married* or *cohabiting* was not mentioned by any of the children. The children's relationships with their fathers' partners were of course significant to the children—and even more prominent in their discussion of problems arising from their parents' new partnerships was the issue of half-siblings—children born to the new relationship between their biological and stepparent. Half the children felt that they came second to the 'new' child of their birth-parent and resident stepparent, for instance, and 45 per cent felt that they came second to their step-parent's own children. It was these issues, rather than the matter of marriage versus cohabitation of parents and stepparents that mattered to the children.

6. CAUTIONS

Three cautions should be noted about generalising from this study. First, the study was based on a sample of children growing up within a relatively stable community, with the majority of non-resident fathers living quite close by, and frequent contact between children and their fathers. It is clearly important not to assume that these findings would generalise to children living in very different family circumstances or communities. The issue of whether quite different patterns of findings might be obtained with families from ethnic minority communities is also important. Thus, a study of adolescents from single-mother families in the US reports that non-resident father involvement had very different significance for the delinquent behaviour of the black and white adolescents (Thomas, Farrell and Barnes, 1996). For the white adolescents, father contact and involvement was linked to *decreased* delinquency, drinking and drug use, while for the black adolescents, there were fewer problems when non-resident fathers were *not* involved with them.

A second caution concerns the age range of the children. Since the children were reporting on their own relationships, this age range is of some concern— the older children were presumably more articulate and able to express their feelings. However the general age pattern found, with older children reporting both less positivity and less negativity in their relationships with their non-resident fathers, was paralleled with the mothers' and stepfathers' reports on their relationships (Dunn *et al*, submitted).

A third limitation concerns the problems in making inferences about direction of effects. As in the great majority of family studies, the causal direction of influence between parental measures and measures of children's behaviour, relationships and adjustment remains unclear, as we have noted.

7. IMPLICATIONS FOR APPLICATION AND PUBLIC POLICY

Among the practical implications of the study, three deserve note. First, the issue of whether contact between children and their non-resident parents should be fostered has been a matter of concern and dispute. The findings of this study indicate that contact with non-resident fathers was associated with children's well-being, and was related to mothers' own contact with their ex-partners and the quality of their relationships. In terms of the two key issues of maintenance of family relationships, and of the welfare of the child (Bainham, this volume), contact with the non-resident parent was important for the majority of children. Most children would have preferred to have more frequent contact. Listening to the children's accounts gives us significant information about children's perspectives on the quality of that contact, and in some cases the children made useful practical suggestions concerning contact arrangements, and how to improve the quality of contact (Dunn and Deater-Deckard, 2001). Their accounts have also shown the importance of the supportive role of grandparents, especially along the matrilineal line (Lussier *et al*, 2002; see also Pryor this volume), and of friends.

However, it has to be recognised that there are some family situations where contact may not be beneficial to children or to their mothers; some children commented explicitly on the relief they experienced at not having to see their fathers. Furthermore, as Marsiglio and colleagues (2000) note, frequent contact provides opportunities for conflict between mothers and their ex-partners, and as such conflict is very stressful to children, contact may reverse the benefits of frequent visitation. Thus, Amato and Rezac (1994) found that contact with non-resident fathers appeared to reduce sons' behaviour problems *when conflict between parents was low*, but increased behaviour problems when conflict between the parents was high (see also Healy, Malley and Stewart, 1990). Clearly the complexity of these inter-relations has to be taken into account in formulating policy. Children's own views on contact should certainly be taken into consideration.

Second, the special significance of the quality of the child-non-resident father relationship for children who were growing up in single-mother families deserves note, and provides further evidence for the vulnerability of such children to a range of risks. Third, it is also important to recognise the risks for children whose parents suffered adverse earlier life experiences; the findings add to the growing literature on the significance of teenage pregnancy as a marker for later problems in family relationships—including relationships with non-resident fathers.

8. APPENDIX

Child's Contact with their Non-resident Father

Three measures were used to assess contact, from maternal interview: (1) A 6-point single item general scale assessing how often children had contact with their non-resident fathers (1 = never, 2 = little—less than once per month, 3 = little—irregular, 4 = moderate—more than once per month—irregular, 5 = moderate—regular, and 6 = very regular, frequent contact—once per week or more); (2) two scales measuring children's specific contact with their non-resident father, assessing (a) how often does child see or talk with his or her non-resident father, and (b) how often does child talk with his or her non-resident father on the telephone (each scale coded: 1 = never, 2 = less than once a year, 3 = 1 to 3 times a year, 4 = 4 to 6 times a year, 5 = once or twice a month, 6 = once a week, 7 = every 2 or 3 days, and 8 = almost every day).

Mother's Contact with Non-resident Father

Three aspects of mothers' contact were assessed: (1) frequency of seeing the father, (2) frequency of talking on the phone, (3) frequency of receiving letters or cards from non-resident fathers (each coded as follows: 1 = never, 2 = less than once a year, 3 = 1 to 3 times a year, 4 = 4 to 6 times a year, 5 = once or twice a month, 6 = once a week, 7 = every 2 or 3 days, and 8 = almost every day). Combined mean scores of these three items were used to create an overall contact score (internal consistency for these was alpha = 0.84); individual scores for the three items are also reported.

Mother's Support from Non-resident fathers

Support reported by mothers was assessed with three items assessing (1) to what extent mothers and non-resident fathers were working together on child discipline (0 = not working together, 1 = occasionally working together, 2 = sometimes working together, 3 = often working together, and 4 = frequently working together), (2) the extent to which the non-resident father provided support (0 = no support, 1 = unreliable support, 2 = low support, 3 = moderate support, and 5 = very reliable support, and (3) the extent to which the non-resident parent took some of the 'parenting load' for the mother (0 = takes no load, 1 = minor load taking, 2 = some load taking, 3 = active load taking, and 5 = major load taking). Mean scores of these items were summed to form a scale. Internal consistency for the scale was alpha = 0.87.

REFERENCES

ACHENBACH, T, *Manual for the Child Behavior Checklist/4-18 and 1991 Profile* (Burlington, VT, University of Vermont, Department of Psychiatry, 1991).

AMATO, PR and REZAC, S, 'Contact with Non-Residential Parents, Interparental Conflict, and Children's Behavior' (1994) 15 *Journal of Family Issues* 191.

AMATO, P and GILBRETH, JG, 'Nonresident Fathers and Children's Well-Being: A Meta-Analysis' (1999) 61 *Journal of Marriage and the Family* 557.

BAKER, D, MORRIS, S and TAYLOR, H, 'A Census Comparison to Assess the Representativeness of the ALSPAC sample' (1997) Unpublished Manuscript, University of Bristol, Bristol.

BOOTH, A and AMATO, P, 'Divorce and Psychological Stress' (1991) 32 *Journal of Health and Social Behavior* 396.

CASPI, A and ELDER, GH, Jr, 'Emergent Family Patterns: The Intergenerational Construction of Problem Behaviour and Relationships' in R Hinde, and J Stevenson-Hinde (eds), *Relationships Within Families: Mutual Influences* (Oxford, UK, Clarendon, 1988).

DENHAM, S, von SALISCH, M, OLTHOF, T, KOCHANOFF, A and CAVERLEY, S, 'Emotional and Social Development in Childhood' in PK Smith, and CH Hart (eds), *Blackwell's Handbook of Social Development* (Oxford, Blackwell Publishers, 2002).

DOWLING, E and GORRELL BARNES, G, *Working with Children and Parents through Separation and Divorce* (London, Macmillan, 2000).

DUNN, J, CHENG, H, O'CONNOR, TG and BRIDGES, L, 'Children's Relationships with their Non-Resident Fathers: Influences, Outcomes, and Implications' (in press).

DUNN, J, DAVIES, LC, O'CONNOR, TG and STURGESS, W, 'Parents' and Partners' Life Course and Family Experiences: Links with Parent-Child Relationships in Different Family Settings' (2000) 41 *Journal of Child Psychology and Psychiatry* 955.

DUNN, J and DEATER-DECKARD, K, *Children's Views of their Changing Families* (York, York Publishing Services/Joseph Rowntree Foundation, 2001).

DUNN, J, DEATER-DECKARD, K, PICKERING, K, O'CONNOR, TG and GOLDING, J, 'Children's Adjustment and Pro-Social Behaviour in Step-Single and Non-Step Family Settings: Findings from a Community Study' (1998) 39 *Journal of Child Psychology and Psychiatry* 1083.

DUNN, J, DEATER-DECKARD, K, PICKERING, K and GOLDING, J, 'Siblings, Parents and Partners: Family Relationships Within a Longitudinal Community Study' (1999) 40 *Journal of Child Psychology and Psychiatry* 1025.

FINE, MA, COLEMAN, M and GANONG, LH, 'A Social Constructionist Multi-Method Approach to Understanding the Stepparent Role' in E Hetherington (ed), *Coping with Divorce, Single Parenting and Remarriage* (Mahwah, NJ, Lawrence Erlbaum Associates, 1999).

FREELY, M, 'Poisonous Parenting' *The Guardian*, 1 October 2002, 16–17.

FUNDER, K, 'Remaking Families: Adaptation of Parents and Children to Divorce' (Melbourne, Victoria, Australian Institute of Family Studies, 1996).

FURSTENBERG, F and CHERLIN, AJ, *Divided Families: What Happens to Children When Parents Part* (Cambridge, MA, Harvard University Press, 1991).

FURSTENBERG, FF and NORD, CW, 'Parenting Apart: Patterns of Childrearing after Marital Dissolution' (1985) 47 *Journal of Marriage and the Family* 893–904.

GOLDING, J, 'Children of the Nineties: A Resource for Assessing the Magnitude of Long-Term Effects of Prenatal and Perinatal Events' (1996) 8 *Contemporary Reviews in Obstetrics and Gynaecology* 89.

GOODMAN, R, 'The Strengths and Difficulties Questionnaire: A Research Note' (1997) 38 *Journal of Child Psychology and Psychiatry* 581.

HARDY, JB, ASTONE, NM, BROOKS-GUNN, J, SHAPIRO, S and MILLER, TL, 'Like Mother, Like Child: Intergenerational Patterns of Age at First Birth and Associations with Childhood and Adolescent Characteristics and Adult Outcomes in the Second Generation' (1998) 34 *Developmental Psychology* 1209.

HEALY, JM, MALLEY, JE and STEWART, AJ, 'Children and their Fathers after Parental Separation' (1990) 60 *American Journal of Orthopsychiatry* 531–43.

HETHERINGTON, EM, HENDERSON, SH and REISS, D 'Adolescent Siblings in Stepfamilies: Family Functioning and Adolescent Adjustment' (1999) 64 *Monographs of the Society for Research in Child Development* 1.

HETHERINGTON, EM, COX, M and COX, R, 'Effects of Divorce on Parents and Children' in ME Lamb (ed), *Nontraditional Families: Parenting and Child Development* (Hillsdale, NJ, Erlbaum, 1982).

HOBBS, T, 'Parent Alienation Syndrome and UK Family Courts. Part 1' (2002a) 32 *Family Law* 182.

HOBBS, T, 'Parent Alienation Syndrome and UK Family Courts. Part 2. The Dilemma' (2002b) 32 *Family Law* 381.

JAFFE, S, 'Pathways to Adversity in Young Adulthood Among Early Childbearers' (in press) *Journal of Family Psychology*.

JAFFE, S, CASPI, A, MOFFITT, TE, BELSKY, J and SILVA, P, 'Why are Children Born to Teen Mothers at Risk for Adverse Outcomes in Young Adulthood?: Results from a 20-year old Longitudinal Study' (2001) 13 *Development and Psychopathology* 377.

LUSSIER, G, DEATER-DECKARD, K, DUNN, J, and DAVIES, L, 'Support across Two Generations: Children's Closeness to Grandparents Following Parental Divorce and Remarriage' (2002) 16 *Journal of Family Psychology* 363.

MACLEAN, M and EEKELAAR, J, *The Parental Obligation: A Study of Parenthood Across Households* (Oxford, Hart Publishing, 1997).

MARSIGLIO, W, AMATO, P, DAY, RD and LAMB, ME, 'Scholarship on Fathers in the 1990s and Beyond' (2000) 62 *Journal of Marriage and the Family* 1173.

MORROW, V, *Understanding Families: Children's Perspectives* (York, Joseph Rowntree Foundation/Children's Bureau, 1998).

MUNSCH, J, WOODWARD, J and DARLING, N, 'Children's Perceptions of Their Relationships with Coresiding and Non-Coresiding Fathers' (1995) 23 *Journal of Divorce and Remarriage* 39.

O'CONNOR, TG, HAWKINS, N, DUNN, J, THORPE, K, GOLDING, J and the ALSPAC Study Team, 'Family Type and Maternal Depression in Pregnancy: Factors Mediating Risk in a Community Sample' (1998) 60 *Journal of Marriage and the Family* 757.

PRYOR, J and RODGERS, B, *Children in Changing Families: Life after Parental Separation* (Oxford, Blackwell Publishers, 2001).

SELTZER, JA, 'Relationships between Fathers and Children who Live Apart: the Father's Role after Separation' (1991) 53 *Journal of Marriage and the Family* 79.

SMART, C, WADE, A and NEALE, B, 'Objects of Concern?—Children and Divorce' (1999) 11 *Child and Family Law Quarterly* 1.

SMITH, M, ROBERTSON, J, DIXON, J, QUIGLEY, M and WHITEHEAD, E, 'A Study of Stepchildren and Step-Parenting' (2002) Unpublished report to the Department of Health.

SWEETING, H, WEST, P and RICHARDS, MPM, 'Teenage Family Life and Lifestyle: Associations with Family Structure, Conflict with Parents and Joint Family Activities' (1998) 12 *International Journal of Law Policy and the Family* 15.

THOMAS, G, FARRELL, MP and BARNES, GM, 'The Effects of Single-Mother Families and Nonresident Fathers on Delinquency and Substance Abuse in Black and White Adolescents' (1996) 58 *Journal of Marriage and the Family* 884.

THOMPSON, RA, 'Fathers and Child's "Best Interests"; Judicial Decision Making in Custody Disputes' in ME Lamb (ed), *The Father's Role: Applied Perspectives* (New York, John Wiley and Sons, 1986).

WALLERSTEIN, JS and KELLY, JB, *Surviving the Breakup: How Children and Parents Cope with Divorce* (New York, Basic Books, 1980).

WHITE, L. and GILBRETH, JG, 'When Children Have Two Fathers: Effects of Relationships with Stepfathers and Noncustodial Fathers on Adolescent Outcomes' (2001) 63 *Journal of Marriage and Family* 155.

WHITESIDE, MF. and BECKER, BJ, 'Parental Factors and the Young Child's Postdivorce Adjustment: A Meta-Analysis with Implications for Parenting Arrangements' (2000) 14 *Journal of Family Psychology* 5.

3

Making and Breaking Relationships: Children and their Families

CLAIRE HUGHES

RELATIONSHIPS ARE OF indisputable importance in shaping children's cognitive and socio-emotional development, and contribute to a wide array of competencies (eg, self-esteem, understanding of emotions, empathy, moral awareness, self-control, sensitivity to criticism, expressive language skills, reading ability and general academic performance—for a review, see Durkin, 1995). Rather than attempting to summarise how each of these areas of development can be affected by children's early close relationships, this chapter opens with a focus on how relationships influence one specific and important area of development, namely children's 'theory of mind' skills. Psychologists use the term 'theory of mind' to refer to the ability to impute mental states (eg, beliefs, desires, intentions and feelings) to others, and to understand how these mental states guide human behaviour. Here, a key milestone is the understanding that beliefs can be mistaken—this understanding makes children much more sophisticated social partners who can engage in jokes, teasing, skilful persuasion and deceit.

The second question to be addressed in this chapter concerns the impact upon children's development of disrupted relationships (resulting from temporary separations from parents, divorce and bereavement). Judy Dunn provides an extended and general answer to this question in her chapter on life in step-families, that in this chapter is complemented by a continued specific focus upon children's theory of mind skills.

The third and final question for this chapter concerns the factors that promote resilience in children: understanding these factors is an important first step towards helping children to cope with disruptions in their close relationships.

1. PSYCHOSOCIAL IMPACT OF RELATIONSHIPS

Relationships figure prominently in a wide variety of theoretical perspectives on development, in particular in Bowlby's attachment theory and in contemporary family-systems theory. This first section begins with an outline of both orthodox and sceptical positions within attachment theory, followed by an overview of how children are affected by their parents' relationships with others, and in particular by marital conflict. Next the importance of children's relationships with other children (in particular with siblings and close friends) is considered. Throughout, examples will be given from work on children's 'theory of mind' skills (that is, children's understanding of how human behaviour is guided by our beliefs, desires, and feelings). The question of how relationships influence children's understanding of mind has attracted considerable research interest, and highlights the many different levels at which relationships matter.

Attachment Relationships

John Bowlby developed his attachment theory after World War II, after observing that children in institutional care who were separated from their mothers showed cycles of protest and despair, eventually becoming detached or indifferent to people. Bowlby also studied juvenile delinquents: many had experienced prolonged maternal separation before the age of two and had 'affectionless' characters. Based on these two sets of observational findings Bowlby (1958) developed his theory of attachment, combining his psychoanalytic training with his interest in ethology. Very simply put, according to attachment theory, ties of affection have a biological basis and are best understood in an evolutionary context. Since children's survival depends on adult care, they are genetically programmed to enhance proximity to their primary caregivers and to elicit their attention and investment. Later, Bowlby (1982) modified his views, highlighting the importance of learned responses to environmental cues and acknowledging that infants can be attached to multiple caregivers. Historically then, there has been a clear shift within attachment theory from a biological to a social definition of family.

Two theoretical claims within attachment theory show the influence of ethology. First, the mother (or primary caregiver) is thought to act as a secure base, from which the child can explore the world (note the contrast with psychoanalytic theory, in which 'dependency' is seen as a sign of immaturity). The second claim is that there is a critical period of contact required soon after birth to enable bonding. On the basis of this claim, babies are now brought to mothers within minutes of delivery, rather than being removed straight after birth as was the practice in the past. However, while immediate contact is of clear benefit for breastfeeding, there is in fact no evidence that it is necessary for 'bonding' which is now seen as a much more gradual psychological process. Again, these research findings have led to a shift from biological to social perspectives on the family, in that attachment to adoptive parents is no longer open to question.

Four early developmental phases can be identified within this more gradual view of attachment. First, between 0–6 weeks the newborn's reflexes (eg, grasping, crying, smiling) help maintain proximity to the caregiver. Second, between

6 weeks to 6 months, infants differentiate family (ie, familiar constant caregivers) from strangers, and begin to show wariness towards unfamiliar people. Third, between 6 to 24 months infants show strong preference for the primary caregiver, and display clear separation anxiety. Fourth, from 2 years, infants begin to understand the caregiver's routine and separation protest declines as the relationship becomes more reciprocal. In particular, from toddler-hood children are thought to develop 'internal working models' of their relationships with caregivers. As a result, children who enjoy satisfying primary attachments think of themselves as lovable, have positive expectations of relationships and so value intimacy with others. Conversely, children who experience harsh or rejecting early relations think of themselves as unworthy of love, expect further rejections, and so may act in ways that elicit rejection from others. That is, when infants experience their social interactions as successful in establishing a reciprocal interchange with the caregiver, an active and happy interaction ensues and a secure attachment relationship develops. Moreover, evidence from longitudinal studies (Fonagy, Redfern and Charman, 1997; Meins, 1997) suggests that securely attached infants later outperform others on standard 'theory of mind' tasks (in which the child is required to attribute a mistaken belief to a character). In its turn, false-belief comprehension is strongly correlated with a range of key social competencies, including connectedness of communication, joint pretend play, emotion understanding and empathy (eg, Hughes and Dunn, 1997; Hughes and Dunn, 1998; Slomkowski and Dunn, 1996; Youngblade and Dunn, 1995). In other words, the quality of infants' early attachment relationships with caregivers is a strong predictor of later social competence.

So far so good, yet attachment theorists face several empirical puzzles and questions. For example, maltreated infants are often securely attached, and this is difficult to explain by attachment theory. In addition, although infants of depressed mothers show the predicted mix of avoidance and ambivalence, so too do children exposed to a transient stress (eg, the birth of a sibling). Indeed, the very notion of stable secure (or insecure) attachment is open to question, since much of the evidence for stable attachment depends upon continuity in children's families rather than in children's posited 'internal working models' of their relationships (Vaughn, Egeland, Sroufe and Waters, 1979). The 'orthodox' view of attachment, in which caregiver sensitivity is seen as the primary determinant of attachment is therefore open to challenge. In particular, it has been argued that attachment is also influenced by other maternal behaviours and general family factors. To resolve this question de Wolff and van Ijzendoorn (1997) carried out a meta-analysis in which they reported that the association between maternal sensitivity and attachment was much weaker for low-income or clinical samples, suggesting that the strains and stresses of financial disadvantage/psychiatric problems may indeed overburden potentially sensitive mothers. In addition, the concept of sensitivity itself may need re-thinking—is it unitary or multi-faceted, and is it a feature of the caregiver, or of the infant-caregiver dyad? (Note that infant temperament, health and cognitive functioning may all interact with maternal sensitivity.) Moreover, as suggested by van den Boom (1997), the relationship between sensitivity and security of attachment may not be linear, but might involve either a threshold function or a curve (indicating diminishing returns).

Meins and colleagues (2001) have suggested an interesting refinement to the construct of maternal sensitivity that she terms 'mind-mindedness'. In her work, mothers of securely attached infants showed more sensitive tutoring, and were more likely to refer to their children's mental characteristics; interestingly the frequency with which mothers made appropriate mind-related comments was an independent predictor of attachment security. Maternal mind-mindedness is therefore a plausible mechanism for explaining later security-related differences in mentalising. Note however that stable within-child characteristics (eg, sociable temperament, good communicative skills) may increase the likelihood of both maternal 'mind-mindedness' and later success in theory of mind tasks, so that causal influences are unlikely to be unidirectional.

Family Discord

An alternative perspective on why relationships matter comes from family systems theory. A central tenet of family systems theory is that families are integrated systems, so that if one part of the family is malfunctioning, other parts of the family will be affected. Unlike attachment theory (which adopts an exclusive focus on infant-caregiver relationships), family systems theory therefore provides a direct means of questioning the impact of marital conflict upon children. This is important, because although we know that one in two children exposed to marital violence will develop serious behavioural problems (Wolfe, Jaffe, Wilson *et al*, 1985), we know much less about the effects of exposure to the more common lower levels of marital conflict (but see Cummings and Davies, 2002 for a recent review). In an early landmark study Cummings and colleagues (Cummings, Zahn-Waxler, and Tadke-Yarrow, 1981) trained mothers to record how their 12- to 30-month-old children responded to witnessing angry exchanges between parents and siblings, and between mother and father. Their findings indicated that, even though only bystanders, children were upset in the majority of incidents (especially those involving physical violence) and showed both generalised distress and rage directed at a particular family member. Repeated exposure appeared to sensitise the children and increase the likelihood of upset. In a follow up study when the children were 6- to 7-years, Cummings *et al* (1985) reported that the children were still aware of and concerned about others' anger (with stable individual differences in sensitivity). However, there were also significant age-related changes; specifically these older children showed almost no aggressive or angry responses, but instead displayed efforts at comforting or distracting participants.

Again there are definitional issues to discuss. Conflict is normal, unavoidable and even healthy. However, when it becomes uncontrollable and violent it presents a threat to the relationship. In addition, family conflicts can vary along several different dimensions, including their duration, their form (eg, stonewalling, verbal, physical), their content (does it involve the child?), whether and how they are resolved, and their relative frequency compared with other forms of family interaction. This leads to the question: What aspect of conflict affects children? In an attempt to answer this question, Jenkins and Smith (1991) interviewed both parents and the child in 119 families with 9- to 12-year olds and examined three aspects of parent conflict: the frequency of overt conflict; the level of covert tension; and discrepancies with respect to child-rearing. Their conclusions were that overt conflicts do the most damage; but covert tension and discrepancies in parental attitudes have a negative effect when combined with overt conflict, although there were wide individual differences and some children in very conflictual families showed no problems. It is worth noting that the child's role in marital conflict can also vary dramatically: in some families the child may be shielded or given compensatory affection; whilst in others the child can become enmeshed as go-between/scapegoat or even become the victim of displaced aggression. There are also a multitude of mechanisms by which a child may be affected by family discord: either directly (through negative arousal or imitative learning) or indirectly (through the impact of the conflict upon the parent-child relationship (as caregivers become strained, depressed, or self-absorbed). Added to this, age effects appear complex: younger children may be protected by their lack of understanding, but older children have better coping strategies.

How might conflict within family relationships influence children's developing understanding of mind? First, Dunn and colleagues have repeatedly noted that young children are acute observers of their social worlds, and show heightened vigilance in situations involving conflict between parent and siblings. The context of conflict provides an ideal opportunity for observing that people have different goals and desires, and so may foster children's understanding of subjective inner states. Second, episodes of conflict are typically emotionally laden and so of extra salience to young children. Third, in order to repair the relationship after a conflict episode, participants may well engage in a reflective discussion of the causes of their disagreement, and this kind of causal talk is thought to be especially conducive to learning about the mind (Dunn and Brown, 1993; Lagattuta and Wellman, 2001). In support of this view, children of parents whose disciplinary strategies highlight the victim's feelings have been shown to develop an early understanding of mind (Ruffman, Perner, and Parkin, 1999; Vinden, 2001). That is, a close relationship with a caregiver who has a propensity to view the world from a mentalistic perspective will, on several different levels (cultural attitude, personal interactional style, biological relatedness), facilitate a child's developing understanding of mind.

Sibling Relationships

Compared with the enormous volume of work (from psycho-analysts, attachment theorists and family systems theorists) on how children are affected by their parents, there is relatively little research into the impact of siblings. And yet sibling relationships are almost universal and are characterised by several features that make them a unique influence upon children's development. For example, the sibling relationship can be described as a 'diagonal' relationship, in comparison with the vertical relation between parents and children, and the horizontal relation between peers. As a result, sibling interactions are characterised by both complementarity and reciprocity. Similarly, sibling interactions include a mixture of sharing and competing (eg, for parental attention); of companionship/support and rivalry/frustration. Finally, sibling relationships are often emotionally intense and typically very enduring. For all of these reasons, sibling relationships are potentially powerful influences on children's development. Their importance is highlighted further by the findings from Judy Dunn's detailed longitudinal studies of striking individual differences in the nature of sibling relationships. As outlined by Dunn (1996b), sibling relationships show marked contrasts along several distinct dimensions, including rivalry (eg, conflict, friendly competition); quality of attachment (child to mother and sibling to sibling); quality of conversations (connectedness, intimacy, humour); frequency of shared pretend play; and reciprocity (the balance of power within the relationship). Yet, however striking, individual differences in sibling relationships are not stable (and so challenge the 'internal working model' hypothesis from attachment theory). This instability reflects both developmental change (as younger siblings become increasingly more active and assertive social partners) and the impact of life events (eg, starting school, parental separation). Importantly, siblings typically become closer in the face of adversity (Dunn, 1996a), and so the sibling relationship is a potential protective factor, although this may depend upon the gender composition and age contrast between siblings (Hetherington, 1989).

Turning to our focal outcome of children's understanding of mind, several studies have reported a dramatic positive effect of siblings upon children's performance on false belief tasks. In particular, Perner, Ruffman and Leekam (1994) argued that this positive effect was equivalent to 6-months in age. Subsequent studies have qualified this claim: Astington and Jenkins (1995) found that having a sibling was only advantageous for children with low verbal ability; Ruffman and colleagues (1998) found that the sibling effect was entirely carried by children with older siblings; and Cutting and Dunn (1999) reported no sibling advantage when a diverse sample was used. Nevertheless, the positive effect of siblings on children's understanding of mind is intriguing, since it contrasts with the usual advantage reported for first-born or singleton children in terms of language development and general academic achievement. So although the presence of a sibling reduces the amount of parental attention a child receives (with a potential negative impact upon general cognitive development), having a sibling also gives children unique insights into how people think, perhaps by providing the opportunity and motivation to outwit, provoke, tease, support and comfort.

Friendships

Friendships also provide a potentially unique influence on children's development, since in many ways they contrast with relationships within the family. For example, friendships are usually chosen, not given. As a related point, friendships will only last if actively maintained. Third, in early childhood, friends are usually the same age and so more egalitarian than sibling relationships. Compared with non-friend peers, friends know each other better, and so can communicate more effectively; have higher expectations of each other, especially with respect to help and support; are more likely to share a 'climate of agreement'; and are more motivated to avoid/negotiate conflict. For each of these reasons friendships provide a chance for children to show themselves at their best. However, it is important to note that friendships do not develop in a vacuum, and typically show strong associations with the quality of family relationships. In particular, several parental traits are correlated with the formation of friendships (and so appear to foster friendships, though again, causal links should be drawn with caution). These include: warmth (the best predictor); moderate control (to limit aggression); involvement (interested and responsive parental style); and a democratic attitude (to foster horizontal skills).

Why do friends matter? One simple and non-trivial answer is that they are a source of companionship and fun. In addition, friends provide the opportunity and incentive for developing social skills (eg, cooperation); a source of knowledge about self, others and the world; experience in handling intimacy and mutual regulation; and emotional support in face of stress. Freud and Dann's (1951) account of six young Jewish orphans provides a dramatic example of how friends can be a source of emotional support. These six children survived a concentration camp together, with little adult contact. After the war, in England, the children were intensely attached to each other; sharing freely, comforting and helping each other and refused to be separated. The importance of close peer relationships is also apparent in studies of non-human primates. For example, Harlow and Zimmermann (1959) reported that monkeys brought up without mothers, but in view of peers, fared better than monkeys brought up in complete isolation, whilst maternally-reared monkeys with *no* peer contact displayed immature play, excessive aggression and fearfulness and less co-operation at maturity.

Research into why friendships matter has progressed from simple rating of children as either 'having' or 'not having' friends to considering (i) the identity of the friend and (ii) the quality of the friendship. The importance of identity is clear: a child may be friends with someone who is outgoing and avoids trouble, or with someone who is antisocial or withdrawn and socially clumsy, and interacting with each type of friend is likely to foster a different manner of social interaction. There are also important indirect effects of social reputation, since children who are perceived as friends are typically also perceived as similar and so children can get tarred with the same brush. In addition, friendships vary in quality almost as much as do sibling relationships. Key dimensions of contrast include: content (the nature of children's shared interests); constructiveness (how is conflict resolved?); symmetry (how egalitarian is the relationship?); and affective substrates (how mutually supportive and secure is the relationship?).

Returning to this chapter's focal outcome, a recent study by Dunn, Cutting and Fisher (2002) provides a clear demonstration of the importance of friendships for children's understanding of mind. Specifically, a cohort of young friendship pairs was followed up across the transition from nursery to primary school. Some of the children were able to maintain their friendship across this change, but in many cases the children moved to different schools or classes from their friends and so lost touch with each other but formed new friendships. Using regression analyses, Dunn and Cutting (2002) demonstrated that the children's level of insight into their new friends was predicted not only by general cognitive ability and early performance on a battery of theory-of-mind tasks, but also showed an independent predictive effect of their *friends'* socio-cognitive competencies. Having a socially skilled friend at nursery appeared to foster children's understanding of their new friends.

2. SEPARATION AND LOSS

In the previous section we emphasised the variety of relationships that have a powerful influence on how children develop. However, research into the impact of separation and loss has centred almost exclusively upon the parent-child relationship, and so this is necessarily our focus here. Most of this research has involved children who were separated from their mothers as a result of an extended hospitalisation (of either mother or child), but we will also consider the literature on early parental divorce and bereavement.

Temporary Separation

According to attachment theory, young children's relationships with their caregivers are so vital to their wellbeing that any severance of these bonds, however temporary, is highly undesirable and indeed, potentially dangerous. Yet empirical support for Bowlby's (1953) claim that a break in the continuity of the mother-child relationship will significantly impair the child's ability to form relationships is surprisingly thin. Even Bowlby's own work with children who experienced early and prolonged separation highlighted the immense variability in child outcome, with only a small minority developing serious personality problems. Similarly, two prospective longitudinal studies with epidemiological samples (reported in papers by Dowdney, Skuse, Rutter *et al*, 1985; Quinton and Rutter, 1976; Quinton and Rutter, 1988; Rutter, Quinton, and Hill, 1990) also highlighted remarkable variability in long-term outcome, although persistent difficulties were reported for a significant minority. For example, men who had spent part of their childhood in care showed an elevated incidence of personality disorders, marital problems and criminal records.

Similarly, mothers who had spent part of their childhood in care were four times as likely as other mothers to show poor sensitivity in handling their own young children's distress and anger. Although the impact of temporary separation upon socio-cognitive skills (such as theory of mind) has not been studied directly, it is noteworthy that this study showed no group differences in maternal warmth, play or discipline. That is, the impact of institutionalised care was most apparent in mothers' (lack of) sensitivity to their children's emotions, suggesting that (for girls at least) socio-cognitive development may be particularly affected by a lack of early close relationships with parents.

Divorce

Here a similar story again emerges: divorce is associated with reduced well-being (in both the short and long term), but there is striking variability in outcome. As a result, the difference between children from divorced and intact families is typically small. There is also a growing recognition that divorce is 'not a single circumscribed event but a multistage process of radically changing family relationships' (Wallerstein, 1991; Wallerstein, Corbin, and Lewis, 1988). Perhaps the clearest support for this view comes from the finding that long before the divorce itself, both children and parents appear significantly different from control families. In particular, Block, Block and Gjerde (1986) reported that children (especially boys) in families that later divorce showed elevated rates of aggression, impulsivity, restlessness and emotional lability, whilst parents who eventually divorce show higher rates of disagreement about child-rearing as long as 11 years before the divorce.

Similarly, recent work has begun to consider the impact of parental divorce on a much longer time-frame. Zill and colleagues have reported that effects of divorce are often still in evidence as much as 22 years after the separation, and are manifest in a variety of ways including low educational attainment, poor relationships with parents (especially fathers) and both internalising and externalising psychiatric symptoms (Zill, 1988, 1994; Zill, Morrison, and Coiro, 1993). Again, however, there was considerable variability in outcome and comparisons with children from intact families produced only modest group differences.

Returning to our focal outcome of children's understanding of mind, a couple of points can be made (although once again there is no direct evidence to report). First, since the enormous variability in outcome suggests that what really matters is family function rather than structure, parental divorce is unlikely to have any simple or direct effect upon children's theory of mind skills. Second, as noted earlier, the frequency of family talk about negative feelings is *positively* associated with later good performance on theory of mind tasks, suggesting that the culture of silence that often develops in stepfamilies may, however well intentioned, do more harm than good to children's socio-cognitive development.

Bereavement

Parental death necessarily exposes children to a more complete loss than does parental divorce. However, the empirical evidence demonstrates that bereavement does not exert the same negative impact as divorce (Amato, 1995), confirming the view that it is conflict rather than loss that carries adverse effects for children. Indeed, for some outcomes (eg, education, adult income, psychiatric symptoms) children from bereaved families do as well as children from intact families.

There is some developmental change in how children respond to bereavement. Infants and toddlers react to separation from an attachment figure by vigorous protest, followed by despair and, eventually, pathological detachment and indifference. For these very young children grief in bereavement is often expressed in bodily reactions: feeding difficulties, constipation, bed-wetting and sleeping difficulties. By five years of age, most children understand that unlike temporary separation, death is irreversible, permanent and universal (although children of this age and older are more likely to understand the changes death brings if they can see the dead parent for themselves). School-aged children therefore respond to loss rather differently from younger children, and typically display both externalising problems (over-activity, attentional problems) and internalising problems (eg, depression, anxiety about survival of remaining parent). The former may lead to learning problems and failure to maintain school progress. With regard to the latter, children may try to 'protect' a parent from their own distress (as a result, their own grief may be missed by adults). In addition, like adults, school-aged children may experience hallucinations involving the dead parent. A longing for reunion is common, and may lead to suicidal thoughts, though these are rarely acted upon.

Emotional problems following the death of a parent are enduring (typically persisting for around 12- to 24-months) and result in a five-fold increase in childhood psychiatric disorder. However, the mechanisms involved in the onset of psychiatric disorder are far from clear, so that there is as yet little guidance to offer professionals working with bereaved children. For example, the classical view of recovery from loss as requiring a period of 'grief work' in order to sever the attachment bond to the deceased (cf Freud's, 1957 'Mourning and

Melancholia') has received very little empirical support (Bonanno and Kaltman, 1999), suggesting that 'failure to grieve' is not necessarily unhealthy, and once again highlighting the importance of recognising individual differences in how children are affected by bereavement. Similarly, there is considerable unpredictability in the nature of children's responses to bereavement: whilst non-specific emotional and behavioural difficulties are common (especially in boys), links with *specific* problems are more uncertain.

3. FACTORS THAT PROMOTE RESILIENCE

A recurring theme in longitudinal studies of the effects of disrupted relationships (through temporary separations, divorce, bereavement) is that a significant minority of individuals continue to thrive despite the most adverse circumstances or life-events. As a result, a key focus for current research is the identification of factors that promote resilience in childhood.

For example, in the long-term follow-up studies of children growing up in care mentioned earlier, a significant proportion (20 per cent of the men and 30 per cent of the women) showed good psychosocial functioning, despite the extended disruption to their early relationships with parents. A favourable home background, positive school experiences and marital support were the three main ameliorating factors noted in this study, suggesting that later positive relationships *can* compensate for a lack of early close relationships.

Similarly, in a review of the divorce literature, Amato (1995) outlined five different factors that contribute to child outcome: loss of a parent, adjustment of the surviving parent, interparental conflict, financial hardship and other stressful life events. Note from this that divorce does not necessarily result in the loss of a parent and often results in many other kinds of stressful changes. Note also that child gender does not appear to influence outcome, although meta-analytic findings (on a total of 13,000 children) indicate a complex age effect, with primary school-aged children showing more negative effects than either pre-schoolers or adolescents (Amato and Keith, 1991).

Taken together, these findings from the divorce literature provide clear and positive messages for caregivers and health professionals—the negative consequences of parental separation for children can be considerably reduced by: (i) mediation to resolve inter-parental conflict, especially for parents of primary school-aged children; (ii) efforts to avoid loss of contact with the non-resident parent (except of course in cases where contact exposes the child to physical or psychological maltreatment); (iii) financial, practical and emotional support for the residential parent. A further encouraging finding from Amato and Keith's (1991) review is that the negative impact of divorce has decreased significantly since the 1950s, probably reflecting the reduced social stigma attached to divorce.

A clear conclusion to emerge from longitudinal research findings is that children are adversely affected by the problems prior to and following from divorce (rather than by parental separation per se); efforts to promote resilience must therefore take a more extended view of family change. Support for the view that conflict rather than loss is what carries adverse effects for children comes from the finding that parental bereavement does not exert the same negative impact as divorce (Amato, 1993). In both cases however, individual differences are striking, and may cast light on the nature of factors that promote resilience. In the case of bereavement, it is worth noting that only 20 per cent of bereaved children are referred to psychiatric services, indicating that the majority of children show remarkable resilience in coping with such a profound loss as the death of a parent (Dowdney, 2000). Related to this, it is worth noting that bereavement studies typically fail to control for associated factors (eg, drop in caregiving, other adverse social and economic changes) that may well be key to a child's outcome. In short, a recurring theme in the field of both divorce and bereavement research is that chronic problems are more disruptive than acute, and it is prolonged adversity rather than isolated events that shape personality. In other words, it is never too late to try to improve the life of a child.

REFERENCES

AMATO, P, 'Children's Adjustment to Divorce: Theories, Hypotheses and Empirical Support' (1995) 55 *Journal of Marriage and the Family* 628.

AMATO, PR and KEITH, B, 'Parental Divorce and the Well-Being of Children: A Meta-Analysis' (1991) 110 *Psychological Bulletin* 26.

ASTINGTON, JW. and JENKINS, JM, 'Theory of Mind Development and Social Understanding' (1995) 9 *Cognition and Emotion* 151.

BLOCK, JH, BLOCK, J and GJERDE, PF, 'The Personality of Children Prior to Divorce: A Prospective Study' (1986) 57 *Child Development* 827.

BONANNO, GA and KALTMAN, S, 'Toward an Integrative Perspective on Bereavement' (1999) 125 *Psychological Bulletin* 760.

BOWLBY, J, *Child Care and the Growth of Maternal Love* (Harmondsworth, Penguin Books, 1953).

BOWLBY, J, 'The Nature of the Child's Tie to his Mother' (1958) 39 *International Journal of Psycho-Analysis* 350.

BOWLBY, J, 'Attachment and Loss: Retrospect and Prospect' (1982) 52 *American Journal of Orthopsychiatry* 664.

CUMMINGS, EM and DAVIES, PT, 'Effects of Marital Conflict on Children: Recent Advances and Emerging Themes in Process-Oriented Research' (2002) 43 *Journal of Child Psychology and Psychiatry and Allied Disciplines*31.

CUMMINGS, EM, IANNOTTI, RJ and ZAHN-WAXLER, C, 'The Influence of Conflict Between Adults on the Emotions and Aggression of Young Children' (1985) 21 *Developmental Psychology* 495.

CUMMINGS, EM, ZAHN-WAXLER, C and TADKE-YARROW, M., 'Young Children's Responses to Expressions of Anger and Affection by Others in the Family' (1981) 52 *Child Development* 1274.

CUTTING, AL and DUNN, J, 'Theory of Mind, Emotion Understanding, Language and Family Background: Individual Differences and Inter-Relations' (1999) 70 *Child Development* 853.

DE WOLFF, M and VAN IJZENDOORN, M, 'Sensitivity and Attachment: A Meta-analysis on Parental Antecedents of Infant Attachment' (1997) 68 *Child Development* 571.

DOWDNEY, L, 'Annotation: Childhood Bereavement following Parental Death' (2000) 41 *Journal of Child Psychology and Psychiatry* 819.

DOWDNEY, L, SKUSE, D, RUTTER, M, QUINTON, D and MRAZEK, D, 'The Nature and Qualities of Parenting Provided by Women Raised in Institutions' (1985) 26 *Journal of Child Psychology and Psychiatry and Allied Disciplines* 599.

DUNN, J, 'Brothers and Sisters in Middle Childhood and Early Adolescence: Continuity and Change in Individual Differences' in G Brody (ed), *Sibling Relationships: Advances in Applied Developmental Psychology* (Norwood, NJ, Ablex, 1996a).

DUNN, J, 'Siblings: The First Society' in N Vanzetti and S Duck (eds), *A Lifetime of Relationships* (Pacific Grove, CA, Brooks Cole, 1996b).

DUNN, J and BROWN, JR, 'Early Conversations about Causality: Content, Pragmatics and Developmental Change' (1993) 11 *British Journal of Developmental Psychology* 107.

DUNN, J, CUTTING, A and FISHER, N, 'Old Friends, New Friends: Predictors of Children's Perspectives on their Friends at School' (2002) 73 *Child Development* 621.

DURKIN, K., *Developmental Social Psychology* (Oxford, Blackwell 1995).

FONAGY, P, REDFERN, S and CHARMAN, A, 'The Relationship between Belief-Desire Reasoning and Projective Measure of Attachment Security' (1997) 15 *British Journal of Developmental Psychology* 51.

FREUD, A and DANN, S, 'An Experiment in Group Upbringing' (1951) *The Psychoanalytic Study of the Child* 127.

FREUD, S, 'Mourning and melancholia' in JAT Strachey (ed), *The Standard Edition of the Complete Psychological Works of Sigmund Freud*. Vol 14, pp 152–70. Original work published 1917 (London, Hogarth Press, 1957).

HARLOW, HF and ZIMMERMANN, RR, 'Affectional Responses in the Infant Monkey' (1959) 13 *Science* 673.

HETHERINGTON, EM, 'Coping with Family Transitions: Winners, Losers, and Survivors' (1989) 60 *Child Development* 1.

HUGHES, C and DUNN, J, ' "Pretend You Didn't Know": Preschoolers' Talk about Mental States in Pretend Play' (1997) 12 *Cognitive Development* 477.

HUGHES, C and DUNN, J, 'Understanding Mind and Emotion: Longitudinal Associations with Mental-State Talk between Young Friends' (1998) 34 *Developmental Psychology* 1026.

JENKINS, J and SMITH, M, 'Marital Disharmony and Children's Behaviour Problems: Aspects of a Poor Marriage that Affect Children Adversely' (1991) 32 *Journal of Child Psychology and Psychiatry* 793.

LAGATTUTA, K and WELLMAN, H, 'Thinking about the Past: Early Knowledge about Links Between Prior Experience, Thinking and Emotion' (2001) 72 *Child Development* 82.

MEINS, E, *Security of Attachment and the Social Development of Cognition* (Hove, Psychology Press, 1997).

MEINS, E, FERNYHOUGH, C, FRADLEY, E and TUCKEY, M., 'Rethinking Maternal Sensitivity: Mothers' Comments on Infants' Mental Processes Predict Security of Attachment at 12-months' (2001) 42 *Journal of Child Psychology and Psychiatry* 637.

PERNER, J, RUFFMAN, T and LEEKAM, SR, 'Theory of Mind is Contagious: You Catch It From Your Sibs' (1994) 65 *Child Development* 1228.

QUINTON, D and RUTTER, M, 'Early Hospital Admissions and Later Disturbances of Behaviour: An Attempted Replication of Douglas' Findings' (1976) 18 *Developmental Medicine and Child Neurology* 447.

QUINTON, D and RUTTER, M, *Parenting Breakdown: The Making and Breaking of Inter Generational Links* (Aldershot, Avebury, 1988).

RUFFMAN, T, PERNER, J, NAITO, M, PARKIN, L and CLEMENTS, W, 'Older but not Younger Siblings Facilitate False Belief Understanding' (1998) 34 *Developmental Psychology* 161.

RUFFMAN, T, PERNER, J and PARKIN, L, 'How Parenting Style Affects False Belief Understanding' (1999) 8 *Social Development* 395.

RUTTER, M, QUINTON, D and HILL, J, 'Adult Outcome of Institution-Reared Children: Males and Females Compared' in LN Robins and M Rutter (eds), *Straight and Devious Pathways from Childhood to Adulthood* (New York, Cambridge University Press, 1990).

SLOMKOWSKI, C and DUNN, J, 'Young Children's Understanding of Other People's Beliefs and Feelings and their Connected Communication with Friends' (1996) 32 *Developmental Psychology*.

VAN DEN BOOM, D, 'Sensitivity and Attachment: Next Steps for Developmentalists' (1997) 68 *Child Development* 592.

VAUGHN, BE, EGELAND, BR, SROUFE, LA and WATERS, E, 'Individual Differences in Infant-Mother Attachment at Twelve and Eighteen Months: Stability and Change in Families Under Stress' (1979) 50 *Child Development* 971.

VINDEN, P, '*Who's in Control?:The Language of Requests, Parenting Style, Mothers' Education and Children's Understanding of Mind*' Paper presented at the Biennial Meeting of the Society for Research in Child Development (Minneapolis, MN 2001).

WALLERSTEIN, J, 'The Long Term Effects Of Divorce On Children: A Review' (1991) 30 *Journal of the American Academy of Child and Adolescent Psychiatry* 349.

WALLERSTEIN, JS, CORBIN, SB and LEWIS, JM, 'Children of Divorce: A 10-Year Study' in EM Hetherington and JD Arasteh (eds), *Impact of Divorce, Single Parenting, and Stepparenting on Children* (Hillsdale, NJ, Lawrence Erlbaum Associates, 1988).

WOLFE, DQ, JAFFE, P, WILSON, SK and ZAK, L, 'Children of Battered Women: The Relation of Child Behavior to Family Violence and Maternal Stress' (1985) 53 *Journal of Consulting and Clinical Psychology* 657.

YOUNGBLADE, M and DUNN, J, 'Social Pretend with Mother and Sibling: Individual Differences and Social Understanding' in A Pellegrini (ed), *The Future of Play Theory: Essays in Honor of Brian Sutton-Smith* (New York, SUNY Press, 1995).

ZILL, N, 'Behavior, Achievement, and Health Problems among Children in Stepfamilies: Findings From a National Survey of Child Health' in EM Hetherington and JD Arasteh (eds), *Impact of Divorce, Single Parenting, and Stepparenting on Children* (Hillsdale, NJ, Erlbaum, 1988).

ZILL, N, 'Understanding Why Children in Stepfamilies Have More Learning and Behavior Problems than Children in Nuclear Families' in A Booth and J Dunn (eds), *Stepfamilies: Who Benefits? Who Does Not?*(Hillsdale, NJ, Erlbaum, 1994).

ZILL, N, MORRISON, DR and COIRO, MJ, 'Long-Term Effects of Parental Divorce on Parent-Child Relationships, Adjustment, and Achievement in Young Adulthood' (1993) 7 *Journal of Family Psychology* 91.

4

Children's Contact with Relatives

JAN PRYOR

My Uncle is important to me because he is funny and kind to me. (12-year-old boy)

My grandma and granddad are important to me because they are very good at listening, which I like. 12-year-old boy (both from Morrow, 1998).

1. INTRODUCTION

RELATIVES ARE A fact of life, so much so that they tend to be taken for granted. Almost all families have them, most know them, yet with the exception of grandparents, family research is spectacularly silent about their possible significance for children. Twentieth and twenty-first century sociologists and psychologists have, in the main, turned their gaze to what have been called beanpole families—the vertical lineage. Why is this? It is driven partly by a strong interest in genealogy and family history (Gillis, 1997); we appear to need historical narratives about our families in order to create the individual identities that are so central to being complete in western societies. And these identities remain heavily reliant on bloodlines (see Richards, this volume). In the past, such knowledge was essential in order to make arrangements about inheritance; today we rely on it in western societies in order to know who we are and from whence we came. In some traditional societies, for example Maori in New Zealand, knowledge of genealogy remains important for spiritual, cultural and economic reasons.

Added to this, at the micro level, is an intense interest in parent-child relationships that occupies family researchers, psychologists, and parents themselves, while horizontal or collateral relationships—those with siblings, aunts, uncles, and cousins—have been taken for granted and largely ignored by scholars. Anthropologists interested in kinship studies have described these relationships to some extent, especially in cross-cultural comparisons. But they do not often illuminate the significance of contact with these relations to individuals, especially to children. Some exceptions to this include the work of Janet Finch (Finch and Mason, 1993) and Schneider (Schneider, 1980; Franklin and McKinnon, 2001), who address changing issues of kinship in western societies.

In contrast, relationships between grandchildren and grandparents are frequent subjects of scrutiny by family researchers. The discipline of gerontology has spawned a raft of studies that consider the impact on elders of grandparenthood, and the literature on divorce and single-parent families has led to enquiries about the involvement of grandparents with children when family transitions occur (see for example Dunn and Deater-Deckard, 2001; Dunn, this volume). More generally, intergenerational relationships remain of interest to sociologists.

In this chapter, children's contact with grandparents, aunts, uncles, cousins and siblings will be addressed (for legal aspects of this contact see chapters by Herring, Bainham and Miles and Lindley, this volume). There is an extant literature on grandparents that will be reviewed briefly. The discussion of aunts, uncles and cousins will be based on what children say about extended family members, and by inference from writing on kinship patterns in cultures other than those that are European-based. Sibling relationships will also be discussed since although they are members of children's intimate families their relationships are of interest to the focus of this chapter. The term 'relatives' will refer to blood or legal kin, and also to 'fictive' kin, identified and claimed as relatives regardless of biological or legal links. As Richards (this volume) points out, kinship involves more than shared DNA sequences, and encompasses social and other connections.

First though, the collateral relationships that exist in non-European cultures will be considered as a way of providing a framework for approaching these in UK families in the twenty-first century.

2. CULTURAL CONSIDERATIONS

The predominant image in modern societies of 'proper' families comprises two married parents and birth children living in one household—the nuclear family. It is a self-sufficient household where resident family members look after each other and rely little on people outside for economic or emotional support. This ideal is undermined by the demographics of households that show that this family form is rapidly diminishing, and historically has had but a brief period of ascendance. It is also in stark contrast to the ways in which the majority of cultures arrange their families and households where extended family members play major roles in the day-to-day lives of children. Oceanic, Caribbean, Asian and Chinese cultures are typical examples. In the last, married couples usually live with the husband's parents who are powerful players in the lives of their children and grandchildren. Children in traditional cultures are not necessarily raised by their birth parents, either. In Maori families in New Zealand the first child is traditionally, and still in some families, offered to grandparents or aunts to raise. In a recent abduction in New Zealand of the child of a prominent Maori Judge and his wife who is a solicitor, their daughter was biologically their niece, born and given to the mother by her sister. Adult siblings, too, play a significant part in the lives of nieces and nephews. In Caribbean families, for example, uncles and aunts are often responsible for the raising and well-being of children (Chamberlain, 1999). These arrangements are not dissimilar to the pragmatic organisation of European families some centuries ago when children were apprenticed to other households and raised by adults who were not their birth parents and often were not related to them.

Migration has been a recent force in strengthening sibling relationships in some cultural groups. In the US, the family reunification programme has meant that related family groups find themselves together in a new country. In this situation extended family members in Italian, Mexican and other groups have relied on each other for support as they have adapted to a new country. In the UK there have been similar processes at work for Caribbean families (Chamberlain, 1999) where members of one generation emigrate, leaving parents behind and joining forces for economic support and childcare in their new home.

In western families, the dominance of the nuclear model in the twentieth century has led to the isolation of many household units. This has been accompanied, and perhaps preceded by, increasing economic well-being and therefore less need for the pooling of resources between households. The rise of the companionate marriage, where each partner is expected to provide intimacy, friendship and support for the other; and the social evolution of intensely child-focused families, have coincided with the diminution of adult sibling and other extended-family ties. The result of the impact of these factors is that for many, especially middle-class families, aunts and uncles and cousins may in effect be distant relatives seen only at Christmas and other family gatherings. Grandparents, on the other hand, appear to have remained significant in the lives of children for reasons that are discussed later in the chapter.

What might be seen as polarisation of kinship patterns by culture, however, is belied by considerable variation in both western and non-western cultural groups. Links with kin in western cultural groups in the UK remain remarkably strong, although they are perhaps more likely to be based on negotiation and choice than on bases of blood ties and obligations. Similarly, it has been suggested that in UK-based Asian families, the nuclear household is increasingly common (Modood, Beishon *et al*, 1994). Kinship patterns, though, probably remain strong and non-western since related households live close to each other and maintain frequent contact.

More generally, household membership is a poor indicator of kin relations. Not only is there consistent and frequent contact across households; divorce and stepfamily formation lead to family members who previously formed nuclear families living in different households. Couples living 'together apart' (LAT families) are also an increasingly common phenomenon, and single-person households have led to a property boom in the UK and other western countries. From children's and adults' perspectives, then, household composition does not necessarily reflect family composition.

The co-existence of different cultures in the same country clearly has the effect of merging boundaries between kinship patterns. In New Zealand, for example, the melding of cultures through mutual inhabitation of a small island and extensive intermarriage has led to considerable blurring of cultural differences. Cohabitation or informal marriage that is characteristic of Maori society is more widespread in both groups there than in other English-speaking countries, and open adoption or 'whanai' has been a characteristic of both Maori and European families for many decades.

Contact with kin, then, can not be easily assumed on the basis of cultural or ethnic group membership. There is wide variation within cultures in the amounts and kinds of contact children have with relatives. This perhaps accounts for more similarities than differences in children's perceptions of families, considered next.

3. CHILDREN'S PERCEPTIONS OF FAMILIES

Children live their families on a day-to-day basis, with only a slowly-developing conception of what Gillis has called 'the families we live by'—the social and cultural images of 'proper' families. Their views on what constitutes 'family' provide an important window onto its meaning and membership. A burgeoning sociology of childhood (see for example James and Prout, 1990) has intersected with legal emphases on children's rights, to fuel a body of research examining children's perspectives on families. The upsurge of concern about children's experiences and well-being associated with transitions such as divorce and step-family formation has also added to the impetus to hear children's views.

Children typically include grandparents, aunts and uncles, cousins and siblings in their definitions of families. Virginia Morrow noted few differences between Asian and white children in her study, who both included extended kin in their definition of family and also described them as important to them (Morrow, 1998). In two recent New Zealand studies, an overwhelming majority of 10–13-year-olds and of adolescents described groupings of people encompassing aunts, uncles, cousins and grandparents as 'family' (Anyan and Pryor, 2002; Rigg and Pryor, unpublished ms).

For children, then, these extended kin are clearly family members. What is not so clear from these studies is what aunts and uncles, for example, actually mean to children. The rupture of households that is brought about by separation and re-partnering serves to highlight the importance or otherwise of extended kin for children. A common finding from studies of children's family configurations following divorce is that matrilineal ties achieve a prominence that is foreshadowed by the nature of kin ties in undisrupted families (Troll, Miller *et al*, 1979; Johnson and Barer, 1987). Kate Funder, for example, found in an Australian study of children whose parents had divorced that following separation one in two included maternal kin in family sculptures, compared with only one in three who included paternal kin (Funder, 1996). Overall an average of 1.8 patrilineal, and 2.3 matrilineal kin were included in these tableaux. This is perhaps unsurprising, given the continuing likelihood that children live mainly with their mothers after divorce. The matrilineal line of kin keeping is in evidence, however, in situations where paternal grandmothers align themselves with ex-daughters-in-law in order to maintain relationships with their grandchildren (Johnson, 1989).

Grandparents were included by a majority of children; aunts and uncles were less often mentioned however. The salience of grandparents is further emphasised by Judy Dunn's findings from the ALSPAC study that grandparents were more likely than parents to be turned to for intimate confiding when parents separated (Dunn and Deater-Deckard, 2001). Children obviously consider extended family members to be part of their families, although their views of families are wonderfully diverse and can include pets as well as friends and other related people. As Kate Funder has said, 'the variety . . . cannot be ignored; children conceive of their family in idiosyncratic ways, and use boundaries that may or may not coincide with standard notions of family relationships.' (Funder, 1996, p 66).

4. AUNTS, UNCLES, AND COUSINS

There is a resounding absence of research that examines avuncular and amitular[1] relationships, especially in western cultural groups. A search of the indices of psychological and sociological texts on families reveals almost no entries for the words 'aunt' and 'uncle' in contrast to their occurrence in common and slang parlance, mostly as terms of familiarity or, sometimes, ridicule. Yet for children, aunts and uncles fill a unique niche. They are of their parents' age group but are *not* their parents, thus providing a once-removed perspective on the generation preceding them without the particular and perhaps restricting prism of the parent-child relationship. They are also made aware of the fact that their parents are siblings to someone else. Thus aunts and uncles are capable of shedding light on parents as individuals rather than as mothers and fathers, and on the previous generation in a way that is rather different from the impressions gained from parents. They provide, too, potential role models that are alternatives to those offered by parents.

The households of uncles and aunts are often the first outside their own to be visited and stayed in by young children. They can serve as an early introduction to the fact that each family micro-culture is unique in its own rules, rituals, and habits. In this sense aunts and uncles can provide a mode of transition to the wider world beyond the family home whilst retaining at least notional familiarity by

[1] Although the word avuncular refers to niece/nephew-uncle relationships, no such word exists for relationships with aunts. However, since 'uncle' is derived from the Latin *avunculum and* 'aunt' is derived from the Latin *'amita'*, in the interests of gender equity I have coined the term 'amitular'.

reason of kinship. It is not surprising, then, that in family sculptures and files aunts and uncles, especially maternal aunts and uncles, are often included in zones depicting close family relationships. And, as we have noted, especially in Asian, Oceanic and Caribbean cultures aunts often have a major role in raising nieces and nephews. Even where families are separated by migration, cheap e-mail, phone and air links enable maintenance of regular contact, for example between Pakistan and the UK.

In a similar juxtaposition, cousins occupy a place midway between siblings and peers. They are not so close as to engender the intense competition often observed between siblings, yet like siblings and unlike friends they are not freely chosen for association. We might expect, then, that they play a similar bridging role between siblings and peers to that provided by aunts and uncles between parents and unrelated adults. And, again, we might expect to find wide variation in the nature of relationships amongst cousins.

Cousin marriage is also common in both western and non-western cultural groups; English upper-class marriage is exemplified by the Darwin and Windsor families, and in ethnic minority groups continues to be a frequent occurrence. Family rituals, such as weddings and funerals, also facilitate contact and familiarity with aunts and uncles and cousins who might not otherwise be well known by children.

5. GRANDPARENTS

The status of elders is as diverse as cultures themselves. They range from precious and revered bearers of cultural wisdom and links with ancestors, as in Maori culture; to dispensable members of society when resources are scarce. Within European-based cultures, too, there is impressive variety in the status of elders. It is probably true, however, that acceleration of change and technological progress means that grandparents as carriers of knowledge and wisdom are not as recognised as they were previously. Increased longevity, too, means that their knowledge will be even more obsolete and irrelevant to the young than it was in past generations. In turn, grandparents may struggle to understand and accept the mores of their grandchildren such as cohabitation, tattoos, and overt homosexuality. More generally, there is a meeting of generations with very different life challenges. As children are growing and expanding their worlds, elders are confronting reduced incomes and power as a result of retirement, and possible reductions in their sense of competency as faculties diminish in acuity. Simultaneously they have more time to invest in relationships and to reflect on their lives.

In migrant cultures where elders are still regarded with respect and reverence, the traditional power of grandparents comes under increasing challenge as their grandchildren embrace the non-traditional values embodied in the culture in which they live. This often leads to dilemmas for young people as they face divided loyalties between their own and the dominant culture.

Nonetheless, grandparents continue to be of considerable significance in the lives of their grandchildren, in quite complex and varied ways. Most obviously, they are the carriers of knowledge and information about recent social history and, specifically, family lineage. Particularly in traditional societies but also in contemporary ones, grandparents are living exemplars of a generation once (or even twice, in the case of great-grandparents) removed. In related fashion, they also represent the other end of the lifespan for children. Depending on the characteristics of elders, they may either inspire respect for, or dread of, old age in younger generations. For children, grandparents also bring another perspective on their own parents. They evoke the realisation that they, too, were children and still are in relation to grandparents. This may be reinforced by anecdotes from their parents' childhood told by grandparents.

At a more specific level, grandparents can serve as role models and confidantes for individual grandchildren. The fact that they are not usually involved directly in parenting means that children can feel liberated to talk to receptive grandparents about problems in their lives, including issues with their parents. The quality of grandchild—grandparent relationships, however, depends to some extent on the nature of other lineal relationships. For example, the quality of the parent-child relationship has been found to be associated with the nature of how grandchildren perceive their grandparents (Shore and Hayslip, 1994). Even more salient is likely to be the relationship between parents and grandparents, which may be a mediator of contact and of the quality of the grandchild-grandparent relationship. And the quality matters; Judy Dunn's data from ALSPAC show that the closeness between grandparents and children makes an independent contribution to the levels of behaviour problems they have, with closeness being associated with fewer problems (Dunn and Deater-Deckard, 2001; and see Dunn, this volume).

Cross-sectional snapshots of grandparent—grandchild relationships fail to capture the changes that occur with time. The relationship between grandparents and their grandchildren is a dynamic one that differs as the ages of both generations vary. Relatively young grandparents are likely to have energy and good health that enables them to be active in their role; older grandparents who may be less mobile will play more restricted roles especially in regard to care-giving for grandchildren. Younger grandchildren may be especially receptive to enjoying the relationship in contrast with adolescents who are likely to be more peer than family orientated. Over time, any one set of grandparents, if they have several children of their own, will be more involved with the earlier-born grandchildren than with those born later when they themselves are older and less active. Grandparenting, then, is as varied as parenting.

The roles of grandparents become especially highlighted when parents separate. Cherlin has referred to them as 'latent fire-fighters' (Cherlin and Furstenberg, 1986) who come into action when needed, and several studies have illustrated the significance of grandparents at times of family transitions. As mentioned above, Judy Dunn's work emphasises that children turn to them in preference to parents and others at the time of separation. In the US, too, the importance of grandparents for young people experiencing transitions has been shown. In one study young adults in stepfamilies reported that they felt closer to grandparents than did those in lone parent households, while those in intact families reported the lowest levels of closeness (Kennedy and Kennedy, 1993). The picture though is not quite as simple as one of all grandparents hovering in the wings waiting to take over when things get difficult; in a recent report for the Nuffield Foundation, Douglas and Murch found that levels of involvement in child care before separation predicted the likelihood of grandparents helping after divorce (Douglas and Murch, 2002). For many elders, too, being called on in these ways is not a straightforwardly positive experience. It calls on resources of time and money that they do not necessarily have. When parents separate the involvement of maternal and paternal grandparents tends to polarise with maternal kin becoming more involved, often in care-taking roles, and paternal kin becoming distanced. Involvement by grandparents is closer if their child is the resident parent for the grandchildren.

A number of single mothers, both never-married and divorced, live with their own mothers bringing grandparents and grandchildren into cohabiting relationships. In the US in 1990 34 per cent of lone-parent families lived with kin, although this varied by ethnicity with 44 per cent Asian, 44 per cent Mexican-American, 40 per cent African-American, and 27 per cent White parents living with kin (usually their mothers) (Amato, 2000). Often this extended family living is through economic necessity, and appears to be of mixed benefit to children. McLanahan and Sandefur reported that 16-year-olds living with mothers and grandmothers were more likely to drop out of high school than those living just with their lone mothers (McLanahan and Sandfur, 1994). Amato (Amato, 2000) has noted, though, that lone mothers living with kin are happier, healthier, and less depressed than those living alone, and less likely to move residence. They also report fewer behaviour problems in their children. Living with their own mothers can mean the provision of material and emotional support for lone parents, as well as on-the-spot child care if they are working and their parents are retired. On the other hand, grandparental involvement in child rearing may interfere with parent-child relationships in ways that are detrimental to children's well-being.

Subsequent family transitions into stepfamilies means that children also have potential or actual relationships with step-grandparents who are even further removed from them than grandparents, having no biological links. Little is known about these contacts although some research suggests that they are enjoyed by elders and grandchildren (Trygstad and Sanders, 1989). We can assume that they are diverse, given the diversity of stepfamilies and their arrangements, and that they will depend on factors that include the availability and closeness to maternal and paternal grandparents, attitudes of step-grandparents, and ages of children.

Finally, it is increasingly common for grandparents to become the main care-givers for their grandchildren when parents are unable or unwilling to take that role themselves. This often means becoming involved in activities associated with schools and sports and other cultural activities, at an age when they might otherwise be joining bowling clubs or travelling. Some countries are making it less difficult than it has been for grandparents to apply for visiting orders or cus-tody of their grandchildren, and grandparental lobby groups are forming in order to support, for example, grandparental claims for financial assistance when they are raising their grandchildren on slender resources.

6. SIBLINGS, STEP-SIBLINGS AND HALF-SIBLINGS

Relationships with siblings are addressed elsewhere in this volume (see chapter by Hughes, this volume) and have been extensively examined by Judy Dunn and others (Dunn, Deater-Deckard *et al*, 1999). Siblings hold the distinction of being the people to whom we are (usually) closely related genetically, and with whom we share the greatest proportion of our lifespan. Siblings experience both shared and non-shared environments (see for example Crosnoe and Elder, 2002) and are the people with whom children try out and practice their earliest social skills apart from those with their parents. Unless they are twins, brothers and sisters are either somewhat older or somewhat younger and hence can be sources of knowledge through prior experience, or a means of feeling responsible as a result of their being younger and less experienced. Not surprisingly, sibling relationships are characterised by being both strongly negative (jealousy, com-petitiveness), and strongly positive.

Stepsiblings enter children's lives when stepfamilies are formed. Children can find themselves sharing bedrooms, meal tables, and parents with children whom they may not have known, have nothing in common, or whom they may know and dislike. Their ages may be nearly identical, or they may range from early infancy to late adolescence in the same household. Despite these unpromising factors, step-brothers and sisters appear to enjoy comparatively benign relationships especially if they are similar in age (Gorrell Barnes, Thompson *et al*, 1998; Fleming and Atkinson ,1999), or they are somewhat disengaged from each other (Coleman and Ganong, 1994; Dunn and Deater-Deckard, 2001). Half-sibling relationships tend to fall somewhere between full and step-siblings in levels of negativity (Dunn and Deater-Deckard, 2001). Younger half-siblings are often welcomed by children, perhaps as symbols of stability of the stepfamily, and as partial kin.

Issues of contact with siblings become salient when parents part and the possi-bility of split residence is considered. Although it seems to be a received truth that siblings should not be separated, some research suggests that in some cases it is an optimal solution. As before, this will depend on a range of factors including geo-graphical considerations, ages of children, and the nature of their relationships both with each other and with their parents.

7. CONCLUSIONS

'Relatives' is a term that can range from pejorative to adulatory. It denotes unwanted duty, obligation, responsibility and entanglement on the one hand; and commitment, support, belongingness and love on the other. I have argued that at some levels they are relations that are taken for granted and unexamined, perhaps because they are so much a part of the fabric of our emotional landscape.

Yet for children they are a powerful and subtle source of identity. They offer unique perspectives on parents and on themselves, in ways that enhance an emerging sense of self within the web of family within which most children develop. Aunts and uncles are also sisters and brothers even though they are grown up; grandparents are parents to their parents who are therefore children even though they are also grown up. These realisations reveal a past for parents that can be compared and contrasted with their own, present childhood. They bring, too, an implicit or sometimes explicit account of recent family history that adds to the developing mosaic of identity. Relatives are also agents of socialisation forming a bridge between proximal family and the outside world. They might be viewed as those with whom children can practise interactive skills with people who are different, but not *that* different, from immediate family members.

There is, too, a sense of circularity in the fact that what might be regarded as practices typical of traditional cultures are also evident in arrangements that arise as a result of modern phenomena such as divorce and artificial reproductive technologies. For example, grandparents become involved in raising their grandchildren when their parents separate. And in issues that arise from infertility, parents are more likely to choose related ovum or sperm donors than strangers. In cases of surrogacy, it is not uncommon for sisters or mothers to bear children for their infertile sisters or daughters. This involvement of extended kin in intimate aspects of childbearing and child rearing is not new, although the reasons for it now reflect aspects of living in the twenty-first century.

It seems, then, that although the importance of biological relationship is consistently challenged by the adoption of fictive kin, and by the fact that unrelated parents are quite as competent and involved with their children as those who are genetically related, biology continues to be significant. Its contemporary nature is summed up by an internationally mobile young adult who said, 'you can always rely on relatives even if you don't know them. They always take you in and you just get on with them.' Contact with relatives is not always that simple or that positive. It is, though, a dimension of families that deserves more consideration in relation to children than it has so far received.

REFERENCES

AMATO, PR, 'Diversity Within Single-Parent Families' in DH Demo, KR Allen and MA Fine (eds), *Handbook of Family Diversity* (New York, Oxford University Press, 2000).

ANYAN, S and PRYOR, J, 'What is in a Family? Adolescent Perceptions' (2002) 16 *Children & Society* 1.

CHAMBERLAIN, M, 'Brothers and Sisters, Uncles and Aunts: A Lateral Perspective on Caribbean Families' in E Silva and C Smart (eds), *The New Family?* (London, Sage, 1999).

CHERLIN, AJ and FURSTENBERG, FF, *The New American Grandparent: A Place in the Family, a Life Apart* (New York, Basic Books, 1986).

COLEMAN, M and GANONG, L, *Remarried Family Relationships* (Thousand Oaks, CA, Sage, 1994).

CROSNOE, R and ELDER, GH, 'Adolescent Twins and Emotional Distress: The Interrelated Influence of Nonshared Environment and Social Structure' (2002) 73 *Child Development* 1761.

DOUGLAS, G and MURCH, M, *The Role of Grandparents in Divorced Families* (Cardiff, Family Studies Research Centre, University of Wales, 2002).

DUNN, J and DEATER-DECKARD, K, *Children's Views of Their Changing Families* (York, Joseph Rowntree Foundation, 2001).

DUNN, J, DEATER-DECKARD, K, PICKERING, K and GOLDING, J, 'Siblings, Parents, and Partners: Family Relationships Within a Longitudinal Community Study' (1999) 40 *Journal of Child Psychology and Psychiatry* 1025.

FINCH, J and MASON, J, *Negotiating Family Responsibilities* (London, Tavistock/Routledge, 1993).

FLEMING, R and ATKINSON, T, *Families of a Different Kind. Life in the Households of Couples who have Children from Previous Marriages or Marriage-Like Relationships* (Waikanae, New Zealand, Families of Remarriage Project, 1999).

FRANKLIN, S and McKINNON, S (eds), *Relative Values. Reconfiguring Kinship Studies* (Durham, NC, Duke University Press, 2001).

FUNDER, K., *Remaking Families* (Melbourne, Australian Institute of Family Studies, 1996).

GILLIS, J, *A World of Their Own Making: A History of Myth and Ritual in Family Life* (Oxford, Oxford University Press, 1997).

GORRELL BARNES, G, THOMPSON, P, DANIEL, G and BURCHARDT, N, *Growing Up in Stepfamilies* (Oxford, Clarendon Press, 1998).

JAMES, A and PROUT, A (eds), *Constructing and Reconstructing Childhood: Contemporary Issues in the Sociological Study of Childhood* (London, Falmer Press, 1990).

JOHNSON, CL, 'In-law Relationships in the American Kinship System: The Impact of Divorce and Remarriage' (1989) 16 *American Ethnologist* 87.

JOHNSON, CL and Barer, BM, 'Marital Instability and the Changing Kinship Networks of Grandparents' (1987) 27 *The Gerontologist* 330.

KENNEDY, GE and KENNEDY, CE, 'Grandparents: A Special Resource for Children in Stepfamilies' (1993) 19 *Journal of Divorce and Remarriage* 45.

McLANAHAN, S and SANDFUR, S, *Growing Up with a Single Parent: What Hurts, What Helps* (Cambridge, MA, Harvard University Press, 1994).

MODOOD, T, BEISHON, S and S. VIRDEE, S, *Changing Ethnic Identities* (London, Policy Studies Institute, 1994).

MORROW, V, *Understanding Families: Children's Perspectives* (London, National Children's Bureau, 1998).

RIGG, A and PRYOR, J, 'Young People's Experiences of Families and Family Change' unpublished manuscript.

SCHNEIDER, D, *Kinship: A Cultural Account* (Chicago, University of Chicago Press, 1980).

SHORE, RJ and HAYSLIP, B, 'Custodial Parenting: Implications for Children's Development' in AE Gottfried and AW Gottfried (eds), *Redefining Families. Implications for Children's Development* (Plenum Press, 1994).

TROLL, LE, MILLER, SE and ATCHLEY, RC, *Families in Later Life* (Belmont, CA, Belmont, 1979).

TRYGSTAD, DW and SANDERS, GF, 'The Significance of Stepgrandparents' (1989) 22 *International Journal of Aging and Human Development* 119.

Section 2:

The Law and its Limits

5

Contact as a Right and Obligation

ANDREW BAINHAM* *(the two are inseparable)*

1. INTRODUCTION

WHAT LAWYERS CALL 'contact' and used to call 'access' is just one aspect of a wider question relating to the role of law in regulating the creation, maintenance and termination of family relationships. This chapter is concerned with that broader role. It is appropriate, as commentators have pointed out (King, 1997), to be sceptical about what the law can achieve in the sphere of human relationships, but we should equally be careful not to underestimate its potential.

A primary function of the law is, it is argued, to assert and defend and, to a degree, enforce the fundamental rights and obligations which arise in connection with the establishment and continuation of family relationships. Specifically, contact between parent and child is both a basic right and obligation of mothers, fathers and children and, importantly, to facilitate it is an obligation of the state.

Rights and obligations in relation to contact are inextricably linked. Thus, to talk of contact as a *right* of anyone is devoid of meaning unless considered alongside the *obligations* which go with that right. These rights and obligations, on one level, are deeply engrained *social norms* which, it is argued, reflect the view of the overwhelming majority (though clearly not everyone) about the importance of the relationship between parent and child. On another level, they have an equally strong legal foundation in international conventions and in English domestic law. In the light of the United Kingdom's obligations under various conventions, most obviously the European Convention on Human Rights and Fundamental Freedoms (ECHR), it will be my contention that those who assert that there is no right or presumption of contact are not merely misguided, but are plainly wrong. Of course, it is quite legitimate to argue that contact *ought not to be* a right or presumption but that is a quite different issue upon which, I concede, reasonable people may disagree.

* I am grateful to the members of the Cambridge Socio-Legal Group and especially my co-editors for their comments and to Belinda Brooks-Gordon for her helpful reactions to an earlier draft. What remains is my sole responsibility.

It is important to make plain at the outset that I am not asserting that any of these rights and obligations are absolute or unqualified. It is clear beyond doubt that they are liable to be displaced by other considerations, most obviously the welfare of the child. No law, international or domestic, has ever suggested otherwise in my view. But neither does this mean that the legal articulation of the right or presumption should be a matter of indifference—far from it. For whether or not the issue of contact should be litigated to what may literally be the bitter end, or vigorously enforced or not, is *not* the crucial question (cf Smart and Neale, 1997). It is argued, rather, that the most important function of the law is a symbolic or hortatory one; to support and underscore the widely held view of the international community that parent and child enjoy a fundamental relationship which ought not to be disrupted without a demonstrably good reason. In this crucial sense, court orders (applying as they do to a minority of cases) and dispute resolution more generally, reflect a *secondary* not primary function of the law. Too great a concentration on the resolution of this minority of disputed cases is therefore misplaced. Indeed, the point has been made many times that the majority of divorcing parents fashion their own contact arrangements without a great deal of assistance from lawyers and the courts or, for that matter, from mediators, though it is also fair to say that this 'settlement culture' has been the subject of a good deal of critical re-evaluation in recent years (Bailey-Harris, Barron and Pearce, 1999; Davis, 2000). The *message* of our legal code is thus critically important in providing the backdrop to the private ordering and reordering of family relationships which clearly occurs on a massive scale.

Yet this is not to say that court orders, and the attempt to enforce them, are unimportant; something acknowledged in a recent report on the facilitation of contact, *Making Contact Work* (Lord Chancellor's Department, 2002). On the contrary, we are right to be concerned about this, not merely from the standpoint of the 'result' achieved for those locked in dispute, but also for the message which is conveyed by the manner in which the legal system responds to these problem cases.

In this chapter I consider first the international obligations on the state regarding family relationships. In the following three sections I look, respectively, at the law's role in creating, maintaining and terminating these relationships. I conclude with a few observations on what we might expect from the law and what changes might be necessary to achieve it.

2.   THE INTERNATIONAL BACKGROUND

The almost relentless 'internationalisation' of family law as the twentieth century drew to a close is a widely recognised phenomenon (Douglas, 1997; Silberman, 2000). It would be possible to find in many international conventions support for the principle of the importance of family relationships and the State's obligations to respect them. But I will confine the discussion to what are probably the two most important international conventions bearing on the issues addressed here—the United Nations Convention on the Rights of the Child (UN Convention) and the ECHR.

The UN Convention

The UN Convention (Le Blanc, 1995) is quite explicit about the state's obligation to uphold the child's right to knowledge of his or her parents and, thereafter, to foster the continuation of their family relations.

Article 7 provides:

> The child shall be registered immediately after birth and shall have the right from birth to a name, the right to acquire a nationality and, as far as possible, the right to know and be cared for by his or her parents.

Two features of this provision are worthy of note. The first is that the child's right to the relationship with the parents arises *from birth*. The second is that no distinction is drawn between *mothers* and *fathers*. The only reference is to the gender-neutral *parent*. It is interesting to note that Australian domestic law contains a not dissimilar, yet more explicit, provision. Under section 60B of the Family Law Act 1975, as amended in 1995, it is stated that

> children have the right to know and be cared for by both parents, regardless of whether their parents are married, separated, have never married or have never lived together.

I will return to both of these features of Article 7 when looking at the State's obligations under the ECHR.

If Article 7 is concerned with the creation of family relationships between a child and his/her parents, Article 8 deals with the *continuation* of those relationships. It provides:

> States parties undertake to respect the right of the child to *preserve* (emphasis added), his or her identity, including nationality, name and family relations as recognized by law without unlawful interference.

It is perhaps significant here that *family relations* extend beyond the parent-child relationship. Again there is no differentiation of mothers and fathers or of the *maternal* and *paternal* family.

Specifically in relation to the question of contact, Article 9 (3) provides:

> State's parties shall respect the right of the child who is separated from one or both parents to maintain personal relations and direct contact with both parents on a regular basis, except if it is contrary to the child's best interests.

These are not provisions which figure prominently in the work of those who seek to argue that contact is not a right. Neither is Article 18 of the Convention likely to appeal greatly to these writers. It provides:

States parties shall use their best efforts to ensure recognition of the principle that *both parents* (emphasis added) have common responsibilities for the upbringing and development of the child.

Again, the aim of the UN Convention to treat the mother and father in an even-handed way is manifest.

The European Convention on Human Rights

There are several obvious distinctions between the UN Convention and the ECHR—not least that the UN Convention is not 'incorporated' into English law (that is, it does not form part of it) in the way that the ECHR has been so entrenched by the Human Rights Act 1998.[1] Another distinction is that the UN Convention is self-evidently about children whereas the ECHR, on its face, is not about them at all. Nevertheless, the ECHR applies as much to children, as it does to adults, while making due allowance for the status of childhood (Kilkelly, 1999). Children therefore have 'convention rights' though the content of these rights is far from clear (Bainham, 2002). One of these rights, arising from Article 8, is a right of contact with parents and other members of the family as an aspect of the right to respect for private and family life. But, importantly, another crucial distinction between the conventions is that the ECHR also upholds *adults'* convention rights, specifically the parent's right to contact which may also be derived from Article 8. While other articles are clearly of great relevance to family relationships (for example Articles 6[2], 12[3] and 14[4]) I will concentrate on what the European Court of Human Rights (the European Court) has said is required by Article 8. It is necessary for this purpose to set out Article 8 in full. It provides:

1. Everyone has the right to respect for his private and family life, his home and his correspondence.
2. There shall be no interference by a public authority with the exercise of this right except such as is in accordance with the law and is necessary in a democratic society in the interests of national security, public safety or the economic well-being of the country, for the prevention of disorder or crime, for the protection of health or morals, or for the protection of the rights and freedoms of others.

Under this provision mothers, fathers, children and other family members all have convention rights to respect for their private and family life. Interferences by the State with these rights must, to be lawful, be *necessary* and *proportion-*

---

[1] Where there is a breach of any of the articles in the ECHR, the 'victim' can apply for damages or injunctive relief in the domestic courts under ss 7–8 HRA (for further discussion, see Miles and Lindley, this volume).

[2] The right to a fair hearing.

[3] The right to marry and found a family.

[4] The right to protection against discrimination in the delivery of convention rights.

ate to one of the legitimate purposes enunciated in Article 8 (2). The key to the operation of Article 8 is therefore *proportionality*. The matter is complicated by the fact that the convention rights of individual members of the family may conflict and, in those circumstances, the courts must in effect determine priorities between them, bearing in mind that the 'scales start even'.[5]

It will be noted that Article 8 makes no express reference to a right of contact between family members. Yet it is now clearly established in the decisions of the European Court that the right of contact between parent and child is a fundamental element in the idea of respect for family life. Hence in a number of decisions, the Court has reiterated the view that 'the mutual enjoyment by parent and child of each other's company constitutes a fundamental element of family life'.[6] Moreover, the Court has explicitly upheld a parent's right of contact in a number of leading decisions (for example *Hokkanen v Finland*[7] (finding for a father) and *Ignaccolo-Zenide v Romania*[8] (finding for a mother) etc). As long ago as 1988, in *W and O, H and B v United Kingdom*,[9] the Court systematically rejected the UK's contentions that contact was the right of the child, and therefore not that of the parent, and that the whole notion of parental rights was outdated.

Where, then, there is family life, the State must respect it unless there is a very good reason for not doing so. For these purposes, it has long been established that family life may exist within or outside marriage.[10] It can also arise between members of the wider family.[11]

The approach of the European Commission has been that whether or not 'family life' exists between grandparents and children for the purposes of the ECHR will depend on an assessment as to whether there are sufficient links between them and the child (Swindells, Neaves, Kushner and Skilbeck, 1999). The position taken both by the European Commission and by the English courts has been to deny an *automatic* right of contact between grandparents, other blood relatives and children but to recognise that contact with such relatives may well be in the best interests of the child in the particular circumstances. Similarly, in the English case of *Re W (Contact: Application by Grandparent)*[12] it was held that a grandmother did not have an automatic right to seek a contact order and was obliged to seek leave under the statutory regime like everyone else who did not have an express statutory right to apply for an order.[13] Moreover, even if the hurdle of obtaining leave was successfully crossed, there would be no automatic legal presumption in favour of contact. The onus would be on the grandparent to demonstrate that contact would be beneficial to the child and

---

[5] *R v Secretary of State for Home Department, Ex parte Gangadeen and Khan* [1998] 1 FLR 762.
[6] See, for example, *Bronda v Italy* [1998] HRCD 641.
[7] (1995) 19 EHRR 139.
[8] (2001) 31 EHRR 7.
[9] (1988) 10 EHRR 29.
[10] *Marckz v Belgium* (1979) 2 EHRR 330, *Johnston v Ireland* (1986) 9 EHRR 203.
[11] Discussed further in section 4 below.
[12] [1997] 1 FLR 793.
[13] See Children Act 1989 s 10 for the categories of applicant.

there was no principle that a member of the family should be allowed contact unless there was a good reason to the contrary.[14]

In the public law there is a statutory duty on local authorities in relation to children looked after by them, to endeavour to promote contact between the child and, inter alia, 'any relative, friend or other person connected with him'. But this does not add up to a right of contact since the duty is expressly qualified in the legislation in that it applies 'unless it is not reasonably practicable or consistent with [the child's] welfare'.

Nevertheless a violation of Article 8 of the ECHR might occur in either the private or public law if there were an unjustified reduction in contact with relatives which threatened the existence of a family relationship. Thus, in *Boyle v United Kingdom*[15] the European Commission found a violation of the rights of an uncle who had known the child from birth and acted as a father-figure. There was found to be an unwarranted failure to consult properly with him after the child had been taken into care bearing in mind the nature of the relationship which he had with the child.

What the case law determines is that whether or not family life is established, and whether a denial of contact could withstand a challenge under the ECHR, will depend not merely on the formal legal relationship arising from blood or affinity but on the nature and quality of the relationship which exists between the relative and the child and a judgement as to its contribution to the child's welfare both at the time and in the future.

In *Z County Council v R*[16] Holman J had to consider these questions in the context of the intended confidential adoption of a child born to an unmarried mother. The mother had concealed her pregnancy from her family and was determined that they should not learn of it, nor of the subsequent birth of the child. The child's guardian ad litem, however, was concerned about the possible implications of the ECHR and sought the Court's guidance on whether the natural relatives should be contacted and asked whether they wished to provide a home for the child. Significantly, Holman J was prepared to find that 'family life' between the child and the extended family could arise by virtue of the blood tie and that it was not necessary to establish an existing social or psychological relationship between them. However, their right to respect for family life had to be balanced against the mother's right to respect for her private life and the welfare of the child. Here the child had already spent a substantial time with his prospective adopters and the balance fell in favour of the mother's decision to press ahead with adoption.

---

[14] But see now *Re J (Leave to Issue Application for Residence Order)* [2003] 1 FLR 114 in which the Court of Appeal emphasized the importance of greater appreciation of what grandparents had to offer and said that minimum protection of grandparents' convention rights required that an application for leave should not be dismissed without a full inquiry.

[15] [1994] 19 EHRR 179.

[16] [2001] 1 FLR 365.

The Court has yet to recognise the 'family life' existing between a gay couple but has accepted that they may have a 'private life'.[17] Family life has been acknowledged to exist between a female-to-male transsexual and children in his household.[18]

At the risk of stating the obvious, there will be no obligation on the State to respect family life where family life does not exist and it is in relation to this matter that the Court has (controversially) drawn distinctions between mothers and fathers which are not found in the ECHR itself and are certainly not found in the UN Convention.

3. THE CREATION OF FAMILY RELATIONSHIPS

The UN Convention upholds the right of the child *from birth*, as far as possible, to know and be cared for by his or her parents. How far can it be said that English law gives effect to these rights and to what extent are they replicated in the ECHR? In attempting to answer this question it will be necessary to distinguish between the child's connection with the *mother* and his or her connection with the *father*.

Maternal Affiliation

As a general proposition, the connection between mother and child will be established at birth through parturition or the fact of giving birth. This is the position taken by English law which recognises as the legal mother the woman who gives birth to the child. This is so whether or not she is also the *genetic* mother.[19] This is the position also taken in most jurisdictions though some give greater recognition to the claims of a commissioning mother in a surrogacy arrangement where her gametes have been used.[20]

Over a quarter of a century ago the European Court of Human Rights (the European Court) also held that for the purposes of the ECHR 'family life' arose between mother and child *at birth*.[21] Belgian law, as it then stood, violated the Convention rights of Ms Marckz and her infant daughter because it required her, inter alia, to undertake a formal act of recognition before maternal affiliation could be established. The Court held that domestic law must render possible, from the moment of birth, the child's integration within the family and that this applied equally to births in and out of marriage. And, most significantly for present purposes, it held that the State's obligations were not merely

---

[17] *Dudgeon v United Kingdom* (1981) 4 EHRR 149. Compare the approach of the House of Lords in *FitzPatrick v Sterling Housing Association* [2000] 1 FLR 271 which held that the survivor of a gay couple might be properly regarded as a member of the deceased's family for the purposes of succeeding to the tenancy of their common home.

[18] *X, Y and Z v The United Kingdom* [1997] 2 FLR 892.

[19] S 27 Human Fertilisation and Embryology Act 1990.

[20] In the United States see particularly *Johnson v Calvert* [1993] 851 P 2d 774.

[21] *Marckz v Belgium* (1979) 2 EHRR 330.

negative viz not to interfere with family life, but *positive* in the sense that the State must act in a manner calculated to allow family ties to develop normally. The extent of these positive obligations is unclear but is an important question to which I must return later.

In essence therefore we might argue that the creation of the legal relationship between mother and child at birth is unproblematic and that both English law and the ECHR have long given effect to this principle. This simple proposition requires some qualification. First, in certain cases of assisted reproduction, there will be instances in which the child will be ignorant about, and remain ignorant about, the absence of a genetic connection between him and his birth mother. There may also be the occasional rare case where the birth register inaccurately records the identity of the mother through fraud or mistake. Thus, in a recent case from Japan, the Tokyo High Court directed DNA tests where a woman registered as the mother wished to deny that she was the natural mother of a deceased woman who was registered as her legal daughter in the Family Registration Book (Minamikata and Tamaki, 2002).

Secondly, there will be cases where the birth mother puts the child up for adoption within a short time of birth. Where a baby is confidentially given over for adoption, that child may quickly lose the legal connection with the birth mother and the wider birth family which arose at the moment of birth. English law, unlike French law (Rubellin-Devichi, 2000) has never given the mother the right to give birth anonymously but it has (until very recently) allowed her to place a child for adoption in circumstances of relative secrecy. Indeed, the introduction of adoption in England by the Adoption Act 1926 was in part influenced by the perceived need to give to unmarried mothers the opportunity to escape the stigma of illegitimate birth (Lowe, 2000). Neither does the child have a legal right to be informed of his or her adoptive status, though the overwhelming majority of adopted children are. Only at 18 does the child have the right to receive information about his or her biological origins[22] but this of course will mean nothing to those who are unaware that they are adopted. Neither is it, clearly, adequate to establish and maintain contact with birth relatives *during childhood*.

This position is rapidly being eroded by human rights obligations which are being taken to require, in most but not all instances, the participation of the natural father in adoption proceedings bearing in mind the presumption that both father and child have a right to establish family life between them.[23] And the courts have begun to question the premise that it is the mother's right to relinquish her parental status, where the effect of this would be to deprive the child of the legal link with her and with the maternal family. In such a case the courts are called upon to conduct a difficult balancing exercise which takes account of the mother's right to respect for her private life.

---

[22] Adoption and Children Act 2002 s 60.
[23] See *Re R (Adoption: Father's Involvement)* [2001] 1 FLR 302, *Re H; Re G (Adoption: Consultation of Unmarried Fathers)* [2001] 1 FLR 646 and *Re M (Adoption: Rights of Natural Father)* [2001] 1 FLR 745.

Paternal Affiliation

The establishment of the child's relationship with the father and the paternal family is altogether more problematic for the self-evident reason that the process of childbirth cannot demonstrate conclusively the identity of the father. Accordingly, the English common law contains a presumption, found almost universally, that the husband of the mother is presumed to be the child's genetic father and is to be treated as the child's legal father. *Pater est quem nuptiae demonstrant.* In a notable exception, the recent legislation in the Netherlands giving effect to gay marriage does not presume that the same-sex spouse of a parent is the child's parent because that would be to deny the all-too-obvious biological reality of the situation (Schrama, 2002). The point is an important one because it demonstrates that it is not the fact of marriage to a mother which gives rise to the presumption of paternity, but rather the fact that being married to the mother gives rise to a presumption that her husband is the genetic father and *from this* legal parentage flows. It is because this genetic connection so obviously does not exist in gay marriage that it is appropriate to deny the legal parentage which normally flows from marriage to the mother. In fact, as we know only too well, many husbands remain as legal fathers only because the presumption of the genetic link arising from marriage has not been rebutted.

The *pater est* rule is reinforced in cases of assisted reproduction where the husband does not object to procedures which involve the use of donated sperm.[24] Here he is treated as the legal father despite the open lack of a genetic connection with the child. Outside marriage there is no corresponding rule, such as exists in some jurisdictions, to the effect that the mother's cohabitant of some specified years' standing is also presumed to be the father of her child.

In the event of a dispute over paternity English law contains procedures which will enable the presumption to be rebutted on the balance of probabilities—a task made infinitely easier by the availability of DNA testing in recent years. Such testing remains discretionary and, in the case of adults, the courts may only *direct* tests and not order them. Where an adult refuses to undergo such a test the court may draw adverse inferences against him or her.[25] In the case of a child, the law has recently changed to empower the courts to *order* a person who has the authority to consent on behalf of a child to produce that child for testing.[26]

[24] S 28(2) Human Fertilisation and Embryology Act 1990.
[25] S 23 Family Law Reform Act 1969 as amended.
[26] S 21(3) Family Law Reform Act 1969 as amended by S82 Child Support, Pensions and Social Security Act 2000 now provides:

A bodily sample may be taken from a person under the age of sixteen years . . .
(a) if the person who has care and control of him consents; or
(b) where that person does not consent, if the court considers that it would be in his best interests for the sample to be taken.

For the difficulties under the law before this amendment see *Re O and J (Paternity: Blood Tests)* [2000] 1 FLR 418. For the most recent decision under the new provision see *Re T (Paternity: Ordering Blood Tests)* [2001] 2 FLR 1190.

The courts have vacillated on the pros and cons of directing tests in individual cases to get at the truth of paternity, bearing in mind that the child also has an interest in having a stable family environment as do the various adults involved.[27] But there can be no doubt that the tide has been flowing strongly in the direction of establishing biological truth where possible.

The current attitude of the English courts to this question is demonstrated by *Re H and A (Paternity: Blood Tests)*[28] where, following an extra-marital affair, the wife gave birth to twins. She informed the man concerned that he was the father and allowed him some contact, but she then fell out with him and he brought a paternity suit which she successfully concealed from her husband for almost a year. The mother refused to consent to blood tests and the husband gave evidence to the effect that he would be likely to leave the family home if blood tests established that he was not the father. The judge refused to give the court's consent to a blood test on the children on the basis of a risk to the stability of the twins' family life.

The Court of Appeal allowed the appeal and remitted the application for retrial on the basis that the judge had given insufficient weight to the benefits of certainty, where there had been much speculation and gossip about the true position, and the judge's conclusion that the twins' family would be destroyed if the application was granted was not substantiated by the evidence—not least because it had been based on the assumption that the marriage was, in any event, sound which was not necessarily borne out by the evidence. Most significantly, the Court gave a clear indication that there would be few cases where the best interests of children would be served by the suppression of truth. The paternity of a child was now to be established by science and not by legal presumption or inference.

The recent English decisions are consistent with the trend elsewhere in Europe. Thus a Dutch law, which allowed only the mother's husband, and not the mother herself, to seek to rebut the *pater est* presumption was found to violate the ECHR.[29]

It should be noted that the mother, while under a statutory obligation to register the birth of the child, is under no such obligation to register the name of the man she believes to be the father[30]—though she will be under a qualified obligation to co-operate with the Child Support Agency where she is receiving state benefits.[31] Where, however, the mother does register a man as the father that man will be presumed to be the father and will be treated as the legal father. Such registration can only take place with the co-operation and attendance of the man concerned.

---

[27] See especially *Re F (A Minor) (Blood Tests: Parental Rights)* [1993] Fam.314. cf *Re H (Paternity: Blood Test)* [1996] 2 FLR 65.

[28] [2002] 1 FLR 1145.

[29] *Kroon v The Netherlands* [1994] 19 EHRR 263.

[30] Births and Deaths Registration Act 1953, s 10.

[31] Child Support Act 1991 s 6(7).

Under the Adoption and Children Act 2002, that man will also acquire parental responsibility when registered as the father of the child.[32] The present position under which the unmarried father does not have parental responsibility, unless he acquires it by agreement with the mother or court order,[33] is well known and I will not rehearse the arguments yet again. We should note however that the rule itself was found by the European Court *not* to violate the ECHR in *B v United Kingdom*[34] because it was thought that valid distinctions could be drawn by the State between the different circumstances in which biological paternity arises. Thus, it could be within the State's margin of appreciation to have a law which differentiated between married and unmarried fathers. Interestingly, the Court has held subsequently that a German law, which at the time differentiated between married and unmarried fathers in the matter of their *right of access* to their children, was in breach of several articles of the ECHR and in particular amounted to unjustified discrimination contrary to Article 14.[35]

This is a hugely significant ruling in the context of this chapter because it clearly means that any attempt by the law to differentiate openly between married and unmarried fathers in relation to contact applications would violate the ECHR.

Returning to the central question, how far can we say that these rules uphold the right of the child, visualised in the UN convention, to a legal connection with the father *from birth*? The picture is far from clear and is clouded further by the difficult question of when exactly 'family life' may be said to arise between the father and the child. What can be stated with absolute conviction is that the *mere fact* that genetic parentage is proved will not be sufficient to establish family life between them. This much is clear from the jurisprudence of the European Court but how much more is required is open to doubt.

The starting point must be the genetic connection itself. If this alone established family life then it would arise between the sperm donor and the child. In *G v The Netherlands*[36] the European Court rejected the argument that it did. We might view this as support for the proposition that family life ought not to arise between the child and the unintentional parent, in the sense that the sperm donor usually has no intention of assuming the responsibilities of parenthood. But we do not generally withhold either family life or the legal status of parenthood from the many who produce children unintentionally from intentional sexual relations. And if there is importance in the genetic connection (a big if) it ought not to matter greatly how that genetic link came into being. Conversely, neither family life nor legal parenthood come about solely on the basis of someone's intention to be a parent. If that were the case the commissioning parents in a surrogacy arrangement would be included.

---

[32] S 4 Children Act 1989, as amended by Adoption and Children Act 2002 s 111.
[33] Children Act 1989 s 4.
[34] [2000] 1 FLR 1.
[35] *Sahin v Germany; Sommerfeld v Germany; Hoffmann v Germany* [2002] 1 FLR 119.
[36] [1990] 16 EHRR 38. Cf Scott Baker J in *Rose v Secretary of State for Health and Human Fertilisation and Embryology Authority* [2002] 2 FLR 962.

What else then is required? The answer which the European Court has thus far given to this question is that 'certain ties' must exist between the father and the child. In the leading case of *Soderback v Sweden*[37] it was established that cohabitation between the mother and father at some point was *not* an essential prerequisite to 'family life'. In that case, a step-parent adoption opposed by the natural father, the court found that certain ties did exist between the father and the child but that interference with the father's family life through adoption could be justified on the basis of the best interests of the child. In *Soderback* the ties in question appear to have been primarily the father's commitment to contact even though little had taken place. In *Kroon v the Netherlands*[38] family life was established on the basis that a relationship of sufficient constancy to create de facto family ties existed. Here the parties had a relationship of considerable duration and four children together but had never cohabited.

The English courts have confronted the issue in a string of cases in which the mother has wanted to place a baby confidentially for adoption without involving the father or indeed, if at all possible, informing him of the birth.[39] The question has been how far the ECHR requires that he be informed of, and allowed to participate in, the proceedings. The background is that under English law the father's consent to adoption is not required unless he has acquired parental responsibility,[40] but the court has a discretion about whether to join him as a party to the proceedings or otherwise allow him to participate. The question is, should it do so, and this may largely turn on whether or not the court feels that family life has arisen between him and the child.

The courts have now given a rather robust signal that the normal rule will be that the father should be informed and given the opportunity to participate. The corollary is that the mother will usually lose her traditional rights of privacy and confidentiality which may be seen as aspects of her wider right to respect for private life. There will however be exceptions. The first is where there has been a track record of violence perpetrated by the father.[41] This exception is entirely consistent with the gathering case law which, in essence and in my view rightly, amounts to saying that the father will forfeit his prima facie right of contact through violence.[42] In this context he may lose his voice to object to adoption. It is consistent also with the thesis in this chapter that rights are accompanied by responsibilities. Failure to discharge the responsibility may lead to loss of the right. The second exception is more controversial. This is that insufficient ties exist between the father and child for them to have established family life.[43] This

---

[37] [1999] 1 FLR 250.
[38] Above n 28.
[39] Above n 21.
[40] Many more such fathers will acquire PR in the future—see n 31 above.
[41] *Re M (Adoption: Rights of Natural Father)* [2001] 1 FLR 745.
[42] The leading decision now being the consolidated appeal in *Re L (A Child) (Contact: Domestic Violence)* [2001] 4 All ER 609.
[43] *Re H; Re G (Adoption: Consultation of Unmarried Fathers)* [2001] 1 FLR 646.

will usually arise because the relationship between the father and mother broke down before the child was born. Perhaps it was no more than a passing sexual encounter, a one-night stand, devoid of any meaning beyond the sudden and temporary flush of sexual excitement. Such a man, kept in the dark about the pregnancy and birth, may find it difficult to argue that there exists between him and the child a relationship which can properly be characterised as family life. Why this is a more controversial situation than the first is that the lack of connection between the child and the father may not have arisen through any culpability on the part of the father (unless it is deemed culpable to have casual sex) but because the mother has chosen, for whatever reason, to cut him out of her life and that of the child. Such a situation requires engagement with some difficult questions of competing human rights.

Perhaps the two central issues which emerge from the legal regime which governs paternal affiliation are as follows. First, to what extent should the legal system embody rules which in effect permit one parent (the mother) to control the extent of the relationship between the child and the other parent (the father)? How far, in other words, is it consistent with the very notion of human rights to make their realisation contingent on actions taken by others? Secondly, what is the State's role in the creation of family relationships? Here the most interesting issue for the future, given that the ECHR is a 'living instrument', will be the extent to which the notion of the *positive* obligations of the State to foster family life is developed.

4. THE MAINTENANCE OF FAMILY RELATIONSHIPS

It will be recalled that the concern of the UN Convention is not simply with the initial right of the child to knowledge of parents but with an ongoing right, as far as possible, to be cared for by them and to maintain direct and regular contact with them when separated from them. How far are these objectives achieved in England?

In broad terms we are concerned here with the principle of contact since the preservation of contact is crucial to the long-term survival of relationships and to the chances of eventual reunification of parent and child.[44] What does this imply in terms of rights and obligations and how enforceable is the right of contact or should it be?

Historically, contact was seen as a right of the *parent*, one aspect of the pre-Children Act concept of parental rights and duties. Then, in 1973, Wrangham J, in a much quoted dictum, described it as a right of the *child*.[45] This was seized upon by those who were keen to find a basis for denying the existence of a

---

[44] A matter clearly recognised by the European Court of Human Rights, especially where the child is in care. See, for example, *K and T v Finland* [2001] 2 FLR 707.
[45] *M v M (Child : Access)* [1973] All ER 81.

parental right of contact despite the evidence that contact disputes always have been and still are about disputed claims brought by *adults*. Notwithstanding, the Children Act 1989 seemed to give added credence to the view of contact as *solely* the right of the child, first by introducing a new form of contact order with child-centred terminology and, secondly, by reconceptualising the parent's legal relationship with the child as one of responsibility rather then rights.[46]

In October 2000 the ECHR became part of English law and it was necessary, rather quickly, to abandon any pretence that parents lacked rights. They quite clearly had them and one of them was a right of contact. This should occasion little surprise. Even before the Children Act, the House of Lords in *Re KD*[47] had made plain its view that, in general, it was correct to state that a parent had a right of access (as it then was) to his or her child and that the normal assumption was that a child would benefit from contact with the natural parent. Both the right and the assumption could, however, be displaced if the welfare of the child required it.

So where do we stand today? The central theoretical standpoint of this chapter is located in what I would call the 'mutuality principle'. According to this, we do not have to choose between the ideas of contact as a right of the child or a right of the parent. It is *both*. The child has a right of contact with the mother and with the father and each of them has a right of contact with the child. These rights carry with them reciprocal duties—reciprocal in two senses. First, a right in one person implies a duty in another. The second is that this right also implies responsibility in the right-holder or, put another way, the right may be forfeited if there is good reason to believe that it will not be exercised responsibly. How might this conceptual framework operate in practice?

Let us take first the correlation of rights in one person and duties in another. Suppose we say that contact is a right of the child. If this is correct it implies duties on the part of each of the parents. In the numerically more common situation of a mother who is primary caretaker and a non-residential father, the child's right to contact with the father implies a duty on the mother to allow it, in so far as it is reasonably exercised. But, it may be objected, if there is to be a duty to allow contact, why is the father not under a duty to exercise it? The answer to this question is straightforward. He *should* be and he is in some jurisdictions. Scots law, unlike English law, provides expressly that a parent has both a right and duty in relation to contact. One of the listed responsibilities of a parent is 'if the child is not living with the parent, to maintain personal relations and direct contact with the child on a regular basis' replicating in Scots law the language of the UN Convention.[48] But surely such an obligation would be unenforceable? Perhaps it would, but its primary function would be to underline society's view of the importance of the continuing relationship between parent

---

[46]   Children Act 1989 s 8 and s 2 respectively.
[47]   *Re KD (A minor) (Ward : Termination of Access)* [1988] AC 806.
[48]   Children (Scotland) Act 1995 s 1.

and child and would not be about rigid enforcement of human relationships, if anyone is naïve enough to believe that were ever possible. In short it would be a message worth conveying in legislation, whether or not capable of enforcement. Neither should we rule out the possibility that there will be human rights based litigation by children seeking to put pressure on their parents to see them.

What about the second aspect? Taking the same example, the exercise of the right of contact by the father should be accompanied by responsible behaviour on his part. This indeed reflects the recent stance of the courts in relation to violent fathers.[49] The violent or abusive father may legitimately be denied contact not, as some have argued, because men have no right of contact with their children but because, although they do have it, they have forfeited it by their adverse conduct.

What other forms of adverse conduct might lead to the right of contact being forfeited? I would suggest that other forms of abuse, such as sexual or emotional abuse, which might not be easily classified as 'violence', can and do result in effect in the forfeiture of contact rights. In these situations a compromise can sometimes be reached in which only *indirect*, or supervised contact is allowed.[50] It is then perhaps the right of *direct* contact which is being forfeited. Beyond violence or abuse it is more difficult to conceive of behaviour which should lead to forfeiture of the right of contact. Although this is not suggested, it is interesting to speculate on whether a culpable failure to provide financial support for the child should have this effect.[51] There has long been a reluctance to accept the association between the payment of child support and the level of contact with the child, yet there does appear to be some evidence from the United States that such an association indeed exists (Seltzer, 2000).

Rights are not absolute. The nature of rights has been the subject of extensive and ongoing debate by philosophers (Simmonds, 2002). In this context they amount, it is suggested, in effect to fundamental presumptions which may be rebutted—but only for good reason. The courts are entirely right to attempt to distinguish between cases in which a mother has a sound reason for refusing the father contact[52] and those in which she does not have one.[53] In the former, the normal duty to allow contact is removed for good cause while in the latter it exists and the law should at least *attempt* to enforce it.

---

[49] N 41 above.

[50] See, for example, *Re S (Violent Parent : Indirect Contact)* [2000] 1 FLR 481 and *Re L (Contact: Genuine Fear)* [2002] 1 FLR 621.

[51] In *Re H (Parental Responsibility : Maintenance)* [1996] 1 FLR 867 the court took the view that failure to pay child support ought not to deprive an otherwise devoted father of parental responsibility even though the court was critical of this failure.

[52] As in *Re L (A Child) (Contact: Domestic Violence)* [2000] 4 All ER 609 and other cases involving violence.

[53] For an admittedly extreme example see *A v N (Committal : Refusal of Contact)* [1997] 1 FLR 533 where the mother, who continued to dispute the father's paternity despite clear DNA results establishing it, was eventually committed to prison for persistent flouting of contact orders.

If fathers and mothers have correlative rights and duties of contact, the question which arises is how to characterise the child's own position. We seem comfortable enough with the notion that the child has a *right* of contact and I have argued elsewhere (Bainham, 1997) that it would not be entirely unreasonable to postulate a corresponding *duty* on the child to co-operate with contact arrangements, though any such duty could only reasonably be imposed on older children. This suggestion has been received with a certain incredulity. Yet, it is a logical enough deduction from everything else. If we say that a parent has a right of contact with a child, how meaningful is such a right unless the child is under a corresponding duty? Again, I am not suggesting that any such duty would be enforceable, or even that attempts should necessarily be made to enforce it. But the principle, I would suggest, is sound. In the case of a baby or young child, the child will lack the autonomy and independent capacity to assert any rights for himself. Such rights have to be urged on his behalf by others—in the above example the father would have to assert the child's right of contact with him as well as his own. The duty of the child to allow contact is then translated into a duty performed for the child by the mother. But if we are talking about 'Gillick-competent' children we may reasonably ask why it is that they have a right to expect growing legal independence without accepting the responsibility which may be thought to go with it.

Finally, there is the question of the State's responsibility in fostering contact, something acknowledged in the UN convention. Where we are concerned with *public law*, there are statutory duties under the Children Act regarding the promotion of contact between children, parents and other relatives.[54] These apply, as we have seen, where the child is being looked after by the local authority and, where the child is in care, there is a statutory code in section 34 of the Act providing for judicial control over the contact question. This code was formulated following decisions of the European Court in which the UK government had sought (unsuccessfully) to argue that contact was no longer a right of the parent.

What is also clear is that the duty on the part of the State to seek reunification of parent and child in this public context is taken very seriously indeed by the European Court.[55] What it has also emphasised, specifically in relation to the maintenance of contact, is the need for *very strict scrutiny* of decisions which would have the effect of curtailing family relationships such as the ending of contact or the placing of a child for adoption. Italy was recently found to be in violation of these principles.[56] Article 6 of the European Convention requires that a legal system provide effective access to the courts for those who may be aggrieved by actions of the state. Following the recent decision of the House of Lords in *Re S (Minors); Re W (Minors)*[57] (Tolson, 2002), which fell just short of

---

[54] Children Act 1989 Sched 2 para 15.
[55] The leading case is *Johansen v Norway* (1996) 23 EHRR33.
[56] *S and G v Italy* [2000] 2 FLR 771.
[57] *Re S (Minors) (Care Order : Implementation of Care Plan); Re W (Minors) (Care Order: Adequacy of Care Plan)* [2002] 1 FLR 815.

finding the public law procedures of the Children Act 1989 incompatible with the Convention, there may need to be amending legislation to give to parents greater opportunity to challenge before the courts important administrative decisions taken in relation to children looked after by the state (see Miles and Lindley, this volume).

What, however, may come as a surprise is the clear view of the European Court that the State has a responsibility also in relation to what we would normally characterise as *private* disputes over contact and, as such, matters of *private law*. What, therefore, we view as private may in this sense be seen as public in that the State may be held accountable for its failure to make appropriate interventions which might have prevented a violation of convention rights. Perhaps the leading case is *Hokkanen v Finland*.[58] Here the state of Finland was found to have violated the rights of a father who, following the death of the mother, had become embroiled in a very long dispute with the maternal grandparents over his daughter. It was found that the national authorities had an obligation to facilitate reunion, especially through the steps taken to enforce the access orders which the grandparents had repeatedly flouted. There was consequently a breach of the father's rights under Article 8. It was recognised in *Hokkanen* that the duty on the State to facilitate the reunion of parent and child was not limitless or absolute. It was rather a matter of evaluating whether a fair balance had been struck between the various interests involved. In the more recent case of *Glaser v UK*[59] the British authorities were found, in contrast, not to have violated convention rights. They had taken all steps they could reasonably have been expected to take (though ultimately unsuccessful) to enforce an English contact order where the mother had managed to disappear to Scotland. As noted earlier, breaches of the ECHR were found in Germany where the State produced laws which discriminated between married and unmarried fathers in relation to contact—again something which we would normally classify as an issue of private law.[60]

In this section I have argued that contact is a right which entails corresponding duties. The fact that it is qualified and may be displaced, especially by considerations of the welfare of the child, is not at all a reason for denying its existence. The maintenance or continuation of family life between parent and child is achieved legally through the contact regime which, at every turn, has important human rights implications. The principle of contact ought also to apply to other familial relationships once established at the social level. It is doubtful, however, whether it can be described as a 'right' enjoyed by people other than parents and children. All those wishing to have contact with the child recognised in law, or otherwise to secure their social relationships with the child, are dependent on the courts' discretion and will usually require leave to

---

[58] [1996] 1 FLR 289.
[59] [2001] 1 FLR 153.
[60] Above n 34.

get before them. It is nonetheless likely that a meaningful social relationship will be reinforced with a contact order and it is clear beyond doubt, from a number of cases involving men who turned out not to be genetic fathers, that contact is not dependent on establishing the genetic link. This is also demonstrated by more than one decision providing for contact between a child and a man who co-operated in techniques of assisted reproduction with the mother. Indeed, in one remarkable case, the court allowed indirect contact between the child and such a man where conception did not occur until after the mother's relationship with him had broken down, by which time she had a new partner.[61] The claim for contact here could not have been based on either a genetic or social link with the child and is perhaps a rare illustration of the law attaching decisive importance to the intention of becoming a parent—albeit a frustrated one.

The Adoption and Children Act 2002 will make further provision for the continuation of social relationships with children by the introduction of a new status of 'special guardianship', the extension of residence orders to the child's 18th birthday and the reduction in the qualification period for local authority foster parents to apply for orders under the Children Act from three years with the child to just one.[62] These measures, which collectively can be viewed as 'alternatives for permanence', recognise the importance of the child's social relationships but, as alternatives to adoption, they will also facilitate the preservation of the child's relationships with the birth parents as opposed to its termination.

5. THE TERMINATION OF FAMILY RELATIONSHIPS

The emphasis in adoption is of course on the *creation* of a new family for a child but the English model of adoption also brings about a legal *termination* of the child's existing family relationships.[63] It is that aspect of adoption which is relevant to this chapter. When the law intervenes in the family, the effect is generally only to restrict the exercise of parental responsibility by those holding it and, in some cases, to give it to others who do not already have it. In general it can be said that the law gives but the law does not take away. The effect of court orders is neither to terminate the status of parent nor the holding of parental responsibility. This, to a large extent, reflects the policy of the Children Act which was to give effect to a notion of 'partnership' between parents, local authorities and others. In these instances, parents remain parents although the question of what exactly they lose under various court orders is a subject worthy of greater attention than it has received.

---

[61] *Re D (Parental Responsibility : IVF Baby)* [2001] 1 FLR 972.
[62] S 9 Children Act as amended by ss 113, 114 and 115 Adoption and Children Act 2002.
[63] S 67 Adoption and Children Act 2002.

Adoption does not sit well with these objectives, nor with the notion that parents and children have increasingly enforceable human rights regarding the preservation of their relationships. It is not surprising, therefore, that adoption is becoming a major battleground on which to fight out some of the conflicts surrounding human rights in the family. The issue of the loss of a parent through adoption and its implications for the human rights of the child came up for consideration by the Court of Appeal and House of Lords in *Re B (Adoption: Natural Parent)*.[64] It should be emphasised that this was not a case in which there was a contest between the father and the mother. *Both* were supporting the adoption of the child by the father. But the Official Solicitor, acting for the child, thought that the child's human rights would be compromised and decided to challenge the adoption plan. The facts were remarkable.

This was one of a number of cases in which, following a short-term relationship, the mother becomes pregnant, decides to have the child but then wishes to place the child for adoption—all without involving the father.[65] In this case the mother said that she had no maternal instincts, did not glance at the child at the time of birth and had no contact with her thereafter. She had previously placed an elder daughter for adoption. She misled the local authority about the whereabouts of the father but things took an unusual turn when a secretary who worked for the authority recognised his name in the adoption papers. The father, with the mother's acquiescence, gave up work, looked after the child and then sought to adopt her. The mother had no lasting interest in the child (beyond wishing to have an annual photograph and progress report) and was not opposed to adoption by the father. Adoption (as the law currently stands) would have the advantage of giving parental responsibility to the father.[66] But, much more significantly, it would also cut the legal link between the mother and the child—something the father badly wanted. He was worried that at some point, and despite her declared intentions to the contrary, the mother might seek to disrupt things by re-entering the child's life.

English law will only permit the adoption of a child by one natural parent to the exclusion of the other in limited circumstances.[67] Except where a parent is dead or missing, it must be shown that there is some reason justifying the exclusion of a parent and the court must make plain what this is. In this case the judge granted the adoption, citing as the reason for excluding the mother her rejection of the child from birth. Ultimately the House of Lords accepted that this was a legitimate exercise of the judge's discretion and restored the adoption order which the Court of Appeal had set aside.

---

[64] [2002] 1 FLR 196.

[65] See cases cited at n 22 above.

[66] The advantages of adoption in this respect will be reduced now that the majority of unmarried fathers will acquire parental responsibility automatically through the process of birth registration. However, a significant number of fathers will still not be registered.

[67] At the time of *Re B* the relevant provision was the Adoption Act 1976 s 15(3). This provision is substantially re-enacted in the Adoption and Children Act 2002 s 51(4).

I want to focus on the Court of Appeal's approach to the issues despite the fact that its decision did not prevail. In my view it represents a much better engagement with the human rights questions in the case. The Court of Appeal[68] (and especially Hale LJ) took the position that it was generally in the best interests of children to have two legal parents and two legal families and that the exclusion of one could only be justified under the ECHR if this was *necessary* in a democratic society. A particular feature of the Court of Appeal's reasoning was that the child would lose the legal link with the mother and the maternal relatives with little corresponding benefit to the child. This was so because the security which the father craved need not involve the use of the 'last resort' remedy of adoption but could be achieved by other means. In this case the Court of Appeal produced a package of measures for the father which included a residence order to last until the child's majority, sole power to apply for a passport for the child and an unfettered right to take her abroad, together with an order prohibiting the mother from making further applications without the court's permission. But to go further and allow the adoption was, for the Court of Appeal, a disproportionate interference with the child's right to respect for her family life with her mother and her mother's family.

What is not clear is whether the Court would have taken the same view if it had been the *mother* seeking to adopt and if it had been the child's link with the father and the paternal family which had been at stake. Hale LJ attached importance to the fact that family life between mother and child arose *at birth*. Were it otherwise, she said, the State could always remove children from mothers at birth with impunity and without fear of contravening the ECHR. That only needed stating for it to be clear how wrong that would be. The point has been made above that the child's relationship with the father *at birth* is viewed differently, though whether this can continue to be defended in an era of commitment to human rights is open to doubt.

Two other features of the Court of Appeal's decision may be highlighted. The first relates to the issue of intentional and unintentional parenthood alluded to above. The Court seemed in no doubt that the law should not allow the abandonment of parental status merely because a parent (in this case the mother) had unintentionally borne a child. This is consistent with the law's general stance on parental responsibility which may not be voluntarily relinquished.[69] It is also the position taken in relation to liability for child support since, as Lady Thatcher once reminded us—'parenthood is for life'. If parents in general were allowed to 'opt out' in cases of unintentional parenthood, the queue of natural fathers wishing to do so would be a very long one indeed. Nonetheless, in the specific case of adoption, courts are only now beginning to impose restraints on the traditional right of unmarried mothers to give their children up for adop-

---

[68] *Re B (Adoption by One Natural Parent to Exclusion of Other)* [2001] 1 FLR 589.
[69] Children Act 1989 s 2(9).

tion. Today this is viewed as something which can no longer be regarded as the exclusive preserve of the mother.

The decision of the House of Lords in *Re B* is dismissive of these human rights considerations, as is the present government whose enthusiasm for adoption evidently knows no bounds (see Eekelaar, this volume). A number of provisions in the recent Adoption and Children Act 2002 warrant close examination from the angle of human rights. There are omissions too, notably the absence of any provisions giving official encouragement to the principle of post-adoption contact, the child's right to be told his or her adoptive status, or to object to adoption at a certain age. These oversights, if such they be, may suggest that the preservation of the child's link with the birth family is being under-valued. For reasons of space I can only concentrate on what is perhaps the most controversial provision in the Act: that the welfare principle (which is to be extended throughout adoption law) is to govern the question of dispensing with a parent's consent. This proposal departs from the recommendations of the Interdepartmental Committee which reviewed adoption law in the early 1990s (Department of Health and Welsh Office, 1992). The Adoption Review thought that adoption ought not to be granted if it was seen to be only *marginally* better than other alternative solutions. It favoured dispensing with consent only where it could be demonstrated that

> the advantages to the child of becoming part of a new family and having a new status are so significantly greater than the advantages of any alternative option as to justify overriding the wishes of the parents.

The key question is whether the unqualified application of the welfare principle to this issue is human rights compliant. Indeed the whole question of the relationship between the welfare principle and human rights obligations has been the subject of recent academic debate (Herring, 1999; Eekelaar, 2002). The government clearly thinks that the application of the welfare principle to the test of dispensing with parental consent would comply with the ECHR but I am not so sure. The position under the Convention was considered by the European Court in *Soderback v Sweden*[70] and *Johansen v Norway*.[71] *Soderback* makes it plain that adoption, though a drastic interference with family life, may be ultimately justified on the basis of the welfare of the child. In that case adoption by the step-father who had a secure social relationship with the child was thought to be consistent with the best interests of the child where there had been very little contact with the natural father. But for present purposes *Johansen v Norway* is more significant since it deals with the adoption of children in public care—the area in which the government is most enthusiastic about driving up the adoption figures (Department of Health, 2000). In *Johansen*, a mother's young child was taken into care and her access (contact) was terminated with a view to

[70] [1999] 1 FLR 250.
[71] (1996) 23 EHRR 33.

permanent placement for adoption. In these circumstances the European Court found a violation of the mother's rights under Article 8. The Court found that the measures taken were particularly far-reaching, they totally deprived the mother of her family life with the child and they were inconsistent with the aim of reuniting them. Such measures should only be applied in 'exceptional circumstances' where there was an 'overriding requirement' pertaining to the child's interests. In simple language the Court saw adoption as a measure of last resort not to be invoked lightly but only where there was a demonstrable necessity for it.

This restriction on the use of adoption was picked up by the English Court of Appeal in the comparatively recent case of *Re B (Adoption Order)*.[72] Here the child had been placed by the mother in foster care but, throughout this arrangement, the child had an excellent relationship with the father and his family. On the father's application for a residence order the Court instead granted a residence order to the foster mother, accompanied by a parental responsibility order and generous contact for the father. The father was prohibited from applying for further orders without the court's permission. Everyone, *except the local authority*, was happy with this result. But the authority pressed the foster mother to apply for adoption which the judge granted.

The Court of Appeal allowed the father's appeal in a decision which shows sensitivity of, and a feel for, the human rights issues involved. The Court's view in essence was that where parties, who lived in close proximity, were in agreement with the inclusive arrangement which had been fashioned, the plans were fundamentally inconsistent with an adoption order. The judge had failed to have proper regard to the interference with the father's family life which adoption would entail and whether it was a *necessary* and *proportionate* response to the situation. The Court reiterated another traditional principle of English adoption law, stretching back for at least 30 years,[73] that there may be more than one reasonable view of whether adoption is in a child's best interests. It was perfectly possible, therefore, that a parent could reasonably disagree with the professional view (also reasonably held) which favoured adoption. The Court said that the judicial licence to override the sustained objection of a natural parent would be stretched to unjustifiable limits if adoption were to be allowed in these circumstances.

It seems that we are about to stretch the limits. The orthodox interpretation of the welfare principle is that disputes should be determined on the basis that the court's *sole* consideration is the best interests of the child.[74] The child's welfare is *paramount*. According to this interpretation any interests or rights of adults are subsumed in the general investigation of the best solution for the child and have no independent status. This is *not* the approach required under the

---

[72] [2001] 2 FLR 26.

[73] The locus classicus being the speech of Lord Hailsham in *Re W (An Infant)* [1971] 682.

[74] According to the long-accepted interpretation of the welfare principle by Lord MacDermott in *J v C* [1970] 668 at 710–11.

ECHR where the rights of all parties have to be carefully weighed and balanced (see Herring, 1999; Eekelaar, 2002). English law has expressly *not* applied an unrestrained welfare test to the question of dispensing with parental consent for similar reasons associated with the rights of parents. The application of the welfare test could now mean that a parent's relationship is terminated with the child merely because, on welfare grounds, the proposed adopters might provide a better home for the child. But the law does not generally sanction the removal of children from their parents just because they are not optimal parents or because someone else could do better than them.[75] In my view, if the welfare principle is to govern this crucial question, it will need to be reinterpreted in a way which openly admits the relevance of parental rights while attaching a good deal of significance to the welfare of the child. The termination of family relationships undoubtedly raises questions of rights as well as welfare, and the law should be seen to be acknowledging this (Eekelaar, 2002).

6. CONCLUDING REMARKS

It is fashionable to say that there are limits to what the law can achieve in the field of family relationships. Relationships between members of the family cannot be forced and if they cannot, so the argument goes, law is redundant. In this chapter I have sought to argue that this is a mistaken view; that the law performs an important role in the creation, maintenance and termination of family relationships. It has an especially crucial part to play in their initial creation. The contrary view seems to me to imply that as a society we only comply with normative rules for fear of punishment if we disobey them. This pays insufficient regard to two factors which, I believe, contribute to compliance with rules of behaviour. The first is a commonly held belief that it is appropriate to comply with legal norms unless there is a very good reason for not doing so. The second is that, for the most part, legal principles will be reflective of the values commonly (admittedly not universally) held in a particular society.

And so it is with contact. The fact that so many parents fashion their own arrangements for contact and that so much contact takes place, probably reflects in part an appreciation that the law expects parents to continue to discharge this most important aspect of their parental responsibility. But, even more, it reflects a prevalent view in society that the relationship of parent and child is indeed a fundamental one which ought to be sustained. I do not believe that a significant number of people see their children, or allow others to see them, because they feel threatened by the prospect of being fined or imprisoned if they do not. In this sense the whole question of the enforcement of contact,

---

[75] The compulsory removal of children on a long-term basis requires that the 'threshold' test in s 31 (2) Children Act 1989 be satisfied. This is essentially a matter of proving that the child is suffering or is at risk of suffering 'significant harm' if a care or supervision order is not made.

and to a lesser extent orders for contact, pales into insignificance alongside the assertion of the principle of contact itself.

I have attempted to draw attention to the ways in which I would argue the law is currently failing to assert and defend sufficiently well the basic human relationship between parent and child. In several respects it is my view that neither English law not the jurisprudence of the European Court go far enough in this respect. At the same time it is important to remember that the ECHR is a 'living instrument' and that we can expect further evolution in the obligations of the State under it. The rather vaguely defined 'positive obligations' will undoubtedly undergo further refinement in the coming years.

What then is wrong and what might we learn from the experience of other jurisdictions? In attempting to answer these questions we have the benchmark of the UN Convention which, as we have seen, asserts the right of the child from birth to know and be cared for by his or her parents as far as possible. In relation to the *creation* of family relationships the key controversies surround paternal affiliation. Under English law whether or not this is conclusively established has a great deal to do with whether the mother wants it to be. In Scandinavia and in many civil law jurisdictions the matter is approached differently. The search for a father for the child is given greater emphasis in Latin America, for example, than it is in England (Pereira, 2002). In the Nordic countries establishing paternity in all cases of childbirth is seen as a responsibility of the State (Eriksson and Saldeen, 1993). Inevitably this must conceptualise the mother as under a legal duty to co-operate. Many civilian jurisdictions stop short of this but do facilitate the establishment of paternity by providing formal mechanisms for a man who believes himself to be the father to 'acknowledge' or 'recognize' the child as his. In some jurisdictions such an acknowledgement can be made *before* as well as after the birth of the child. Some form of acknowledgement or recognition applies in many countries in continental Europe, Latin America and Francophone Africa (Teshome, 2002). Where the identity of the father is known, the approach of English law, in common with that in many other jurisdictions, has been to withhold a full parental status by giving parental responsibility only to the mother. The Adoption and Children Act 2002 changes the position radically and a large number of unmarried fathers will henceforth acquire parental responsibility on being registered as the father.

This reform will not however address those cases which have thrown up the most serious human rights issues. These have often arisen where the father is not cohabiting with the mother and may not even be aware of the initial pregnancy and subsequent birth of the child. The reforms will not engage with this problem because these men will not very often be registered as fathers. The solution would be to confer automatic parental responsibility *on proof of paternity* whether or not the man in question is registered as the father. This is the solution which has commended itself to most of the countries of Eastern Europe in the post-war period and to Australia in 1975. It has the distinct advantage that the status of illegitimacy may be conclusively abolished alongside it.

Yet, according to the European Court, 'family life' may or may not arise between the father and child on proof of paternity. This gender-specific approach to the commencement of family life is also something which should be re-evaluated in the light of the gender-neutral commitment in the UN Convention to the child's relationship with *both* mother and father *from birth*. It should be added that no convincing reason has yet been advanced for distinguishing in this way between the wider *maternal* and *paternal* families in terms of the contribution which they might make to the child's life.

In relation to the *maintenance* of family relationships through ongoing contact, there needs to be a sharper awareness that contact is a right with accompanying duties. The law is correct to uphold the principle that primary caretakers should be obliged to allow contact between the child and the non-residential parent and the courts should at least attempt to enforce it, if only to underline the seriousness with which the issue is viewed (Lord Chancellor's Department, 2002). But, equally, there needs to be a clear understanding that both the right and the duty may be displaced by adverse behaviour which threatens the well-being of the primary caretaker or the child. The law again has an important function to perform in distinguishing between legitimate and illegitimate reasons for refusal of contact. One relatively straightforward reform which ought to be introduced would be, as in Scotland, to place the non-residential parent under a statutory duty to exercise contact regularly and responsibly. Commentators have rightly pointed out that the much larger problem posed by non-residential fathers is *indifference* rather than *interference*. The new Austrian child law which came into force in 2001 (Vershraegen, 2002) recognises these principles by withdrawing the parent's right to be consulted on matters of upbringing where contact has been abused.

The characterisation of contact as a right has however been subjected to a powerful critique by certain feminist writers who see a gendered aspect to the issue (Smart and Neale, 1999). According to this view, mothers following divorce see their position with their children in terms of *needs* and seldom mention *rights*, whereas fathers talk a great deal about rights and are conceptualised by the legal system as the possessors of rights (see Day Sclater and Kaganas, this volume). It is not my intention here to dispute these perceptions which do appear to be supported by empirical evidence. While men and women have formal equality in the sense that, with very few exceptions, domestic legislation and international conventions refer to the gender neutral *parent* as opposed to the gender specific *mother* or *father*,[76] these writers would maintain that the reality is different. Equal rights for men, especially in the formal retention of parental responsibility following divorce, means in many cases giving out rights

---

[76] A rare exception being Children Act 1989 s 2 which governs the allocation of parental responsibility and distinguishes between mothers and fathers in the context of the unmarried family. But even this distinction will be substantially eroded in practice by the Adoption and Children Act 2002 which will give automatic parental responsibility to unmarried fathers whose paternity is registered—see n 31 above.

without responsibility. Smart and Neale are, from this perspective, critical of current legislation which may be seen as supporting a free-floating concept of rights which has no commensurate presumption about responsibilities or quality of fathering and which is capable of enhancing 'gendered power without accountability' (Smart and Neale, 1999).

It is impossible to argue with the evidence that the overwhelming majority of primary carers are women or that many men fail, for whatever reason, to discharge the responsibilities of parenthood following separation and divorce. But, the solution is not to abandon the concept of rights or to deny the role which law can play in sustaining fundamental relationships in difficult circumstances. One necessary reform, as argued above, is rather to place men under clearer legal duties to remain involved with their children and to seek out ways of facilitating this continued involvement. Rights should not exist without responsibility, but the answer is not to remove the rights but to promote and if necessary attempt to enforce the obligations which go with them. It should also be said that although the concept of rights may be perceived to be gendered, there are quite a number of reported instances in which *mothers* have sought to invoke their right of contact with their children. We ought not to forget that two of the leading cases in English law on rights of contact *both* involved *mothers*.[77] And, as the case of *Ignaccollo-Zenide v Romania*[78] demonstrates, it may be the mother who is seeking to enforce her rights under the ECHR against the father. There are also many examples of mothers attempting to recover abducted children from the possession of their fathers under the Hague Convention governing child abduction (Smith, this volume). It would therefore be a mistake to view rights as a concept which can only benefit men as against women. The evidence is otherwise.

Where the issue of terminating the relationship of parent and child arises in adoption proceedings there needs to be an ever-vigilant appreciation of rights. The severing of the parental tie has always been regarded as a grave issue and it should continue to be regarded as such. The ECHR *requires* that adoption be seen as a last resort where reunification of parent and child has ultimately proved impossible. It must be a necessary and proportionate response to the child's situation. There is nothing in the ECHR or in the decisions of the European Court capable of justifying the cavalier attitude to rights displayed by the present government in the Adoption and Children Act 2002 (Department of Health, 2000) and by the judicial committee of the House of Lords in *Re* B. This basic disregard for rights is liable to result in a series of challenges to the new legislation. And so it should. The relationship of parent and child is fundamental to both. The law should be defending it strongly and vigorously—and be seen to be doing so.

---

[77] *Re KD (A Minor) (Ward : Termination of Access)* [1988] AC 806 and *Re M (Contact: Welfare Test)* [1995] 1 FLR 274.
[78] (2001) 31 EHRR 7.

REFERENCES

BAILEY-HARRIS, R, BARRON, J and PEARCE, J, 'Settlement Culture and the Use of The "No Order" Principle under the Children Act 1989' (1999) 11 *Child and Family Law Quarterly* 53.

BAINHAM, A, 'Honour Thy Father and Thy Mother': Children's Rights and Children's Duties' in G Douglas and LSebba (eds), *Children's Rights and Traditional Values* (Aldershot, Ashgate, 1998).

—— 'Can We Protect Children and Protect their Rights?' (2002) 32 *Family Law* 279.

DAVIS, G, 'Love in a Cold Climate—Disputes About Children in the Aftermath of Parental Separation' in S Cretney (ed.), *Family Law: Essays for the New Millennium* (Bristol, Family Law, 2000).

Department of Health and Welsh Office, *Review of Adoption Law* (London, HMSO, 1992).

Department of Health, *Adoption: A New Approach* (Cm 5017, 2000).

DOUGLAS, G, 'The Significance of International Law for the Development of Family Law in England and Wales' in C Bridge (ed), *Family Law Towards the Millennium: Essays for P M Bromley* (London, Butterworths, 1997).

EEKELAAR, J, 'Beyond the Welfare Principle' (2002) 14 *Child and Family Law Quarterly* 237.

ERIKSSON, A and SALDEEN, A, 'Parenthood and Science' in J Eekelaar and P Sarcevic (eds), *Parenthood in Modern Society* (Dordrecht, Martinus Nijhoff, 1993).

HERRING, J, 'The Human Rights Act and the Welfare Principle in Family Law—Conflicting or Complementary?' (1999) 11 *Child and Family Law Quarterly* 223.

KILKELLY, U, *The Child and the European Convention on Human Rights* (Aldershot, Ashgate, 1999).

KING, M, *A Better World for Children?* (London and New York, Routledge, 1997).

LE BLANC, LJ, *The Convention on the Rights of the Child* (Lincoln and London, University of Nebraska Press, 1995).

Lord Chancellor's Department, *Making Contact Work: A Report to the Lord Chancellor on the Facilitation of Arrangements for Contact Between Children and Their Non-Residential Parents and the Enforcement of Court Orders for Contact* (Lord Chancellor's Department, 2002).

LOWE, NV, 'English Adoption Law: Past, Present and Future' in SN Katz, J Eekelaar and M Maclean (eds), *Cross Currents: Family Law and Policy in the US and England* (Oxford, Oxford University Press, 2000).

MINAMIKATA, S and TAMAKI, T, 'Family Law in Japan during 2000', *The International Survey of Family Law* (Bristol, Family Law, 2000 edn).

PEREIRA, R DA CUNHA, 'Brazilian Family Law in the Twenty-first Century and Psychoanalysis', *International Survey of Family Law* (Bristol, Family Law, 2002 edn.).

RUBELLIN-DEVICHI, J, 'France: How Matters Stand Now in Relation to Family Law Reform', *International Survey of Family Law* (Bristol, Family Law, 2000 edn).

SCHRAMA, W, 'Reforms in Dutch Family Law during the Course of 2001: Increased Pluriformity and Complexity', *International Survey of Family Law* (Bristol, Family Law, 2002 edn).

SELTZER, JA, 'Child Support and Child Access: Experiences of Divorced and Non-Marital Families' in JT Oldham and MS Melli (eds), *Child Support: The Next Frontier* (Ann Arbor, University of Michigan Press, 2000).

SILBERMAN, L, 'The Hague Children's Conventions: The Internationalization of Child Law' in SN Katz, J Eekelaar and M Maclean (eds), *Cross Currents: Family Law and Policy in the US and England* (Oxford, Oxford University Press, 2000).

SIMMONDS, NE, *Central Issues in Jurisprudence: Justice, Law and Rights* (2nd edn, London, Sweet and Maxwell, 2002).

SMART, C and NEALE, B, 'Arguments against Virtue—Must Contact be Enforced?' (1997) 27 *Family Law* 332.

——*Family Fragments?* (Cambridge, Polity Press, 1999).

SWINDELLS, H, NEAVES, A, KUSHNER, M and SKILBECK, R, *Family Law and the Human Rights Act 1998* (Bristol, Family Law, 1999).

TESHOME, T, 'Ethiopia: Reflections on the Revised Family Code of 2000', *International Survey of Family Law* (Bristol, Family Law, 2002 edn).

TOLSON, R, *Care Plans and the Human Rights Act* (Bristol, Family Law, 2002).

VERSHRAEGEN, B, 'The New Austrian Child Law 2001', *International Survey of Family Law* (Bristol, Family Law, 2002 edn).

6

Connecting Contact: Contact in a Private Law Context

JONATHAN HERRING

INTRODUCTION

CONTACT IS A cold word. It suggests a brief, casual, perhaps unwanted, connection with another. When a court orders that there be contact between a parent and child this will only offer benefits if it is part of a constructive relationship between them (Emery, 1994; Poussin and Martin-Lebrun, 2002; Hetherington and Kelly, 2002). But there is little that the law can do to ensure that such a relationship develops. As Lord Justice Thorpe has commented:

> It must be recognised that contact is no more than a mechanism for the maintenance and development of relationships and the court's powers are restricted to regulating the mechanism and do not extend to the underlying relationships.[1]

In a sense the actual law on contact in a private context is straightforward. The definition of a contact order is found in section 8 Children Act 1989:

> an order requiring the person with whom a child lives, or is to live, to allow the child to visit or stay with the person named in the order, or for that person and the child otherwise to have contact with each other.

As this definition makes clear a non-resident parent cannot be compelled to have contact with his child (see Bainham, this volume). A judge deciding whether to order contact is bound by section 1 Children Act 1989:

> When a court determines any question with respect to –
> (a) the upbringing of a child . . .
> the child's welfare shall be the court's paramount consideration.[2]

The 'simple' question, then, for a judge is to decide whether it would or would not be in the child's welfare to make a contact order. It might well be said

---

[1] *Re L, V, M, H (Contact: Domestic Violence)* [2000] 2 FLR 334.
[2] Children Act 1989, section 1(3) provides a 'checklist of factors' to be taken into account when considering the child's welfare.

that little more can usefully be added, apart from the obvious point that each case depends on its own special facts. In the past there was talk of children having a right of contact with each parent,[3] or at least there being a presumption in favour of contact between a child and a parent.[4] However, recently the Court of Appeal has stated that there is no legal right to contact or even presumption in favour of contact.[5] The most that can be said is that there is an assumption that contact between a child and parent is beneficial. Each case must be examined on its particular merits, the benefits and disadvantages of contact weighed to determine what order, if any, would promote the child's welfare.[6] In respect of other relatives the court will examine the quality of the particular relationship between the individual and child when deciding whether contact will be beneficial.[7]

It is natural for a lawyer considering the issue of contact to focus on contact orders. However, the aim of this chapter is to consider the way that the law can influence the quality and extent of contact between parents and children, apart from contact orders. It will explore two important points:

1. Contact must be seen as but one of the legal mechanisms governing the relationship between the child and non-resident parent. There are a variety of other ways that the law can seek to reinforce, shape or indeed undermine that relationship, apart from contact orders.
2. It will be argued that contact between a non-resident parent and child cannot be viewed in isolation from the relationship between the resident and non-resident parent, and the relationship between the resident parent and the child (see Dunn, this volume). If contact is to work successfully this trio of relationships must operate effectively. This chapter will seek to outline the way in which the law (outside the context of contact applications) can affect these relationships and thereby influence contact.

1. THE WIDER LEGAL RELATIONSHIP BETWEEN THE CHILD
AND THE NON-RESIDENT PARENT

On the separation of parents, the relationship between the non-resident parent and each child requires re-negotiation and re-developing (Smart and Neale,

---

[3] M v M [1973] 2 All ER 81; Re W (A Minor) (Contact) [1994] 2 FLR 441.

[4] Re M (Contact: Welfare Test) [1995] 1 FLR 274.

[5] Re L, V, M, H (Contact: Domestic Violence) [2000] 2 FLR 334. With respect, in the light of the Human Rights Act 1998 and the interpretation of Article 8 of the European Convention on Human Rights, in Sahin v Germany [2002] 1 FLR 119 it is hard to deny that parents have a right to contact with their children. See further Bainham, this volume.

[6] Whether or not we can assume that contact benefits children is highly controversial. Compare Maclean and Eekelaar (1998); Kaganas (1999); Eekelaar (2002); Willbourne and Stanley (2002). However the benefits of contact are usually assumed by court welfare officers (Sawyers, 2000) and legal practitioners (Neale and Smart, 1997).

[7] See eg Re A (Section 8 Order: Grandparent Application) [1995] 2 FLR 153.

1999). Although a few non-resident fathers report seeing more of their children (and spending more money on them) after the separation than before, in many cases the relationship will be strained and even effectively come to an end (Bradshaw *et al*, 1999). Key to the relationship is, of course, direct communication, with which contact orders are concerned. But the potential impact of the law on the relationship is not restricted to that (for further discussion of fathers' attitudes to contact see Simpson, Jessop and McCarthy, this volume). Here are four other ways that the law might impact on it:

(a) The Granting of Parental Responsibility

Section 3 of the Children Act defines parental responsibility as 'all the rights, duties, powers, responsibilities and authority which by law a parent of a child has in relation to the child and his property'. The mother of a child automatically has parental responsibility for her. A child's father will have it if he was married to the mother at the time of the birth or has since married her; or has obtained an order of the court granting parental responsibility; or has been registered as the father on the child's birth certificate; or has reached a parental responsibility agreement with the mother which has been lodged at the court.[8] Parents retain parental responsibility even following their separation or divorce.

The courts have made it clear that contact and parental responsibility are to be treated as separate questions. It is quite possible to make a contact order in favour of a father who does not have parental responsibility; or give him parental responsibility, but not a contact order.[9] Whether a father has parental responsibility is significant in the context of adoption proceedings and child abduction (see Smith, this volume). Although this has often been confirmed by the courts it is not by any means self-evident. If a father has no contact with the child does it make sense to grant him 'all the rights . . . powers . . . and authority' which by law a parent has over a child? Is he in any position to make important decisions for the child, if he has not seen her for years?

The answer to this apparent oddity is that the Court of Appeal has interpreted parental responsibility in a surprising way. In some cases[10] the courts have understood parental responsibility as merely recognising a man's position as a father, rather than giving the father rights to make decisions over the upbringing of the child. In *Re C and V*[11] Ward LJ explained:

> . . . it should be understood by now that a parental responsibility order is one designed not to do more than confer on the natural father the status of fatherhood which a

---

[8] Children Act 1989, s 2. For a detailed discussion of the law see Herring (2001: 290–92).
[9] *Re C and V* [1998] 1 FLR 392; *Re H (A Child: Parental Responsibility)* [2002] EWCA Civ 542.
[10] In other cases the courts have emphasised that parental responsibility does grant the father the power to make decisions: eg *M v M* [1999] 2 FLR 737. Note also the apparent duty on the resident parent to consult over important issues with anyone else with parental responsibility (see below).
[11] *Re C and V* [1998] 1 FLR 392, at 397.

father would have when married to the mother. There is also a sad failure fully to appreciate, when looking at the best interests of the child (which are paramount in this application, as elsewhere) that a child needs for its self-esteem to grow up, wherever it can, having a favourable positive image of an absent parent; and it is important that, wherever possible, the law should confer on a concerned father that stamp of approval because he has shown himself willing and anxious to pick up the responsibility of fatherhood and not to deny or avoid it.[12]

Seen in this way the distinction between contact and parental responsibility makes some sense. A father may well deserve a 'stamp of approval'[13] for being a committed father, even if it would not promote the welfare of the child for him to have contact with her.

In the passage quoted above the Court of Appeal represented parental respon- sibility as an attempt by the court to foster a positive image of a father in the mind of a child. The hope is that this positive image may encourage contact to take place at a later date, even if that is not possible now. Conversely the denial of parental responsibility may create in the child a negative image of her father, which may scupper any hope of contact in the future. It must be added that whether children are aware who has parental responsibility for them, or, even if they are, whether that creates the positive image intended by the courts is doubt- ful. More likely it will operate on the mind of the father as an affirmation of his parental status by the courts.

(b) Post-separation Decision-making Over Children

One of the things that clearly distinguishes a parental relationship from any other relationship an adult may have with a child, is the power the parent has to make decisions for or with the child. The ability of a non-resident parent to be involved in decisions concerning the upbringing of the child is therefore a sig- nificant aspect of his or her relationship with the child. Where the child lives with one parent, a tension inevitably arises over who is in a position to make decisions concerning the child's upbringing. There are issues which all parents face: what kind of food should the child eat? What time should the child go to bed? What attitude towards discipline should be taken? To the resident parent such issues should be for her to resolve: the resident parent knows the child bet- ter than the non-resident parent and her right to private life would be severely affected if the non-resident parent could, for example, insist that the child was taken to particular religious activities or eat particular kinds of food. To the non-resident parent, not being allowed any say in how the child is raised means that his parental status has become diminished. Although, under the Children Act, the separation of the parents does not technically affect the parental

---

[12] To similar effect see *Re S (Parental Responsibility)* [1995] 2 FLR 648.
[13] *Re S (Parental Responsibility)* [1995] 2 FLR 648, at 657.

responsibility each parent owes to the child, if the non-resident parent is not able to exercise that responsibility in making decisions about the child's upbringing he may feel that he has been effectively sidelined (Bainham, 1990).

The answer to these difficulties adopted by the courts, in brief, is that day-to-day issues are to be resolved by the resident parent,[14] whereas on fundamental issues the resident parent should consult with the non-resident parent.[15] Although the non-resident parent can seek to challenge the primary carer's day-to-day care of the child in the court, such a challenge is unlikely to be successful unless there is clear evidence that the child is being harmed. For example, in *Re W (Minors) (Residence Order)*[16] the resident parent and her new partner were naturists who were regularly naked in front of the children. The non-resident parent sought an order stopping such nudity. The Court of Appeal held that in the absence of clear evidence that the children were suffering harm it would not intervene and make the order sought. It seems also that a resident parent should not seek to interfere in the day-to-day issues which arise while the non-resident parent was caring for a child during a contact visit. In *Re D (Children) (Shared Residence Orders)*[17] it was explained:

> A cardinal feature [of the Children Act] was that when children are being looked after by either parent that parent needs to be in a position to take the decisions that have to be taken while the parent is having their care; that is part of care and part of responsibility. Parents should not be seeking to interfere with one another in matters which are taking place while they do not have the care of children.

This suggests that a resident parent could not, for example, seek to prevent the non-resident parent taking the child to a Macdonald's 'restaurant' during a contact visit on the basis of moral, political or dietary concerns. Similarly the non-resident parent could not require the resident parent to feed the child with vegetarian food.

Where the issue is one of 'fundamental importance', the parents must consult and reach agreement before either of them can act. In the absence of agreement the parties must apply to a court for resolution of their conflict.[18] It is not possible to provide anything like a complete list of what issues will be fundamental, but they include the changing of a child's name, removing the child from the jurisdiction, changing the child's school or circumcising a male child.[19]

This requirement to consult is significant, because as mentioned earlier, involvement in making decisions about a child is one of the elements of a

---

[14] *Re M (Handicapped Child: Parental Responsibility)* [2001] 3 FCR 454. See the discussion in Eekelaar (2001).

[15] *Re H (Parental Responsibility)* [1998] 1 FLR 855; *Re J (Specific Issue Orders: Child's Religious Upbringing and Circumcision)* [2000] 1 FLR 571. This is despite Children Act 1989, s 2(7) which states that each parent can exercise parental responsibility independently.

[16] [1998] 1 FCR 75.

[17] [2001] 1 FCR 147.

[18] *Re J (Specific Issue Orders: Child's Religious Upbringing and Circumcision)* [2000] 1 FLR 571.

[19] *Ibid.*

child-parent relationship which clearly distinguishes it from other family relationships. A parent deprived of that power may feel this a direct challenge to his status as a parent. A child's awareness that her father has no power to make decisions about her upbringing may affect her attitude towards him. As the child grows up a healthy parent-child relationship involves finding ways of negotiating and discussing issues of dispute. If the non-resident parent has no decision-making role that aspect of the parent-child relations (with all its difficulties as well as benefits) will be lost. The point being made here is not to argue in favour of a particular distribution of power between parents on separation in relation to decision-making, but to note that what distribution is made can have a significant impact on the nature of the relationship between the non-resident parent and the child (Smart and Neale, 1999).

(c) Names

The mother of a child on birth is required to register the birth of the child and select a surname for the child.[20] The father has no right to have his name as the registered name, although he could apply to court for an order that the child has his surname. If such an application were made the court would have to decide which name would best promote the child's welfare.[21] The Court of Appeal has recently advocated the use of children's surnames that contain elements of both the father's and mother's surname.[22] Once the child's name has been registered, the resident parent should only change the child's name with the non-resident parent's consent, or the leave of the court. This is because, to the surprise of some, the surname of the child has been regarded as an issue of 'crucial importance' for a child's upbringing. So much so that the House of Lords have been willing to hear an appeal on the naming of children.[23]

It is clear that the surname of the child is seen by some fathers as forming an exceptionally important link between father and child. The changing of that surname, particularly from that of the father to the surname of the mother's new partner, is felt particularly keenly as the severing of a fundamental link. These feelings have, to some extent been recognised by the courts. Lord Jauncey stated in the House of Lords in *Dawson v Wearmouth*:[24]

> A surname which is given to a child at birth is not simply a name plucked out of the air. Where the parents are married the child will normally be given the surname or patronymic of the father, thereby demonstrating its relationship to him. The surname

[20] For detail on the law of names see Herring (2001: 418–22).
[21] A father does not have a right that his child bear his surname (*Dawson v Wearmouth* [1999] AC 308).
[22] *Re R (A Child)* [2002] 1 FCR 170.
[23] *Dawson v Wearmouth* [1999] AC 308. In *Re R (A Child)* [2002] 1 FCR 170 Thorpe LJ described surnames as a 'comparatively small issue' (para 1).
[24] [1999] 1 FLR 1167, at 1175.

is thus a biological label which tells the world at large that the blood of the name flows in its veins.

The name may be thought not only to establish a link with the father himself, but also between the child and the father's religious and cultural heritage.[25]

Whether surnames should have this significance or not is another matter. As Hale LJ has commented:

> It is also a matter of great sadness to me that it is so often assumed, and even sometimes argued, that fathers need that outward and visible link in order to retain their relationship with, and commitment to, their child. That should not be the case. It is a poor sort of parent whose interest in and commitment to his child depends upon that child bearing his name. After all, that is a privilege which is not enjoyed by many mothers, even if they are not living with the child. They have to depend upon other more substantial things.[26]

(d) Contact and Financial Support of Children

Some fathers regard the financial support of their child as a crucial aspect of their relationship with him or her. Indeed there is evidence that some fathers see financial support as more important than contact (Bradshaw *et al*, 1999), although this might be thought to be very much a minority view given the low rates of payment of child support. Interviews with non-resident fathers demonstrate that the payments of child support are regarded by many fathers as carrying symbolic significance, beyond the mere provision of money (Bradshaw, 1999; Waller, 2002). Here are the meanings that some fathers attach to the payment of child support:

(i)   Some fathers see the role of being the primary 'bread winner' for the child as an important part of being a father. Significantly to many fathers it is important that the child is aware that he is performing that role. They therefore object to the operation of the Child Support Act where payments received by the Child Support Agency from the father are usually paid to the mother through the benefits system, meaning that the child is not made aware of the link between the money and the father. In other words, there are objections that the father's role as bread winner is not reinforced in the child's mind (Lewis, 2002).

(ii) To some fathers it is significant that payments of child support are seen by their children as a 'gift'; rather than an enforced payment. Voluntary payments are seen by some fathers (and it is assumed the children perceive

---

[25] *Re S (Change of Names: Cultural Factors)* [2001] 3 FCR 648.
[26] Hale LJ in *Re R (A Child)* [2002] 1 FCR 170 at para 13. In that case the Court of Appeal wisely recommended that the child's surname should be a combination of the father's and mother's surname, rather than the surname of the mother's new partner, as the mother wished.

them in the same way[27]) as their way of caring about the child; expressing love; and fulfilling a proper fatherly role.[28] Again, studies looking at the operation of the Child Support Act have found fathers objecting to the Act in that it restricts this expression of their care for children.

(iii) There are reports that financial support is used by fathers as a way of making up for not being with a child, payments perhaps even being driven by guilt (Bradshaw, Stimson, Skinner *et al*, 1999). It could be noted that this is perhaps not restricted to fathers who have separated from the child. Resident fathers may use a similar excuse to compensate for their absences from the home while over-working.

In these different ways it is clear that financial support is seen by some non-resident parents, and maybe some children[29] as conveying love for a child; being a means of caring for a child; and re-inforcing the father's role as a 'good father'. It should be stressed that I am not arguing that such an understanding is worthy or to be encouraged, it is simply that at least to some fathers payment of child support is an important aspect of the non-resident father-child relationship.

Conclusion

It is, then, not just contact that in legal terms constitutes the relationship between the non-resident parent and child. Through the allocation of parental responsibility, the division of decision-making powers, the regulation of surnames and the payment of child support, the law is able to influence the relationship. This may be significant for two reasons. The first is that one of the most common explanations offered by fathers who cease contact is that they feel unable to fulfil a proper paternal role (Bradshaw *et al*, 1999). It *may be* through the issues discussed in this section that the father can be re-inforced in his role and thereby encouraged to maintain contact. Whether contact can be encouraged in this way is a matter of debate. Further, the image of fatherhood sought by some fathers: having his name as the name of the child; reinforcement of the 'primary breadwinner role'; the right to have a say in 'important' decisions may well not be the kind of fatherhood our society wishes to encourage.[30] Second, it must not be assumed that if the court does not order contact, any link between child and father is completely severed.[31] As these matters show, through pay-

---

[27] For wider discussion of children's perspectives on their relationships with parents see Dunn this volume.

[28] Davis, Wikeley and Young (1998) explain that women are used to not being able to control family finances. See further Lewis (2002).

[29] Although little research has been carried out on children's perception of financial support.

[30] On notions of new fatherhood see Herlth (2002).

[31] If direct contact is not possible then the court will consider whether to order indirect contact (eg by way of telephone, e-mails or letters): *A v L (Contact)* [1998] 2 FCR 204.

ment of financial support, the awarding of parental responsibility or use of sur-names, a link of some kind can be maintained.

2. RELATIONSHIP BETWEEN PARENTS

It is all too easy to see the issue of contact simply in terms of the relationship between the non-resident parent and child (Masson, 2000). However, where the relationship between the parents has broken down completely contact is going to be ineffective (Hester, 2002). Indeed there is strong evidence that contact where the parents are still in bitter conflict can harm the child (Pryor and Rogers, 1998).[32] Successful long-term contact requires trust and co-operation between the two parents (Maccoby and Mnookin, 1992). Indeed, it is often overlooked that for most very young children contact is in fact very difficult unless the resident parent is involved in the contact sessions.[33] As Dame Elizabeth Butler Sloss puts it:

> If his [the father's] relationship with the mother is not friendly, then it will be almost impossible to remove the child from the mother for the purpose of contact (even super-vised contact) until the child is of an age when she would not cling to her mother.[34]

Further, in relation to older children, whatever the court orders the child is likely to decide for him or herself whether to pursue contact.[35] Most signif-icantly, focussing on contact orders deals with only one half of the 'problem of contact': resident parents who oppose contact. It ignores the much more numer-ically significant 'problem' of fathers who do not seek contact. It is argued in this chapter that if the law wishes to facilitate and encourage contact it would do far better in seeking to do the little it can to build up and establish trust between parents, than focus on the enforcement of contact orders.

It is worth at this point contrasting the position in private law with that where a parent seeks contact with a child in care. Section 34 of the Children Act 1989 cre-ates a presumption in favour of contact between a parent and child in care.[36] Contrast this with the private law position where a non-resident parent seeks con-tact with his child, where there is no such presumption. The distinction in part may be explained by the increased need for a child in care to have links with his family. But it may also reflect the fact that public law cases lack any need to accommodate the benefits of contact with the interests and views of the resident parent, and con-cerns over negative impact on a child that a contested contact order can have (see

---

[32] See, for further discussion, Trinder, this volume; James, this volume, and Buchanan and Hunt, this volume.

[33] *Re D (A Child) (IVF Treatment)* [2001] 1 FCR 481.

[34] *Ibid.* She suggested this would be until the child reached the age of three.

[35] *Re S (Contact) (Children's Views)* [2002] 1 FLR 1157. Pearce, Davis and Barron (1999) found many older children in their study did this.

[36] *Re E (A Minor) (Care Order: Contact)* [1994] 1 FLR 146.

Lindley and Miles, this volume, for further discussion of the public law). The requirement of a degree of co-operation between the parents, which is essential if a private law contact order is to be effective, is absent in the public law cases, making it easier to declare the presumption in favour of there being contact.

One controversial issue which indicates the need for co-operation as the basis of successful contact is what has been called 'parental alienation syndrome' (see Willbourne and Cull, 1997; Hobbs, 2002). There is much debate over whether the syndrome exists (Kelly and Johnston, 2001). Proponents allege that it arises where a child has been so influenced by one parent against the other that the child refuses to have anything to do with the other parent. The majority view in Britain seems to be that the syndrome does not exist.[37] It is not denied that children can be turned against their parents, but there is much debate over whether or not this is accurately described as a syndrome. Although those who wish to raise the court's awareness of the alleged syndrome normally do so to encourage the courts to take a strict approach against resident parents who oppose contact, in fact the evidence is that it is far more common for non-resident fathers to seek to turn children against their resident mothers than vice versa (Berns, 2001). Leaving aside the debate over whether there is a syndrome, the discussions reveal the grave dangers in enforcing contact where the parents are still at war themselves.

First, I will seek to explain why the enforcement of contact is ineffective. Then I will consider whether there are other ways that the law might more efficiently encourage contact.

(a) The Ineffectiveness of Contact Orders

It will be argued that as a means of ensuring there is contact between a child and a non-resident parent a contact order is largely ineffective.[38] The courts are naturally reluctant to make and enforce orders against resident parents who strongly oppose contact. Further they are understandably unwilling to restrict the resident parent's freedom of movement.

(i) Contact and the 'Obdurate Parent'

Courts face great difficulties in cases where the resident parent strongly opposes contact.[39] On the one hand there are those who are concerned that paying too

---

[37] Sturge and Glaser (2000) did not recognise Parental Alienation Syndrome (see further Williams, 2002; Birch, 2001). The courts are so far reluctant to accept the existence of the syndrome see *Re L (Contact: Genuine Fear)* [2002] 1 FLR 621; *Re S (Contact: Children's Views)* [2002] 1 FLR 1156; *Re C (Prohibition on Further Applications)* [2002] 1 FLR 1136.

[38] See Bainham (this volume) who emphasises the symbolic value that such an order may nevertheless have.

[39] In *Nuutinen v Finland* 27 June 2000 ECtHR and *Glaser v UK* [2000] 3 FCR 193 the European Court of Human Rights has confirmed that there is not an absolute obligation to enforce contact. In *Glaser v UK* [2000] 3 FCR 193 the European Court of Human Rights did not think that the state was

much attention to the objections of the mother[40] will create a 'selfish parents' charter'[41] where mothers who are most vocal in their opposition to contact have the best chance of persuading a court to deny contact.[42] On the other hand, commentators who are more sympathetic to mothers opposing contact argue that such opposition is nearly always based on sound reasons, such as a past history of domestic violence or allegations of sexual or physical abuse of the child (Rhodes, 2002; Day Sclater and Kaganas, this volume). Especially in cases where there has been a history of domestic violence, evidence suggests that fears that contact may be used as a means of continuing to exercise power over the mother and child are well founded (Rhodes, 2002; Radford, 1999).

At one time the courts took a strict approach toward 'obdurate parents' and readily enforced contact against them, arguing that contact with the non-resident parent was the right of the child which should not be lost, because of the mother's opposition.[43] More recently the courts have taken a different approach.[44] There are now two circumstances in which the resident parent's opposition may be relevant:

(i) Judges must carefully consider the reasons for the mother's opposition.[45] If the reasons for the opposition were reasonable they should be taken into account in deciding whether contact would promote the child's welfare.[46] However, the courts have left unclear what constitutes a reasonable ground of objection here. If a mother believes that a child will be sexually abused or that she will be the victim of continuing domestic violence then surely that is a good reason for refusing contact. But it seems the courts require the mother to demonstrate that such beliefs are reasonably held. The view taken here is that contact enforced on the basis of a relationship between parents involving such mistrust (even if unfounded mistrust) is doomed to failure; a failure which will harm children.

(ii) Occasionally the courts have accepted that the mother will suffer such emotional or psychological harm that it would not be in the child's interests for contact to take place.[47]

required under the European Convention on Human Rights to imprison a mother who refused to permit contact with a father, nor to change the residence of the child.

[40] I will assume, as is most common, that the resident parent is the mother.

[41] *Re H (A Minor) (Contact)* [1994] 2 FLR 776.

[42] *Re O* [1995] 2 FLR 124.

[43] Even where there were genuine reasons to fear that contact would cause harm to the child. See eg *Re F (Minors) (Contact: Mother's Anxiety)* [1993] 2 FLR 830.

[44] The Children Act Sub-Committee of the Lord Chancellor's Advisory Board on Family Law has produced guidelines on cases of contact where there has been domestic violence (2001).

[45] *Re D (Contact: Reasons for Refusal)* [1997] 2 FLR 48.

[46] *Re H (Contact: Domestic Violence)* [1998] 2 FLR 42.

[47] *Re J (A minor)* [1994] 1 FLR 729; *Re M and B* [2001] 1 FCR 116; *Re L (Contact: Genuine Fear)* [2002] 1 FLR 621. Although at least one district judge is cynical of what he labels 'self-traumatic conditioning' Gerlis (2002), there is clear evidence that the psychological well-being of the primary carer affects the welfare of the child (Pryor and Rogers, 1998).

If neither of these arguments applied, then contact should be ordered, despite the mother's 'implacable hostility'.[48] The courts have been willing to enforce contact through imprisonment of the mother[49] or to consider changing the residence of the child from the mother to the father (Gerlis, 1998).

Such cases have lead to ferocious arguments amongst commentators (Piper, 1996). Some approve of the court's tough approach. Simon Jolly (1995: 234) has argued that:

> . . . any judicial decision must ultimately be supported with (the threat of) coercion. If this threat is seen to be empty, then law is seen to be brutal and proud—prepared to sacrifice the child's welfare to protect its own dignity. The choice is a stark one—the ultimate weapon which may be used to sustain the enforcement of a contact order is that of imprisonment.[50]

Many others object to the court's approach: in the name of promoting the welfare of the child, vulnerable women are being subjected to the law's strongest compulsion providing a result which will ultimately harm the child (Smart and Neale, 1997). The case against such enforcement is considered particularly strong by those who believe the benefits of contact are speculative (Eekelaar, 2002) or argue that given the high rates of breakdown of contact the benefits are unlikely to be realised. There is also a notable distinction between the law's response to mothers who prevent a father seeing his child and a father who decides not to see his child. It has been argued that the approach taken by the courts has labelled the mother as a 'bad mother' for preventing what is seen as beneficial contact with the father (Smart, 1991). Contrast the position of a father who does not seek contact with the child. He, as much as the mother, would be denying the child the benefit of contact. While the law would be willing to imprison the mother and label her obdurate, the father who refused to see his child would receive no opprobrium and the law would make no effort to compel him to contact the child (see further Bainham, this volume).

As the discussion of these issues demonstrates, if the resident parent is not co-operative contact is unlikely to succeed. Although the courts have been willing to threaten punishment and even imprison mothers who have refused to consent to contact, these are exceptional cases. It is hard to believe that in many of the cases where contact has taken place following threats of imprisonment or pressure from judges or professionals, beneficial long-term contact has taken place.[51] It is highly unlikely that court compulsion will remove the underlying

---

[48] [1994] 2 FLR 441.

[49] *F v P (Contact: Committal)* [1998] 2 FLR 237. Contrast *Re C (Children: Contact)* [2002] 3 FCR 183.

[50] The Advisory Board on Family Law: Children Act Sub-Committee (Lord Chancellor's Department, 2002) at para 14.10 explained that the majority of respondents to their consultation paper thought the rule of law and proper administration of justice required that courts be able to fine or imprison to enforce contact. However, the Board noted that imprisonment was rarely used, 'rightly so' (para 14.10).

[51] See the discussion in Advisory Board on Family Law: Children Act Sub-Committee (Lord Chancellor's Department, 2002), para 1.13.

animosity or tension between the parents. We have ample studies which teach us that raising children in situations where there is tension and conflict harms them.[52]

In some of the most recent cases the courts have moved towards an approach which seeks to avoid enforcement through legal mechanisms and instead prefers to use psychological, counselling and mediation services to enable the parties to reach an appropriate solution.[53] Indeed *Making Contact Work*,[54] has recommended that courts have power to direct parties to attend mediation and counselling services to resolve contact disputes.[55] I have grave reservations about these proposals. Leaving aside all the debates over the suitability of mediation to resolve disputes between parents, one issue on which nearly everyone involved in mediation is agreed is that it is unsuitable in cases where there has been domestic violence or where one party is in fear of the other (Piper and Kaganas, 1997). Yet nearly all the cases where a resident parent has refused contact occur where there have been allegations of domestic violence or sexual abuse (Radford, 1999). Mediation would seem a suitable solution in only a very few contact cases (see Maclean and Mueller, this volume).

(ii) Contact and Restraining the Resident Parent's Movement

Of course, contact is not a one off issue. The making of the contact order is only the start of the process. Even if the courts force the initial making of the order, it is practically impossible to ensure that contact continues. The question which most clearly highlights the issues is where one parent wishes to move from the jurisdiction with the child, or while staying in the UK, move a long way away from the non-resident parent.[56]

A resident parent who wishes to remove a child from the jurisdiction must obtain the consent of all those with parental responsibility or apply for the court's leave before doing so.[57] In the face of such an application the court must use the welfare principle in section 1, Children Act 1989 to decide whether to grant leave. The general approach which the courts have adopted is that if the proposals of the resident parent are reasonable then the parent will be able to

---

[52] For a useful review see Buchanan, Hunt, Bretherton and Bream (2001).

[53] *Re H (A Child) (Contact: Mother's opposition)* [2001] 1 FCR 59; *Re L, V, M, H (Contact: Domestic Violence)* [2000] 2 FLR 334.

[54] The Advisory Board on Family Law: Children Act Sub-Committee (2002) at para 14.53 preferred the option of directing the resident parent to attend a parenting programme or an information meeting or counselling or suffering a Community Service Order, to imprisonment.

[55] For a discussion of the way mediation can assist in contact cases see: Cottingham and Slade (2000).

[56] For a discussion of child abduction see Smith, this volume.

[57] Children Act 1989, s 13(1). Although the section on its terms only applies where there is a residence order in force, by analogy with the approach the courts have taken in respect of cases of surnames (eg *Re PC (Change of Surname)* [1997] 2 FLR 93), the requirements apply to children who are not subject to residence orders.

remove the child from the jurisdiction.[58] The court, in particular, will consider why the resident parent wishes to leave the country. It is clear that if the main reason for leaving the jurisdiction is in order to prevent the other party from having contact then leave will be refused. Leave will be granted, however, if the reason for leaving the jurisdiction is, for example, to take up a new job or to marry someone living abroad.[59] As Thorpe LJ in *Payne v Payne*[60] explained:

(a) the welfare of the child is the paramount consideration;
(b) refusing the primary carer's reasonable proposals for the relocation of her family life is likely to impact detrimentally on the welfare of her dependent children. Therefore her application to relocate will be granted unless the court concludes that it is incompatible with the welfare of the children.[61]

Although the Court of Appeal in *Payne v Payne* has emphasised there is no pre-sumption in favour of allowing a reasonable resident parent to leave the juris-diction, in effect the burden of proof in such applications appears to be reversed: the burden lies on the non-resident parent to persuade the court that the pro-posed action in relation to the child is contrary to the interests of the child, rather than demonstrating that the proposed order is in the interests of the child.[62]

In an analogous line of cases, non-resident parents have sought orders to restrict the movement of the resident parent within the United Kingdom. For example, in *Re S (A Child) (Residence Order: Conditions)*[63] the father sought an order that the mother remain in Croydon and not move to Cornwall, argu-ing that the move to Cornwall would effectively end the contact between the father and the child, which would harm the child's welfare.[64] The Court of Appeal said that such restrictions on the freedom of movement of the resident parent should only be granted in exceptional cases.

So why might it be that these cases appear to depart from a straightforward application of the welfare principle? There are two possible explanations:

(i) If the resident parent's application for leave is refused she will suffer such great distress that the child herself will suffer. It is then argued that the child's welfare is dependent upon the security and stability of the resident parent and so unless there is a good reason to the contrary leave will be granted. As Thorpe LJ put it in *Payne v Payne*:

---

[58] *Re H (Application to Remove from Jurisdiction)* [1998] 1 FLR 848; *Re M (Leave to Remove from Jurisdiction)* [1999] 2 FLR 334. Contrast the decision of the Supreme Court in Canada in *Gordon v Goertz* (1996) 19 RFL (4th) 177.
[59] See Herring (2001: 424) for a more detailed discussion of the factors to be taken into account. See also *Re H (Children) (Residence Order: Condition)* [2001] 3 FCR 182 where the main reason for refusing leave to take a child out of the jurisdiction (in effect) was because it was yet to be decided who was to have long-term residence of the child.
[60] [2001] EWCA Civ 166; [2001] 1 FCR 425.
[61] Para 26.
[62] *Re B (Children) (Removal from the Jurisdiction)* [2001] 1 FCR 108.
[63] [2001] 3 FCR 154.
[64] Similarly the courts have refused to restrict with whom the resident parent can live: *Re D (Minors) (Residence: Conditions)* [1996] 2 FCR 820.

In a broad sense the health and well-being of a child depends upon emotional and psychological stability and security. Both security and stability come from the child's emotional and psychological dependency upon the primary carer. The extent of that dependency will depend upon many factors including its duration and the extent to which it is tempered by or shared with other dependencies . . . Logically and as a matter of experience the child cannot draw emotional and psychological security from the dependency unless the primary carer herself is emotionally and psychologically stable and secure. The parent cannot give what she herself lacks.[65]

This appears perhaps inconsistent with the position taken in cases of contact disputes where the courts have been very reluctant to accept an argument that the emotional harm caused to the resident parent of allowing contact is a good reason for denying contact.[66] So contact is of such importance to a child that the court will order it almost regardless of the strength of opposition of the resident parent, but then will not stop the resident parent moving to a remote part of the country effectively rendering contact impossible. Is protection of the right of free movement of a resident parent a better reason than protecting psychological or emotional well-being?[67] Or is Thorpe LJ's emphasis on the importance of the emotional well-being of the resident parent on the welfare of the child an approach which has been overlooked in cases of disputed contact?

(ii) The resident parent's right of free movement should only be restricted if there is clear evidence that the child will be significantly harmed by the removal.[68] This approach has come to the fore with arguments based on the Human Rights Act 1998. The Courts have suggested that the Human Rights Act 1998 leads to a balance between the non-resident parent's right to family and private life (in the shape of the contact with the children) and the resident parent's right of family and private life (in the shape of being able to choose where to live). These rights had to be balanced against each other.[69] In *Payne*, it was held, that in balancing these rights the child's interests were of crucial importance and therefore the present approach could be supported. Bainham (2002), although supporting the result reached in that case, asks:

If we break the decision down in terms of competing values, the court apparently attached more significance to the security and stability of the child with her mother, than it did to the preservation of the child's relationship with the father, as secondary carer, and the father's family. This, again, might be criticised as an inadequate response to the child's identity rights under the UN Convention.

---

[65] Para 31.

[66] Unless that emotional distress is such as to amount to a specific psychiatric illness.

[67] Those who would restrict the resident parent's movements must explain why the law does not restrict the non-resident parent's freedom of movement, even if contact with the child is in the welfare of the child (Thomas Oldham, 2001).

[68] For a discussion of an argument that under American law the resident parent has a constitutional right to move, see LaFrance (1995).

[69] *Re A (Permission to Remove Child from Jurisdiction: Human Rights)* [2000] 2 FLR 225.

To others, there will be no controversy in valuing the security and stability of the attachment with the resident parent more highly than the right of contact to the non-resident parent.

Whichever view is taken it is clear that there are grave difficulties in enforcing the contact order; in preventing the resident parent from acting in a way which effectively prevents the contact taking place. We now turn to the ways the law may seek to encourage contact, outside the context of contact applications.

(b) Contact and Domestic Violence

The Court of Appeal in the highly influential case of *Re L, V, M, H (Contact: Domestic Violence)*[70] has emphasised the importance that should be attached to the fact that there has been domestic violence in a case of contact.[71] It acknowledged that in the past the courts[72] might not have paid sufficient attention to the significance of domestic violence in cases of contact.[73] The old attitude that domestic violence may be a relevant issue between the two parents but was not relevant for child issues such as contact has been firmly rejected. Although the Court of Appeal emphasised that the law did not create a presumption against contact in cases where there had been domestic violence,[74] the existence of domestic violence was an important factor in deciding whether contact was in the best interests of the child. They referred to evidence that children who witness violence suffer in a variety of ways (Maccoby and Mnookin, 1992; Hester and Pearson, 1997; Sturge and Glaser, 2000). Although contact in such cases can help to heal these wounds, contact in other cases may exacerbate the harms suffered by the child and pose risks to the child and her primary carer.[75] The court emphasised that it is crucial also to ensure that contact did not put the child or primary carer at risk.[76]

The court's acknowledgement of the significance of the impact of domestic violence on children in contact cases is to be welcomed.[77] However, with

[70] [2000] 2 FLR 334.

[71] For discussion of the research on the effects on children of domestic violence between the parents see Hughes (1988); Hester, Pearson and Harrison (2000); and C Sturge and D Glaser (2000).

[72] There is evidence that solicitors and barristers similarly encouraged parties to think that domestic violence was not a relevant issue in contact disputes: Barnett (2000).

[73] In *Re P* [1996] 2 FLR 314 the Court of Appeal ordered supervised contact in favour of a man who had allegedly threatened to kill the children and had been jailed after attempting to strangle the mother.

[74] Lemon (2001) discusses attempts in the United States to put such a presumption on a statutory footing.

[75] In Hester and Radford's (1996) sample all post-separation violence was linked to contact. Mirrlees-Black (1995) found that domestic violence was prevalent following separation, especially where children were involved.

[76] Eg *Re H (Children) (Contact Order)* [2001] 1 FCR 49 (see also *Re H (Contact Order) (No 2)* [2001] FL 795).

[77] Although there are concerns that the bitterness that surrounds contact disputes may only be worsened if there are allegations and counter-allegations of domestic violence. Barnett (2000) argues that some mothers are reluctant to raise concerns about domestic violence for fear of increasing hostility. By contrast the pressure group Families Need Fathers argue that allegations are frequently made solely in order to frustrate contact (Families Need Fathers, 1999).

respect, the Court of Appeal's approach involves a sleight of hand. Asking 'should there be a presumption against contact where there has been domestic violence' is to skew the answer. Many people would accept that there are cases where despite domestic violence in the past, contact may be beneficial where both parents agree to there being contact. However, the real question is: 'where there has been domestic violence *and the mother who has been subjected to that violence opposes contact*, should an order forcing her to permit contact be made?' This is the real question and one to which it is far harder to answer 'yes'. This is true, particularly with evidence that in 76 per cent of cases where courts ordered contact in favour of a violent father, children or mothers suffered further abuse at the father's hands.[78] In the face of such evidence even a presumption against contact where there has been a history of domestic violence seems a rather weak response.[79] It risks enabling an abusive man to use contact as a tool to continue exercising power over his former partner and children (Hester and Harne, 1999; Hester, 2002). It should be added that many women involved in contact disputes are reluctant to raise the issue of domestic violence for fear of it aggravating a tense situation (Barnett, 1999; Hester, 2002).

Those who wish to support contact in cases of domestic violence should be arguing for tougher, faster and more effective responses to domestic violence to minimise its impact on the victim and thereby increase the possibility of a trust-filled relationship between the parties which can form the basis of a relationship between the parents upon which contact can rest.[80] The Court of Appeal in *Re L, V, M , H (Domestic Violence: Contact)*[81] has, at last, recognised the significance of domestic violence in contact issues. In particular it has recognised the harmful impact that domestic violence can have on children. However, this realisation has failed to impact on decisions relating to domestic violence. Domestic violence law, governed by the Family Law Act 1996, Part IV, notably does not state that in applications for orders under the Act the interests of the children are to be paramount. Indeed the interests of children are not weighted as any more significant than the interests of adults. Space prevents a detailed argument in favour of putting the interests of children first in domestic violence cases. However, even accepting that interests of children rank equally with those of adults[82] the courts have not shown an appreciation of the effects of witnessing

---

[78] Radford (1999). Hall (1997) cites research that between 40 and 60% of cases involving domestic violence may also involve the physical abuse of children by one or other adult partner.

[79] The lack of such a presumption at the stage of interim orders, awaiting a full hearing on the facts has led in Australia to mothers being left in a vulnerable situation: Harrison (2002). Nor must it be assumed that supervised contact provides the answer as *Making Contact Work* (at para 13.11–23) indicated there are real concerns over the level of professionalism at some contact centres.

[80] Harrison (2002) discusses Australian research on the problems faced in achieving successful co-operative parenting following domestic violence.

[81] [2000] 2 FLR 334.

[82] Arguably they are not even equal because if the harm the respondent will suffer if an order is made is equal to the harm the child will suffer if an order is not made the court is not required to make an occupation order under the balance of harm test (Family Law Act 1996, s 33(7)).

violence or living in a violent household.[83] Consider, for example, the facts of *Re Y (Children) (Occupation Order)*,[84] involving 'a family divided among itself and at war with itself.'[85] The relationships between the parents and two children were described as 'pretty appalling': there was 'hatred in the house'; 'constant fighting' and there were 'frequent rows and fights between father and daughter'.[86] However the court declined to make an occupation order, explaining that such an order was 'a Draconian order. It is a last resort and is not an order lightly to be made'.[87] Sedley LJ argued that an occupation order should be used 'as a last resort in an intolerable situation, not as a move in a game of matrimonial chess'.[88] It must be admitted that there were complicating factors in that case (such as the absence of alternative accommodation for the father); nevertheless the court seems to have shown scant attention to the harm being caused to the children by living in such a hostile atmosphere, nor to the impact of non-intervention on the prospects for future contact.[89] The appropriate response to domestic violence is far too big and important a topic to be adequately dealt with here, but the point is that if contact is to work, rapid and effective response to claims for protection from domestic violence is required.

(c) Child Support and Contact

In English law the issues of contact and child support have traditionally been quite separate. A parent is obliged to support his or her child whether or not they have contact; a contact order can be made even if the non-resident parent is refusing to pay child support. The law has been strongly opposed to any kind of argument along the lines: 'because I do not see my child I do not have to pay child support' or 'because the father does not pay child support he does not deserve contact'. The view that contact can be paid for, is not surprisingly abhorred by many. Nevertheless at least one District Judge believes it rational to question the sincerity and commitment of a non-resident father who fails to pay child support towards his child (Brasse, 2002).

Despite the denials of a link between child support and contact there are links both in the law and in practice.

---

[83] It is important when considering this area not to restrict violence to physical threats. Emotional abuse and threatening behaviour can do as much to undermine the relationship between the parents as physical violence: Kaganas and Day Sclater (2000). Parliament has acknowledged this to some extent in the Adoption and Children Act 2002 which amends the definition of 'harm' for the purposes of public law orders under the Children Act to include 'impairment suffered from seeing or hearing the ill-treatment of another'.

[84] [2000] 2 FCR 470.

[85] Para 5.

[86] Para 9.

[87] Para 27.

[88] Para 41.

[89] See also *G v G (Occupation Order)* [2000] 3 FCR 53.

The Link Between Child Support and Contact in the Law

There are three main ways in which the law now acknowledges a link between contact and payment of child support:

(a) Contact expenses reducing child support.

If a non-resident parent has financial expenses connected with contact with a child he can claim a departure requiring a reduction in the level of child support payable.[90] The aim of this provision is to ensure that a non-resident parent will not be put in a position where because of his child support obligations he cannot afford to contact his child (DSS, 1999). That said, unless the parties live a long way apart, it would be a most exceptional case where contact would be unaffordable. One leading study on the operation of the 1991 Act found that

> whilst we acknowledge the possibility that absent parents' ability to maintain contact with their children may be affected by the amounts demanded of them by the Agency, we are not convinced that the level of maintenance demanded has had this effect other than, perhaps, in some men's imagination. (Davis, Wikeley and Young, 1998).

As the amounts payable under the new scheme[91] will be lower than those under the old scheme the argument is even less likely to apply in the future.[92]

(b) Overnight contact reducing child support levels.

More significantly the new child support scheme provides for a direct reduction where a non-resident parent has contact with the child for at least on average one night a week.[93] Basically child support is reduced by one seventh for every night per week that a child spends with the non-resident parent; up to a 3/7 reduction if the child stays with the non-resident parent three nights per week.[94] The explanation for this provision is unclear. Two arguments can be made:

(i) An attempt to affect people's behaviour

The legislation can be seen as a way of encouraging contact, particularly overnight contact. Evidence from the United States indicates that following a similar kind of statutory amendment there was a dramatic increase in the rate of overnight contact (Maccoby, 1999). A cynic might argue many men will be attracted by the bargain of obtaining a one seventh reduction in child support by paying for a burger and a video. Even

---

[90] Child Support Act 1991, s 28A–H. It is possible to require the resident parent to pay the contact expenses of the non-resident parent by means of a condition attached to the contact order under s 11(7): *Re K (Minors)* unrep 25.1.99.

[91] Found in the Child Support Act 1991, as amended by the Child Support, Pensions and Social Security Act 2000.

[92] See *Logan v UK* (1996) 22 EHRR CD 178.

[93] Child Support Act 1991, Sch 1 (which is yet to come into force).

[94] Child Support Act 1991, Sch 1, para 7.

if contact is initially encouraged as a money-saving device, it is presumably hoped that subsequently it will be persuaded for the benefits of the relationship.

(ii) Fairness

It could be argued that the proposal is a fair way of allocating the cost of child care. If the child is cared for one night a week by the non-resident parent then the cost of child care will be lower for the resident parent, and there will be an increased expense for the non-resident parent. The Government admitted the one-seventh figure was a compromise between two arguments. On the one hand fathers' groups argued that the reduction should be more than one seventh. The argument is most clear where the father shares care equally with the mother. In such a case fathers' groups argue that the father should pay nothing rather than having to pay half of the child support formula because both parents are sharing the costs of care equally. On the other hand there were others who argued a one seventh reduction was too great pointing out that most of the costs of raising the child (providing accommodation, laundry, clothing etc.) would have to be paid by the mother regardless of how many nights were spent with the father. It will rarely be in the mother's financial interests to have the child cared for by the father at night under the new scheme.

It should be pointed out that there are other aspects of the proposals that cannot be dealt with here in detail, such as whether it is desirable to encourage *overnight* contact (Solomon and Biringen, 2001; Lamb and Kelly, 2001); the effect of such proposals on levels of poverty among lone parent families (Maclean and Eekelaar, 1998:145); or the consequences of the provision on the apparent housing shortage.

(c) The relevance of child support to questions of residence or contact.

The issue of child support can be relevant in cases of residence or contact. For example, in *Re R (Residence Order: Finance)*[95] the Court of Appeal preferred to make a joint residence order whereby both parents were able to work full-time, than to give sole residence to the mother, who had offered to give up her work. The Court of Appeal accepted that the judge was entitled to decide that the effect of the mother giving up her job (she would become dependent on benefits and the Child Support Agency would become involved) was more harmful than the difficulties caused by a joint residence order. In *Re H (Children) (Residence Order: Condition)*[96] a resident father sought leave to take the child to Northern Ireland. The Court of Appeal accepted that an important reason for refusing leave was that the psychological effect on the non-resident mother if leave were granted might be such

---

[95] [1995] 2 FLR 612.
[96] [2001] 3 FCR 182.

that she would have to give up her job and hence the children would lose the benefit of the substantial payments under the CSA that she was making.

A more significant issue, and one which the courts tend to avoid discussing is whether in residence disputes a parent who is willing to be a 'stay-at-home' parent is to be preferred over a parent who is intending to go to work and rely on childcare. In *Re D (A Child) (Residence: Ability to Parent)*[97] Thorpe LJ suggested that in residence disputes the availability of a full time carer was described as an 'important consideration and in some cases an overwhelming one'.

The Link Between Child Support and Contact in Practice

Even though there are now some legal links between contact and child support the two questions are still largely seen as separate by family lawyers. It is clear, however, that many parents see a clear link between the two. Indeed there is strong evidence that where the non-resident parent has contact with the child, it is more likely that the non-resident parent will pay child support (Seltzer, 2000; Maclean and Eekelaar, 1998; Seltzer, Schaeffer and Charng, 1989; Seltzer, 1991; Bradshaw *et al*, 1999; DSS, 1999: 45). The payment of child support can 'oil the wheels' of contact.[98] Mothers who receive child support may feel more ready to enable contact to take place. Conversely, the fact that no child support is paid may increase a mother's reluctance to permit contact. As Davis and Wikeley's survey (Davis and Wikeley, 2002) demonstrates, the level of contact and quality of relationship between the father and child can play an important role in determining whether the level of child support required is regarded as fair by the parents.

There is an element of negotiated commitment in the parents' post-separation relationship (Bradshaw *et al*, 1999; Davis and Wikeley, 2002). Some couples regarded the relationship as based on balanced reciprocity (Finch and Mason, 1993). Those cases where child support was paid were likely to be cases where there was a reasonable relationship between the parties and such cases were similarly likely to be ones where there was contact. Bradshaw *et al* go on to explain:

> The resultant attitude tended to be that there was no point in paying maintenance because the children would not know their fathers were supporting them, there was no guarantee that the money would be spent for the children's benefit and the fathers were 'paying for a child they were not seeing'. Thus not only would fathers get 'nothing back' in return for maintenance (contact with their children), but payment was meaningless because the fathers' act of giving was rendered invisible to the children themselves. Children would be unaware of the symbolic expression of love and care embedded within the act of giving maintenance money, particularly when, in the

---

[97] [2001] 2 FCR 751.
[98] To use the phrase of Theo (a respondent in Bradshaw *et al*'s sample): Bradshaw *et al* (1999: 192).

absence of contact, there was no other means through which fathers could demonstrate their affections to children directly. Therefore the obligation to pay maintenance was intimately linked with contact through the relationship with the mother, and the different outcomes of the process of negotiation (payment or non-payment) primarily hinged upon this relationship.

It would be wrong to think that the payment of child support is in this sense a one way process. Neale and Smart (2002) argue:

> When fathers pay maintenance they are engaging in more than a utilitarian transfer of cash to support their children's upbringing. They are paying . . . for the privilege of seeing their children, for a share of parental authority and for the mother's day-to-day responsibilities for childcare. If the transfer of money is imbued with symbolic significance, so too is the transfer of the children. Mothers are not simply handing over the children for contact but are giving up some of their time with and authority over their children in exchange for financial support and what they hope will be valued input into their children's lives. In other words, the parents are engaging in, resisting or otherwise negotiating a moral contract over their respective responsibilities and commitments.

Accepting then that many parents perceive a link between contact and child support,[99] there are two issues. The first is whether this perception is one which the law should seek to encourage or one which the law should seek to challenge. The majority view among family lawyers seems to be that child support should be regarded as a right of the child, or at least an essential responsibility of parenthood, which exists quite independently of any question of contact. Certainly from the child's point of view it could certainly be the case that although it is in the child's interests to receive financial support, it might not be to have contact with the non-resident parent.

The second issue is whether, nevertheless, the perceived link between child support and contact is one upon which the law wishes to build. For example, Maclean and Eekelaar (1998) argue that the law is more likely to be effective if it builds on social obligations, rather than seeking to work against them. This is in the context of debating whether a man should be primarily financially responsible for the child with whom he is living or his birth children who are living apart from him. For some there is perhaps an issue of pragmatism versus realism here. Even if you decry the link that many parents make between contact and support it must still be asked whether it is a link upon which the law should seek to rely to achieve desirable goals.

To clarify the issue it is important to appreciate that if it was decided to seek to build on the link it could be used in at least five ways:

1. The law could seek to increase levels of contact by offering a reduction in child support where contact takes place.

---

[99] Wallerstein and Lewis (1998). Seltzer (2000) also discusses the evidence that child support and contact are linked although there is not unanimity on this issue:

2. The law could penalise no contact by offering an increase in child support where contact does not take place.
3. The law could seek to increase levels of contact by more vigorously enforcing child support obligations.
4. The law could seek to increase levels of child support by compelling greater levels of contact.
5. The law could decrease the amount of benefit received by mothers who refuse to permit contact.

Of course, these options would need to be fleshed out in far greater detail than just summarised. The Government has essentially pursued the first option, but that was only one way to build on the perceived link between contact and child support. In choosing between these options a key question is: do non-resident parents seek contact because they have been obliged to pay support; or do non-resident parents pay support because they have had contact? Research to date does not provide a clear answer to this. It is probably a complex mixture of the two.

I would suggest that if a father is having contact solely because of the financial benefits (or to avoid a financial disbenefit) the effectiveness of that contact could be questioned. As the research emphasises, it is not the fact of contact that potentially benefits a child, but the quality of it. Even if that is not the reason for contact, an astute child, aware that contact is saving his father money, may find that knowledge undermines the relationship.[100] I would recommend the third approach, outlined above. It avoids any open link between the two issues and upholds the key principle of financial support for children. Any improvement in contact would be a desirable side-product and provide an incentive towards effective enforcement of obligations to children.

CONCLUSION

Katharine Bartlett has written:

> The law is given both too much blame for what goes wrong at divorce, and too much credit for how it might make things better. The law cannot prevent embittered or adversarial adults from waging battle over children. It cannot guarantee the future behaviours of adults or responses by children. Most of all, the law cannot guarantee that children will obtain the love and nurture that they most need. (Bartlett, 1999: 97)

While accepting the severe limits on what the law can do in cases of dispute over contact, this chapter has sought to argue that the law can try and do something (see also James, this volume). However, this is not at the obvious stage of

---

[100] According to the Advisory Board on Family Law: Children Act Sub-Committee (Lord Chancellor's Department, 2002: 14.41): some men's groups contrast the rigour with which the CSA enforced with the lack of rigour of enforcement of contact.

arranging and enforcing contact. Rather it is to encourage parents to develop and maintain a co-operative relationship after divorce. In particular two suggestions have been made. It has been argued that the law on domestic violence needs to appreciate the harm children suffer by witnessing violence and living with hostility. The swift and effective intervention of the court will protect children from these harms and increase the possibility of beneficial contact in the future. It has also been suggested that the effective enforcement of child support might lead to an increase in the number of fathers seeking contact and the number of mothers willing to permit contact. It should be emphasised that I have not recommended directly linking contact and child support. It is, perhaps, ironic that the organisations[101] which have been most vocal in their support of increased contact between fathers and children have also been some of the most vociferous in their objections to the Child Support Act and most wary of the court's use of domestic violence orders. I would suggest the opposite: those who wish to encourage contact should seek greater use of domestic violence and child support legislation.

REFERENCES

BAINHAM, A, 'The Privatisation of the Public Interest in Children' (1990) 53 *Modern Law Review* 206.
——'Can We Protect Children and Protect their Rights?' (2002) 32 *Family Law* 279.
BARNETT, A, 'Disclosure of Domestic Violence by Women involved in Child Contact Disputes' (1999) 29 *Family Law* 104.
BARNETT, A, 'Contact and the Domestic Violence: The Ideological Divide' in J Bridgeman and D Monk (eds), *Feminist Perspectives on Child Law* (London, Cavendish, 2000).
BARTLETT, K, 'Improving the Law Relating to Post-divorce Arrangements for Children' in R Thompson and P Amato (eds), *The Post Divorce Family* (Thousand Oaks, CA, Sage, 1999).
BERNS, S, 'Parents Behaving Badly: Parental Alienation Syndrome in the Family Court— Magic Bullet or Poisoned Chalice' (2001) *Australian Journal of Family Law* 6.
BIRCH, C, 'Parental Alienation Syndrome and Parental Alienation: Getting it Wrong in Child Custody Cases' (2001) 35 *Family Law Quarterly* 527.
BRADSHAW, J, STIMSON, C, SKINNER, C, and WILLIAMS, J, *Absent Fathers?* (London, Routledge, 1999).
BRASSE, G, 'Contact and Money' (2002) 32 *Family Law* 691.
BUCHANAN, A, HUNT, J, BRETHERTON, H and BREAM, V, 'Families in Conflict— Perspectives of Children and Parents on the Family Court Welfare Service' (2001) 31 *Family Law* 900.
Children Act Sub-committee of the Lord Chancellor's Advisory Board on Family Law, *Guidelines for Good Practice on Parental Contact in Cases where there is Domestic Violence* (London, Lord Chancellor's Department, 2002).

---

[101] Eg Families need Fathers (www.fnf.org.uk).

COTTINGHAM, U and SLADE, A, 'Mediating in Child Contact: A Multidisciplinary Approach' (2000) 30 *Family Law* 933.

DAVIS, G and WIKELEY, N, 'National Survey of Child Support Agency Clients—The Relationship Dimension' (2002) 32 *Family Law* 522.

DAVIS, G and WIKELEY, N and YOUNG, R, *Child Support in Action* (Oxford, Hart, 1998).

Department of Health, *The Children Act Report 2001* (London, Department of Health, 2002).

Department of Social Security, *Children First* (London, Department of Social Security, 1998).

——*Children's Rights and Parents' Responsibilities* (London, Department of Social Security, 1999).

EEKELAAR, J, 'Rethinking Parental Responsibility' (2001) 31 *Family Law* 426.

——'Contact—Over the Limit' (2002) 32 *Family Law* 271.

EMERY, R, *Renegotiating Family Relationships: Divorce, Child Custody and Mediation* (NY, Guilford Press, 1994).

Families Need Fathers, *Response to the Consultation Paper. Contact Between Children and Violent Parents* (Families Need Fathers, 1999).

FERRI, E and SMITH, K, *Parenting in the 1990s* (London, Family Policy Studies Centre, 1996).

FINCH, J and MASON, J, *Negotiating Family Responsibilities* (London, Routledge, 1993).

GERLIS, S, 'Contact—Pernicious Poison' (1998) 28 *Family Law* 695.

——'Contact—Name Your Poison' (2002) 32 *Family Law* 68.

GOLDSTEIN, J, SOLNIT, A, GOLDSTEIN, S and FREUD, A, *The Best Interests of the Child* (New York, Free Press, 1996).

HALL, His Honour Judge, 'Domestic Violence and Contact' (1997) 27 *Family Law* 813.

HARRISON, M, 'Australia's Family Law Act: The First Twenty-Five Years' (2002) 16 *International Journal of Law Policy and the Family* 1.

HERLTH, A, 'The New Fathers: What Does it Mean for Children, Marriage and for Family Policy?' in F-X Kaufmann, A Kuijsten, H-J Schulze and K Strohmeier (eds), *Family Policies and Family Policies in Europe* (Oxford, Oxford University Press, 2002).

HERRING, J, *Family Law* (Harlow, Longman, 2001).

HESTER, M, 'One Step Forward and Three Steps Back? Children, Abuse and Parental Contact in Denmark' (2002) 14 *Child and Family Law Quarterly* 267.

HESTER, M and HARNE, L, 'Fatherhood, Children and Violence: Placing England in an International Context' in S Watson and L Doyal (eds), *Engendering Social Policy* (Buckingham, Open University Press, 1999).

HESTER, M and PEARSON, C, 'Domestic Violence and Children—The Practice of Family Court Welfare Officers' (1997) 9 *Child and Family Law Quarterly* 281.

HESTER, M and PEARSON, C and HARRISON, M, *Making an Impact, Children and Domestic Violence* (London, Kingsley Publishers Ltd, 2000).

HESTER, M and RADFORD, L, *Domestic Violence and Child Contact Arrangements in England and Wales* (Bristol, Polity Press, 1996).

HETHERINGTON, M and KELLY, J, *For Better or For Worse: Divorce Reconsidered* (New York, WW Norton & Co, 2002).

HOBBS, T, 'Parental Alienation Syndrome and UK Family Courts' (2002) 32 *Family Law* 182 and 381.

HUGHES, H, 'Psychological and Behavioural Correlates of Family Violence In Child Witnesses and Victims' (1988) 58 *American Journal of Ortho-Psychiatry* 77.

JOLLY, S, 'Implacable Hostility, Contact and the Limits of Law' (1995) 16 *Journal of Social Welfare and Family Law* 299.

KAGANAS, F, 'Contact, Conflict and Risk' in S Day Sclater and C Piper (eds), *Undercurrents of Divorce* (Aldershot, Ashgate, 1999).

KAGANAS, F and DAY SCLATER S, 'Contact and Domestic Violence—The Winds of Change?' (2000) 30 *Family Law* 630.

KELLY J and JOHNSTON, J, 'Alienated Children in Divorce: The Alienated Child: A Reformulation of Parental Alienation Syndrome' (2001) 39 *Family Court Review* 249.

LAFRANCE, A, 'Child Custody and Relocation' (1995) 34 *Journal of Family Law* 1.

LAMB, M and KELLY, J, 'The Continuing Debate about Overnight Visitation' (2001) 39 *Family Court Review* 365.

LEMON, N, 'Statutes Creating Rebuttable Presumptions Against Custody to Batterers: How Effective Are They?' (2001) 28 *William Mitchell Law Review* 601.

LEWIS, J, 'The Problem with Fathers: Policy and Behaviour in Britain' in B. Hobson (ed.), *Making Men into Fathers* (Cambridge, Cambridge University Press, 2002).

Lord Chancellor's Department, The Advisory Board on Family Law: Children Act Sub-committee, *Making Contact Work* (London, Lord Chancellor's Department, 2002).

MACLEAN, M and EEKELAAR, J, *The Parental Obligation* (Oxford, Hart, 1998).

MACCOBY, E, 'The Custody of Children of Divorcing Families' in R Thompson and P Amato (eds), *The Post-Divorce Family* (Thousand Oaks, California, Sage, 1999).

MACCOBY, E and MNOOKIN, R, *Dividing the Child* (Cambridge, Harvard University Press, 1992).

MASSON, J, 'Thinking About Contact—a Social or a Legal Problem?' (2000) 12 *Child and Family Law Quarterly* 15.

MIRRLEES-BLACK, C, *Estimating the Extent of Domestic Violence Findings from the 1992 BCS Research Bulletin No 37* (London, Whiting and Birch, 1995).

NEALE, B and SMART, C, 'Good and Bad Lawyers? Struggling in the Shadow of the New Law?' (1997) 19 *Journal of Social Welfare and Family Law* 377.

NEALE, B and SMART, C, 'Caring, Earning and Changing' in A Carling, S Dunacan and R Edwards (eds), *Analysing Families* (London, Routledge, 2002).

PEARCE, J, DAVIS, G and BARRON, J, 'Love in a Cold Climate—Section 8 Applications under the Children Act 1989' (1999) 29 *Family Law* 22.

PIPER, C, 'Norms and Negotiation in Mediation and Divorce' in M Freeman (ed.) *Divorce: Where Next?* (Aldershot, Dartmouth, 1996).

PIPER, C and KAGANAS, F, 'Family Law Act 1996, Section 1(d)—How Will "They" Know there is a Risk of Violence' (1997) 9 *Child and Family Law Quarterly* 269.

POUSSIN, G and MARTIN-LEBRUN, E, 'A French Study of Children's Self-Esteem after Parental Separation' (2002) 16 *International Journal of Law Policy and the Family* 313.

PRYOR, J and ROGERS, B, *Divorce and Separation* (York, Joseph Rowntree Foundation, 1998).

RADFORD, L, *Unreasonable Fears? Child Contact in the Context of Domestic Violence* (London, Women's Aid, 1999).

RHODES, H, 'The "No Contact Mother": Reconstructions of Motherhood in the Era of the "New Father"' ' (2002) 16 *International Journal of Law Policy and the Family* 71.

SAWYERS, C, 'An Inside Story. Ascertaining Child's Wishes and Feelings' (2000) 30 *Family Law* 170.

SELTZER, J 'Relationships between Fathers and Children who Live Apart: The Father's Role after Separation' (1991) 53 *Journal of Marriage and the Family* 79.

—— 'Child Support and Child Access: Experiences of Divorced and Nonmarital Families' in J Thomas Oldham and M Melli (eds), *Child Support: The Next Frontier* (Ann Arbor, University of Michigan Press, 2000).

SELTZER, J, SCHAEFFER, N and CHARING, H, 'Family Ties after Divorce. The Relationship between Visiting and Paying Child Support' (1989) 51 *Journal of Marriage and the Family* 1013.

SMART, C, 'The Legal and Moral Ordering of Child Custody' (1991) 19 *Journal of Law and Society* 485.

SMART, C and NEALE, B, 'Arguments Against Virtue—Must Contact be Enforced' (1997) 27 *Family Law* 332.

SMART, C and NEALE, B, *Family Fragments?* (Cambridge, Polity Press, 1999).

SOLOMON, J and BIRINGEN, Z, 'The Continuing Debate about Overnight Visitation' (2001) 39 *Family Court Review* 355.

STURGE, C and GLASER, D, 'Contact and Domestic Violence—The Experts' Court Report' (2000) 30 *Family Law* 615.

THOMAS OLDHAM, J, 'Limitations Imposed by Family Law on a Separated Parent's Ability to Make Significant Life Decisions: A Comparison of Relocation and Income Imputation' (2001) 8 *Duke Journal of Gender Law & Policy* 333.

WALLER, M, *My Baby's Father: Unmarried Parents and Paternal Responsibility* (Ithaca NY, Cornell University Press, 2002).

WALLERSTEIN, J and LEWIS, J, 'The Long-term Impact of Divorce on Children' (1998) *Family and Conciliation Courts Review* 368.

WILLIAMS, C, 'Parental Alienation Syndrome' (2002) 32 *Family Law* 410.

WILLBOURNE, C and CULL, L, 'The Emerging Problem of Parental Alienation' (1997) 27 *Family Law* 807.

WILLBOURNE, C and STANLEY, G, 'Contact under the Microscope' (2002) 32 *Family Law* 687.

7

Supporting Cross-Household Parenting: Ideas about 'the Family', Policy Formation and Service Development across Jurisdictions

MAVIS MACLEAN and KATRIN MUELLER-JOHNSON

1. INTRODUCTION

IN THIS CHAPTER we look at the different ways in which the on-going relationship between children and their parents who live outside the home is regarded in different jurisdictions, and the policy formulation and service development which subsequently flow from this, focusing particularly on development of contact centres. We comment on the way in which support for contact is conceptualised in the UK, the USA and in Continental Europe. We then make a more detailed comparison between recent developments in England and Wales and in Germany of the way these service developments may serve children and their parents. The contact support services provided have developed in response to the need for help following a private law dispute between parents. But their use is not restricted to private law cases; they can also be used by families trying to maintain or rebuild a relationship with a child who is being looked after by the state following a public law hearing.

The authors' understanding of the need for support to parents having difficulty in arranging for them both to have a meaningful ongoing relationship with their children is as follows: *parenting* is a good thing, and children need as much of it as they can have, UNLESS there are strong contraindications such as conflict which the child is drawn into or troubled by, or fear of pressure or harm, or where uncertainty over contact, particularly when not discussed with or explained to the child, may have an impact on the child's confidence and self esteem. *Loss* is a bad thing for children, and they may need help in maintaining a relationship which they value but is difficult for them, or their parents, to manage, particularly in the early stages of a separation when emotions are running high. Kathleen Funder (1996) demonstrated, using family sculpture techniques, how children find it far easier to accept new family members than we had thought, but far harder to lose anyone, even family pets. But it is also important to remember that over-zealous attempts to avoid losing contact with an external parent may lead to a loss of stability and security in the primary home.

These are personal assumptions, and we still lack a body of empirical research to answer all our queries. But the research, as can be seen from this volume, is beginning to offer both hard data and clear and constructive analysis on contact in cases following a separation where the dispute between parents is a private matter, and in cases where there is a public interest in that there have been questions about the child's safety and well-being involving local authority social services. It is important to remember that, although the legal consequences of a private or public dispute are very different, it is not unusual for the same children to be involved in both.

We have evidence that conflict and violence are bad for children (Hester, Pearson and Harwin, 2000; Buchanan *et al*, 2001), and that uncertainty is damaging to the child's self-esteem (Poussin and Martin-Lebrun, 2002). Judy Dunn's work (this volume) finds clear evidence of the benefits of contact. But the research evidence on the links between contact and the child's well being is not conclusive and does need to be contextualised. In a study of looked after adolescents in foster care, contact with biological parents was found to be unhelpful (Sinclair *et al*, 2002). A recent large-scale study by Marjorie Smith (Smith *et al*, 2001) of children living in stepfamilies, with a sample drawn from local schools rather than any therapeutic or court related setting, found that contact with a non-resident parent had no discernible effect on development or welfare. The best predictor of the child's development and welfare in this study lay in the quality of relationships in the home where the child lived. This is not a surprising finding, but it is an aspect of the child's situation which is not often discussed. Contact disputes tend to focus on the two parents, and say less about the wider context of 'home'. If we are thinking of the well-being of the child as the starting point, home is a primary factor. An approach which concentrates on the dispute between the two parents reflects a preoccupation with the rights of the adults as the starting point, rather than the needs of the child.

2. UNITED KINGDOM

In the UK, as in other jurisdictions, the issue of contact is discussed in terms of the benefit to the child. Our model of the family is traditionally of a small, nuclear, two-generation unit, whose function is to provide the best start in life for the children. This statement is a vast over-simplification, particularly in view of the increasingly diverse nature of our society, but may serve as a starting point for the discussion.

Increasing the amount of contact between children and non-resident parents has become a primary aim of both family law and government family policy in England and Wales, albeit with the caveat that this must be consistent with the welfare of the child. In order to achieve this aim the government has been considering a number of options to bring into play when one parent is adamant in objecting to contact with the other. These include developing the powers of the court, which can already order a custodial sentence for a hostile parent. There is at the time of writing discussion of alternative interventions, such as obligatory parenting classes (see Lord Chancellor's Department, 2002). All of these options are raised in the context of making it possible for a father to see the child even where the mother, and possibly the child, does not wish it. The reverse situation, when the child and the mother wish the father to see the child and he refuses is not discussed often enough in England and Wales, even though the assumption should still hold that contact is a good thing (see Bainham, this volume). There is also little discussion of the question of continuing access for parents where a child has been taken into care, fostered or adopted.

Our concern, then, is selective. Women's groups have pointed out that the policy debate appears to be dominated by the question of how to secure access for fathers to the children of reluctant mothers. Sadly, as so often in family law matters, the agenda has become a battleground defined by gender. We need to keep the children centre stage in these discussions, recognising that the well-being of children and their parents are not unrelated, but also are not identical. Perhaps we also need to bear in mind the changing definitions of parenthood. The contact disputes driven by unhappy non-resident biological fathers may have been underestimating the growing importance and acceptance of social parenthood whereby those who perform the parenting tasks assume the role and need to be supported in doing so. An extreme example lies in the appearance of a biological father who has no pre-existing relationship with the child and wishes to develop one. Repartnered parents and their partners may fear disruption of their family life, but the courts have in the past been sympathetic to the biological father's claims. To establish a new relationship may well be beneficial to the child. But we need also to pay attention to the value of the status quo, and to be cautious about bringing legal sanctions into play in order to pressure a family into new untried situations (see Eekelaar, this volume). In the past, stability was usually the overriding factor in custody disputes. Eekelaar and Clive (1977) described how reluctant courts were at that time to submit a child to a major change in home circumstances unless there were overwhelming reasons to do so. The issue of stability is currently, by contrast, less often discussed in contact disputes.

The role of law is inevitably limited. It cannot use sanctions to require people under stress to behave better than 'OK'. That is, the law may require them to refrain from infringing the rights of others, but it cannot make them behave extremely well. As Liz Trinder (this volume) has demonstrated, successful contact makes demands on both parents to trust and work together as parents in a new way after their relationship as a couple has broken down. This requires a long-term commitment of time and emotional energy. Arranging contact is not like making a property settlement, where an asset can be handed over or withheld. It is a continuing and demanding process fraught with difficulty. Failure requires support rather than sanction, a willingness to accept that success may not be possible in every case and it is unhelpful to frame the parties as guilty or innocent. We now accept the no-fault but stressful character of the divorce process. Perhaps it is time to think of the stressful but no-fault nature of the process of contact. The UK policy discourse is presented in welfare terms and dominated by the requirement to avoid loss for the child. The legal framework, the Children Act 1989, looks firmly towards private ordering of residence and contact after divorce or separation. Where the public interest is not involved, when two parents cease to live together the role of the court is not to prescribe where the child should live. It is limited to intervening to resolve a dispute. The presumption is clear that there should be no court order unless it is better for the child that an order is made and such orders are not set in stone. The Act is based on the recognition that children grow, that circumstances change, and that the court can be approached at any stage to vary an order. Our recent study of the work of divorce solicitors bears this out, in that the lawyers were anxious to avoid becoming involved in contact disputes and frequently sought to persuade clients that these were issues for them as parents to resolve and were not best helped by coming before a court (Eekelaar *et al*, 2001). But on closer examination, if we take away the rhetoric and look at the events, what we see, in the main, is parents with care, mainly mothers, wishing to maintain their status quo. And we see non-resident parents, mainly fathers, seeking more contact, with some of them looking to the courts and lawyers to help them achieve this. The pro-contact stance of the courts, combined with the policy aims of the Child Support Act to increase parental involvement and acceptance of financial responsibility after divorce, did mean, for a time, that the question of safety for mothers and children was overlooked in domestic violence cases. Recent moves to remedy this have taken place (see Lord Chancellor's Department, 1999).

Service development, based on the need to make contact work primarily in private law cases, has been rapid over the last few years. The Family Law Act 1996 drew attention to the importance of providing information for those with family issues to resolve. We have great hopes of the new Children and Family Advice and Support Service (CAFCASS), which despite a troubled beginning has great potential to bring together advice and support for parents and children. The contact centre movement continues to develop rapidly. There is discussion of increasing the advice available through schools and family centres. The Legal Services Commission is piloting Family Advice and Information Networks (FAINS), based initially in solicitors' offices, to offer support and advice, and encourage use of mediation and counselling as well as helping to identify which issues require legal advice or action. It is to be hoped that the service providers will be able to maintain their focus on the welfare of children, while also finding a way to deal with the father's wishes, claims, or rights (see Eekelaar, this volume, for a fuller discussion of the implications of the Human Rights Act in this respect).

3. UNITED STATES OF AMERICA

In the UK thinking about support for parenting, as in so many other social policy issues, stands midway between the US and our European neighbours. Before turning to Continental Europe we therefore comment briefly on the American approach. If we again employ generalisation, or 'models' of the family, as we did for the UK, let us consider the possibility that in the US there is a more individualistic and rights-based approach to life, including family life and that this is reflected in family law.

In the US the legal framework for divorce has long been directed more towards distribution of individual assets and establishment of visitation (contact) rights at the end of the relationship. In contrast the UK divorce law looks to the future needs of both parties and their children and sees the parenting relationship as a continuing one. This individualistic rights-based approach to life after divorce, which is present but lying a little below the surface in the UK and may indeed develop following the Human Rights Act 1998, has been more clearly visible in relation to contact in the US. Carol Bruch (2001) has described the level of control over the parent with care and the child that has been laid down and enforced in the detail of visitation arrangements provided for fathers by some courts, a position that might seem surprising to European eyes. Services for supporting or supervising these arrangements have developed in response to domestic violence and child sexual abuse issues as a means to provide a way for fathers to exercise their visitation rights while at the same time ensuring the safety of the child and residential parent. Although there is considerable variation between services, access programmes are generally run with a high degree of professionalism and the profit-making services levy charges for the service provided. In total, 63 per cent of providers in a recent survey charged fees, on average $20–25 per hour[1] (Pearson and Thoennes, 1997). The centres work with the courts, and provide reports to referrers or to the courts covering facts like attendances and brief notes on what occurred during the sessions. UK centres rarely charge fees, and are much more hesitant about providing reports back to referrers, not only because this might undermine their neutrality, but also because they cover a less conflicted population and perhaps lack the professional assessment and reporting skills required (Dickens, 1999). The regulation of supervised visitation in the United States is at state level, and in most cases forms part of specific domestic violence legislation (see, for example, Code of Alabama 30–3–135). In some states specific criteria for ordering supervised contact are restricted to child abuse or neglect (see, for example, the Code of Maryland Family Law 9–101). In a few states the norms for ordering supervised visitation are part of the regulation of marriage dissolution and include the

---

[1] This average fee is calculated from information which includes data from non-profit making institutions.

supervision of visitation in circumstances other than family violence. In Kansas, for example, supervised visitation can be ordered where a parent is impaired with respect to his parenting capacity due to mental disability, mental illness or substance abuse (see Kansas Statutes 75–720–c). Thirteen states and Washington DC had no specific criteria for ordering supervised visitation at the time of writing.

The survey by Pearson and Thoennes (1997) found that US centres tend to have paid staff, whether part-time employees or independent contractors. Nearly all centres also have volunteers who supervise visits. About half the programmes have postgraduate and senior undergraduate students as volunteers and about a quarter to a third of centres also use community volunteers. About half of the visitation programmes in the study placed restrictions on the type of cases that volunteers are allowed to supervise, typically excluding cases where there is a risk of violence.

Although 13 per cent of the agencies in this sample were profit making, nearly two-thirds (60 per cent) were private, non-profit agencies, while 14 per cent were part of public agencies and 9 per cent were individuals who provided supervision services.

The main difference between US and UK providers seems to be that in the United States access programmes concentrate on providing supervised visitation on a one-to-one basis. The type of service in which a group of parents and children is supervised by one volunteer in a less closely monitored setting, in US terminology, group supervision, is provided by only one fifth of the access programmes in the survey. Few centres seem to offer only group supervision. This contrasts with the UK situation, where supervised contact is rarely offered and supported contact (or 'group supervision') is the norm.

Further options for access programmes in the US are 'facilitative or supportive supervised visitation' and 'therapeutic supervision', in both of which a supervisor steps out of his or her neutral role and explicitly tries to help improve the visiting parent's behaviour towards the child, through advice and modelling of behaviour. Although such supervisors are specially trained to provide this sort of education, 'therapeutic supervised visitation' can be provided only by a mental health professional. Therapeutic supervision may be indicated where there has been past trauma (Marsh, 2000). About 35 per cent of access programmes offer such a service.

As can be inferred from these differences, contact services in the US seem to be targeted at a clientele perceived to be in need of higher levels of intervention. This is not to say that all access programmes in the US provide a more professional and individualised service aimed at high conflict or high risk cases. One centre described by Pearson and Thoennes (1997) appeared to be quite similar to the average UK centre. It provided supported contact almost exclusively and was staffed by two adult supervisors and several teenagers who were in charge of taking the children to the toilet. In addition, and this is a typical US feature, it had a security officer onsite. The sessions were described as similar to day care experience, ie in which children and parents join others in play and supervisors remain in the background. But though this centre superficially seems quite similar to a typical UK centre, the clientele had a more conflicted/higher risk background than that of the average UK centre. About one quarter of families at this centre reported allegations of physical abuse and in about the same number of families there were allegations of child sexual abuse. Furniss (2000) shows in her survey of UK centres that 29 per cent of centres would not accept families with allegations of inappropriate behaviour towards the child and 41 per cent would refuse families with child sexual abuse allegations. So, while US centres generally seem to be run in a more professional manner and are more intervention-oriented, there are also some that provide a lower key service although they seem to deal with a higher risk population.

4. CONTINENTAL EUROPE

France

If we return to Europe we find a very different picture of family life, family law and ideas about how to support cross-household parenting. If we continue our practice of setting up a model to start our discussion, we might suggest that in France the family is traditionally highly valued and seen as a cross-generational institution at the heart of society. Following from this it is fascinating to note that there is a strong school of thought in France that the purpose of contact lies in maintaining the concept of the family over time, through a line which flows from generation to generation. This conceptualisation of the relationship between parent and child argues for the provision of help and support in maintaining this relationship where there is no common household. But in order for this to work the former couple must be helped to work together as continuing parents, as a 'couple parental'. In France the work of supporting contact developed from within the mediation movement. From this perspective there comes the view that it is not sensible to place a child in the middle of a conflicted couple and expect her to sustain a valuable relationship with two key adults who are not co-operating with each other. The strain on the child is thought to be harmful. An adult conflict is no place for a child. In a survey conducted by Benoit Bastard and Laura Cardia Voneche of 45 contact centres in 1998 this view was predominant in two thirds of those responding. But there is also a group of contact centres who take a different view and who place more emphasis on the need to establish the relationship between parent and child irrespective of the relationship between the parental couple. This approach was developed at the Point-Rencontre de Bordeaux where the non-resident parent and child are given time and space to be together with support at hand (see Bastard, 1998).

To sum up, in France support for parents is based on more developed theorising about the relationship between parents and children across generations, as well as across households and takes a therapeutic approach rather than merely facilitating or helping to enforce the requirements of the court. The pragmatic British service provides the basic amenities of a place to meet and has been widely used by the courts as the solution to a difficult problem, but has been slow to develop a more professional approach to the more complex cases. In the US there is a strong connection between the insistence of fathers on the right to see their children and the development of a private market in places where safety can be guaranteed.

Germany

Finally we turn to Germany, where the concept of contact facilitation is relatively new, and has taken the new form of high quality state provision, free at the point of delivery, which has been added to the existing child welfare services with a requirement also for parental counselling. To continue our generalisations, we might suggest that in Germany the conflicted family is defined as 'sick' and in need, not of conflict resolution, but of therapeutic intervention. We find almost a medicalisation of the problem with the state taking responsibility, not for punishing individuals for failure to comply with contact orders, but instead being proactive in providing treatment for the non-functioning post-separation family. Many providers have begun work in response to this recent change in law, which explicitly granted courts the option of ordering supported and supervised contact and made it a responsibility of the social services to pay for contact supervision as part of their provisions for families and children in need and in crisis. Paragraph 1684 IV, Sentences 3 and 4 of the Civil Code introduced in 1998, enable the family court to require contact to take place under the supervision of a third party. Children, adolescents and parents are entitled to state assistance in connection with post-divorce contact (I 18 Social Security Code VII, the comprehensive codification of all social insurance and welfare legislation). This assistance is to come from the social services youth welfare service when a court order for supervised contact is made. The social services are also required by law to make sure that there are enough supervised contact places available.

Much of the service is still in flux: preliminary standards for contact supervision were only set out in summer 2001 and are currently under review before they are being voted on in the summer of 2002. But it is possible to distinguish two distinct approaches to contact provision in Germany. One more pragmatic approach, which has similarities to the UK model, provides supported contact for groups of families by trained volunteers supervised by a social worker or psychologist (eg as provided by the Kinderschutzbund). Members of this type of centre were already providing contact before the legislative introduction of contact facilitation. The other approach is reminiscent of the French model. In fact, it takes the idea of intervention even further: it provides contact supervision on an individual rather than a group level, regardless of the amount of supervision needed (in the UK one-to-one supervision is also available, but only for supervised contact). Contact supervision is provided by highly qualified professionals, who are usually psychologists or social workers, with an additional qualification in family mediation, family therapy or divorce and separation counselling. Contact visits are accompanied by parallel counselling sessions for parents, either jointly or separately. Facilitating contact is regarded as pointless unless the relationship between the parents—as parents—is addressed (Haid-Loh, Normann-Kossak and Walter, 2000).

The current preliminary legislative standards favour the interventionist approach and the provision of services by professionals rather than volunteers. To a substantial extent this move away from low-key centres to professionally managed individual interventions may also be associated with the change in funding for contact. The legislative change of 1998 made the provision of supervised contact a standard responsibility of the social services, just like assistance with child rearing or counselling for children in crisis. These services were being provided by psychologists and social workers. It appears therefore to be a logical development to entrust the facilities and institutions that provided those earlier services for the state with the additional provision of contact supervision.

When a family approaches the contact provider, whether ordered by the court, sent by the social services or through self referral, the facility draws up an individual plan for the contact intervention and sends it for approval to the social services who assess the need for contact facilitation on a case-by-case basis. By contrast, centres which were already providing contact before the legislative change were mainly run by charitable organisations (eg Kinderschutzbund, Red Cross) and were largely independent of state funding. They were also independent of direct state supervision and of the need for the provision of services for each individual family to be approved by the social services.

It has been argued in Germany that families move onto independent contact more quickly when they undergo counselling at the same time. Also there may be a hope that families will move out of the court and the contact support system once and for all, rather than reappearing again and again for newly arising conflicts. Volunteers are not generally qualified to conduct such counselling, which makes it understandable that the state would want to fund professionals to do contact facilitation. But such services are expensive. Some projects have two counsellors (if possible one male, one female) to conduct the sessions with the parents and one fixed contact supervisor for all contact visits. In high-risk cases it has been reported that providers would consider having two contact supervisors for a family. At the moment, the demand for contact facilitation is still at the start-up stage, and many facilities are working with qualified contractors rather than permanent staff, or are not used to full capacity. As demand increases it remains to be seen whether it will be possible to maintain such cost-intensive services.

Closely related to this aspect of professionalisation of services is the question of mandatory parental counselling. The majority of providers at the annual contact facilitators' conference regarded parental counselling as an important aspect of contact facilitation, although some institutions were not able to provide it due to lack of staff. Most projects offer joint or separate counselling and also believe that contact facilitation makes sense only if it is accompanied by parallel counselling sessions with the parents (Haid-Loh *et al*, 2000). Parents referred to the projects are usually highly conflicted. It is believed that counselling for both parents is the best way to de-escalate conflict and change attitudes in a way that enables them to have independent contact in future (Haid-Loh *et al*, 2000). Still, even though most projects regard the combination of counselling and contact as desirable, counselling sessions tend to take place only irregularly while the family uses its services. Some larger institutions have an even stronger focus on counselling. Here contact is facilitated only at the beginning of the process and families are encouraged to move to independent contact as soon as possible, while continuing counselling at the project to support their efforts and talk through what went well and what did not.

It has been reported that long-term use of a project by families may be partly due to the fact that attribution of fault, or lack of parental aptitude, may be reinforced (Haid-Loh *et al*, 2000). Counselling is believed to work on these aspects and to decrease the time that families need to attend the project. A counterargument has been voiced that there may be families who do not want to undergo mandatory counselling and they should be given a choice in the model of contact facilitation that they would like to use. Volunteer run centres can be a useful alternative here, because they do not usually provide counselling services.

The issue of reporting back to courts is being debated in Germany, just as it has been in the UK. Facilities differ in how far they co-operate with the court system. Some services work very closely with the courts and provide court reports after a specified number of visits. In addition, the social services, which in many cases are the funding source for contact facilitation, get a brief factual report of the contact intervention in the cases they fund. As a member of the social services always takes part in the contact proceedings, as was the case for the family court welfare officer in the UK, facilities' reports may be introduced in court proceedings by the representative of the social services.

Families are usually referred by the courts or the social services (the German equivalent of the former UK family court welfare officer). Lawyers or experts, who assessed the child or the parental fitness for the court, only rarely made referrals. There are some self-referrals. Data from a well established contact facilitation programme run by a charity shows that about 35 per cent of referrals to this particular centre were made by social services, 31 per cent by the family court and 25 per cent by lawyers or mental health experts involved in the case. Nine percent of families were self-referrals. In contrast in the UK, most families are referred by lawyers for supported contact. In 1999, 70 per cent of referrals were from lawyers, 21 per cent from family court welfare officers, 4 per cent from the Social Services and 2.6 per cent were self-referrals. Referrals for supervised contact came less often from lawyers, only around 50 per cent, and 35 per cent were made by family court welfare officers. We have the impression that families who use contact facilitation in Germany tend to be more like families using supervised contact in the UK than those using supported contact centres. The standard service offered by German contact providers looks like the few highly professional centres which provide supervised contact in the UK. Similarly, German contact providers see a high proportion of families with allegations of physical or sexual abuse, with domestic violence allegations or risk of abduction. In the UK allegations of physical or sexual violence towards the child are regarded as reasons for many centres to refuse to accept the families.

In the typical UK setting, centres conduct short intake interviews with the parents and have them sign an agreement to abide by the ground rules of the centre. Centres have restricted opening times, such as, for instance, every other Saturday. Usually several families will share the room in which contact takes place. Most centres have restrictions in the activities they can offer for children, only a few have gardens (due to safety considerations) and toys and games are usually more geared to younger children. In Germany, by contrast, contact takes place on an individual level. At the first meetings, parents work out a plan for how contact is to take place. They negotiate times, frequency and location of contact. Depending on the child's age, his or her wishes about contact activities are taken into account. Because each family has 'their own' facilitator it is possible to have supervised visits to places other than the contact facility, such as the playground or the zoo. In this way contact can take place at times best suited to parents and, as far as safety considerations permit, with activities that the child really enjoys.

At these initial meetings parents also agree that they will undergo parent counselling at the facility to work on their conflicts about contact and they draw up a set of responses and sanctions to possible behaviours by the other parent (e.g. what should happen if one parent comes repeatedly late or cancels the visits).

In the UK centres often offer the opportunity for the child to make a preliminary visit to the centre in order to familiarise him or herself with the place and the staff. Families find this very helpful for the child (Furniss, 2000). In Germany, this is taken even further: before the child meets the visiting parent for the first time, he or she attends one or two play sessions at the contact service, in order to get to know and bond with the contact facilitator. This is very much in contrast to US approaches, where some centres rotate staff on purpose to minimise the possibility of a family's dependency upon staff.

In the UK, families who start with supervised contact can move to supported contact after sufficient progress is made. This decision is usually taken by the centre staff together with the parents. In Germany, this decision is also made by parents with the staff but only with permission of the social services, and this is regarded as an additional safety provision. In both the UK and Germany, contact facilitation is regarded as a temporary solution. However, contact centres in the UK do not place a limit on how often families can come. The average period is about 10 visits per family for supported contact and they then move on to independent contact.

In Germany, a case by case plan, drawn up with the social services before visits start, determines for how many visits funding is approved. It has been reported that families visit an average of 20 times. In Berlin, facilitators (personal communication) reported that facilitation is usually approved for about six months and then it is possible to apply for renewal, which so far has usually been granted (bearing in mind that numbers of applications for contact facilitations are still relatively small). The bureaucracy involved in contact facilitation is much higher here than in the UK system. As stated above, parents have to agree to co-operate in counselling and contact-related mediation. It is not necessary, however, that they agree to joint sessions, although this is the ideal form of these sessions.

Counselling is typically provided by a person other than the contact facilitator, but some programmes do not have enough staff to keep these roles separate, bringing both advantages and disadvantages. The division or non-division of labour is one of the additional points that is still being discussed. Overall there is a much higher ratio of staff to families in the German system, as favoured by the preliminary standards, than in the UK system. In the UK, there are several families per session, say eight families with four volunteers and a co-ordinator. In Germany there is one family, one contact facilitator, one or two counsellors (often a male and a female staff member at counselling sessions, to show the fairness of the process to the parents). In high-risk cases, a second staff member needs to be present at contact sessions to cover eventualities, such as the contact facilitator having to leave the contact room. Thus, the ratio of staff to families is easily twice as high in Germany as it is in the UK. Of course, this comes at a high financial cost, while the majority of contact centres in the UK manage to survive on very modest budgets indeed.

With the financing comes the question of neutrality, which is strongly emphasised in UK contact centres. While German centres also regard themselves as neutral places, they are at least financially dependent on the social services and for decisions such as whether to proceed from supervised to supported contact. While UK contact centres can choose or decline to write court reports, German centres who receive funding from the social services have to write brief factual reports for the social services. The social services take part in the court proceedings, so families could be concerned about information being reported to the courts, even if the programmes themselves do not write special court reports.

Once families have progressed far enough to have unsupported contact, they tend to just stop coming to the centre in the UK, sometimes without giving feedback or a reason for not showing up anymore. In Germany, parents get together to draw up another, final, written agreement, with details of how contact is to take place in future and with agreed reactions to cancellation of visits. It is hoped that in this way families will be enabled to stay away from the court and regulate contact on their own. The German system is very new. It is ambitious and expensive in times of tight state finances. Future evaluations will have to show whether the German system is successful .

5. CONCLUDING OBSERVATIONS

Over the past 15 years there has been rapid development of new ways of intervening to support contact for families going through divorce and separation and for families where children have been removed from home following abuse or neglect. A range of services have been developing variously known as 'meeting places', contact centres and supervised visitation programmes. These vary across a number of dimensions: the degree of professionalism or informality, closeness to the legal system, whether provided by the state, voluntary or private sector, and whether they deal with private conflicts between parents only or deal also with child protection issues involving a public interest.

Each of these dimensions can be broken down into constituent elements:

—The level of professionalism may indicate whether or not the service is prepared to deal with high-risk situations involving questions of violence or abuse. A high degree of professionalism may also be an indicator of a therapeutic aim for the service rather than just facilitation. A non-professional ambiance on the other hand may be valued by families, particularly the visiting parents, as being more 'normal' and avoiding any question of stigma.

—The relationship of the service to the legal system, if close and willing to provide reports on visits to the courts, may indicate either a centre lacking in the confidence to refuse such requests, or a highly professional centre used by the courts for diagnostic or therapeutic purposes. For families it is of the highest importance to be clear about this relationship.

—The model of service delivery may be related to the approach to contact—countries with different approaches have also different models of service delivery.

The greater part of our provision of contact centres in the UK is in the voluntary sector, and are merely locations, typically a church hall with orange squash and biscuits. Now as fathers' demands increase and courts are pressed to find solutions, the contact centre is a tempting option to employ even where the court has little clear understanding of to what it is sending the family. Expectations are frequently unduly high about the level of support or vigilance. No disasters have happened yet, but could do so any day. Fears of abduction were especially marked among minority ethnic families where an alternative life is available, perhaps in the Asian subcontinent.

What can we learn from this cross-jurisdictional discussion? There is little point in the 'Cook's tour' approach, which tells us that in Germany contact workers are usually highly qualified and in the UK they are usually not. What we have tried to do is to bring together our simple models of the meaning of 'family' in the different settings and show how this works through into policy thinking and service provision. Such an approach may help to avoid 'cherry picking' expeditions to other settings in search of speedy solutions to local problems.

Where the family is an institution valued for its continuity across generations and state responsibility for maintaining it, the approach to supporting the parent child relationship will differ from where the legal rights of individual adults are the starting point and privacy is highly valued. We suggest, in addition, that seeing how grounded in social norms and expectations policy and practice are in this highly emotive area, any future attempt at evaluation must also be context-specific. Finally we offer some observations which seem to hold across the different settings:

—Contact is not an event or a good but an ongoing process fraught with difficulty.
—It is time to move away from the court-based concept of guilty parties and fault in contact, as we have done in divorce. Punishing parents is punishing children.
—Remember the demands on the child who has to handle transfers, questions about the other parent's household and to cope with new partners and siblings.

We would argue for caution. Contact is not necessarily always good in itself. It is a marker for what is happening in a child's life. Where there is conflict, we favour the Continental European approach which requires that the parents deal with their own problems before the child is expected to enter the arena. But we would like to keep some of the informality of the British approach, which can help to normalise a difficult situation. We are cautious about the rights-based approach which seems to derive from the demands of adults rather than the needs of children.

REFERENCES

BASTARD, B, 'De l'experience a la maturite: les lieux d'accueil pour l'exercise du droit de visite B' Paper to the *Premier Colloque International sur les services d'accueil du droit de visite* (Paris, November, 1998).

BRUCH, C, 'Public Policy and the Relocation of Custodial Households in the United States' in M Sottmayor and M Tome (eds), *Direito da Familia e Politica Social* (Porto, Publicacoes Universidad Catolica, 2001).

BUCHANAN, A, HUNT, J, BRETHERTON, H and BREAM, V, *Families in Conflict: The Family Court Welfare Service: The Perspectives of Children and Parents* (Bristol, The Policy Press, 2001).

DICKENS, J, 'International and UK Perspectives on Child Contact Centres' (1999) 21 *Journal of Social Welfare and Family Law* 180.

EEKELAAR, J and CLIVE, E, *Custody after Divorce* (Oxford, SSRC Centre for Legal Studies, 1977).

EEKELAAR, J, MACLEAN, M and BEINART, S, *Family Lawyers* (Hart, Oxford, 2001).

FUNDER, K, *Remaking Families* (Melbourne, Australian Institute of Family Studies, 1996).

FURNISS, C, 'Research Findings', in *Child Contact Centres in the New Millennium* (Nottingham, National Association of Child Contact Centres, 2000).

HAID-LOH, A, NORMANN-KOSSAK, K and WALTER, E, *Begleiteter Umgang—Konzepte, Probleme und Chancen der Umsetzung des reformierten §18 SGB VIII* (Berlin, EZI-Eigenverlag, 2000).

HESTER, M, PEARSON, C and HARWIN, N, *Making an Impact: Children and domestic violence. A Reader* (London, Barnardos in Association with Department of Health, 2000).

Lord Chancellor's Department, The Advisory Board on Family Law: Children Act Sub-committee, *Contact Between Children and Violent Parents* (London, Lord Chancellor's Department, 1999).

——*Making Contact Work. A Report to the Lord Chancellor on the Facilitation of Arrangements for Contact Between Children and their Non-Residential Parents and the Enforcement of Court Orders for Contact* (London, Lord Chancellor's Department, 2002).

MARSH, K, 'The Services' in A Reiniger (ed), *Professionals' Handbook on providing supervised visitation* (New York, NYSPCC, 2000).

MUELLER, K, *The Management of Conflicted Post-Divorce Parenting: The Contribution of Child Contact Centres to the Facilitation of Contact with Special Reference to Families having a Background of Domestic Violence* (Unpublished Masters thesis, University of Oxford, 2000).

PEARSON, J and THOENESS, N, *Supervised Visitation: A Portrait of Programs and Clients* (Denver, Colorado, Center for Policy Research, 1997).

POUSSIN, G and MARTIN-LEBRUN, E, 'A French Study of Children's Self esteem after Parental Separation' (2002) 16 *International Journal of Law Policy and the Family* 313.

SINCLAIR, I, GIBBS, I and WILSON, K, *Contacts Between Birth Families and Foster Children: Some Evidence on Their Effects.* Unpublished mimeograph (York, University of York, March 2002).

SKINNER, C and LOCKWOOD, G, 'Discussion Group 3. Safety and Risk in Child Contact Centres' in *Child Contact Centres in the New Millennium* (Nottingham, National Association of Child Contact Centres, 2000).

SMITH, M, ROBERTSON, J, DIXON, J and QUIGLEY, M, *A Study of Step Children and Step Parenting.* Report to the Department of Health (London, Thomas Coram Research Unit, 2001).

8

Squaring the Circle—the Social, Legal and Welfare Organisation of Contact

ADRIAN L JAMES*

THE DETERMINATION OF issues surrounding post-separation and divorce contact between non-resident parents and children has never been simple and the problems encountered have never been easy to resolve. In seeking to tackle such issues and difficulties, those working within the family justice system have understandably looked first and foremost at finding practical solutions to such problems, followed by reviewing the way in which the system works. Too often, however, such approaches have failed to address one fundamentally important question—viz 'How do people organise their understanding of and responses to issues concerning contact?' This chapter offers some thoughts that might begin to answer this question and therefore, perhaps, to identify some new approaches to addressing these problems.

The debate about contact is dominated primarily by the framework provided by the Children Act 1989 and the principles that underpin the Act. Prominent among these in terms of more recent debate, and in the context of the increasing attention now being given to the provisions of the UN Convention on the Rights of the Child, is the 'right' for the child's voice to be heard in such proceedings, an issue to which I shall return later. It is within this legal framework that the social and organisational issues that also shape the debate about contact are located in terms of the professional and academic discourses surrounding contact between children and their parents, post-separation and divorce. Given the apparent dominance in England and Wales of the legal (and adversarial) paradigm for dealing with divorce—evidenced, for example, by the non-implementation of key sections of the Family Law Act 1996, the resistance to any major extension of private ordering and the recent development of CAFCASS as a dedicated support service for the courts (rather than for families)—there might be grounds for assuming that the family justice system is accorded a degree of legitimacy by those who use it and that it is therefore well equipped for dealing with such issues. This is not, however, necessarily the case.

* I would like to acknowledge the helpful comments of Dr Allison James on an earlier draft of this paper. However, blame for any shortcomings that remain are the responsibility of the author alone.

As the recent report *Making Contact Work* (Lord Chancellor's Department, 2002) makes clear, the full extent of the problems surrounding contact is not, in fact, known. This is because most separating parents make their own arrangements. The fact that the majority of parents *are* able to deal with such issues without recourse to law therefore suggests that the legal paradigm may, in terms of social practices, be less widely supported than is suggested by the prominence of those cases that *do* cause such difficulties. Even though highly problematic contact cases represent only the minority of situations, however, it is clear that the family justice system still cannot adequately deal with the complexity of the issues they raise, given their apparent resistance to resolution, by means of the mechanisms that are currently available for dealing with such disputes.

Ideally, we should be able to learn from those cases where contact issues do *not* end up in court but, because so little is known about these, detailed and systematic analysis of why they 'work' is not possible. The fact that many people do *not* resort to litigation, however, taken in conjunction with the fact that, for those who do, the system often struggles to deal effectively with their problems, suggests that the legal framework itself might be part of the problem. An alternative approach to understanding this situation, therefore, is to infer why this might be so by considering the social processes and practices that surround relationship breakdown. In addition, however, we must also consider the way in which such social practices are framed and processed by the law; the tensions between these different processes; the systems that are in place to deal with them; and the implications of these factors, both for legal and welfare practitioners and for those who use the services they offer. Central to such a consideration is an understanding of the differing perspectives of parents, their children, the courts, and those who work within them, alongside competing discourses concerning 'the best interests of the child'.

1. THE SOCIAL ORGANISATION OF DISPUTES OVER CONTACT

The starting point for such an analysis must surely be with the lived-experience of those whose relationships with their partners break down. Unless we keep sight of this when such situations become legal disputes and we attempt to understand the social realities of post-divorce conflict and the problems of 'making contact work', we shall be doomed to fail in our attempt to understand why such situations have the potential to become intractable disputes in which any kind of resolution seems beyond hope.

The failure of a close couple relationship is never easy, even when those involved manage to be 'civilised' about it and to agree how to reconstruct their lives and those of their children without recourse to law. Indeed, the very fact that the word we so often use in connection with such events is 'failure' gives an important clue as to why this should be so. For the vast majority who form such partnerships, whether through marriage or not, the expectation is that it will 'succeed'—that is, it will not only endure for some time (and even 'til death do us part'), but that it will satisfy most if not all of our emotional, personal, developmental and economic needs. Our view of 'successful' partnerships is invariably rooted in some combination of these factors and when a relationship breaks down or 'fails', it is not only the fact that it is *seen* to have 'failed' that is so distressing, it is the fact that such failure is so often perceived and experienced by one or both partners as *personal* failure. Failure is an experience that is never comfortable and one that few of us relish or find easy to deal with in any aspects of our lives, least of all in such a deeply personal relationship in which so much of our selves is invested.

So it is not only that *ideas* of 'success' and 'failure' run through our thinking about couple relationships, it is also that the words themselves play a key part in both the personal and the public construction and reconstruction of the social and legal situations that follow from their breakdown, as well as the discourses that surround them. Why else should the idea of 'no-fault' divorce be such a socially and politically contentious one, unless it is the fact that the idea of 'fault' is deeply rooted in the thinking of many about marital breakdown and that if a relationship 'fails', someone must be to 'blame'? And, of course, if someone is to blame, there must also be at least some level of culpability and 'guilt' that can be attributed, and where there is culpability and guilt, our punitive instincts lurk not far behind. So in terms of the lived experience of relationship breakdown, of its emotional impact on individuals, and how this shapes their attempts to cope with such a fundamentally distressing and psychologically (not to mention socially and economically) threatening life experience, the language, perception and experience of fault, blame, and guilt combine to create uncertainty, confusion, ambiguity, ambivalence and paradox. For some, as Gathorne-Hardy (1981) put it so eloquently, this means that:

> each partner is part rejected, part rejecter. Each is bounded by remorse, pain, and residual love. Anger and cruelty set them free from these bonds: force their spouses to leave them, consume the stubborn stumps of their love, make guilt vanish . . . and from anger grows hate. (171–74)

Similarly, in their application of psychodynamic theory to the experience of divorce, Brown and Day Sclater have taken the view that:

> From a psychoanalytic perspective, our relationships from infancy onwards are coloured by a strong vacillation between love and hate and ambivalent, contradictory feelings. The ambivalence between love and hate is particularly acute, according to this perspective, when we are faced with separation . . . it is separation which tests our ability to cope with conflict, as feelings of hate, jealously, betrayal, and so on are potentially unleashed. (Brown and Day Sclater, 1999: 148)

As Smart and Neale (1999) point out, however, there are considerable difficulties caused by the prevailing dominant paradigm of child welfare in divorce—ie that there should be co-operative post-divorce parenting, a paradigm that is clearly reflected in *Making Contact Work* but that fails to acknowledge:

the difficulties and problems associated with ongoing parenting relationships. It seems to be taken for granted that such relationships will thrive just so long as parents are sufficiently committed to the welfare of their children. (Smart and Neale, 1999: 68)

However, as they argue, the social reality of post-divorce parenting is somewhat different. Echoing the psychodynamic perspective on separation, they observe that:

> In order to reconstitute the self on divorce . . . it was necessary for many women to disconnect themselves and to cease to be bound up with their former partners . . . Yet the conditions under which they were making this transition was still one of connectedness—through their children. They had to construct a boundary against the father while remaining connected to the father. (Smart and Neale, 1999: 141)

Intractable cases of post-divorce conflict are therefore rooted in the rich soil provided by the detritus of failed relationships, in the struggle to construct separate lives from what was once shared, including the struggle to address the needs of the children and also to achieve what both parties can accept as an equitable financial separation (Arthur *et al*, 2001). Importantly, however, such disputes are also rooted in our very psychological foundations and in the difficult task of reconstructing an identity as a single person that is separate and distinct from the previous identity as part of a couple. In the process, however, those involved also have to cope with the demands that emerge from the prevailing wisdom about child welfare. Bolstered by the principles that underpin the present framework of family law, this requires the construction of a continuing working relationship between *parents* whose personal relationships as *partners* did not work. Such a demand, for many, flies in the face of the psychological adjustments that they are struggling to make post-separation and confounds their attempts to achieve a 'clean break'. Thus although we may despair at the unwillingness or inability of some couples to agree about post-divorce family relationships, we should not be surprised at the failure of mediation (for the minority of the divorcing population who make it through the doors of a mediation provider) to make a sustained impact more often than it does. We must not forget the emotional soil in which such conflicts are rooted.

As Day Sclater's research has so convincingly illustrated, the narratives developed by those who have gone through divorce revolve around wrongs done, blame, and revenge, narratives that reflect powerful feelings of vulnerability. Against such a background, 'issues of rights, and justice loom large' whilst in spite of the efforts of the Children Act 1989 to reduce conflict between divorcing parents, the disputes constructed around such histories and issues continue to create 'winners' and 'losers' (Day Sclater and Yates, 1999: 278. See also Day Sclater and Kaganas in this volume). Viewed from this perspective, the past is too profoundly important, too all-pervasive to be set aside—indeed it actually *comprises* the relationship that has failed. Thus to expect a process that is concerned only with the immediate dispute and its resolution—that is focused primarily on the future and that prefers to ignore the past—to resolve the disagreements around which such conflict revolves, let alone the causes of these, is to expect more than it can possibly deliver.

A further part of the social context of relationship breakdown is the impact this has on wider family and social networks. Again, although there is nothing new in this observation, it is crucially important not to forget that the process of destruction and reconstruction that is divorce also involves families and friends, who will also interpret events often using the same language of 'failure', 'fault', 'blame' and 'guilt'. In coping with their own sense of loss, often magnified by their own feelings of inadequacy when it comes to supporting someone about whom they care, they will often feel torn between the individuals they have previously known as a couple. Consequently, when faced with the challenge of coping with their own uncertainty, confusion, ambiguity and ambivalence, they will often resort to 'taking sides', thereby further reinforcing, sometimes implicitly but also too often explicitly, the emerging conflict, the fight to attribute successfully 'blame' and 'fault' to 'the other side'.

Such processes and such language are, of course, richly redolent of what is seen as the traditional adversarial world of law and lawyers. This world, however much it has changed in recent years in terms of family law in particular, is still viewed, understood and valued in these terms by the public. However, their detailed knowledge of law and the legal process can be extremely partial, and often known only either through the disputes of others or through the lens provided by cultural or artistic constructions such as films like *Kramer v Kramer*. Such depictions of lawyers offer beleaguered and blamed individuals the prospect of a someone unequivocally on 'their side', a champion, a partisan, a fighter against injustice, a defender of rights (Davis, 1988). In the lived reality of the family justice system, however, things turn out to be not quite so clear-cut.

To the language of fault and blame, however, we must also add the language of ownership. Close couple relationships accumulate 'belongings', things that belong to the couple as individuals but also to the couple *qua* couple. When a relationship ends, those belongings, the accumulated goods and chattels, have to be redistributed, their ownership renegotiated and redefined. Historically, it is not that long since children were also treated in the same way as goods and chattels, although of course they cannot be redistributed in quite the same manner. But although children are now no longer viewed as goods and chattels, the language of ownership and possession persists—indeed, it is fundamental to the way in which *all* parents talk about and construct their relationship with their children, both socially and interpersonally. This is unproblematic in the context of an intact couple relationship—references to 'our' children, or to 'my' daughter or son are wholly unexceptional. Sometimes, when tensions emerge in such relationships, such references can become emotionally loaded as, for example, in a demand to 'do something about *your* son/daughter', a rhetorical device used to dissociate one parent from the behaviour or personality attributes of the other that are being attributed to a child. Such use of language is commonplace and is, indeed, fundamental to our construction of family life.

When a relationship breaks down, however, such language immediately becomes problematic in that joint ownership by two individuals is inherently more problematic than joint ownership by a couple. Instead of parents talking of 'our' children, family breakdown sees the emergence of separate parents, a mother and a father, each of whom can legitimately refer to 'my' child(ren)— the same words, but words now used in a situation that engenders competing claims in relation to those children (see also Geldof in this volume). Indeed, the attempt to move away from the emotiveness of such language was implicit in the Children Act 1989, which introduced a deliberate shift away from the language of custody and access, with all that they implied about relative claims of ownership, towards the more descriptive terms of residence and contact. But this is legal language—the language of ownership that is used to construct and describe parent/child relationships is not just about words or terms. It reflects the very fundamentals of biological and family relationships and it has long been the case that disputes over matters of kinship have been some of the most bitter in human experience.

Much of this is obvious, given a moment's reflection. It is nonetheless important sometimes to restate the obvious and in this case, the justification for doing so lies in the fact that these words reflect the immensely powerful personal feelings and experiences of relationship breakdown—it is this emotive language that is used to construct, organise, define and symbolise the social and behavioural dimensions of divorce. This language therefore becomes the hard currency of those interpersonal and social conflicts that become transformed into the most intractable of legal disputes. And in such conflicts these words, which are often passionately held and of profound importance to the individuals involved, become stripped of their significance in the context of dispassionate legal processes. This is the first circle that has to be squared.

2. THE LEGAL ORGANISATION OF DISPUTES OVER CONTACT

In considering separately the legal organisation of disputes over contact, there is no implication that the social and the legal do not overlap. Certainly the legal system is discrete and clearly identifiable in organisational and structural terms, and law as a discrete system of thought, as a way of understanding, organising and doing things, is clearly identifiable in epistemological terms. But law is also socially constituted, not only in terms of its epistemology and practice but also in terms of how it informs and is informed by our everyday experiences. As Ewick and Silbey (1998) argue, law (or what they refer to as legality):

> is an emergent feature of social relations rather than an external apparatus acting upon social life . . . it embodies the diversity of the situations out of which it emerges and that it helps to structure . . . Legality is not sustained solely by the formal law . . . Rather it is enduring because it relies on and invokes the commonplace schemas of everyday life'. (p 17)

Indeed, they go on to suggest that:

the law does not simply work on social life (to define and to shape it). [It] also operates through social life as persons and groups deliberately interpret and invoke law's
language, authority and procedures to organize their lives and manage their relationships. In short, the commonplace operation of law in daily life makes us all legal
agents insofar as we actively make law, even when no formal legal agent is involved
. . . Because law is both an embedded and an emergent feature of social life, it collab-
orates with other social structures ([eg] religion, family and gender) to infuse meaning
and constrain social action . . . Legality operates, then, as both an interpretive framework and a set of resources with which and through which the social world (including that part that is known as the law) is constituted. (pp 20–3)

Divorce is thus readily also understood by most people as a dispute that
requires legal remedy. This is the dominant paradigm informing everyday
understandings of the consequences of marital breakdown (see, for example,
Davis, 1988; Eekelaar *et al*, 2000). Indeed, as Walker (2001) commented at the
conclusion of the information meetings pilot, conducted as part of the ill-fated
attempt to introduce the Family Law Act 1996:

To a large extent, solicitors and divorce go hand in hand . . . For the majority of people
who pursue a divorce there appears to be some inevitability about using a solicitor
during the process. Neither information meetings nor mediators replace lawyers as a
source of legal advice . . . Solicitors are regarded as a legitimate and authoritative
source of information and advice. (Walker, 2001: 42)

It is partly because of this that the language used in the social construction of
the divorce experience maps so well onto the legal language of disputes. Indeed,
part of the social construction of the disputes surrounding divorce involves the
deployment of 'legal' concepts and the use of 'legal' language as those involved
'deliberately interpret and invoke law's language, authority and procedures to
organize their lives and manage their relationships' (Ewick and Silbey, 1998)
and to assert the 'legality' and thus the morality of their claims.

A significant part of the social organisation of divorce, therefore, also
involves the use of legal concepts and language such as 'rights' and 'justice', both
of which buttress the language of ownership and are central to attempts to
organise social outcomes that can be seen and experienced as 'fair' (see also Day
Sclater and Kaganas, this volume). Unfortunately, however, these 'commonplace' and common-sense constructions of law do not always match with the
meaning they have for lawyers and others in the context of the formal processes
of the family justice system. This is because the process of transformation from
the social to the legal context is one of 'conceptual cleansing',[1] which involves
tidying up the messiness of the social realities of divorce. As King (1990) argues,
the social function of law is normative—it serves:

---

[1] I am indebted to Allison James for this particularly helpful description.

to organise people's expectations in order to manage and control social conflict. This it does by the imposition of binary categories, such as legal/illegal and right/wrong, even though such classifications often make the settlement of disputes more difficult. (James, 1992: 272)

Thus Teubner (1989) suggests, in his discussion of law as an autopoietic system, that such systems make it impossible for there to be any real merging or integration, for even where information produced by one discourse is apparently incorporated into another, it is 'reconstructed' to fit in with the host discourse. Therefore, not only does the law give both a meaning and a precision to concepts of 'rights' and 'justice' that are lacking in the common-sense deployment of such terms, it reconstructs disputes in a way that removes them from their discursive social context and simultaneously renders them incomprehensible to those seeking legal redress.

This enables us to identify a second circle that must be squared, since a key element in understanding intractable disputes over contact is the failure of law to deliver what it appears to promise. In many cases, those who have recourse to law find that their expectations in terms of rights and justice are not met, that they do not understand the process, and that their common-sense understanding of law often does not equate with that of legal professionals. As Davis put it some years ago:

> If either party feels that they need the court's protection, they have little option other than to seek legal advice. Thereafter, an issue that they may regard as essentially straightforward is transformed into a highly technical and inaccessible legal matter. The result is that they do not understand what is going on, and secondly, they are not allowed to contribute directly to the resolution of their quarrel. This . . . was at the heart of much of the criticism of the legal process which we encountered. (Davis, 1988: 126)

It may be that such expectations are unreasonable or based on a lack of understanding of law but if those who go to law expect solutions to social problems that they understand as requiring legal resolution, and if the law fails to provide these, in the absence of other remedies they have few options. Either they abandon their search for what they believe to be a just outcome, or they keep returning to law in the hope that it will, eventually, fulfill the promise it appears to hold out.

Such issues also need to be understood in the context of the increasing 'reach' of law in recent decades. This is reflected in the creation of a thriving market for law and with it, a customer-base comprised of phalanxes of increasingly legally-aware and litigious citizens, keen to pursue their 'rights' as consumers of legal services.[2] Such consumers expect the law to provide the answers to those

---

[2] Simultaneously, however, we should note the apparent paradox that pressures on the *court system* have led increasingly to a search for alternatives to litigation (especially if this is funded out of the public purse, as are a substantial proportion of family proceedings) in the shape of various forms of alternative dispute resolution.

problems over which the law and lawyers claim to have control, a change that bears comparison with similar developments in relation to attitudes towards the medical profession.

There are also signs of what might be described as a growing legal imperialism or colonisation in recent decades, with the increasing dominance of law and legal discourse in fields that were once dominated by other discourses. Specific evidence for this might be found, for example, in the ousting of medical discourse in favour of legal discourse in the context of child protection practice (Parton, 2001). It is also evident in the development of conciliation and mediation in the UK and its eventual incorporation into the sphere of law and legality. Thus over a decade ago, at a critical stage in the development of conciliation (subsequently termed mediation), it was noted that the endorsement of the Family Mediators' Association by the Law Society might 'be viewed as a means of incorporating conciliation to bring it under the control of the legal profession' (James, 1990: 24). In the same volume, a lawyer disagreed with this view, asserting that she did not believe 'that conciliation and/or mediation will be "taken over" by the legal profession' (White, 1990: 52). Now, with family mediation funded, franchised and effectively controlled by the Legal Services Commission and provided increasingly by lawyers, those earlier concerns appear to be well founded. Those committed to nurturing the development of child contact centres might be well advised to bear this history in mind as they ponder the development of such centres and possible future sources of core funding.

The most recent evidence of such a process is to be found in the newly created Family Advice and Information Networks (FAINs), currently being piloted by the 'product champions' of the legal profession in this expanding market, the Legal Services Commission (LSC). Announced in 2001 by the Lord Chancellor (in the same year that he expressed his disappointment with the lack of impact of the information meetings pilot and announced his decision not to implement the remainder of the Act), FAINs are to be developed around a network of suppliers that will act as gateways to services provided by other agencies. These suppliers will, for the most part if not exclusively, be family lawyers, operating under franchises awarded and quality assured by the LSC.

In effect, FAINs are the descendents of information meetings and the topics on which information was to be given under section 8 (9) of the Family Law Act 1996 in the context of the information meetings can be subsumed without difficulty under the aims of the FAINs (LSC, 2001a). The difference is that the LSC and the legal profession will be at the fore in terms of their development. It is also interesting to observe in this context that, although the Children and Family Courts Advisory and Support Service (CAFCASS) was launched in April that year, the new service receives only passing mention in the FAINs Consultation Paper published just 3 months later (LSC, 2001b) and none at all in the Specification and Invitation to Tender document for the evaluation of the FAINs project (LSC, 2001a).

This important service for those contemplating divorce, is intended:

> to facilitate the dissolution of broken relationships in ways which minimise distress to parents and children and which promote ongoing family relationships and co-operative parenting . . . [and to] also provide tailored information and access to services that may assist in resolving disputes and/or assist those who may wish to consider saving or reconciling their relationship. (LSC, 2001b: para 2.1)

The services of family lawyers and the contribution they make to the divorce process have been described on the basis of recent research (Eekelaar *et al*, 2000) in positive terms, findings that have undoubtedly furthered a process of rehabilitation in the wake of the largely negative critique of their work over recent decades that was part of the context in which mediation developed. Whatever one's views about the services provided by family lawyers, however, it is arguable that the provision of the services envisaged by the FAINs project will require the kind of skills and practice perspectives more traditionally found within the welfare discourse. Regardless, therefore, of the results of the LSC's latest project, it is important to acknowledge that such developments, by giving a pivotal role to the legal profession, serve to reinforce the view of divorce as a justiciable event rather than a social/emotional process. This reinforces the location of such issues within the legal system even though, as *Making Contact Work* confirms, it cannot cope with the most difficult cases.

We should also note, however, that *Making Contact Work* takes a somewhat broader approach to the provision of information than that of the LSC. It recommends, *inter alia*, that the Lord Chancellor's Department should involve CAFCASS, along with other organisations such as the National Family and Parenting Institute, in the development of a co-ordinated approach to the provision of comprehensive information. This 'should be available at the widest possible number of outlets possible, including video and the internet' (Lord Chancellor's Department, 2002: 113). Such an approach seems somewhat at odds with the LSC's strategy for the development of FAINs and invites speculation that this might shed further light on the difficulties identified in *Making Contact Work*. In spite of the current emphasis in government on joined-up-thinking, a lack of coordination or perhaps even rivalry seems to exist between different components of the machinery of State. This can frustrate substantive policy developments such as how most effectively to disseminate information to families and children experiencing the trauma of divorce.

3. THE WELFARE ORGANISATION OF DISPUTES OVER CONTACT

Once contact disputes are brought into the legal system, as suggested above, they are likely, as part of the process of trying to achieve a resolution, to experience another transformation, in the course of which they are further reframed, reprocessed and reorganised—this time within the context of the welfare perspective. Because family law is structured by and revolves around the principle that the child's welfare is paramount, in disputes over children that are referred to CAFCASS, disputed issues will be determined primarily in the context of the welfare discourse. Thus, parents find that the disputes they have constructed in terms of 'fairness', 'rights' and 'justice' are being challenged in terms of notions of 'parental responsibility' and the *child's* 'right' to maintain contact with both parents. And, rather than being given the opportunity to construct narratives of dispute, they find themselves being encouraged to minimise differences and to seek the reduction of conflict through reaching agreements, whilst also being exhorted to listen to the wishes and feelings of their children.

Such an approach, in practice, provides a sub-text to the Act that is embedded in the rhetoric of 'the best interests of the child'. Although this concept is widely used to inform practice in the context of the Children Act 1989, two points are worthy of note. The first is that once a case has been referred to a Children and Family Reporter, there is a strong presumption that the court will follow any recommendation made. Thus parents who sought to be empowered by going to law and having a lawyer 'on their side' suddenly find that, in reality, they seem to be dependent upon the power and influence of a welfare professional. The second is that, although widely used, the concept of 'the best interests of the child' is not defined in the Act itself—rather, it is embedded in various references to decision making in respect of children in the extensive volumes of guidance that accompany and interpret the provisions of the Act, which are drafted with welfare, as much as legal, practice in mind. Thus, apart from inferences that might be drawn from the so-called welfare 'check list' in section 1(3) of the Children Act, there is no single, unambiguous definition of what *are* 'the best interests of the child'.

Whilst this may not be a problem to legal and welfare professionals, whose practice is located and understood within the inherent ambiguities and relativities of the legal system, it leaves this crucially important concept undefined and therefore wide open both to ambiguity and contestation within the context of the *social* organisation of disputes over contact. Crucially, therefore, as a result of this ambiguity parents are able to resort to 'legality' (to return to Ewick and Silbey's description of law) and to develop narratives and therefore, importantly, *disputes* about what constitute the most appropriate post-divorce arrangements for children, arrangements that often incorporate morally and, in common-sense terms, legally defensible claims based on what is in 'the best interests' of *their* child (see also in this volume Day Sclater and Kaganas).

In attempting to find a way through such competing claims, however, welfare professionals necessarily reconstruct people's stories into their own discursive frames of reference. And since two conflicting constructions of what is in 'the best interest of the child' cannot both be right (in practice), the validity of the experiences on the basis of which at least one parent has constructed their version of a dispute over contact must inevitably be seen to be being denied. To the parent concerned, this may well seem to be the antithesis of 'justice'—the failure of law to uphold not only their 'rights' as a parent but also to acknowledge competing constructions of what might be in 'the best interests of the child'. Thus, for example, Davis' observation, made in relation to mediators in his research (1988), can be applied more generally to the way in which welfare professionals organise disputes over access, in the sense that they are:

> committed to one particular standpoint (that access should take place) without fully understanding all the circumstances of the case. It is clear therefore that to identify a shared goal—the child's best interests—does not in itself take one very far. There is still the problem of agreeing what those interests are, and it is this that is likely to prove contentious. (Davis, 1988: 82)

In 1988, Davis' research revealed 'a somewhat unflattering image of the divorce court welfare service' (1988: 142), with welfare officers' practice displaying a lack of understanding and a readiness to impose their own viewpoint on parents, who clearly regarded them as very powerful. Most recently, Buchanan *et al* (2001) have revealed a slightly more diverse picture in which:

> many parents spoke of their experiences with great depth and strength of feeling. Many described anger, bitterness, betrayal, frustration and anxiety. Others talked of being supported and understood. (2001: 28)

The main criticism made by parents, however, the majority of whom were not satisfied with the process of welfare report preparation, was that 'the investigation was not thorough enough, both in the amount of time spent and the number of professionals and other family members who were contacted' (2001: 42). Such a perception is rooted in a common-sense view of what the preparation of a welfare report might mean and often a lack of understanding of the way in which welfare officers understand and define their task as professionals. As Buchanan *et al* also point out, however:

> Each parent will have their own view about what is 'in the best interests of their child'. The decision to apply to the court will usually be taken by one parent with the other a reluctant participant. The applicant may be looking for 'justice' from the court and for their rights as a parent to be upheld; instead they find that the court regards the welfare of the child as paramount . . . [and] the parent may take a very different view from the court of what is best for their child . . . Entry to the court arena will produce uncertainty and a sense of alienation as personal histories are translated into legal discourse. (Buchanan *et al*, 2001: 54)

The introduction of CAFCASS, although it has altered the organisational—ie social and institutional—context in which those welfare professionals who have to deal with contact disputes are employed, has, as yet, done nothing to alter either the professional practices or the welfare discourse which, between them, construct and comprise the prevailing conceptual framework within which disputes over contact are organised. Thus, although research (Buchanan *et al*, 2001) reveals that parents expect more thorough investigation, this continues to be limited by lack of resources and the minimum delay principle, which underpins the Children Act and bolsters previous National Standards that required reports to be completed within 10 weeks. It is also limited by an approach to practice that favours the resolution of problems and the reaching of agreements over the kind of investigation that parents expect.

It is also, perhaps, important to note that a significant feature of the social, legal and welfare organisation of disputes over contact is that each of these frameworks is about adults organising the adult world for adults. Divorce is perceived and defined almost exclusively as an adult issue that requires solutions to be found by and for adults. In such a context, despite the provisions of the Children Act and the UNCRC, children are in practice predominantly treated as 'victims' requiring protection, rather than as actors. Thus, the voice of the child often does not feature prominently in the organisation of contact. From the point of view of many parents, which finds expression in the emotional language of ownership, the social reality is that children 'belong' to and with one parent or the other. If, in addition, from the welfare practitioner's point of view, as new research would suggest (James *et al*, 2002), 'the child' is nearly always conceived of as a product of *parenting* and 'childhood' is generally assumed to be about the experience of *being parented*, then there is little room in such conceptualisations for 'the child' to be seen as having an identity in his/her own right—ie there is little room for the agency of children.

This brings us back to the issue raised at the start of this chapter—the increasing attention now being given to the 'right' of the child's voice to be heard in such proceedings. Unless the child *is* conceptualised as having agency, it may be hard for practitioners to give real credence to the importance of children's thoughts, wishes and feelings when making decisions on children's behalf, because it is precisely these things that express each child's individuality and agency. In practice, because the process revolves around disputes (both social and legal) between and constructed by adults—disputes that ultimately can only be resolved by the adults involved—children's ability to participate fully and effectively is heavily circumscribed. Assessments are made and 'expert' advice is offered based on constructions of childhood and children in general (often derived from the developmental paradigm championed by Piaget and others) and on the process of parenting and children's experiences of being parented, rather than on the experiences of individual children.

Such constructions of childhood effectively deny children a voice because they are unable to acknowledge sufficiently, if at all, what being a child means in terms of an individual child's experience, agency and personhood. Rather, what is offered is an adult construction of what is in 'the best interests of the child' that is rooted in adult concepts defining the nature of childhood. Based upon a set of adult-orientated and legally-endorsed assumptions that attempt to resolve the ambiguity inherent in the task of allowing the child's wishes and feelings to be heard, whilst also responding to parents' claims for justice, such constructions serve to drown out the sound of the child's voice in a system that struggles, but largely fails, to acknowledge the individual child as a competent actor with agency.

That children's competence may vary cannot, of course, be disputed, but nei- ther can the fact that children have much greater competency and agency than they are given credit for in the context of the family justice system (see, for example, the wide range of research conducted under the ESRC 'Children 5–16' initiative that demonstrates this). This is not, of course, to argue that children should be given or forced to accept the responsibility of *choosing* where they want to live. Not only may some children not wish to express a view (Smart and Neale, 2000) but, as Bainham argues elsewhere in this volume, the child's view should not be the only factor to be considered in making such decisions. However, as Smart *et al* (2001) have so clearly demonstrated, children *do* have views that may differ from adults and although they understand that their views may not necessarily be adopted, *some* children *do* wish to express opinions on such matters and have such opinions listened to and respected, even though adults (not only parents) may find it hard to do so. As Smith et. al. comment:

> Our research, and that of many others . . . suggests that children are indeed competent social actors who reflect and devise their own ideas and strategies for coping with family life after their parents separate, and that their views are worth listening to. (Smith *et al*, 2003)

Their research also suggests 'that almost all children, whatever their age, are able to express what is important to them' (Smith *et al*, 2003—forthcoming) and should therefore be given the option of expressing their views if they so wish, although they should be helped to understand why these are being sought and why their perspective is important, so that they can decide whether they want to be involved. In the light of such arguments, Smith *et al* suggest that the legal pre- sumptions underpinning a child's participation in family proceedings should be changed in order to allow them to 'opt-out' of the process, rather than having to wait for a judgement to be made as to whether they are old enough or of suf- ficient maturity to be given the right to participate and express their views. Such an approach, they argue, would 'rightly place the onus on adults to justify the overriding of the child's competence' (Smith *et al*, 2003), although it may also require that welfare reports are produced less quickly, so that sufficient time is available in order to establish the necessary degree of trust with the child(ren) concerned. Practice might also need to be changed to ensure that in every case, children's views are, if they wish them to be, reported directly and verbatim to the court. Only by adopting such approaches can we respond adequately to the concerns raised by Dunn elsewhere in this volume about the need to understand children's concerns about the quality of their relationships with both resident and non-resident parents.

In some cases, however, we may even need to allow for the possibility of a child expressing the wish to have *no* contact with the non-residential parent since this can also be a rational choice, made 'for a variety of normal, realistic, and/or developmentally expectable reasons', rather than because of 'parental alienation syndrome' (Kelly and Johnston, 2001; 251). Certainly such a view should not necessarily be determinative but neither should it be dismissed solely because parents believe they have a right to contact (see Herring, this volume), or because the adults concerned think the child too young to understand, not competent to form such an opinion, or may disagree on the basis that they believe they know better than the child what is in their interests. Indeed, not until a child is given the right to express the wish to have no contact shall we be able to say that this situation has changed. As Glaser (2001) has argued, the legal system can be very adversarial, particularly in cases where there are allegations of domestic violence or sexual abuse, since:

> these are the cases where the adversarial system comes into its own in a way which entirely overlooks the children. It overlooks the children either in terms of finding out what their wishes and feelings are, but in a sense even worse, discounting the child's feelings when these feelings are clearly stated by dismissing the child's feelings as being suggested by the resident parent. (2001: 22)

Thus as a consequence of the way in which childhood is currently constructed and understood, the pervasive and much-used concept of 'the best interests of the child' represents yet another circle that remains unsquared. Having been incorporated into and become central to the social, legal and welfare discourses of adults in the construction of disputes over contact, it is now at risk of being devalued and of becoming simply a generalised and disputed socio-legal concept, rather than an important, individualised human concept. It therefore risks becoming little more than a rhetorical device that is given meaning by reference to the generalities of 'children' and 'childhood', from which is then derived what is, in effect, no more than an inferential understanding of the interests of any particular 'child'.

4. CONCLUSIONS

In this consideration of the various and complex ways in which we can view the organisation of disputes over contact, much ground has not been covered. It has not been possible, for example, to consider issues about contact in public law cases, although these could undoubtedly have been considered from similar perspectives, with the important caveat that the element of 'failure' in public law cases is far more profound, since it involves 'failure' as a parent and not simply failure as a spouse or partner. The nature of the 'failure' therefore significantly alters the social, legal and welfare organisation of disputes over contact, and how these are constructed and understood by all concerned, as well as bringing about a fundamental realignment of the power issues that lie at the heart of such disputes.

It has also not been possible to consider the much larger issue of the *cultural* organisation of disputes. The ideas outlined above are clearly culturally rooted in and supported by research that seeks to understand the significance of the organisation of disputes over contact in the context of the racial, ethnic and cultural background of the majority of the population in Britain. We cannot, however, make any necessarily valid assumptions about either the significance or the organisation of such disputes for other ethnic groups, in the context of which religion, family structure, and a range of other factors may well produce a very different set of parameters within which such disputes might be organised. The approach of large parts of the family justice system to the organisation of contact takes little substantive account of ethnicity and it can be argued that the dominant model of family mediation, for example, may well be unsuited to the needs of many South Asian families in Britain who experience marital breakdown (see, for example, Shah-Kazemi, 2001). Importantly in this context, ethnicity is an issue that was noticeable by its absence from the LSC's proposals for the provision of information about contact and related issues through FAINs (Legal Services Commission, 2001a).

In this analysis, however, I have sought to demonstrate that the social processes of family breakdown and divorce are not adequately addressed by the legal and welfare processes that are provided to deal with them and, indeed, that there is in fact a profound mismatch between the professional view of law, marriage and the family and the common-place experience of these. Fortunately, for a great many people, this is not a major issue—they confront and successfully resolve the ambiguities and challenges that arise for them as individuals when their marriages and partnerships break down, often with a lot of support from friends and family and with only minimal recourse to law, although we have no way of knowing how hard they might have to struggle in order to do so.

For those who find it hard to resolve such issues without recourse to law, however, this mismatch is pervasive in its effects and it is apparent that the law can often be of only limited effect, especially if it fails to deliver the promise of justice to parents who, for whatever reason, feel wronged, especially if that wrong concerns the denial of 'justice' in the form of the frustration of their 'natural' 'right' as a parent to have contact with 'their' child(ren). Such concerns, in many cases, lie at the heart of what *Making Contact Work* describes as the 'general dissatisfaction with the legal process as a mechanism for resolving and enforcing contact disputes' (Lord Chancellor's Department, 2002: 10). If we are to ameliorate the conflict such disputes generate, therefore, every effort must be made to bring the legal and welfare construction of such disputes closer to the social reality that underpins them and we should note with concern the continued and strengthening discursive construction of divorce and family problems as primarily legal problems requiring legal solutions.

The strength of *Making Contact Work* lies in the fact that it implicitly recognises this and that new ways of thinking are necessary in order to begin to address the problem of intractable disputes over contact. It does so by recommending the development of a range of measures that will offer the opportunity to consider these different perspectives and that will simultaneously, to varying degrees, take such disputes out of the immediate confines of the legal arena. As Eekelaar (2002) has argued, however, the emphasis of the Report on the *enforcement* of contact rests not only upon some important and questionable assumptions about the desirability of contact in all cases and the effects of contact upon children but also, importantly, on the ability of the law to influence such situations. Herein lies the Report's main weakness, therefore, for until such time as the different perspectives explored above are acknowledged, it seems inevitable that bitter disputes will continue to perplex those working in a system that does not appear to recognise the limits of and constraints upon its sphere of influence, or understand that legal remedies cannot always be effective and that the law does not, and *can not*, work for those individuals who feel their needs remain unmet by it.

Thus the notion implicit in the Report that such problems can be addressed and overcome by explaining to litigants how the law works may well be naïve and misconceived. We should not assume that the provision of information *per se* would necessarily encourage rational decision-making on the part of parents (see also Barlow and Duncan, 2000), since the profound psychological impact of separation and divorce is not conducive to rationality. Nor will information necessarily help to transform the common-sense view of law and justice, unless it can successfully modify the high and perhaps unrealistic expectations that the law appears to offer to those in search of justice and the enforcement of their 'rights'. It is therefore important to recognise that, regardless of whatever mechanisms for the education of parents and the enforcement of court orders are devised, the power to make contact work or not ultimately rests with parents, and 'The law must recognise that some things are beyond its limits to achieve' (Eekelaar, 2002: 274).

It also seems certain, given the psychological impact of divorce, that the tension between the demands of constructing a new self-image and a new social identity post-separation, and the dominant welfare paradigm, which demands continuing contact between ex-spouses in 'the best interests of the child', will continue to be a rich source of conflict. Indeed, it is clear that here there are, in fact, irreconcilable tensions between the social and the legal organisation of disputes that serve to perpetuate rather than to ameliorate problems over contact. Thus although much can be done to seek to minimise these problems, unless and until these circles can be squared, continued conflict will be an inevitable feature of a system that promises to provide family justice since, in the final analysis, it is justice itself that is contested in the context of such disputes.

REFERENCES

Arthur, S, Lewis, J, Fitzgerald, R, Maclean, M and Finch, S, *Settling Up: Financial Arrangements After Separation and Divorce: Report of Interim Findings* (London, National Centre for Social Research, 2001).

Barlow, A and Duncan, S, 'New Labour's Communitarianism, Supporting Families and the "Rationality Mistake", Parts I and II' (2000) 22 *Journal of Social Welfare and Family Law* 23 and 129.

BROWN, J and DAY SCLATER, S, 'Divorce: A Pschodynamic Perspective' in S Day Sclater and C Piper (eds), *Undercurrents of Divorce* (Dartmouth, Aldershot, 1999).

BUCHANAN, A, HUNT, J, BRETHERTON, H and BREAM, V, *Families in Conflict: Perspectives of Children and Parents on the Family Court Welfare Service* (Bristol, Policy Press/Nuffield Foundation, 2001).

DAVIS, G, *Partisans and Mediators: The Resolution of Divorce Disputes* (Oxford, Clarendon Press, 1988).

DAY SCLATER, S and YATES, C, 'The Pyscho-Politics of Post-Divorce Parenting' in A Bainham, S Day Sclater and M Richards (eds), *What is a Parent?: A Socio-Legal Analysis* (Oxford, Hart, 1999).

EEKELAAR, J, 'Contact—Over the Limit' (2002) 32 *Family Law* 271.

EEKELAAR, J, MACLEAN, M and BEINART, S, *Family Lawyers: The Divorce Work of Solicitors* (Oxford, Hart, 2000).

EWICK, P and SILBEY, S, *The Common Place of Law* (London, University of Chicago Press, 1998).

GATHORNE-HARDY, J, *Love, Sex, Marriage and Divorce* (London, Cape, 1981).

GLASER, D, 'The Implications of Domestic Violence' Paper presented at the Family Courts Consortium Conference on *Making Contact Work*, November (proceedings published by the Family Courts Consortium, 2001).

JAMES, AL, 'Conciliation and Social Change' in T Fisher (ed), *Family Conciliation within the UK: Policy and Practice* (Bristol, Family Law/Jordans, 1990).

—— 'An Open or Shut Case? Law as an Autopoietic System' (1992) 19 *Journal of Law and Society* 271.

JAMES, AL, JAMES, A and McNAMEE, S, 'The Legal and Social Construction of Childhood' (paper presented to the Socio-Legal Studies Association Annual Conference, Aberystwyth, 3–5 April, 2002).

KELLY, J and JOHNSTON, J, 'The Alienated Child' (2001) 39 *Family Court Review* 249.

KING, M. 'Child Welfare Within Law: The Emergence of a Hybrid Discourse' (1990) 18 *Journal of Law and Society* 303.

Legal Services Commission, *Specification and Invitation to Tender for the Family Advice and Information Networks Pilot Project Research Programme* (London, Legal Services Commission, 2001a).

—— *Family Advice and Information Networks Consultation Paper* (London, Legal Services Commission, 2001b).

Lord Chancellor's Department, Advisory Board on Family Law: Children Act Sub-committee, *Making Contact Work: A Report to the Lord Chancellor on the Facilitation of Arrangements for Contact Between Children and their Non-Residential Parents and the Enforcement of Court Orders for Contact* (London, Lord Chancellor's Department, 2002).

PARTON, N, 'Protecting Children: A Socio-Historical Analysis' in K Wilson and A James (eds), *The Child Protection Handbook* (2nd edn, London, Ballière Tindall, 2001).

SHAH-KAZEMI, S, *Untying the Knot: Muslim Women, Divorce and the Shariah* (London, University of Westminster, 2001).

SMART, C and NEALE, B, *Family Fragments?* (Cambridge, Polity Press, 1999).

—— ' "It's My Life Too"—Children's Perspectives on Post-Divorce Parenting' (2000) 30 *Family Law* 163.

SMART, C, NEALE, B and WADE, A, *The Changing Experience of Childhood: Families and Divorce* (Cambridge, Polity Press, 2001).

SMITH, A, TAYLOR, N and TAPP, P, 'Rethinking Children's Involvement in Decision-Making after Parental Separation' (forthcoming, 2003—Special Issue on Childhood and Divorce) 10 *Childhood*.

TEUBNER, G, 'How the Law Thinks: Towards a Constructivist Epistemology of Law' (1989) 23 *Law and Society Review* 727.

WALKER, J, *Information Meetings and Associated Provisions within the Family Law Act 1996: Summary of the Final Evaluation Report* (London, Lord Chancellor's Department, 2001).

WHITE, F, 'Conciliation and the Legal Profession' in T Fisher (ed), *Family Conciliation within the UK: Policy and Practice* (Bristol, Family Law/Jordans, 1990).

Section 3:

Mothers, Fathers and Children

9

Contact: Mothers, Welfare and Rights

SHELLEY DAY SCLATER and FELICITY KAGANAS

1. INTRODUCTION[1]

THE CHILDREN ACT 1989 introduced a new concept into family law—that of Parental Responsibility (PR). The legislation provides that married parents[2] automatically acquire PR[3] and, with it, equal status and equal 'rights' in relation to their children. Each can autonomously exercise PR in the absence of the other. Moreover, PR is inalienable—it cannot be taken away.[4] In divorce cases, this new concept reflected an emphasis on 'responsibility', and so children's welfare, rather than 'rights'.[5] The codification of 'responsibility' in the Children Act was new, but the emphasis on responsibility was not. Rather, it simply reflected a trend in the case law leading to a weakening of 'rights' and consequent strengthening of welfare,[6] a trend that has survived the advent of the Human Rights Act 1998.[7]

However, it was hoped that to enshrine the concept of PR in legislation might have some instrumental value. It was suggested by the Law Commission (1988) that giving 'equal' status to parents would further a general aim to encourage both to feel 'concerned and responsible' for their children, and would help to reduce conflict and litigation. Many thought that the new scheme would abolish 'winners' and 'losers', leaving parents less to fight over (para. 4.5). Also, it was hoped this would address the concerns of the non-custodial fathers who felt aggrieved by the perceived bias of the old law in favour of mothers. Finally it

---

[1] This section of the paper draws extensively on Kaganas and Piper (2002). We would also like to thank Christine Piper for her helpful comments on an earlier draft of this chapter.

[2] And unmarried fathers, by agreement with the mother, or by order of the court (s 4(1) Children Act 1989). S 111 of the Adoption and Children Act 2002 makes provision for the amendment of s 4 of the Children Act 1989 to enhance the legal position of unmarried fathers. It adds another means by which they can acquire parental responsibility: registration as the child's father.

[3] Parental responsibility gives rise, in effect, to automatic 'joint custody', although the concept of 'custody' was abolished by the Children Act 1989.

[4] See Roche (1991). In the case of PR acquired under s 4 Children Act 1989, however, the court may terminate a parental responsibility order or agreement (s 4(3)).

[5] See, eg Law Commission (1986) para 4.53(d).

[6] See, eg the judgment of Lord MacDermott in *J v C* [1970] AC 668.

[7] See, eg *Payne v Payne* [2001] 1 FLR 1052, *Dawson v Wearmouth* [1999] 1 FLR 1167. See, for discussion of the case law in the context of the Human Rights Act, Kaganas and Piper (2001).

was hoped that the enduring and inalienable nature of PR would encourage fathers to remain involved with their children after separation and divorce.

With the benefit of hindsight, these hopes were unrealistic, and were not to be realised. As King (1987) predicted, the changes have proved to be largely symbolic in nature; the law failed in its attempt to change human behaviour. Evidence suggests that parental co-operation, in the form of joint parenting and joint decision-making are far from the norm (Smart and Neale, 1999), and many fathers still continue to lose touch with their children altogether (Simpson *et al*, 1995). Bitterness and conflict have not been reduced and, on the contrary, the volume of disputes has increased and they are taking longer to resolve (Bailey-Harris *et al*, 1998). Fathers' rights groups[8] in particular have been vociferous in their condemnation of the current dispensation, arguing that non-resident fathers are not given sufficient powers to make decisions affecting their children and that the contact they are afforded is inadequate. They criticise the courts' reluctance to award joint residence orders and their failure to enforce rigorously the contact orders that they make.

Once again, reform of the law is being considered. A recent Consultation Paper issued by the Children Act Sub-Committee of the Lord Chancellor's Advisory Board on Family Law (Lord Chancellor's Department, 2001, para 1.4) notes widespread concern that court orders have failed to facilitate contact between children and non-resident parents and that enforcement of orders has proved a problem. In the Report, *Making Contact Work* (Lord Chancellor's Department, 2002) which outlines the results of the consultation and sets out recommendations, emphasis is placed on providing education, information and therapeutic measures for separating parents designed to persuade them of the benefits of contact. However, the Report also documents the responses to the consultation paper made by three groups representing, primarily, fathers' interests: Families Need Fathers, The Equal Parenting Council and The Association for Shared Parenting. These groups suggest that, in order to counter the 'idea that "winner takes all"' and to promote parental involvement in the least adversarial way possible, a presumption of 'shared parenting' should be introduced into the law. This would not necessarily mean that there should be an equal division of time. Rather its purpose would be to accord recognition of both parents as important. It would also inform negotiations and would remove 'obstacles' to contact.

The Lord Chancellor's Department report (2002) makes no recommendations on a presumption of shared parenting, stating that such a radical change went beyond its remit (*ibid* Preface para 9). It also expresses some doubts as to the usefulness of such a presumption in practice, suggesting that, for example, financial constraints might preclude the setting up of two suitable homes within travelling distance of each other (*ibid* Appendix 3 para 13). Also, it points out, one parent or the child might need protection from the other parent (*ibid*

---

[8] See, eg the website of Families Need Fathers: www.fnf.org.uk

Appendix, para 14). Nevertheless, the report states, shared parenting should be encouraged and it goes on to suggest that the government might consider setting up a pilot scheme to test the effects of such orders (*ibid* Appendix, para 16).

While the report gives only qualified support to shared parenting, it is an idea that appears to be gaining ground. At a conference organised by the Family Courts Consortium and the Lord Chancellor's Department, a consultant child psychiatrist advocated the introduction of a framework for shared parenting that entailed the courts operating a presumptive split, possibly 70/30, which would be applied in section 8 applications.[9] An international conference, chaired by Dame Margaret Booth, was organised to consider the possibility of a legal presumption, rebuttable only for good reason (Sealy, 2002). A psychologist has published a piece in a law journal (Hobbs, 2002) suggesting that the way to solve the problem of 'parental alienation syndrome'[10] might be to develop a 'satisfactory form of legal "default" position, whereby child-parent contact continues to be shared, unless there is a valid reason to the contrary' (Hobbs, 2002, p 386). The debate has even reached the pages of the popular press (Driscoll, 2002; Freely, 2002). See also the chapter by Geldof (this volume).

This growing support for a presumption of shared parenting as the solution to the problem of intractable contact disputes and as a way of safeguarding the best interests of children is somewhat surprising. The possibility of introducing a very similar measure into the law, a presumption of joint custody, was extensively canvassed in the 1980s and rejected. A 1986 Report of the Law Commission found that the case for such a reform had not been made out (Law Commission, 1986, para 4.46). It expressed concern that imposed joint custody could create new power imbalances and increase the likelihood of litigation. Moreover, where care was not shared in reality, such orders would be largely only symbolic (*ibid* para 4.40 and 4.43). In its 1988 Report, the Law Commission was equally unenthusiastic and explicitly rejected the idea that the court should specify how a child's time should be divided (para 4.10). Why a presumption of shared parenting would be any more effective a solution to difficult contact disputes is not clear.

Indeed it is not self-evident that the law in any form can provide a panacea; it is too blunt an instrument with which to address the profound emotional forces that underlie family litigation.[11] There can be no simple solution to the problem of contact, because parental motivations in seeking or opposing contact are complex—both psychologically and strategically. And these are precisely two

---

[9] 'Sanctions of the Last Resort' (talk given at a conference, 'Making Contact Work', 20 November 2001). See now Conference Report by the Family Courts Consortium, 2002.

[10] The Court of Appeal accepted expert evidence that the existence of such a syndrome is not generally accepted in *Re L (Contact: Domestic Violence); Re V (Contact: Domestic Violence); Re M (Contact: Domestic Violence); Re H (Contact: Domestic Violence)* [2000] 2 FLR 334. Hobbs (2002) asserts that the Court of Appeal did recognise PAS in a subsequent case: *Re C (Prohibition on Further Applications)* [2002] 1 FLR 1136. However, this interpretation is questioned and dismissed by other commentators: Masson (2002); Williams (2002).

[11] See Day Sclater (1999).

dimensions of the problem that have tended to be sidelined in debates about contact. If we look closely at how parents themselves talk about their involvement in contact disputes, we can see some of the complexities that disrupt the smooth operation of the law. We can also begin to understand why it might be, as King (1987) observed, that law has such a tenuous influence on human behaviour.

In 1999/2000 we collected personal narrative accounts from parents who had been involved in protracted disputes (lasting at least a year) over contact.[12] A narrative approach[13] is designed to research the ways in which individuals—conceived of as active human agents—themselves make sense of their lives, drawing on the range of biographical experiences and cultural resources that are available to them (Andrews *et al*, 2000). Narrative work is interdisciplinary; it moves away from traditional (discipline-based) practices in the social sciences that have focussed on the problems of standardisation—how to ask all respondents the same question, and how to analyse their responses with standardised coding systems—to embrace issues of diversity, complexity and contradiction, and to confront, instead, problems of language, meaning and context (Mishler, 1986). Narrative work is a way of finding out about how people frame, remember and report their experiences; it illuminates both individual lives and broader social processes (Rustin, 2000). It generates knowledge about how people negotiate social structures and manage institutional demands (Andrews *et al*, 2003). In our work, we used narrative analysis to look at the ways in which mothers framed their thoughts, feelings and actions in contact disputes, with particular reference to welfare discourse. In what follows, we draw on data from eight of the mothers in the study.

While parenting has been framed in law in terms of 'responsibilities', separating and divorcing parents themselves continue to invoke notions of 'rights' or something akin to rights. It is clear from our data from both mothers and fathers that engagement in a contact dispute is about making or resisting a moral claim.[14] However parents are obliged to formulate their arguments within a range of discourses that explicitly exclude 'rights'. The dominant discourses that disputing parents encounter in the legal process provide no space for rights-talk, and instead 'welfare' is the favoured lexicon. The disputants accordingly seek to position[15] themselves as 'good' fathers and 'good' mothers, a position from which they consider they can legitimately assert moral claims. It is the fact that they are based on welfare arguments that renders these moral claims legitimate. So, the reasoning, sometimes implicit, of many fathers appears to be

[12] The work was supported by a Fellowship grant from the Leverhulme Trust.

[13] See, for example, Riessman (1993; 2001).

[14] The moral dimension of parents' talk was also evident in the interview material collected by Carol Smart and her co-authors. See, for example, Smart and Neale (1999).

[15] The concept of 'positioning' refers to the ways in which human subjects align themselves in relation to the discourses that circulate in culture. It assumes, not passive individuals, but active human agents who will, variously, take up, negotiate or resist the 'positions' (such as that of the 'good parent') that discourses offer. See, for example, Davies and Harré (1990).

along the following lines. Since they care about their children, they are good fathers. Good fathers have the capacity to influence their children's development positively and their involvement is necessary for the welfare of their offspring. Such fathers ought therefore to have liberal contact. Good mothers, on the other hand, indicate that they have proved their devotion by caring for their children and know what is best for them. They, therefore, argue that they ought to be in a position to decide how their children should be raised and, among other things, whether there ought to be paternal contact and, if so, how much. Parents assert what they see as morally justified entitlements stemming from welfare considerations and in this way, are not forced to rely on rights talk. In our study, mothers negotiated the tensions between 'rights' or 'entitlements' and 'welfare' in a number of ways.

2. INTERNALISING THE WELFARE DISCOURSE

By and large, the mothers we interviewed eschewed direct references to rights and instead tended to frame their arguments and their opposition to contact within the parameters of the dominant welfare discourse. Indeed, they tended to accept, at least in abstract terms, that contact is beneficial for children. They took pains to emphasise that they were not maliciously or irrationally seeking to destroy the links between the children and their fathers and, in confirming their support for the principle of contact, positioned themselves firmly within the dominant, and their own, conception of the good mother. In particular, they distanced themselves from the image of the vindictive mother who looms large in the notion of parental alienation syndrome.

Implicit in Cora's story, for example, is an ambivalent acceptance that there should be contact between father and child. At the same time, she frames her resistance to contact within a welfare discourse that prioritises her child's interests. In so doing, she endeavours to maintain her position in her own eyes as a 'good' mother:

> I don't want her to feel bitter because—I don't want it to be where it is like mother telling daughter. You know I don't want her to feel any way about him because, at the end of the day, he would probably change, like, God knows, maybe, maybe not, I don't know. She may see him in a different way. And I don't want to poison her mind against the father because at the end of the day, you know, whatever the case may be, she'll probably think I'm trying to—I don't want to do that. It's between me and him. It is nothing to do with her. . . . And I want her to know him as well because at the end of the day I don't want her to say 'look, you took me away from my dad' . . . But at the same time, right now, she is not even close to him. She goes to see him. She comes away. Great. But most of the time she gets frightened. . . . She still doesn't like going . . . So I take her mind off whatever she is thinking. It's hard you know. And that's how it is. And that is how we have to live. And I don't like it. I don't like it at all. This is going back in time. Back in time . . . She doesn't like it at all. I wish this wasn't there. I wish it wasn't there.

Gina had two children, aged 4 and 18 months when her partner Roy, a social worker, left her for another woman. Gina tells that, at first, Roy would come to see the children frequently—almost every evening he would call to bath them and put them to bed. One day the eldest child began refusing to see him, and indicated that there had been inappropriate sexual contact with her father. At the time of the interview, Gina was trying to stop contact and was waiting for a 'risk assessment'. Gina underlines her claim to be a reasonable person and a good mother by showing that she has always had her children's interests at heart. She feels resentful that she has, in her view, been wrongly categorised in the legal process as a vindictive woman:

> I can be as horrible as anybody else . . . but I tried to bend over backwards and I think—I do think, most women—if you're half sensible, because the children would hate me if I was saying, you know 'Right, you're not seeing your dad', you know, trying to poison their minds and stuff . . . and obviously it's not a very nice thing to do, and it is their daddy after all. And I think I was always driven very much by the fact, I think, I thought they'd lost enough when he left . . . I wanted them to know so much that their daddy still loved them and I think I was really driven by that. And then it's so funny how the legal system immediately view it as you're a bitter woman who's trying to keep them away . . .

Both Cora's and Gina's endorsement of the dominant discourse is undermined by more critical welfare-centred remarks. Gina, for instance, voices concern about sexual abuse and Cora describes her daughter's negative response to contact. It was not unusual for mothers to explain their opposition to contact as an attempt to promote their children's best interests.

3. PROTECTION

For some mothers, the welfare of their children had to take second place to or was closely tied up with issues of safety. Nathalie, for example, said:

> Initially I was happy for whatever was best for my son David. But, again, I was frightened that he'd divulge—you know, divulge where we lived [refuge] and I was so frightened physically because of all the violence[16] . . . I did say to her (CWO) in the end that whatever is best for David I was happy to have provided we were kept safe . . .

In Nathalie's case, it is her perceived need for physical safety for herself and her son that counters her acceptance of the idea that her son should have contact with his father. These concerns for safety appeared in the narratives of all the mothers we interviewed. But safety was not the only qualification that mothers cited to oppose contact in spite of their acknowledgement that it was normally desirable. For some mothers, contact, far from serving the best interests of their

---

[16] The outcome of Nathalie's case was indirect contact (a letter each month and an exchange of photographs), but the father failed to send anything to the child.

children, was a source of damaging emotional distress to them. Cora, for example, is torn between wanting to do the 'right thing' by facilitating contact, and the need to question whether contact is, in fact, the right thing, in view of the history of her relationship. In this extract, Cora is telling about the first contact at the contact centre:

> Now we have to wait ages for this contact centre because it was too full up and I wanted a place where I could go near, not far . . . On the first day after so many months we went on (date) . . . And (child) started to bawl, (child) started to cry. As soon as she sees his face she wants to go home, and she's screaming down the place . . . I felt so sorry for (child). She had confidence in me and that day it kind of broke . . . 'I don't want to stay here. I want to go home. I want to go home.' And she is clinging onto me so hard. She didn't want to let me go. And he's just standing watching it. He's got the most biggest bag of sweets you've ever seen in your life for a child . . . She was screaming so badly I had to take her to the toilet because it was echoing the whole place and she was really screaming . . . And I literally nearly went home, because I said I can't take this, I can't see this child suffer so. Because I think all the things that had happened—it came back to her. Because she was happy, happy, happy, happy, and then when she left that day she—. . . I said to him 'don't just sit there, talk to her'. He opened the bag and he said 'look what daddy brought you' and she didn't want to take it. She didn't want to know. So I said 'here, here' and I had to coax her. Can you imagine coaxing a child? So she sat on my lap and she was burying her head in my neck and she kept looking like that and turning away, and looking like that . . . But I think this contact centre is—I think it's like—it's like going back in time. I wish it wasn't there at all. I wish it would just carry on and when the child is old enough to say, you know, stand up for herself . . . she should say 'well I am going to see my dad' and then he could present himself better because she's older. And he could present himself more better to the child, because the child is old enough to handle herself. And he can't talk any rubbish to the child, because the child would know. Do you understand?

Bernice:

> I wasn't going to bundle screaming children into a car just because the court had said this is what should happen . . .'

Clara's story portrays her fight as one to 'defend' her children's interests:

> I've tried to defend their best interests all along . . . Sarah was saying 'Can we speak to the—, I want to go and see the judge', and of course you don't get to.

4. UNINVOLVED FATHERS

Apart from their perceived need to protect their children from the harm engendered by contact, mothers pointed in general terms to the deficiencies of fathers. In particular, the mothers highlighted fathers' lack of experience in childcare, their lack of commitment to their children in the past and their scant potential to act as good fathers in the future.

Cora's description of the first visit at the contact centre makes it clear that, in her view, her former partner's understanding of and relationship with his child are tenuous:

> I said 'try and coax her and take her to see the teletubbies' because they had all these pictures on the wall. So I had to tell him what to do now. But anyway he took her. He goes 'come and look at the teletubbies, come and see'. So I had to take her first and he followed us behind. And I said 'look at the teletubbies' and he said 'yes look at the teletubbies', because he don't know how to react to the child anyway, because he's never had hold of her. He's never bathed her in his life. He's never seen to her nor nothing . . .

Cora positions herself as a good mother, mediating the father's relationship with the child. At the same time, she undermines the assumptions underlying the law when she tells us that the father doesn't 'know how to react to the child anyway'.

Nathalie too questions the value of the fathering that her child, severely disabled, has received and is likely to receive:

> He was never there regularly for David, he was never there on a daily basis, never ever fed David which was two and a half [years], never fed him a meal or gave him drinks, bathed him, never did any of that . . . The husband should have to say why they can have contact when they've never cared for the child, never washed, dressed them, sung to them or been with them, or taking them to the childminder, or have any sort of contact . . . And here he was wanting to look after . . . its all right, it's the cat . . .

And Bernice:

> He still doesn't want to make—As a responsible parent you care about the children's schooling, you care about their social life, their out of school activities. But he never even questions me . . . and it would be so easy to get a copy of the school report. But in all the years, he's never once, you know, gone along these lines. So it seems as it was a bit of the, well, the Victorian father perhaps who has produced these children . . .

And Clara's experience:

> He never asks about the children. He doesn't say anything about them.

For these mothers, contact is a moral issue that has its roots in the practical realities of relationships and childcare. In these narratives we see mothers making implicit claims that there is something 'special' about their relationships with their children that the father-child relationship simply does not have. Motherhood, in this talk, is about 'caring for', with all that that entails, on an everyday basis. Fatherhood, by contrast, is about 'caring about'—something that is emotional, not necessarily devoid of self-interest, and that lacks evidence of any practical engagement or commitment (Smart, 1991). There are inevitably moral dimensions to narratively positioning yourself as a good mother, particularly when the stories simultaneously construct the father as wanting or even as bad—the good mother takes shape by contrast and sometimes even by default.

These are mothers whose narratives tell us that they are trying to get things right for their children's sake. In contrast, according to some mothers' accounts, contact is sought by fathers less out of love or concern for their children than for ulterior motives.

5. CONTROLLING OR VINDICTIVE FATHERS

Underlying Bernice's words is a judgment of her former partner as selfish and manipulative:

> I think he was being vindictive. I still say that to this day. I don't think that he was for one minute thinking of the children, because you wouldn't do that to children . . . From his point of view, I don't doubt for one minute that he loves his children without any doubt, and he has always loved them. But I think he was very selfish in the way he went about it and, rather than bring the children closer, he's really turned the children away from him . . . He didn't ever take any interest . . . but just seemed to be absolutely obsessed by getting the children away from me and I really think that the crux of the matter was he felt that if he got the children, I would follow because like any mother, you would fight tooth and nail. . . . I would feel rightly or wrongly that they needed me and by getting them out of the country he would be able to get me out of the country.

And Clara:

> The whole thing is a charade to have access to me . . . I think the courts have violated my view and those of my children, by the way they've continued this procedure, because he clearly demonstrates no interest . . . Clearly if he was interested in his children he wouldn't want to keep wanting to punish me, because that has an effect on them inevitably . . .

6. PRESENTING AS THE 'GOOD MOTHER' IN LAW

Despite their scepticism about their former partners' abilities as caretakers and the genuineness of their concern about their children, the mothers felt constrained to operate within the framework of legal assumptions about how good and 'sensible' mothers behave. So, while they evidently doubted the value of contact in their own particular cases, they were careful not to appear obdurate or unreasonable.

Cora's story about the first time at the contact centre presents an image of herself as a mother who, against her will, is facilitating contact. What we have here is a verbal performance of a mother who is trying to do the 'right' thing.

> I do it by the law. I am going by the law. I don't want nothing to fall back on me, to make me look the bad one. So I try and do everything by law . . . I do everything by the law.

The moral message of Gina's story focuses on the different interpretations of welfare and her children's interests made by the professionals, the court, herself as mother and Roy as father. Her narrative shows the centrality of the welfare discourse about contact and does not dispute its general validity. Yet she sees her own children's best interests as lying elsewhere. Nevertheless, she is compelled to conform to the law's expectations of good mothers. For our present purposes, the 'performative' aspect of Gina's engagement is apparent in the following extract:

They've (the counsellor) said to me 'You have to go along with everything. You have to be seen to be going along with everything, to be like trying every angle.' It's a whole game you have to play and it seems just so unfair. . . . So I've had to sit in so many meetings. I've had to go to mediation with him, which is basically an opportunity for him to be very abusive.

Gina is telling here of the personal cost to herself of 'toeing the line'. Gina 'toes the line' and so proves herself to be a 'good' mother in law. Clearly, however, she feels a sense of grievance at having to do so. Indeed, most of the mothers interviewed expressed dissatisfaction with the legal process.

7. THE LEGAL PROCESS AND RIGHTS TALK

It is only in their critical comments about the legal system and the legal process that mothers adverted to the concept of rights and largely they did so in negative terms. Rights were seen in contradistinction to responsibility; they were weapons deployed by irresponsible and even dangerous fathers, fathers with no moral standing, in a legal battle that left no room for children's welfare. And the legal system, in adjudicating this contest, was seen as concerned primarily to uphold those fathers' rights while riding roughshod over the interests of the children as well as those of the mothers. Mothers' complaints were generally not framed in terms of a clash of parental rights. Rather they saw the law with its support for fathers as an impediment to their efforts to fulfil their role as good mothers who had only their children's well being at heart. Locating their arguments firmly within the discourses of welfare and morality, in a sense of fairness, these mothers indicated that rights should play no part in contact disputes at all.

Cora clearly considered the law to be gender biased:

All the laws are for men, not for the women. All the laws are for the men, she (solicitor) already warned me . . .

This is how Nathalie put it:

It's very difficult because I feel the court systems do very much support the men in many ways and, erm, his *rights*, but he was never a father there. . . We shouldn't have to produce all these forms and things, having to prove why we think contact is not suitable. It should be the other way around. . . . Yes it does seem the wrong way that there I was having to prove why contact wouldn't be in David's best interests. It was very difficult to do that.

Gina's description of the legal process also emphasised unfairness and injustice but went further. The law's unfairness towards her had consequences for her family; its failure to heed her views and take her seriously left her struggling to protect her children, alone and without support. In her view, the law, while it paid lip service to good mothering, was in effect sabotaging her attempts to be a good mother.

> I went to court on Monday, and finally the judge agreed, though it was very touch and go, that he needed to have a risk assessment before anything else could be done, before he could get contact. But I noticed, even then through the court process, I've noticed so much that it was stacked against me from the start, that I was the villain. I had to prove—It was almost like I'm guilty until proven innocent. I was the kind of vicious ex-wife who's trying to paint all these—you know, say all these things about him . . . There's no support at all, you're left completely to your own devices, really . . . The whole thing has been a total ordeal, a total ordeal. And it does seem so much that the legal system is so stacked against women . . . What I've been through isn't about the children at all, it's about his *rights* . . . So it seems really kind of incongruous, the two things, and when you're the mother and unable to kind of tie the two up together. Because they're saying it's up to you to protect your children, you have to do everything to protect your children, of course, you can't do anything but that, as a mother. But then you go to court, and there's no opportunity, almost . . . But it's a whole game you have to play, and it seems just so unfair, so absurd, really . . . It seems to me with the legal system, there's no protection, there doesn't seem to be any protection for the woman or for the children. But as long as they all pander to the man's *rights*, and the man's kind of life, his *right* to see the children, despite whatever else is happening . . . (authors' emphasis) . . . To me it seems as if in this case that there isn't a lot of justice . . .

Here we see Gina taking the moral high ground, interpreting what Roy is doing as evidence, not of his concern about the children, but as an assertion of his own 'rights'. Implicit in her talk is the idea that parental 'rights' should have nothing to do with it. But she sees the legal process as an opportunity for Roy to pursue those rights, disguised as welfare. This talk is persuasive; through it we are pulled into the dominant discourse in which Gina occupies the position of a right-thinking but not a rights-thinking parent—a good mother, whose own interests are second to those of the children, in contrast to a morally dubious father who puts his own interests first.

Clara's criticisms were even more wide ranging. She attacked the very basis of the law's approach to contact disputes. In her view, the assumption that contact is best for children does not always hold good; it is a generalisation that fails to take account of particular circumstances and personalities. Its indiscriminate application prejudices individual children:

> Because he's legally aided and I'm not, he penalises me at every single stage and the courts, as far as I'm concerned, whatever myth they choose to support through the

Children Act, have just totally violated my rights and colluded with him as the perpe-
trator . . . As I said, if he really wanted to see the children, he would have started by
putting in place some of the things that he was asked to do. He never has . . . The
Children Act, I guess, is based on some kind of fallacy about the natural parents somehow being wonderful. And of course, they often are, however, not always. And it is a
shame that the Act claimed to take into consideration the children's best interests. And
the only best interest they serve really are some particularly middle class perception of
what is important to those children, as opposed to how those children feel, or their
personal experience of their parents. I think it is a mistake not to consider more
strongly evidence of abuse against the mother. I think the part that plays is very very—
. . . It tends to be biased in favour of fathers.

Unusually, Clara does refer explicitly to her own rights and contends that these
have been violated. However, she is quick to re-establish her position as a good
mother by accepting that her rights are less important than and even sub-
ordinate to her children's welfare:

So you know, even if it is not my *rights* that are considered . . . I really don't think the
children have been considered at all.

8. CONCLUSION

The women we interviewed clearly wanted to see themselves, and to be seen, as
'good' mothers. This meant that they were obliged to engage in complex negotiations of competing discourses that are not easily amenable to a single interpretation. As 'good' mothers they have to put the 'welfare' of their children first
and they have to accept the premise of the dominant welfare discourse that contact is good for children. That they had internalised the messages emanating
from the child welfare discourse emerges from their insistence that they did not
wish to alienate their children from their former partners and that, as 'good'
mothers, had striven to co-operate with contact arrangements.

However, whilst these mothers accept that contact might be beneficial for
children generally, they are, at the same time, convinced that it is not good for
their particular children. Positioning[17] as a 'good' mother means knowing what
is best for your children, and being prepared to fight for it, even when the odds
seem stacked against you, even when the legal system, in your eyes, favours men.
The knowledge about what is best for one's own children comes not from what
Court Welfare Officers[18] recommend, nor from what judges say, nor from social
science research, but comes instead, in these mothers' views, from the intuition
and the intimacy born of nurturing a child throughout life. Fatherhood, it
seems, can claim no such credentials. Disputing mothers, then, interpret welfare
from privileged vantage points that only mothers can occupy.

---

[17] See n 15 above.
[18] Now Children and Family Reporters.

These women not only believe that they intuitively know all that needs to be known about their children, but they also speak as people who have had (sometimes still have) unique knowledge about the father's shortcomings, his inadequacy or even his badness; they alone know what their former partners are 'really' like. This is knowledge that the courts cannot have, and one of which the Court Welfare Officers, as outsiders, will usually be deprived. Yet, in the experience of these women, the legal system does not readily accept or attach credence to the information they seek to convey; instead they are branded as vengeful or vindictive if they resolutely oppose contact. So, in order to maintain their standing in law as 'good' mothers, they are compelled, despite their misgivings, to present themselves as reasonable and as conforming to the law's and the legal system's expectations. This strategic behaviour is not simply a cynical ploy. It is designed to persuade legal and welfare personnel that, because they are 'good' mothers, their views should be taken seriously. Their hope is that, eventually, they will be vindicated instead of having their objections dismissed out of hand. Psychologically, they are impelled to fight on to protect their children's welfare[19] but tactically they must 'go by the book' in doing so.

The women we interviewed felt the need to continue their resistance despite pronouncements by the courts to the contrary. In a sense, the decisions of the courts were regarded as illegitimate; they were unfair and they ignored mothers' moral claims, as victims of abuse, as mothers and as primary caretakers, to make decisions about contact. More importantly, they ignored the children's 'real' best interests. The mothers we interviewed saw 'rights' as being in opposition to 'welfare' and morality. Their former partners were regarded as exercising paternal rights that had no basis in either welfare or morality; to uphold their claims was to damage children, to reward dereliction of duty and to perpetrate injustice. They saw the law as fundamentally unfair and interpreted law's construction of welfare as simple bias in favour of fathers' rights.

It is, of course, now something of a commonplace to say that men's and women's parenting activities are 'gendered'. Neale and Smart (1999), for example, draw a useful distinction between parental care ('caring for') and parental authority ('caring about') in relation to the post-divorce parenting activities of, respectively, women and men. They examine the range of moral codes that underlie different post-divorce parenting arrangements. The dominant ethical framework articulated by mothers tends to be that of an 'ethic of care'[20] whilst fathers tend to favour one of 'justice'. Whilst it is beyond the scope of this chapter to discuss the narratives of the fathers in our study,[21] it is worth pointing out that we found a similar gendered patterning in the deployment of

---

[19] For discussion of the psychological imperatives that underlie fathers' involvement in contact disputes, see Day Sclater and Yates (1999).

[20] See Sevenhuijsen (1998).

[21] These are discussed elsewhere. See, for example, Day Sclater and Yates (1999) and Kaganas and Day Sclater (2000a).

the welfare discourse, with mothers at pains to emphasise 'welfare' and fathers less circumspect in invoking 'rights' talk. As we have seen, however, concerns about 'rights' constitute a powerful sub-script in mothers' talk too, and contact disputes, for both mothers and fathers, imply an inevitable moral positioning.[22]

In the legal arena, the welfare principle has been interpreted in a way that prioritises the separate but continuing post-separation family; children fare best when parents maintain a co-operative, conflict-free relationship with the aim of maximising the participation of both in the upbringing of their offspring. However, this single, oversimplified image of children's interests fails to take account of the multiple interpretations that parents make as they try to accommodate and live with a whole range of discourses that seem, somehow, very far removed from reality as they know it. The dominant welfare discourse generates images of good and bad parents, and it is surely no small irony that mothers and fathers then engage in prolonged disputes in order to attach those images to themselves and simultaneously dismiss the other parent as wanting. Despite law's interpretations, the welfare principle remains potentially open to myriad meanings and is in that sense indeterminate. When it is sought to be applied to particular cases, its very abstraction invites parents who are intent on disputing to fill it with their own meanings.

Our argument is that those meanings are highly significant, the more so when they are at odds with the prescriptions for 'good' parenting implicit in the dominant discourses. For it is parents' own meanings that drive disputes, and that sustain them, sometimes over years and at great emotional and financial cost. The law would do well to recognise that welfare means different things to different people and that it necessarily has a moral dimension. It has meaning for disputing parents only insofar as it can be used to justify and to further their own moral claims.

It is very unlikely that a presumption of shared parenting will somehow alter parental moral reasoning and, indeed, behaviour. It will, undoubtedly, increase fathers' bargaining power and strengthen their position in court. Since shared parenting is being presented as both fair and as 'good' for children, a presumption would fortify fathers' sense of entitlement. As long as they cannot be shown to be 'bad' fathers, they ought to get an order. And, not surprisingly, fathers do not readily categorise themselves as 'bad' fathers, a reluctance mirrored, to a degree, by the courts. To warrant judicial criticism, a father would have to be

---

[22] Discussion of the impact of the Human Rights Act on contact disputes is beyond the scope of this chapter, since our fieldwork was done before the Act came into force. Neither mothers nor fathers invoked notions of human rights in their talk about contact disputes. We would anticipate, however, that as the Human Rights Act becomes a more prominent part of British culture, notions of 'human rights' will increasingly enter as a dominant discourse, in competition with that of 'welfare', in the narratives of disputing parents. We would also anticipate that notions of 'human rights' will be subject to similar patterns of negotiation and interpretation by parents as we have reported in relation to the currently dominant welfare discourse in this chapter and elsewhere. In short, human rights legislation will not 'solve' the problem of disputing parents any more than the Parental Responsibility of the Children Act 1989 did.

shown to have behaved violently, cruelly or completely irresponsibly.[23] Yet there is no reason to assume that mothers will be led by a shared parenting presumption to accept paternal perceptions or judicial prescriptions any more than they do under the current dispensation. For them, there will still be no moral or welfare justification for giving symbolic affirmation to fathers whom they see as abusive or simply as uninvolved and as contributing little to caretaking duties. Such a presumption is likely to heighten mothers' perceptions that the law is unfair and impervious to real children's needs. And they will continue to resist in the same way that they do now.

REFERENCES

ANDREWS, M, DAY SCLATER, S, SQUIRE, C and TREACHER, A (eds), *Lines of Narrative: Psychosocial Perspectives* (London, Routledge, 2000).

ANDREWS, M, DAY SCLATER, S, SQUIRE, C and TAMBOUKOU, M, 'Narrative Analysis' in C Seale, G Gobo, JF Gubrium and D Silverman (eds), *Qualitative Research Practice* (London, Sage, 2003).

BAILEY-HARRIS, R, DAVIS, G, BARRON, J and PEARCE, J, *Monitoring Private Law Applications under the Children Act: A Research Report to the Nuffield Foundation* (Bristol, University of Bristol, 1998).

DAVIES, B and HARRÉ, R, 'Positioning: The Discursive Construction of Selves' (1990) 20 *Journal for the Theory of Social Behaviour* 43.

DAY SCLATER, S, *Divorce: A Psychosocial Study* (Aldershot, Ashgate, 1999).

DAY SCLATER, S and YATES, C, 'The Psycho-Politics of Post-Divorce Parenting' in A Bainham, S Day Sclater and M Richards (eds), *What is a Parent?: A Socio-Legal Analysis* (Oxford, Hart, 1999).

DRISCOLL, M, 'After the Split, the Marrying of Minds' *The Sunday Times*, 17 February 2002.

FREELY, M, 'Children First' *The Guardian*, 27 March 2002.

HOBBS, T, 'Parental Alienation Syndrome and the UK Family Court—The Dilemma' (2002) 32 *Family Law* 381.

KAGANAS, F, 'Responsible or Feckless Fathers?—Re S (Parental Responsibility)' (1996) 8 *Child and Family Law Quarterly* 165.

KAGANAS, F and DAY SCLATER, S, 'Contact Disputes: Narrative Constructions of 'Good' Parents' (Paper presented at the annual conference of the Socio-Legal Studies Association, Dublin, April 2000a).

—— 'Contact and Domestic Violence—The Winds of Change?' (2000b) 32 *Family Law* 630.

KAGANAS, F and PIPER, C, 'Grandparents and Contact: "Rights v Welfare" Revisited' (2001) 15 *International Journal of Law, Policy and the Family* 250.

—— 'Shared Parenting: A 70% Solution?' (2002) 14 *Child and Family Law Quarterly* 365.

---

[23] See eg *Re D (A Minor) (Contact: Mother's Hostility)* [1993] 2 FLR 1. Compare *Re H (Contact: Domestic Violence)* [1998] 2 FLR 42; *Re M (Contact: Violent Parent)* [1999] 2 FLR 321. See also Kaganas and Day Sclater (2000b). For a discussion of the 'bad' father in the context of PR, see Kaganas (1996).

King, M, 'Playing the Symbols: Custody and the Law Commission' (1987) 17 *Family Law* 186.

Law Commission, *Family Law, Review of Child Law: Custody Working Paper No 96* (London, HMSO, 1986).

——*Family Law, Review of Child Law: Guardianship and Custody, Law Com. No 172* (London, HMSO, 1988).

Lord Chancellor's Department, *Making Contact Work. The Facilitation of Arrangements for Contact between Children and their Non-Residential Parents and the Enforcement of Court Orders for Contact. Consultation Paper* (London, Lord Chancellor's Department, 2001).

——The Advisory Board on Family Law: Children Act Sub-committee, *Making Contact Work. A Report to the Lord Chancellor on the Facilitation of Arrangements for Contact Between Children and their Non-Residential Parents and the Enforcement of Court Orders for Contact* (London, Lord Chancellor's Department, 2002).

Masson, J, 'Parental Alienation Syndrome', Letters (2002) 32 *Family Law* 568.

Mishler, E, 'The Analysis of Interview-Narratives' in T Sarbin (ed), *Narrative Psychology: The Storied Nature of Human Conduct* (New York, Praeger, 1986).

Neale, B and Smart, C, 'In Whose Best Interests? Theorising Family Life Following Parental Separation or Divorce' in S Day Sclater and C Piper (eds), *Undercurrents of Divorce* (Aldershot, Dartmouth, 1999).

Riessman, CK, *Narrative Analysis* (London, Sage, 1993).

——'Analysis of Personal Narratives' in JF Gubrium and JA Holstein (eds), *Handbook of Interviewing* (London, Sage, 2001), available at http://www.uel.ac.uk/cnr/forthcom.htm

Roche, J, 'The Children Act 1989: Once a Parent Always a Parent' (1991) 5 *Journal of Social Welfare and Family Law* 345.

Rustin, M, 'Reflections on the Biographical Turn in Social Science' in P Chamberlayne, J Bornat and T Wengraf (eds), *The Turn to Biographical Methods in Social Science* (London, Routledge, 2000).

Sealy, A, 'A Different Framework for Contact' (2002) 32 *Family Law* 88.

Sevenhuijsen, S, *Citizenship and the Ethics of Care: Feminist Considerations on Justice, Morality and Politics* (London, Routledge, 1998).

Simpson, B, McCarthy, P and Walker, J, *Being There: Fathers after Divorce* (University of Newcastle, Relate Centre for Family Studies, 1995).

Smart, C, 'The Legal and Moral Ordering of Child Custody' (1991) 18 *Journal of Law and Society* 485.

Smart, C and Neale, B, *Family Fragments?* (Cambridge, Polity Press, 1999).

Williams, C, 'Parental Alienation Syndrome' (2002) 32 *Family Law* 410.

10

The Real Love that Dare Not Speak its Name:

A Sometimes Coherent Rant

BOB GELDOF

Because of statements I have made on TV and elsewhere, I was invited by the editors to participate in the seminars convened by the Cambridge Socio-Legal Group, and to write what can clearly only be a lay view for this book.

If my contribution is of any use, it will be, I suppose, in the shape of the amateur absolutist and iconoclast. The kicking up of an impassioned, but informed, fuss is the role Nature seems to have assigned me. Family law is not my field of expertise but it is certainly my field of experience and like many, many men in this country, it left me feeling criminalised, belittled, worthless, powerless and irrelevant. I wrote this chapter very quickly, allowing those emotions to determine the outcome.

I had no idea, and did not even care, whether it made sense or had any basis in fact but it was all true, and was what I and thousands more had experienced and found wanting. I assumed that my eminent collaborators in this work would be embarrassed by me and unwittingly patronising. They were not. They were in fact hugely tolerant, sympathetic and often, to my dismay, in agreement with my inchoate groping towards the dark heart of this matter. I learned much from them.

They sent me papers which put solid, researched fact behind my assumptions and observations. They argued amongst themselves, and with me, over parts of the piece. In the end, however, I have changed nothing because I believe still that what I wrote is true and just. Its emotional tone is what is required to change this hugely destructive assault on our personal lives, which in turn endangers this society through an onerous and disgraceful Family Law and the system that must implement it.

I have tried incorporating supportive texts and arguments into the body of the piece to lend a greater credibility or weight—texts which my colleagues sent me, arguments which were thrashed out in the seminar—but it seemed presumptuous. I do not want to give the impression that I am an expert or pseudo-professional. I am not. But maybe, unlike them, I am someone lacerated by this law, which contributed massively to the misery of my family. That is expert enough. Instead, claiming, and being allowed privileged, non-academic and profoundly unprofessional behaviour by my weary editors, I have included in an addendum the relevant texts, quotes, arguments and statistics (referring to them in the main text by number, with the references I have come across). I hope they serve three functions: firstly, they give credence to my uninformed thought; secondly, they make me appear a little less extreme or idiotic; and finally they may help force the sure and soon day that these baleful diktats will be scornfully shoved aside.

* * *

Family Law as it currently stands does not work. It is rarely of benefit to the child, and promotes injustice, conflict and unhappiness on a massive scale.[29,43,45]

This law will not work for the reason that society itself and society's expectations have changed utterly.

Law must constantly evolve in order to keep pace with the dynamics of the society within which it is framed.

Social law, specifically that governing human relationships, will need to evolve ever faster particularly in an age of unprecedented and confusing change. Deeply cherished nostrums of the ages are as nothing when confronted with a different moral structure to that in which those beliefs took root.

The endless proposed adjustments with Family Law will not do. They do not eliminate the injustices or aid the intended beneficiaries. An unthinking tinkering with Family Law becomes unjustified tampering with peoples lives.

Adjustments imply satisfaction with the core structure, but in the case of Family Law, my view is that this is inappropriate on the basis that this same law promotes pain, hurt and broken families in direct and unintended contradiction to its purpose.[33,43,44,45] It serves merely to compound the self-inflicted damage done to the individuals who come before it.

Therefore, just as society appears to be in a state of fundamental and perhaps revolutionary change, the professionals of the law must be prepared to think afresh, and act boldly.[38,44]

This would mean new basic law.

I understand few believe this is necessary, and that it is too drastic or dangerously radical or just silly but I will try to give my, no doubt, poorly conceived notions a rationale.

Sometimes my attempt at being dispassionate will fail and I will be seized by the actual deep rage I feel at what the system has done to my family, myself and many others I know personally or from the over 70 plastic bin liners of letters I have received from individuals unknown to me. This amounts to thousands of letters. Many more than I ever received during Live Aid or the Boomtown Rats or at any other period of my 'public life'. As Bob Dylan might have said 'Something's going on and you don't know what it is. Do you Lord Chief Justice Whatever-your-name-is?'

We'd better find out.

I will try and break down the factors that I believe have changed and which, as a result, require a change of law. Beyond that this is the story of those 70 bin liners—the love of fathers for their children.

1. SOCIETY

Given that the birth of children through the institution of marriage and the desired end result of Family as the basic block of society is of cardinal importance to our stability and social coherence we must start here.[60,61] All of the assumptions in the above sentence however are now up for grabs.[50,63]

Today, Government tries to deal with differing views of what is Family, and each view insists upon equal validity. This is perhaps inevitable in an age of moral relativism, itself an adjunct to our secular times. This alone is a massive change and something some members of the judiciary seem to be unable to grasp.

The real and significant change that occurred however, the paradigm shift as an American might say, was of course, the 'emancipation' of women.[1,34,36,38]

Financial freedom, and the end of biological determinism, produced an overdue and welcome balance in society. Its disruptive consequences to the status quo however, could not be predicted but it has been massive and it has not stopped yet.

Economics determine social arrangements. It has affected all areas of society but most profoundly and inevitably in the relationship between the sexes and, as a result, Family. There have been other exogenous factors contributing to societal shifts but the effect of women free to enter the workplace has given rise to consumerism, altered production, home ownership and house building models, and whole areas of law and sentiment within society itself. Very little has been left unchanged by this huge and positive social movement and most of those changes have strained the old glues that bound the family into the breadwinner/nurturer/children model.[38]

This model worked well enough for centuries and where it can still be sustained works well today. The cardinal and excellent difference between now and the past is that it is not clear until it is determined by the couples in question who will do the breadwinning and who the nurturing or whether it will be both simultaneously.

And yet while individuals struggle with these difficult new conundrums the law governing the, if you will, 'intimate' parts of society, the 'personal' laws, remain (though some are fairly recently drafted) resolutely unaltered in their presumptions, save for the pathetic pretence that they are gender neutral. This is a grotesque lie that all Family Law professionals have tacitly agreed to be party to, as willingly acknowledged by nearly all the lawyers I have talked to on this issue.[26,28] And regardless of whether the professionals acknowledge it to be or not, the vast majority of my correspondents, friends and others regard it to be so. If this is the commonly held view then the law *will* change. It is simply a question of when.

The law appears unwilling or unable to accept the change in the way we now barter our relationships. The altered state of women has of course produced the altered state of men. Men cannot be the same because women are not.[5] The law will not acknowledge this and it must.[4] It appears bewildered, as indeed famously do the men in question. What is their new role? What is expected of them? How do they now define themselves in this more fluid brave new world? And if the world is more fluid, if it now flexes, bends and warps like morality itself, why is the law so rigid, so inflexible and fixed that its application to individuals binds them to an overweening and restrictive State of Orwellian proportions—the common experience of those who find themselves as victims of the secret world of Family Law.

Divorcees are not criminals, women are not angels, men are not ogres. Recent rulings have produced two classic examples of the bewildering and blinkered confusion at the inflexible heart of the law. One ruling was given against the man who had successfully raised his children at home for 5 years while his wife went to work. She got the children??? She got them because she was a woman. The eminent male judge in question said so.[4] Two weeks later, another ruling by the same judge was given *against* a woman who sought potential lovers on the Internet. The children were given to the man??? These rulings show no understanding of contemporary society, they appear flagrantly prejudiced and discriminatory in clear breach of any 'gender neutral' guidelines or law, and perfectly illustrate the law's inability to come to terms with the modern age. The law must now root itself in reality and not social work theorising or emotive or traditional notions of men and women's roles. I am not the first to call for this: a recent report published by the Work Foundation, which argues for father-friendly workplaces, notes that:

> Older fathers—the dinosaur dads—are currently the ones in the most senior positions and so have a disproportionate influence. Most continue to see the world through the lens of their own generation's experience i.e. a world of bread winning men and child-rearing women. (Reeves, 2002).

Something like 51 per cent of the workforce are women. The implication of this figure is staggering and yet does not appear to be considered in relation to family law. In addition men now hold a completely different view of the parenting role than before. Again this is a huge philosophical shift which has enormous implications.[11,16,28]

There are no studies which suggest that a child brought up by a man (as I was) display any marked psychological or emotional characteristics different to one raised by a woman.[3]

The contention that women are inherently better nurturers is wrong.[3,4,7,22,23,28] Rulings appear to be based on the 'sugar and spice and all things nice' school of Biological Determinism rather than on anything more significant. The law to its eternal discredit stands in the way of great and important cultural and social progression and as such will be swept aside despite the legal Luddites who opine secretly from their benches. Kimmell (2002) is entirely correct in asserting that if the later twentieth century saw the transformation of women's lives then the transformation of the twenty-first century involves the transformation of men's lives, and by definition the lives of their children.

My complaints are not the moans of the unsuccessful litigant. I, in fact, was 'successful'. This was someone dismayed by the inappropriateness of the law to the everyday.

Nor is this the complaint of the proto-misogynist, indeed the law is so inept it produces misandrists in equal measure, but rather the irritation and anger of someone who sees exact parallels with women's struggle against assumptions, bias and prejudice.

2. LANGUAGE

We have indeed been here before. Female emancipationists of the 60s and 70s found, as they set out their agenda for change, that the very language militated against them. The issue of language becomes incredibly potent as attitudes change. Words once used frequently become freshly freighted with meaning, emotion and unintended insult and need to be changed. This of course can escalate to the realms of madness and the thought police (rather like the consequences of Family Law) but in the everyday use and their meaning, and therefore import, they carry whole ideas that when heard afresh from a different perspective need to be adjusted. This is never more true than in the language used in Family Law.

In this new era of 'Family Liberation' as it were, where the law itself and its officers, attendants and practitioners are the instruments of reaction and discrimination, the language used to discuss the personal appears to have been deliberately chosen to be as cold, deadening and hopeless as possible in the hope of appearing neutral. In fact it becomes heartbreaking, hurtful, rage inducing and an instrument of absolute harm in the entire process.

I cannot even say the words. A huge emptiness would well in my stomach, a deep loathing for those who would deign to tell me they would ALLOW me ACCESS to my children—those I loved above all, those I created, those who gave meaning to everything I did, those that were the very best of us two and the absolute physical manifestation of our once blinding love. Who the fuck are they that they should ALLOW anything? REASONABLE CONTACT!!! Is the law mad? Am I a criminal? An ABSENT parent. A RESIDENT/

NON-RESIDENT parent. This Lawspeak which you all speak so fluently, so unthinkingly, so hurtfully, must go.

Indeed, like the law returning to a wholesale root and branch re-drafting as I believe it must, we should look while we're here at the two most basic words that permeate this issue: Mother and Father.

If a woman 'mothers' a child an entire warm universe of nurturing is conjured. If a man 'fathers' a child it implies nothing more than the swift biological function involved in the procreative act. The importance of language is critical. It expresses whole ideas for us and, in the case of the above loaded examples come with assumptions upon which laws are based and judgments made that can destroy people and their lives.

So society, ideas, language itself has changed but the law has not. This law framed by people, albeit 'experts', of other generations and classes have imbued the drafting with their own prejudices, theories and philosophies. Of course it was done with benign intent but so were all laws of previous times which have subsequently been abandoned.[43,44]

Laws which no longer apply to society, notoriously become widely ignored and therefore impossible to implement. Punishment is redundant in something not recognised as a breach viz the current debate on drug legalisation upsetting generations of hitherto accepted nostrums.

Some professionals within the law accept this or at least feel an as yet inchoate discontent and anxiety towards the law on the part of huge numbers of people who fall under its intolerable weight. They seek to tinker, modify, add or subtract and adjust but it is pointless. These legalistic tweakings are utterly impotent against this growing tide of ill-feeling and anger against the law itself. We have all moved on from its assumptions and the law must now be re-appraised and torn open to its heart, for it has no soul.

It is the movement of society that determines law, not its draftees and implementers. Society will always move forward re-inventing the moral parameters in which it needs to operate in order to facilitate its new thinking and consequently different modes of behaviour. The law runs after society—a legal pooper-scooper—sweeping up its unasked for droppings and disposing of them. The law seeks to put a legal frame around where society has already gone in order to protect it from the often unanticipated consequences of its moral behaviour.[44,46,48,50]

3. MARRIAGE

Marriage has become meaningless. It may retain its romantic ideal connotations but has it any import beyond the dress, the cake, the speech and the drunk uncle?[60]

The law gives it no value whatsoever save the occasional and typical denial of a man's parental rights when he is an unmarried father.[59] Some financial considerations are taken on board but these can be augmented by the courts, generally in favour of the woman, should it be required. And . . . that's it.[41,46,60]

But if the law has devalued its view of marriage to be as nothing, what does it mean outside of that view. When during a long-term relationship your girlfriend annoyingly and inevitably raises the issue of 'commitment' she means it. She means the commitment that couple will make to bring children into the world and raise them as useful members of society. It is this that gives the man pause for thought. If he decides to 'commit' it must be that, inherent in this compact, is the real, desired expectation that he, like the mother, will have the privilege of raising that child to adulthood. She in turn desires the 'commitment'. Simply having a child isn't a problem; but the commitment gives the sure and probably innate knowledge that the child will have better chances of survival with the two parents and their respective roles than the one. This is the real weight behind marriage which the law seems to have opted out from. How odd that we should have to repeat the obvious and the commonplace. Except that this too can no longer be assumed. Single parent families become a more frequent option.[61] With economic freedom some women feel they can now raise the child single-handedly. But so can men.[3,8] What's sauce for the goose as they say is sauce for the gander (except of course in the eyes of Family Law). However if these assumptions are correct, then this removes the absolute rationale behind marriage.

Nonetheless society accepts that the ideal of the two parents is more beneficial and we therefore try to encourage the continuation of the institution of marriage while doing nothing legally or economically to support it.[41] An act of grotesque moral hypocrisy.[44,48–50,54,61]

While we appear to encourage our young to get married we rarely explain to them what its consequences will be. This has disastrous results. Bombarded as we are with all sorts of cultural messages, we have learned, through TV, the main cultural arbiter, and its populist programmes, a childlike and naive view of marriage with extremely high and unsustainable levels of expectation.

The happiness of the wedding day will be assumed to continue unaltered through life, as we fondly imagine it once did. And still today most of us long for and strive for a lifelong relationship with the one partner. We view this with moral approval and we're probably right. Unfortunately today with a near 50 per cent divorce rate, it is increasingly unlikely to be the case.

We should support this institution and educate people again to the true meaning and nature of marriage. That which our parents had explained to them, those examples of a 'normal' marriage which were all around and clearly visible to the participants in another age, has dissolved in our more fractured society.[46,60] Equally the law must stop pretending and insisting that the dissolution of a relationship is fault-free—it never is.[17,42,58] This again is convenient but it is another disastrous moral failure on the part of the law. One understands what the law is trying to do, but in pretending it is non-judgemental (ie morally neutral) it lessens the importance of the institution and allows its dissolution to be that much easier, which is not, as I've argued, in society's interest and by extension, not in the interest of the child.[44,50,54] This failure becomes full-blown when divorce is embarked upon, which I will discuss shortly.

The nullity of marriage becomes a Potemkin Village of the heart upon signature of the marriage contract and the utterance of the oath.

This is the great act of State betrayal. The moment the great pantomime or charade begins. At this point the man ceases to be an equal partner in anything but name. And he'd better hang in there or risk losing everything he's had and be forced under pain of pursuit, prosecution and imprisonment, using the full panoply of the State, to be sometimes in effect nothing better than a wage slave for life.

For both the oath and the contract are void and meaningless. What are they for? In life when one signs a contract one reasonably expects the other person to uphold their end of the deal. That is the contract's purpose. A legal thrashing-out of obligations between the parties, failure of which to uphold results in sanctions. Certainly in business, should one fail in one's contractual obligation, one would face dire consequences.[49,54,58,59,62]

And there's the cardinal mistake—marriage has obligations and responsibilities. It's a grown-up's game. But if the consequences of marriage become tiresome why not escape them? Divorce for a large number of women, but not for the man and children, is consequence free.[42,62] So what of obligation and responsibility? What of the oath, the contract? What of sanction? The law is silent.[59]

At this point the initial moral failure of the law is compounded into a freefall of hypocrisy, gender- biased assumptions, discrimination, suspension of rights and all the other baleful results of a morally neutral law.[58] How can such a thing exist? It is impossible to have judgement with neutral consequence. Family Law is a sophist's delight. No law is morally neutral and when it pretends to be, and behaves as though it were, it has, by definition, become a travesty of justice.[43]

What may be done?

The contract must have weight and meaning and it should spell out what is expected of the parties in the case of children and also the terms under which a marriage may be dissolved.[53]

At the point of misgivings in a relationship there should be mandatory discussions with an authority who cannot recommend the dissolution of the contract.[48,51,52,57]

It should spell out the consequences, which are null should it simply be two individuals who are involved, but if there are young children involved, the matter should be thoroughly dwelt upon, all help given to the participants and the consequences of divorce spelt out and they must be equally onerous to both parties. It would be helpful were this to be spelt out in pre-marriage meetings also.[49,52,53]

It makes clear that this marriage is a serious thing, society takes it seriously. It is not to be entered into and dissolved on whim, making light of it is a profound mistake, this contract says so and this contract will be upheld.[49,58,59]

Again this process should re-occur before the separation of a partnership and the dissolution of a contract. When the initial stage has ended and the participants still wish to proceed with divorce, fully cognizant of its consequences, then and only then at this point should it go to law with the judge being obliged to take full weight of the arbitrator's view.[51,52,57]

Marriage must become real and meaningful again.[44,60,61] It must be taught in school as the relationship paradigm with good parenting being the desired peak of social approval, which it is not at present.[21]

The durability or otherwise of the romantic ideal of love and its development to more profound emotional depths needs to be explained and illustrated. The social dynamic between men and women talked about with regard to their school, family and the wider community and what its purpose is.[61]

This is not social engineering—this is picking up the slack that modern society has thought unimportant. This is doing the job that was self-evident to most people, pre-divorce meltdown.[40,56]

It may not make much difference, but it may begin to alter the view of responsibility and re-introduce peer group pressure to behave in a certain way in order to obtain societal approval.[46]

4. DIVORCE

Sometimes, for whatever reason, Britain becomes the lightning rod for social change. Who could have predicted the disastrous levels of divorce unique to the UK?[45] What great failure is at work here? There is much hand wringing and soul searching and everyone has their theories. I think it's because we're more stupid and our schools suck and as a society we no longer care enough . It's called decadence.[46]

Certainly from the once seemingly homogenous vertical society that once pertained we have become more fissiparous and horizontal. (Like me really). And it happened very quickly as things tend to do in small islands with large populations.[20,44] In more coherent or classically homogenous societies like my home country of Ireland, only 11,000 people have sought divorce since it was permitted seven years ago, though this too is changing. Secularism, and its twins materialism and consumerism, have not yet taken root so much there, extended families still play an important function, it is more of a child-centred society and parental authority is for most still considered absolute. Finally, the moral value of promise and its concomitant social disapproval of separation is strong. 'Yiv made yer own bed, now lie on it!' is often heard and is ill-disguised code for Grow Up.[46,58]

Other societies teach recommended relationship behaviour earlier and this seems to have some effect but what is sure is that other modern philosophical and moral ideas have become the motor of social change here.[60]

The mutual dependency that was the glue to previous generations and their marriages no longer pertains in the financially independent world. So what is to replace it now? Why not divorce when things get boring, sticky, sulky, difficult, predictable, you've changed, I've changed, you need to change, I can't change etc.?

Why not divorce when there's no downside? If I was a woman I would. Indeed were I a woman and realised I could hop off with the new man/men, keep the house, keep the kids, give up work AND get paid . . . forever . . . well, Hello Opportunity Knocks![13,42,53,54,59,62,64]

If he becomes irritating about the kids I can have the courts stop him phoning them. I can stop him seeing them without any consequence; even if the court orders me to I'll just refuse to do it and if he doesn't pay, why I'll just get the court to order the CSA to rifle his accounts and seize whatever assets he has left and if all else fails they'll put him in jail for me . . . And then maybe I'll leave the area and change the child's surname while I'm at it. Yep the ol' divorce-as-career move.[13,37,42,48,52,54,55,59,62,64]

No doubt some readers will view the above as 'unhelpful'. That's too bad because that is what's going on in too many cases. It's true, we never talk about it, we know it's going on, it's become normal because of its ubiquity but we should talk long and hard about it. We should drag it out into the light because that same ubiquity will never make it right and its reality makes it a hindrance to reform and a barrier to stemming the divorce tide.

There is a very grave injustice happening here and I suggest it is high time that it was addressed.

Many will read Bob the embittered, abandoned husband in this. They will be quite wrong. My personal response to my situation was shock and dismay, pain, emptiness and loss. I was embittered only with the law and my consequent lack of rights as a man.

This is not the right way to behave in supposed fault-free, gender neutral, consequence-free divorce law. I am only too aware of the pain and hurt and loss that women suffer in divorce but it is equally and empirically true that it is as nothing compared to the physical, financial and emotional loss of men. She may lose her man, he loses the lot. There must be an equality of burden. Neither gender neutral nor consequence free but consequence balanced.[37,39,42,49,52,59,62,64]

If he is the offending party people believe it's right he should leave the house and kids and pay for them. He has, after all, in effect abandoned them for his own selfish needs and therefore he should pay. He even half thinks this is his guilt.[37]

But rarely does he think I've got a new woman, I'm happier, so I'll just take the kids and go off to this new life. Indeed society would view it askance if he took the kids. Why? We don't if she does precisely the same. Why? If he took the kids it would be viewed as abduction, but not if she does. Why?

If she is unhappy she asks him to leave the house. We think that's ok. If he's unhappy and he demanded she leave we'd think it was weird and unmanly. Why? And indeed if she did leave we'd think she was a slut who'd abandoned her kids to that bastard. Why?

The gross imbalance that leads to this manifestly, gender based and discriminatory injustice is based on the original sin of the Family Law, page one, chapter one.

The law is currently heavily weighted in favour of women. This is acknowledged by most commentators and lawyers when they are being honest. I can accept that this was not the intent, but it is the inevitable and unjust end logic to a set of prejudiced assumptions.[2,5,28,30]

The first correct assumption is that the law should always act in the best interests of the child. Fine, we can all agree with that. But, though it's heresy to say it and for fear of being thought a heartless, ill-feeling brute, I guess philosophically there's an argument as to why any one group's rights and interests should have paramountcy over another's, particularly if those other parties' rights are ignored or denied in order to support the others. I raise the question here because at last the advent of the Human Rights Act legitimises a rights-based debate within the child welfare discourse (see Bainham, this volume).

Extrapolating the logic of that into wider areas takes one to frightening places. And again if we are to look at all aspects of this law we should particularly examine in detail its base assumption, especially if the group around whom the assumptions were made, and the law framed initially to defend, may suffer as a direct result of the law's intent. In other words the instrument set up to act in a child's interests has the exact opposite effect.

Certainly in centuries to come all our laws will appear fairly comical and none more so than those struggling to cope with social change and its consequences. I wonder whether they will consider us dewy-eyed and emotional, blinding ourselves to reason to the detriment of all concerned and the benefit of nobody.

Will they make a joke of this blinding of reason and contrast it with the emblematic portrayal of blind Justice itself and the absolute reversal of its meaning.

Still we've agreed. Where we begin to disagree comes next in the unwritten and unspoken but clearly understood corollary of that first assumption and that is: that the law believes that the interests of the child are nearly always best served by the presence of the mother.[24,28,30] This is simply wrong. It is emotive and traditional and does not bear scrutiny.[2,3,7] What flows from this well meaning but intellectually flabby cardinal mistake is a catalogue of injustice, misery and cack-handed interference by an overweening state assuming for itself onerous responsibility over free born citizens.

Obviously, though it is unspoken and unwritten, we know this corollary to exist because only in rare cases, and then in exceptional circumstances, will a man be allowed to raise his children,[8,11,16,39] something that outside the justice system and within society is assumed to be inalienable upon his child's birth.

The professionals will argue that this in fact pertains, and is indeed, their very raison d'etre. This would of course be disingenuous nonsense.[25,26,28] The law in reality exists to favour and facilitate the mother-and-child construct, to the almost total exclusion of the father.[24–28,30] The father is viewed as being, and certainly is given the impression of being, a tiresome irrelevance.[2,6,9,23–26,28,30] Or at least of tertiary importance. The hurdles that the courts put in the father's way become so tortuous and painful to negotiate that most 'good' fathers give up within two years. For to continue is to invite chronic health problems to a futile end.

The law must know it is contributing to the problem. It is creating vast wells of misery, massive discontent, an unstable society of feral children and feckless adolescents who have no understanding of authority or ultimate sanction, no knowledge of a man's love and how it is different but equal to a woman's, irresponsible mothers, drifting, hopeless fathers, problem and violent ill-educated sons and daughters, a disconnect from the extended family and society at large, vast swathes of cynicism and repeat pattern behaviour in subsequent adult relationships. So many of us are hurting and yet the law will treat the man in court (if my case is typical) with contempt, suspicion, disdain and hostility and not as its ally and the second leg of this now crippled corpus without whom the whole thing falls over.[11,24,28,30]

The further injustices of loss pertaining to men all flow from the above. He has already lost his wife—the person he loved, his children—prized above all, the house in which to keep the children, his home—that metaphysical place of being, signifying rest and comfort and belonging, his right to be a parent and its concomitant authority—for that now goes to the State and, of course, his money, often his health and frequently his job. Good, eh? And still we believe this law works. It is a disgrace.

When the marriage contract is a cynical worthless sham, when divorce for a lot of women is either relatively painless or consequence-free, then marriage can become a one-stop shop to self-fulfilment and divorce a career move.[53,62] On the other hand, for men it is a zero sum game with (literally) a 50-50 gamble. The resulting mess is the Family industry's (of which this volume is simply another branch) sole raison d'être.

No doubt professionals will decry this view. But it is a commonly held one, it is certainly mine and my acquaintances, men and women alike, and I would be supported by the large bulk of the thousands of letters I have received. Indeed, if everything in the garden were so rosy why this book, why the Lord Chancellor's report and the endless stream of surveys, studies and reports all categorising the failures I have just articulated, So many of you out there tinkering and foostering (as my father might say) Why? Rip it down. Start again. It's broke. Get a new car.

5. POST-DIVORCE

Seeing Your Children

Everything can be tolerable until the children are taken from you. I cannot begin to describe the pain, the awful eviscerating pain of being handed a note, sanctioned by your (still) wife with whom you had made these little things, with whom you had been present at their birth and previously had felt grow and kick and tumble and turn and watched the scans and felt intense manly pride and profound love for before they were even born, had changed them, taught them to talk, read and add, wrestled and played with, walked them to school, picked them up, made tea with, bathed and dressed, put them to bed, cuddled and lay with in your arms and sang to sleep, felt them and smelt them around you at all times, alert even in sleep to the slightest shift in their breathing . . . a note that will ALLOW you ACCESS to these things who are the best of you . . . ALLOW mark you, REASONABLE !!!! ACCESS?!?!!! to those whom two weeks ago you couldn't wait for to walk in the door at home.[23,25]

What have you done? Why are you being punished (for that's what it appears)? How can she be allowed to dictate what I can or can't do with regard to MY children? When did she assume control? Why do I have no authority any longer?[6,13,24,26] What's going on? She wants to leave. OK there's nothing I can do about that. What's that got to do with the kids and me? Were I to issue her a similar note what would happen? What then the assumptions?

I still ask these questions. Why is one treated as a criminal? Why is the language that of the prison visit? Why is the person (and I'm being restrained because it is nearly always the woman but we're actually not meant to say that for fear of being labelled misogynist and to maintain Family Laws fig-leaf of fiction) who has taken the children, or been left with them, suddenly given immense emotional, legal and financial power over the other party. Yes, yes I know in theory that until certain procedural moves have occurred one has equal dibs but in practice you don't because they've gone.[24,39]

It is easy to see why women resist intrusion in parenting by men.[11] Why give up the one monopoly you have.[6,16] A key part of gender equality has to be improving the deal on offer to men.[1,2,39,40]

The children have immediately become the weapon and the shield. It is at this juncture that things spiral into acrimony, bitterness, loathing, hate and rage.

It is of course the power that is the intoxicant. Where hitherto it had been a partnership of equals now the party with the children can largely control events. The resulting feeling of helplessness, hopelessness and powerlessness on the other side results in either withdrawal into weary defeat and supine acceptance of being beaten—being raped actually, for it shares the symptoms of being overwhelmed hopelessly in the face of brute hatred and power—or like endless examples of powerless peoples you fight viciously, for you have nothing left to lose. There is nothing more desperate than the impotent. Losing control of one's life is a desperate experience, having someone else being able to exert control over it is worse.

The Weapon and the Shield

The Weapon: 'Do as I say or you won't see the children.'
The Shield: 'Don't do that to me or you won't see the children'.

'Behave well or I'll report it. Don't telephone, it's harassment. I don't care you wish to say goodnight. I don't want you to and neither do the children. Stop now before I have it forbidden. If you do it again I'll call the police. Don't write to them. It upsets them. They think it's weird.'[17–19]

'You look a mess. It's not my fault you're not sleeping, obviously you're incapable of looking after them, no, you can't take them. I know we agreed but I'm not having them see you like this. Stop pleading it's pathetic. Go home or I'll call the police.'

And so you turn from your own door. Dismissed peremptorily like a penitent tramp. Inside—inches away, is your family, the key to the door is still in your pocket. It still fits. Your key, your house, your family. That night you must see them. You must touch them and smell them. You drive, fear rising to hysterical levels near to the house. Not too near—she'll see or hear. You walk to the door. Utter panic rising. Fear of this girl you loved beyond reason. Everything's weird. Disconnected. Unreal beyond imagination. There's the door. In front of it you pause. You raise your hand. You feel like a madman but you only want to say goodnight to your babies. You lift the doorknocker and listen hard. Inside—inches from you, you hear them laughing. Your family. That you made. You worked for everything they're sitting on, sleeping in, eating. They're telling some story or joke that you can't hear. A joke that two weeks ago you'd have been laughing at too. They're inside. You're outside—why? Too scared you gently lower the knocker and retreat to the car. You park near the house and turn off the lights and engine. You sit and wait 'til all the bedroom lights go out. As each one goes you whisper 'goodnight' to yourself like a madman. After the last light has gone you sit and sob, hoping no-one sees you, waiting 'til you're able to drive again.

Why is that allowed to happen?[29]

This disgusting law that imposes that fear and panic on people must be destroyed. In your loss and grief how is this supportable? And why should it be so. Who are these people that impose this law and how dare they?[16,25,26,30]

Some readers will know better than I the incidence of serious illness in men arising from divorce. It is far higher than in women. Why is this? Everyone knows the effect of divorce in terms of employment and homelessness. Again far greater than for women. Why? Everyone knows the relationship between alcoholism and divorce, again greater for men. Why? Don't you think this is serious enough to insist on change?[41] Count the economic and social cost if that means more to you than the human, but when you finally achieve a negative sum, ask Why?

What more is required to make men the same in the eyes of the law as they are in the eyes of their children. To avoid all the foregoing is relatively simple. Men must be accorded equal status under the law. Currently they are not and presently they must be. No bromides or platitudes should be acceptable from now on.[2,30,38,40]

The first way to achieve this, to put meat on the marriage contract and render divorce as significant for women as it is for men, is to give men the same status as parent immediately upon separation.

There must be an immediate presumption, as there has been in Denmark since January 2002 that the children, where possible, will live with the father 50 per cent of the time. Should this prove impossible the children must be free to be with their dads 50 per cent of the time or allow a mutually acceptable arrangement to be arrived at by both parties. Isn't that eminently civilised?

In the course of the seminars which informed this book, we discussed a cultural, and therefore legal, bias that men shouldn't raise their children if they're toddlers. Why not?[3,14,15,23,33,63] Who do you think looked after them when Mum was at work or otherwise out? Who changed their nappies or did the bottles. What period of time do some of you live in? And if a man doesn't know how to do it initially, like most first time mothers, it is easily learned.[20,22,23] Relationship courses within school and during the mandatory pre-marriage classes could helpfully incorporate babycare and parenting skills within their agenda.[3,20,21] Clearly there may be difficulties with breast-fed babies but these are not insurmountable, and some allowances would have to be made in this and several other circumstances, but these are details in the overall concept and can be dealt with. The principle remains and it is that principle of equality that must be central.[40]

Herring (this volume) reports cases in which women who wished to move out of the area or even territory or jurisdiction were allowed to, because, well it's obvious innit, she'll be-unhappy-if-we-don't-let-her-and-that's-clearly-not-in-the-best-interest-of-the-child-now-is-it? . . . and therefore she should be allowed!!![30,33]

Am I the only one who reads this and thinks this is a world gone insane? Even if I take the utterly warped logic of the courts, how can they believe that the child never seeing their father again until they meet a stranger some day as an adult is in the best interest of anyone. While of course he pays for this child who he will never see. A particularly futile way of living I would venture—I don't think I'd bother.[29]

Herring also reports judicial disapproval for a man who objected to a woman who wished to change the child's surname.[30] 'A poor sort of parent' is what this unfortunate was called, whose child would at least know who she and her father were before the past and her identity were stripped, like a Stalinist photograph, out of her family's history. He was not allowed even to give her his name. Her family name. So a man is to be stripped of even that. He is to be utterly expunged from the past. The past and he never happened. The child was a miracle birth. The father of no consequence. A figment of a time. Best forgotten. Let's move on. Year Zero is now and forever.[24,29,30,33,38]

It is unfortunate in these people's eyes, but ultimately academic, that children are genetically 50 per cent of the man and perhaps that selfish gene which drove this man to express genetic infinity with his partner through their children should just go away and conveniently disappear. But I doubt he will. The contempt shown to the father is nonetheless, you will agree, utterly breathtaking. Or will you?

The principle of 50 per cent of everything, the same for mother and father, must pertain. We have seen the rise of dual-career couples; now we need dual-carer couples. The best people to provide this care are almost always parents. And we mean parents—not just mothers,[3,14,15] Indeed the reality of this would help to neutralise the divorce advantage I describe above. Advantage is, of course, a non-issue where there's economic equality between the parties. In poverty, divorce simply exacerbates the penury, in wealth it is academic. But, whether in cases of poverty or wealth, an equal child-sharing arrangement would be advantageous. Hopefully, it would help both parents to be free to earn a living and pursue their independent lives, and achieve and maintain greater amicability bewteen them, which will in turn benefit their children. I am not blind to the impact this will have on the demand for affordable housing, but this is essentially no different to the already huge housing crisis caused by divorce and other factors now busily chewing up the green belt.

Seven million people live alone today as opposed to 1.5 million 50 years ago. This change has been driven partly by the fivefold increase in divorce during the same period and which, in turn, has driven the huge demand for housing and the concomitant rise in price. 80 per cent of all new social housing is for single parents. The government must address this core feature of the housing crisis and aid those who care for their children to do so, especially in lower income cases, whether it be through more shared ownership schemes run by local authorities, greater investment in housing development, or tax relief, etc. The detail of this can come later. However it is clear that the social and economic cost benefits of such policies will far outweigh the current price of social disintegration.

As to those who can't or won't or don't want to participate in this arrangement, then the parties can work out something of mutual convenience and benefit to the children.

Work patterns have altered considerably: flexi-time, work-from-home, the 35 hour week, and, with increasingly aware employers, will alter further. Should new legislation be enacted allowing equal time as a norm, as increasingly happens elsewhere, it would become necessary for employers to accommodate this.

Working hours are stuck in the industrial era. They are also stuck in an age where few employees had to worry about school runs or nursery pick-ups. The Work Foundation (2001) has already called for legislation giving all employees the right to request a change of working conditions (which will be granted to the parents of young children from April 2003). It is now time the government recognised that granting employees more control over their hours increases productivity (Knell and Savage, 2001), and that, according to a recent survey of respondents views about their 'work-life' balance, fathers want flexitime, a compressed working week and the chance to work at home (O'Brien and Schemilt, 2002).

Obviously I have not dealt with domestic violence or abuse of any kind. However it should be understood as a given that there will be a small minority of circumstances in which the 50-50 presumption should not apply and may not even be safe—we have a child protection system which should and must deal with those cases – but in all others, the presumption should prevail. However, even in such cases, as with many aspects of family law, it should not be overlooked that the assumptions and biases pertaining to abuse and violence—that perpetrators in the main are men—are often overwhelmingly contradicted by empirical and surprising fact which I have cited in the Addendum.[32–36]

So the marriage contract is meaningless. Divorce is consequence free. The law is biased and its premise discriminatory. What is left of this hollow sham? The thing that makes any law a laughing stock and worthless—the utter moral failure or lack of will or inability to implement its own orders or impose its authority with all the powers and sanctions it has awarded itself. Except in the case of male non-compliance of course.

The Reality of 'Contact'

The implication of any order determining the father's allotted time with his children is that he was always of secondary importance within the household.[2,8,9,10,11,28] Indeed this would appear to be again the unspoken assumption underpinning the whole farrago. The weasel words 'gender neutral', and the oft stated pieties of equality occur so frequently one would be forgiven for thinking that if one says them often enough we could convince ourselves we actually are administering a fair system. But these words, like all the other alibi utterances such as REASONABLE CONTACT, will never disguise the underlying reality of painful discriminatory practice.

Reasonable contact is an oxymoron. The fact that as a father you are forbidden from seeing your children except (like a visit to the dentist) at State-appointed moments is by definition UNreasonable. The fact that you must VISIT your family as opposed to live with them is unreasonable. I suppose CONTACT as an idea works. One does become like a visitor from Mars, infrequent and odd, making contact with strangers in an alien landscape with all the concomitant emotion of excitement, fear, anticipation, suspicion and dislocation. But hardly the ideal emotions involved in being with your children or them with you. In the end there is emptiness, loneliness and an overwhelming sense of failure and loss. This wasn't a Dad with his kids. This was an awkward visiting Uncle in false fleeting situations of amity.

A man (like a woman) must be allowed to LIVE with his children where possible, to raise them as he should, and as he desires, in co-operation with his ex-partner. Once what the court deems appropriate orders (orders?) have been made, the man enters the emotional marathon that is trying to retain your sense of family and fatherhood with your children. It may well be that he was the type of person who read his Sunday paper throughout the morning apparently oblivious to anything but what was in front of him. ('He was never a very good father'.) The children would come in playing some game or other scrambling over him. He continued impassively reading. The children climbed over him and then buggered off.

This was the Dad they knew and loved. Now the Sunday morning papers and the games are gone. Forever. There is no house. There's an embarrassing bedsit or small flat. 'Well they can't stay there can they. It's not suitable. Don't be stupid, there's no space'. The children are embarrassed for their Dad. They don't want to see him down on his luck. They feel somehow guilty, like they're partly to blame. Dad should be in a big house again. Then they'd like to come over. Come over. Like a visit to another person but not a Dad. Dad looks sad in this place; they don't want to see that. He looks like Dad, a little tired, a little crushed, still he looks like him but he doesn't feel like him. There's nothing to do here. It's boring. It's weird Dad playing Monopoly and stuff . . . and drawing and . . .What's going on?

In Battersea Park on Sunday. Watch the single men with the children drag themselves through the false hours in a frantic panic of activity. The build-up. The excitement of being with them. The all-week anticipation. The fear of the pick-up. The coldness. The stranger's voice. The peremptory instructions. The 'have them back at . . .' It's Sunday. You remember the quiet papers and the tumbling bodies about you. The serenity. But they're here and the other thing has gone. Not now the excitement, its not now the couple of hours together, now it's only the 2 hours and 58, 57, 56 etc, minutes left. Time dripping too fast, decaying. Every second measured and weighed in the balance of loss, losing, going away and fading. Everything must be crammed into this space. Life in an hour. Love in a measured fragment of State-permitted time.

Now, oh boy, yeah you're Action Dad! Yessiree kick that ball, push that swing higher than those other Dads. You're much better than them aren't you? Feed them ducks . . . again. Go to that movie . . . in the afternoon? Madame Tussauds, the London Dungeon, the Eye, the Circus, Funfair . . . Hey Johnny every day with Dad is Treat Day. Birthday party time. They've finally forced me into being . . . Hurrah for the State . . . New Model Dad!!!!!!!! and maybe if I keep it up they'll let you stay just one night . . . Just one night. 'But don't tell them we'll share the bed like we used to before . . . they think it's different now, they won't like it.' Weird minds. 'It's the best thing that's ever happened to him. He's a much better Father now. He used to do NOTHING before. Nothing'. McDad in McDonalds. Sunday lunchtime. Where else do you go? Contact centres?

Long benches and institutionalised coffee. 'I want to go home Dad'. So do you, but unlike him you can't. You don't have one to go to, remember? What do you talk about? The silences must be filled. So much to say. Your heart bursts with things to say. But shut up. It's too much. Too grown-up. Too heavy. Too burdensome on someone so small. 'How's school?' brightly, cheerily. 'Fine'. 'Great'. 'How's Pete?' 'Pete? Who's Pete?' 'Y'know Pete. Your mate' 'Oh Simon, yeah he's good'. 'Good'. Everything to say, no way or nowhere to say it. Those easy silences, that casual to and fro talking of the past gone. Now there must be subjects to fill in the spaces. And never get angry, or cross or raise your voice or shout . . . it'll be reported. No discipline whatever you do.

'Why, Mum lets me.' 'Yeah well I'm telling you not to.' 'You're not the boss. Mum is' 'You still must do as I tell you.' 'Why?' Yeah he's right . . . why? Next week. 'Don't you ever speak to him like that again. Who do you think you are?'[17–19]

None of this is working. It is not the best we can do. The law itself is to blame for these consequences of divorce. It is the clumsy, cack-handed law that imposes this life on people. It is not right.

I note in the Lord Chancellor's report, *Making Contact Work*, the desire to create even more layers of State administration, tax money and bureaucracy by creating a network of 'Contact Centres'. Of course this is as nothing to their solution for non-compliance with contact orders. Vast areas of advisors, mediators, consultants and persuaders are to be set up to please ask the 'resident' parent to go on . . . oh, go on, please let him see his kids. Don't be so mean. Don't be so horrible. Pretty please.

It is a cliché that the bureaucrat when confronted with a problem of his own making will seize upon the opportunity to create even further layers of bureaucracy and contribute to the State apparatus even further. As the man said 'It'll end in tiers'—it always does. But that seems to be the sum total of their creativity. That's the big conclusion of the Lord Chancellor's report: in principle everything's ok but could we have more money please to set up lots more levels of interference. Thank you everyone who has contributed. Your comments have been noted and duly ignored.

6. STATUS QUO

Upon separation, the system is slow and delay occurs immediately. This allows the *status quo* to be established. As the process labours on it becomes impossible to alter. This is unfair. It is nearly always possible for the resident parent (let's face it, the girl) to establish a pattern. It is then deemed in the child's interest not to break this routine. But at the cost of losing sight and touch of their father, we must really examine all our assumptions without fear. Then we can move to building a more equitable system benefiting all equally.

Again a presumption of 50-50 rids one of the *status quo* problems.

Equally, 50-50 deals with the non-compliance issue. There would be no need for sanctions under this regime. And no need for the laborious and unjust proposals in the Lord Chancellor's report which is a reductionist brief in a bid to make CAFCASS into the overarching State implementor of Family Law. Perhaps we should call it KAFKASS. This provides for an interminable round of increasing sanctions to a recalcitrant parent who will not allow access to the child though so ordered. Under the proposed regime it would literally take months and possibly years before the other parent could see his child. At which point he would meet a virtual stranger, possibly poisoned with prejudice (also a problem in the *status quo* issue) against him.[17–19] Why is this permitted?

If the parent cannot see his child because of the refusal of the other parent to allow it in breach of the court order, they should be arrested and jailed. The end.[12,47]

It is not much different from that other mother who was found to be harming her children by not making them attend school. She went to jail. The children went to school. She says it will never happen again, she was stupid. Previously truanting children around the country, shocked by the visible hand of authority have started showing up again. Try it. Is it any more harmful that someone spends a brief period in jail because she is harming her children by not letting them see their Dad? Or is it less harmful that they never see their Dad?[26]   Sometimes I also pose this question to you academics and researchers because you are all part of this vast industry. And you are all tinkering.

I know what I've written is a mess. I know it spills from coherent thought into pain and anger. I know it sprawls across assumptions and anecdote and imaginary and real conversations. Had I time I would whittle it all down to your polite, empirical language. The problem is that this issue is bound up with pain that spills its tears across your politesse and renders your language null.

The law is profoundly flawed. When there is absolute wrong it is permissible, indeed imperative to be absolutist in your thinking. Do chuck out the baby with the bath water. (Perhaps an unfortunate expression given the subject matter.) Think fresh. Tabula rasa. Clean slate. Blank paper. Re-examine cause and effect, for whatever the cause in the past, it is a different one today.

As we have seen, Society has changed profoundly. Marriage is meaningless because it has no contractually enforceable consequences. Divorce is the same. It should not be a 'one bound and I'm free' construct when there are children involved. In the past people found a different freedom within their own chosen chains of marriage.[48,50,56,60,61]

Some pressure groups advocate a 'Shared Parenting' presumption at separation (see Buchanan and Hunt, this volume) and cosy up to the Family Law Establishment by saying that this in no way implies an equal time situation, far less a split residence one.

I insist on the latter. There is no harm in being radical when the status quo breeds injustice. I have suggested:

—education in schools that would lead to an understanding of relationships and familial responsibility;
—marriage classes which outline the consequences of a marriage contract (with teeth), and the consequences of having children within that marriage and their impact upon that agreement;
—at separation, and before divorce can be contemplated, a mandatory arbitrator who could insist on staged withdrawal or conciliation before the dispute may be permitted to go to court where due weight would be given to the arbitrator's recommendations, and

—should proceedings move to divorce, a presumption of equal parenting, implying shared responsibility and equal residency, would be assumed even if not acted upon, but from which other formulae that suit the particular couples could emerge, save those arrangements so flagrantly ridiculous that it would not be in the clear best interest of the child.

Currently my proposition has already begun to be assimilated into the mainstream; in Denmark since 2001, more frequently in the US and other places.[55,56]

I myself fought for it in this country. I had always worked from home. I had money. I took care of the children. I lived beside the school; had ample accommodation; a stable relationship with a woman they knew and liked. My ex-wife worked etc. Why couldn't they be with me 50 per cent of the time? I understand my circumstances were exceptional but I could not and still don't understand why there was so much opposition to this perfectly reasonable request. This is not being naive or disingenuous. Eventually I succeeded but I had to nearly bankrupt myself in the process simply to be able to live with my children. How is that in their interests? Finally I was granted full custody. But I never wanted or asked for that. My ex-wife was not a criminal so why this punitive measure of taking our children from her. If I disagree with it happening to men, equally so with women. I was given full custody because the professionals involved would not agree that split residence was acceptable, despite the urging of the judge in the case who had sat on international benches, making those judgments daily.

Once he asked 'If it works in those countries, why not here?' Answer came there none. What is it with you people? I was granted my children, but this humane man told us should we wish to arrive at something more conducive to us both he would welcome that. 50-50 worked fairly well for us. The only problems in our case were the personal and finally tragic circumstances. In a normal household I cannot see why, after perhaps some initial dislocation, this would not work.

The children are fine now, I'm fine . . . but the things your industry put us through almost destroyed us. My children will remember your unwarranted intrusions and heavy-handedness, save for a few gentle souls we encountered along the way—all professionals—working inside or outside the state apparatus, who were kind and sympathetic. But Lord how I hated you, and what you did to us.

Allow men their dignity. Let them be with their children. The sting is drawn that way. The financial issue is laid aside. Co-operation, if not amity, would be the norm. Issues of power and control and their attendant responses of impotence and hopelessness which fuel the anger and rage are redundant.

Of course it will work for some and not for others. But that's now. When it becomes the social norm—and it will, children will meet their peers who will have the same or expected experience. Just as divorce was shaming for children in the schoolyard once and is now a commonplace, albeit still painful. Allow men to reclaim their fatherhood and their children.

All the other papers in this book are ignoring this central critical issue. It is tinkering with the already redundant. We have all changed. Think anew.

> Right now the agenda around Fatherhood is a modest 'add-on' to initiatives. It is at best a sideshow. But the truth is that only changes in men's lives can generate genuine equality. Fatherhood is now the key to feminism. (Reeves, 2002)

Women changed their circumstance and so must men. By definition their children must too occupy a different world—a different idea of family. For better or worse? Who knows. But the law must as an imperative, recognise it and act. There has been too much destruction. Too much pain.

As I entered court on my first day someone leaned over who felt they were doing me a favour. 'Whatever you do' he said 'for Chrissakes never say you love your children.' Bewildered I replied 'Why not?' The answer was as shocking as it is illustrative 'The court thinks you're being unhealthily extreme if, being a man, you express your love for a child.'

For two years I shut up while I heard the presumptions in favour of a mother's love.

Finally I began articulating the real love that dare not speak its name—that of a father for his child.

No law should stand that serves to stifle this.

ADDENDUM

Fathers and Mothers' Changing Roles

1. 'Feminists point to increased father participation as essential in the realisation of women's equality of opportunity' (Rich, 1971).
2. 'Currently, child care is seen as a women's issue; it is rare indeed to find any commentaries which frame the question within the context of women and men. Perhaps while the question continues to be dismissed as a women's issue that is what will remain' (Russell, 1983, p 219).
3. 'There is a natural expectation that a woman's biological capacity to bear children carries with it an exclusive obligation to actually rear children. However, there is no justifiable reason for the quantum leap between the two functions—parental behaviours such as feeding, protecting, grooming, playing, reading, education, putting to bed, washing and comforting are not sex specific tasks' (Opie, 2002, p 2).
4. 'The idea that motherhood is a holy vocation managed to oppress women by its impossible demands and unwarranted assumptions about femininity; but it also oppressed men by excluding them from the home and consigning them to a life of work, conflict and politics' (Seel, 1987).

5. 'By locking women inside the home, the Victorians effectively locked the men out. Just as women were deprived of experiences relating to production (power, creativity, economic independence, excitement), so men were excluded from experiences relating to reproduction (nurturing, caring, supporting and loving relationships with their children)' (Opie, 2002, p 8).

6. 'Children are universally seen as being owned by women. This leads to a motherhood monopoly of childcare. The father, as a participating parent, is chronically disadvantaged.' (Opie, 2002, p 10).

7. 'There is no evidence for a maternal instinct.' (Opie, 2002, p 11).

8. 'Contrary to the expectations of many, that only fathers would suffer identity problems with reversing roles and would feel threatened by mothers taking over the breadwinning job, the evidence indicates quite clearly that mothers experience considerable difficulty in adjusting to the father being the primary parent.' (Russell, 1987, p 176).

9. 'Mothers felt threatened when fathers were intimate with their children' (New and David, 1985).

10. 'Mothers felt threatened by their husband's participation in the traditionally female domain' (Russell, 1987, p 121).

11. 'The answer [to why women do not want male involvement] may lie in the traditional patterns of female power and privilege. Some women may fear losing their traditional power over home activities if they allow men to relieve them of even part of the home and family work' (Polternick, 1987, p 112).

12. 'Where involvement and responsibility are shared so is the decision-making. A father's involvement in the domestic sphere means that the number of decisions that have to be negotiated greatly increases. Hence, in order to keep to a minimum the child-centred decisions and the inevitable conflicts, the father's participation is restricted by the mother' (Hoffman, 1977, cited in New and David, 1985, p 205).

13. 'It has been suggested that mothers do not want to abdicate any childcare responsibility because by doing so they would place themselves in a less favourable position with regard to custody of the child in the event of a divorce' (Lamb, *et al*, 1987, p 115).

14. 'Fathers are as sensitive and responsive to their young children as mothers are. For example when fathers feed their young babies they respond appropriately when the baby wants to pause or needs to splutter after taking too much milk. They also manage to get as much milk into the baby as mothers do' (Parke, 1981).

15. 'Babies usually bond as easily with their fathers as with their mothers. Many studies have compared the ways in which 1–2 year olds relate to their attachment figures and have found that the closeness of father and baby is almost identical to that of mother and baby' (Lewis, 1982).

16. 'For various reasons, mothers resent active father involvement in child care' (Biller, 1993).

Mothers' Influence over the Father-child Relationship

17. 'Mothers are gatekeepers, capable of enhancing or dampening father-infant attachment' (Braselton and Cremer, 1991).
18. 'If a mother's attitude to the father is negative she may wish the children to reflect the same feelings towards him' (Opie, 2002, p 17).
19. 'In all too many families, children's perceptions of fathers are heavily weighted by information provided by mothers . . . if a mother continually uses derogatory terms in describing the father, the children may come to believe her and begin to withdraw their respect for him' (Biller, 1993 at p 23).

Education and Parenting

20. 'It (the curriculum) regrettably undervalues the father's role to accept that, while the girl is educated to be a mother, the boys do not need preparation for parenting' (Sutherland, 1981).
21. 'Formal education ignores fathering. One researcher found that only 1% of his interviewees had received a school lesson on the subject of fathering. It has been repeatedly found that parenting classes are dominated by female staff and aimed specifically at girls' (Lewis, C, 1986, pp 33–4).
22. 'Most hospitals show mothers how to bathe, dress, change, carry and feed their babies, but these skills were seldom shown to fathers, even though they needed to be taught more than the mothers did' (Lewis, 1983, p 252).
23. 'Mothers must learn to love their babies, to change nappies, bath and feed them. Fathers who try to do these things at visiting time [in hospital] are often discouraged and the idea that they might need to hold their new-born is new. One father was told to stop bonding—"it isn't fair on the mother"' (New and David, 1985, p 210).

Family Service Professionals' View of Fathers

24. 'Child and family centred professionals perpetuate the ideological division between mothers and fathers by positively underwriting the mother's owner-ship of the children and negatively marginalizing fathers' (Opie, 2002, p 18).
25. 'Other child care professionals are resistant to father's involvement. In America a survey showed that only 50% of workers in a pre-school pro-gram supported fathers' involvement.' (Burgess, 1997).
26. 'It is important to bear in mind that the professional denial of father's role is widespread.' (Rowe *et al*, 1984).

27. 'Social work practice and research has not appreciated the role of the father, he is dealt with as a 'problematic figure' rather than a full partner in social service delivery.' Bolton, 1986).

28. 'By holding negative attitudes to all fathers and thereby ignoring them, child-centred professionals are actually endangering the children they are meant to protect. It may be speculated that this anti-father attitude is created from the combination of two-factors—the ideological elements in training and the current negative image of men in society . . . the whole culture of such professionals needs to be addressed . . . Prejudice against fathers appears to be manifest amongst child-centred professionals, whose attitude and behaviour promote the ideology that mothers should have a monopoly on childcare.' (Opie, 2002, p 22 and IPPR, 2000).

29. 'Fathers are exalted as breadwinner and scorned as parents by a system that relentlessly promotes child care by mothers and role defines the father out of the home' (Opie, 2002, pp 26–28).

30. 'The dominance of women in family services, and the corresponding scarcity of men, is among the most powerful of all the forces which exclude fathers from the lives of their children today for in this we see the outward and visible sign of what begins to be perceived as an essential truth: that in family life, men are an irrelevance at best, and at worst a danger.' (Delaney and Delaney, 1990, p 156).

31. 'There is no legislation or encouragement to introduce male quotas in the female ghettos of child centred occupations, as there has been for females in male ghettos.' (Opie, 2002, p 27).

Some Evidence about the Perpetrators of Child Abuse

32. 'A sample of workers from the Australian Family Services were asked what percentage of fathers abuse their own children. The answer was an astonishing 25%. The actual figure was only 2%.' (Clare, 2000, p 185).

33. 'The biological father is the least likely person to abuse his children and all types of abuse increase significantly when biological fathers are absent from the family.' (Clare, 2000, p 186).

34. '[In] the neglect, physical and sexual abuse cases, [the children] were over twice as likely to be living with their natural mother alone.' (NSPCC, 1988–90).

35. 'In one American study it was found that mothers were the physical aggressors in 62% of the abuse cases that were reported to the child protection services.' (Wright and Leroux, cited in Fillion, 1997, p 233).

36. 'Greater father participation in child rearing is unlikely to lead to more child sexual abuse. Provided that the father is intimately involved from the very beginning, there seems to be a protection from sexual abuse' (Kremer, 1995, p 12).

Policy Implications

37. 'The child support agency . . . clearly indicates to society that the government considers the father's role only as a breadwinner. The agency should link maintenance payments to non-residential father contact with his children, thereby making a public acknowledgement that fathers have a physical presence in their children's lives, a right to be involved parents and not just carry financial responsibility.' (Opie, 2002, p 29).
38. 'The movement for men to be parentally equal at home is as revolutionary as the demand of women to be politically and economically equal outside the home. Indeed it is probably more so because it involves a more fundamental cultural, social, economic and political change . . . It is not surprising that men who seek a fair share of power in the family are incurring as much opposition as women who seek their fair share of power in the market place.' (Opie, 2002, p 31).
39. 'A woman who is denied a job because of her sex can always seek redress and compensation through the numerous Sexual Discrimination Acts. But a father who is denied his child has no legislative support or recompense. He has lost them forever.' (Opie, 2002, p 31).
40. 'We need equality for women and for men—particularly for men because we won't have real equality until men are able to take on their caring responsibilities.' (Mellor, 2000).
41. 'The growth of marital dissolution witnessed in recent decades has imposed increasing costs on the tax payer . . . and imposed a range of extra demands on the welfare state. (Dnes and Rowthorn, 2002, p 2).
42. 'Specialists frequently observe that modern family law creates an incentive structure that encourages opportunism and facilitates interpersonal obligations'(Dnes and Rowthorn, 2002, p 2).
43. 'A badly designed divorce law may undermine the fabric of trust upon which stable marriages depend. If it is badly designed, the law itself may stimulate divorce and contribute to a great deal of human misery.' (Dnes and Rowthorn, 2002, p 2).
44. 'How far was legal reform a causal factor in the growth of divorce? Statistics provide compelling evidence that the liberalisation of divorce law had a permanent impact on divorce rates.' (Dnes and Rowthorn, 2002, p 2).
45. 'The law has a significant effect on divorce rates' (Dnes and Rowthorn citing Zelder, 2002, p 8).
46. 'Much can be claimed for the older reliance on informal social sanctions and the good moral sense of the parties. Our modern need to wrestle with settlement issues may stem from losing this traditional set of checks and loosening the moral value of promise.' (Dnes and Rowthorn citing Cohen, 2002, p 3).

47. 'A failure to enforce quasi-contractual obligations between marriage partners encourages opportunistic behaviour' (Dnes and Rowthorn citing Cohen, 2002, p 3).

48. 'One does not have to be conservative to support legal restrictions on divorce. The legal enforcement of marital commitments is consistent with the legal principles and may enhance the freedom of individuals to pursue their life goals.' (Dnes and Rowthorn citing Scott, 2002, p 4).

49. 'In marriage as in commercial contracts, legal commitment can promote co-operation and protect investment in the relationship to the mutual benefit of the parties concerned.' (Dnes and Rowthorn citing Scott, 2002, p 4).

50. 'Family law reforms since the 1960s have increased the freedom of individuals to leave a marriage, but in so doing they have restricted the freedom of individuals to bind themselves so as to achieve the long term goals they desire.' (Dens and Rowthorn citing Scott, 2002, p 4).

51. 'Amongst the possibilities that would facilitate personal commitment consistent with liberal principles, are mandatory pre-marital and pre-divorce counselling, and mandatory waiting period of 2–3 years before divorce.' (Dnes and Rowthorn citing Scott, 2002, p 4).

52. 'Primary grounds for divorce should be mutual consent. A marriage should be dissolved only if both spouses agree it is a failure.' (Dnes and Rowthorn citing Parkman, 2002, p 5).

53. 'A spouse who wishes to terminate a marriage against the initial desire of the other spouse will have to win the consent of the latter. This suggestion mirrors the standard of specific performance remedy for breach of contract, which obliges a party wishing to be released from a contract to pay full compensation. Bargaining over terms of dissolution might require concessions on such issues as custody, alimony or division of the family assets. Such a provision protects spouses against expropriation of their investments in a marriage, since it deters opportunistic desertion and forces a departing spouse to pay full compensation. But to limit this power, unilateral, penalty-free divorce should be available early in the marriage when there are no children.' (Dnes and Rowthorn citing Parkman, 2002, p 5).

54. 'In the absence of legal penalties, partners may avoid investing in the marriage. '(Dnes and Rowthorn citing Rasmusden, 2002, p 5).

55. 'Louisiana couples can now choose between two types of marriage: the conventional type, which permits easy divorce with few penalties and the new common marriage, in which divorce is obtainable only after substantial delay or on proof of fault. Before entering a covenant marriage, couples must undergo counselling, and they must agree to mandatory counselling in the event of difficulties that threaten the marriage. Moreover a spouse who is guilty of serious misconduct, such as adultery or physical abuse, may be compelled to pay damages in the event of divorce. There may also be damages if the divorce follows a refusal to take

'reasonable steps to preserve the marriage including counselling' (Dnes and Rowthorn citing Spat, 2002, p 6).

56. ' The covenant marriage law unites two distinct strands of thought: it is consistent with the liberal notion that individuals should have the right to make binding commitments if they so choose. This choice is denied to them in states that offer liberal, no-fault divorce. At the same time it embodies the communitarian notion that marriage serves important social functions and that marriage law should embody moral principles consistent with these functions.' (Dnes and Rowthorn citing Spat, 2002, p 6).

57. 'Under the covenant law the primary purpose of counselling is to save marriages, and counsellors are not expected to be neutral with regard to divorce.' (Dnes and Rowthorn citing Spat, 2002, p 6).

58. 'Marriage law like ordinary contract law, should embody the moral notion of personal responsibility. Fault is no more difficult to establish in the case of divorce than in many other legal contexts.' (Dnes and Rowthorn citing Spat, 2002, p 6).

59. '. . . apply normal contractual principles to marriage so that damages would be payable for a unilateral breach of the marriage contract' (Dnes and Rowthorn citing Dnes, 2002, p 7).

60. 'In Western culture, marriage helps individuals to signal to each other and to the outside world, their desire for a sexually permanent union. However, modern legal and social trends have greatly reduced the credibility of this signal. As a result, marriage is no longer an effective signal of commitment.' (Dnes and Rowthorn citing Rowthorn 2002, p 7).

61. 'The degree of commitment is still higher, on average, amongst married couples than among cohabiting couples, and marriage is still the best predictor of the durability of a relationship.' (Dnes and Rowthorn citing Rowthorn, 2002, p 7).

62. 'Insulating women from the adverse consequences of divorce may reinforce incentives for marital dissolution.' (Dnes and Rowthorn citing Smith, 2002, p 9).

63. 'People may choose to cohabit because marriage law is dysfunctional and offers inadequate protection for spouses who invest in their marriage' (Dnes and Rowthorn citing Dnes, 2002, p 7).

64. 'Marriage bargaining is . . . a co-operative game in which the outcome is efficient, in the sense that one spouse could not be made better off without making the other worse off' (Dnes and Rowthorn citing Zelder, 2002, p 8).

REFERENCES

BILLER, HB, *Fathers and Families: Paternal Factors in Child Development* (Auburn, House, 1993).
BRAZELTON, TB and CREMER, BG, *The Earliest Relationship* (London, Karnoc, 1991).

BOLTON, FG, 'Negative Paternal Stereotyping in Social Service Delivery' in ME Lamb, *The Father's Role: Applied Perspectives* (Chichester, Wiley, 1986).

BURGESS, A, *Fatherhood Reclaimed: The Making of the Modern Father* (London, Vermilion, 1997).

CLARE, A, *On Men: Masculinity in Crisis* (Chatto and Windus, 2000).

COHEN, L, 'Marriage: the Long term Contract' in A Dnes and R Rowthorn, *The Law and Economics of Marriage and Divorce* (Cambridge, Cambridge University Press, 2002).

CREIGHTON, SJ, *Child Abuse Trends in England and Wales, 1988–90* (London, NSPCC, 1992).

DELANEY, TJ and DELANEY CC, 'Managers as Fathers: Hope on the Home Front' in LR Meth, *Men in Therapy: the Challenge of Change* (New York, Guildford Press, 1990), cited in A Burgess, *Fatherhood Reclaimed: The Making of the Modern Father* (Vermillion, 1997).

DNES, A and ROWTHORN, R, *The Law and Economics of Marriage and Divorce* (Cambridge, Cambridge University Press, 2002).

DNES, A, 'Cohabitation and Marriage' in A Dnes and R Rowthorn, *The Law and Economics of Marriage and Divorce* (Cambridge, Cambridge University Press, 2002).

HOFFMAN, LW, 'Increased Fathering; Effects on the Mother' 1977 cited in C New and M David, *For the Children's Sake: Making Children more than Women's Business* (Harmondsworth, Penguin, 1985).

KIMMELL, M, *The Gendered Society* (Oxford, OUP, 2002).

KNELL, J and SAVAGE, C, *Desperately Seeking Flexibility* (London, Resource Connection, 2001).

KREMER, S, *Active Fathering for the Future* (Working paper No 7, Demos, 1995).

Institute for Public Policy Research, *Father Figure: Fathers' Groups in Family Policy* (London, Institute for Public Policy Research, 2000).

LAMB, M, PLECK, J and LEVINE, J, 'Effects of Increased Paternal Involvement on Fathers and Mothers' in C Lewis and M O'Brien (eds), *Re-assessing Fatherhood: New Observations on Fathers and the Modern Family* (London, Sage, 1987).

LEWIS, C, cited in M Lamb and A Sagi (eds), *Fatherhood and Family Policy* (New Jersey, Lawrence Erlbaum, 1983).

LEWIS, C (1982) cited in 'father facts' www.fathersdirect.com.

—— *Becoming a Father* (Milton Keynes, Open University Press, 1986).

MELLOR, J, Chair of Equal Opportunities Commission *The Times*, 13 March 2000.

NEW, C and DAVID, M, *For the Children's Sake: Making Children more than Women's Business* (Harmondsworth, Penguin, 1985).

O'BRIEN, M and SHEMILT, I, *Dads on Dads: Needs and Expectations at Home and at Work* (London, EOC, 2002).

OPIE, W, *Barriers to Father's Involvement in Child Care Within the Two Parent Family and Policy Suggestions to Remove Them* (Unpublished Masters thesis, University of Bristol, 2002).

PARKE, R, *Fathering* (London, Collins, 1981) cited in 'father facts' www.fathersdirect.com.

PARKMAN, A, 'Mutual Consent Divorce' in A Dnes, and R Rowthorn, *The Law and Economics of Marriage and Divorce* (Cambridge, Cambridge University Press, 2002).

POLTERNICK, N, 'Why Men Don't Rear Children: A Power Analysis' (1974) cited in C Lewis and M O'Brien, *Re-assessing Fatherhood: New Observations of Fathers and the Modern Family* (London, Sage, 1987), p 112.

RASMUSDEN, E, 'An Economic Approach to Adultery Law' in A Dnes and R Rowthorn, *The Law and Economics of Marriage and Divorce* (Cambridge, Cambridge University Press, 2002).

REEVES, R, *Dad's Army: The Case for Father-Friendly Workplaces* (The Work Foundation, 2002).

RICH, A, *Of Woman Born: Motherhood as Experience and Institution* (London, Virago, 1977).

ROWE, J, CAIN, H, HUNDLEBY, M and KEANE, A, 'Long Term Foster Care' (London, Batsford, 1984), cited in C Lewis and M O'Brien, *Re-assessing Fatherhood: New Observations of Fathers and the Modern Family* (Sage, 1987).

ROWTHORN, A, 'Marriage as a Signal' in A Dnes and R Rowthorn, *The Law and Economics of Marriage and Divorce* (Cambridge, Cambridge University Press, 2002).

RUSSELL, G, *The Changing Role of Fathers* (Milton Keynes, Open University Press, 1983).

RUSSELL, G, 'Problems in Role-Reversed Families' in C Lewis and M O'Brien, *Re-assessing Fatherhood: New Observations of Fathers and the Modern Family* (London, Sage, 1987).

SCOTT, E, 'Marital Commitment and the Legal Regulation of Divorce' in A Dnes and R Rowthorn, *The Law and Economics of Marriage and Divorce* (Cambridge, Cambridge University Press, 2002).

SEEL, R. *The Uncertain Father: Exploring Modern Fatherhood* (Bath, Gateway Books, 1987).

SMITH, I, 'European Divorce Laws, Divorce Rates and their Consequences' in A Dnes and R Rowthorn, *The Law and Economics of Marriage and Divorce* (Cambridge, Cambridge University Press, 2002).

SPAT, K, 'Louisiana Covenant Law: Recapturing the Meaning of Marriage for the Sake of the Children' in A Dnes and R Rowthorn, *The Law and Economics of Marriage and Divorce* (Cambridge, Cambridge University Press, 2002).

SUTHERLAND, M, *Sex Bias in Education* (Oxford, Basil Blackwell, 1981).

The Work Foundation, *Cool Contracts: Modernising Employment Contracts*, Industrial Society Policy Brief (London, The Work Foundation, 2001).

WRIGHT, C, and LEROUX, P, 'Children as Victims of Violent Crime' in Juristat Bulletin 11, p 12, cited in K Fillion, *Lip Service* (Harper Collins, 1997).

ZELDER, M. 'For Better or for Worse? Is Bargaining in Marriage and Divorce Efficient?' in A Dnes and R Rowthorn, *The Law and Economics of Marriage and Divorce* (Cambridge, Cambridge University Press, 2002).

11

Fathers After Divorce

BOB SIMPSON, JULIE A JESSOP and PETER McCARTHY

It is not so strange that I love you with my whole heart, for being a father is not a tie which can be ignored. Nature in her wisdom has attached the parent to the child and bound them together with a Herculean knot . . . (Sir Thomas More 1517—quoted in Tomalin, 1981)

Basically, the only thing I can do, is be there for whenever he wants me. For him to take from the relationship what he needs at any given time . . . you're left to feel rather cold, that you're not living with the person, you're not providing on a daily basis, and therefore the expectations from you are not that you can resolve or sort out any of the problems or difficulties, or you don't make any of the decisions, there is no decision that you will be asked to make, that would directly affect or involve your children— you're not required to . . . I'm afraid I haven't got the responsibility have I? I mean you know, if he gets into trouble, or he needs an appointment for X, I don't have to worry about that. She and her partner worry about it, so the obligation has gone (non-resident father in the study by Simpson *et al*, 1995).

1. INTRODUCTION

OVER THE LAST 40 years the organisation of families and households in Western societies has undergone a series of fundamental and far-reaching transformations. Perhaps the most spectacular of these is the way that the 'Herculean knot' referred to by More has for many men and their children been loosened and undone. Fundamental shifts in gender relations and the changing economic order of western societies has re-configured the nuclear family and associated patterns of domestic organisation which hitherto revolved around a male bread-winner and household head. Divorce and separation, in particular, have resulted in a profound dislocation of fathers in relation to their children. The rise in the number of 'lone' and 'single' mother households over the last two decades is a clear indicator that after relationship breakdown few fathers end up being the parent with whom children live (Berthoud *et al*, 1999). Once the social, emotional and economic foundations of the nuclear family begin to shake, fathers typically find themselves parenting at a distance, or not at all. As a result, far from being bound to the nuclear family by a 'Herculean knot' many fathers have found themselves hanging on by a thread; in danger of becoming ever more marginal in the lives of their children. Under such circumstances, it would appear that the thread all too easily snaps.

Breakdown in contact need not be irreparable but, over time, the net effect is for fathers to move out of, rather than into, the lives of their children after divorce. Such tendencies have given rise to the charge that fathers are callous, fickle, 'dead-beat dads' who are far too quick to assume emotional and economic 'absence' from their children's lives. Throughout the 1980s, social and political concerns grew around the position of fathers in families after divorce with attempts being made to reinforce their economic and social relationships with their children through legislation, notably the Child Support Act 1991 and the Children Act 1989. In the early 1990s, it was estimated that 35 per cent of non-resident parents did not maintain contact with their children after divorce (Bradshaw and Millar, 1991) and that some three-quarters of a million children in England and Wales no longer had contact with their father (Wicks, 1991). More recently, research has indicated that children and non-resident fathers may be seeing more of one another (Dunn, this volume; Maclean and Eekelaar, 1997). However, the contact conundrum persists: how best to bring about the discontinuity of adult relationships without causing damage to the quality of parent-child relationships? The 'clean break' can end up being more clean than anyone wished for and likewise regular contact with frequent communication between parents may do nothing to dislodge the conjugal dynamics that were the root of marital dissatisfaction in the first place (Smart and Neale, 1999). How families negotiate the painful disentanglement is clearly not just about the simple re-configuration of roles but about the much more demanding process of re-negotiating fundamental relationships. The majority of parents achieve this with greater or lesser degrees of success and without recourse to law or specialist intervention.

In this chapter we focus specifically on the experience of fathers within this process. This is not because fathers and their actions, wishes, grievances and aspirations are any more or less important than anyone else's after divorce. On the contrary, the experience of fathers is but one element to be considered in the complex and deeply painful tangle of rights, attachments and obligations that lie beneath the success or failure of contact arrangements. Here we draw attention to the broader frameworks within which fathers' experience currently unfolds and provide an overview of the constraints and possibilities that attach to being a non-resident father. The chapter is based on two pieces of research into post-divorce fathers carried out by the authors (Simpson *et al*, 1995; Jessop, 2001) as well as drawing on other recent studies of this important topic (Bradshaw *et al*, 1999; Stark *et al*, 2001).

Our general conclusion is that despite a growing acceptance and assimilation of familial arrangements that extend in novel ways beyond single nuclear family households (Simpson, 1998), there is still an extremely powerful social, legal and economic momentum that pre-disposes mothers and fathers to replicate the emotional and economic division of labour that existed in the marriage. In marriage, mothers are generally presumed to have principal responsibility for home and childcare whereas men are viewed primarily in terms of their role as providers and protectors. Such arrangements make for a markedly gendered experience of parenting within marriage (Backett, 1987; de Singly, 1993), as well as when a marriage comes to an end. For men who experience divorce, the implications of this simple observation are profound. Leaving marriage on the tramlines laid down in domestic arrangements that were in place long before separation was even contemplated, many experience a series of 'double whammies' (Chiriboga *et al*, 1979). Having failed to read the signs that suggest a partner's dissatisfaction with arrangements in marriage (Jessop, 2001), a man might not only face a shock transformation in his life circumstances but also have to deal with the expectation of ex-wife, children and indeed of himself that he will suddenly take on new and unfamiliar parenting roles and responsibilities. Furthermore, separation is likely to bring the loss of the person to whom he is closest and the person, by virtue of this closeness, who is most likely to help him deal with such loss and personal crisis. Finally, in cases where an ex-wife withdraws her support, either overtly or tacitly, for a man in his relationship with his children (eg in relation to contact and the validation of his relationship with the children) a man's efforts to maintain continuity will be rendered considerably more difficult.

Despite the installation of a government committed to supporting families and children regardless of their domestic arrangements, the institutional tramlines that carry divorcing couples towards traditional parenting outcomes are still firmly in place. Child support legislation continues to cast fathers as absent providers and it is still broadly the case that men who choose to give up work to look after their children are likely to be seen as aberrant; as Collier points out, 'legislation continues to construct fatherhood in terms of economics and not quality of interaction' (Collier, 1995: 259). The debate around men's abilities to do anything other than earn a wage was rekindled once again as a result of the recent pronouncement by Lord Justice Thorpe, by which the Court of Appeal rejected a man's residence application which seemed to 'ignore the realities involving the different roles and functions of men and women' (*Guardian*, 20 April 2002). However, despite the considerable pressure on parents to conform to these realities by replicating the classic allocation of roles and responsibilities in relation to children after divorce (and, perhaps even in circumstances where alternative arrangements prevailed in the marriage) the research which we have carried out has drawn attention to the rather less spectacular circumstances of the majority of couples who simply get on with it, devising for themselves their own strategies to ensure 'good relations' all round. We suggest that despite the many problems that come with parenting at a distance, increasing numbers of men do create, negotiate and maintain new kinds of relationship with their children and their former partners. In other words, some families are able to escape their 'feudal gender fates' (Beck and Beck-Gernsheim, 1995) after divorce and overturn an opposition which defines men through a rhetoric of rights, autonomy and entitlement and women through an ethic of care and responsibility for others (cf Gilligan, 1982 and Okin, 1989 for critique). In practice, these two dimensions of kinship become imbricated in novel ways and open up possibilities for how men might go about the business of 'doing' fatherhood rather than simply 'being' a father. First however, we consider the circumstances in which the attempts to manage the transformation of role and circumstance which divorce brings results in the breakdown of contact.

2. LOSING CONTACT

Conventional wisdom would have us believe that fathers who do not have contact with their children have simply dropped out, lost interest and abandoned their responsibilities for care and support of their children. However, in the research conducted by Simpson *et al* (1995) some 60 per cent of the divorced fathers who never or rarely saw their children said they were in dispute with their ex-wives about the absence of contact. Most of these men wished to change what was, for them, an unsatisfactory state of affairs. Nearly all of those who had no contact with their children claimed they had made considerable efforts to maintain positive relationships, and that they had only given up contact because of serious frustrations and wrangles. Many non-resident fathers identified their ex-wives as the principal impediment to contact. Words like 'vindictive' and 'manipulative' were common as was the allegation that ex-wives had deliberately turned children against them or sought to 'poison' the relationship. Likewise, Bradshaw *et al* (1999) found that the most common reason fathers gave for having lost contact was that the mother of the child had 'obstructed access'. Indeed, some have suggested that such behaviour is so prevalent as to constitute a 'parental-alienation syndrome' (Cartwright, 1993; Gardener, 1993; Vassiliou, 1998) in which there is a systematic denigration and undermining of the non-resident parent in order to ensure that contact does not take place. Others, however, have suggested that this is a particularly unhelpful concept, preferring to describe the circumstances in terms of 'implacable hostility' (Sturge and Glaser, 2000; Dunn, this volume). Either way, the inference is clear: a mother has considerable influence on how a father's role develops after divorce and indeed, whether the father has a role at all.

It would seem that in the studies by both Simpson *et al* (1995) and Bradshaw *et al* (1999) some of the fathers who were not in contact had reached the point where the emotional, physical and financial costs of pursuing contact had to be weighed against the benefits of abandoning the struggle. One of them put it as follows:

> I would like to see more of my children, but due to all the hassles and complications at my last attempt, I think it would be a waste of time.

Although this might be seen as opting out, the fathers were more apt to describe their actions in terms of making a sacrifice in order to alleviate suffering not just for themselves but for their children and indeed their ex-wives. They typically talked about not being keen to 'drag the kids through the courts' but had perhaps also realised that the law was a particularly blunt and largely ineffective instrument when hurled at what they perceived as the sheer dogged incalcitrance of their partners.

Needless to say, women's perceptions of the problems in such cases are rather different (see Day Sclater and Kaganas, this volume). Where contact arrangements have broken down, ex-wives describe fathers as irresponsible, hypocritical and selfish. Their accounts of the past tend to dwell on ex-husbands arriving late for contact visits, being erratic in maintaining contact, and being insensitive or oblivious to the impact of their behaviour on their children. As Bradshaw *et al* (1999) suggest, fathers who act in this way often fail to see why their behaviour should lead to contact with their children being denied. Similarly, Stark *et al* (2001) found that even in cases where contact is continuing, almost one in four (23 per cent) resident parents were dissatisfied with childcare arrangements and that much of this dissatisfaction related to the feeling that non-resident parents were not taking enough responsibility. In this study, dissatisfied resident parents appeared as likely to want their children to have more contact with the other parent as they were to want them to have less. The following remarks made by resident mothers illustrate their frustrations about their ex-husband's reluctance to accept responsibility:

> I am dissatisfied with the fact that he will not have both children together—my son goes one Saturday and my daughter the next—so I never get time on my own. Also, when the children are not at school because of sickness or teacher training days he won't look after them, even though he doesn't work and I do.

> He had the choice (as to whether) to see his son, and stopped for months. This is unsettling for my son and confuses him now.

> He begrudges coming here to look after the children. I think he feels he is doing me a favour. He invariably threatens to stop doing it. He values his free time, and says he has 'not been put on this earth to be a babysitter'.

Comments from mothers also identify children themselves as being resistant to contact in circumstances where, for example, they are frequently let down by their father; they are bored when with him; they are troubled by his distress at the breakdown of the marriage; they resent being interrogated by him about what their mother is up to, or they feel uncomfortable in the presence of stepmothers, step-children or new girlfriends. Where parental relationships are not good, mothers are unlikely to show continuing support for children's contact with a father who is perceived to be causing them upset. However, as many solicitors and mediators will no doubt attest, one man's protests that he is being excluded on the grounds of expedience, revenge or punishment is another woman's claim to have taken decisive action to protect children from harmful situations. In cases of disputed contact there is a thus a fine line between children suffering because their contact with the non-resident parent is disrupted and attenuated (Hetherington, 1979; Wallerstein and Kelly, 1980) and them suffering when contact with both parents places them in the middle of severe conflict (Maccoby and Mnookin, 1992). Finally, a mother's withdrawal of support for contact may not just be about the quality of father-child interaction. As Smart (1999) suggests, resident mothers also have to make transitions, and putting energy into helping an ex-husband deal with his might hinder the exercise of making her own.

Separating continuing parental relations from discontinuing spousal relations is undoubtedly a complex and challenging business. The accounts of non-resident fathers make it clear that the relationship between fathers and mothers is a crucial factor in determining both the quantity and the quality of fathers' contact with their children after separation. However, relational dynamics are not the only determinants of post-divorce contact. Other variables have been identified as crucial to contact with the non-resident parent.

Fathers' Employment Status

Unemployed fathers, who might be thought to have more time available for child-care, tend to have less contact with their children than their counterparts who are in work. Bradshaw *et al* (1999) found that employed fathers were twice as likely as unemployed ones to have regular contact with their children. Three-quarters of the unemployed fathers involved in the study by Simpson *et al* (1995) rarely or never had contact with their children, while the fathers in non-manual jobs tended to have more regular contact with their children than the manual workers.

Employment status is clearly linked to income and it is interesting to note that fathers on higher incomes tend to report more frequent contact. This observation is in part explained by the fact that keeping up contact is in itself an expensive business often involving travel costs, gifts and treats. Looking at the bigger picture, however, it may well be that the ability for a father to emulate successfully the role of breadwinner and provider through the payment of regular and adequate child support does ensure that, however instrumental, the cash-contact nexus is maintained (Simpson, 1998).

Fathers' Housing Circumstances

There is an active equal-parenting lobby in the UK which argues for shared residence, with children spending approximately equal time in each parental home (Baker and Townsend, 1996; Ricci, 1980). Such an arrangement, however, depends on both parents having a home of their own and more specifically being able to offer a child space within which the routines of eating, sleeping, playing and simply being around can be established on a stable and ongoing basis. Being able to afford what amounts to a doubling up of home and contents after divorce is something which is beyond the reach of many parents, and particularly if the security offered to children by continued residence in the matrimonial home is to be preserved. The rupture in personal living circumstances is likely to be particularly acute in the period immediately following separation. When fathers initially leave the marital home, they tend to move into temporary housing, either in the private-rented sector, or in the homes of relatives or friends (McCarthy, 1996; McCarthy and Simpson, 1991). If they return to the home of their parents, there may be positive implications for the continuation of parenting, in that contact may take place in the grandparental home. However, given a tendency for parents to move to smaller housing when grown-up children leave home, accommodation may be less than adequate for staying contact to take place.

When the move is into the home of friends, contact with children is particularly problematic. Friendships are apt to be put to the test when children come to visit. Similar problems arise following moves into the private-rented sector, which is a marginal provider of residential accommodation in Britain, comprising just 10 per cent of the total housing supply. Although such moves are usually intended to be temporary, the arrangements can last a long time. In some cases, these 'temporary' arrangements last long enough for the father's contact with his children to break down because there is nowhere for him to take them. For instance, one father who had moved into private-rented accommodation told McCarthy and Simpson (1991):

> Most of the places I have lived in (six in all) were unsuitable for children to visit, because it was only one room. (My wife) has stopped access now. Most of the places I have moved to have had just one room, and a shared kitchen, toilet and bathroom. All very unsuitable but I couldn't afford anything else.

The owners of privately-rented property often impose restrictions on tenants which create difficulties for parents who desire to have contact with their children. One father said:

> All I've got for the money I pay is one room. It has a bed in it, a wardrobe, a chest of drawers, a television, and a video. The rest is downstairs and shared with others. You never know what kind of people they are going to bring back, so you are never at ease in the shared part . . . can't have friends to stay, I can't have the kids to stop. She doesn't like it anyway, the landlady . . . Even if you are desperate, she doesn't like anybody stopping.

The disruptive effects of having accommodation which is unsuitable for contact to take place are captured by one of Jessop's informants (2001), who spoke of having:

> . . . two kinda separate lives, I had my life without the kids and then I had my weekends with the kids . . . when I had the kids, I'd go up to my mum's, so I like had my life over there too. And it was really strange, artificial kind of a situation and at the end of the weekend I'd go back to my life.

Moreover, as one of the fathers who participated in the study by Simpson *et al* (1995) remarked:

> Having your own house makes the difference between being a father and being like a bachelor uncle to your kids.

Significantly, although this study found no direct link between income and contact in itself, they did find a distinctive connection between income and staying contact. Fathers on higher incomes, who were much more likely to be able to afford housing with extra rooms, were also much more likely to have children staying with them on a regular basis and thereby at least aspire to something like equal parenting.

Children's Gender

Although the dynamics are inevitably complex, it would appear that children's gender does play a role in determining the likelihood of ongoing contact taking place. Put in broad terms, fathers can make alliances with sons in ways that they may not be able to do with daughters. Simpson *et al* (1995) found that fathers were more likely to keep up contact with sons than with daughters: 56 per cent of fathers who had only female children had little or no contact with their children, as against 19 per cent of those who had only male children and 39 per cent of those who had male and female children. Similarly, Jessop (2001), reveals how some of her informants were apprehensive about their contact with daughters, particularly as they approached adolescence. Bradshaw *et al* (1999) found that fathers were most likely to maintain contact if they had both male and female children.

Simpson *et al* (1995) suggest that attempts by fathers to re-position themselves as friends and equals with their children is an important factor in understanding the gender differential in contact. As Burgess points out, during the first part of the twentieth century the 'image of the father as his children's pal and confidante was relentlessly promoted' (Burgess, 1997). It seems, however, that fathers feel more comfortable in this role when it is sons, rather than daughters, who are in this role. Having once been boys themselves, men may well be able to relate to their sons in ways that they would find difficult with their daughters (Sharpe, 1994). It seems that fathers feel a son can be a 'mate', whereas the relationship with a daughter is somehow more inscrutable. For instance, one father in the study by Simpson *et al* (1995) commented:

> (I am) very, very close (to my son) . . . I have tried to treat him appropriate(ly) to his age, rather than as a baby or anything. So, now that he is sixteen, he is more like a mate than a son. We have a lot of laughs, but there is an unbridgeable gap between me and (daughter), partly as I say because she is a different sex, and partly because we missed out on that bit, because of the state of the marriage . . . Unfortunately (contact visits) tend to involve (son) more than (daughter), I am afraid. But I think it is the bond. That

makes her sound like a second-class citizen, but I don't mean that. It is just that there is a rapport between (son) and I, which there isn't between (daughter) and I . . . Now and again it happens, and it is very rewarding when it does, but it is almost an exception, whereas with (son) it is almost normal.

Finally, some of the men in this study intimated concern about their sons growing up in female-dominated households, leading them to speculate that men's greater interest and efforts where sons were concerned may have been rooted in anxieties about the development of an appropriate sense of masculinity. Without suitable 'role models' boys might not be appropriately loosed from their mother's apron strings and experience damage to their growth into 'proper' men.

Fathers and New Partners

The arrival of new partners, who may themselves also have children, significantly adds to the challenge of managing relationships after divorce. It would seem that in circumstances where a father forms a new relationship/family before having worked through the consequences of the demise of the previous one, contact can be rendered problematic. Bradshaw *et al* (1999) found that fathers who lived alone were more than twice as likely as those who lived with a new partner, and almost three times more likely than those who lived in a household containing other children, to have regular contact with their children after separation. The presence of a new partner provides someone with whom childcare can be shared and Jessop cites the instance of one man seeking out a new partner precisely in order to compensate for what he felt he himself could not provide (Jessop, 2001). However, despite the best of intentions, new partners are apt to create tensions over contact arrangements, as the following remarks addressed by resident mothers in the study by Stark *et al* (2001) attest:

(My ex-husband) would like (the children) to spend weekends with him and his new partner but the children have no wish to do this because of her presence. Although this means I am caring for the children alone 95 per cent of the time this arrangement suits me, because I have no wish for them to be with her either.

I feel at home with the children living with me and resent them liking their dad's new partner.

In this section we have highlighted some of the key factors present in the demise of father-child contact after divorce and separation. Poor relations with a former partner, inappropriate housing circumstances, inadequate income, the presence of new partners, to say nothing of lack of insight and imagination, all play their part in propelling fathers, albeit reluctantly, into absence from their children's lives. To a large extent the opposite also holds true. The chances of contact being maintained and assimilated as part of normal day to day family life are likely to be maximised in circumstances where parents can get along reasonably well; that is, where they have a shared concern over the children matched by a civil disinterest in one another. Similarly, the availability of reasonable housing and adequate finance to spend on children directly (in looking after them and as gifts and treats) and indirectly (as child support paid to a former partner) also augur well for positive relationships after divorce. However, it would be a mistake to assume that these circumstances alone will ensure satisfactory continuity of contact: they are necessary rather than sufficient causes. The way that men themselves manage the transition to non-resident fatherhood is a crucial determinant of the outcomes. In the next section we turn to a discussion of the way that men themselves experience their role as fathers after divorce.

3. ON CEASING TO BE AN 'IN-HOUSE' FATHER

However committed men may be to their children, the studies by Simpson *et al* (1995) and Jessop (2001) both reveal the considerable struggle that is involved in creating and maintaining this relationship after divorce. Being a father after divorce is not, as yet, a socially prescribed role (Lund, 1987; Daly, 1995; Ferri and Smith, 1998). Whereas fatherhood within marriage is based on complementarity and is generally mediated through wives/mothers, on divorce men are placed in a position, not only of having to negotiate fatherhood directly with their children but also being under conditions where the time of contact is usually limited and outside their control. This adjustment is often undertaken as the full realisation of what it is to lose 'home' and 'family' begins to dawn (cf Kruk, 1989). For many men the growing sense of loss is deeply painful and disorientating.

Loss of Control

In Western society, the role of the father is integrally linked with ideas of power, authority and the maintenance of order within the family. Whether fathers do in practice exercise control over the conjugal family in quite this way is another matter. Nevertheless, becoming a non-resident father with weekly or fortnightly contact means that the arena in which this sense of power was exercised becomes less accessible; by lack of physical proximity, if nothing else. The net result is that power is in effect dislocated and a father's input in terms of control over the child is greatly diminished. This is particularly felt in areas of decision-making which are explicit and public, for example, with regard to education, schooling and health care. Fathers in the study by Simpson *et al* (1995) regularly complained that, intentionally or by neglect, they were informed about important events regarding the children only after the event, if at all. As one man commented:

: . . . she never tells me when the parents' evenings are, she never tells me how they are doing at school. The little one, when he had his toilet problem, she never told me he was ill, and she sent him round here with measles one day.

Jessop (2001) points out that such attitudes are often compounded by schools and surgeries that insist on dealing with the mother as the primary parent and thus distancing men from their role in decision-making. She cites the predicament of one of her informants:

I've got a conflict at the moment with the head mistress of (daughter's) school because I had an occasion where—I had to pick (daughter) up 'cos I take the children to the dentist, that's something I've always done . . . An' at first they were a bit hesitant and then she said, 'oh it'll be alright, just let me make a phone call' . . . their procedure was to phone my wife because we were divorced. And, er, I—didn't ask me about it, they just did it. And then (ex-wife) gave the OK and (daughter) could leave . . . and then when I got home (ex-wife) tells me, oh I don't want the school phoning me up, how embarrassing, blah, blah, blah. An' I said well hang on a minute, how should, how should I feel about that.

However, loss of control is not just experienced in relation to the practicalities of schooling and healthcare but also in relation to the more abstract enterprise of passing on identity from parents to children. Issues such as religion, manners, morals and values, which might have been of little consequence in the marriage, often become highly charged and contested afterwards. Disputes over events such as baptism, confirmation or circumcision point to the broader questions of which parent gets to stamp the child with their own identity. Given that the process of moving out of marriage often involves a powerful assertion of separate identities by a husband and wife, such conflicts can become emotive in ways that they never would whilst safely under the umbrella of marriage. Men usually feel distinctly disadvantaged when it comes to asserting their influence. Quite simply, the mother spends, or is believed to spend, time with the child which is quantitatively greater and qualitatively better. The non-resident father at best sees himself as a passive spectator in the child's growth and development or at worst sees the child being consciously influenced away from him.

Such issues become highly explicit in relation to discipline. Parental inability to harmonise rules, boundaries and sanctions across the conjugal divide can be the cause of conflict and misunderstanding which passes round and round the over-charged circuitry of post-divorce family life. A mother may be brought into conflict with her children because she is 'trying to be both mother and father at once'. A step-father may compound the issue because whilst he has the power to discipline he may not, in the eyes of the child, have the authority to do so. The father may experience difficulties because whilst he has the authority, his absence denies him the occasion to implement it. He may wish to bring power and authority together yet the last thing he wishes to do with limited access time is be a stout disciplinarian. Consequently, children are apt to experience a sense of empowerment vis à vis their fathers. This could lead to development of a mature and respectful relationship between individuals who hold one another in high esteem but it could also lead to one in which the child exploits the father's distance from day-to-day routines and disciplines. One father who contributed to the study by Simpson *et al* (1995) captures this dilemma:

> He seems to be, from what I can see, a little bit out of control. His eating habits are terrible. That's the main battle with him for me, getting him to eat proper food . . . it's all junk food. I can't get him to eat anything. It's impossible. I say it's impossible because—I can't handle it 'cos I'm not there with him all the time. He's not influenced by me as to what eating habits he should have. That's really his mum and whoever he's living with—they're the main controllers aren't they. I can't very well, when I just have him for one day, change his whole weekly pattern, and say this is what you should eat . . . you just have to accept it. Sometimes you might say something to him and you just hope for the best that he might pick it up and he might be alright.

This particular father felt that there was only a very small amount of pressure that could be applied to his son before he had to 'back off'.

Discrepancies in the levels of discipline and authority might well be exploited by both fathers and children at the cost of the mother. Avoidance of taking a strong line on discipline may be seen by the father as an effective strategy to bolster a weak position. Thus, in effect, killing two birds with one stone, by undermining a mother's authority on the one hand and indulging the child on the other.

The child might also exploit the discrepancy for his or her own ends, being a model child when with the father during limited and non-ordinary contact times and playing up when with the mother during the week. Unfortunately, some fathers' assessment of this situation often took the form of 'I can't understand what the problem is because he/she is perfectly alright when with me!' Problems of discipline arising outside of contact time were therefore apt to be re-framed as a deficiency of the ex-partner. As one of Jessop's (2001) informants commented:

> Em, when the kids weren't living with me I did what all non-resident parents do, and this is the thing that people don't understand, don't make allowances for, when you see them each weekend, er, only once a fortnight, unconsciously or consciously you make allowances, you do things, you're the nice parent, em, and you have to be because at the end of the day you don't want to be the bad parent, so . . . you give in and the other parent who they're residing with gets the worst of it because they go back and they think, oh you're an absolute so and so, em, my mum or dad, whatever they've visited, is great, y'know.

Loss of Intimacy

Closely related to the loss of control is the loss of intimacy. Many fathers in the study by Simpson *et al* (1995) alluded to the sense of emotional distance that existed between them and their children, they described going through the motions of fatherhood and their children becoming strangers to them. Try as they might their relationships developed an artificiality which was hard to counter. In the early stages this was clearly linked to the practical circumstances in which contact took place; perhaps a down-market bed-sit, the house of a friend or relative, or even in a public place. However, the sense of distance and artificiality was apt to remain and authentic feelings of closeness and intimacy remained elusive.[1]

The true extent of this distancing was brought home in the case of one man whose ex-wife had died very suddenly. Her death necessitated the return of his children to live with him after six years of being a non-resident father. Despite having always had regular and positive contact with his children, he spoke of how he and his children had to get to know each other all over again. Significantly, he likened the process to one of adoption rather than a resumption of parental responsibilities.

Loss of Routine

For many fathers the loss of intimacy is acutely linked to the loss of daily routines of child care and home-making centred on the children. With the move from the matrimonial home fathers often experience a separation from the daily routines of family life which are basic to ongoing relationships within the family. As one man commented in the study by Simpson *et al* (1995):

> . . . I was always involved with changing nappies, bathing, reading stories with both of them. I feel I have always done my fair share of that, so you sort of build, it is almost an internal bond. I feel I did my fair share of the domestic side of it.

The loss of these routines was a powerful theme to emerge amongst the men in this particular study, and even amongst fathers who appeared to have had relatively little involvement in domestic activities during their marriage. Bath-times, meal-times, nappy-changing, bed-times, taking children to school, bringing them home, helping with homework—and a host of other minor, daily routines were recalled with great sense of loss and sadness. This was particularly so where young children were involved and where fathers had actively taken responsibilities for child-care. For example, several fathers in this study described looking after children in the evenings and at weekends whilst their partners were out at work. Routines such as these, were seen as an important element in the 'bonding' between a father and his children.

> . . . I think there would be a stronger bond if I was there all the time. It would be nice to take N. to Cubs and B. to Brownies and that sort of thing. Pick 'em up from school. It's the little things like that you miss really.

[1] Stewart (1999) in a study of parenting styles of both non-resident fathers and mothers argues that artificiality of the situation rather than gender is the salient factor in non-resident parent-child interaction patterns (see also Jessop, 2001).

Being outside of the rhythms of child care was felt most poignantly by those who had not remarried. For fathers in this position the periods in between access were often crammed with work, sport and a full social calendar in order to avoid confronting the practical implications of their isolation from their children.

> . . . now I have 13 days between the times I see them. I have to divert my attention to other things to fill the gap . . . other relationships, sport and other minor ways. Whereas when I was there full-time the children imposed limits on what you could and could not do, which wasn't burdensome, it was something you accept as a parent. When they are removed from your midst you can't just go out and walk the streets, you certainly have to consciously find things to do.

The problems that many fathers identified in this respect were essentially one of time, and how, when removed from the security of domestic routines, a relationship with a child could or should be conducted. Family relationships are fashioned out of the minutiae of daily commerce and interaction and with this comes mutual familiarity and predictability. It is this fine grain interaction which is lost for many fathers after divorce. Their interaction loses continuity and takes on a highly irregular and contrived aspect. Typical in this respect was the father in the study by Simpson *et al* (1995) who described his fortnightly access as 'hectic' and how each weekend he frantically struggled to pack in as much activity and stimulation as he possibly could for his two sons. At the same time, however, he felt misgivings about this because he also felt the need to spend quiet, ordinary and uneventful time with his children. This dilemma was expressed by many fathers who felt that they were missing out on a more natural level of communication with their children. Such communications could not be planned or predetermined but were spontaneous and often seen as linked to the development of the child—such as first day at a new school or cutting second teeth etc. One man spoke of his children's experiences coming to him 'second hand', that is, through other people, usually long after the event and rarely from the children themselves for whom the moment of excitement had quickly passed. The general feeling appeared to be that access arrangements operated rather like time-lapse photography, replacing child growth and development with a series of crude and fragmented images.

> . . . it's like not seeing his school report, not seeing the school photograph, or the recent photograph of your child, not having one. Quite often there are sudden jumps at this time of life, last time I saw him I was quite shocked, he was really growing up and you miss that continuity . . . it's like shots taken every so often, little pieces you have.

It is important also to recognise that communications flow in the opposite direction. Daily intimate contact with children also creates the possibility for fathers to pass on things to their children. Again these cannot be scheduled or pre-meditated but flow from interaction. Timing is of the essence. As one father said:

It's not so much anything that's specific but if you've got the opportunity to pass on any pearls of wisdom at the appropriate time, the appropriate time might not come as easily when you're racing up and down the motorway.

Loss of Role

With the move out of marriage and out of the household comes a loss of role. Roles can easily be recreated elsewhere but in relation to the children of an earlier marriage there is a considerable ambiguity of role. This sense of ambiguity may well be a critical factor in fathers making the decision not to pursue their relationship with their children. The prospect of becoming a relative who is more like an uncle, or, indeed anything that is less than a father in the traditional sense—the 'sturdy oaks and strong pillars' of family life (Benson, 1968)—is for many men unacceptably second best. On becoming a non-resident father the traditional accoutrements of fatherhood are quickly stripped away. The occasions upon which a father might be called upon to fulfil the role of guide and preceptor may well prove few and far between. Indeed, the dispensability implied by this failure of mothers and children to evoke the father figure in times of need is cause for considerable loss of self esteem. It is no doubt a factor in explaining the deterioration in physical and mental health, inability to establish new relationships and increased reliance on drugs and alcohol and the sense of personal failure reported by fathers who participated in the study by Simpson *et al* (1995).

4. DISCUSSION—FATHERHOOD: A SENSE OF GROWTH

It is as mistaken to assume that divorce means paternal 'absence' as it is to assume that marriage always means paternal 'presence'. Whereas in conventional family settings fathers may be physically close to their children their role is apt to leave them emotionally distant from them (cf Lewis and O'Brien, 1987). Conversely, and somewhat paradoxically, divorce usually results in fathers being physically separated but does create the possibility that kinds of emotional closeness can develop which might not have been possible in marriage. The new role is far less clear cut than that of the 'in-house father' and one that many of the fathers in the study by Simpson *et al* (1995) characterised as simply 'being there' should the children ever need them. This ranged from 'being there' to help with homework over the phone (cf Bell, 2001) to the rather more drastic 'being there' to provide an alternative home should a crisis befall the child's relationship with his or her mother or the mother herself become unable to look after the child. However, for almost all the fathers who contributed to the study by Simpson *et al* (1995) the message was the same; it was important that their children knew that they had a second parent who loved them dearly and upon whom they could make claims in times of difficulty and who would become an active, rather than a passive, parent should this ever be required. This knowledge provided an important counter to the feelings of marginality felt by non-resident fathers and the sense of guilt and impotence which this was likely to engender. It also opened up the possibility for men to experience a more direct and immediate relationship. Fathers often spoke of developing a heightened sense of focus and attention on their children. One man in the study spoke of 'living' for his children and the fortnightly contact he had with them. Respondents in the study by Jessop (2001) also spoke of their newly found dedication:

> Er, I think that possibly I haven't actually (ha ha) managed (having a social life). Er, to some extent I think that, y'know, parenting is a full-time job so it's not possible to— let's say I have the kids every other weekend from Friday to Sunday, it's not, it it doesn't start at 5 o'clock Friday evening and stop at 6 o'clock Sunday evening. Er, from the practical point of view, y'know, you have to get prepared, you have to think of some—what you're gonna do with the children, y'know . . . Em, so yes I mean I do, I do visit my friends and do keep in touch, but, er, in terms of finding a second partner I think that's much more difficult, much more difficult. Especially with someone who would need to accept the fact that, y'know, I've got two kids who are, maybe not living here physically, but they are definitely a part of this, er, house, very much so.

In such cases, it would appear that men are making a choice between being a 'good father' and having a new relationship. This observation perhaps goes some way to explaining why fathers in the study by Simpson *et al* (1995) who reported good communication with their ex-wives and good relationships with their children also reported high levels of loneliness.

For many fathers it would therefore seem that the typical condition of post-divorce fatherhood is one of resignation and acceptance. There are fathers, however, for whom this state is never reached and who go on to join a dangerously embittered and misogynist minority. For others, acceptance comes after a long period of attrition in which they have battled for illusory 'fathers' rights'. However, for many of the men interviewed by Simpson *et al* (1995) and Jessop (2001), the point of acceptance seems to have been reached at a relatively early stage. Men had, in many respects, let go of the complex of ideas, values and assumptions which go to make up the role of 'father' rather than trying to hang on to this complex in its entirety. In other words, divorce splinters fatherhood into many fragments and it is the ability to make something of these fragments, rather than to carry on regardless, which offers the best prospects for satisfying relationships. In effect, resolution amounted to giving up attempts to achieve 'normal' fatherhood in an abnormal situation and the acceptance of 'abnormal' fatherhood in what had become a normal situation. One of the more intriguing developments in this regard is the re-positioning of fathers into a role more akin to friendship with their children. Several men in the study by Simpson *et al* (1995) were quick to point out that they were not 'like a father' and how they had eschewed an authoritarian role; their children were often described in terms such as 'good friends', 'mates' and 'pals'. Whilst no doubt part of a more widespread flattening out of kinship hierarchies, it is nonetheless significant that this equalisation should centre on what was hitherto the most formal and distant of family relations. For some couples, this transformation of role opens the way for both parents to derive benefits from post-divorce parenting arrangements. The contact-residence conundrum need not be a zero-sum game. Although this outcome clearly requires time, energy and resources to sustain, workable arrangements are possible. As one man in the study by Simpson *et al* (1995) commented:

> I think how it's occurred now I can only say I'm really pleased with the outcome for the children. It's their character as well as ours but I don't think I could have hoped for any better. They're great, they're slightly unruly, they're polite, they haven't been squeezed dry and they're considerate lively kids. Part of that's my ex-wife's doing and part of that's mine and part of it is the kids. So generally I think it's worked out really, really well. Certainly had we been together and arguing I think we'd have had real problems. . . . I'm not advocating divorce and separation as a method of bringing up your kids but it does have its positive sides as well.

The positive sides to which this man referred, apart from the children themselves, were the mid-week break which he got from the children and the weekend break which his ex-wife got from them. Both parents therefore had 'space' in which they could pursue their own interests. As far as the children were concerned the alternating pattern of parenting meant that each parent came at the children with fresh energy. The children thus benefitted from the stimulation and focused interest of each individual parent—'they get double the experience in some ways!' Indeed, when fathers were asked if they felt that their children had benefited in any way from the separation a typical response was as follows:

> They now have two life-styles from which to gain experience. My ex-wife's approach to things is totally different to mine. I do like to try and do a wide range of things with them . . . broadening them, yes.

Ironically, the sad fact of divergent interests and growing incompatibility upon which marriages foundered becomes reformulated as the basis of a richer experience of parental diversity for children following divorce.

REFERENCES

BACKETT, K, 'The Negotiation of Fatherhood' in C Lewis and M O'Brien (eds), *Reassessing Fatherhood* (London, Sage Publications, 1987).
BAKER, A and TOWNSEND, P, 'Post Divorce Parenting—Rethinking Shared Residence' (1996) 8 *Child and Family Law Quarterly* 217.
BECK, U and BECK-GERSHEIM, E, *The Normal Chaos of Love* (Cambridge, Polity Press, 1995).
BELL, V, 'The Phone, the Father and Other Becomings: On Households (and Theories) That No Longer Hold' (2001) 5 *Cultural Values* 383.

BERTHOUD, R, MCKAY, S and ROWLINGSON, K, 'Becoming a Single Mother' in S McCrae (ed), *Changing Britain: Families and Households in 1990s* (Oxford, Oxford University Press, 1999).

BENSON, L, *Fatherhood: A Sociological Perspective* (New York, Random House, 1968).

BRADSHAW, J and MILLAR, J, *Lone-Parent Families in the UK* (London, HMSO, 1991).

BRADSHAW, J, STIMSON, C, SKINNER, C and WILLIAMS, J, *Absent Fathers?* (London, Routledge, 1999).

BURGESS, A, *Fatherhood Reclaimed: The making of the modern father* (London, Vermilion, 1997).

CARTWRIGHT, GF, 'Expanding the Parameters of Parental Alienation Syndrome' (1993) 21 *American Journal of Family Therapy* 205.

CHIRIBOGA, DA, ROBERTS, J and STEIN, J, 'Divorce, Stress and Social Supports: A Study of Helpseeking Behaviour' (1979) 2 *Journal of Divorce* 121.

COLLIER, R, *Masculinity, Law and the Family* (London, Routledge, 1995).

DALY, KJ, 'Reshaping Fatherhood: Finding the Models' in W Marsiglio (ed), *Fatherhood: Contemporary Theory, Research and Social Policy* (Thousand Oaks, CA, Sage Publications, 1995).

DE SINGLY, F, 'The Social Construction of a New Paternal Identity' in *Conference Report: Fathers of Tomorrow* (Denmark, Ministry of Social Affairs, 1993).

FERRI, E and SMITH, K, *Step-parenting in the 1990s* (London, Family Policy Studies Centre, 1998).

GARDENER, RA, *The Parental Alienation Syndrome: A Guide for Mental Health and Legal Professionals* (Creskill, NJ, Creative Therapeutics, 1993).

GILLIGAN, C, *In a Different Voice* (Cambridge, MA, Harvard University Press, 1982).

HETHERINGTON, EM, 'Divorce: A Child's Perspective' (1979) 34 *American Psychologist* 851.

JESSOP, JA, *Psychosocial Dynamics of Post-Divorce Parenting: Pleasures, Pitfalls and New Partners* (University of Cambridge, Unpublished PhD Thesis, 2001).

KRUK, E, *Impact of Divorce on Non-Custodial Fathers: Psychological and Structural Factors Contributing to Disengagement* (University of Edinburgh, Unpublished PhD Thesis, 1989).

LEWIS, C and O'BRIEN, M, 'Constraints on Fathers: Research, Theory and Clinical Practice' in C Lewis and M O'Brien (eds), *Reassessing Fatherhood* (London, Sage Publications, 1987).

LUND, M, 'The Non-Custodial Father: Common Challenges in Parenting after Divorce' in C Lewis and M O'Brien (eds), *Reassessing Fatherhood* (London, Sage Publications, 1987).

MACCOBY, E and MNOOKIN, RH, *Dividing the Child: Social and Legal Dilemmas of Custody* (Cambridge, MA, Harvard University Press, 1992).

MACLEAN, M and EEKELAAR, J, *The Parental Obligation: A Study of Parenthood Across Households* (Oxford, Hart Publishing, 1997).

MCCARTHY, P, 'Housing and Post-divorce Parenting' in H Jones and J Millar (eds), *The Politics of the Family* (Aldershot, Avebury, 1996).

MCCARTHY, P and SIMPSON, R., *Issues in Post-Divorce Housing: Family Policy or Housing Policy?* (Aldershot, Avebury, 1991).

OKIN, SM, *Justice, Gender and the Family* (New York, Basic Books, 1989).

RICCI, I, *Mom's House—Dad's House: Making Shared Custody Work* (London, Collier-Macmillan, 1980).

SHARPE, S, *Fathers and Daughters* (London, Routledge, 1994).

SIMPSON, B, 'On Gifts, Payments and Disputes: Divorce and Changing Family Structures in Contemporary Britain' (1977) 3 *Journal of the Royal Anthropological Institute* 731.

—— *Changing Families: An Ethnographic Approach to Divorce and Separation* (Oxford, Berg, 1998).

SIMPSON, B, MCCARTHY, P and WALKER, J, *Being There: Fathers After Divorce* (Newcastle upon Tyne, Relate Centre for Family Studies, 1995).

SMART, C, 'The New Parenthood: Fathers and Mothers after Divorce' in EB Silva and C Smart (eds), *The New Family?* (London, Sage Publications, 1999).

SMART, C and NEALE, B, *Family Fragments* (Oxford, Polity Press, 1999).

STARK, C, LAING, K and MCCARTHY, P, 'Giving Information to Parents' in J Walker (ed), *Information Meetings and Associated Provisions within the Family Law Act 1996: Final Report, Vol 2* (London, Lord Chancellor's Department, 2001).

STEWART, SD, 'Disneyland Dads, Disneyland Moms?: How Non-Resident Parents Spend Time with Absent Children' (1999) 20 *Journal of Family Issues* 539.

STURGE, C and GLASER, D, 'Contact and Domestic Violence: The Expert's Court Report' (2000) 30 *Family Law* 615.

TOMALIN, C, *Parents and Children* (Oxford, Oxford University Press, 1981).

VASSILIOU, D, *Parental Alienation Syndrome: The Lost Parents' Perspective* (1998) http://www.education.mcgill.ca/pain/thesis.htm.

WALLERSTEIN, J and KELLY, J, *Surviving the Break-up* (London, Grant McIntyre, 1998).

WALLERSTEIN, JS and KELLY, J, 'California's Children of Divorce' (1980) 13 *Psychology Today* 71.

WICKS, M, 'Research Results of Lone Parent Families' Letter to *The Independent*, March 1991.

Section 4:
The Hand of the State

12

Contact for Children Subject to State Intervention

JO MILES and BRIDGET LINDLEY

WHEN A CHILD is looked after in the care system as a result of social services' intervention, whether on a compulsory or voluntary basis, contact between the child and his/her parents and other members of the family is a key issue. Research carried out in the 1980s strongly suggested that it is very important for the well-being and development of children who are away from home to maintain contact with their families (Department of Health, 1991a, at p 24). The pattern of contact established at the outset can have a substantial influence on both the future contact arrangements and the plans and outcomes for the child generally: for those children who have a realistic chance of returning to live with their family, maintaining contact is the key to *early* discharge from care; for those children who are destined to remain in a long-term placement away from their birth family, frequent changes of placement and social worker may mean that contact with that family provides the only element of continuity in the child's life, (Millham et al, 1986, ch 7). And even once the child is in a permanent placement, that placement's success may depend upon ongoing, good quality contact with family members, (Macaskill, 2002; contrast findings of research discussed in Browne and Moloney, 2002).

In response to this evidence, one of the core principles of the public law provisions of the Children Act 1989 (CA) is that all children subject to protective intervention by the State[1] should be allowed contact with their families, unless this is considered to be contrary to their welfare. However, although this principle is now firmly established in law, reinforced by the jurisprudence of the recently incorporated European Convention on Human Rights (ECHR), its application in practice varies. The existence of statutory presumptions in favour of contact and contact orders provide one piece of the jigsaw, but cannot themselves determine the *quality* of contact between parents and children in care.

In the private law context, parents generally make decisions about contact arrangements between the basic triad of parents and child, and between the

---

[1] The lead agency responsible for this intervention is the Social Services department of the local authority.

child and other relatives (unless there is a defined contact order). In the public law context, most decisions about contact are in practice made by social workers, who are bound to take account of the complex network of relationships impacting on contact in this context. These include the relationships between any or all of the following: the parent(s), social workers, the child and foster carers or residential home staff, (and in many cases a non-resident parent, siblings, other relatives, and prospective adoptive parents). It is important to analyse how both courts and social workers exercise the power that they enjoy under the legal framework in order to get a real picture of the way contact is managed in these cases, and, most importantly, to determine whether the human rights of those involved are being respected.

The aims of this chapter are therefore, firstly, to examine the legal and practice framework for decision-making at the different stages of state intervention in a public law context; secondly, to explore the factors which impact on implementation of that framework in practice (so far as they can be ascertained); and, thirdly, to identify how law and practice may be improved to promote the best possible contact for children in public law cases.

1. THE LEGAL FRAMEWORK FOR CONTACT IN PUBLIC LAW CASES

Although the law promotes contact with family members for all children subject to state intervention, the extent and manner in which this occurs varies according to the nature of the intervention. We therefore explore in this section the decision-making processes about contact created by the CA across the different stages of state intervention. However, before turning to the detail of domestic law, we examine the human rights jurisprudence underpinning this area.

1.1. Jurisprudence of the European Convention on Human Rights

The ECHR has already had an impact on English child care law as one of the driving forces behind the Children Act 1989 (CA). But since the incorporation of the ECHR into domestic law by the Human Rights Act 1998 (HRA), it is necessary to re-examine domestic child protection law and practice. Under the HRA, it is 'unlawful for a public authority to act in a way which is incompatible with a Convention right'.[2] All decisions about, and actions relating to, contact, whether made by the local authority in an administrative context or by the courts in a judicial framework, must therefore not breach any of the rights established by the Convention. Various remedies—injunctive relief and damages awards, as well as public law remedies available via judicial review—

---

[2] Save where primary legislation requires otherwise: see s 6.

are now available directly to victims.[3] The main effect of these provisions in this context is that local authority planning and decision-making in relation to children who are subject to child protection enquiries and those who are looked after by the local authority must be compatible with the Convention rights of those affected. Otherwise, local authorities will find that their decisions are under closer judicial scrutiny than previously.[4]

The provisions of the ECHR most relevant to contact in public law cases are:

—Article 6, which confers procedural rights in order to guarantee a fair trial where there is a "determination" of an individual's "civil rights and obligations". This has been interpreted to include the mutual rights of family members to their family life;[5] and

—Article 8, which has been interpreted to confer both substantive and procedural guarantees implicit in the concept of the 'right to respect for family life' which it protects.[6]

Much of the European case law on contact concerns the application of Article 8. Key to this article is the scope of 'family life'. The European Court has not concretely defined that concept by reference to particular classes of familial relationship. Whether family life is enjoyed between given parties may depend as much on their social and emotional ties as it does on the existence of a blood or legal tie. But it is clear that most mothers and children,[7] and many fathers and children[8] will share a family life together for these purposes; siblings, grandparents and other blood relatives may also fall within the scope of Article 8.[9] Indeed, contact with these members of the extended family may become increasingly valuable to children in public law cases, where relations with one or both parents may be difficult, (see Pryor, this volume).

Any interference by the state in family life is likely to involve a prima facie violation of Article 8(1). Taking the child into care certainly does; imposing restrictions on when and how a child may see members of its family does too. Any such restriction, in order to be lawful, must satisfy the familiar requirements of Article

---

[3] Ss 6–8 HRA.

[4] Prior to implementation of the HRA, the only possibilities for challenging local authority decision-making (other than via applications under the Children Act regarding contact and discharge of care orders) were either to apply for judicial review, which was only successful in rare cases (see *R v East Sussex CC ex parte R* [1995] 1 WLR 680 discussed below), or to apply to the European Court for a decision that there had been a violation of the applicants' rights under the ECHR (see for example *R v UK* (1987) 10 EHRR 74). Neither were particularly accessible or available. The HRA now provides not only for direct remedies in the domestic courts where there has been a breach, but also places a duty on such decision-makers to observe the Convention rights of those affected by the decision throughout their involvement with the child.

[5] *R v UK* (1987) 10 EHRR 74.

[6] *W v UK* (1987) 10 EHRR 29; *McMichael v UK* (1995) 20 EHRR 205.

[7] *Marckx v Belgium* (1979) 2 EHRR 330.

[8] Contrast the findings on this point in the two cases reported at *Re H, Re G (Adoption: consultation of unmarried fathers)* [2001] 1 FLR 646.

[9] See *Marckx v Belgium* (1979) 2 EHRR 330, para 45; *Boyle v UK* (1994) 19 EHRR 179.

8(2), that any 'interference by a public authority with the exercise of this right' be 'in accordance with the law' and 'necessary in a democratic society . . . for the protection of health or morals, or for the protection of the rights and freedoms of others.'[10] The debate in most cases centres on this last point—is the restriction a proportionate one, or is it too intrusive? (see Bainham and Herring, this volume).

The vast majority of cases which have come before the European Court concerning children in care have related to the *implementation* of those care orders, in particular in relation to contact, which is regarded by the European Court as vitally important. Restrictions on contact are accordingly subjected to strict scrutiny. Having interfered so dramatically in family life by removing the child, the state is required (negatively) to ensure that that interference goes no further than is necessary for the protection of the child, such that it will usually be required to *allow* contact of some form and frequency. A key aspect of Article 8, which poses difficulties for English child law generally, is the requirement that the child's rights and interests be balanced against those of the parents'.[11] This exercise sits uneasily alongside English law's position that the child's best interests are the paramount (or, one might say, only) consideration. The ECHR, unlike some statements of modern English law,[12] recognises that parents (and other family members) themselves have rights to contact and family life with their children, as well as children having a right to, or welfare interest in, contact with their parents and other relatives. In many cases, contact between child and parent may benefit the parent but not the child, in which case any restriction on the parent's Article 8 right to respect for his or her family life with the child must be justified under Article 8(2). Whilst Article 8(2) supports a presumption in favour (if *not* a paramount weighting[13]) of the child's interests, the state has a persuasive burden to demonstrate that denying contact is a proportionate restriction on the relevant party's rights.

Moreover, it is clear from case law in the private law context that the state is also subject to *positive* obligations to promote contact between child and parents. Whilst in the private law case, *Hokkanen v Finland*, the state's breach of those positive obligations lay in its failure to take adequate steps to enforce a contact order obtained by one parent against the other,[14] in the public law context under discussion here, the nature and extent of the state's positive obligations may justifiably be more onerous. In many cases, the state (in the

---

[10] Less relevant passages omitted.

[11] For a typical statement from the European Court indicating this position, see *Johansen v Norway* (1997) 23 EHRR 33, para 78.

[12] See for example comments of Thorpe LJ in *Re L, Re V, Re M, Re H (Contact: Domestic Violence)* [2000] 1 FLR 334 at 364, doubting the utility of describing even children as having rights in relation to contact, instead preferring a welfare framework.

[13] Some English judges have been dangerously selective in their quotations from, and so understandings of, European case law in this regard: see for example Thorpe LJ in *Payne v Payne* [2001] EWCA Civ 166; [2001] Fam 373, para 36, omitting essential, qualifying wording from the original text in *Johansen v Norway*. This omission was highlighted by Shazia Choudhry in a paper delivered at the SPTL conference, September 2002.

[14] [1996] 1 FLR 289.

form of the local authority) has physical control of the child; even where it does not, it may have parental responsibility and/or a statutory duty to make protective plans for the child. This de facto and de jure control enables the state to influence the child's contacts on a day-to-day basis. As outlined above, there is strong research evidence to suggest that it should use this control to promote contact between the child and family because it is vital for the successful rehabilitation of the child in its home environment, and even where return home is not planned (or achieved), contact with family members may still be valuable for the child's development and well-being in the long term. Recent domestic case law highlights the dangers of drift faced by children when links to the birth family are lost without any permanent replacement being found.[15] A failure by the state to promote contact and/or rehabilitation may therefore cause its intervention to be regarded as a disproportionate interference in family life, in violation of Article 8.

1.2. Domestic Law on Contact in Public Law Cases

Having set out the requirements of human rights law in relation to contact, we now turn our attention to the domestic legal framework. The key statutory provisions relating to contact, found in the CA, closely reflect the European Court's philosophy in relation to contact: protecting the independence and integrity of the family, and limiting the power of local authorities to terminate contact without judicial sanction (in compulsory cases).

Several statutory provisions in the CA promote on-going contact and rehabilitation of the family unit, and the courts have generally supported the maintenance of contact unless there is a real need for it to be terminated.[16] Indeed, the statutory presumption in favour of contact in public law cases and the courts' approach to contact may be thought to be as much protective of the parents' rights as it is of the child's, if not formally conceptualised in those terms. So while the ECHR jurisprudence provides a useful reminder of the importance of contact in these cases, it may not in fact lead to a major change in domestic courts' decisions on contact.

However, the courts are only called on to make a decision about contact in a minority of cases. Local authorities make many more, on-going decisions about contact for the child. We therefore set out below the legal framework for contact, identifying the extent of the powers and duties of the key decision-makers at the different stages of state intervention. We begin with the first stages of child protection, which take place outside the courtroom.

---

[15] *Re F; F v Lambeth LBC* [2002] 1 FLR 217.

[16] Though the cases do not go uncriticised: see for example Masson (2000) pp 25–6 on *Re T (Termination of contact: discharge of order)* [1997] 1 All ER 65.

1.2.1. Child Protection

The first level of state intervention in a child's life occurs where it is suspected that the child is suffering significant harm. Section 47 CA provides that where the local authority have reasonable cause to suspect that a child is suffering, or is likely to suffer significant harm, they must make enquiries to enable them to decide whether they should take any action to safeguard or promote the child's welfare.[17] These enquiries are carried out under the auspices of the Area Child Protection Committee (ACPC). They do not confer parental responsibility (PR) on the local authority. In the course of these enquiries, the local authority must see the child, unless they are satisfied that they already have sufficient information about him.[18] If these enquiries reveal that the child is at continuing risk of significant harm, a formal child protection plan must be drawn up to secure the child's future safety and protection, (Department of Health, 1999, at para 5.64). This plan may specify who the child may, and perhaps more crucially who the child may *not* live with or see.

Indeed, a typical example of a (perceived) risk might be that the child is in contact with someone who is alleged to have harmed him or another child. But if the parents do not agree with the local authority's view that the child's contact with that person must cease, the local authority are unable to impose and enforce any restrictions on such contact for two reasons: firstly they do not usually have physical control of the child—the parents do; and secondly they do not have parental responsibility—the parents do. Agreement by, and between, the parents about restrictions on the child's contacts, and the protection plan generally, is therefore essential.

This reflects the implicit and fundamental expectation that parents and local authority will work in co-operative partnership during the course of these enquiries, with the aim that any subsequent protective plans for the children concerned are agreed between them. Not only has such partnership been found to be a key factor for the successful protection of children over the last decade (Department of Health, 1995, p 45), but it also has clear pragmatic value, since an estimated 82 per cent of children on the child protection register remain with their parents or within their family environment (Department of Health, 1997).[19] The day-to-day protection of children is therefore, in practice, the task of parents and family members, not Social Services. However, if children are to be successfully protected within the family, Social Services need to be confident that family members understand the risk to the child and agree with their view

---

[17] Cases may also reach the attention of the LA via private family law proceedings, for example in cases (including private law contact disputes) involving domestic violence—see s 37 CA. Note also the amendment of the public law threshold test in s 31(9) CA to include harm caused by 'seeing or hearing the ill-treatment of another' (s 120 Adoption and Children Act 2002).

[18] S 47(4) CA.

[19] To date it has not yet been possible to obtain more up to date statistics from the Department of Health.

of how the child may best be safeguarded in the future. In the event that the parents do not agree to act in the way the authority would wish, the local authority may have no choice but to proceed to the second level of intervention—applying for a compulsory order—in order to acquire the legal authority to override the parents' exercise of parental responsibility (PR), and, where necessary, to empower them to remove the child from the home situation.

1.2.2. Accommodation Cases

However, before proceeding to compulsory intervention, contact arises as an important issue in another voluntary context: where the local authority, with the agreement with the parents/carers, accommodate the child.[20] The legal framework in accommodation cases—in terms of the theoretical status of the parent and the local authority in relation to the child—is not dissimilar to that in section 47 cases, in that arrangements for contact must be discussed and agreed between the parent and the local authority. When a child is accommodated, the local authority do not acquire PR for the child. The parents retain full PR, including the right to remove a child from accommodation without notice (unless there is a residence order (RO) in force in which case the right to remove is confined to the person with the RO). However, although the local authority lack PR, they do have a duty to safeguard and promote the child's welfare.[21] In making such arrangements, they must consult with the child, parents and significant others in relation to all decision-making,[22] and agree a plan detailing the arrangements with one person with PR.[23] The plan should include the arrangements for the child to have contact with the family.[24] The statutory principle underpinning contact for accommodated children is that the local authority must *promote* contact between a child who is looked after and their parents, relatives and other significant people in their lives, unless it is not reasonably practicable or consistent with the child's welfare.[25] Crucially, as is the case during the course of section 47 inquiries, the local authority has no legal power to refuse contact between the child and any family member, even if it is agreed in the plan, since these plans are not (directly at least) legally binding.

These provisions mean that, in theory at least, when a child is accommodated, the family unit retains its integrity and independence, the child and its parent (or primary carer) retain an uninterrupted relationship with each other, and the parent remains able to determine the contacts that the child has. However, the practical reality of these and child protection cases is not always as cosy as was intended when the CA was enacted. As will be seen in Part 2, the

---

[20] S 20, CA 1989.
[21] S 22, CA 1989.
[22] S 22(4), CA 1989.
[23] Regulation 3, Arrangement for Placement of Children Regulations 1991 SI No 890.
[24] Schedule 1, Arrangement for Placement of Children Regulations 1991 SI No 890.
[25] Schedule 2, para 15 CA 1989.

extent to which parents remain truly autonomous in making decisions about contact is far removed from that theoretical position.

1.2.3. Compulsory Cases

Contact Where the Child is Subject to a CAO or EPO

The result of enquiries under section 47, or concerns about a child whom they are accommodating, may lead the local authority to abandon the voluntary approach and to seek enhanced, compulsory legal powers, if only short-term ones, via a court order. Initially, this may be under a child assessment order (CAO), where they need greater investigative powers; or, in urgent cases, where there is some immediate concern for the child's safety, via an emergency protection order (EPO).

In both cases, the CA makes express provision for the regulation of contact for the duration of the order, in recognition of the fact that, unless warranted by a concern for the child's safety, even an apparently short-term cessation of contact can have a huge impact on the long term outcome (Department of Health 1991b, at para 4.10). Where the child is, unusually, to be kept away from home under a CAO, section 43(10) *requires* that the order contain such directions as the court thinks fit with regard to contact arrangements for the child during that period. Where a child is subject to an EPO, under which the local authority acquire limited PR (section 44(4)(5)), the starting point is that the local authority are under a duty identical to that imposed where a care order has been made, to allow the child reasonable contact with several categories of person.[26] In addition, however, the court *may* make directions regarding the contact which is, *or is not*, to be allowed between the child and any named person: section 44(6).

Contact Where the Child is in Compulsory Care

A care order, whether made on a full or interim basis, confers parental responsibility on the local authority,[27] which is shared with that of the parents. The local authority have the power to determine the extent to which the parents exercise their parental responsibility, according to the authority's judgement as to what is necessary to safeguard or promote the child's welfare.[28] The local authority therefore has full power to make decisions about, and plans for, a child in care whether or not the parents agree, and the court has no power to impose conditions on the implementation of the care order, for example requiring that the child be allowed to remain in the family home.[29] Once made, a full

---

[26] S 44(13): parents, PR holders, anyone with whom child was living before the order, persons in whose favour a contact was allowed pursuant to s 34 or a private law order.

[27] Some matters ordinarily falling within the jurisdiction of holders of parental responsibility are expressly denied to the local authority: s 33(6)(7).

[28] S 33(3)–(5).

[29] *Re T (A Minor) (Care Order: Conditions)* [1994] 2 FLR 423.

care order therefore passes effective control over most issues to the local authority. However, the key exception to this is contact. This issue remains a matter within the control of the courts. As such, it is perhaps the only aspect of the public law provisions of the CA in which the balance of power has been shifted away from local authority and towards the court, right from the inception of the order.[30]

The statutory regime for the regulation of contact, specifically designed for public law cases, is weighted in favour of on-going contact. Contact in relation to children in care is governed by section 34, regulations made under it, and Schedule 2 paragraph 15, CA. There are two forums in which contact decisions are made: the local authority and the court.

The local authority: The starting point for determining contact arrangements is section 34(1). This provision places a duty on the local authority to allow 'reasonable contact' between a child in care and his parents and other specified persons (referred to here as the 'privileged category'). It is interesting to note a contrast here with private law. In private law cases, contact, like all other issues relating to the child's upbringing, is left at large by the statute (if not by case law), a matter to be determined by the judges (and more usually parents) in exercising their discretion to act in the child's 'best interests'.[31] In the public law context, by contrast, we find a clear *statutory* norm promoting reasonable contact with a privileged category of persons. Crucially, the local authority may not terminate contact between the child and this privileged category in section 34(1) without court approval, other than for a very short period[32] (and in accordance with regulations[33]). However, the local authority have the power otherwise to decide what amounts to reasonable contact, taking account always of their over-arching duty to safeguard and promote the welfare of the child concerned, unless or until any court order is made.[34] If the local authority wish to refuse contact with a privileged person *outright* for more than seven days, they must obtain prior court authorisation. However, wherever the dispute relates to the *level* or *nature* of contact being permitted, the onus will be on the aggrieved individual(s) to bring the matter to court.

It is notable that, despite the accepted potential importance of these contacts to a child, and the finding in Macaskill's survey (2002) that siblings contact was the most prevalent contact arrangement for children in permanent (including

---

[30] See s 34(11) regarding the scrutiny of contact plans prior to the making of an order; if the court doesn't like the plans, it can impose different plans, or even withhold the order. For discussion of the balance of power between court and LA in these cases, see *Re B (Termination of contact: paramount consideration)* [1993] Fam 301; *Re S (A Minor) (Care: contact order)* [1994] 2 FLR 222, and cases mentioned in text below; see Dewar (1995).

[31] Cf the never brought into force s 11(4)(c), Family Law Act 1996, which would for the first time have created an equivalent presumption in favour of on-going contact between parents, other family members and child in the private law context.

[32] S 34(6).

[33] Contact with Children Regulations 1991, SI 1991/891, Reg 3.

[34] S 22(3)(a).

adoptive) placements, siblings and many other relatives are not included amongst the privileged category in relation to whom reasonable contact *must* be allowed. Instead, Schedule 2 para 15, requires the local authority to endeavour to *promote* contact not only with the privileged category, but also with any relative, friend or other person connected with the child, unless it is not reasonably practicable or consistent with the child's welfare to do so. This at least places a requirement on the authority to consider arranging contact with relatives, unless it would be contrary to the child's welfare. However, if the local authority wish to *refuse* contact between the child and one of these non-privileged individuals—such as a sibling or grandparent—they may do so without court sanction. The onus is then on that individual (or the child) to challenge the local authority's decision in court, rather than for the local authority to seek prior court authorisation, as it has to in the section 34(1) cases. And since they do not fall within the privileged category, such individuals (though not the child herself[35]) will require the leave of the court to make the application at all.[36] However, this is an improvement on the previous law. Prior to the CA, such relatives did not even have the right to apply to court for contact, and the regime instituted by the 1989 Act has been implicitly accepted by the European Court as being compatible with the Article 8 rights of such relatives.[37]

The court: Once the court is seized of the matter, it determines what contact is reasonable in the circumstances, applying the welfare principle. It can attach conditions in relation to the contact (for example regarding the location and/or supervision, whether it should be direct or indirect, and so on).[38] It is also empowered by section 34(4), on an application made by the authority or the child, to make an order authorising the authority to refuse to allow contact between the child and any privileged category individuals named in the order. It is interesting to note that such an order does not *require* the local authority to refuse contact,[39] but simply gives them the power to do so where they consider this is necessary for the benefit of the child.[40] Case law indicates that the court's power to make this order should be used with as much circumspection as the power to make a care order, since the termination of contact is a serious step in the child and parents' lives, bringing them one step closer to adoption, and so to the complete severance of their familial relationship in law. Before the court hands over this last contact-card to the local authority, the latter should be

---

[35] Contrast the position in private law, where the child needs leave to apply for s 8 orders.

[36] See for example *Re M (Care: contact: grandmother's application)* [1995] 2 FLR 86, where the court had regard to criteria similar to those used under s 10(9) to grant leave to make private law applications, together with the assumption implicit in Sched 2 para 15 that contact with relatives is beneficial, in granting the grandmother leave to apply for a contact order with the child whose foster parents wished to adopt.

[37] *Boyle v UK* (1994) 19 EHRR 179.

[38] S 34(7).

[39] Contrast orders made under EPOs, where the court may apparently direct that contact is not to take place: s.44(6)(a).

[40] *Re W (Section 34(2) Orders)* [2000] 1 FLR 502.

required to demonstrate a foreseeable and probable need to terminate contact.[41] Section 34(4) orders will therefore not be made as a matter of course to give the local authority at the outset the power to refuse contact later should they wish to do so. Critics have, however, expressed concern that the 'foreseeable and probable need' test puts children at a substantial risk of being left in limbo if, as is apparently often the case, the hoped-for permanent placement fails to materialise or breaks down.[42]

It is important to emphasise that the courts' role in these cases is entirely to *maximise* desirable contact in accordance with the statutory norm. As we have seen, they have no power to *prohibit* contact, only to authorise the local authority to do so where this is necessary to safeguard the child's welfare; and case law determines that such authority should only be given where there is a real need. However, it would be misleading to suggest that this issue does not arise frequently, particularly in cases where children are being placed permanently with a new family. It is therefore important to examine the courts' general attitude to contact cases and their philosophy about the value of contact, a project usefully begun by Jolly (1994).

The courts recognise the importance of maintaining links in the short term. It has been held that the courts have jurisdiction to make contact orders, including section 34(4) orders, on an interim basis, as a holding position, even if a final care order has been made.[43] However, pending a final hearing, save in circumstances of exceptional and severe risk, contact should be maintained. It should be very rare to give leave to terminate contact under section 34(4) to parents of children subject to interim care orders pending a final hearing as this has the effect of pre-judging the final hearing, at least at the welfare stage of the inquiry.[44]

In the long term, it is clear that contact can be regarded as serving more than one purpose, or indeed may have a negative impact on the child's overall welfare. In *Berkshire CC v B*, the judge plotted a spectrum of cases illustrating these differences; a judge's decision about the given case's location on the spectrum will clearly be crucial.[45] At one end, lies the child who has no future with his natural family and needs a new family life; contact with the natural family will bring little or no benefit to (or may positively harm) the child and is likely to impede the establishment of the new family unit. Here, contact is viewed as disruptive and possibly as a deterrent to potential adopters who may prefer a closed adoption with no on-going contact. In some cases, on-going contact with

---

[41] *Re T (Termination of contact: discharge of order)* [1997] 1 All ER 65.

[42] Cf Masson, (2000) pp 24–5 for criticism of the court's failure in that case to take back control (by ordering a resumption of contact) of the case of the younger child who had gone 16 months without a permanent placement being found.

[43] *West Glamorgan CC v P* [1992] 2 FLR 369; *Re B (A Minor) (Care order: review)* [1993] 1 FLR 421.

[44] *A & M v Walsall MBC* [1993] 2 FLR 244.

[45] [1997] 1 FLR 171.

the parents will only further disturb an already emotionally damaged child and jeopardise the success of therapy being given to the child. Terminating contact in these cases may be readily justifiable under Article 8(2).

In the middle of the spectrum lie cases where the child is unlikely to be returned home and so needs a long-term, stable placement, but the relationships he has with his natural family are so important to him, providing continuity in a context of change, that they should be maintained. Simon Brown LJ has identified four reasons for favouring on-going contact in such cases:[46]

(i)   it can give the child the security of knowing that his parents love him and are interested in his welfare;
(ii) it can avoid the damaging sense of loss to the child in seeing himself abandoned by his parents;
(iii) it can enable the child to commit himself to the new carers with the seal of approval of his natural parents;
(iv) it can give the child a sense of family and personal identity.

All these factors may reinforce, and increase the chances of success for, the new permanent placement, (Macaskill, 2002). But in some cases, despite the potential value of contact, events may have overtaken that possibility. Where contact has been terminated with a view to adoption but the placement has failed with no long term resolution in sight, a resumption of contact may not be in the child's best interests; it may cause the child grave distress to see the parent again after having had a goodbye visit, and yet have to face the risk of losing that parent again at some point in the future.[47] It will be necessary in each case to weigh the advantages and disadvantages likely to accrue from contact, and so to identify the location of the case on the spectrum.[48]

At the other end of the spectrum, where the child is likely to return home in the short to medium term, contact will be essential to facilitate that return. Here, contact is viewed as a means to the end of rehabilitation. *Re B* illustrates this type of case.[49] The mother was seeking contact with a view to rehabilitation with the child. The local authority had planned that the child should be adopted by prospective adopters who were known to be unwilling for the birth mother to have on-going contact; any such contact was therefore likely to destabilise the placement. However, despite this, the court refused the local authority's application to terminate contact, on the basis that the mother's ability to parent the child had not been properly assessed in the light of recent good progress that she had made with her new baby. So the court was able, via its decision on contact, in effect to force the local authority fundamentally to reconsider their care plan for the child in circumstances where it felt that those plans should be reassessed.

---

[46] *Re E (A Minor) (Care order: contact)* [1994] 1 FLR 146.
[47] *Greenwich LBC v H* [1996] 2 FLR 736.
[48] *Re D and H (Care: termination of contact)* [1997] 1 FLR 841.
[49] [1993] Fam 301.

1.2.4. One Flaw in the Law

Whatever the practice on the ground, much of the *legal framework* outlined above gives courts and local authorities plenty of scope for protecting and respecting the Convention rights of the parties concerned. As we have seen, the emphasis is very much on promoting contact. But there is one flaw in the legal framework itself which merits attention before we turn our attention to implementation: the representation of children. If a family member is dissatisfied with the way in which the local authority are implementing a care plan, whether in terms of the level or nature of contact being permitted, or otherwise, he or she may bring the matter before the court. Since the HRA came into force, the remedies open to that person are in theory quite extensive: applications for a contact order, judicial review, discharge of the care order, or, where Convention rights are at stake (as they generally will be in these cases), for a remedy under the HRA, which may take the form of injunctive relief, compelling the LA to act (or to abstain from acting) in a particular way.

However, the same is not true for children. The recent decision of the House of Lords in *Re S* highlighted a serious gap in the legal framework, concerning an unrepresented child who is not *Gillick* competent to make an application him or herself.[50] Several provisions of the CA envisage applications being made by the *child* in relation to contact. But where that child is incompetent, that option is available only if an interested person brings proceedings on the child's behalf.[51] In a contact case, one might expect that the person with whom contact would be beneficial for the child will be ready and willing to bring proceedings. However, as we shall see below, that other party may, although technically competent, in practice not feel able to apply to the court. In the absence of the Children's Guardian, who is *functus officio* once the care order is made, there may therefore be no one willing to make representations on this child's, or this family's, behalf. So it falls in practice upon the local authority to ensure that Convention rights are being protected. It would perhaps be going too far to draw an analogy with a fox guarding geese, but there is clearly a need for some independent person to be appointed whose role it is to ensure that the authority are implementing the care order in a way that protects the parties' rights, and to launch proceedings where necessary to enforce those rights. Indeed, the contact issue is so important, bearing as it does so essentially on the child's future relationship with its natural family, that this is an area where Article 6 of the Convention requires judicial protection. Without enhancing the mechanisms available for bringing these children's cases to a judicial forum, English law is in

---

[50] *Re S (Children) (Care Order: Implementation of Care Plan); Re W (Children) (Care Order: Adequacy of Care Plan)* [2002] UKHL 10; [2002] 2 AC 291.

[51] Civil Procedure Rule 21 allows for such applications to be brought in the child's name. This possibility is not discussed in *Re S*, or in the recent case concerning the Children's Guardian's power to bring proceedings—see next note.

breach of the Convention.[52] It remains to be seen whether the Government's attempt to redress this problem by introducing a review mechanism for the implementation of care plans in the Adoption and Children Act 2002 will work in practice.[53]

2. PROMOTING CONTACT IN PRACTICE: THE RESEARCH EVIDENCE ABOUT BARRIERS TO CONTACT

The legal framework outlined above establishes the different decision-making processes about contact at the different stages of state intervention in respect of children at risk of harm. In child protection and accommodation cases, it is the parents who decide, in the exercise of their PR, who the child will see; but in practice, their decisions are usually subject to clear (if theoretically non-binding) stipulations from the local authority in the child protection plan about who the child may and may not see. In compulsory care cases, it is primarily the local authority which implements the statutory duty of promoting contact, and, where this is challenged by one of the parties, the arrangements for contact specified by the court in any contact order (although such orders may still give the local authority considerable flexibility (Gallagher, 2001).[54] The common denominator in all these cases is the local authority. In practice, social workers are responsible for making the vast majority of decisions about contact in public law cases. They do so within a framework which requires them to:

—comply with the statutory norm of allowing reasonable contact unless welfare considerations require contact to be restricted;
—apply to the court for authority to refuse contact where they consider it should be terminated for the benefit of the child; and
—protect the child and family members' Convention rights in accordance with the HRA.

However, despite the clarity of this legal framework, law and practice are sometimes at odds. Whilst there is evidence that the *amount* of contact which fostered children have with their parents has increased considerably since the

---

[52] *Re S*; but no declaration of incompatibility could be made, since no statute was at fault—there is a gap in the legislative framework which cannot be attributed to any one statutory provision.

[53] S 121 of the Act amends the CA by requiring local authorities to conduct independent reviews of care plans. A member of the authority who is not part of the line management of the case will be required to review the case, and if he or she sees fit, could refer the case to CAFCASS. Accompanying regulations may additionally be required to provide some mechanism for the reappointment of the Children's Guardian, and to ensure that that officer has standing to make the relevant court application since Guidance and case law currently suggests that the CAFCASS officer has no standing to make an application on behalf of a child under the Human Rights Act—see *C v Bury MBC* [2002] EWHC 1438; [2002] 2 FLR 868.

[54] Gallagher (2001) reports a tendency by courts to abdicate their responsibility for controlling contact by acceding to the request of local authorities that 'contact should be at the discretion of the local authority'.

CA was implemented (Cleaver, 2002, at p 178), there is still plenty of evidence suggesting room for improvement in social work practice to maximise the quality and so sustainability of that contact. There is also evidence that social workers are ill-informed about the law relating to their work (Ball *et al*, CCETSW reports, cited by Masson, 2000), and may see the law as just one possible resource to use, or avoid, according to their objectives (Grace, 1995, at p 6). Moreover, the possibilities created by the CA and HRA for challenging local authority decisions are only valuable to family members if they have the knowledge and empowerment to assert the rights that that legislation confers. We therefore now look at research evidence to see how non-legal factors influence implementation of public law contact, and may do so in a way that raises human rights concerns.

2.1. Child Protection and Accommodation Cases: the Reality

The legal framework for child protection implies a cooperative partnership between local authority and parent, the latter apparently having the upper hand, by exclusively holding parental responsibility for the duration. However, it takes little imagination to appreciate that the power dynamic is rather different in reality. Parents retain their PR during the course of section 47 enquiries and when a child is accommodated by the local authority, and the local authority do not acquire it. However, parents often feel coerced to comply with the local authority's plans for their child, whether or not they agree with them, because if they do not, the local authority may apply for a court order against them. Parents therefore find that, despite having PR, they cannot make decisions without reference to Social Services. This can skew the power balance against them in favour of Social Services (Corby, Millar, and Young, 1996; Bell, 1999). This imbalance can be exacerbated by the fact that the enquiry process and planning for an accommodated child is administrative rather than judicial. This means there is no independent forum in which the parents may challenge the evidence on which decisions are being made, or the plans, unless they make an application for a section 8 order, or there are grounds for judicial review[55] or for an application under the HRA, or an application is made by the LA for a compulsory order under Part IV CA (in which case there is a judicial forum to challenge these decisions). However, in most cases, there are no court proceedings (even if there are grounds for bringing them) which means that the parents'

---

[55] Although technically possible, such applications are rarely successful. In the case of *R v East Sussex CC ex parte R* [1995] 1 WLR 680, in which, Sir Stephen Brown P said, refusing an application for judicial review regarding registration on the CPR, that 'recourse to judicial review of decisions which do not involve removal from the parents should be rare and only adopted in exceptional circumstances'. It remains to be seen whether the advent of the HRA will make any difference here.

only opportunity to challenge the local authority's view is within the core group in child protection cases, or at review meetings in accommodation cases.[56]

One area in which this imbalance of power is evident is contact. Generally, parents make decisions about who has contact with their child, unless the child is old enough to make those decisions himself, or the court has made an order regarding contact (on contact in the private law context see Herring, this volume). However, when child protection enquiries are pending, social services may in practice be able to dictate the contact arrangements, though they have no *legal* power to do so, either verbally or in the child protection plan. This might involve preventing the child from having contact with, for example, the parent's new partner where allegations have been made against him or her, even if the parent does not believe them. The effect of this is that although the parent still has the right, in theory, to stipulate any contact arrangements, he or she is in fact a mouthpiece for Social Services, because defiance of those arrangements will almost certainly trigger an application for an EPO.

Likewise, the theoretically voluntary nature of accommodation is belied by reality.[57] Children about whom the authority have some 'concerns' (often unspecified) may be placed or kept in accommodation, under threat of court proceedings if the parents do not agree to it, even in cases where the statutory criteria for an EPO or care order could not be established (Hunt and McLeod, 1999; Brandon *et al*, 1999). This means that in reality the power to make decisions about accommodated children lies broadly with Social Services in an administrative context. Whilst there is some scope for parents to challenge these decisions either by withholding agreement to the plan with which they disagree, or by exercising their right to remove their child from accommodation,[58] many decline to do so for fear of precipitating an application for a compulsory order. The 'agreed' plan will detail the contact arrangements, but many parents and other family members find that arrangements for contact are dictated to them by the local authority, even though the latter have no legitimate statutory basis for doing so. These cases may be described then as 'quasi-compulsory'. Family members have the possibility of challenging these arrangements in that they can apply for a section 8 contact order,[59] but, as we shall discuss below, many are too stressed or intimidated to do so.

---

[56] The core group is convened by the key worker following registration of a child's name on the child protection register. Its task is to draw up the child protection plan. See para 5.75–5.82, Department of Health (1999).

[57] For discussion of the various uses to which voluntary accommodation is put, and the difficulties which these cases, and the law governing them, can generate for local authorities and for families, in particular in relation to contact, see Schofield (2000).

[58] Children Act 1989, s 20(7), (8).

[59] Parents may apply as of right, but other relatives and friends need leave to make such an application see Children Act 1989, s 9.

2.2. Compulsory (and Quasi-compulsory) Cases: an Examination of the Barriers to Contact

Prior to the Children Act, the research of Millham *et al* (1986), highlighted many de facto barriers to contact, the existence of which undermined any theoretical legal provision. This research found that in two fifths of cases where the child had been in care for three years or more, there was no contact with the birth family after two years. Perhaps more disturbing was the finding that in the majority of *those* cases, there was no cogent social work reason for that contact to have withered (Millham *et al*, 1986), yet no permanent placement for the child may have been found (Department of Health, 1991a, at p 26). The research identified both specific and non-specific restrictions on contact: those that were placed by social workers on contact as a matter of routine and conscious decision; and those that were simply inherent in placements, and which affected a larger proportion of children, (for a useful summary, see Department of Health and Social Security, 1985, at pp 26–7). The clear message from this research was that these de facto barriers to contact needed to be addressed if the valuable objective of promoting contact was to be attained.

Has the picture changed since implementation of the Children Act in 1991? The quantity of research evidence from the 1990s is increasing, with three recent in-depth studies (Cleaver, 2000, Macaskill, 2002, Schofield *et al*, 2000), to augment previous findings. The existing evidence suggests that, although there are examples of good practice, many of the problems identified by the Millham (1986) research have yet to be resolved. Indeed, Freeman and Hunt (1996) concluded that 'the accumulation of knowledge since contact issues were highlighted in research in the 1980s . . . has had less impact than might have been expected or hoped'. Many of these problems, which would be classified by Millham *et al* as 'non-specific' barriers, seem to fall into three distinct groups: practical, psychological and professional. All of these problems call into question the compatibility of Social Services' management of these cases with the family members' right to respect for their family life.

2.2.1. Practical Problems

For many parents, the most basic barriers to satisfactory contact with their child are *practical*. The child may be placed some distance from the family home, a practice which necessarily incurs travel costs for the parents and others wishing to visit the child where, as is often the case, they are required to visit the child at the foster home. The local authority has a power to help meet the costs associated with contact visits.[60] However, it appears that in some cases assistance of this nature is refused, even to parents in receipt of welfare benefits (Lindley,

---

[60] Children Act 1989, Sched 2 para 16.

1994, at para 3.4). And the parents may be unwilling to press their case for support too far, out of pride, or for fear of appearing to rely on the social workers (Freeman and Hunt, 1996).

These problems are exacerbated where one of a sibling set is being looked after, or a set of siblings looked after by the local authority, is separated, (Freeman and Hunt, 1996). As noted above, sibling contact can be extremely important to a child's sense of continuity and emotional security. Where both siblings are looked after, the presumption is that they should be placed together,[61] but this is not always possible, (though in some cases it would seem that the impossibility is the product of poor planning on the part of the authority (Beckett and Herschman, 2001). Where siblings are not placed together, contact between them therefore assumes vital importance, and the costs associated with that contact ought clearly to be for the authority to pay. But geographical distance is often the biggest barrier to sibling contact (Macaskill, 2002).

Timing and frequency of contact visits appears also to be problematic for some parents. Visits may be perceived to be scheduled more at the convenience of the foster carers than the parents. The amount and type of contact may change frequently in the course of an individual case (Lindley, 1994). Freeman and Hunt (1996) report complaints about contact not being synchronised with significant dates such as family birthdays and national holidays. Though, viewed from another perspective, Macaskill (2002) reports that having contact at such emotive times can actually be counter-productive for the child. What parents want may therefore not be beneficial to the child.

The location in which contact occurs is often a source of problems. Where the child is, as is common, placed in a foster home, contact is (subject to safety concerns (Macaskill, 2002)) likely to occur there. The Department of Health Guidance advocates this pattern on the basis that it provides continuity for the child in that setting and enables the parent and carers to meet (Department of Health, 1991b, para 4.18). However, the Guidance also encourages contact in the family home from the earliest possible stage where family reunification is planned, and research evidence suggests that such home visits are valued by children and parents. The reality is that home-based contact occurs in a minority of cases (Cleaver, 2002). Contact with children living in institutional settings raises special problems, particularly if contact is to occur in the institution. Millham *et al* (1986) describe the 'chilling' effect of 'totality' of the residential context on contact. However, Bilson and Barker (1995) found that regular contact was more likely for children in residential homes than in foster care, and that those children were also more likely than fostered children to have contact in the family home.[62]

---

[61] S 23(7), CA 1989.

[62] Though this may reflect different reasons behind each population of children's being 'looked after', which renders more contact, and more home contact, more appropriate for residential rather than fostered children.

2.2.2. *Psychological Problems*

In addition to, and in consequence of, some of these practical problems, parents and children suffering the trauma of separation face psychological problems in attempting to maintain meaningful contact. The parents may very often feel inadequate, unaware of their legal rights and obligations, and uncertain of the role that they are now required to play in their child's life. They may therefore wait for a prompt from the social worker that does not come. Alternatively, a lack of preparation and support with contact may lead parents to attempt to relate to the child at contact meetings in a way that the child finds upsetting and unsettling, thereby damaging the prospects for successful contact in future, and/or contributing to placement breakdown (Macaskill, 2002). Foster carers may thus become unhappy about, and unsupportive of, contact if there are problems associated with contact visits which disturb the child and so threaten the stability of the placement.[63] The foster carers may also be perceived by the parents to be in a powerful position, especially where they are co-opted by the local authority in effect to supervise the contact sessions which occur in their home.[64] Many parents involved in child protection may be suffering depression, a factor which necessarily aggravates the feelings of disempowerment experienced by parents in these cases (Sheppard 2002).

In turn, Masson (2000) notes that fostered children may be reluctant to have contact with parents for various reasons: negative attitudes to the parents, and loyalty to, or fear of rejection by, the foster carers. Other children may want more contact than their emotional resilience can sustain, but if the decisions made are not explored appropriately with the child, the resentment and misunderstanding felt by the child may impact negatively on contact relationships that would otherwise be valuable to and wanted by the child, thereby jeopardising their future. Macaskill's research (2002) indicates that failure to explain decisions about placement and contact to children in a child-appropriate way may therefore also cause problems.

Some evidence suggests that parents who deal directly with social workers regarding contact arrangements, rather than via a solicitor or court order, feel particularly disempowered (Lindley, 1994). By contrast, Masson (2000) suggests that parents who deal directly with social workers may establish a more satisfactory contact regime. Similarly, Freeman and Hunt (1996) found that parents with voluntary contact arrangements were comfortable without a court order, whilst some of those parents whose contact *was* regulated by a court order felt far more confident about their position and satisfied with the contact they had with the child than they would have done without the order. Such parents were found to be distrustful of social workers' '[prejudiced] whims . . . , lack

---

[63] See work discussed in Browne and Moloney (2002).

[64] Contrast the findings of the Birmingham Foster Care Association, (2000), discussed by Gallagher, (2001), that foster carers feel uncomfortable about having to supervise contact visits, and may be deterred by that prospect from fostering at all.

of resources and general muddle', whereas the court was perceived as an impartial source of control over the local authority. Freeman and Hunt tentatively concluded from their sample, and the varied research findings on this point suggest, that court orders were being used only where necessary, and not routinely.

A particular source of psychological difficulty for parents is the circumstances in which contact sessions are conducted. Venue is very important. Macaskill (2002) concludes that the venue chosen for contact can convey a very strong message to the child and others about the perceived value of the relationship: a poor quality venue will inevitably impact negatively on the contact relationship. But there is a dearth of suitably resourced, neutral contact venues. Where contact is supervised, the presence of a third party during the visit may be, or may be perceived by the parents to be, for the purposes of assessment, rather than mere monitoring to make sure that nothing untoward occurs during the visit. The stress of such 'supervision' can cause a lack of spontaneity in the interactions between parent and child, with the result that some parents may be discouraged from continuing with the contact. Evidence about parents' experiences suggests that such arrangements can feel very unnatural and uncomfortable, particularly where the visit occurs in the foster home (Lindley, 1994; Freeman and Hunt, 1996).[65] Yet the opportunity for parents to challenge the manner in which 'supervision' occurs may be severely limited by the fact that parents who are still being assessed for rehabilitation with the child may not want to rock the boat by complaining. Holland (2000) has noted the importance that may be attached to parents complying with social workers' demands in this respect. Parents who are apparently willing to subscribe to the social worker's perception of the problem and identification of solution are likely to do better than those who are not.

2.2.3. Professional Problems

This brings us on to the social workers themselves, and aspects of their practice which may impact negatively on contact, or which could be altered in order to enhance the quality of contact. The potential importance of the social workers' role is suggested by various recent research findings. For example, Browne and Moloney (2002) found a correlation between placement ambiguity (ie where there were perceived to be underlying problems with the placement which had yet to come to crisis point) and infrequent contact (ie where visits did not follow any set pattern, making it difficult to prepare for contact). It is important to examine the causes of infrequent (and other poor quality) contact, and to investigate whether greater efforts can be made by social workers to monitor the patterns and quality of contact taking place, and intervene as appropriate to improve the situation, whether by promoting more frequent contact where

[65] Though this may also be a source of concern for the foster parents themselves: see Gallagher (2001).

possible, or, if continued contact is going to be detrimental to the child, taking steps to terminate it. It is clearly arguable that infrequency of contact, and the problems it generates for placement stability, may in part be a product of a lack of proper support.

Indeed, in Schofield's study (Schofield *et al*, 2000, see also Cleaver, 2002), factors associated with positive contact experiences were continuity of social work support and the involvement of foster carers in planning the arrangements for contact. By contrast, the most unsatisfactory contact arrangements in their sample were where contact plans were made between the social worker and the birth family, the foster carers only being subsequently informed. Concern has also been expressed that social workers may pay insufficient attention to encouraging uncertain parents and children to maintain contact in the new situation in which they find themselves. Bilson and Barker (1995) found that contact between the social worker and the parents and child respectively tended to fade once the child had been admitted into care or accommodation, especially contact with the parent. If so, the social worker is unlikely to pick up on the difficulties that the parent and child are facing in maintaining contact, and so will not be in a position to intervene positively to improve matters. Similarly, Macaskill (2002) found that the work done (or not done) by social workers to prepare all parties (parents, children and foster carers) for the practicalities and emotional impact of contact was crucial to the success of visits. On a more mundane level, where contact is required to be supervised, the unavailability of a supervisor may mean that a contact session has to be cancelled (Lindley, 1994). There are clearly resource issues at play here that need to be addressed.

Moreover, when social workers are still actively involved, it seems that in some cases they misconstrue signals from the parents and child, in a way that may cause them to proceed on the assumption that the parent is uninterested in the child. Millham *et al* (1986) expressed concern about social work having self-fulfilling tendencies, the system itself creating the client, and this tendency apparently persists post-Children Act. For example, if the parent is unable to visit the child frequently because of difficulties in meeting travel costs, he or she may be perceived as being uninterested in the child, (Lindley, 1994).[66] Holland (2000) has noted that passivity and indifference presented by a parent, who feels powerless and lacks articulacy, may be construed negatively by social workers. In the case of depressed parents this is exacerbated further, and if contact fades away, the depression is liable to worsen, so creating a negative spiral. Sheppard (2002) notes that parents in such a situation are unable to engage in the partnership envisaged by the CA without significant support from social workers and others.

---

[66] This research post-dates the publication of *Patterns and Outcomes*, (DoH, 1991a) which urged social workers to beware of simplistically equating levels of contact with levels of concern: p 120.

3. MAKING CONTACT WORK IN THE PUBLIC LAW CASES

If contact is going to work, these obstacles (some legal, in the case of children's representation, but mostly non-legal) have to be overcome. Otherwise parents may not act on a contact order that has been made for the benefit of the child. Or where an order has not been made already, the parents may simply drift away, not encouraged by the social workers and foster parents to do otherwise, and lacking the confidence and empowerment proactively to seek contact or to challenge the existing contact arrangements. Such an outcome goes against the clear intention of the Children Act Guidance, which states that:

> it cannot be in the interests of the child and it is no service to the parents to allow them to drift to the periphery of the child's life, without reminding them of the possible implications of this course to the plan for their child and the child's relationship with them (Department of Health, 1991b, para 4.38).

Case law suggests that the courts are largely supportive[67] of continuing family life where it is likely to be beneficial to the child, even in some cases if rehabilitation seems unlikely.[68] However, where decision-making about contact occurs within the local authority, whether in implementing a court order, or in managing a voluntary case, there is far greater scope for different ideology, assumptions and relationship-dynamics to influence the contact arrangements. As has been noted already, the law may have limited impact on social workers. Masson (2000) suggests that other forms of control, such as recording practices and 'funding levers', may be more effective means of engineering social workers' decision-making, though these can be tailored to accord with legal requirements in order to allow the law indirectly to control social work activity. Moreover, the courts, which themselves only have a limited range of orders available to them, cannot *directly* alter the attitudes and actions of social workers, foster carers and family members in relation to contact, nor provide support to facilitate the rebuilding of relationships after the order has been made.[69] Even now that the Human Rights Act has increased the powers of the courts to review the manner in which local authorities exercise their powers in this field, social work practice remains central to the success of contact relationships.

But, given these caveats, is there anything more that the current law and the courts, and social work policy, could do to respond to the problems highlighted above? There seem to be two issues: firstly, the implementation of the positive obligations incumbent on the state; and secondly, (actually a specific example

---

[67] Individual cases of course may be open to criticism: see for example Masson (2000) pp 25–6 on *Re T (Termination of contact: discharge of order)* [1997] 1 FLR 517.

[68] *Re E (A Minor) (Care order: contact)* [1994] 1 FLR 146.

[69] Masson contrasts the availability in the private law sphere of family assistance orders. The court can prescribe the frequency, location and nature of contact by way of conditions, but ultimately the implementation of contact is a matter for the social workers and their delegates.

of the first issue) the empowerment of parents (and other family members) through procedural rights and advocacy.

3.1. Emphasising the Obligations Incumbent on the State

The Children Act regime leaves social workers with wide, low-level discretion in the management of contact, the effect of which on families can be profound. But that discretion is not untrammelled. As has been outlined already, the ECHR places the state under negative obligations not to interfere disproportionately in family life, and positive obligations to foster family life in care situations, and to maximise the chances of reunification or continuity of relationships taking place in the long term.

There has been much focus recently on both public[70] and private law's apparent impotence in dealing with cases where a family member, for what may be a variety of reasons, seems not to want contact with a child for whom that contact could be beneficial (see Bainham and Herring, this volume). Although the law may find it difficult, even inappropriate, to impose and to enforce on the unwilling individual a duty to have a relationship with the child, in the public law context at least, the law *can* try to maximise the chances of that relationship being fostered by placing a duty on *social workers* to take reasonable steps to manage these cases in a manner which promotes and supports such relationships. And that is arguably what Article 8's positive obligations require, raising serious issues for social work practice. The law cannot be too prescriptive about steps to be taken to this end; every case is different, and research findings can offer new ways of approaching familiar problems. What is crucial is that contact relationships are properly supported, and that the management of these relationships is regularly reviewed in order to ensure that the support being offered is the most appropriate and beneficial possible for the individuals concerned.

The objective of family unification, or at least of maintaining an on-going relationship between child and other family members where that would be beneficial to the former, cannot be fulfilled unless that goal is internalised by social workers (and courts) and manifested in their handling of cases. This is particularly important in the non-compulsory stages of a case where there is no a priori court involvement, and so the onus falls more heavily on the local authority to ensure compliance with the parties' rights. Failure to manage a case in the light of this goal may violate Article 8, and so generate an application from the parents, child, and/or other affected family members under the Human Rights Act.[71] Pending the possible empowerment of independent Children's

---

[70] *Re F (Contact: child in care)* [1995] 1 FLR 510: a court cannot require any private party to participate in contact which the local authority is obliged by a s 34(2) order to permit to a child in care.

[71] See *Re S (Children) (Care order: implementation of care plan)* [2002] UKHL 10; [2002] 2 AC 291.

Guardians to bring such cases,[72] the onus for promoting contact rests with the local authority, unless parents or children take the initiative to move the court where the contact regime is perceived to be unsatisfactory (which in many of the sorts of cases under discussion may be an unrealistic expectation). And in any event, it is preferable that the initial management of the case is compatible with the parties' rights, to avoid the distress and expense of litigation, and to ensure substantive protection of the rights at stake, rather than the somewhat futile retrospective award of damages to remedy otherwise irremediable breaches.

A *legal framework* for fulfilling these positive obligations already exists, in the sense that local authorities' and courts' existing powers under the Children Act are more than adequate to meet the task. For example, even though siblings and other relatives with whom contact may be vital to a child's sense of continuity and identity are not in the 'privileged' category of contacts, local authorities have the power to ensure that those contacts are maximised. Moreover, courts could more frequently make specific orders in relation to siblings in order to emphasise this, rather than, as Masson (2000) reports is currently the practice, leaving sibling contact as an implicit adjunct to parental contact or, where both children are in care, as an aspect of day-to-day case management for the authority to determine.

The state could also act to reduce some of the barriers to contact discussed above. The dearth of suitable neutral contact venues must be addressed, (as discussed in MacLean and Mueller, this volume). So too must the routine use of supervised contact, and there are lessons here for both courts and social workers. The research discussed above demonstrates that, owing to the potentially detrimental psychological effects of supervision described above, careful justification should have to be demonstrated before *supervised* contact is required at all. It has been complained that courts too quickly accede to local authorities' requests for supervision of contact with parents, and with family members from whom there is no risk to the child at all (Gallagher, 2001). The courts clearly have a role to play here, which it seems would be valued by parents, in paying closer attention to proposed contact arrangements, not least because an automatic *assumption* that contact in these cases should be supervised violates the rights of the parties under Article 8. Freeman and Hunt (1996) suggest that where supervision *is* required for the child's safety, the *manner* in which contact is supervised could be made rather less hostile. There is a potential role here for properly resourced contact centres. As Freeman and Hunt note,

> the quality of contact is often a key factor in decision-making in care cases, and reports on contact sessions frequently form part of the LA evidence. At the moment it seems parents may, however, unintentionally, be being set up to fail.

If contact is a key part of the assessment of the parent/child relationship, and if we are to operate a child protection system which is best geared towards max-

---

[72] See n 53.

imising the chances of family reunification, it is only fair that that the assessment visit is identified and separate from the rest of the contact arrangements, which should be permitted to occur in the least unnatural circumstances possible.

But one remaining difficulty, as ever, is *resources*, without which the sort of support envisaged here will simply not materialise, though there are some possible savings to be made as well as investments. For example, the current practice of routine supervision of contact where it is not strictly necessary should be ended, not least since it is likely to infringe the rights of the family members involved, intruding disproportionately into their family life. The consequent savings could be invested in the infrastructure necessary to ensure that where supervision *is* required, it can be effected as unobtrusively as possible. Another area of practice which should change, but which has significant resources implications, relates to the subsidy of travel costs incurred by parents and other family members visiting a child in care. Local authorities should more frequently exercise their power to make these subsidies.[73] But they require more resources with which to do so. In *Olsson v Sweden* the Swedish authorities were found to be in violation of Article 8 by virtue of having placed siblings separately and some considerable distance apart from each other and from the parents, thereby substantially limiting opportunities for contact to take place.[74] It is noteworthy that the European Court was unsympathetic to the state's plea of lack of resources, such as a limited supply of suitable foster homes, a factor which contributed to the less than ideal placements in that case. The Court remarked that administrative difficulties of this sort could play only a secondary role in determining the legality of the agency's actions.[75]

English courts do not take a rose-tinted view of local authorities' resources[76] in determining the extent of their positive obligations, so this is a matter ultimately for central government to address.[77] But the courts will expect authorities to dig into their pockets. In one recent case,[78] the placement of the child in a specialist residential centre some 350 miles away from the mother's current home meant that the authority would have to pay the travel and accommodation costs incurred by the mother, the child's only known relative, in order to facilitate the required monthly contact. It was implicit from the President's judgment in that case that the authority would have to do this in order for the

---

[73] Under Schedule 2, para 16, Children Act 1989.

[74] (1988) 11 EHRR 259.

[75] *Ibid* para 82.

[76] Per Hale LJ in *Re W (Children) (Care Plan), Re W & B (Children) (Care Plan)* [2001] EWCA Civ 757; [2001] 2 FLR 582, para 60; see also Brooke LJ in *W v Lambeth LBC* [2002] EWCA Civ 613; [2002] 2 All ER 901, para 83, holding the authority to have acted lawfully in failing to exercise a power under Part III of the Children Act 1989 in favour of the applicants: '[the authority] has given intelligible and adequate reasons why it is not willing to exercise its power in this case, given all the other pressures on its resources'. The courts, it seems, will be satisfied that there are no grounds for quashing a decision where a cogent explanation of resource allocation can be given.

[77] For fuller analysis of the question of resource allocation and positive legal obligations, see Miles, (2001) at 437–41.

[78] *C v Bury MBC* [2002] EWHC 1438; [2002] 2 FLR 868.

substantial infringement on the mother and child's family life entailed in the placement to be proportionate. Where contact is required, it can be costly, and the necessary investment of funds cannot be avoided.

3.2. Empowerment of Parents

The second, related issue is the empowerment of parents and other family members. Parents are generally parties to, and are represented in, *court* proceedings relating to questions about contact. However, given that most decision-making about contact occurs within *local authorities*, it is important to consider parents' involvement in this forum too, particularly in non-compulsory cases where almost *all* decision-making takes place in an administrative forum unless the decision can be challenged under section 8 CA, the HRA or in judicial review proceedings. This issue is important to the psychology of parents. Given a proper voice and adequate opportunity to have their views heard and understood by the decision-makers, they may in turn have a better understanding of the situation, and so one of the barriers to contact discussed in part 2 may thereby be lowered.

Given the procedural obligations of Articles 6 and 8 of the Convention, parents cannot be marginalised and excluded from such decision-making processes without good reason. Not only is this clearly established in the Children Act[79] itself, and in regulations and guidance about child protection case conferences,[80] planning meetings and/or reviews,[81] but it has also been confirmed by the courts in several cases. For example, in the case of *Re M*,[82] the decision of a permanency planning meeting (to which the father was not invited), which effectively ruled out any chance of the child being reunited with him, was quashed because the local authority had unwittingly failed to involve the father at a crucial moment. In the case of *TP and KM v United Kingdom*,[83] the European Court held that the local authority's failure to submit to the court the question as to whether to disclose to the mother a video containing crucial evidence as to the identity of the alleged abuser, amounted to a breach of Article 8. The non-disclosure of that material had deprived the mother of adequate involvement in decision-making about her daughter's case, most importantly,

---

[79] See s 22(4) & (5) which places a duty on local authorities to ascertain and give due consideration to the wishes and feelings of parents, the child and significant others in relation to all decisions about children who are looked after.

[80] There is a clear expectation in *Working Together* (DoH, 1999) that parents and wider family members will normally attend child protection conferences (para 5.57). However, it is acknowledged that, exceptionally, the chair may decide to exclude a family member, in whole or in part, following criteria set out in a protocol drawn up by the ACPC (para 5.58 and 4.13). The guidance adds that they should be 'helped fully to participate' (para 5.57) and that their involvement should be planned carefully (para 5.58). Moreover, the social worker should explain that they may bring an advocate friend or supporter to the conference (para 5.57).

[81] Reg 7, Review of Children's Cases Regulations 1991 SI No 895.

[82] *Re M (Care: challenging Decisions by the Local Authority)* [2001] 2 FLR 1300.

[83] [2001] 2 FLR 612; for comment, Miles (2001).

the opportunity to offer an alternative interpretation of that key evidence. Most recently, a domestic court has held that the right to a fair trial (Article 6) is not confined to the purely judicial part of the proceedings; unfairness at any stage in the litigation process might involve not merely a breach of Article 8, but also of Article 6. Munby J's judgment gives guidance on how local authorities can avoid unfairness in their decision-making, to ensure compatibility with both Articles.[84]

The parents' right to be *involved* is therefore fairly unequivocal. But the key question is how best to empower parents in a process which is not governed by rules of evidence, which reserves an element of procedural discretion to the authority making the decision, and in which the power imbalance is such that parents may feel intimidated about articulating their views for fear of destabilising their working relationship with the social worker, a concern which is particularly inhibiting where there is an assessment pending. Evidence suggests that where there is a divergence of perceptions between the parent and the social worker about what is best for the child, the social worker's dual role safeguarding the child's welfare and working with, and acting as an advocate for, the family becomes untenable (Bell, 1999; Corby, Millar and Young, 1996; Thoburn, Lewis and Shemmings, 1995). In these circumstances, parents may need an independent advocate to formulate and express their views (Hunt and McLeod, 1999; Freeman and Hunt, 1996). There is some evidence to suggest that the involvement of an advocate on parents' behalf, certainly within child protection decision-making, can be very helpful (Lindley, Richards and Freeman, 2001a, 2001b). However, parents still lack a *right* to advocacy in such a context,[85] with associated public funding. Until they do,[86] it may continue to be difficult for parents to participate equally in local authority decision-making about contact arrangements, with the result that their experience of disempowerment persists.

4. CONCLUDING THOUGHTS

There is a problematic clash within the Children Act between child protection and family welfare concerns which can be extremely difficult to negotiate in the individual case. Contact provides a focal point for these tensions. An entirely child protection-focused approach risks neglecting the value of links with the birth family. Article 8 clearly requires attention to be paid to the family life

---

[84] *Re L (Care: Assessment: Fair Trial)* [2002] EWHC 1379 (Fam); [2002] 2 FLR 730.

[85] The question of whether parents involved in child protection cases should have a right to involve an advocate is also addressed in Lindley, Herring and Wyld, 2001, at pp 170–200.

[86] Although there has not, to date, been a case which has established whether or not the parents have a right to advocacy within the internal decision-making processes in the local authority, the recent case of *Re L* (n 84 above) raises a strong presumption that they should: Munby J said that, in order to avoid procedural unfairness, parents should be allowed to attend and *be represented* [emphasis added] at professionals meetings if they wish.

shared by all the parties. Managing contact in child protection cases is perhaps one of the most difficult and, if taken seriously, potentially time-consuming tasks faced by child protection social workers. Already heavy work-loads are not compatible with the sorts of sustained work required to achieve this. As Sheppard (2002) notes, the social worker really needs to be acting for the parents as well as the child, but, as we have seen above, there is an inevitable stage in the process when this becomes impossible if provided by one person alone.

It is clearly important not to focus exclusively on empowering the parties simply by way of legal rights and representation, since those are of limited use, for example, to a parent who psychologically feels unable to assert herself. Masson (2000) advocates a 'social' approach to contact problems, in preference to a 'legal' approach, in recognition of the limitations of the dispute-centred focus of the latter. The social approach emphasises the importance of social workers acting to avoid or remove the sorts of barriers to contact outlined in part 2 of this chapter, in relation to which the law can seem somewhat impotent. The growing body of research literature offers valuable lessons as to how contact may best be managed. Masson suggests that a new agency should be specifically dedicated to making contact work in public law cases, leaving social workers to concentrate on child protection and family support. This may be necessary to avoid the impossible task, identified above, that is otherwise faced by one social worker. But whether a given case is ultimately resolved with or without legal process, it is crucial that this sort of 'social' work is done. It is clear from the research evidence that proper support, careful planning and proper resourcing are absolutely key to the success and quality of contact. This approach is likely to improve the understanding and confidence of parents in the process. In addition, social workers and from them, the courts, may develop a greater awareness of the difficulties experienced by the individuals involved and so be less likely to draw erroneous conclusions from the ambivalent, apparently uninterested or hostile behaviour of adults and children. With this sort of support, resort to the legal process may not be necessary. Without it, resort to the legal process may in practice be rendered impossible for many families, and their rights in this most invasive of state interferences in family life may thereby go unprotected.

REFERENCES

BECKETT, S and HERSCHMANN, D, 'The Human Rights Implications for Looked after Siblings' (2001) 31 *Family Law* 288.

BELL, M, 'Working in Partnership in Child Protection: the Conflicts' (1999) 29 *British Journal of Social Work* 437.

BILSON, M and BARKER, R, 'Parental Contact with Children Fostered and in Residential Care after the Children Act 1989' (1995) 25 *British Journal of Social Work* 367.

Birmingham Foster Care Association, *Contact in Foster Care* (Birmingham, BFCA 2000).

BRANDON, M, THOBURN, J, LEWIS, A and WAY, A, *Safeguarding Children with the Children Act 1989* (London, The Stationery Office, 1999).

BROWNE, D and MOLONEY, A, ' "Contact Irregular": a Qualitative Analysis of the Impact of Visiting Patterns of Natural Parents on Foster Placements' (2002) 7 *Child and Family Social Work* 35.

CLEAVER, H, 'Fostering Family Contact: A Study of Children, Parents and Foster Carers' in Department of Health, *Children Act Now* (London, The Stationery Office, 2002).

CORBY, B, MILLAR, M and YOUNG, L, 'Parental Participation in Child Protection Work: Rethinking the Rhetoric' (1996) 26 *British Journal of Social Work* 475.

Department of Health and Social Security, *Social Work Decisions in Child Care: Recent Research Findings and their Implications* (London, HMSO, 1985).

Department of Health, *Patterns and Outcomes in Child Placement* (London, HMSO, 1991a).

——*Children Act Guidance and Regulations, Volume 4: Residential Care,* (London, HMSO, 1991b).

——*Children Act Guidance and Regulations, Volume 3: Family Placements* (London, HMSO, 1991c).

——*Child Protection: Messages from Research,* (London, HMSO, 1995).

——*Children and Young Persons on Child Protection Registers Year Ending 31/3/97* (London, Government Statistical Office, 1997).

——*Working Together to Safeguard Children: A Guide to Inter-agency Working to Safeguard and Promote the Welfare of Children* (London, The Stationery Office, 1999).

——*Children Act Now* (London, The Stationery Office, 2002).

DEWAR, J, 'The Courts and Local Authority Autonomy' (1995) 7 *Child and Family Law Quarterly* 15.

FREEMAN, P and HUNT, J, *Parental Perspectives on Care Proceedings* (Bristol, Centre for Socio-Legal Studies, 1996).

GALLAGHER, P, 'Contact with a Child in Care and the Human Rights Act 1998' (2001) 31 *Family Law* 686.

GRACE, C, *Social Workers, Children and the Law* (Oxford, Clarendon Press, 1995).

HOLLAND, S, 'The Assessment Relationship: Interactions between Social Workers and Parents in Child Protection Assessments' (2000) 30 *British Journal of Social Work* 149.

HUNT, J and McLEOD, A, *The Last Resort: Child Protection the Courts and the Children Act* (London, HMSO, 1999).

JOLLY, S, 'Cutting the Ties—The Termination of Contact in Care' (1994) 15 *Journal of Social Welfare Law* 299.

LINDLEY, B, *On the Receiving End* (London, Family Rights Group, 1994).

LINDLEY, B, RICHARDS, M and FREEMAN, P, 'Advice and Advocacy for Parents in Child Protection Cases—What's Happening in Current Practice?' (2001a) 13 *Child and Family Law Quarterly* 167.

——'Advice and Advocacy for Parents in Child Protection Cases—An Exploration of Conceptual and Policy Issues, Ethical Dilemmas and Future Directions' (2001b) 13 *Child and Family Law Quarterly* 311.

LINDLEY, B, HERRING, J and WYLD, N, 'Public Law Children's Cases: Whose Decision is it Anyway?' in J Herring (ed), *Family Law: Issues, Debates, Policy,* (Cullompton, Willan Publishing, 2001).

MACASKILL, C, *Safe Contact? Children in Permanent Placement and Contact with their Birth Relatives* (Lyme Regis, Russell House, 2002).

MASSON, J, 'Thinking About Contact—A Social or a Legal Problem' (2000) 12 *Child and Family Law Quarterly* 15.

MILES, J, 'Human Rights and Child Protection' (2001) 13 *Child and Family Law Quarterly* 431.

MILLHAM, S, BULLOCK, R, HOSIE, K and HAAK, M, *Lost in Care* (Aldershot, Gower, 1986).

MILLHAM, S, BULLOCK, R, HOSIE, K and LITTLE, M, *Access Disputes in Child Care* (Aldershot, Gower, 1989).

SCHOFIELD, G, BEEK, M, SARGENT, K with THOBURN, J, *Growing up in Foster Care* (London, British Agencies for Adoption and Fostering, 2000a).

SCHOFIELD, G, 'Parental Responsibility and Parenting—The Needs of Accommodated Children in Long-Term Foster-Care' (2000) 12 *Child and Family Law Quarterly* 345.

SHEPPARD, M, 'Depressed Mothers' Experience of Partnership in Child and Family Care' (2002) 32 *British Journal of Social Work* 93.

THOBURN, J, LEWIS, A and SHEMMINGS, D, *Paternalism or Partnership? Family Involvement in the Child Protection Process* (London, HMSO, 1995).

13

Contact and the Adoption Reform

JOHN EEKELAAR*

1. INTRODUCTION

THE FIRST OF the set of recommendations at the beginning of the
Government White Paper, *Adoption—A New Approach* (Department of
Health, 2000, hereafter 'the 2000 White Paper') published in December 2000, is
breathtaking: 'The Government **will** invest **£66.5m** over three years to secure
sustained improvements in adoption services'.[1] There it is: cash up front; something usually buried, sometimes never to be revealed, in most family law reform
proposals. Compare this with the previous Government's White Paper of 1993
(Department of Health *et al*, 1993, hereafter 'the 1993 White Paper'). It is actually quite difficult to detect clear recommendations in it. But Chapter 2 sets out
the 'main thrust' of the then Government's 'intentions'. These take the form of
something like a set of principles, which are expanded discursively in subsequent chapters. On money, the only comment is:

> The Government does not intend that they [the 'approaches' to adoption described in
> the document] will create extra costs and will have regard to the need for cost-
> neutrality in working further on the details.[2]

The speed with which the present government has acted is also remarkable.
In February 2000 the Prime Minister commissioned the Performance and
Innovation Unit (PIU) of the Cabinet Office to 'conduct a study and assess the
evidence' on adoption, and to make recommendations on policy options. The
PIU reported in July (Performance and Innovation Unit, 2000, hereafter referred
to as PIU Report); the White Paper followed in December. This contained a
detailed timetable for implementing its recommendations. A Bill was introduced by April 2001, and, although it fell with the general election in May, it
was speedily reintroduced and enacted in November 2002 as the Adoption and
Children Act 2002. In striking contrast, the *1993 White Paper* concluded: 'The
Government will bring forward the necessary legislation when the legislative

---

* I would like to thank, besides the editors and participants in the seminars, Professor Mervyn
Murch, for helpful comments. The views expressed are, of course, my own.
[1] Bold type in original.
[2] *1993 White Paper*, para 7.4.

timetable permits . . .'.[3] It is perhaps not surprising that a draft Bill appeared only three years later.

What can account for such a dramatic change? Of course, there had been a change of political administration after the Conservatives lost the 1997 election. The new administration, concerned about the state of public children's services, rapidly launched a three-year programme (subsequently extended by two years), called *Quality Protects*, which, through the introduction of new management regimes and additional resources, was designed to 'transform the management and delivery of social services for children.'[4] The new urgency over adoption is part of that drive for improvement, but this does not explain why it was that *adoption* should be seen as such a key component. We may not know exactly why, but the answer must at least include a new perception of the nature of the problem to which adoption was thought to provide an answer. It will not be my purpose to argue for or against the use, or increased use, of adoption of children in public care. But it is necessary to examine the evidence relied on by government sources which advocated an increased role for adoption. I will suggest that the use of adoption raises some serious difficulties, and that these arise most visibly around the issue of contact between the child and its birth family.

2. ADOPTION AND CONTACT

I have elsewhere expressed the view that the law should be slow to intervene in private-law contact issues unless it is clear that a parent is behaving in a way which directly harms a child, and that the potential benefit to a child of face-to-face contact with a non-residential parent with whom the child has no, or only a slight, relationship is too speculative to justify coercive intervention (Eekelaar, 2002). Such matters, I say, should be dealt with by persuasion and consent. But contact in the context of adoption raises issues of an entirely different order. Here the state will have *already* intervened in the parental relationship, often coercively through child protection law. Maintaining contact between a very young child and its parents is often an essential prelude to returning the child to live permanently with the parents rather than with a foster or adoptive family. This is far from the objectives of trying to build up a relationship between a child and a non-residential parent. For older children the situations are more similar, because in both cases the problem is one of preventing disruption to a child's existing relationships. But these are the types of case where I believe there is a stronger case for intervening in private law because of the direct damage caused by such disruption.[5]

---

[3] Para 7.5.
[4] See LAC (98) 28.
[5] See Eekelaar (2002).

Contact issues can arise in relation to adoption in two senses. One, which is not the main focus of this chapter, concerns the opportunities for adopted children to begin contact with a natural parent after they have reached majority. An Adoption Contact Register was introduced in England and Wales on 1 May 1991. Up to 30 June 2001, just under 20,000 adoptees and 8,500 relatives (mostly parents and siblings) had placed their names on the register. So more adoptees wish to contact their relatives after they grow up than the other way around. But relatively few succeed. During that period, 539 pairs of records were linked. A small number of relatives put their name on the register during the child's minority (although adopted children have to wait until they are 18 before doing so: most wait until they are about 30). Female relatives on the register are almost twice as likely to be mothers as male relatives are to be fathers of the sought-for adopted child, whereas male relatives were more than twice as likely as female relatives to be siblings or half siblings (Haskey, 2001). This system only works to the extent that both parents and child wish to make contact. Adopted children have no right to trace their birth parents, though they may manage to do so through their birth certificate which they are entitled to receive unless the Registrar-General believes this would put the parents at significant risk.[6] The Government has attempted to rationalise the basis upon which information is provided to adult adopted children: they will retain the right to the birth certificate (though the High Court *may* disallow it), and will be able to acquire information about their family at the discretion of the agency.[7]

These attempts to track down blood relatives would not be necessary in cases in which contact was maintained between the adopted child and its natural family during childhood. Such contact is by no means rare. Contact of some kind (and there are many variations) is exercised by some 70 per cent of adopted children.[8] Nor is the judicial attitude hostile to so-called 'open' adoption. If adoptive parents agree, even informally, that they will allow contact between the adopted child and its natural family, they may find themselves held to it unless they have good reasons to withdraw their agreement.[9] On the other hand, the judiciary is unwilling to *impose* a contact requirement on adoptive parents, which they see as unduly interfering with their freedom to bring up the child,[10] and inconsistent with the unconditional nature of the natural parents' consent to the adoption.[11] Thus if the adoption is threatened by pressing the contact claim, the claim will fail. This is in sharp contrast to the presumption of contact which applies when a child is looked after by a local authority,[12] and the general approach under private law. Yet as I have suggested, the significance of contact

---

[6] Adoption Act 1976, s. 51; *R v Registrar-General, ex p Smith* [1991] 2 All ER 88.

[7] Adoption and Children Act 2002, ss 60 (2) and 61.

[8] *PIU Report*, para 3.141.

[9] *Re T (Adopted Children: Contact)* [1995] 2 FLR 251; *Re T (Adopted Children: Contact)* [1995] 2 FLR 792.

[10] *Re C (A Minor) (Adoption Order: Conditions)* [1989] AC 1.

[11] *Re T (Adopted Children: Contact)* [1995] 2 FLR 251.

[12] Children Act 1989, s 34.

for the child is probably greater in the circumstances of adoption. So it is surprising that so little attention was paid to the issue of contact in the adoption reform. But before discussing the issue of contact, it is necessary to look more closely at the nature of the reform.

3. THE CONSTRUCTION OF A PROBLEM

The Children Act 1989 had been a major achievement. It had been the product of consultation and development at least since 1984 (Social Services Committee, 1984). It dealt primarily with private law matters concerning children and with the powers and duties of public authorities regarding child care and child protection. But it did not cover adoption, which had last been investigated by the Houghton Committee, which reported in 1972 (Departmental Committee on the Adoption of Children, 1972). So in July 1989 an interdepartmental group was set up to look at it again, and it produced a Consultation Document in October 1992 (Department of Health and Welsh Office, 1992). The subsequent *1993 White Paper* was the government's response.

As regards 'domestic' adoptions (which are distinguished from 'overseas' adoptions[13]) the *1993 White Paper* starts by saying that the balance of rights and interests between the child, the adoptive parents and the birth parents will be 'defined afresh', and issues such as the test for choosing permanency over other options (it must have a 'clear and significant advantage to the child'), the extent of recognition of the child's wishes (to be given 'great weight'), contact between the child and the birth family (a 'careful judgement' was necessary), information to adopted children about their origins (to be 'encouraged') are mentioned first, followed by reference to the desirability of 'commonsense' judgments and values in making placements.[14] Then the White Paper states that 'in addition' there will be 'separate procedures through which **families already caring for children other than their own** may adopt them' which will, 'in suitable cases give special recognition of the role of some foster parents and caring relatives', 'simpler ways' by which step-parents can acquire parental responsibility and 'other ways than adoption in which the relationship and the responsibilities of **carers and relatives** can be recognised'.[15] The subsequent chapters deal with these matters in greater detail.

It should be observed that there is no special emphasis on the adoption of children who are already looked after by public authorities. The issues raised first are general to all adoptions. Only later is there specific reference to that group, and it is introduced by the phrase: 'In addition'. This is not the language which identifies a priority issue. The *1993 White Paper* does, in chapter 3, acknowledge

[13] The latter had been giving rise for concern, but this issue will not be considered further in this chapter.

[14] *1993 White Paper*, para 2.6.

[15] *1993 White Paper*, para 2.7. Bold type in original.

the decrease in 'baby' adoptions both absolutely and relative to the adoption of older children, but this is seen in the general context of step-parent and inter-country adoptions. There is acknowledgment of

> some concern that local authorities may sometimes work to keep a child with an unsatisfactory family for too long when it would be better to apply to the court for an order authorising an alternative family placement with perhaps a view to adoption. [And] some feeling that planning for a child who needs a permanent new family can be more difficult because of the emphasis in the [Children] Act on maintaining contact with birth families.[16]

But the immediately following comment dispels any sense of urgency about the matter:

> It is no part of the Government's objective to discourage agencies from seeking secure placements, including adoptions, away from birth families for those children who need them. In suitable cases, adoption has a good record in its outcome compared with other options.[17]

The negative language ('no' policy to 'discourage') and the cautious assessment of success ('in suitable cases') serves to sum up the tenor of the official thinking of the time. This is not to say that the administration was complacent. It commissioned research. But this was published only at the end of the decade (Department of Health, 1999, hereafter referred to as *Messages*, 1999 and Lowe *et al*, 1999).

We will consider later how far this research may have warranted the difference in response.

In contrast, the *2000 White Paper* immediately proclaims a 'vision' (rather than the *1993 White Paper*'s 'objectives'): that of 'permanent, secure family life.'[18] Setting the scene in the context of the provision of 'opportunities for all' and equality, it rapidly focuses on 'children and the public services'. 'Adoption', it states, 'has traditionally been a means of providing a permanent alternative home for some of the children unable to *return to* their birth parents'.[19] The Government then proclaimed its belief 'that more can and should be done to promote wider use of adoption for looked after children who cannot return to their birth parents.'[20] This led to its second goal, stated up-front just after its commitment of public money, and no less startling: it is to

---

[16] *1993 White Paper*, para 3.16.

[17] *1993 White Paper*, para 3.17.

[18] *2000 White Paper*, title of ch 1.

[19] *2000 White Paper*, para 1.12 (emphasis supplied). The truth is more complex. Nigel Lowe has shown that, while in the early part of the last century adoption was largely used to legitimise existing (private) arrangements (de facto adoptions), in the first two decades after the Second World War, adoption was overwhelmingly used as a means for the voluntary placement of (illegitimate) babies. At all times, adoption of children out of public care was rare. (See Lowe, 2000, an outstanding review of adoption law and policy over the twentieth century.)

[20] *2000 White Paper*, para 1.13.

set a target of **increasing by 40%** by 2004–05 the number of looked after children adopted, by improving councils' practices on adoption, and aim to exceed this by achieving, if possible, a 50% increase.[21]

So in 2000 the overwhelming concern of policy regarding adoption was directed at children who were already in public care. The desirability of moving such children into adoption is no longer hedged by such expressions as 'where suitable', but is promoted as an end in itself. To reach such a firm direction, policy makers must have been convinced, both, that the current situation was in some way detrimental, and also that the new policy would achieve improvements. Since the justifications are given in terms of the children's interests, I will proceed on the assumption that the perceived detriments and improvements are of the children concerned, rather than, say, the adults or the state. Of course, detriments and benefits are largely two sides of the same coin. But for analysis it is convenient to separate them.

(a) Perceived Wrongs of the Current Position

The period immediately prior to the commissioning of the review by the PIU saw an increase in public criticism of the use by local authorities of adoption as a way of dealing with looked after children. So, on 4 March 1999 the press published 'league tables' giving relative percentages of children adopted out of state care between local authorities in an attempt to 'shame' those with 'poor' records;[22] and the following year (after the review was commissioned) it was reported that Members of Parliament were demanding 'hit squads' to take over adoption services which were not placing a sufficient number of children for adoption.[23] There were allegations that social workers were rejecting applicants out of 'political correctness', for example, by refusing transracial placements or placements with smokers. Perhaps because no evidence of this emerged,[24] the Government characterised the problem largely in procedural terms. Shortfalls in adoptions were seen primarily as systems failures, both within Social Services departments and in the legal process. 'The Government wants to change this,' says the White Paper, 'and will overhaul the adoption process so that it makes more sense, moves more quickly and delivers for children the outcome they want: a new family.'[25]

What was the evidence that systems failures were impeding adoption? The first question to ask is whether there exists a pool of 'adoptable' children who

---

[21] *2000 White Paper*, p 5. Bold type in original.

[22] See *The Independent*, 4 March 1999.

[23] See *The Independent*, 13 April 2000.

[24] *PIU Report*, para 3.33; *2000 White Paper*, para 2.16. This did not prevent the Secretary of State for Health, when re-introducing the Bill, from asserting that the main problem was to change the 'culture' prevalent in social services: Hansard, 29 October 2001, col. 649.

[25] *2000 White Paper*, para 1.18.

were not being adopted, or who were being adopted too slowly, and, if so, how big the pool is. June Thoburn, who reviewed the research literature for the government review of 1992 (Department of Health and Welsh Office, 1992, Appendix C), thought it was very small. She refers to the assessment that only around six per cent of children who came into care in Millham's 1986 sample (Millham, Bullock, Hosie *et al*, 1986) 'could possibly be candidates for adoption by non-relatives' (Department of Health and Welsh Office, 1992, p.136). She added that two overviews (Parker, 1980; Social Services Committee, 1984) had expressed concern that adoption might be being used 'inappropriately'. In the 1990s the percentage of such children who were adopted clustered around four per cent.[26] The main reason is that most children coming into public care are expected to return to their natural families. Hence it is immediately obvious that we are dealing with what *Messages 1999* referred to as a 'minor activity' taking place 'at the margins of the local authority's child care services'.[27]

If this is correct, there seems to be relatively little room for manoeuvre. But the *PIU Report* claimed that there was scope for greater use of adoption. This was based on three factors:[28] information on the 'stock' of children spending a long time (understood as meaning over two years) in care; evidence of the 'effectiveness' of adoption and 'the variable level of local authority performance' (between one and 14 per cent of looked after children being adopted). I will return to the issue of 'effectiveness', because that concerns benefits. The other two factors seem to tell us little, for merely giving the crude figures of the totality of children being looked after and the length of time this happens does not address the issue of the circumstances or of the merits of fostering as opposed to adoption. The mere fact of variability between local authorities of course raises questions, but could equally suggest that adoption is used *too much* by some authorities as that it is too little by others. A study published after the *PIU Report* and the *2000 White Paper* (Lowe and Murch, 2002) designed to discover the reasons for such variations was disappointingly unable to come up with convincing explanations: the most likely cause seemed to be that some had some unstated policy favouring adoption while others did not.[29] But that does not mean that high use of adoption rather than long-term fostering was *necessarily* better for the children. The *PIU Report* noted that the rate of adoption from public care varied extensively between twelve selected countries, from 6.6 per cent in the United States to 0.2 per cent in Sweden (it is almost unknown in the Netherlands, and below 1 per cent in 8 countries, including New Zealand and Australia). The rate in England and Wales (4 per cent) is high by international standards.[30] Can it be assumed that low rates necessarily serve children

---

[26] *Messages 1999*, pp 96–7; *PIU Report*, para 3.1.
[27] *Messages 1999*, pp 97 and 109.
[28] *PIU Report*, para 3.3.
[29] It is possible that availability of resources played a part, for these also varied widely between authorities.
[30] *PIU Report*, Annex 4.

worse? In the United States large numbers of children have had the legal ties with their birth families broken without later adoption occurring (Cashmore, 2001). This seems a flimsy basis on which to set targets for a 40–50 per cent increase in adoptions of these children. In any event, the numbers of such children adopted are rising slowly: in 1998/9, 2,200 children were adopted from a total of 55,300 looked after children, a small rise on the previous year, and in the same year 2,900 children were placed for adoption.[31]

What, then, about problems of delay? The evidence showed that the average time a child was looked after *before a decision was made* that adoption was in the child's best interests was one year and four months, varying significantly according to the child's age from nine months for children under one month old to nearly two years for children aged over six months.[32] It takes an average of one year and nine months from that decision to the making of an adoption order, with older children taking longer.[33] But since the child has to have lived with prospective adopters for twelve months before the adoption can be made,[34] this should not be looked upon only as a 'delay'.[35] The main problem, if problem there be, seems to be in the time taken to reach a decision about adoption (one year and four months), and the time (average 6 months) from that decision to finding a match. In an effort to speed up the former, the *PIU Report* observes that:

> once a child has been admitted into local authority care the focus can too often tend to be exclusively on rehabilitation with the birth family. This is clearly the most desirable outcome but, if it turns out not to be achievable, a permanent home for the child may be delayed if contingency plans, including options for placement with extended family and for adoption or planned long-term fostering have not been considered.[36]

The Report concedes that restraints upon the vigorous pursuit of the adoption alternative do not arise from an anti-adoption culture, but instead result from the fact that social workers and their managers:

> are (properly) highly committed to working to reunite children with their birth parents and the structures and procedures are not in place to ensure that they think more widely than that.[37]

This is not surprising given the strong winds blowing from the courts, especially since the Human Rights Act 1998, proclaiming that intervention must be 'proportionate' and, as Hale LJ put it,

---

[31] *PIU Report*, para 2.4–5.
[32] *PIU Report*, para 3.22.
[33] *PIU Report*, para 3.49.
[34] Adoption Act 1976, s 13(2).
[35] Lowe and Murch (2002), at p 4, draw a distinction between 'purposeful' and 'detrimental' delay.
[36] *PIU Report*, para 3.27.
[37] *PIU Report*, para 3.33.

the principle has to be that the local authority works to support, and eventually to re-unite, the family, unless the risks are so high that the child requires alternative family care.[38]

The Government has however taken up the cause of reducing timescales, setting them out in new National Standards, which require (in general) a plan for 'permanence' (which might include return home or adoption) to be made before a child has been continuously looked after for four months.[39]

This chapter does not attempt to evaluate the effects of such management devices, which include more active judicial case management.[40] No institution or practice can claim to be without the need for improvement. But institutional changes seldom come without some costs, either directly financially, or in other ways, including costs or time-savings elsewhere in the system. The calculation as to overall benefits and detriments must therefore include a judgement about the extent of the problem and the extent to which the changes address it. So we start with the fact that the overwhelming majority of looked after children return home, 70 per cent within a year.[41] It is therefore hardly surprising that local authorities will work on the assumption that the child will, eventually, return home. The devotion of large amounts of resources to the low risk that the child will not return home may jeopardise work on actually returning children. And we have seen that the scope for increasing the numbers of children adopted is problematic. Although the *PIU Report* thought there was 'scope for improvement', that report itself did not feel confident enough to recommend a 'precise target' for adoptions of looked after children.[42] The government, however, has set targets of 40–50 per cent increase. This is despite the fact that the *PIU Report* noted that the needs of looked after children were becoming more challenging (for example, those being looked after as a result of abuse or neglect, or on care orders, have been rising).[43] Even so, the numbers of children potentially involved remain small, about 1,000 a year (ie about 40 per cent of the 2,900 children per year now currently adopted out of care).

(b) Perceived Benefits of Adoption

But it may be that the advantages of adoption over the alternatives are so great that they justify significant resources to be devoted, switched or created to achieve it for this relatively small number of children who would otherwise not

---

[38] *Re C & B* [2001] 1 FLR 611.
[39] Department of Health (2001), A. Children, para 2 (a): 'Whenever plans for permanence are being considered, they will be made on the basis of the needs of each looked after child, and within the following timescales: (a) The child's need for a permanent home will be addressed at the four month review and a plan for permanence made;'
[40] Adoption and Children Act 2002, s 109.
[41] *2000 White Paper*, para 2.1.
[42] *PIU Report*, Annex 7.
[43] *PIU Report*, Annex 5.

be adopted. Was there, then, convincing evidence about this which accounts for the dramatic change in approach between 1993 and 2000?

The government in 1993 had the benefit of a thorough review of the research evidence then available undertaken by June Thoburn for the Interdepartmental Working Group (Department of Health and Welsh Office, 1992, Appendix C). The picture which emerges of the effectiveness of adoption is difficult to evaluate, partly because 'success' is often expressed in terms of 'breakdown' rates. But a child's well-being is not represented only through that measure. On the favourable side are the following statements:

> . . . American studies show clearly that breakdown rates are lower if a child and foster family, even if their relationship started off as temporary, become so attached that an application to adopt seems appropriate.

> Hill and Triseliotis (1989) reported that long-term foster children who were subsequently adopted said that they much preferred their adoptive status.

The conclusions to be drawn from this are limited. They say little more than that when adoption is appropriate (that is the relationships are already good), it may give value added. Against them must be put the following:

> However, Macaskill (1985), in a small-scale study of some especially difficult placements . . . found that adoption did not solve the problems, and in some cases made them worse.

> Borgman (1981) considers the impact of involuntary adoption on 29 older abused and neglected children, and concludes that adoption against parental wishes and without parental contact was a high risk enterprise. Morris (1984) also counsels caution and suggests that some social workers do not listen adequately to the reservations of the children themselves.

These last references advert specifically to children of the kind which are likely to be candidates for adoption if the targeted expansion occurs.

Did the research on which the *PIU Report* was able to draw present any different picture? Among the studies which were available to it was a set summarised by Roy Parker and an advisory group referred to earlier as *Messages 1999*. The report developed a theme also evident in Thoburn's review that the younger the child when adopted, the less likelihood was there for a poor outcome and that special risks had to be confronted when considering adoption for older children who had been in care for longer periods. These risks include not only risks for the child (disruption; the child's needs not being met and his problems exacerbated) but

> there is evidence that others in the adoptive family may be exposed to a variety of risks. The parents may risk long periods of stress, frustration or despair. Other children in the family may be put at risk of unhappiness or in some cases, abuse. They may feel that they risk the loss of their parents' attention or affection. The family as a whole may risk turbulence, upheaval and discord.[44]

[44] *Messages 1999*, p 18.

Messages 1999 reports that studies which had mixed samples of adopted and fostered children found no significant differences in outcomes.[45] Drawing on this, and some other, research, the *PIU Report* concluded that:

> there is no clear evidence of a difference in the rates of disruption between adoption and long term fostering, once the differing age of the children is taken into account.

But it does refer to 'some indications' from qualitative studies (in particular, Triseliotis, Shireman and Hundleby, 1997: 111) that:

> children generally prefer the sense of security that adoption gives them over long term foster placements, even if these are intended to be permanent

But the report also noted the

> presence of a group of children, mainly older, in need of permanent placement, but who do not wish to make the absolute legal break with their birth family associated with adoption.[46]

So we find that the research evidence is unable to detect any significant advantages to adoption over long-term fostering. There is evidence that some children prefer it, but against that should be placed the clear statement of risks, not only to the child, but also to the adoptive family set out in *Messages 1999*. None of this, however, stood in the way of the breezy optimism of the *2000 White Paper* which proclaims:

> Research shows that children who are adopted when they are over six months old generally make very good progress through their childhood and into adulthood and do considerably better than children who have remained in the care system throughout most of their childhood.[47]

This is a reference to a sentence by David Howe which reads:

> . . . their (i.e. children adopted over six months) overall levels of adjustment are much better than those of children who remain in institutional settings and children who have been returned to and raised by their disadvantaged birth families. (Howe, 1998: 86)

This of course does not compare children who are adopted with those who are fostered.

4. THE SPECIFIC CHALLENGES TO ADOPTION

The *PIU Report* revealed that 'the looked after population is becoming younger.'[48] The average age fell from 11 years 3 months in 1994 to 10 years 4 months in 1999. So while, in 1994, 63 per cent of looked after children were aged

---

[45] *Messages 1999*, p 125.
[46] *PIU Report*, paras. 2.16–17.
[47] *2000 White Paper*, para 1.12.
[48] *PIU Report*, Annex 5.

over 10, and 14 per cent were under four, in 1999 56 per cent were over 10 and 21 per cent were under four. At the same time the age of looked after children who were adopted also fell. In 1995, 40 per cent were between one and four and 15 per cent between 10 and 15. In 1999, 57 per cent were between one and four and only 7 per cent from 10 to 15.[49] Surprisingly, these trends were not followed up in the *2000 White Paper*, but they are important because the studies show clearly that the 'success' of adoption of younger children (and in particular, those placed under the age of 10) is higher than for older children (Howe, 1998, ch 5; Triseliotis, Shireman and Hundleby, 1997: 27–33). So it is possible that, if the age of 'looked after' children falls, the increased push towards adoption will be exerted with respect to children under, say, four, rather than for older children. Indeed, Lowe and Murch (2002) found that age was a key factor in the likelihood that an adoption plan would be made: the younger the child, the more likely adoption was to be chosen. This has advantages in terms of likely success of the placement, but, since such children are less likely to maintain contact with their birth families, it increases the risk of parents having the relationship with their child completely severed. This risk is enhanced by the desire to reach rapid decisions, when birth parents can come to be seen as a nuisance, and to speed up processes.

The first challenge then is to overcome obstacles without prejudicing the position of parents unfairly. The second challenge lies in the fact that the pressure towards more adoption will be felt also for older children. Here the distinction between adoption and long-term fostering may not be so clear. Contact with the birth family is likely to continue, and Lowe and Murch (2002) found that this factor was a key determinant for fostering to be chosen over adoption. If it is wished to change this pattern, the challenge will be to ensure that adoption is used only in appropriate cases, and that the institution, originally designed for babies and very young children, operates in an appropriate way for these older children.

(a) The First Challenge: Younger Children and Parents

Some alarm had been expressed (see for example, Barton, 2001) that the statement in the *2000 White Paper* of an intention to align the adoption legislation with the Children Act 1989[50] could lead to children being forcibly removed from their parents simply on a judgement that this was in the children's best interests. There were good reasons for this concern. Under the previous government's Draft Adoption Bill it would have been possible for an adoption agency to place a child for adoption either with the parents' consent or, under a placement order, without it if the court were to be satisfied that the consent should be

---

[49] Figures taken from the bar chart at Figure 2.3, *PIU Report*, p 13.
[50] *2000 White Paper*, pp. 5, 16.

dispensed with. Such dispensation could occur if 'the court is satisfied that the welfare of the child requires the consent to be dispensed with.' (Department of Health and Welsh Office, 1996, Draft Bill, clauses 23 and 46). Far from being consistent with the 1989 Act, this appeared to allow an authority to by-pass the policy which requires all non-voluntary state intervention into the parent-child relationship to enter via the 'gateway' which requires the establishment of significant harm or its likelihood.[51] There is, however, no such cause for alarm this time. The new provisions stipulate that a court may only make a placement order if the child is already subject to a care order (and thus the 'gateway' has been passed), or if the court is satisfied that the conditions set out in the 'gateway' are met.[52] Only then may the court dispense with the parents' consent if it is not freely given.[53] Since the effect of the order is to authorise the local authority to place a child for adoption 'with any prospective adopters who may be chosen by the authority', and to terminate contact with the birth parents, and the parents may only intervene later to object to the adoption if there is a subsequent change in circumstances,[54] this provision allows a court to make a disposal in favour of adoption at the same time as it finds the grounds for making a care order are established. This will facilitate decisions about adoption to be made at a very early stage in the intervention.[55] It is, however, difficult to see this working except in rare and extreme cases. This is because of the imperative under both human rights law[56] and current policy that the presumption must be to work to rehabilitation of the child in the family. Although agencies are urged to develop contingency plans for permanent placement while attempting rehabilitation, it may be difficult to make efforts at rehabilitation look convincing once the agency has obtained a placement order.

It will be particularly difficult to know what to do about contact in such cases. Where a placement order is made, the new Act removes the presumption of the Children Act 1989[57] that a child looked after under a care order should remain in contact with its birth parents. Instead, the court is permitted to regulate contact.[58] But what should it do? In *K & T v Finland*,[59] the authorities had ruled

---

[51] Children Act 1989, s 31.

[52] Adoption and Children Act 2002, s 21(2). See Special Standing Committee, 20 November 2001, Memorandum from Department of Health, paras 14–16.

[53] Consent may be dispensed with only if the parent cannot be found or is incapable of giving it, or if 'the welfare of the child requires the consent to be dispensed with' (s 52(1)(b)). The child's welfare is 'paramount' s 1(2)). These provisions are unlikely to affect the pre-existing test, [whether the advantages to the child of adoption are sufficient to justify such dispensation (*re F* [2000] 2 FLR 505)], which conforms to the proportionality requirement of the Human Rights Act 1998.

[54] Adoption and Children Act 2002, s 21(1), 24 and 47(7).

[55] Indeed, if adoption forms part of the care plan for the child, the authority *must* apply for a placement order: Adoption and Children Act 2002, ss 22(2).

[56] See especially the decision of the Grand Chamber of the European Court of Human Rights in *K & T v Finland* [2001] 2 FLR 707.

[57] Children Act 1989, s 34

[58] Adoption and Children Act 2002, ss 26 & 27.

[59] Above n 56.

out rehabilitation, and therefore allowed only very restricted contact. The Grand Chamber saw these restrictions as part of the failure of any 'serious effort towards reunification':

> The possibilities of reunification will be progressively diminished and eventually destroyed if the biological parents and the children are not allowed to meet each other at all, or only so rarely that no natural bonding between them is likely to occur.[60]

Possibly contact could be maintained despite the placement order, so as to avoid criticism that reunification has been ruled out prematurely, but terminated later if rehabilitation fails. But this retains the suspicion that a decision in favour of adoption has already been reached (see Jolly, 1994). Furthermore, the child could hardly be placed with prospective adopters because it would be neither feasible nor fair to expect them to co-operate with the attempts at rehabilitation. So the child would need to go to temporary fostercarers, despite the placement order, until rehabilitation had been ruled out. There is another possible approach. Where it is felt that the chances of rehabilitation are very slim, the agency might forego attempting it and proceed rapidly to adoption through a placement order, but accept that contact should continue despite the adoption. In other words, the plan from the start is for adoption, but an open adoption. This might satisfy the human rights demands that the intervention be proportionate, for the parents will not have been potentially deprived of any relationship with the child. There is some evidence (reported by Elsbeth Neil, this volume, see also Lindley, 1997 citing some examples from research by Fratter and Ryburn and Smith and Logan, 2002) that adoption can succeed despite the continuation of contact with the birth parents, even if they are initially opposed to the adoption, and even in the case of young children. Smith and Logan (2002) suggest that adoption can even make contact easier, because the adoptive parents feel more in control. This important observation may well have force *over time*, but it may be difficult to find adoptive parents who are willing to accept young children who from the outset are maintaining contact with their birth parents, and especially if the birth parents oppose the adoption. (Lowe and Murch, 2002: 62–64).

It therefore seems probable that agencies will apply for placement orders at some time after a care order has been made. The National Adoption Standards for England (Department of Health, 2001, A. Children. Para.2 (a)) state that a child's need for a permanent home will be addressed at the four month review 'and a plan for permanence made'. If adoption is the option, an application for a placement order might be made at this stage and contact regulated or denied accordingly. This has a better chance of satisfying the requirement of showing that strenuous efforts at rehabilitation had been made prior to this decision. Nevertheless, it may be doubted whether assessment of the viability of returning the child will always be possible within pre-set timescales.

---

[60] At para 179.

(b) The Second Challenge: Older Children

Contact is also a difficult issue in the case of older children, though for a differ-ent reason. It is less likely to revolve around the question of rehabilitation, for in these cases the children may already have been living away from their birth family for some time. The question is rather, given that rehabilitation is unlikely, or even ruled out, whether contact should continue if adoption is pur-sued as the framework for permanent placement. Smith and Logan (2002) rely on Grotevant and McRoy's (1998) US research in concluding that the evidence demonstrates neither harm nor benefits from 'openness' in adoption, but that study was confined to children adopted under the age of one, and who were under 12 at the time of assessment. The evidence regarding older children is summarised by Triseliotis, Shireman and Hundleby (1997) in this way:

> From the research evidence available, it appears that provided the parties involved can handle the situation in a constructive and positive manner without acrimony and recriminations, there is no reason why contact should be harmful to the child. On the contrary, the maintenance of existing meaningful links, especially for the older adopted child, appears to be beneficial to children, to their sense of identity and self-esteem and for gaining a better understanding of their genealogical background and adoption circumstances. In effect, contact has to be seen as being of value to the child and not introduced in order to create a parent-child relationship that was not there before . . . The research studies support a cautious move towards semi-openness until more is known. This cautious approach will also be reflected in the new English adop-tion legislation.

Howe (1998) is rather more positive, pointing out that the studies show that maintaining contact, especially in the case of late-placed children, 'generally appears to be a good thing', and that when contact is not allowed, 'problematic behaviour and adoption breakdowns are more likely.' (Much of the evidence is discussed by Lindley, 1997.) Neil (this volume) is rather more cautious, recog-nising that, while contact may improve adopted children's well-being, many other factors can affect outcomes.

The *PIU Report* recommended that provisions for contact should form part of local authorities' post-adoption support duties, and also that guidance on the issue might be provided in the National Standards.[61] The National Adoption Standards in fact offer very little guidance about contact beyond saying that the child's

> wishes and feelings, and their welfare and safety are the most important concerns when considering links or contact with birth parents, wider birth family members and other people who are significant to them

and that such people should be involved in discussions on the issue. The Adoption and Children Act 2002 is generally silent on the issue, so the legal

[61] *PIU Report*, p 61.

framework for providing for contact will remain section 8 of the Children Act 1989. There are, however, new provisions for judicial regulation of contact in the case of placement orders (discussed above) and special guardianship (discussed below).

On the basis of the research evidence, it seems improbable that an adoption can be successful if contact is maintained in a conflictual situation. So, if the adoptive parents object to the contact, or the birth parents object to the adoption, contact is likely to be harmful. The solution could be either to maintain contact and eschew adoption, or pursue adoption and prevent contact. As explained earlier, the judicial solution has been to favour adoption over contact in cases where the adoptive parents have objected to contact. The real question should be whether contact is desirable for the child, not whether it would make adoption unworkable. For even if adoption and contact can co-exist, as Neil (this volume) and Smith and Logan (2002) indicate they can, when it is decided in a particular case that they are incompatible, then it is adoption which should be set aside, not contact.

It is presumably with problems such as these in mind that the 2002 Act creates the institution of Special Guardianship. The *PIU Report* had suggested following up the idea of creating an 'intermediate legal status', which would provide greater security than long-term fostering (by, for example, removing the degree of social services supervision) without the full status of adoption.[62] The *2000 White Paper* took this up, referring to cases where children might not wish to be legally separated from their birth parents, or where the adults looking after them are members of the wider birth family, or where there were religious or cultural objections to adoption.[63] No doubt these are all types of situation where adoption would be inappropriate, or difficult. But so might be cases where contact is desirable, but could not be sustained well in an adoption context. It is interesting that the new provisions for Special Guardianship expressly require the court, before making a Special Guardianship order, to 'consider whether, if the order were made, a contact order should also be made with respect to the child.'[64] There is no equivalent provision regarding the making of an adoption order. A Special Guardianship order can, effectively, be made in favour of anyone who could apply for a section 8 order under the Children Act 1989. The effect is very similar to a Residence Order, except that:

1. The special guardian is entitled to exercise parental responsibility 'to the exclusion of any other person with parental responsibility for the child (apart from another special guardian)'. But whether this gives the special guardian greater power than someone with a Residence Order is unclear because it is subject to 'the operation of any enactment *or rule of law* which requires the consent of more than one person with parental responsibility in a matter

---

[62] *PIU Report*, paras 8.5–7.
[63] *2000 White Paper*, para 5.8.
[64] Adoption and Children Act 2002, s 115 (inserting s 14B into the Children Act 1989).

affecting the child'.[65] It is possible that judicial decisions suggesting that all persons with parental responsibility have a right to be consulted on significant issues concerning the child constitute such a rule of law (see Eekelaar, 2001).

2. A parent may apply to vary a Special Guardianship order only with leave of the court, and this may only be given if there has been a 'significant change in circumstances' since making the order, and in any event not before a year after making the order.[66]

These provisions are almost identical to those of the Children Act 1975, where the orders were called 'custodianship orders' and the beneficiary, perhaps unfortunately, the child's 'custodian'.[67] Those provisions, though little used, were abolished by the Children Act 1989 shortly after their implementation. It seems to have been the intention to replace them with 'custody orders' to be attached to supervision orders unless the court thought this was unnecessary (Department of Health and Social Security, 1987, para 63). In the event, this was not done, probably because it was thought that anyone in whose favour a supervision order was made could, if they so wished, apply for one of the new section 8 orders, probably a residence order. But that lost the idea, advocated by the Curtis Committee as long ago as 1946 (Committee on the Care of Children, 1946, para 425, seeking a means to make possible a stable relationship short of adoption between a foster-parent and a child), and re-iterated by the Houghton Committee in 1972 (Departmental Committee on the Adoption of Children, 1972, ch.6) that a means of securing the de facto position of the child should be available without necessarily moving the child legally from one family to another.

5. CONCLUSIONS

This chapter has sought to examine the evidence given and arguments used for the significant pressure to increase the use of adoption as an instrument of child care policy. It has suggested that they do not, in themselves, provide a compelling case. One perhaps needs, therefore, to look to other factors for an explanation. For example, ideological pressure groups, like the Institute of Economic Affairs (see Morgan, 1998), and the influence of American policy, may have played a role. That is a matter for another paper. This one is concerned with the immediate impact of present policies. It is perhaps unfortunate that legal outcomes in this area come in packages, for these distract attention

---

[65] Children Act 1989, s 14C(1)(b) & (2)(a). A person with a residence order may also exercise parental responsibility by acting 'alone and without the other (or others) [who also hold parental responsibility]'. But this has been restrictively interpreted.

[66] Children Act 1989, s 14F.

[67] Children Act 1975, ss 33–35.

from the reality of relationships towards legal incidents of the packages. It is interesting to observe that older adopted children, who maintain contact with their birth families, are capable of seeing themselves as belonging to two sets of families at the same time, their birth parents being seen as a kind of 'extended' family like an aunt or uncle (Triseliotis, Shireman and Hundleby, 1997: 6). Yet this does not correspond to the legal situation which moves them from one family to another, severing legal ties not only with the parents but with siblings and grandparents. Section 1(4) of the 2002 Act expressly requires courts, when making decisions pertaining to adoption, to take into account the likely effect on a child 'throughout his life . . . having ceased to be a member of the original family'. Although some might argue that this does not matter, it seems undesirable that there should be disjuncture between reality and the legalities. For example, why should the child lose succession rights within its family of origin in such circumstances? Furthermore, there is a danger that pressure to opt for the adoption route by obtaining a placement order at an early stage could leave children having legal ties with their birth family broken without the benefit of later adoption. These criticisms were a major factor behind the abandonment in 2001 of an initiative very similar to (and indeed influenced by) the policy described here in New South Wales (see Parkinson, 2002).

In these types of case, two things should be fixed points: stability (Lowe and Murch, 2002: 7, favour this term over 'permanence') of the child's residence with the current carers and (subject to the child's welfare and particularly for older adopted children) continued contact of some kind with the birth family. At some point independence from local authority surveillance and control also becomes an issue. But this and other matters should be the subject of negotiation, as, indeed, was found to be the case in *Messages 1999*. In the case of younger children, then, the dilemma over contact revolves around the problem of how to achieve stability for a child while at the same time making the efforts needed to reunite the child with the birth parents. It is a problem which is aggravated by the early use of adoption, or authorisation of placement for adoption, as the mechanism for achieving permanent placement outside the home.

One could imagine a very different legal scenario for dealing with this group of children (against the wishes of the parents). This would run as follows:

1. On establishing grounds for intervention, the court makes a care order *transferring*[68] parental rights to the local authority. The authority is under a duty to pursue rehabilitation and to take such steps as necessary to do this. The child may be placed with foster carers on an interim basis.
2. On successful rehabilitation the care order is discharged.

---

[68] This would avoid the difficulties caused by the present law under which the parents share parental responsibility with the local authority, raising a potential human rights issue if the authority (as it may do) restricts the exercise of parental rights without legal process: *Re S (minor) (Care Order: Implementation of Care Plan); Re W (minors) (Care Order: Adequacy of Care Plan)* [2002] 1 FLR 815, para 76.

3. A decision to abandon rehabilitation and opt for permanence elsewhere is made at the discretion of the authority. When made, the child is moved to long-term carers. This may or may not involve terminating contact. No additional legal authority is needed to achieve this.
4. The matter is reviewed by the court if the care order is still in place after a year.
5. The question of adoption of the child, or some alternative, by the long-term carers is dealt with on a case by case basis, at the time of the year-end review, outside the pressures of the initial decision-making, but subject to the judicial review one year from that date.

On 20 March 2002 the Health Minister, Jacqui Smith, announced a major review of fostering and placement choice for looked after children and a better framework of reward and support for foster carers. This is welcome because, in the case of older children, where permanence is secured, but contact continued, the question of adoption should be a matter for negotiation in each case. *Messages 1999*[69] observed that, from the carers' point of view,

> an important difference [between adoption and fostering] . . . seems to lie in the degree to which the carers [who have adopted] feel (and are considered by others to be) *wholly* responsible for the child's behaviour or education, for their successes or shortcomings.

Foster carers saw their responsibility as shared with the authority, in contrast to adopters, who felt they had real control over the child. As Smith and Logan (2002) point out, this should not necessarily be viewed as undesirable: after all, good parents want to accept full responsibility for their child. So adoption could be the right solution. But it has to be balanced against all the factors, and a solution reached by agreement if possible. It would be unfortunate if the desire of local authorities to meet adoption targets set by central planners as a result of political pressures disposes them against other outcomes which might be more appropriate for individual children. But the signs are hopeful that a more balanced approach might emerge.[70]

REFERENCES

Barton, J, 'Adoption Strategy' (2001) 31 *Family Law* 89.
Borgman, R, 'Antecedents and Consequences of Parental Rights Termination for Abused and Neglected Children' (1981) 60 *Child Welfare* 391.
Cashmore, J, 'What Can we Learn from the US Experience on Permanency Planning' (2001) 15 *Australian Journal of Family Law* 215.
Committee on the Care of Children, *Curtis Report*. Cmnd 6922 (London, HMSO, 1946).

---

[69] Pp 125–6.
[70] As indeed occurred in New South Wales when the original strongly pro-adoption Bill was withdrawn in 2001 and substituted by a more balanced one: Parkinson (2002).

Department of Health, *Adoption Now: Messages from Research* (London, John Wiley, 1999).

——*Adoption—A New Approach: A White Paper*. Cm 5017 (London, The Stationery Office, December 2000).

——*National Adoption Standards for England* (Department of Health, August 2001).

Department of Health and Social Security, Home Office, Lord Chancellor's Department, Department of Education and Science, Welsh office, Scottish Office, *The Law on Child Care and Family Services*. Cm 62 (London, HMSO, 1987).

Department of Health and Welsh Office, *Report to Ministers of an Interdepartmental Working Group, Review of Adoption Law* (London, Department of Health and Welsh Office, October 1992).

——*Adoption—A Service for Children*. Draft Bill (Department of Health and Welsh Office, March 1996).

Department of Health, Welsh Office, Home Office, Lord Chancellor's Department, *Adoption: The Future*. Cm 2288 (London, HMSO, November 1993).

Departmental Committee on the Adoption of Children, *Houghton Report*. Cmnd 5107 (London, HMSO, 1972).

EEKELAAR, J, 'Re-thinking Parental Responsibility' (2001) 31 *Family Law* 426.

——'Contact—Over the Limit' (2002) 32 *Family Law* 271.

GROTEVANT, HD and McROY, RG, *Openness in Adoption: Exploring Family Connections* (London, Sage, 1998).

HASKEY, J, 'Adoptees and Relatives who wish to Contact one Another using the Adoption Contact Register: Trends, Relationships and Proportions of Records Matched' (2001) 106 *Population Trends* 15.

HILL, M and TRISELIOTIS, J, 'The Transition from Long-Term Care to Adoption' in J Hudson and B Galloway (eds), *The State as Parent* (The Hague, Kluwer, 1989).

HOWE, D, *Patterns of Adoption* (Oxford, Blackwell, 1998).

JOLLY, S, 'Cutting the Ties—the Termination of Contact in Care' (1994) *Journal of Social Welfare and Family Law* 299.

LINDLEY, B, 'Open Adoption—Is the Door Ajar?' (1997) 9 *Child & Family Law Quarterly* 115.

LOWE, NV, 'English Adoption Law: Past, Present, and Future' in SN Katz, J Eekelaar and M Maclean (eds), *Cross Currents: Family Law and Policy in the US and England* (Oxford, Oxford University Press, 2000).

LOWE, N, MURCH, M, BORKOWSKI, M, WEAVER, A, BECKFORD, V with THOMAS, C, *Supporting Adoption: Reframing the Approach* (London, British Agencies for Adoption and Fostering, 1999).

LOWE, N and MURCH, M, *The Plan for the Child: Adoption or Long Term Fostering?* (London, British Agencies for Adoption and Fostering, 2002).

MACASKILL, C, *Against the odds: Adopting mentally handicapped children* (London, British Agencies for Adoption and Fostering, 1985).

MILLHAM, S, BULLOCK, R, HOSIE, K and HAAK, M, *Lost in Care* (Aldershot, Gower, 1986).

MORRIS, C, *The Permanency Principle in Child Care Social Work* (Norwich, University of East Anglia, 1984).

MORGAN, P, *Adoption and the Care of Children* (London, Institute for Economic Affairs, 1998).

PARKER, RA, *Caring for Separated Children* (London, Macmillan, 1980).

Performance and Innovation Unit, *Prime Minister's Review: Adoption: Issued for Consultation* (London, Cabinet Office, July 2000).

PARKINSON, P, 'Child Protection, Permanency Planning and Children's Rights to Family Life' (2003) 17 *International Journal of Law, Policy and the Family* 147.

SMITH, C and LOGAN, J, 'Adoptive Parenthood as a "Legal Fiction"—Its Consequences for Direct Post-Adoption Contact' (2002) 14 *Child and Family Law Quarterly* 281.

Social Services Committee, *Children in Care*. Short Report, HC 36 (London, HMSO, 1984).

TRISELIOTIS, J, SHIREMAN, J and HUNDLEBY, M, *Adoption: Theory, Policy and Practice* (London, Cassell, 1997).

14

Adoption and Contact:
A Research Review

1. INTRODUCTION

IN ENGLAND AND Wales over 3,000 children a year are currently being adopted outside of their family of origin, and government policy is to achieve a 40 per cent increase in this figure by 2004 (see Eekelaar, this volume). The vast majority of these children will have been in the care system and most are adopted under the age of five (Department of Health, 2001). Since the first Adoption Act in 1926, adoption has been used in different ways, for different types of children and with varying levels of openness (Triseliotis *et al*, 1997). In the earlier part of this century adoption was largely perceived as a means of providing care for children in need but after World War II the focus switched to providing babies for childless couples. This came to be known as 'the era of the "perfect baby" for the "perfect couple"' (Triseliotis *et al*, 1997 p 7). Children were only considered to be 'adoptable' if they were young babies, white, developmentally normal and from an 'acceptable' background. The rise in the birth of children to unmarried women, brought about by changing sexual mores, meant that during the 1960s and 70s, when the social disincentives against rearing a child outside of marriage were still high, many such babies were available for adoption. The numbers of children adopted peaked in 1968 when 24,831 were adopted in England and Wales. Excluding stepparent adoptions, almost all of these children were adopted as babies (General Register Office, 1970). Secrecy was seen as necessary in order to protect all parties from the stigma of illegitimacy and to protect the adoptive family from interference by the birth family (Home Office, 1972). Following the Adoption of Children Act in 1949 the identity of adopters could be concealed from birth parents. Adopted adults could not access information enabling them to identify their birth parents, adopters were told very little about the child's background and all contact ceased once the child was placed. It has been argued that closed practices in family placement followed on from the Poor Law tradition of viewing the birth families of illegitimate and destitute children as a bad influence (Millham *et al*, 1986; Triseliotis *et al*, 1997).

During the 1980s changes in social attitudes towards single mothers, together with the greater availability of birth control methods, resulted in far fewer babies being available for adoption. The plight of children in care had been highlighted by research such as that of Rowe and Lambert (1973) and social workers began to widen considerably their view of which children could benefit from adoption. The model of adoption moved again towards it being seen as a means of providing homes for children needing families. Today, not only are far fewer children being adopted than in the past, but their backgrounds and needs are very different. Ivaldi (2000) undertook a comprehensive analysis of local authority adoptions in 1998–9. This study of 1,801 children found that four in 10 had initially been taken into care because of abuse or neglect. The mean age at which the children were placed with their adopters was just over three years, indicating that adoption is most commonly used for children at the younger end of the 'in care' age range. Seventeen percent of the children had developmental delay and/or learning difficulties and 18 per cent were described as presenting hereditary risks, eg having a parent with schizophrenia. Ten percent of the children were of minority ethnicity, most of these being children of mixed parentage. Although children adopted from care rarely fit the profile of a healthy baby that most adopters would desire, it is still the case that adoption continues to provide a service to adults wishing to become parents. The majority (about three-quarters) of adoptive parents are childless couples seeking to start a family (Ivaldi, 2000; Neil, 2000a).

These changes in the types of children being adopted has, in part, led to a more open approach: children placed at older ages bring with them family loyalties and memories and many are reluctant to make a clean break. Moves towards more openness in adoption have also been driven by concerns about the longer-term difficulties of a closed system. Research focusing on the perspectives of adult adopted people highlighted the difficulty some adopted people had in establishing a coherent sense of identity without information about where they came from (Triseliotis, 1973; Haimes and Timms, 1985). Many adopted people reported that their parents were reluctant to share with them even what little background information they did have. An atmosphere of secrecy stifled discussion of adoption related issues in some families, leaving the adopted person with the impression that adoption was a dirty word or a subject that their parents could not bear to talk about (McWhinnie, 1967; Triseliotis, 1973). Research also identified the long-term anxiety and misery experienced by many birth mothers whose children were placed under the closed system. In the absence of information about their child's subsequent welfare, some women reported that they could not follow advice to forget what had happened and get on with their lives. Many reported a deep sense of loss enduring for many years, and in some cases the experience of having the child adopted led to long term psychological difficulties (Winkler and Van Keppel, 1984).

These difficulties of a totally closed model are now generally recognised and most current adoptions depart from the completely closed form that dominated adoption practices from the 1950s to the 1980s (Triseliotis *et al*, 1997; Parker, 1999; Neil, 2000b). The Children Act 1975, consolidated in the Adoption Act 1976, gave English and Welsh adopted people the right on reaching the age of 18 to information enabling them to identify their birth parents. This act also introduced the Adoption Contact Register (section 51A(1)), a means by which adopted people and birth relatives can indicate willingness to make contact with each other, although this service was not formally set up until 1991.

These two changes have made it easier for adopted people to seek out their birth relatives when contact has been lost but there is also evidence that the numbers of children *retaining* links with their birth families has increased. Fratter *et al* (1991) collected information about contact arrangements directly from placing agencies. Of their large sample of children permanently placed in the early 1980s, 30 per cent were having some ongoing contact with birth relatives after adoption. However, children having contact were mainly those older at the time of placement and only 8 per cent of those under age five had any such contact. Approximately a decade later, of the children placed for adoption who were studied by Lowe *et al* (1999), three-quarters (77 per cent) were said to have some post-adoption contact with a birth relative and in 39 per cent of cases this contact was face-to-face. The Social Services Inspectorate reported on post-adoption arrangements for 371 children placed between 1993–4 (SSI, 1995). They found that 27 per cent of children were having direct contact with birth relatives, 41 per cent only indirect contact, and 31 per cent no contact at all. Neil (2000b) found that only 11 per cent of a sample of 168 children placed in 1996–7 when under the age of four were not going to have any contact with birth relatives, indirect letter contact being the most usual plan for this group of children. Parker (1999), in an overview of 10 studies, concluded that although reliable estimates of the prevalence of contact are hard to come by, the amount of post-adoption contact had certainly increased during the 1990s. A likely estimate of current rates of contact, and one used in the Prime Minister's Review (PIU, 2000) seems to be that about 70 per cent of adopted children are likely to have some kind of plan for direct or indirect contact after adoption.

In the matter of contact after adoption, practice is ahead of research. What *doesn't* work is accepted, but what *does* remains unclear; research leaves many questions unanswered and ideological perspectives abound as can be seen in a recent series of five linked articles debating the issue (Quinton *et al*, 1997; Quinton and Selwyn, 1998; Quinton *et al*, 1999; Ryburn, 1998; Ryburn, 1999). Decisions about the advisability, type, frequency and management of post-adoption contact need to be made by social workers, the judiciary, adoptive families and birth families in the absence of longitudinal data about how contact arrangements work out, especially in terms of how they affect children over time. This paper will review what is known about the outcomes of contact, by summarising the available literature and through reporting relevant findings from the author's study of post adoption contact for recently adopted young children (the '*Contact after Adoption*' study).

2. THE 'CONTACT AFTER ADOPTION' STUDY

This study, summarised briefly here but described in greater detail elsewhere (Neil, 1999; 2000a; 2000b; 2002a; 2002b), was the first stage of a longitudinal project and used both qualitative and quantitative methods to examine post-adoption birth relative contact for children placed under the age of four. Ten adoption agencies participated in the research and a cohort of children, placed for adoption or adopted during 1996–7 was identified. Social workers provided detailed, non-identifying information about 168 children by means of a postal questionnaire. The main aim of the questionnaire was to determine current practice in relation to contact after adoption. An interview study followed up the cases of 36 children whose adoption included a plan to have ongoing face-to-face contact with adult birth relatives. The adoptive parents of 35 of the children were interviewed, as were 19 birth relatives of 15 children. Sixty-one per cent (22 of 36) of these children had contact with a birthparent, and in some cases other relatives too. The remaining children had contact with other adult relatives, usually grandparents. A wide variety of face-to-face arrangements were taking place ranging from very frequent informal meetings in the adopters' home, to once a year brief supervised contacts.

3. PSYCHOLOGICAL TASKS IN ADOPTION

It is generally accepted that for adopted children, birth relatives and adoptive parents, certain psychological challenges need to be negotiated. As these challenges do not occur in families where children are raised by their birth parents, they are often described as 'additional tasks' (Triseliotis *et al*, 1997). These tasks will first be outlined; subsequently the impact of various contact arrangements on the capacity of children and families to manage these tasks will be considered.

For adopted children the first task is to form an attachment to their new parents. For a child placed in early infancy this relationship may be their first attachment, but for those placed beyond the second half of the first year this process involves also coping with the loss of previous attachment figures. Children's capacity to make and sustain relationships is negatively affected by previous poor quality care. There is a consensus in the research that those who are older at placement, who have experienced abuse or neglect, or who have had many changes in caregiving arrangements are at greater risk of their adoptive placements failing (Howe, 1998). Adopted children may also face struggles to achieve a satisfactory sense of personal identity. In the absence of information about their backgrounds, many adopted people have reported that they feel a sense of incompleteness, of not knowing *who they are* (Triseliotis, 1973; Haimes and Timms, 1985; McWhinnie, 1967). Being adopted constitutes a minority, marginal status; the adopted individual is 'different' and may have to answer their own questions, or the queries of others, as to *why* they are adopted (Haimes and Timms, 1985). Triseliotis (1973) reported that the people in his sample were, in almost all cases, hoping to discover that their birth parents had loved and wanted them, but had given them up for reasons beyond their control. Brodzinsky (1990) argues that even when placed in early infancy adopted children are vulnerable to feelings of loss and rejection because of the difficulty in making sense of why they were adopted. In the 'Contact after Adoption' sample, most children were found to have a multiplicity of difficulties in their backgrounds; the reasons why the children needed to be adopted frequently involved sad and painful stories of parental incapacity, socioeconomic deprivation, maltreatment, and, in some cases, what the adopted person may fear most—outright rejection (Neil, 2000b). As these children and others like them grow up, achieving a healthy sense of self-esteem and identity in the knowledge of these facts may pose significant challenges.

For adoptive parents, as with children, the initial task when the child is placed is that of relationship building. Adopters may not only have to try to get close to a child they do not know and who finds it hard to trust others, but may also have to manage their own feelings of loss of the birth child they could not have; under such circumstances achieving a sense of 'entitlement' to parent someone else's child is not straightforward (Jaffee and Fanshel, 1970). Adopters also need to help their child sort out any questions and confused feelings about their history and identity. It is important to the child's development that adopters are able to be open in discussing adoption related issues, and that they are able to present the birth family in a sympathetic but realistic way. When adopters convey negative views of the child's heritage, or when they wish to exclude the child's past by never talking about it, this can bring about feelings of anxiety and shame in the child, as well as resulting in poorer relationships between parent and child, lower satisfaction with the adoption experience and poorer child functioning (Jaffee and Fanshel, 1970; McWhinnie, 1967; Raynor, 1980; Triseliotis, 1973).

Turning now to the perspective of birth relatives, it is clear that for many people having a child adopted, whether or not the adoption was requested or consented to, is a profoundly painful loss that can have long term detrimental psychological outcomes. The loss is made worse by not hearing about the child's subsequent welfare in spite of their continued existence, lack of support and opportunities to talk through the experience and the stigma that arises from either 'giving away' a child or having them 'taken away'. Most research has been done on birth *mothers*, mainly those who relinquished their child for adoption (eg Winkler and Van Keppel, 1984; Howe *et al*, 1992; Bouchier *et al*, 1991). The very limited research on the experiences of birth fathers (Deykin *et al*, 1988; Cicchini, 1993; Clapton, 2000) indicates that many men also experience an array of negative feelings, and that they often had even less control over the adoption decision than the birth mother. Relatives, other than birthparents, have received almost no research attention, but Tingle (1994; 1995) writes about the views of grandparents, again, similar to birth parents, describing the experience as 'a living loss'. There is very little significant research that explores the feelings of birth relatives whose children are adopted *from care*. The small scale research that has been done indicates that feelings of anger and powerlessness, engendered by going unsupported though a stigmatising, adversarial process, further hampers the capacity of birth parents to come to terms with the loss of their child (Ryburn, 1994b; Lindley, 1994; Charlton *et al*, 1998; Mason and Selman, 1997).

4. THE RESEARCH REVIEWED

Contact and Attachment

Many children adopted today have experienced adverse caregiving environments and it is appropriate that the tasks for all concerned in making new relationships are not underestimated. Thoburn (1996) describes how, in the 1980s, child placement practice was based around the theory that in order for children to make new attachments it was seen as necessary for them to separate totally from their previous carers. The need to break the child's links with the birth family was also seen as being essential for the new parents, in order that they had, 'a "clear run" unimpeded by reminders of the child's first family and earlier attachments' (Thoburn, 1996 p 131). This argument that contact was likely to be disruptive to the formation of new relationships has been called the 'disruption model' and it is argued that even post Children Act this model is strongly favored by courts (Jolly, 1994). Were contact with members of the birth family likely to upset children attaching to new carers, it would be expected that placements with such arrangements would break down more frequently. In fact research studies focusing on placement breakdown have indicated that ongoing contact with birth relatives has a positive or neutral effect on placement stability (Fratter *et al*, 1991; Borland *et al*, 1991; Barth and Berry, 1988). Barth and Berry's (1988) interview study of 120 families who had adopted children over the age of three found no difference between rates of disruption according to whether children had contact with birth relatives or not. They assert however, that the overall 'no difference' finding masks different outcomes according to the difficulty of the placement with contact enhancing the success of straightforward adoptions but disturbing higher risk placements. This suggests it is useful to consider two types of situation: contact where children have established relationships with birth relatives (this is generally the case with older placed children), and contact where the child does not really know and remember his birth relatives (usually the case for children placed age three and under).

Children with Established Relationships

For children who know and remember birth relatives, the loss, anxiety and guilt caused by having to relinquish important relationships may undermine the process of settling in a new family (Borland *et al*, 1991). Ryburn (1996), in a questionnaire study of the views of adopters having direct contact with birth families after contested adoptions, found that children *without* birth family contact were often described by adopters as showing confusion and divided loyalties, but that children who stayed in contact with their family of origin were not upset in this way. Adoption involves many manifestations of loss for children. For children who have established relationships with birth relatives, the fact that such relatives were not able to meet all the child's needs often does not diminish the strength of this relationship or the distress that the child may feel if the relationship is not allowed to continue. The feelings of children about contact, gleaned from a number of qualitative studies, attest to children's desire to stay in touch with significant birth relatives (eg Thomas *et al*, 1999; Owen, 1999; Fratter, 1996; Thoburn *et al*, 2000; Macaskill, 2002). However, children do show discrimination between different birth relatives and may wish to cease contact with some people in their family. This is especially so where the relative concerned has been abusive, rejecting or hostile. In fact, in a recent study of fostered children by Sinclair *et al* at York University (undated), it was found that when children had been abused, outcomes were better when at least one person was forbidden from having contact with them (this finding did not hold for children who had not been abused).

Most children (80–90 per cent) placed for adoption will have siblings in their birth family (Kosonen, 1996; Rushton *et al*, 2001). In many cases, because of the fractured nature of birth families, not all these siblings will have lived with the adopted child, or even be known to him or her (Neil, 1999). The views of children in care who have been separated from familiar siblings show that many children desperately do not want to lose contact with their brothers and sisters (Harrison, 1999; Sinclair and Gibbs, 1998; Macaskill, 2002). Harrison (1999) argues that for some children losing touch with a sibling can bring about grief as great as losing a parent. Children who had been maltreated worried about any siblings left at home. For some children interviewed in her study, feelings about siblings were much less ambivalent than feelings about birth parents. Even when people have been adopted in infancy and have grown up never knowing their birth siblings, some adopted people experience this as a loss and seek out their siblings in adulthood (Howe and Feast, 2000).

Despite this evidence that many children regret losing contact with siblings, it is still very unusual that an adopted child will remain in contact with *all* of his or her siblings after adoption. In the 'Contact after Adoption' sample only five per cent of those children who had siblings were placed for adoption with *all* of their brothers or sisters and 58 per cent of children had at least one sibling living elsewhere with whom there was no contact plan (Neil, 1999). In this sample, as was also found in the research by Rushton *et al* (2001) and Lowe (1999), adopted children were more likely to have face-to-face contact with siblings who were also fostered or adopted, as opposed to those remaining in the birth family. This suggests that anxieties about contact with adult birth relatives often drive decisions about sibling contact. Regarding the outcomes of sibling contact, some research suggests that adopters find sibling contact easier than birth parent contact, though not necessarily always straightforward (Lowe *et al*, 1999; Rushton *et al*, 2001). The 15 adopted children interviewed by Fratter (1996) all expressed very positive views of sibling contact. Mackaskill (2002), in her study of direct contact arrangements, reported that most sibling contact seemed to work well and was greatly valued by the children. However she found that contact could be problematic and needed careful management in certain circumstances, for example after placement disruptions and in situations where children had very negative behaviour patterns with each other. Rushton *et al* (2001) found that between 62 and 79 per cent of sibling contact arrangements were viewed positively by adoptive and foster parents. The proportion of families reporting mixed or negative evaluations of contact declined over the first year of placement, as people adjusted to their new circumstances. Arrangements that continued to be seen as negative by parents were cases where children were exposed to mixed messages or undesirable lifestyles, or where they were frightened by their siblings. Safety issues may also need to be considered in managing contact for siblings where sexual abuse had taken place in the family as siblings can be involved in abusing each other, or in reintroducing sexually abusive adults (Head and Elgar, 1999; Farmer and Pollock, 1998).

Where relationships with siblings and adult birth relatives have been largely positive, there would seem to be more risks involved in ceasing face-to-face contact than in continuing it. Contact can be a source of continuity in the child's life. With placement for adoption, almost everything in a child's day-to-day life will alter and maintaining contact with birth relatives can be something familiar. In most cases, therefore, the fact that the birth relatives have sufficient commitment to the child that they wish to continue to visit should be seen as a resource for the child in the new family, not as a disadvantage.

Although children may have relationships with birth relatives, attachments are often insecure. For such children contact meetings can be highly charged emotional events. Difficulties between the child and the birth relative that pre-dated adoption remain evident when they meet again. The child can be left with a mixture of positive and negative feelings which may emerge as difficult behaviours (Schofield *et al*, 2000; Lowe *et al*, 1999; Macaskill, 2002). Where this is the case it is essential that *all* parties feel supported. From the child's point of view, especially for young children, he or she may need the adopters to be fully involved in such meetings to provide a sense of safety and security (Neil, 2002b; Neil *et al*, in press). Birth relatives may need help and advice about how to talk to and play with the child, as well as emotional support. Potentially difficult contacts need to be firmly controlled to prevent children experiencing further harm and there will be situations where it is necessary to cease contact (Macaskill, 2002; Schofield *et al*, 2000). The impact of birth relative's behaviour and attitudes on the ease and value of contact for the child is an important consideration, and is explored further below.

Children Who Do Not Know and Remember Birth Relatives

The research evidence is quite clear that when children are placed at young ages, and when they do not have attachment relationships with birth relatives, contact does not interfere with attachment relationships with adopters and is likely to be relatively straightforward for children to manage (Grotevant and McRoy, 1998). A study by Fratter (1996) found that face-to-face birth parent contact, even at a high frequency, was not reported to have interfered with the relationship between adopters and the child in any cases of children placed under the age of seven years. My own research looking at face-to-face contact with adult birth relatives also supports this (Neil, 2000a; 2002b). Based on ratings from adoptive parent interviews, 91 per cent of the children in my study (32 of 35) had developed close relationships with their adopters by the time of interview (on average interviews were two and a half years post placement). Although some adopters reported that it had not been straightforward for their child to attach to them, in none of the cases did they feel that birth family contact had in any way influenced the process. The mean age at placement was 21 months (sd = 16 months) and twenty five (69 per cent) of the children had lived in their birth family before placement for adoption, but the mean age at which such children finally left home was 11 months. By the time of placement therefore, most children had either not had the opportunity to develop attachment relationships to birth relatives, or had already transferred their attachment to foster carers. Contact meetings did not have the same intensity as they can have for children who are highly invested in relationships with their birth relatives; three-quarters of the children responded to meetings in a neutral or positive manner, and a quarter showed mixed reactions (Neil, 2002b). My research suggests that social workers tend to think of face-to-face contact as being needed *only* when children have established attachments to birth relatives, face-to-face contact being planned for only 17 per cent of the 168 children in my sample (Neil, 2000b; 2002a). However, this lack of an attachment between the child and birth relatives may well be the factor that makes contact relatively straightforward.

5. IDENTITY ISSUES FOR CHILDREN

Contact as a Means of Providing the Child with Information

Both face-to-face and indirect forms of contact provide opportunities for all parties to receive updated information about each other. This easier access to information the child may need for identity purposes is commonly identified by adopters as a benefit of both face-to-face and indirect contact. In terms of children's views of the information they could obtain through various forms of contact, the picture that emerges is complex. Ryburn found that children who had contact with birth relatives after adoption were reported by their parents as having different identity and information needs than those who did not have contact (Ryburn, 1995). Those who had face-to-face contact made more frequent requests for information, wanted more sophisticated types of information and were more likely to complain about the quality of available information than those children without contact. Ryburn concluded from this that the children with direct contact were better able to communicate their information needs than were those children without such contact. Less than half the sample (47 per cent) said their adopted child was happy with the amount of information available to them and this did not differ according to the contact arrangements the child had. In the same sample adoptive parents said that access to fuller and more accurate information about the child's background, including medical information, was a major advantage of having contact (contact being defined as letters or face-to-face meetings with adult relatives or siblings). In some respects the findings from Grotevant and McRoy's (1998) study of 190 infant adoptions concur with those of Ryburn. They too found that children's curiosity about their background was not assuaged by contact, but that once they had the basic information they then wanted more specific, detailed material.

A one-off meeting between adopters and birth relatives can have advantages in providing adopters with information they feel will be useful to pass onto the child at a later date (Siegel, 1993; Dominick, 1988). In my questionnaire sample, one-off meetings around the time of placement between adopters and birth relatives had taken place in 53 per cent of cases. In many more cases there was also a plan for ongoing agency mediated letter contact between adult birth relatives (usually the birth mother) and adopters. This was the most usual form of contact after adoption, 82 per cent of children having such a plan (Neil, 2000b). There is some evidence that letterbox contact is viewed as helpful by adopters in assisting children with identity tasks (Logan, 1999; Rajan and Lister, 1998) but it cannot be assumed that such contact will be 'easy'. People find it hard to write to other people who they do not know. Managing feelings involved can be difficult and a proportion of indirect contacts wither over time, most commonly because birth relatives do not maintain contact (Rajan and Lister, 1998; Logan, 1999; Berry et al, 1998). As one birth parent in my study put it;

I don't really know what to write and say. What can I write and say for them to read to my children? What can I say in a letter? I'm not a letter writer as it is so I don't really know what to put in a letter to my children.

Grotevant and McRoy (1998) found that adoptive parents having contact did not always pass on information to children about their birth family but that the more children were included in open adoption arrangements the greater was their understanding of adoption. They also report that in some cases of indirect, mediated contact adopters and birth parents made incorrect assumptions about each other and could find letters cold or uninformative. In this study which compared four different levels of openness in adoption, generally people who were dissatisfied with contact arrangements wanted more contact, not less. These findings suggest that 'letterbox' contact is not guaranteed to be successful, especially without agency support. Because of the high levels of personal and social difficulties faced by birth relatives, many people will require assistance, practical and/or emotional, to enable them to keep up letter contact with their child.

Looking now at face-to-face contact, Fratter (1996) reports that with very few exceptions adoptive parents felt that contact had assisted their child with identity tasks. Interviews with 15 young people confirmed this. For some black children who had been placed transracially, contact with black birth relatives had helped them develop a sense of, and pride in, a black identity. Increased understanding of the circumstances of adoption was described as a benefit of having direct, usually face-to-face, contact after adoption by the young people and all demonstrated a good knowledge of the reasons why they were adopted. Ten people explicitly stated that having contact had helped them to understand their own adoption story. In a small scale study (12 children in 7 families) of face-to-face contact with birth parents, all seven adoptive couples said that they thought contact was good for the child because it enhanced the child's identity, especially as in many cases it provided a route to information about other relatives and about the family medical history (Beek, 1994). In the 'Contact after Adoption' study, I found that one of the major advantages of contact for adoptive parents was that they could see birth relatives for themselves and form their own impressions, as well as having an easier, more direct means of obtaining information.

Contact as a Means of Helping the Child Understand Why He Was Adopted and Helping Him Not To Feel Unwanted or Rejected

Many children placed for adoption have not been rejected or parted with because of any absence of love or concern on the birth parent's part: it is often a lack of parental capacity rather than lack of affection that leads to the need for children to be adopted. For example, in my interview sample, almost half of birth mothers had a mental health problem, a quarter had learning disabilities and 40 per cent had substance abuse problems (Neil, 2000b). Contact could be beneficial to children in as much as it affords the birth relatives opportunities to demonstrate that they care *about* the child even though they cannot care *for* the child. This was found to be one potential benefit of contact in Fratter's (1996) study where the young people were reported to have a good understanding of their parents' difficulties and to be able to describe these without being judgmental. In some cases this had lessened children's self blame for their adoption. On the other hand, if contact is terminated it may be very difficult for a child to understand why his relatives have stopped coming to see him. From his point of view, regardless of explanations offered, this may be experienced as a rejection or a result of his own bad behaviour (Fahlberg, 1991). Thoburn *et al* (2000) in a longitudinal follow up of children in permanent placements, report that children who had ongoing contact with birth relatives often, in the longer term, were enabled to understand the reasons why they needed to be adopted. Because of difficulties in the birth family, which could include a rejecting or unreliable attitude towards the child, contact was not necessarily straightforward over the years. Some children did experience disappointment and upset, but they could be helped to deal with this, bit by bit, in the safe context of the adoptive family. In talking to adopters and the adopted young people it was found that:

> Those who remained in contact with one or both parents throughout the placement made both positive and negative comments about them, but they dealt in reality, not fantasy . . . Painful feelings about the experiences that led to them having to leave their first families never went away, but they could be talked about and worked through with both sets of parents. . . For some, the contact helped the young people to feel less badly about their early lives and to understand the predicament of their parents. For others, it reinforced the reasons why they could not be at home. (pp 101–2).

Children who had no contact after adoption were reported to have experienced more difficulties in resolving issues about what had happened to them. A number of children did not have any birth family contact for many years, but resumed this at a later stage, often in adolescence, at the adopted person's initiative and at a time when relationships with adopters were strained. The most common outcome of this pattern of contact was that the young person's reunion with birth relatives was often painful and over time led to further rejection (Thoburn *et al*, 2000). The value of contact in helping children develop realistic views is also described by Andersson (1999) in her study of children in permanent foster homes in Sweden. Exposure to parents' difficulties meant that children understood why they could not go home. Children were realistic and showed a preference for living in the foster family.

Studies of children in the care system that have included measures of child well-being give some indications of whether children are helped to adjust to the substitute care situation if they continue to see their parents. For example, Fanshel and Shinn (1978) found that children who were visited consistently by their birth family were better adjusted, even though contact could cause temporary upset. They suggest this is because such children were 'more at peace with themselves' (p 409) and that even good quality substitute care could not fully mitigate against the profound insult of believing that parents cared so little that they could not be bothered to keep in contact. Other foster care studies by Weinstein (1960) and the UK replication of this by Thorpe (1980) also found that children who retained contact with birth relatives were better adjusted, were less likely to feel rejected and had less insecurity about their identity than those who lost contact. A more recent study of older children in permanent placement failed to find any association between contact and the children's well-being, but the sample was small (only 19 children were having face-to-face contact with a birth parent) and frequency of contact highly varied (Quinton *et al*, 1998). The majority of adopters said that they felt contact had a beneficial or neutral effect on the child and where this was not the case, it was usually when adopters felt that children were receiving mixed or inappropriate messages from birth parents. The importance of good relationships between substitute parents and birth relatives was also discussed in a study of the adjustment of 74 foster children (Cantos *et al*, 1997). In this research children who were visited regularly showed fewer externalising behaviour problems and the authors suggest that this may be because they were less angry. However, when children were well integrated into the foster family, contact with birth relatives led to slightly higher levels of internalising behaviour problems. It was suggested that this was because contact in such circumstances could lead to children feeling more ambivalence and guilt, and that this was likely to be especially so when foster parents and birth relatives did not get on. Long term foster children whose foster carers had been positive about, and inclusive of the birth family, were most likely to have good overall adjustment in the study by Triseliotis (1980). In Cleaver's (2000) study of 152 fostered children, those who retained contact with their mother were found to be better adjusted to living in foster care than those who had no maternal contact.

Although the studies mentioned above do provide some evidence that contact can improve the well-being of permanently placed children, the relationship between contact and children's adjustment is far from clear cut. A huge number of factors aside from contact are likely to affect outcomes such as behavioral and emotional functioning and self esteem, and separating out the effects of contact from these other variables is nigh on impossible. It is also clear that 'contact' is not a uniform concept; not only are there many types of contact, but the quality of any contact is a vital consideration.

6. CONTACT: THE IMPACT ON ADOPTERS

Parent/Child Relationships

In the past it was often felt that a closed approach would help adopters to feel secure in their role as the child's parents and increase their feelings of 'entitlement'. This approach does not serve adopted children well, but neither is it particularly helpful to adopters. From a large study of adoptions with no ongoing contact, Raynor (1980) found:

> Very striking indeed was the sense of insecurity in adoptive parents when it came to talking about background and birth parents. Even when things had gone well, and they had a close relationship with the young adult they had brought up from infancy, they still feared the power of the birth mother to wean him away and felt they might lose his affection. (p 147).

Adopters can fear birth family contact, their main worry being that it will interfere with their relationship with the child (eg Belpas, 1987; Iwanek, 1987; Logan and Smith, 1999; Siegel, 1993; Sykes, 2000). However, contact rarely proves adoptive parents fears to be founded and there is evidence that positive contact can help adopters feel confirmed in their parenting role. For example, in Grotevant and McRoy's (1998) study adopters having unmediated face-to-face contact with birth mothers were those who were *least* likely to feel insecure about the birth mother trying to reclaim the child, their sense of security being based on the reality of their mutual understanding with her. Neither indirect nor face-to-face contact negatively affected adoptive parents' sense of permanence in their relationship with the child or their sense of entitlement. Other studies of infant adoptions with some level of contact between adopters and birth relatives report very similar results (eg Iwanek, 1987; Dominick, 1988; Berry *et al*, 1988; Belpas, 1987; Etter, 1993; Gross, 1993). Similar findings also apply to studies of children placed from the care system (Fratter, 1996; Logan and Smith, 1999; Sykes, 2000; Ryburn, 1994; 1996; Neil, in press).

Recognising and Meeting the Child's Needs as an Adopted Person

Contact can help adoptive parents recognise and meet the child's needs as an adopted person. Adoptive parents have the often challenging task of helping the child feel OK about their background, and adoptive parents' own capacity to understand the situation of birth relatives will influence the extent to which they can help the child. A number of studies have found that various forms of contact can help adoptive parents come to a more positive view of the birth family. This has been found to be a benefit of pre-placement meetings between adopters and birth relatives, even if no further face-to-face contact occurs (Lee and Thwaite, 1997; Dominick, 1988; Belpas, 1987; Siegel , 1993; Silverstein and Demick , 1994; Baumann, 1999). In most of these studies, meetings with birth relatives did not necessarily continue post-adoption, and so it is unclear whether ongoing contact has benefits over and above one-off meetings. The only study that has systematically explored this issue is the Texas/Minnesota project. In this research adopters in fully disclosed adoptions (these involved ongoing, direct face-to-face meetings) were found to show significantly higher empathy for the child, higher empathy for the birth parents' feelings, and greater communication with the child about adoption than adopters with less open arrangements (Grotevant and McRoy, 1998; Grotevant *et al*, 1994).

The implications of having contact with relatives who have high levels of personal difficulties, who have not requested adoption, and who may have mal-treated the child need to be considered. Fratter (1996) reported that ongoing contact with birth relatives enabled adopters to see positive qualities that they had not anticipated as well as the difficulties that they had already imagined. In most of these adoptions being able to have ongoing contact had deterred birth-parents from their intention to contest the adoption. This, in turn, helped adopters feel more positive about birth relatives and about themselves. Through meeting birth relatives, in some cases adopters saw first hand the difficulties many people had. The usual effect of this was that they felt it was the right thing that the child had been adopted. Sykes (2000) also reports that in many cases adopters described how their empathy had increased through having ongoing contact with birth relatives. Some adoptive parents harbored lingering feelings of anger towards birthparents because of the poor care given to the child, although these feelings did become somewhat more manageable over time. In the longitudinal Californian research, it was also found that adopters were less comfortable with birth family contact when the child had been maltreated (Berry, 1993; Berry *et al*, 1998). Ryburn (1994a) found that the feelings of adop-tive parents towards birth relatives were likely to change over time, usually in a positive direction. Adopters reported that the time of the court case was highly stressful and that emotions about the birth relatives could be quite intense.

In the 'Contact after Adoption' study the capacity of adoptive parents to empathise with the birth relatives and with the child as an adopted person was studied in detail. Building on the 'empathy for birth relative' and 'empathy for child' ratings used by Grotevant and McRoy (1998), researcher ratings were developed and applied to adoptive parent interview transcripts (Neil, 2000a; Neil *et al*, in print; Neil, in press). Over 70 per cent of these adopters having face-to-face contact showed 'good enough' empathy for birth relatives. This meant they that they did not deny any problems that the birth relative presented, but they considered such problems with reference to the difficulties and disadvan-tages that people had faced and the issues of loss the adoption occasioned. There were many examples of adopters able to hold this position even when birth rel-atives could be difficult. For example, one adoptive mother described how when she first met the birth mother, 'her language was appalling and her vocabulary consisted of "they are not having my f-ing children" '. However, she went on to say:

> I sometimes look at her and think, 'what must she be feeling, looking at us and feeling this is the couple that can give my kids everything?' It is not surprising that she is the way she is . . . she has lost her kids whichever way you look at it . . .

In all cases of 'good enough' empathy it was clear that the experience of face-to-face contact had positively impacted on adoptive parents' ability to understand the perspectives of birth relatives, in many cases this change taking place because contact helped adopters to manage their own anxieties. In some families contact helped adopters to understand that the birth relatives were not rivals for the child's affection. Once relieved of this anxiety, adopters were free to adopt a more positive view of birth relatives. As one adopter put it:

> Maybe if we didn't have contact I would feel threatened by her, because it's the unknown isn't it? It doesn't affect the love [the children] give to me . . . even in one way I feel less threatened because they are quite happy to leave at the end of the contact visit. They don't ask to stay longer, they don't say 'can I go back to mum?'.

In other cases adopters felt good about contact and about the birth family because they received messages of approval:

> [the birthparents] never come out with anything negative about us, they have always said from day one that they feel they have done the right thing, which is pleasing for us. It makes you feel better about it.

Some adopters found that contact helped them understand the very real difficulties the birth relatives had, and therefore reassured them that it was the right thing that the child was adopted:

> If there wasn't contact we wouldn't know that the birth mother is currently in hospital again. And having met [the birthfather] we know he couldn't look after [the child].

Finally, some adopters found that the reality of birth relatives was far more positive than any fantasies they had before meeting them:

> It is very easy to be prejudiced against a birthparent because of what they have done or neglected to do . . . we don't pre-judge as much now. And in fact as time goes on my feelings towards the birthmum, I just feel sorry that she was just immature . . . we have got no bad feelings about her.

As others have described (eg Fratter, 1996; Sykes, 2000; Lowe *et al*, 1999; Berry *et al*, 1998) I found that the success or otherwise of face-to-face contact arrangements seemed to be more closely related to the attitudes and beliefs of adoptive parents about the value of such contact, than to characteristics of the birth relatives or the detail of contact arrangements. Adopters who had an open, empathic attitude were more positive about contact, and were more likely to sustain or increase contact, altering arrangements when problems occurred as opposed to stopping contact altogether. Positive attitudes towards birth family contact are related to more successful contact, but, as I illustrated earlier, positive contact experiences can create and reinforce such attitudes in adopters. Clearly it is important that for contact to work well adopters must feel positive about it, but it can also be argued that all adoptive parents need to have this open and understanding attitude, regardless of the plans for contact. This is firstly because such attitudes are related to a positive experience of adoption for the child and secondly, because a child's need for contact may well change over time—adoptions that begin 'closed' may need to be 'opened' and vice versa. A number of studies, including my own, suggest that adopters feel most comfortable with contact arrangements when they are fully involved in negotiating such arrangements and have control over the plans for their child (Neil, 2002a). The attitudes of agencies about contact after adoption can clearly influence the attitude of adopters (Silverstein and Demick , 1994; Gross, 1993; Neil, 2002a).

6. BIRTH RELATIVES AND CONTACT

Studies of relinquishing birth mothers indicate that ongoing contact with the child can promote adjustment to the loss (Christian *et al*, 1997; Cushman *et al*, 1997; Etter, 1993; Iwanek, 1987). There is hardly any research looking at the impact of contact on people whose children have been adopted from care, but it is plain that such people have similar needs and desires for information about their child's welfare (Charlton *et al*, 1998). The welfare of birth relatives after adoption ought to be considered in its own right, but also because of the link between birth relative adjustment and the usefulness of contact for the child. Two problems are evident in the literature. Firstly that it is hard for birth relatives always to sustain contact because of practical and emotional barriers (eg Miles and Lindley, this volume; Berry *et al*, 1998; Masson *et al*, 1997; Etter, 1993; Millham *et al*, 1986; Aldgate, 1980). Secondly, that contact can be of poor quality both because of poor parent/child relationships and because birth relatives may have unresolved feelings of deprivation, guilt and anger which can be directed at agencies or adopters (Ryburn, 1994b; Charlton *et al*, 1998). The benefit to the child of contact is likely to be related to the quality of such contact, in particular the capacity of birth relatives to adopt a supportive position towards the child and to work collaboratively with adoptive parents (Festinger, 1986; Grotevant *et al*, 1999; Logan and Smith, 1999; Lowe *et al*, 1999; Triseliotis 1980).

The findings from my interviews with birth relatives in the 'Contact after Adoption' study (Neil, 2000a; Neil, in press), reinforce those of Fratter (1996) and Ryburn (1994b) that birth relatives can be accepting of an adoptive placement, even though their child may have been in care and the birth relative had neither requested, desired nor consented to the adoption. Using the data from my 15 interviews with 19 birth relatives, ratings were made on the extent to which birth relatives showed a realistic appraisal and acceptance of the changes brought about by the child's adoption. In this sample, remembering that three quarters of children were adopted from care, two thirds of birth relatives (11 of 15) were coded as 'realistic and accepting'. In 14 out of 15 interviews birth relatives were positive about the adopters, and expressed that they would not wish to disturb the placement in any way. For example, one mother said 'I couldn't take him now because he is so settled . . . and he is happy . . . and that makes me happy'. As with adoptive parents, birth relatives frequently described a process of change in their feelings since the time of placement, a change very much influenced by the experience of having face-to-face contact with the adopters and child. For some people what helped them to accept the adoption was being reassured of their child's welfare, as the previous quotation illustrates. In other cases birth relatives were relieved to find that they liked the adopters:

> I wanted to hate the adopters . . . but they were nice . . . I saw how the kids were with them and that reassured me. If I hadn't met them I would have seen them as monsters . . . it would have done my head in.

Birth relatives were also unable to fantasise about their relationship with the child. As I have described, most of these very young children did not have close relationships with their birth relatives. Seeing the child clearly attached to the adopters was a very painful experience, but ultimately seemed to help some people move on:

> Last time I went to see [my daughter] I tried to pick her up and she just pushed me off, she didn't want to know. I was upset, but that's to be expected. I said to [the adoptive mother] it's nice to see her so happy . . . it's true—she's taken to [the adoptive mother] like a duck to water.

Because the reality of contact is very painful for birth relatives, the availability of support is likely to be vital to the maintenance of contact in many cases.

The findings of my study about birth relatives' levels of acceptance may not apply equally to adoptions of older children. It may be harder for birth relatives to let go when they have firmly established relationships with their child, especially when the child's feelings and loyalties may reinforce those of the parent. It also may be harder for parents to accept the adoption as a good thing when children continue to experience high levels of behavioural or emotional problems. Nevertheless it is clear that it cannot be assumed that birth relatives in contested adoptions will not be able to support new placements, neither should it be taken for granted that the views people express at the time of placement will remain fixed over time.

6. CONCLUSION

Research indicates that benefits follow from sensitively managed post-adoption contact. This applies to all significant parties; the adopted child, the adoptive parents and the birth relatives. By its very nature, quality of contact will be something that is continually evolving; what works at one point in time may not necessarily work at another. Research findings, therefore, do not support a blanket policy about contact. The question 'is post adoption contact a good thing?' is not really the best question to be asking. The better starting point is to give detailed thought to what the child needs or is likely to need, both now and later in his or her life, to deal with maturing issues of loss and identity. Once an idea of the child's needs has been reasonably clarified, it should be possible to develop more sensitive and effective strategies for contact.

Many older children who have made relationships with birth relatives will not readily accept the breaking of these; to do so, without regard to the child's feelings, may do more harm than good. If birth relatives can maintain positive contact with the child and support him or her in their new family this can be of immeasurable benefit to the child's sense of self worth and personal identity and their willingness to invest in new relationships. However the situation becomes more problematic where birth relatives give the child messages implying they do not approve of the adoption; where relationships between the child and birth relative are difficult or abusive; or when birth relatives are experiencing serious personal difficulties. In some such situations contact may have too unsettling an effect on the child, and if the quality of contact cannot be improved, prevailing arrangements may need to be altered or stopped. In other cases, if sufficiently supported, children may still benefit from seeing members of their birth family because they will be helped to develop a realistic picture of why they were adopted.

The right solution for each child can only be made on a case by case basis taking into account the individual wishes, feelings and circumstances of all involved. Flexibility is important as contact plans made at the time of placement are unlikely to last the duration of the child's minority without changes to accommodate the evolving needs of all concerned. Many, though not all, contact arrangements are likely to need some level of support and it is vital that agencies offer this to all parties. Without good quality support many contact arrangements will be set up to fail, with the danger that people will experience a further sense of loss, failure and bitterness towards other parties. If direct or indirect contact is not feasible, then it is especially important that the child's needs are met in other ways. Information kept on file, given to the adopters, or prepared for the child to access when older, needs to be both accurate and detailed. Records must avoid as far as possible reproducing any judgements or opinions about moral character that may threaten the child's ability to come to their own conclusions about their own history. Both before and after placement the child and adoptive parents may need help with dealing with difficult questions and feelings that arise from thinking about the child's past. Children may need answers to questions about their background before they are legally entitled to access their files. Adoption practices should allow for this and be prepared to help children at earlier ages. Birth relatives who cannot or will not maintain contact with their child should not be left to manage their pain without support.

Regardless of what contact a child may have or need, *all* adoptive parents must be comfortable with discussing the birth family, able to understand their child's needs as an adopted person and capable of taking the perspective of birth relatives. When prospective adopters, in spite of education and support, take an intransigent stance against contact regardless of the case situation, social workers need to consider whether such people will make good *adoptive* parents. Children's contact requirements may need to be thought about in relation to the question of which type of permanent placement may be best. Permanent foster placements can, if managed and supported appropriately, be as successful as adoption in providing a 'family for life' for looked after children, and some children, carers and birth relatives prefer this route (Thoburn *et al*, 2000). Some foster carers may have superior experience in working with birth families and they may be more accepting of the child's need for contact than will prospective adopters. In some cases, especially where children are assessed as requiring a lot of birth family contact, it will be necessary to select new parents firstly on the basis of the skills and attitudes they have that will help them meet the child's needs; finding the *right* parents will be more important than whether they are *foster* parents or *adoptive* parents.

Some professionals are unconvinced about the value of contact after adoption, and the research is clear that contact can be a complex and difficult matter. It is important however to remember that *not* having contact can also be complex and difficult. Anxieties about the advisability of having contact must always be weighed against the possible detriment to the child of having none.

REFERENCES

ALDGATE, J, 'Identification of Factors Influencing Children's Length of Stay in Care' in J Triseliotis (ed), *New Developments in Adoption and Fostering* (London, Routledge and Kegan Paul, 1980).

ANDERSSON, G, 'Children in Permanent Foster Care in Sweden' (1999) 4 *Child and Family Social Work* 175.

BARTH, RP and BERRY, M, *Adoption and Disruption: Rates, Risks and Responses* (New York, Aldine de Gruyter, 1988).

BAUMANN, C, 'Adoptive Fathers and Birthfathers: A Study of Attitudes' (1999) 16 *Child and Adolescent Social Work Journal* 373.

BEEK, M, 'The Reality of Face to Face Contact after Adoption' (1994) 18 *Adoption and Fostering* 39.

BELPAS, NF, 'Staying in Touch: Empathy in Open Adoptions' (1987) 57 *Smith College Studies in Social Work* 184.

BERRY, M, 'Adoptive Parents' Perceptions of, and Comfort with, Open Adoption' (1993) 72 *Child Welfare* 231.

BERRY, M, CAVAZOS DYLLA, DJ, BARTH, RP and NEEDELL, B, 'The Role of Open Adoption in the Adjustment of Adopted Children and Their Families' (1998) 20 *Children and Youth Services Review* 151.

BORLAND, M, O'HARA, G and TRISELIOTIS, J, 'Placement Outcomes for Children with Special Needs' (1991) 15 *Adoption and Fostering* 18.

BOUCHIER, P, LAMBERT, L and TRISELIOTIS, J, *Parting with a Child for Adoption: The Mother's Perspective* (London, BAAF, 1991).

BRODZINSKY, DM, 'A Stress and Coping Model of Adoption Adjustment' in DM Brodzinsky and MD Schechter (eds), *The Psychology of Adoption* (New York, Oxford University Press, 1990).

CANTOS, AL, GRIES, LT and SLIS, V, 'Behavioural Correlates of Parental Visiting during Family Foster Care' (1997) 76 *Child Welfare* 309.

CHARLTON, L, CRANK, M, KANSARA, K and OLIVER, C, *Still Screaming: Birth Parents Compulsorily Separated from their Children* (Manchester, After Adoption, 1998).

CHRISTIAN, CL, McROY, RG, GROTEVANT, HD and BRYANT, CM, 'The Grief Resolution of Birth Mothers in Confidential, Time-Limited Mediated, Ongoing Mediated and Fully Disclosed Adoptions' (1997) 1 *Adoption Quarterly* 35.

CICCHINI, M, *The Development of Responsibility: The Experience of Birth Fathers in Adoption* (Mount Lawley, Western Australia, West Australia, Adoption Research and Counselling Service, 1993).

CLAPTON, G, 'Perceptions of Fatherhood: Birth Fathers and their Adoption Experience' (2000) 24 *Adoption and Fostering* 69.

CLEAVER, H, *Fostering Family Contact* (London, The Stationery Office, 2000).

CUSHMAN, LF, KALMUSS, D and BRICKNER NAMEROW, P, 'Openness in Adoption: Experiences and Psychological Outcomes Among Birth Mothers' (1997) 25 *Marriage and Family Review* 7.

Department of Health, *Children Looked after in England and Wales: 2000/2001 (Bulletin 2000/25*, 2001) On-line http://www.doh.gov.uk/public/sb0125.htm

DEYKIN, EY, PATTI, P and RYAN, J, 'Fathers of Adopted Children: A Study of the Impact of Surrender on Birth Fathers' (1988) 58 *American Journal of Orthopsychiatry* 240.

DOMINICK, C, *Early Contact in Adoption: Contact Between Birthmothers and Adopters at the Time of and After the Adoption* (Wellington, New Zealand, Department of Social Welfare, 1988).

ETTER, J. 'Levels of Co-operation and Satisfaction in 56 Open Adoptions' (1993) 72 *Child Welfare* 257.

FAHLBERG, V, *A Child's Journey through Placement* (London, BAAF, 1991).

FANSHEL, D and SHINN, EB, *Children in Foster Care: A Longitudinal Investigation* (New York, Columbia University Press, 1978).

FARMER, E and POLLOCK, S, *Sexually Abused and Abusing Children in Substitute Care* (Chichester, Wiley, 1998).

FESTINGER, T, *Necessary Risk—A Study of Adoptions and Disrupted Adoptive Placements* (Washington DC, The Child Welfare League of America, 1986).

FRATTER, J, *Adoption with Contact: Implications for Policy and Practice* (London, BAAF, 1996).

FRATTER, J, ROWE, J, SAPSFORD, D and THOBURN, J, *Permanent Family Placement: A Decade of Experience* (London, BAAF, 1991).

General Register Office, *The Registrar General's Statistical Review of England and Wales for the Year 1968* (London, HMSO, 1970).

GROSS, HE, 'Open Adoption: A Research-Based Literature Review and New Data' (1993) 72 *Child Welfare* 269.

GROTEVANT, HD and McROY, RG, *Openness in Adoption: Exploring Family Connections* (Thousand Oaks CA, Sage, 1998).

GROTEVANT, HD, McROY, RG, ELDE, CL and FRAVEL, DL, 'Adoptive Family System Dynamics: Variations by Level of Openness in the Adoption' (1994) 33 *Family Process* 125.

GROTEVANT, HD, ROSS, NM, MARCEL, MA and McROY, RG, 'Adaptive Behaviour in Adopted Children: Predictors from Early Risk, Collaboration in Relationships Within the Adoptive Kinship Network, and Openness Arrangements' (1999) 14 *Journal of Adolescent Research* 231.

HAIMES, E and TIMMS, N, *Adoption Identity and Social Policy: The Search for Distant Relatives* (London, Gower, 1985).

HARRISON, C, 'Children being Looked After and their Sibling Relationships: The Experiences of Children in the Working in Partnership with "Lost" Parents Research' in M Mullender (ed), *We are Family: Sibling Relationships in Placement and Beyond* (London, BAAF, 1999).

HEAD, A and ELGAR, M, 'The Placement of Sexually Abused and Abusing Siblings' in M Mullender (ed.), *We are Family: Sibling Relationships in Placement and Beyond* (London, BAAF, 1999).

Home Office, *Report of the Departmental Committee on the Adoption of Children* (Chaired by Sir William Houghton) (London, HMSO, 1972).

HOWE, D, *Patterns of Adoption* (Oxford, Blackwell Science, 1998).

HOWE, D and FEAST, J, *Adoption, Search and Reunion* (London, The Children's Society, 2000).

HOWE, D, SAWBRIDGE, P and HININGS, D, *Half a Million Women. Mothers who Lose Their Children by Adoption* (London, Penguin, 1992).

IVALDI, G, *Surveying Adoption: A Comprehensive Analysis of Local Authority Adoptions 1998–1999 (England)* (London, BAAF, 2000)

IWANEK, M, *A Study of Open Adoption Placements* (14 Emerson Street, Petone, New Zealand, unpublished, 1987).

JAFFEE, B and FANSHEL, D, *How They Fared in Adoption: A Follow-Up Study* (New York, Columbia University Press, 1970).

JOLLY, SC, 'Cutting the Ties—The Termination of Contact in Care' (1994) 3 *Journal of Social Welfare and Family Law* 299.

KOSONEN, M, 'Maintaining Sibling Relationships—A Neglected Dimension in Childcare Practice' (1996) 26 *British Journal of Social Work* 809.

LEE, JS and THWAITE, JA, 'Open Adoption and Adoptive Mothers: Attitudes Towards Birthmothers, Adopted Children, and Parenting' (1997) 67 *American Journal of Orthopsychiatry* 576.

LINDLEY, B, *On the Receiving End: Families Experiences of the Court process in Care and Supervision Proceedings under the Children Act 1989* (London, Family Rights Group, 1994).

LOGAN, J, 'Exchanging Information Post Adoption: Views of Adoptive Parents and Birth Parents' (1999) 23 *Adoption and Fostering* 27.

LOGAN, J and SMITH, C, 'Adoption and Direct Post-Adoption Contact' (1999) 23 *Adoption and Fostering* 58.

LOWE, N, MURCH, M, BORKOWSKI, M, WEAVER, A, BECKFORD, V and THOMAS, C, *Supporting Adoption: Reframing the Approach* (London, BAAF, 1999).

MACASKILL, C, *Safe Contact? Children in Permanent Placement and Contact with their Birth Relatives* (Lyme Regis, Russell House Publishing, 2002).

MASON, K and SELMAN, P, 'Birth Parents' Experiences of Contested Adoptions' (1997) 21 *Adoption and Fostering* 21.

MASSON, J, HARRISON, C and PAVLOVIC, A, *Working with Children and 'Lost' Parents: Putting Partnership into Practice* (York, York Publishing Services, 1997).

McWHINNIE, AM, *Adopted Children: How they Grow Up* (London, Routledge and Kegan Paul, 1967).

MILLHAM, S, BULLOCK, R, HOSIE, K and HAAK, M, *Lost in Care* (Aldershot, Gower, 1986).

NEIL, E, 'The Sibling Relationships of Adopted Children and Patterns of Contact after Adoption' in M Mullender (ed), *We are Family: Sibling Relationships in Placement and Beyond* (London, BAAF, 1999).

——*Contact with Birth Relatives after Adoption: A Study of Young, Recently Placed Children* (Norwich, UEA, Unpublished Ph.D. Thesis, 2000a).

——'The Reasons Why Young Children are Placed for Adoption: Findings from a Recently Placed Sample and Implications for Future Identity Issues' (2000b) 5 *Child and Family Social Work* 303.

——'Contact after Adoption: The Role of Agencies in Making and Supporting Plans' (2002a) 26 *Adoption and Fostering* 25.

——'Managing Face to Face Contact for Young Adopted Children' in H Argent (ed), *Staying Connected: Managing Contact Arrangements In Adoption* (London, BAAF, 2002b).

——'Accepting the Reality of Adoption: Birth Relatives' Experiences of Face-to-Face Contact' *Adoption and Fostering* (in press).

——'Understanding Other People's Perspectives: Tasks for Adopters in Open Adoption' *Adoption Quarterly* (in press).

NEIL, E, BEEK, M and SCHOFIELD, G, 'Thinking About and Managing Contact in Permanent Placements: The Differences and Similarities Between Adoptive Parents and Foster Carers' *Clinical Child Psychology and Psychiatry* (in press).

OWEN, M, *Novices, Old Hands and Professionals: Adoption by Single People* (London, BAAF, 1999).

PARKER, R, *Adoption Now: Messages from Research* (London, The Stationery Office, 1999).

Performance and Innovation Unit, *The Prime Minister's Review of Adoption* (London, The Cabinet Office, 2000)

QUINTON, D, RUSHTON, A, DANCE, C and MAYES, D, 'Contact between Children Placed Away From Home and Their Birth Parents: Research Issues and Evidence' (1997) 2 *Clinical Child Psychology and Psychiatry* 393.

——*Joining New Families: A Study of Adoption and Fostering in Middle Childhood* (Chichester, Wiley, 1998).

QUINTON, D and SELWYN, J, 'Contact with Birth Parents after Adoption—A Response to Ryburn' (1998) 10 *Child and Family Law Quarterly* 349.

QUINTON, D, SELWYN, J, RUSHTON, A and DANCE, C, 'Contact Between Children Placed Away From Home and their Birth Parents: Ryburn's "Reanalysis" Analysed' (1999) 4 *Clinical Child Psychology and Psychiatry* 519.

RAJAN, P and LISTER, L, 'Nottinghamshire's Letterbox Contact Service' (1998) 22 *Adoption and Fostering* 46.

RAYNOR, L, *The Adopted Child Comes of Age* (London, George Allen and Unwin, 1980).

ROWE, J and LAMBERT, L, *Children Who Wait* (London, ABAFA, 1973).

RUSHTON, A, DANCE, C, QUINTON, D. and MAYES, D, *Siblings in Late Permanent Placement* (London, BAAF, 2001).

RYBURN, M, 'The Use of an Adversarial Process in Contested Adoptions' in M Ryburn (ed), *Contested Adoptions: Research, Law, Policy and Practice* (Aldershot, Arena, 1994a)

——'Contested Adoption—The Perspectives of Birth Parents' in M Ryburn (ed), *Contested Adoptions: Research, Law, Policy and Practice* (Aldershot, Arena, 1994b).

RYBURN, M, 'Adopted Children's Identity and Information Needs' (1995) 9 *Children and Society* 41.

—— 'A Study of Post-Adoption Contact in Compulsory Adoptions' (1996) 26 *British Journal of Social Work* 627.

—— 'In Whose Best Interests?—Post Adoption Contact with the Birth Family' (1998) 10 *Child and Family Law Quarterly* 53.

—— 'Contact Between Children Placed Away from Home and their Birth Parents: A Reanalysis of the Evidence in Relation to Permanent Placements' (1999) 4 *Clinical Child Psychology and Psychiatry* 505.

SCHOFIELD, G, BEEK, M, SARGENT, K with THOBURN, J, *Growing Up in Foster Care* (London, BAAF, 2000).

SIEGEL, DH, 'Open Adoption of Infants: Adoptive Parents' Perceptions of Advantages and Disadvantages' (1993) 38 *Social Work* 15.

SILVERSTEIN, DR and DEMICK, J, 'Toward an Organisational-Relational Model of Open Adoption ' (1994) 33 *Family Process* 111.

SINCLAIR, I, BAKER, C, GIBBS, I and WILSON, K, *Supporting Foster Placements* (York, Social Work Research Development Unit, University of York, undated).

SINCLAIR, I and GIBBS, I, *Children's Homes: A Study in Diversity* (Chichester, Wiley, 1998).

Social Services Inspectorate, '*Moving Goalposts': a Study of Post-Adoption Contact in the North of England* (London, Department of Health, 1995).

SYKES, M., 'Adoption With Contact. A Study of Adoptive Parents and the Impact of Continuing Contact with Families of Origin' (2000) 24 *Adoption and Fostering* 20.

THOBURN, J, 'Psychological Parenting and Child Placement: "But we want to have our cake and eat it" ' in D Howe (ed), *Attachment and Loss in Child and Family Social Work* (Aldershot, Avebury, 1996).

THOBURN, J, NORFORD, L and RASHID, S, *Permanent Family Placement for Children of Minority Ethnic Origin* (London, Jessica Kingsley, 2000).

THOMAS, C, BECKFORD, V, LOWE, N and MURCH, M, *Adopted Children Speaking* (London, BAAF, 1999).

THORPE, R, 'The Experiences of Children and Parents Living Apart: Implications and Guidelines for Practice' in J Triseliotis (ed), *New Developments in Adoption and Fostering* (London, Routledge and Kegan Paul, 1980).

TINGLE, N, 'A View of Wider Family Perspectives in Contested Adoptions' in M Ryburn (ed), *Contested Adoptions: Research, Law, Policy and Practice* (Aldershot, Arena, 1994).

TINGLE, N, 'Grandparents Speak' in H Argent (ed), *See You Soon: Contact with Children Looked After by Local Authorities* (London, BAAF, 1995).

TRISELIOTIS, J, *In Search of Origins* (London, Routledge and Kegan Paul, 1973).

—— 'Growing Up in Foster Care and After' in J Triseliotis (ed), *New Developments in Adoption and Fostering* (London, Routledge and Kegan Paul, 1980).

TRISELIOTIS, J, SHIREMAN, J and HUNDLEBY, M, *Adoption: Theory, Policy and Practice* (London, Cassell, 1997).

WEINSTEIN, E, *The Self Image of the Foster Child* (New York, Russell Sage Foundation, 1960).

WINKLER, R and VAN KEPPEL, M, *Relinquishing Mothers in Adoption: Their Long Term Adjustment* (Melbourne, Institute of Family Studies, 1984).

Section 5:

Challenging Contact

15

Assisted Reproduction and Parental Relationships

MARTIN RICHARDS*

1. INTRODUCTION

IN ORDER TO consider questions of parent-child relationships, it is necessary to know who is a parent. When assisted reproductive techniques are employed to produce a child more than two adults may be involved (Johnson, 1999). Does parenthood rest with those whose intentions led to the conception of the child and who are likely to rear the child, or those who provided the necessary gametes, or the womb in which gestation took place, or perhaps all of these?[1]

Assisted reproduction has a long history. The first clinical use of artificial insemination by a husband was recorded by John Hunter in 1790, while the insemination by donor[2] followed a century later (Bartholomew, 1958). During the 1930s and 1940s a small but growing number of clinics in Britain offered artificial insemination by donor (AID), as it was then called, to infertile couples or those where the husband was at risk of transmitting an inherited disease. The practice was encouraged by some eugenicists who saw 'eutelegenesis' (Brewer, 1935) or 'germinal choice' (Muller, 1936) as a method of improving the human stock without constraining marital choices or indeed some men's marital prospects. However, it was widely condemned by sections of the public, many doctors and the church, and was often seen as a form of adultery. In 1948, for example, the Archbishop of Canterbury's Commission recommended that AID should be criminalised because it was adulterous and it involved masturbation and created an illegitimate child.[3] In this climate it was not surprising that the

---

* I would like to thank a number of colleagues including Dr Andrew Bainham and Baroness O'Neill for their helpful comments on an earlier version of this chapter though I must make clear that the views I express are my own and not necessarily shared by these generous friends.

[1] With the development of new techniques this list will grow. Where nuclear transfer ('cloning') techniques are employed, there is the provider of the egg which is enucleated, as well as the provider of the egg or other cell from which the nucleus is taken.

[2] By convention the providers of eggs and sperm are referred to as donors whether or not they receive expenses, a fee or both. For convenience I will follow this convention which is often a socially convenient fiction.

[3] As a possible way of avoiding the first of these difficulties the Commission considered a suggestion that semen could be collected from the donor's wife's vagina (see Haimes, 1993).

whole matter was dealt with in secret; donation was usually anonymous and couples very rarely told their children about the manner of their conception or their biological parentage. In cases of infertility, semen from the husband was often mixed with that of the donor and the couple were encouraged to have sexual intercourse after the insemination so that there was always a possibility that the child might be conceived by the social father. While the child was technically illegitimate if conceived by AID, couples would usually register the birth as their own and the husband would, in any event, be presumed in law to be the father.

2. THE NEW REPRODUCTIVE TECHNOLOGIES

The first IVF baby was born in 1978 (Steptoe and Edwards, 1978) and this was followed by the first case of egg donation in 1984. These developments led to legal changes and following the Family Law Reform Act of 1987 and the Human Fertilization and Embryology Act 1990 (HFE Act), children produced with the use of donated sperm, eggs or embryos can be registered on a birth certificate as the child of the couple, or individual, being treated in a (registered) clinic. Eighteen thousand such children have been born in Britain since 1991. In following the practice that has grown up in the pre-war period, the HFE Act takes a somewhat unusual view of parentage, confirming it on men who simply accompany a woman being treated in a clinic (independently of their relationship), and on the same basis, if a woman on her own (and unmarried) is given treatment, her child is legally fatherless. Donation is anonymous. To avoid unwitting genetic incest, at age 16 a young person can enquire from the Human Fertilization and Embryology Authority (HFEA) whether he or she is genetically related to someone they intend to marry. At 18 anyone can ask whether they were born as the result of infertility treatment using donated gametes or embryos and, if regulations are made (these are currently the subject of a consultation, Department of Health, 2001), may receive some or all of the very limited non-identifying information that the HFEA holds on each donor.[4] These arrangements only apply to those who use the services of a licensed clinic. An unknown number of people make their own arrangements for DIY insemination. In this situation the donor has the same status as any other unmarried (biological) father. Some would-be parents use the web to find clinics and vendors in countries where trade in gametes and surrogacy is unregulated and join the growing numbers of medical tourists.

In effect, most of the adult actors in the British system of assisted reproduction using donated gametes and embryos treat these as biological tissue, or as the HFE Act terms it, 'genetic material' regarding this in much the same way as

---

[4] This is height, weight, ethnic group, eye colour, hair colour, skin colour, occupation, interests and whether they have other (non-donation conceived) children. There is also an optional section of the form which invites donors to give 'a brief description of yourself as a person'; however, relatively few donors provide this.

organs used for transplantation. Gametes are not accorded with the symbolic properties that those conceived with them are likely to perceive. As Rachel Cook (2002) has pointed out, to all intents and purposes people own their own gametes (see also Herring, 2002). Those who chose to 'donate' them (in the UK) for others to use receive a small fee plus expenses, and can attach conditions about who may use them. Donors typically do not tell their partners (though HFEA guidelines suggest that donors should be advised to tell their wives and partners) or other relatives what they have done (Cook and Golombok, 1995). Donation is anonymous and donors have no rights or duties towards any children born of their donation or indeed have any right to know whether any such children have been born.[5] Only a minority of heterosexual couples using these methods set out with the expectation of telling their children about the manner of their conception and even fewer fulfil such expectations once a child is born (Cook, 2002; Golombok *et al*, 2002). However, we should note that this is not the situation in all countries. In Sweden, for example, when adult, children conceived with donor gametes have the right to know the identity of their biological fathers. However, the evidence suggests that only a small percentage of parents tell their child of their donor insemination (DI) origins (Gottlieb *et al*, 2000). In contrast to these ways in which heterosexual couples use the technologies, most lesbian and gay couples and single women are open with their children about their origins (Sparks and Hamilton, 1991; Cook, 2002; Richards, 2002). In the USA commercial companies offering gametes for sale usually provide extensive information about donors. In some cases parents know the identity of the donors and there is a continuing relationship between the donors, recipient couples and their children. Those who treat the gametes or embryos simply as biological material and do not tell their children about their conception may be regarded as normalising their families, 'as if' they were reproducing in the traditional way. This parallels accounts of the 'fictive' family of adoption (Modell, 1994). Alternatively, where the parentage is open and known to the child, the gamete provider may be incorporated into the family as a godparent or a fictive aunt, uncle or parent. In this situation the family is normalised by modifying the kinship relationships, rather than creating an 'as if' family (Richards, 2002; see also Bharadwaj, 2003). Kinship is never purely a matter of sex and blood but in these situations may involve some careful and conscious social construction.

As might be expected, the practice of ARTs is fundamentally gendered. Haimes (1993) has pointed out this may be seen in different attitudes toward sperm and egg donors. In the realm of traditional procreation, parenthood for fathers does not simply follow from biology; paternal parental rights, as one American judge once put it, 'do not spring full blown from the biological

---

[5] Assuming that they have been conceived after treatment in a licensed clinic. As mentioned above, these regulations do not apply to the unknown number of people who make their own private arrangements for AID or seek treatment in a clinic outside the UK where there may be no such regulations.

connection' (Dolgin, 1995). When a mother bears a child, maternity and maternal rights and duties follow; but parenthood for men has more the characteristics of an opportunity to be grasped or a status that must be achieved. Though,
as I have argued elsewhere (Richards, 2002, 2003), things may be changing a little in the 'century of the genome'. Under the Child Support Act 1991 a man is
liable for support of any child with whom he shares DNA sequences.[6] In English
law, married and unmarried fathers have always been treated differently. While
a married father assumes parentage and parenthood of any child of the family,
an unmarried father does have a duty to support his (biological) children financially but he has to go to court to seek a parental responsibility order. This will
change when the Adoption and Children Act 2002 comes into force. The Act
amends section 4 Children Act 1989, to the effect that, in addition to acquiring
parental rights by agreement with the mother or by court order, he will also
acquire them by being registered as the child's father.[7] Gendered notions of
parenthood are reflected in the regulation of ARTs. A woman who is commissioned by a couple to carry a child for them, whether or not it is conceived using
her eggs, retains maternal rights over the child. So, if she becomes pregnant following IVF using another couples' gametes, she retains maternity until or unless
she agrees for it to be transferred to the commissioning parents (under the
Surrogacy Arrangements Act 1985 and the HFE Act 1990).

3.   WHAT SHOULD CHILDREN KNOW?

With the development of ARTs there has been a continuing debate about
whether or not a child should know, or has a right to know, the manner of their
conception and perhaps the identity of the gamete provider(s). A great deal has
been written on this subject. On one side it is argued that a child has a right or
a need to know of their origins, including their genetic origin, so that they are
able to place themselves socially in terms of a genealogy by knowing who has
come before and who may follow them. More recently it has been claimed that
knowledge of biological parentage is an essential part of 'genetic identity'. On
the other side, it is asserted that social parents (and donors) should be able to
keep matters secret for a number of social, commercial and pragmatic reasons
(see discussion by Wilson, 1997; O'Donovan, 1989; Freeman, 1996; Maclean
and Maclean, 1996; Cook, 1999; Blyth, 1998).

What has been established by research with children conceived with donated
gametes is that most children are not told of the manner of their conception
(Golombok, 2002). They are allowed to believe that they are conceived by the
traditional method and so with gametes from their social parents. However,
because most parents tell some friends or family about the child's conception,

---

[6] Unless conceived with donated eggs or sperm or a donated embryo in a licensed clinic.
[7] S 111 Adoption and Children Act 2002.

there is a likelihood that children may discover the truth. Children themselves, or others, may notice a lack of physical resemblance which can cause suspicions. Such suspicions can now be simply and easily confirmed, or disconfirmed, with DNA testing which can be done with samples collected without the knowledge of the adults involved.[8] The growing use of DNA tests for genetic disease which may reveal what geneticists usually refer to as 'non paternity' provides another route by which someone may learn of their genetic parentage.[9] While research suggests that children growing up aware that donated gametes were used for their conception are not particularly troubled by this, inadvertent discovery or being told in adulthood may lead to prolonged distress, anger and resentment of the social parents' lack of honesty. Part of young people's upset may stem from the knowledge that others—their social parents and perhaps family and the clinic involved in their conception—have intimate knowledge about them to which they have been denied access (Blyth, 1998). The argument for children to know of their origins broadly parallels that for children of adoption (see Neil, this volume), though there are some differences. Almost all adopted children are told of their origins and are given information about their birth parents. At 18 adopted children have access to their birth certificates and significant numbers use this information to trace their birth parents. The most common motive given for doing this is for a sense of identity and connectedness with forebears (Howe and Feast, 2000; see also Carsten, 2000). In many societies, but not our own, open adoption is the norm and children grow up knowing and having contact with their birth mother, and occasionally father.

Follow up studies of children conceived by donor insemination (who do not know of their origins) show that they are, in general, as well adjusted in their social and emotional development as comparable groups of children conceived conventionally. In donor insemination families, mothers have been found to show slightly more expressive warmth toward their children and fathers to be less involved in discipline as compared to adoptive or naturally conceived families. It has been suggested that these findings reflect the 'genetic imbalance' in these families (Golombok *et al*, 2002). In their studies of children at age 12 these authors found no evidence of ill effects of the secrecy surrounding DI in the children.

In addition to the arguments about a child wanting to know their origins and the possible inadvertent discovery of the manner of their conception, the case for openness has been argued on the basis of children's rights. Michael Freeman (1996) states that a children's rights perspective (see also Maclean and Maclean, 1996) has been neglected in relation to ARTs. He suggests that the longstanding policy of relative openness to avoid 'genealogical bewilderment' in adoption

[8] In the UK there are Department of Health guidelines for DNA paternity testing which should ensure that consent is always obtained. However, testing is also widely available via the web and there are sites which promote themselves by advertising that they will test samples without questions about their origin or consent of the parties involved. These tests are usually based on samples of hair roots which are easy to collect from someone without their knowledge or consent.

[9] A further route is the growing use of techniques based on mitochondrial DNA or Y chromosome analysis for tracing lineages in family histories (see Richards, 2003).

may be the result of the social workers' involvement in that practice, while the medical control and framing of ARTs has led to policies of secrecy, only tempered by concerns about genetic incest and inter-marriage. He argues that there are few more basic rights than that to one's identity and he assumes that this involves knowledge of the manner of conception and the identity of all those involved, including gamete or embryo donors. A right to know who one's parents are is enshrined in the UN Convention on the Rights of the Child. Others, who wish to maintain the current status quo, have suggested that this position reflects a kind of 'geneticisation' and an over-emphasis on blood ties.

While there are good reasons to suppose that any child may have a strong interest in their origins, the manner of their conception and the history of their family, the claim that a knowledge of parentage may be essential to a person's 'genetic identity' may be flawed. Indeed, the notion of genetic identity is not one that stands up to close scrutiny as O'Neill (2002) has helpfully pointed out. Indeed, the claim seems to be based on a version of genetic exceptionalism that increasingly pervades our culture in this 'century of the gene'. Of course, knowledge of genetic parentage may well be of particular interest and concern if there are questions about inherited disease. And for a number of diseases even with DNA predictive genetic testing, knowledge of the family history of a disease may assist in the assessment of risk and the likely expression of the disease. However, the claim of genetic identity goes much beyond this and seems to rest on a notion that our self depends on our genetic make up and our connections to our genetic forebears. In effect, it reduces notions of social identity, kinship, family connection and history to DNA sequences.

O'Neill distinguishes three claims implicit in notions of genetic identity. The first is that genetic make up individuates persons. As is clear from the case of so-called 'identical' (monozygotic) twins, the claim is false as twins are obviously distinct persons. So clearly, sharing the same genome is not sufficient to make people the same. The second point is that genetic information can be used to identify people (except in the case of monozygotic twins); indeed this is the purpose of forensic DNA data bases which can be used to match DNA from a crime scene with DNA from a suspect. But here it is important to point out that DNA, in itself, does not identify a person; rather identical DNA sequences in two or more samples indicate that all these came from the same person (or a monozygotic twin). In the same way shared DNA sequences can determine whether or not two people are parent and child, but of course this does not indicate anything about the nature of the parental relationship between them. The two may be a father and son who have always lived together and stand in that social relationship, or they could be two individuals who might pass each other in the street without either having any knowledge of any connection between each other.

The third possibility is that genetic information may give us a sense of identity in the same way as an ethnic identity may give us a sense of belonging to a particular social group. In a few rare cases there may indeed be groups who share a sense of genetic identity—all those in a support group who carry a mutation associated with a particular genetic disease, for example. But generally people do not see themselves as members of groups defined by genetic make up. Once again, it is important to notice that families are not genetic groups and that kinship is defined by blood, marriage and social relationship and mutual recognition.

Those who argue against giving information about gamete providers or about the manner of their conception to children say that secrecy protects the family from public knowledge of the father's infertility, or genetic problems; and the child from possible adverse consequences of knowledge of circumstances of their conception. It also protects the donor from having to take any responsibility for the child.[10] There are further pragmatic and commercial arguments. Those involved in the provision of services (which are largely in the private sector) suggest that it would be difficult to find sufficient donors in an open system. They also point to the fact that most (current) donors wish to remain anonymous.[11] Experience in Sweden, where the system became open and parents are given information about the identity of the donors, was that numbers of sperm donors initially dropped but later recovered. Similarly, a Californian sperm bank which provides donor children with details of the genetic father's identity when they are 18 does not lack donors (BBC World News, 8 Nov 2002). Clearly gamete provision may appeal to rather different people under open and closed systems. Studies of UK donors suggest that, at the time of donation, most are young and childless and they have little interest in the children that may be conceived and their major motive is the small amount of money they earn (Cook and Golombok, 1995). However, there are indications that some sperm providers, especially after they have had children of their own, may come to regret what they have done and may become interested in the children they may have fathered (Baran and Pannar, 1989). While there have been recommendations that clinics should attempt to recruit older men in stable relationships who already have children of their own[12] and who might wish to donate for more altruistic reasons,[13] practice in selecting donors has not changed. Interestingly, a recent study of Swedish donors suggests that under that open system donors are older, more altruistic in their motives, and are not motivated by money (Lalos *et al*, 2003).

O'Donovan (1989) and others have argued that the ARTs situation is not like adoption because there is no pre-existing child with a history and documentation

---

[10] This protection is afforded by the Family Law Reform Act (1987) and the HFE Act (1990) if licensed clinics are used.

[11] In fact, in situations where an anonymous system has become open, such as Victoria, Australia, past donors have been approached to see if they would be willing for identifying information to be passed on to their children. A majority agreed to this.

[12] In France there is a requirement that donors should already be parents.

[13] It has been remarked that eugenicists would be unlikely to approve of the use of donors who are solely interested in the payments they receive and that they would wish to see the use of more altruistically inclined donors.

and because in the usual ARTs situation one parent will be genetically related to the child.[14] She also suggests the idea of a relationship between the child and a donor is 'socially constructed'. Of course there are usually very different motives involved in providing gametes for ARTs and conceiving and then surrendering a child for adoption. However, O'Donovan's argument seems to miss the point made about a child's need to know something of their origins. The claims and arguments about such a need see the genetic connection as part of, but certainly not the whole story of a child's origins. The suggestion that the link is socially constructed (or simply a matter of geneticisation) seems to be effectively an argument that reduces the status of the gametes to that of any tissue that might be used in organ transplantation. It ignores the symbolic and biological properties of gametes. The story of a child's origins would be incomplete and potentially misleading if the origin of the gametes used was not included. Suppose a child required a blood transfusion after birth, the parents might (much later) tell the child this in discussing their birth. However, it seems unlikely that many children or young people would lose much sleep wondering who the blood donor was. But I would suggest that if donated gametes are used in conception, because of their role in reproduction (and in law) and our cultural attitudes and values about them, children and young people are likely to be very interested in the fact that gametes from another have led to their conception, and in the identity of that person. For some the shared substance linking parent and child is significant. Of course, O'Donovan is right in saying that social construction is involved in that story. That is the case in any discussion of our origins, kinship and reproduction. But in our culture, the act of donating blood (or kidneys or corneas) is not the same as providing eggs or sperm.[15] As emphasised earlier, kinship is not simply a matter of blood and sex (Yanagisako and Delany, 1995). Nor, as we have pointed out, is it solely determined by shared DNA sequences. However, the identity of the people involved in acts of conception, whether these take place in a body or petri dish, are part of our social origins.

4. CONCLUSIONS

The conception of children using assisted reproductive technologies can take place in different circumstances with different arrangements and relationships between the would-be social parents of the child and those who may be involved in providing gametes or gestational surrogacy. Sometimes, as in some cases in the unregulated clinics of California, or by private arrangements between those involved in Britain, the gamete provider becomes, not simply a person known to

---

[14] That, of course, parallels the stepparent situation where adoption is generally discouraged.

[15] This argument is not intended to imply that there are no social consequences of giving blood or tissue. As concerns about the fate of postmortem samples has demonstrated, even when medical samples are anonymised and dehumanised they may not lose their social significance for relatives.

the child, but a part of their kin. But in Britain at least, the great majority of children conceived with gametes from others than those who rear them, know nothing of their origins and are led to believe they are the natural children of those whom they regard as their parents. As I have described, a small number of these children do subsequently discover that the facts of their conception were not as they supposed and this may cause continued distress and disruption of family relationships. Easy access to DNA testing is making such unintended discovery more likely. Should the regulated system for ARTs in the UK go over to the use of open donation of gametes as some others have? I would suggest that on the balance of the evidence I have described, it should. At present, most parents who have children using donated eggs, sperm or embryos do not tell those children that this is how they have been conceived. I would suggest that parents should be encouraged to tell their children this in age appropriate ways early in childhood. There are several books for both parents and their DI children which engage the issues (Anon, 1991; McWinnie, 1996; Donor Conception Support Group of Australia, 1997; Blyth, Crawshaw and Speirs, 1998).

As far as the identity of the donor(s) is concerned there are two possible ways forward. The first, which would parallel the current British adoption situation, would allow young people access to identifying information at 18, or to provide them with this information (as some Californian sperm banks do, for example). The second way would be to take a further step in addition, and would also give the information to the parents at the birth of their child, so that they could decide when to pass on this information.

Knowing the manner of your conception and the identity, and perhaps some other information, about the gamete provider is not, of course, the same thing as having a social relationship with that person. Again, there may be some parallels with the adoption situation. Research on adoption reunion (Howe and Feast, 2000; Neil, this volume) suggests that there is a significant group of adoptive children who have knowledge of their birth parents but do not wish to meet them. Any system of open gamete provision (and presumably the same would apply for surrogacy) would allow the possibility of provider and (adult) child meeting but that would depend on the wishes of both parties. Also implicit in such a system is the idea that gamete providers would receive information about children that may be conceived.

Clearly, such a change in the system is likely to bring about a change in the kinds of motives that may lead people to provide gametes, but that seems more of an argument for, than against, change. And as the situation in other countries has demonstrated, the supply of gametes does not disappear if a system is made open. Our current system reflects the immediate interests of infertile would-be parents and the clinics that offer them 'treatment'. While, of course, these needs should be taken into account in any system of regulation, I think we need to give more weight to the needs of the next generation and the children who are conceived through the use of ARTs involving donated gametes or embryos. The evidence suggests that an open system would best serve their need to grow up with knowledge of their origins. The point is sometimes made that some children conceived by conventional sexual intercourse grow up with a false belief about who provided the sperm. That is, of course, true and family histories do not always follow bloodlines. However, that point does not seem to justify a system of the employment of ARTs which systematically denies children knowledge of their origins.

REFERENCES

ANON, *My Story* (Sheffield Infertility Research Trust, 1991).

BARAN, A and PANNAR, R, *Lethal Secrets: The Psychology of Donor Insemination* (New York, Amisted, 1989).

BARTHOLOMEW, GW., 'The Development and Use of Artificial Insemination' (1958) 49 *The Eugenics Review* 187.

BHARADWAJ, A, 'Why Adoption is Not an Option in India: the Visibility of Infertility, the Secrecy of Donor Insemination and Other Cultural Complexities' (2003) 56 *Social Science and Medicine* 1867.

BLYTH, E, CRAWSHAW, M and SPEIRS, J, *Truth and the Child 10 Years On: Information Exchange in Donor Assisted Conception* (Birmingham, British Association of Social Workers, 1998).

BLYTH, E, 'Donor Assisted Conception and Donor Offspring Rights to Genetic Origin Information' (1998) 6 *International Journal of Children's Rights* 237.

BLYTH, E and HUNT, J, 'Sharing Genetic Origin Information in Donor Assisted Conception. Views from Licensed Centres on HFEA Donor Information Form' (1998) 13 *Human Reproduction* 3274.

BREWER, H, 'Eutelegenesis' (1935) 27 *The Eugenics Review* 121.

CARSTEN, J, ' "Knowing Where You've Come From": Ruptures and Continuities of Time and Kinship in Narratives of Adoption Reunions' (2000) 6 *Journal of the Royal Anthropological Institute (NS)* 687.

CARTER, CO, 'Eugenic Implications of New Techniques'. in CO Carter (ed), *Developments in Human Reproduction and their Eugenic/Ethical Implications* (London, Academic Press, 1983).

COOK, R and GOLOMBOK, S, 'A Survey of Semen Donation: Phase 2—The View of Donors' (1995) 10 *Human Reproduction* 951.

COOK, R, 'Donating Parenthood: Perspectives on Parenthood from Surrogacy and Gamete Donation' in A Bainham, S Day Sclater, and M Richards (eds), *What is a Parent? A Socio-Legal Analysis* (Oxford, Hart Publishing, 1999).

——'Villain, Hero or Masked Stranger: Ambivalence in Transactions with Human Gametes' in A Bainham, S Day Sclater and M Richards (eds), *Body Lore and Laws* (Hart, Oxford, 2002).

Department of Health, Donor Information Consultation, (2001) http://www.doh.gov.uk/gametedonors.

DOLGIN, JL, 'Family Law and the Facts of Family' in S Yanagisako and C Delaney (eds), *Naturalizing Power* (New York, Routledge, 1995).

Donor Conception Support Group of Australia Inc, *Let the Offspring Speak* (Georges Hall, NSW, The DC Support Group of Australia, 1997).

FREEMAN, M, 'The New Birth Right?' (1996) 4 *International Journal of Children's Rights* 273.

GOLOMBOK, S, 'Parenting and Contemporary Reproductive Technologies' in MH Bornstein (ed), *Handbook of Parenting* (Mahwah NJ, Erlbaum, 2002).

GOLOMBOK, S, MACCALLUM, FM, GOODMAN, E and RUTTER, M, 'Families with Children Conceived by Donor Insemination: A Follow Up at Age Twelve' (2002) 73 *Child Development* 952.

GOTTLIEB, C, LALOS, O and LINDBLAD, E, 'Disclosure of Donor Insemination to the Child: the Impact of Swedish Legislation' (2000) 15 *Human Reproduction* 2052.

HAIMES, E, 'Issues of Gender in Gamete Donation' (1993) 36 *Social Science and Medicine* 85.

HERRING, J, 'Giving, Selling and Sharing Bodies' in A Bainham, S Day Sclater, and M Richards (eds), *Body Lore and Laws* (Oxford, Hart Publishing, 2002).

HOWE, D and FEAST, J, *Adoption, Search and Reunion* (London, The Children's Society, 2000).

JOHNSON, M, 'A Biomedical Perspective on Parenthood' in A Bainham, S Day Sclater, and M Richards (eds), *What is a Parent? A Socio-Legal Analysis* (Oxford, Hart Publishing, 1999).

LALOS, A, DANIELS, K, GOTTLIEB, C and LALOS, O, 'Recruitment and motivation of semen providers in Sweden' (2003) 18 *Human Reproduction* 212.

MACLEAN, S and MACLEAN, M, 'Secrets in Assisted Reproduction—The Tension Between Donor Anonymity and the Need of the Child for Information' (1996) 8 *Child and Family Law Quarterly* 243.

MCWINNIE, J, *Families Following Assisted Conception. What Do We Tell Our Child?* (Dundee, Dept of Law, University of Dundee, 1996).

MODELL, JS, *Kinship with Strangers. Adoption and Interpretation of Kinship in American Culture* (Berkeley, University of California Press, 1994).

MULLER, HJ, *Out of the Night: A Biologist's View of the Future* (New York, Garland, 1984, originally published in 1936).

O'DONOVAN, K, 'What Shall We Tell the Children? Reflections on Children's Perspectives and the Reproduction Revolution' in R Lee and D Morgan (eds), *Birthright, Law and Ethics and the Beginning of Life* (London, Routledge, 1989).

O'NEILL, O, What is Genetic Identity? (Unpublished, 2002) Newnham College, Cambridge.

RICHARDS, M, 'Future Bodies: Some History and Future Prospects for Human Genetic Selection' in A Bainham, S Day Sclater, and M Richards (eds), *Body Lore and Laws* (Oxford, Hart Publishing, 2002).

RICHARDS, MPM, 'Assisted Reproduction and Genetic Technologies and Family Life' in J Scott, J Treas, and MPM Richards (eds), *Blackwell Companion to the Sociology of Families* (Oxford, Blackwell, 2003).

SPARKS, C and HAMILTON, JA, 'Psychological Issues related to Alternative Insemination' (1991) 22 *Professional Psychology Research and Practice* 308.

STEPTOE, P and EDWARDS, RG, 'Birth after the Replacement of a Human Embryo' (1978) ii *Lancet* 366.

WILSON, S, 'Identity, Genealogy and the Social Family: The Case of Donor Insemination' (1997) 11 *International Journal of Law, Policy & The Family* 270.

YANAGISAKO, S and DELANEY, C (eds), *Naturalizing Power* (New York, Routledge, 1995).

16

Contact in Containment

BELINDA BROOKS-GORDON*

Prison rule 31. Special attention should be paid to maintaining contacts between prisoners and their families, and that a prisoner should be 'encouraged' to develop contacts with the outside world which best promote the interests of his family and his own social rehabilitation. (Livingstone and Owen, 1999).

THE NUMBER OF people contained in prison in the UK has reached the highest level ever and yet prisoners' contact with members of their family has decreased, in the number of visitors received, over the last five years of the past decade (Prison Reform Trust, 2001). Why might this be? Indeed, it seems especially serious in the light of the official policy in the prison rules above and of the evidence in this volume that highlights the value of, and rights to, contact between children, their parents and family (see Hughes, Dunn, and Pryor, this volume). One suggestion has been that the decline is due to the difficulties in booking visits and the long distances visitors have to travel (Prison Reform Trust, 2001). But is this the whole story? Visits are not the only way of maintaining contact, nor is direct contact the only way for prisoners to maintain family ties. Is the decline in visits therefore part of a deeper problem surrounding the maintenance of contact for prisoners' families?

In order to answer this question I propose to explore the contemporary policy for establishing and maintaining family ties for people held in containment. Containment, broadly speaking, is coercive control by the State in what Goffman (1961) called total institutions and for these purposes 'containment' will include prisoners and asylum seekers[1] held in prison accommodation in England and Wales, the secure accommodation of juveniles and of psychiatric patients. This chapter is specifically concerned with changes in prison practice and policy regarding contact in the past decade. During this period broad social influences such as the decline of the rehabilitative ideal (Livingstone and Owen, 1999) and

* I thank John Eekelaar for an informative and helpful discussion on adoption, and Martin Richards for kindly providing personal copies of his research papers. I am grateful to Andrew Bainham for many a long discussion on children's rights and for drawing my attention to the *Mellor* case.

[1] Prisoners and asylum seekers are not distinct groups in this respect. For example, of the 1,370 people being detained under Immigration Act powers in March 2002, 8% (n = 105) of detainees are held in prisons (Home Office Asylum Statistics, 1st Quarter 2002, UK).

more specific influences such as the Woodcock Report in 1995 and the Fallon Inquiry in 1999, have constrained the amount and quality of family contact in prisoners' lives. At the same time the implementation of the Human Rights Act 1998 in 2000 has given prisoners and their families new rights which have had to be balanced not just against each other but also against the Prison Rules.

In order to address the issue of contact for prisoners' families, I intend to explore the questions policy makers need to consider when making decisions regarding contact. These include: What provision can be made for prisoners to maintain family ties? Is contact provision evenly and justly distributed amongst prisoners? What are the risks of allowing contact? What are the rights of prisoners and their families? In exploring these issues I will also aim to address further questions such as whether the exercise of rights is gendered in a penal context.

1. PREVALENCE OF PARENTS AND CHILDREN AFFECTED BY IMPRISONMENT

A thorough account of the issues concerning contact for prisoners' children can be found in Shaw (1992). This chapter is concerned with the period *since* that review; a period in which a steady increase of the prison population occurred from 1993 to reach a record high by 2002.[2] This increase can be seen in Table 1, which also shows that yet further increase is projected and by 2008, the total prison population will have risen more than a fifth (21 per cent).

Table 1. Prison Population of England and Wales

	1993	1996	2001	2002	2008[3]
Men	43,010	53,020	65,560	65,580	73,800
Women	1,560	2,260	3,740	4,210	5,390
Total[4]	44,570	55,280	69,300	69,780	79,190

The size of the prison population is relevant to the family contact issue because studies have shown that 61 per cent of women in prison in England and Wales are mothers (Caddle and Crisp, 1997) and at least 100,000 children in England and Wales are thought to be affected by a father in prison (Lloyd, 1995). The actual figures could be much higher as some prisoners do not reveal their parental status for fear that the children will be put into care. But using the present rate of imprisonment the increase in the number of children whose mother is in prison means that this impinges on the lives of over 11,000 children.

---

[2] This population measure underestimates the number of people who experience imprisonment. For example in 1998 the average prison population of women was 3,105 but there were 10,000 receptions of women in custody during the year.

[3] This projected figure is based on the impact of policy and changes in legislation which assume custody rates will rise but sentence lengths do not increase further (HMP RDS, March 2002).

[4] Figures may not sum due to rounding.

Imprisonment may impact upon the lives of nearly 124,000 children whose fathers are in prison.

Children affected by parental imprisonment comprise those whose parents are convicted and those on remand. A typology of prisoners' children was suggested by Lloyd (1995) who made the following categorisation: 1) children who remain with the other parent or close relative and retain some form of contact—these tend to be the children of male prisoners, 2) children in the same situation but who have little contact with the imprisoned parent—these tend to be children of female prisoners, 3) children who live with their mothers in prison, 4) children looked after by the local authority, and 5) children themselves in prison as juvenile offenders and separated from their own parents. I would suggest a further category, 6) children themselves in prison as juvenile offenders and who are themselves parents. The vast majority of children remain outside when the parent is imprisoned; the rest are held with their mothers in a mother and baby unit in prison. This chapter focuses on the situation of the first two categories before considering group three. Later in the chapter I will go on to consider children in categories four and six.[5]

2. CHILDREN'S CONTACT WITH THEIR IMPRISONED PARENTS

There are numerous ways that family ties may be forged, maintained and strengthened in families who enjoy freedom. For example, as technology advances families can use an increasing variety of digital equipment and computers to maintain contact. There are few means open however to prisoner-parents seeking to maintain contact with their children in the outside world. Contact in prison comprises visits by family to the prison, temporary release of the prisoner, telephone and mail. The next section illustrates the policy and the provision that governs contact, and discusses the constraints under which these operate as well as demonstrating how the situation has slowly worsened for prisoners' families over the past decade.

Prisoners are allowed one visit upon reception into prison and then two visits every four weeks thereafter. This single 'statutory' visit should be at least 30 minutes long.[6] More visits may be earned through compliant behaviour. A prisoner who is a long way from home may request a temporary transfer to take all their visits in one week at a prison nearer home. Alternatively, a contribution towards the costs of visiting may be given under the 'assisted visiting scheme' to low-income families.

All social visits are subject to a visiting order (VO), which is sent to the visitor who presents it on arrival at the prison. When children arrive after a long journey they may be hungry, tired and fractious and extended visits and visitor's

---

[5] For further information on children in category five however see Goldson (2002) or Neustatter (2002).

[6] Prison Rule 34(2) b1.

centres are provisions that were developed with the intention of relieving the worst effects of custody on prisoner families. Extended visits were begun in HMP Holloway whereby children could come in to the prison and spend a whole day with their mothers and Government commitment to this was shown in the 1991 White Paper *Custody, Care and Justice*. The 1992 Home Office Guidelines *Regimes for Women* further supported these schemes and they were extended to other prisons, some of which have since had to end them. There has also been a commitment since 1990 to set up visitors' centres in all new or refurbished prisons (Lloyd, 1995). Visitors' centres are special areas for family visiting and core services include a supervised play area, canteen facilities, a quiet room where confidential matters can be discussed and advice on welfare benefits and the criminal justice system can be given. However, a recent survey for the Prison Reform Trust (PRT) found that facilities ranged from bare halls with no staff to busy well-staffed resource centres (PRT, 2001). Thus there is a tension between official policy at the start of the decade and the subsequent quality of provision for families that exists now.

The Impact of Security and Risk Management on Contact 1992–2002

Early in the 1990s, The Woolf Report highlighted visits as a key obligation to those in prison care and prisons became more committed to improving visiting conditions, especially for children, both in England and Wales. However, following the escape of three men from Parkhurst prison in 1993 and the escape of six men from the Special Secure Unit (SSU) at Whitemoor prison in September 1994 two subsequent reports influenced the heightening and tightening of security across the prison system: the Woodcock Report (1995) and the Learmont Report. The influence of Woodcock was reflected in reports shortly afterwards:

> the effects that the break out from the SSU and subsequent Enquiry by Sir John Woodcock had had on the establishment and on the Prison Service in general were profound. The security systems in place at Whitemoor and the attitude of the staff we met towards security had increased out of all recognition. (Report of an unannounced inspection of Whitemoor, HMIP 1996)

At the same time complaints to the Board of Visitors revolved around the searching of visitors and one of the most common complaints of inmates was that the searching of children had not been carried out sensitively (HMIP, 1996). Thus the focus on security had begun to impact upon contact.

By contrast, the Ashworth Inquiry focused on a series of events at a special hospital in Liverpool. The inquiry team found that a father had taken a female child of eight to visit a patient with a long history of violent sexual assaults on little girls. She was undressed by this man and had inappropriate physical contact with him. Leave of absence visits also took place with a nurse escort during which inappropriate photographs of the little girl were taken at her home. During searches pornographic videos were found (including ones involving children and bestiality) and the inquiry found that the female child was being groomed for paedophile purposes. Since the findings of the Ashworth Inquiry (1999) were reported, the prevailing ethos has been that concerns of risk take precedence above all else in relation to the contact a child has with those in prison.[7] Throughout the same period, changes to the Mental Health Act of 1983 to include increased powers for detention have been under discussion.[8] Because it has been described as a lottery as to whether someone ends up in secure hospital or in the prison system[9] and because the majority of legal psychopaths are long-term and difficult-to-manage it has been suggested that psychiatrists are tempted to consider them untreatable, which results in those diagnosed with psychopathy going to prison (West, 2000). The increase of sex offenders in prison in addition to the longer sentences they now receive has resulted in changes to the demography of prison populations, resulting in less of the prison population being allowed contact with children.[10] The Prison Service is now expected to work with other agencies to assess the risk of prisoners both during sentence and pre-release.[11] This emphasis on safety would partially account for reductions in visits over time and suggests that this issue is part of a wider problem for the Prison Service.

Searching Constraints in the Wake of Ashworth and Woodcock

Both prisoners and their visitors can be searched. A full rub-down search is usual and a strip-search can be carried out with consent or by calling the police. The following excerpt from The Prisoners' Handbook illustrates what families might expect:

[7] *Guidance on the Visiting of Psychiatric Patients by Children* (HSC1999/222 LAC (99) 32) to NHS trusts contained guidance on the implementation of the recommendations. Further guidance is included in the White Paper Part I, 2000 (para 2.16).

[8] Discussion papers include *Managing Dangerous People with Severe Personality Disorder: Proposals for Policy Development* (HMSO,1999), and *Reforming the Mental Health Act* (2000) Cm 5016, Vol I and Vol II. *Directions and Associated Guidance to Ashworth, Broadmoor and Rampton Hospital Authorities* (HSC/160) sets out the procedure for deciding whether a child may visit a patient at these establishments.

[9] The Mental Health Act 1983 required that a person diagnosed with psychopathy must be 'treatable'. This depends on whether a) the offender is assessed, b) assessed by a clinician who is 'pro-treatment' or not, c) if 'treatable' whether a bed is available, 4) if a bed is available it depends on whether the judge accepts the diagnosis, and finally 5) if an offender gets to hospital on a hospital order with restrictions without limit of time. An individual committed to hospital on a section 37/41 hospital order may never be regarded as safe enough to leave hospital. S 46 of Crime (Sentences) Act 1997 amended the Mental Health Act 1983 to give the Crown power to admit to hospital instead of passing sentence after conviction.

[10] The percentage of sex offenders in the system may continue to rise given the recommendations of the Sentencing Advisory Panel for more severe sentences regarding child pornography. This, when balanced with calls for increases in electronic tagging and community sentences for other low risk offences, will cause a change in the present balance of prisoners.

[11] Prison Service Order 440 introduced child protection measures in Nov 1998 to 'minimise the risks from certain prisoners, particularly those convicted of, or charged with, sexual offences against children while in prison' (Creighton and King, 2000).

A strip search involves being asked to empty pockets and have the contents searched, removal and searching of headgear, search of hair, ear, nose and mouth, removal of clothing from the waist up—at which point you will be given a pre-searched dressing gown to wear. You will then be asked to remove your lower half clothing which will be searched. You will be asked to stand with your legs apart and take one step to the side—to make sure you are not standing on anything. For females wearing external sanitary towels, you may be asked to remove it: 'an appropriate container' will be available for disposal and a replacement towel will be provided. No prison officer has the right to remove, or ask that you remove, internally fitted tampons. (p 254)

This uncomfortable and humiliating procedure can place a strain on contact and parents have stated that they were prepared to be strip-searched after visits if it meant their children could be left alone. Further pressure can come when officers intimidate family as a means of controlling the prisoners.[12] If an illegal substance is passed to a prisoner the person can be passed to police, banned for three months, at the end of which closed visits will operate and (strip) searching will occur every time until the risk is deemed to be gone (Leech and Cheney, 2001). Given that 40 per cent of female and 17 per cent of male prisoners are in prison for drug offences the search is thus a regular feature of contact, and likely to be another reason why visits have decreased.

One of the most obvious constraints on contact, however, is the distance and inaccessibility of many prisons by public transport (PRT, 2001). Women's prisons in particular tend to be in remote parts of the country and the cost of journeys makes family visits difficult (National Association for the Care and Rehabilitation of Offenders—NACRO, 1996). The relatively small number of women's prisons means that temporary transfer to a local prison is less feasible than for men and nearly 20 per cent of women are held over 100 miles from their committal court town. As the average round trip of a visit is seven hours and no more than a quarter of this is for the visit itself, this can cause dislocation from family.[13] Given the increase in women prisoners, this distance is likely to have had a negative impact upon visits over the past decade.

It is not unusual for families to arrive for a visit and be told that the prisoner has been moved to another part of the country; or, for families to be turned away when there has been a 'lock-down' owing to threat, riot or fire (NACRO, 1996). This can act as a disincentive to families to visit again. Booking systems vary across prisons and a common complaint is the frustration caused by the booking system (HMIP, 2001). Every visit must take place within sight of an officer.[14] Directions may be given regarding the day and time a prisoner may be

---

[12] However an HMIP review deemed search procedures adequate against misuse (i.e. as a means of intimidation and control) (HMIP, 2001).

[13] Only 17 of 138 prisons hold women. Despite plans for two new women's prisons, one in Middlesex and one in Peterborough, neither will extend the geographical concentration of prisons that results in dislocation.

[14] Prison Rules 34(2) and Prison Rules 34(5) and (6).

visited.[15] No prisons allow visits on Christmas Day, Boxing Day or Good Friday and some prisons do not allow visiting on Sundays (Leech and Cheney, 2001).

There are constraints as to *who* may have contact. These include spouses, partners, parents, siblings, fiancées, and people in *loco parentis*. Anybody can be prohibited from visiting.[16] Ordinary visits take place at a table and high-risk prisoners have closed visits through a glass screen—this makes contact with children particularly difficult. Visitors are not allowed to take any personal possessions with them into prison. This includes children's drawings and models and children visiting are not allowed to carry a fur toy or comfort blanket.

A quarter of male juveniles in prison are fathers and the effect of the juvenile prison on young fathers was studied by Nurse (2001), who found that although 22 per cent saw their children weekly, one third did not see their children at all throughout their entire period in prison. The three main reasons given were lack of transport, the visiting list and the conditions of entry into prison. The visiting list dictates who is allowed to visit. The limits on the number of adult visitors makes things problematic for men whose girlfriends are not the mothers of their children and men who have children from multiple relationships may have to choose which children they will see. Few can resist seeing their girlfriends so they may miss substantial parts of their children's lives. Others arrange for their mothers or a sibling to bring the children but this is dependent upon good relationships with the children's mother. The conditions of entry into some prisons require compliance with a dress code. Twenty per cent of men in the study had families turned away for these reasons. Nurse (2001) states that all these formal policies stand in the way of men's ability to *build* a relationship with their children.

Two further elements prevent young men in prison from developing and sustaining contact. 'Hard timing' is when a young man is first received into prison and finds it hard to deal with the difficulties inside *and* outside, so he cuts off the outside to deal with the pressures within the prison walls (Nurse, 2001:379). Incarcerated young men then feel guilty and powerless at the same time and find it better not to know about the problems outside at all. It is possible that 'hard timing' can cause resentment in the family and harm family relationships. This element is related to safety, and, because of this, contact with family is not the most important thing for *all* prisoners. For example, when male inmates were asked what their three wishes in prison would be, the most popular answer was safety and support from staff and other inmates. Contact with family came second, and third was purposeful activity (Koch, 1992). Prison is not always a safe place and getting through the day uninjured in the prison system can be the most important concern for an inmate. Thus contact for the male prisoner is often secondary to personal safety. Only when safety is assured does contact become the most important priority. And regimes, as understood by male prisons, are

---

[15] Prison Rules 34(7).
[16] Except JPs, Board of Visitors, and lawyers. Prison Rule (73)(1) and (2).

not transferable to the female prisons where the main concern for the woman arriving in prison *is* her children (NACRO, 1996). Just as the prison service has to balance the priority of contact with good order and security then the (male) prisoner has to balance his priority of contact with his personal safety. So it can be argued that an important restraint on contact is its relationship to safety inside the prison for the prisoner.

Constraints on Temporary Release

An important way for prisoners to maintain quality contact with their children can be through temporary release. There are three types of temporary release: compassionate licence, for example to attend a family funeral; facility licence, for work experience or for an educational reason; resettlement licence, the main purpose of which is to enable prisoners to maintain family ties and links with the community. In all cases a risk assessment is made and the main factors are the risk to the public, whether the licence will be adhered to, suitable accommodation, and whether the purpose of release is likely to be acceptable to reasonable public opinion (Creighton and King, 1999). Many temporary release schemes, which operated successfully before *Woodcock* and *Ashworth* have now been curtailed.

Prior to the Woodcock Enquiry women were only handcuffed in exceptional cases where there was a high risk of escape. But following the publicity of some temporary release failures involving men who committed further offences or abused the 'privilege', women were also subject to this restraint. This has had a negative impact on the maintenance of family ties as women have stated that they could not face going out of prison for family funerals when they had to be handcuffed to an officer (NACRO, 1996). This was also found in a follow-up inspection by HMIP (2001) where women did not attend child custody hearings for the same reason. Whilst women prisoners are no longer chained during childbirth, women are still routinely handcuffed up to arrival at hospital and upon leaving the hospital.[17] There can be few greater barriers to contact for a mother nursing her newborn than manacles.

Wider Social Constraints on Contact and Gendered Experience

Wider social factors that constrain contact include financial hardship, as the children of imprisoned parents in this country are not entitled to benefits that are otherwise available to single-parent families (Lloyd, 1995). There may be

---

[17] PS Instruction 5/97: women admitted to NHS hospitals should not be handcuffed from the time they arrive at hospital until they leave. See HMIP (2001) for specific criticism of the practice of cuffing women and recommendations for best practice.

increased stress and tension in the house, increased responsibility for the care of the children, and loss of contact with other family members. There is a stigma attached to imprisonment that can cause isolation and hostility in the community and Girschick (1996) argues that imprisonment is different from loss through separation or by any other means, as other types of separation have social approval whereas imprisonment never does and she refers to loss of family through incarceration as family 'dismemberment'.

There are gender differences in the constraints on contact and the loss is considered to be greater if a mother is sent to prison as often she is the child's primary carer. In this situation, other changes may follow; father, partner, or older sibling becomes the primary carer, or the child moves in with relatives or friends, or the child is taken into care and may be fostered or adopted causing permanent loss of contact in some cases. If prisoners lose their home when in prison they also lose all their possessions. It is most often women who lose homes and everything they own and the curb on temporary release makes it harder for these prisoners to secure a home (NACRO, 2001).[18] Children may continue living with relatives and this lessens a woman's priority for housing with the local authority. To gain priority a woman must have her children with her but cannot do so without housing so she is caught in a housing trap.[19] Women are more likely to lose contact in this way than men. The situation for foreign nationals is worse than for home prisoners as few of the provisions for visits apply to them since their children are unlikely to be visiting them. Indeed as Richards *et al* (1995) point out, extensive provision for home prisoners may make the separation of foreign national prisoners from their own children even more painful. Foreign nationals also have special contact needs as there may be language difficulties and lack of familiarity with the English legal process. The PRT provide a foreign prisoner's resource pack and the Prison Service provides a 24-hour telephone interpreting service along with free letters on reception into prison, but there is no other specific provision for foreign nationals with children (HMP, 1999).

The gender differences of prisoner's experiences go beyond the English legal system and in 1997 the President of the Republic of South Africa exercised his right to free certain prisoners by freeing mothers with children under 12 years old. Hugo was a male prisoner in prison in South Africa when he became sole carer of his children on the death of his wife. He challenged this exercise in *President of Republic of South Africa v Hugo*[20] on the basis that it discriminated against him on the grounds of sex/gender and indirectly against his son because the sole parent was not a woman. Following full scrutiny under the Bill of Rights

[18] One survey found that 81% of women had a home before prison but 48% expected to be homeless on release (NACRO, 2001).

[19] The Wedderburn Committee for NACRO (2001) recommended small geographically dispersed custodial units to ensure support for women after release. These would enable women to keep their children after release.

[20] 1997 (4) SA 1 (CC).

a judicial review found that, although the exercise of such powers may have been discriminatory, the discrimination was not unfair and therefore did not violate the equality clause in the Constitution. Sinclair (2002) argues that the 'trail of confusion' this judgment has caused derives from the court's failure to acknowledge Hugo as a single parent, and the court's denial to single fathers who were prisoners of the same benefits accorded to single mothers who were prisoners. The court claimed that male prisoners were denied the right, not because of the presidential pardon to women but because of their own criminality. This case privileges a female parent over a male parent, and provides evidence that the courts (in South Africa) do not see parental rights as equal rights.

Constraints on Indirect Contact: Telephone and Correspondence

The telephone also represents an important medium of contact for prisoners especially when the literacy difficulties of the average prisoner are considered. For foreign nationals in prison the telephone may be the only way of maintaining family ties. Telephone provision varies however throughout the prison estate[21] and prisoners are limited to 15 numbers of family and friends. These numbers may not be changed more than once a month—even though a child in care can have three or four different homes during a mother's sentence and foreign national prisoners who as Richards *et al* (1995) illustrate, have more dependent children, and cannot make use of other opportunities for contact for these prisoners.[22] Some prisoners are allowed a free call on reception into prison; for others it will depend on the private 'spends' they have. In the case of those women imprisoned for drug offences, money is seized as part of the crime. This means that some prisoners will be unable to maintain contact with their children or even make plans for childcare when being remanded into custody. All of these issues show that contact is part of a wider problem than visits alone.

Convicted prisoners are allowed one 'statutory' letter a week.[23] Prisoners should also be allowed at least one 'privilege' letter per week and as many above that with which the prison has staff to cope.[24] All communication can be listened to, opened and examined.[25] The formal policy and rules on correspon-

---

[21] See HMIP (2001) for examples of security measures that have been questioned by HM Inspectorate of Prisons and for examples of good practice.

[22] This is supported by NACRO (1996) who found that Nigerian prisoners in particular had problems with the telephone as few families had telephones and therefore calls had to be to neighbours necessitating two calls.

[23] Prison Rules 34(2)(a).

[24] Such letters are paid for out of prison earnings or private 'spends'. PSO 5 B (6A) (2).

[25] Routine censorship occurs for category A prisoners and those on the 'escape' list unless grounds exist that a prisoner is breaking rules on correspondence. *All* letters are routinely opened however to check for illegal enclosures (Leech and Cheney, 2001). Prison Standing Order (PSO) (34) States that all mail may be read but PSO 5 B (31) (2) suggests this should only be done in open conditions if it is suspected of containing illicit enclosures.

dence are a result of the decision in *Silver* (1980/1983) whereby a prisoners' mail was withheld by the prison under the 'prior ventilation' rule which required a prisoner to raise an issue with the prison before taking the matter outside. In *Golder v UK*[26] a prison officer had stopped a prisoner's correspondence to his solicitor. The European Court held that this violated his right under Article 8(1) to respect for correspondence and also Article 6(1) right of access to a court, and in so doing identified the principle for correspondence (for further discussion of these articles see Bainham this volume). Both of these cases have obvious implications for wider contact.

Constraints Imposed by the Incentives and Earned Privileges Scheme and 'Volumetric Control'

Eligibility to receive visits and send mail is linked to the incentives and earned privileges scheme (IEP) which was imposed following *Woodcock*. The IEP has a hierarchy of three levels: basic, standard and enhanced. Prisoners on 'enhanced' receive more visits than those on standard or basic. They can also earn better visits in improved surroundings, for longer, with more choice over the time of day. There are implications for children's rights of contact being linked to a family member's status on the IEP scheme. Following *Ashworth* it became necessary for the frequent cell searches to be carried out easily and efficiently, and all prisoners' belongings must now fit into two prison issue boxes of 1m[3]. This 'volumetric control' places limits on the amount of children's drawings, school reports and family photographs prisoners can keep in their possession. It also limits the amount of hobby items or knitting a prisoner may have in their possession in order to make a present for a child. As the giving and receiving of gifts is a common way of showing feelings and care, this has direct implications for the quality of contact a prisoner has with their child.

No statutory agency or service is responsible for the children or family of prisoners and it is usually only when child protection has to be considered that social services get involved (Ramsden, 1998). Under paragraph 10 schedule 2 of the Children Act 1989, there is an obligation on the the local authority to help maintain contact for children who are not looked after but are living apart from their family either to enable the child to live with their family or to promote contact if necessary to promote or safeguard the child's welfare. However, it is not clear how 'family' is defined, and the obligation to foster links with family is seldom invoked when a family member is sent to prison.

It can be seen that a variety of practical and legal constraints is imposed on *every* form of prisoner-family contact and that many of these restrictions are the direct result of specific incidents such as those at Ashworth and Whitemoor and their analysis, as well as wider social policies such as sentencing. Not

---

[26] (1975) 1 EHRR 524.

surprisingly then, considering the above constraints on contact, the extension of units in which prisoners may look after their children *within* prison has been advocated, for example, NACRO (2001) and HMIP (2001). In the next section I examine the question of mother and baby units and also explore the nature of parental rights and contact in this context.

3. CHILDREN LIVING WITH PARENTS IN PRISON

> The prison, which could spoil so many things, had tainted Little Dorrit's mind no more than this. Engendered as the confusion was, in compassion for the poor little prisoner . . . it was the last speck Clennam ever saw, of the prison atmosphere upon her. (*Little Dorrit*, ch 10, p 353)

It is not a recent phenomenon for children to be brought up in prison. Notwithstanding the fictional example of the child of Marshalsea Prison[27] a number of historical prison biographies illustrate children in prison with their parents (see for example Priestley, 1985). Before the formal establishment of mother and baby units (MBUs), mothers in closed conditions could keep their babies until they were toddlers when they had to hand them over to families or agencies to care for outside prison. In open prisons, the first of which, Askham Grange, was opened in 1947 children were allowed to stay until three years of age. Provision for mothers and babies in prison has increased by over a third in the past decade while the age at which the child is allowed to be in prison has been reduced to 18 months. There were places for 39 babies in three institutions in England and Wales in 1992 (Catan, 1992). There are now 65 places in four institutions in England and Wales and a fifth is planned (House of Commons written answers 27 January 2000). A mother admitted to an MBU may stay until her baby is 18 months old and then a separation plan is drawn up to aid the child's transition to a carer outside prison. In the most recent Prison Service Report, *Report of a Review of Principles, Policies and Procedures on Mothers and Babies in Prison* (1999) some of the most salient recommendations for policy were:

—that the interests of the child should be the primary consideration at every level;
—the MBU must have a strategy that supports 'family ties';
—to review policy that bars foreign national women from open conditions.

Further down the list was the consideration of the: 'importance for fathers as well as for mothers to maintain family relationships'. Way down the list was the investigation of the needs of male prisoners who are fathers, have parental responsibility, or were primary carers before imprisonment and I will show later how this hierarchy of gender is further borne out in case law.

---

[27] Dickens' novel of a child born in prison was based on his own experience of his father's imprisonment in 1824.

Mother's Rights, Children's Rights and Arguments in Favour of MBUs

The main arguments for mother and baby units in prisons are that close contact between mother and child encourages the bonding process because of the key role of the mother in the child's development, and that separation causes long term emotional damage (Caddle, 1998). For example, Catan's (1989, 1992) comparison of the development of babies inside and outside prison found that although both groups had normal healthy physical growth, babies in units for over four months showed a slight decline in some cognitive and locomotor skills. As children became more mobile there was less opportunity to use skills in confinement. This study gave support to the fixing of 18 months as an upper age limit in MBUs in England and Wales (Caddle, 1998). There is variability across Europe in the upper age limits of children who may stay with their mothers in prison[28] and children at Ter Peel prison in the Netherlands have shown normal development owing to the space provided by its woodland setting.

The arguments against mothers having their babies in prison in MBUs are numerous. The most commonly used is that prisons are unsuitable places for children; the overall rates of mental illness are higher than in the community for example,[29] and in prison substance abuse is approximately 40 per cent higher than in the community (Blaauw, 2001). There is also inferior health care in prisons.[30] For example, the nursing staff are security officers first and nurses second. Further arguments include the view that the environment shapes those growing inside in the formation of future criminogenic attitudes. Violence in prisons is another factor which will impact on a child. Another argument relates to the dislocation; when a mother is in an MBU she can be even further from her other children and the baby's siblings thus denying the baby contact with their siblings.[31] In an MBU the IEP scheme means that babies' contact with the outside world can be tied to their mothers' compliance with the system. If the mother loses 'privilege' visits this violates the child's right to contact with the family. It can be argued that the very existence of MBUs privileges the mother's role with the child and denies the father's right of contact. Although the debate continues as to whether children should be in containment at all, it is clear that parental rights are gendered in this respect.

---

[28] For example in Spain and Germany the upper limit is 6 years of age whereas in Sweden and Ireland it is one year old. For further comparison see Caddle (1998).

[29] Although studies produce different rates, the overall rate of psychotic disorder is 5% higher than in the community (Blaauw, 2001).

[30] It is argued that this separate system lags behind the NHS (in terms of delivery, quality and funding) and is providing a worse system. Recommendations have been made by both the Royal College of Psychiatrists (from 1979) and the Chief Inspector of Prisons (1996) that the NHS should take over the prison medical service.

[31] For example in a HMIP Review (2001) only one woman residing in the open unit at Askham Grange lived within 50 miles of her home; two thirds lived more than 100 miles away.

4. PRISONERS' RIGHTS AND THE FORFEIT OF RIGHTS TO CONTACT

How then do these provisions and constraints translate into rights, and what rights do prisoner parents have to maintain family ties when these rights are tested in court? A commonly used dictum is that of Lord Wilberforce in *Raymond v Honey* (1982)[32] who stated:

> Under English law, a convicted prisoner, in spite of his imprisonment, retains all civil rights which are not taken away expressly or by implication.

The statutory provision for the power of the court to make a contact order in the private sphere comes in Section 8 of the Children Act 1989 and section 34 enables the court to make contact orders when children are in care. To explore how prisoners' rights to contact have been interpreted by the courts, the following section will examine specific cases where rights have been balanced against good order and security as well as against the rights of those of other family members.

The case of *Birmingham City Council v H (No 3)*[33] involved an application for contact with a child in care. Both the mother and child were 'children' under the Children Act 1989 and both subject to care orders. The mother had the baby at 14 years old and when the baby was a year old the mother was thought to be 'rough handling' him. The baby was placed with foster parents and the mother applied for contact. The Lords had to decide who was the child in this case. They decided that it was the baby and therefore, applying the welfare principle, it was held that it was the baby's welfare which was paramount. And in *R v Secretary of State ex p Hinckling and JH (minor)* (1986)[34] a mother's disruptive behaviour in an MBU at Askham Grange prison in open conditions had prompted her removal from the unit and a transfer to Bullwood Hall, a closed prison without any mother and baby unit. The baby was removed from its mother and put into care. Both mother and baby were denied contact as a disciplinary act towards the mother. The Court of Appeal turned down an application for judicial review of procedures relating to the Governor's decision. The Governor's decision in the light of the security and operation of the unit was enough to dismiss any claim that he had acted unreasonably. In both of these cases the decisions would require further consideration in a post-Human Rights Act environment, and the decision in the second case might be overruled as it arguably violates the mother's and the child's rights.

In 1995 the Court of Appeal refused leave in *R v Secretary of State ex P Togher* (1995) for a judicial review challenge by a prisoner mother of a two month old child, who had been classified as provisional category A due to a drugs importing charge. She was refused a place in an MBU despite medical

---

[32] *Raymond v Honey* [1983] 1 AC 1.
[33] House of Lords [1994] 1 FLR 224.
[34] [1986] 1FLR 543.

advice that she was still breastfeeding. Hirst LJ decreed that the Secretary of State had not acted unreasonably after hearing evidence that the mother was part of a drugs ring with sufficient contacts to mount an escape attempt in which violence might be used. In this case, the good order and security of the prison again took precedence over the child's right to contact. However in later cases, *The Queen on the Application of P and Q and QB v Secretary of State for the Home Department and Another*,[35] there were appeals brought by two mothers who asked that their babies stay with them for longer than the 18 month limit. P was a Jamaican woman sentenced to 8 years for importing drugs. Her baby PB was 20 months old at the time of the appeal. P had three other children in Jamaica and she was likely to be deported following her sentence. She could not stay on the MBU and although the most ideal solution would have been a place in open conditions, P as a deportee, was not entitled to live in open conditions under Prison Service policy.

In the case of Q she had given birth while on bail for offences involving class B drugs. She was sentenced to five years when her baby QB was nine months old and so did not have as much of her sentence to run. Mother and baby were at Askham Grange, which has large grounds to which prisoners have free access. A report from a social worker stated that the child would suffer significant harm if separated from her mother and the best result would be to have day care during the week whilst living with her mother in open conditions. There was also a problem finding a suitable and culturally appropriate foster carer.

In both cases it was clear that family life had been established and compulsory separation was a serious interference by the State with the children's right to that. The cases presented a complex dilemma in balancing the competing interests of the State in the proper management of prisons with those of mothers and their right to family life, together with the interests of the children's right to family life and also of their best interests. Importantly too, it was considered that the Prison Service had declared that the objective of its policies and practice in relation to MBUs was to 'promote the welfare of the child'. It was accepted that the Prison Service was entitled to have a policy but, having declared a policy, it was the view of the Court of Appeal that the policy should be more flexible for two reasons. Firstly, the policy's own aim was to promote the welfare of the child, and, if the effect of that policy was to have a catastrophic effect on the welfare of a child, then the policy was not meeting its own objectives. Secondly, the interference with the child's right to family life, which the Prison Service had allowed and encouraged to develop, must be justified. The Prison Service has to strike a balance between the necessary limitations on the mother's rights and freedoms in prison, the extent to which a relaxation in policy would cause problems for the good order of the prison and service as a whole, and the welfare of the individual child. The court thus allowed Q's appeal and she was permitted to keep her child with her until the end of her sentence. P's appeal was dismissed

---

[35] [2001] 2 FLR 1122.

on the grounds that a culturally appropriate and suitable foster home had been found. The Court made it clear that such challenges to prison policy would have little prospect of success unless brought on behalf of a child whose welfare is seriously at risk from separation through incarceration.

In the more recent case of *Kleuver v Norway*,[36] a mother on remand for drug smuggling in Norway claimed her parental rights were breached when her newborn baby was removed after birth to a nearby centre and then, following her conviction, to the maternal grandmother in the Netherlands. It was held that there was no infringement of Article 8. No infringement of Article 8 was found either regarding the presence of officers during her pre-natal scans or in the use of escape chains when she visited her baby in hospital.

The Rights of Prisoners in Contested Contact

In private law cases of contested contact, the rights of prisoners have had to be balanced against the rights and obligations of the other parent and also the rights of the child in question. In *Re M (Contact Conditions)*[37] the child was three years old and the parents separated when the child was one year old. The mother alleged that the father had been violent to her and she left without informing him of her whereabouts. The father was in prison on serious criminal charges and wished to see the child while in prison. The magistrates made a contact order for indirect contact by post which the mother would have to read to the child along with sending progress reports to the father. The mother appealed the decision. The decision was upheld on the grounds that the justices failed to assess the burden on the mother of such contact. The Court of Appeal held that the mother must have power of censorship over correspondence. In this case such an order should only have been made with the consent of the mother. Nor was it in the court's jurisdiction in ordering contact to order the parents to have contact with each other and thus there were limits to the duties that could be imposed on the mother. The court had the power to prevent a parent from impeding a contact order but not the coercive power to compel a parent to undertake a facilitative act. This case sets boundaries and limits to a father's rights and a mother's obligations.

In *S v P (Contact)*[38] a father in prison for three years applied for direct contact with two children. The mother opposed contact as she feared for her new family if their address was discovered, nor was anyone able to escort the children to visit the father. The judge made an order for indirect contact with an order for the mother to send photographs and progress reports. The court could not make a direct contact order without the consent of the local authority and

---

[36]   Application No 45837/99/Decision 30.4.2002.
[37]   [1994] 1 FLR 272.
[38]   [1997] 2 FLR 277.

there was none. The father had to wait for release before being able to make a direct contact application. However, in *Re O (Contact: Imposition of Conditions)*[39] the parents' relationship broke up during the pregnancy amidst the man's violence towards the child's mother. The father, who was in prison, applied for indirect contact with his three-year-old son. The court accepted that the child should not know his biological parent until later in life. But the father appealed and the appeal was upheld on the grounds that to do otherwise was storing up trouble for the future. On appeal the court held that it was very important for a child to have some knowledge and some contact with his natural father. It was therefore both a fundamental right of the child and in the child's welfare to have contact with both his parents. The father was given indirect contact through the mother's solicitors and allowed to send letters and small presents. It was interesting that the court did not factor in the mother's right to a private life nor the father's right to family life although the case was admittedly decided before the HRA. In both this case and *S v P* there was no State obligation to facilitate contact.

In a further case of indirect contact a father had been violent to the mother, which the 12-year-old child remembered witnessing. In *Re P (contact: indirect contact)*[40] the father was in prison for armed robbery. The child had been to see the father in prison and the child told the court that he would not mind having some written contact with his father. While magistrates dismissed the father's application, the Family Division upheld his appeal for indirect contact on the grounds that the magistrates did not understand how limited indirect contact was. This was to be restricted to sending birthday and Christmas cards and was enough to remind the child that he had a father and to give the father the opportunity of showing the boy he did care for him. It can be seen from these cases that the courts hold a father's right to indirect contact with his children as important irrespective of whether or not he is in prison.

Ironically, the judicial system has incarcerated parents for refusing to allow contact to the other parent. In *A v N (Committal: Refusal of Contact)*[41] a father requested contact with his four-year-old daughter with whom family life had been established. The court granted supervised contact on the grounds of the mother's fears of the father's previous violence but the mother refused to accept the contact order. The court finally and reluctantly imprisoned her for six months. However, Herring (2001) points out that more recent cases have tried to avoid such a drastic step. In such cases as *Re F (Contact: Enforcement: Representation of Child)*[42] and *(Re L (A Child) (Contact: Domestic Violence)*[43] the judge recommended that treatment such as family therapy might be more

[39] [1995] 2 FLR 124.
[40] [1999] 2 FLR 893.
[41] [1997] 1 FLR 553.
[42] [1998] 1 FLR 691.
[43] [2000] 2 FCR 42.

effective than imprisonment; an approach that is more in keeping with the HRA (Herring, 2001) (see discussion by Bainham, Herring, and Lindley and Miles, this volume).

5. THE FORFEIT OF PRISONER RIGHTS IN ADOPTION

The lack of prisoners' parental rights may well also impact upon a child's right to freedom from harm/torture. In the US, the Adoption and Safe Families Act 1997 allows courts to begin terminating parental rights if a child is in foster care for 15 months in any 22 month period. However, it is possible for an accused person to wait that long to come to trial. Given that the US female prison population alone has risen 650 per cent in the past two decades this constitutes a serious problem for those who are parents. This reduction in the rights of parent-prisoners may also be a reason why the adoption rates in the US are comparatively large (see Eekelaar and Lindley and Miles, this volume). Indeed, many non-relative foster families express concern about parental incarceration and carers question the parenting capacities of incarcerated parents, the likelihood of rehabilitation and the advisability of parent-child contact in a prison setting (Seymour and Finney Hairston, 2001).[44] Fear of losing their children forever in this way is one reason why women have left their children with the same family in which they themselves were abused. Because leaving a child with family increased the chance of a woman retaining custody of, and contact with, her children after release, women felt that putting their children with their own past abuser was the lesser of two evils (Sharp and Marcus-Mendoza, 2001).

Prisoner-fathers' rights fare even worse than mothers' where adoption is concerned. In *Re M (Adoption: rights of father)*[45] the mother wanted to place the child for adoption. The father had spent many years in prison. The local authority had a duty to contact the father but the mother applied to the court for an order that no contact should be made with the father. The court decided that the local authority did not have to locate the father as there had never been any 'established family life' between the father, mother and child. *If* there was a failure to respect his family life this was justified in order to protect the rights of the mother and the two children. This case suggests however, that those men who are in custody and unable to *establish* family life then have their rights as a father eroded.

---

[44] These fears are not grounded in research evidence. Boswell (2002) explored children's views of visiting their father in prison and found that all of the children had positive feelings about visiting their father. Johnston (1995) found no long-term negative effects from visiting although short term ones such as excitability were found.

[45] [2001] 1 FLR 745.

6. IMPLICATIONS FOR PRISON AND EDUCATION POLICY

There is a growing recognition of the plight of prisoners' children as the successive penal policies mentioned above have made things more difficult with regard to contact. There is clearly a need to balance long-term outcomes of various measures with short-term cost and acceptability as the long-term benefits may outweigh the short-term costs of policies that improve contact. For example, a new post, that of Family Development Contact Officer, has been initiated in the Prison Service to facilitate family contact and look after family needs in a proactive way. But as yet there is only one of these officers in England. The Prison Service should consider a more proactive policy with regard to recruitment and development of staff in this role. Other less formal resources that could profitably be considered include materials and books for teachers who may have prisoners' children in class and storybooks for children to help them to understand why contact is intermittent if it occurs at all (see Ramsden, 1998).

Given that the demographic and social features of the prison population are related to wider issues of parent-children contact such as age (the male population in particular are young), and high frequency of disrupted relationships with their own parents (compared with the general population), there are serious risks of disrupted relationships with children (see Dunn, this volume). The prison could be a suitable place to foster 'quality' contact and the Prison Service might do well to target this group who may never have learnt 'how to parent'. One project found to help the quality of father-child contact was carried out in Nottingham at Holme House Prison when a 'storysack' project was set up (Cashman, 2001). In this study, offenders wrote or read a story for their child and then recorded it. The outcome was positive. It provided a way for the father and child to share a book together which they may not have done before.

On a more fundamental level some limited research to date suggests that positive attitudes to fathering *can* be fostered within the prison environment. A 'young men as fathers' programme runs at four institutions with the aims of promoting active fathering (which would enable men to create a relationship with children) and also to decrease violence against children (Nurse, 2001):

> [previously] I didn't know nothing about the baby shaking syndrome or whatever. And I used to . . . like a little rough horseplay. I figured he was laughing, there wasn't nothing wrong with it. After going through that class, that's how lots of babies are injured. Also, I know a lot of people who before I went to YA, I used to do it to, give babies alcohol to put them to sleep, and blowing marijuana smoke in their face and I thought it was cool, I thought it was funny until I realised what could actually happen to the baby. Their system isn't as developed as ours, you know. A little alcohol can kill a baby. I realize a lot about child safety, being there for the child is more important than giving them money.

This study shows that groups that educate fathers in prison about parenting may have a beneficial effect on their subsequent knowledge and behaviour during contact. The expansion of such projects and fathering classes could be explored within the prison estate.

7. CONCLUSIONS

In this chapter I have shown many of the reasons why contact in containment has decreased despite the growing prison population. This decline is due not only to difficulties in booking visits and long distances but is also likely to be part of wider policies such as those on sentencing, sex offending, safety and security that have impacted upon prisoner-family contact. The legacy of *Woodcock* and *Ashworth* set in train many powerful constraints and restraints on visitors with regard to searching and curbs on temporary release and visits. The exploration of rights has shown that men may be disadvantaged by not being allowed to establish contact in the first place, that direct contact rights are highly gendered in a penal context and that access to new technologies still remain beyond the prisoner who wishes to become a parent. In doing this I have also shown, implicitly, how prisoner parents differ from parents and carers discussed elsewhere in the book, in for example, the denial of contact used as a disciplinary act against disruptive prisoners.

The Blair administration has been criticised for its 'continuing love affair with custody' and the current political trend will ensure that even greater numbers of men and women will be contained in prison.[46] Although the prison environment can militate against the quantity and quality of parent-child contact, it can also be a place in which positive attitudes to contact and parent education can be promoted. The research evidence shows that there are some innovative ways of promoting and maintaining contact, especially with regard to fathering. It might be worthwhile for the prison services to consider some of these further.

REFERENCES

BLAAUW, E, 'Suicide in Prison'. Conference Paper delivered at The Assessment and Treatment of Sex Offenders Conference, University of Leicester, April 2001.
BOSWELL, G, 'Imprisoned Fathers: the Children's View' (2002) 41 *Howard Journal of Criminal Justice* 14.
CADDLE, D, *Age Limits for Babies in Prison—Some Lessons from Abroad.* Research Findings No 80 (London, HMSO, 1998).
CADDLE, D and CRISP, D, *Mothers in Prison.* Research Findings No 38 (London, HMSO, 1997).

[46] Director General of the Prison Service Martin Narey was reported to have referred to the Government's policy on imprisonment in this way during a Downing Street seminar (*The Guardian*, 14 May 2002).

CASEMENT, P, *On Learning from the Patient* (London, Tavistock, 1986).

CASHMAN, H, 'Time for Kids: A Story-Sack Project at a Local Prison', (134) *Prison Service Journal*; Mar 2001, pp 39–41.

CATAN, L, 'Infants with Mothers in Prison' in R Shaw (ed), *Prisoners' Children: What are the Issues?* (London, Routledge, 1992).

—— The Development of Young Children in Mother and Baby Units (London, Home Office Research and Planning Unit, 1989).

CREIGHTON, S and KING, V, *Prisoners and the Law* (2nd edn, London, Butterworths, 2000).

COUNCELL, R and SIMES, J, *Projection of Long Term Trends in the Prison Population to 2009*. Home Office Statistical Bulletin 14/02. http://www.homeoffice.gov.uk/rds/index.html

DICKENS, C, *Little Dorritt* (Oxford, Oxford University Press, re-issued 1999).

Department of Health, 'Inspection of Facilities for Mothers and Babies in Prison'. Third inspection (London, Dept of Health, 1996).

—— Consultation on Draft Mental Health Bill. 18 June 2002.

FALLON, P, BLUEGLASS, R, EDWARDS, B, DANIELS, G, Report of the Committee of Inquiry into the Personality Disorder Unit, Ashworth Special Hospital (London, The Stationery Office). Cm 4194–ii, 1999.

GIRSCHICK, LB, *Soledad Women. Wives of Prisoners Speak Out* (Westport, Connecticut, 1996).

GOFFMAN, E, *Asylums* (London, Penguin, 1961).

GOLDSON, B, *Vulnerable Inside. Children in Secure and Penal Settings* (London, The Children's Society, 2002).

HERRING, J, *Family Law* (Harlow, Longman, 2001).

HM Prison Service, *Report of a Review of Principles, Policies and Procedures on Mothers and Babies/Children in Prison* (London, HM Prison Service, 1999).

HMIP, *Women in Prison: A Thematic Review by HM Chief Inspector of Prisons* (London, HMSO, 1997).

HMIP, *Follow-up to Women in Prison: A Thematic Review by HM Chief Inspector of Prisons* (London, HMSO, 2001).

HMIP, *Report of Unannounced Inspection of HMP Whitemoor* (HMIP, 1996).

Home Office, *Prison Population Brief England and Wales* June 2002 (Home Office, London, 2002).

House of Commons Written Answers, 27 January 2000 (pt 4) http://www.parliament. the-stationery-office.co.uk/pa/cm199900/cmhan.../00127wo4.ht)

Howard League for Penal Reform, *'I Thought Babies Weren't Prisoners': Why are They being Deprived in Prison Mother and Baby Units?* (London, Howard League for Penal Reform, 1995).

JOHNSTONE, D, 'Child Custody Issues of Women Prisoners. A Preliminary Report from the CHICAS project' (1995) 75 *The Prison Journal* 222.

LEECH, M and CHENEY, D, *The Prisons Handbook* (Winchester, Waterside Press, 2001).

LIVINGSTONE, S and OWEN, T, *Prison Law* (2nd edn, Oxford, Oxford University Press, 1999).

LOUCKS, N, *Prison Rules: A Working Guide. Millennium Edition* (London, Prison Reform Trust, 2000).

LLOYD, E, *UK Prisoners' Children* (London, Save the Children Fund, 1998).

—— (ed), *Children Visiting Holloway Prison* (London, Save the Children, 1995).

NACRO, *Women Beyond Bars: A Positive Agenda for Women Prisoners' Resettlement* (London, National Association for the Care and Resettlement of Offenders, 2001).

NACRO, *Women Prisoners. Towards a New Millennium* (London, National Association for the Care and Resettlement of Offenders, 1996).

NEUSTATTER, A, *Locked In, Locked Out* (London, Turnaround Ltd, 2002).

NURSE, AM, 'The Structure of the Juvenile Prison: Constructing the Inmate Father' (2001) 32 *Youth and Society* 360.

PRIESTLY, P, *Victorian Prison Lives. English Prison Biography 1830–1914* (London, Methuen, 1985).

Prison Reform Trust, *Justice for Women* (Report by D Wedderburn) (London, Prison Reform Trust, 2000).

——*Justice for Women: the Need for Reform. The Report of the Committee on Women's Imprisonment* (London, Prison Reform Trust, 2000).

——*Just Visiting? A Review of the Role of Visitors' Centres* (London, Prison Reform Trust, 2001).

RAMSDEN, S, *Working with Children of Prisoners. A Resource for Children* (London, Save the Children, 1998).

RICHARDS, MPM, 'The Separation of Children and Parents: Some Issues and Problems' in R Shaw (ed), *Prisoners' Children. What are the Issues?* (London, Routledge, 1992).

RICHARDS, MPM, MCWILLIAMS, B, BATTEN, N, CAMERON, C and CUTLER, J, 'Foreign Nationals in UK Prisons: I. Family Ties and their Maintenance' (1995) 34 *Howard Journal of Criminal Justice* 158.

——'Foreign Nationals in UK Prisons: II. Some Policy Issues' (1995) *Howard Journal of Criminal Justice* 195.

Sentencing Advisory Panel *Offences During Child Pornography*. 15 January 2002 Downloaded 9/05/02 httpPwww.sentencing-advisory-anel.gov.uk/c_and_a/consult/child_offences/page_07.htm

SEYMOUR, C and FINNEY HAIRSTON, C (eds), *Children with Parents in Prison* (London/New York, Transaction, 2001).

SHARP, SF and MARCUS-MENDOZA, ST, 'It's a Family Affair: Incarcerated Women and Their Families', (2001) 12 *Women and Criminal Justice* 21.

SHAW, R (ed), *Prisoners' Children: What are the Issues?* (London, Routledge, 1992).

SINCLAIR, J, 'Ebb and Flow: The Retreat of the Legislature and Development of a Constitutional Jurisprudence to Reshape Family Law' in A Bainham (ed), *International Survey of Family Law* (Bristol, Jordans, 2002).

TOCH, H, *Living in Prison* (Washington, APA Books, 1993).

WEST, D, 'Paedophilia: Plague or Panic?' (2000) 11 *Journal of Forensic Psychiatry* 511.

WOLFE, T, *Counting the Cost. The Social and Financial Consequences of Women's Imprisonment*. Report presented to Wedderburn committee on women's imprisonment. March 1999.

WOODCOCK, SIR JOHN, The Escape from Whitemoor Prison on Friday 9th September 1994 (Cmnd 2741) (London, HMSO, 1994).

17

Making Contact Work in International Cases: Promoting Contact Whilst Preventing International Parental Child Abduction

DONNA SMITH

1. INTRODUCTION

THE CHALLENGES TO 'making contact work' in domestic cases have been extremely well documented by the government consultation on contact which culminated in the *Making Contact Work* report to the Lord Chancellor (Lord Chancellor's Department, 2002), and indeed by several authors within this volume. In this chapter I consider the challenges to making contact work in *international* cases: those cases where a parent remains resident in England/ Wales following separation from the other parent but has links with another country, for example family or business interests, and those cases where a parent becomes resident outside England/Wales following separation from the other parent.

Of course contact might 'work' in international cases without any intervention by the legal system, just as it does in many domestic cases, and it will often mean just what it does in domestic cases, with the attendant aims and challenges. However, in cases where contact is likely to be problematic, an international dimension might be an exacerbating factor or at least an additional challenge. Firstly, barriers to achieving meaningful contact in the domestic arena might be amplified in cases where one separated parent is resident in or has connections with another country. Moreover, securing, facilitating and enforcing contact in such cases is likely to be much more difficult than in domestic cases due to practical, financial and legal difficulties. Secondly, making contact work in international cases (or indeed failing to do so) might increase the risk of international parental child abduction, that is where one parent removes the child from England/Wales without the consent of the other parent, usually to a country with which they have a connection, or where a parent who is now resident outside England/Wales retains the child abroad after a lawful period of contact. Safeguarding contact and minimising the risk of international parental child abduction is likely to be much more difficult in cases where one parent has connections with another country or is resident in another country.

This chapter will demonstrate that making contact work in such cases will entail promoting it where this is consistent with the welfare of the child, whilst simultaneously preventing international parental child abduction. I begin with an analysis of the problem of international parental child abduction in order to illustrate the paramountcy of prevention. Thereafter I focus on the ways in which the legal system might assist parents in making contact work in international cases: how the non-resident parent may secure, facilitate and (if necessary) enforce contact in order to promote a continuing and meaningful relationship with their child(ren), and how the resident parent[1] may safeguard contact in order to prevent, reduce the risk of, or at least not cause, international parental child abduction.

2. INTERNATIONAL PARENTAL CHILD ABDUCTION

Reunite International Child Abduction Centre[2] ('*Reunite*') received reports of 365 children having been abducted from the United Kingdom by one of their parents in 2000 (Reunite, 2001). This figure represented a 64 per cent increase in the number of children abducted from the United Kingdom during the period 1995 to 2000. Whilst *Reunite* is the only United Kingdom-based charity specialising in international child abduction, it is of course unlikely that all cases are reported to it, hence the true figure will be higher.[3] There is no reason to suspect that this is a phenomenon peculiar to the United Kingdom and not a global trend and, moreover, the number of families affected by international parental child abduction is likely to continue to rise due to the increasing number of dual-nationality relationships on the one hand, and increasing rates of relationship breakdown on the other. It is therefore essential that the international community is equipped with the means to address this growing problem.

The Hague Convention on the Civil Aspects of International Child Abduction 1980[4] ('the Hague Convention') constitutes a very powerful weapon in the war against international child abduction. Where a child under 16 who is

---

[1] Throughout this chapter the term 'resident parent' is used to denote the parent with whom the child lives full time or the majority of time. This parent will not necessarily have a residence order since the living arrangements for many children are not contained in court orders.

[2] See further *www.reunite.org*

[3] A more accurate assessment of the extent of the problem would require a survey akin to that of Finkelhor, Hotaling and Sedlak (1991) in which an estimate of the national incidence of family abductions in the United States of America was calculated by telephoning 10,544 randomly selected households and enquiring about family abduction episodes. See *www.missingkids.com* for details of more recent studies based on this method.

[4] Adopted on 25 October 1980 at the Fourteenth Session of the Hague Conference on Private International Law and given force of law in England and Wales by the Child Abduction and Custody Act 1985.

habitually resident in one contracting state[5] ('the requesting state') has been wrongfully removed to or retained in another contracting state ('the requested state'), the court of the requested state must order the return of the child to the requesting state (Article 12). The removal or retention of the child will be wrongful where it breaches the custody rights of the other parent or, less frequently, another body or institution (Article 3).

The court of the requested state applies the law of the child's habitual residence state in order to determine whether the left behind parent has 'rights of custody' capable of being breached under the Convention. Accordingly, where a child has been abducted (removed or retained) *from* England/Wales, the parties with rights of custody for the purposes of the Convention are those with parental responsibility for the child, as determined by the Children Act 1989 ('CA'). In the case of married parents, both have parental responsibility under section 2(1); in the case of unmarried parents, the mother has parental responsibility automatically under section 2(2)(a), whereas the father acquires it only by court order or agreement with the mother under section 4(1).[6] Others with parental responsibility include guardians by virtue of section 5(6); those with a residence order by virtue of section 12(2); and the local authority where a care order has been made by virtue of section 33(3). Adoptive parents also acquire parental responsibility under section 12(1) of the Adoption Act 1976.

The custody rights of many parents will not be contained in a court order, not least due to the operation of the 'no order' principle contained in section 1(5) CA. However, this does not necessarily deprive them of rights of custody for the purposes of the Convention: under Article 3, rights of custody may arise by 'operation of the law' or by 'an agreement with legal effect', in addition to a 'judicial decision' such as the making of a residence order. Moreover, there is a tradition of broad and purposive interpretation of the concept of 'rights of custody' in order to give effect to the aims of the Convention. Hence in *Re B (A Minor) (Child Abduction: Consent)*,[7] the English court held that an unmarried father with no custody rights under Australian law (the child's habitual residence) nevertheless had rights of custody for the purposes of the Convention.[8] Where a mother has sole *legal* rights of custody but has delegated the primary care of the child to the father (and/or another person), they may be deemed to

---

[5] The Hague Convention is currently in force between the United Kingdom and 66 contracting states, a full list of which is contained in the Child Abduction and Custody (Parties to Conventions) (Amendment) Order 2001 (SI 2001/3923). An application for the return of an abducted child under the Convention is made via the Central Authority of the child's state of habitual residence. In England/Wales this is the Child Abduction Unit of the Lord Chancellor's Department. See further *www.offsol.demon.co.uk*

[6] Note however that s 4 of the Children Act has been amended by s 111 of the Adoption and Children Act 2002, to the effect that a man who is registered as the father of the child will acquire parental responsibility for that child whether he is married or not.

[7] [1994] 2 FLR 249.

[8] See further Practice Note: Hague Convention—Applications by Fathers without Parental Responsibility [1998] 1 FLR 491 and Harris (1999) for discussion/criticism.

have rights of custody for the purposes of the Convention.[9] However, this is not the case where a mother with sole legal rights of custody remains the primary carer, or care is shared with the father (and/or another person).[10]

If the court of the requested state deems that the removal or retention of the child within its jurisdiction has breached rights of custody in the child's habitual residence state, then it must order the return of the child to the requesting state (Article 12). The court does not consider the merits of the dispute: the Convention presupposes that the court of the requesting state is best placed to make decisions concerning custody of the child. Moreover the circumstances in which the court can set aside the central rule contained in Article 12 are extremely limited. Accordingly the courts of Hague Convention contracting states must order the return of abducted children in almost all cases: in 1999 only 10 per cent of the Hague Convention applications made by contracting states for the return of abducted children were judicially refused (Lowe, Armstrong and Mathias, 2001).

The Convention is widely acknowledged to have been a great success in combating international child abduction (Permanent Bureau of the Hague Conference on Private International Law, 2001; Bruch, 1996). Nevertheless, in 1999 only 50.2 per cent of applications made under the Hague Convention resulted in either the voluntary or judicially ordered return of the abducted child (Lowe, Armstrong and Mathias, 2001). Moreover the true figure will be lower since a judicial order alone will not necessarily secure the return of an abducted child, for example in cases where there are subsequent problems with enforcement or where a re-abduction occurs. Of the applications that did not result in the return of the abducted child, 10 per cent were accounted for by judicial refusal in cases where one of the exceptions to return was invoked and accepted. More disconcerting however is the 20 per cent of applications that were either rejected, for example where the child could not be located or had moved to another country, or withdrawn, for example where the applicant experienced legal aid difficulties or ceased communication with their lawyer.

The outlook is bleaker still for parents whose children have been abducted to countries which are not signatories to the Hague Convention.[11] In 2000, 26 per cent of the abduction cases reported to *Reunite* concerned non-Hague Convention countries (Reunite, 2001).[12] The left behind parent will often have limited, if any, redress, even in cases where the parent who has abducted the child has committed a criminal offence under the Child Abduction Act

---

[9] *Re O (Child Abduction: Custody Rights)* [1997] 2 FLR 702; *Re G (Abduction: Rights of Custody)* [2002] 2 FLR 703.

[10] *Re C (Child Abduction) (Unmarried Father: Rights of Custody)* [2003] 1 FLR 252.

[11] A US study of 371 left behind parents who had consulted missing children's organisations found that there was an 84% chance of abducted children being recovered from Hague Convention countries as opposed to a 43% chance from non-Hague Convention countries (Greif and Hegar, 1993).

[12] It is of course extremely difficult to gauge the true level of abduction to non-Hague Convention countries as there is no official institution to report abductions to, unlike the Central Authority for Hague Convention cases.

1984[13] ('the CAA') and/or breached a Children Act order. Indeed the left behind parent might face insurmountable practical problems before the legal issues can be tackled: even to trace a child can be virtually impossible without the co-operation of institutions abroad, particularly where there are language and/or financial barriers. The Foreign and Commonwealth Office may assist to the extent that they can approach Interpol in the United Kingdom and the relevant authorities overseas to try to trace the child.[14]

If the child is found but an agreement between the parents cannot be reached, it is likely that the only recourse will be to bring proceedings in the foreign court. The foreign court is not obliged to recognise the order of the domestic court relating to custody, for example residence or wardship, if indeed one has been made, and so the left behind parent must bring proceedings under the foreign law, often in spite of language barriers and/or financial constraints. Again the Foreign and Commonwealth Office may assist in bringing the existence of any court order to the attention of the relevant authorities in the country to which the child has been taken (with the permission of the court which made the order) and providing details of English-speaking lawyers there. Nevertheless success-fully negotiating these hurdles will not always result in a solution for left behind parents whose children have been abducted to non-Convention countries: for example, in some Islamic countries non-Muslim mothers have very little chance of winning custody and so the return of an abducted child is unlikely (Foreign and Commonwealth Office, 2001).

In view of the fact that many left behind parents either have no remedy or have a remedy which is ineffective, some commentators recommend encourag-ing non-Convention countries to become signatories and reform of the Hague Convention respectively (Banotti and Hennon, 1999). Nevertheless, even if the Convention was in force in every country around the world and even if it oper-ated perfectly, it is highly unlikely that it would provide a complete solution to the problem of international parental child abduction because it cannot be invoked unless the whereabouts of the abducted child is known. In cases where abducted children cannot be located, left behind parents have no remedy, notwithstanding the existence or indeed the efficacy of the Hague Convention. Accordingly it remains axiomatic that prevention is better than cure.

Moreover the fact that a remedy might or might not exist, and indeed might or might not be effective, does not detract from the obligation based on rights and/or welfare-based considerations to prevent international parental child

---

[13] S 1(1): it is an offence for a person connected with a child under the age of 16 to take or send the child out of the United Kingdom without the appropriate consent. An abducting parent commits the offence as they are 'connected' with the child and have failed to gain 'appropriate consent' from the other parent. Note however that s 1(4) permits a parent with a residence order to remove the child for up to one month without committing the offence, provided this does not breach a Children Act 1989 order. Since it is based upon the act of taking the child out of the United Kingdom this Act would not assist a left behind parent whose child is retained abroad at the end of a lawful contact visit.

[14] See generally Foreign and Commonwealth Office (2001) and *www.fco.gov.uk*

abduction whilst promoting contact. Firstly, parents and children have *rights* as regards both contact and international child abduction (see Bainham, this volume). The United Nations Convention on the Rights of the Child 1989 ('the UN Convention') accords a child the right to contact[15] but also obliges States Parties to take measures to combat and prevent child abduction.[16] However, it is not directly incorporated into domestic law so does not accord rights in the sense that they might be directly enforceable by an individual child via the courts. The European Convention for the Protection of Human Rights and Fundamental Freedoms 1950 ('the ECHR') was however directly incorporated into English law by the Human Rights Act 1998. Article 8(1) stipulates that, 'Everyone has the right to respect for his private and family life . . .'. This comprises a parent's right to contact with their children: see for example *Hokkanen v Finland*[17] wherein the court held that Mr Hokkanen's right to respect for his family life had been breached by the Finnish authorities' consistent failure to enforce his right of access to his daughter. Similarly in *Ignaccolo-Zenide v Romania*[18] the court held that a mother's right to respect for her family life had been breached by the Romanian authorities' failure to enforce the Hague Convention return order in respect of her abducted children and to facilitate contact with them. Children have their own right to respect for their private and family life too.[19] Where there is conflict between the parents' rights and those of the child, the interests of the child prevail.[20]

Secondly, there are *welfare* considerations for parents and children in the context of both making contact work and preventing international child abduction. It is well established that contact is extremely important in terms of the well-being of children separated from their parents, albeit with certain caveats (see Dunn, this volume). Thus English case law reflects the view that a continuing relationship between non-resident parent and child is usually in the child's best interests and direct contact should be ordered unless there are cogent reasons not to.[21] At the same time it is true to say that child abduction has the potential to be so devastating that notwithstanding the existence (or not) of a remedy, it must be prevented wherever possible. US research studies have shown that abduction is psychologically damaging in all kinds of ways, to all parties and in both the short and long term (Terr, 1983; Agopian, 1984; Finkelhor, Hotaling and Sedlak, 1991; Hatcher, Barton and Brooks, 1992; Greif and Hegar, 1993). It is of course extremely difficult to make generalisations when the subject under consid-

---

[15] Art 9(3): States Parties shall respect the right of the child who is separated from one or both parents to maintain personal relations and direct contact with both parents on a regular basis, except if it is contrary to the child's best interests.

[16] Ar 11(1): States Parties shall take measures to combat the illicit transfer and non-return of children abroad, and Art 35: States Parties shall take all appropriate national, bilateral and multilateral measures to prevent the abduction of . . . children for any purpose or in any form.

[17] [1996] 1 FLR 289.

[18] [2000] 1 IFL 77.

[19] *Marckz v Belgium* (1979) 2 EHRR 330.

[20] *Hendricks v Netherlands* (1983) 5 EHRR 223.

[21] *Re H (Contact Principles)* [1994] 2 FLR 969.

eration comprises a plethora of circumstances and emotions. Nevertheless, even if such research was shown to be flawed, contradictory, inconclusive (Freeman, 1998), or simply inapplicable, the notion that child abduction is a 'domestic' matter and that an abducted child cannot come to any harm since they are with one of their parents has been completely disproved by cases in Italy and the Republic of Ireland where the abductor parents killed their children and themselves.

Both rights and welfare considerations indicate that the prevention of international parental child abduction is vital notwithstanding the existence or not of any remedy. Making contact work in international cases will therefore mean securing, facilitating and enforcing contact arrangements which are safe, and which also reduce the risk of, or at least do not cause, international parental child abduction. This applies equally to the non-resident parent and the resident parent. I now consider each in turn.

3. THE NON-RESIDENT PARENT'S PERSPECTIVE

Successful contact provides an opportunity for a continuing and meaningful relationship between the non-resident parent and child. Achieving it is nonetheless highly problematic for many families and this might be exacerbated where there is a perceived and/or actual risk of parental abduction. In this section I examine the ways in which the non-resident parent might seek to address these problems via the legal system, firstly in cases where both non-resident parent and child live in England/Wales and secondly in cases where the child now lives abroad.

(a) Contact Arrangements Where the Child Lives in England/Wales

Securing the Arrangements for Contact

Arrangements for contact with a child are often made by mutual agreement between the parents. It goes without saying that the success of these informal arrangements depends upon co-operation between the parties, clearly not always possible in the aftermath of a relationship breakdown. Accordingly many non-resident parents will make an application to the court for a contact order, defined in section 8(1) CA as an order requiring the person with whom the child lives, or is to live, to allow the child to visit or stay with the person named in the order, or for that person and the child otherwise to have contact with each other (see Herring, this volume, for ways in which the law can affect contact other than by the use of contact orders). A parent can make an application for a contact order as of right.[22]

---

[22] S 10(4)(a) Children Act 1989. Hence an unmarried father can make an application regardless of whether or not he has parental responsibility by virtue of a court order or agreement—see n 6 above.

In considering an application for a contact order, the court will apply the principles contained in section 1 CA: the child's welfare is the court's paramount consideration when determining any question with respect to the upbringing of the child; delay is likely to prejudice the welfare of the child; the court will not make an order unless it considers that doing so would be better for the child than making no order at all; and if the application is opposed by any party, the court must have regard to the statutory checklist of factors contained in section 1(3). In *Re M (Contact: Welfare Test)*,[23] Wilson J said that the test is,

> whether the fundamental emotional need of every child to have an enduring relationship with both his parents [Section 1(3)(b)] is outweighed by the depth of harm which in the light inter alia of his wishes and feelings [Section 1(3)(a)] this child would be at risk of suffering [Section 1(3)(c)] by virtue of a contact order.

Facilitating Contact

In some cases, obtaining a contact order will not necessarily mean securing contact. Contact arrangements, even if contained in a court order, are dependent upon a degree of co-operation and compromise between the parents and there are all kinds of reasons why this might not be achieved. Disputes or difficulties with the contact arrangements might then be dealt with by further recourse to the court to re-negotiate the terms of the contact order.

Of particular use in international cases will be the court's powers under section 11(7)(a) CA to specify certain *directions* about how the contact order is to be carried into effect. In so doing the court might 'encourage' compliance with the contact order and facilitate contact. So for example, in cases where the resident parent is obstructing contact due to fears that the non-resident parent will abduct the child, based perhaps on their family or business connections with another country, the court might direct that the contact takes place in a contact centre and is supervised. The success of this approach might however be dependent upon the availability of resources and facilities in the locality, as highlighted in the report to the Lord Chancellor *Making Contact Work*. We will return to this point in our discussion of facilitating contact from the *resident* parent's perspective.

Enforcing Contact

The theory of contact as the right of the child breaks down in practice if the resident parent is unwilling to co-operate with contact arrangements (or indeed the non-resident parent does not wish to exercise contact). Furthermore, the enforcement of contact even with a contact order is notoriously difficult. If it has not been possible to encourage compliance by negotiating the terms of the contact order; varying the terms of the contact order; and/or specifying directions

---

[23] [1995] 1 FLR 274 at 278–9.

as to how it is to be carried out, the court might also consider using its powers under section 11(7)(b) CA to impose *conditions*. In *Re O (Contact: Imposition of Conditions)*[24] the Court of Appeal held that the court may impose positive obligations on the resident parent: in this case the court made an order for indirect contact and imposed conditions that the resident mother who was hostile to contact send the non-resident father photographs of the child and accept delivery of cards and presents for the child.

In cases where the resident parent continues to be hostile to contact, the court might order that a penal notice be attached to the contact order. Disobedience of the order might then lead to committal proceedings and a fine or imprisonment, although the ultimate sanction of imprisonment has seldom been used. Traditionally the courts held the view that imprisonment was inappropriate because it would not be in the child's best interests.[25] The child's welfare is likely to be adversely affected by being deprived of the resident parent and the child might well blame the non-resident parent for this. Moreover imprisonment will often be counter-productive, leading to an escalation of conflict between the parents rather than assisting in resolving their problems. That said, more recent case law might suggest a tougher stance. In *A v N (Committal: Refusal of Contact)*[26] the court held that the question of whether a defaulting parent should be imprisoned is not a question relating to the upbringing of a child and therefore section 1(1)(a) CA (the child's welfare shall be the court's paramount consideration) does not apply. The child's welfare is an important but not paramount consideration.[27]

Ultimately however, the law cannot force the resident parent to behave in a particular manner to facilitate contact, regardless of whether imprisonment is available as a sanction or not. This highlights a much wider debate about the role of law in issues involving personal relationships: ultimately the law cannot force people to behave in a particular way (the research carried out by Day Scalter and Kaganas, this volume, is particularly illuminating in this regard). Hence the role of the law in this context might be more symbolic than tangible. In the *Making Contact Work* consultation, the majority of respondents favoured retaining the sanctions of fines and/or imprisonment but only for flagrant, blatant and inexcusable breaches of a court order (Lord Chancellor's Department, 2002). The general feeling was that such a sanction is needed to deliver the message that the law is not to be willfully flouted, although a more therapeutic approach might be more appropriate in terms of *actually* making contact work, for example resolving disputes and problems by dealing with the emotional consequences of the ending of the relationship (see Buchanan and Hunt, this volume).

---

[24] [1995] 2 FLR 124.
[25] See for example *Churchard v Churchard* [1984] FLR 635.
[26] [1997] 1 FLR 533.
[27] See also *F v F (Contact: Committal)* [1998] 2 FLR 237.

There are particular concerns about enforcing contact in cases involving domestic violence. Contact may enable a violent non-resident parent to continue to access the resident parent thereby exposing them to the risk of further violence (although that does not preclude the possibility that the non-resident parent also has a genuine desire to maintain their relationship with the child). Accordingly, resident parents who have been subjected to domestic violence might sabotage contact through fear of the consequences for themselves and their children.[28] To make contact work in those cases is extremely difficult, and the failure to provide adequate protection has in the past proved fatal for parents and children (Saunders, 2001). Increasing recognition of the seriousness of this issue has led to contact in domestic violence cases being the focus of a great deal of attention in recent times, not least due to the government consultation (Lord Chancellor's Department, 1999) and the decision of the Court of Appeal in *Re L, Re V, Re M and Re H*.[29]

The issue of domestic violence has particular resonance in the context of international parental child abduction (Kaye, 1999; Reddaway and Keating, 1997). An increasing number of abducting parents are female: 70 per cent of taking persons in the Hague Convention applications for 1999 were female (Lowe, Armstrong and Mathias, 2001). Given that research shows domestic violence to be particularly prevalent in international parental child abduction cases,[30] it follows that a proportion of abductions by females might be accounted for by cases where the resident parent is trying to escape from a violent non-resident parent and effectively sever all ties. It is of course extremely difficult to show a direct causal link, not least because gaining access to abductors in order to study their motivations would be extremely difficult. Nevertheless in the analysis of applications made in 1999 under the Hague Convention (Lowe, Armstrong and Mathias, 2001), 26.4 per cent of the cases where the court refused to order the return of the child were based on Article 13b, which contains the exception to return that is most likely to capture cases of domestic violence: 'there is a grave risk that his or her return would expose the child to physical or psychological harm or otherwise place the child in an intolerable situation'. Moreover Hague Convention jurisprudence shows that this defence would be accepted in extreme cases only (Caldwell, 2001; Freeman, 2001).

Therein lies the dilemma presented in international cases: how simultaneously to make contact work *and* not cause parental abductions. Satisfactory contact arrangements from a non-resident parent's perspective may prevent abduction borne of the desire to see more of the child. However, in cases where

---

[28] See generally Sturge (2000), concerning the effects on children of domestic violence. Even if the violence is perpetrated solely against the parent, the child will be adversely affected by witnessing it and/or the victim parent's fear. Moreover, children are at far greater risk of abuse themselves if they have a violent parent.

[29] All (*Contact: Domestic Violence*) [2000] 2 FLR 334.

[30] For example, in the study carried out by Greif and Hegar (1993), more than half of the parents indicated that they were the victims of violence. This was thought to be an unusually high rate of violence, notwithstanding the fact that the rate of violence in divorcing couples is higher.

domestic violence is an issue, contact might be detrimental or even dangerous for both resident parent and child, and might therefore precipitate *resident* parental abductions borne of the need to escape from the violence. Accordingly, the need to make contact work will be inextricably linked with the need to make the contact arrangements safe, a point I shall return to in the context of the resident parent's perspective.

(b) Contact Arrangements Where the Child is Now Resident Abroad

When a relationship breaks down, many resident parents who have family and/or connections with another country decide to emigrate or return home. Others might wish to make a new start in another country, where they have better employment prospects for example. Clearly it is likely to be much more difficult to secure and, if necessary, enforce contact when a resident parent takes the child to live in another country. In those cases the arrangements made for contact, and their success, will depend firstly upon the circumstances of the move abroad (whether it be by agreement between the parents, permission from the court or abduction), and secondly on the country to which the resident parent and child move. I now examine each of these factors in turn.

The Circumstances of the Move Abroad

(i) Agreement Between the Parents

Where a residence order is in place with respect to a child, the resident parent who wishes to move abroad with the child must have the permission of the non-resident parent, unless the non-resident parent is an unmarried father without parental responsibility. Section 13(1)(b) CA stipulates that where a residence order is in place, no person can remove the child from the United Kingdom without either the written consent of every person who has parental responsibility or the leave of the court. The only exception to this is contained in section 13(2): the parent with a residence order may remove the child for one month without permission. Even where there is no residence order in place, the resident parent's move abroad without the non-resident parent's consent is not permitted: to do so constitutes an abduction for the purposes of the Hague Convention (provided of course that they have moved to a contracting state and that the left behind parent has 'rights of custody') and/or the CAA.

In cases where the non-resident parent's consent to the move abroad is forthcoming, it is nonetheless wise to formalise arrangements for contact. Application might be made to the court for a contact order, as discussed earlier. This order will not be enforceable in the foreign jurisdiction and so the non-resident parent's consent to the move abroad might be made conditional upon the arrangements contained within it being 'mirrored' by an order of the court in the country to which the resident parent is moving. Whilst this constitutes a safeguard for the non-resident parent, it must be borne in mind that its efficacy is dependant upon the mechanisms available for enforcement in the new jurisdiction.

(ii) Permission From the Court

If the non-resident parent vetoes the removal of a child from the jurisdiction, the resident parent might make an application to the court for leave in the form of a specific issue order, defined in section 8 CA as:

> an order giving directions for the purpose of determining a specific question which has arisen, or which may arise, in connection with any aspect of parental responsibility for a child.

As with other applications the court will apply the principles of section 1. In *Payne v Payne*[31] the Court of Appeal held that section 13(1)(b) does not create a presumption in favour of an applicant parent: the welfare of the child is paramount. In practice however there is a tradition of relative leniency by the English courts in granting leave to resident parents,[32] founded on the view that refusing the reasonable proposals of a primary carer would adversely affect their emotional and psychological welfare and this would impact detrimentally upon the welfare of the child.

Nevertheless the removal of the child from the jurisdiction will inevitably have a huge impact on the relationship between non-resident parent and child. Moreover contact in the international setting is likely to be more difficult than that in the domestic arena due to distance, cost and other practicalities. Whilst one could argue that a restrictive approach is justified on the grounds that the resident parent and child moving abroad will have a detrimental effect on the relationship between non-resident parent and child, it is unlikely that this would be consistent with human rights legislation. In *Re A (Permission to Remove Child from Jurisdiction: Human Rights)*,[33] the father appealed the court's decision to grant leave for the mother and their child to move abroad on the grounds that it breached his right to family life under Article 8 of the ECHR. The Court of Appeal upheld the decision because whilst Article 8 accords the father and child the right to family life, it also gives the mother the right to her private life. Furthermore, Article 8(2) requires the court to balance conflicting rights, in this case the right of the father to maintain contact with the child and the mother's right to choose where she lives and works.

In cases where the resident parent obtains permission to move abroad with the child, the contact rights of the non-resident parent might be preserved by the use of undertakings. In *Re A (Permission to Remove Child from Jurisdiction:*

---

[31] [2001] 1 FLR 1052.
[32] See Webster (2000) for a table of the last 30 years of case law.
[33] [2000] 2 FLR 225 CA.

Human Rights)[34] the court's permission to remove the child from the jurisdiction was granted on the basis of the mother's undertakings to facilitate meaningful and regular contact, so far as possible. Nevertheless the non-resident parent's prospects of securing and enforcing contact are jeopardised if the foreign jurisdiction is unable or unwilling to enforce the undertakings. A more effective course of action for a non-resident parent might therefore be to obtain a mirror order from the court of the country the resident parent and child are moving to. So for example in the case of *Re S (Removal from Jurisdiction)*,[35] leave to remove the child to Chile was granted subject to the High Court's contact arrangements being authenticated by the court in the new jurisdiction.

(iii) Abduction

It must be borne in mind that the non-resident parent is just as vulnerable to abduction as the resident parent, as demonstrated by the changing demography of international parental child abduction. As previously noted, some 70 per cent of Hague Convention applications in 1999 concerned abductions carried out by women (Lowe, Armstrong and Mathias, 2001).[36] Of course female abductors will not necessarily be resident parents but it is likely that the majority are, given that in terms of Hague Convention countries, 84.2 per cent of respondents (parents with care of the child) in access applications for 1999 were female (Lowe, Armstrong and Mathias, 2001). The Hague Convention was drafted with non-resident parental abduction in mind since abductions by resident mothers is a relatively recent phenomenon. In 1987 the Central Authority for England and Wales dealt with 40 applications of which 45 per cent concerned abductions by mothers and 48 per cent by fathers: by 1996 there were 372 applications and the ratio was 70 per cent mothers and 27 per cent fathers (Lowe and Perry, 1999).

As already discussed, one possible explanation for resident mother abductions is to escape from violence. Another might be that a resident parent who has been living in the country of origin of the non-resident parent is more likely to want to return to their own country of origin when the relationship ends. Both non-resident and resident parental abductions can be accounted for by 'going home': 49.4 per cent of Hague Convention applications in 1999 involved a taking person who was of the same nationality as the requested state, i.e. 'going home' (Lowe, Armstrong and Mathias, 2001). In some of these cases the abductor parent might remove or retain the child in flagrant disregard for the law and in others the abductor parent might simply be unaware that they are in fact abducting their child by removing them from the jurisdiction without the necessary permission.[37]

---

[34] [2000] 2 FLR 225 CA.

[35] [1999] 1 FLR 850.

[36] Note however that the demography of abductions to non-Hague Convention countries might be quite different. Unfortunately due to the nature of such abductions there is a dearth of research and statistics.

[37] See for example the study carried out by Johnston, Sagatun-Edwards, Blomquist and Girdner (2001): Profile 6 of the Profiles of Parents at Risk for Abducting their Children was parents who feel

In abduction cases it goes without saying that it will be extremely difficult, if not impossible, to make contact work from the non-resident's perspective, even if the whereabouts of the resident parent and child are known. Even where the left behind non-resident parent succeeds in having the abducted child returned, an extremely disruptive 'yo-yo' situation might then ensue: the child is removed by the resident parent in disregard or ignorance of the law; if removed to a Hague Convention country the child will almost certainly be ordered to be returned; the resident parent then makes an application for leave to remove the child from the jurisdiction and if granted removes the child again, this time lawfully. Nevertheless from the perspective of a non-resident parent, an application for leave to move abroad is an opportunity to put mechanisms into place for securing, facilitating and enforcing contact, as already discussed.

The Country to Which the Resident Parent and Child Move

Whatever the circumstances of the resident parent and child moving abroad, the prospects of making contact[38] work for the other parent are of course reduced once the child is resident in another jurisdiction, in both practical and legal terms. If difficulties or disputes arise, the options available for securing and/or enforcing access depend upon where the child is now resident. In this section I confine my discussion to the Conventions that are currently in force and that give the parent a remedy—the Hague Convention and the European Convention on Recognition and Enforcement of Decisions Concerning Custody of Children and the Restoration of Custody of Children of 20 May 1980 ('the European Convention') which was incorporated into English law by the Child Abduction and Custody Act 1985 ('the CACA'). We should however note that this area of law is subject to a plethora of initiatives emanating from Europe,[39] some of which contain peripheral access provisions.[40] Moreover, as previously discussed, the UN Convention accords the child rights relating to access but these are not directly enforceable by the child under English law.

(i) A Hague Convention Country

The primary aim of the Hague Convention is to bring about the return of abducted children to their country of habitual residence. However, the Convention also aims, 'to ensure that the rights of access under the law of one

---

alienated from the legal system and have family/social support in another community. In their study that group of parents comprised those who had no knowledge of custody laws and the need to gain permission; those who were too poor to have access to the court system; and those mothers who never married the father and thought of the child as their property.

[38] Hereinafter referred to as 'access' in the context of international law as opposed to 'contact' in the domestic setting.

[39] See Lowe (2001) for a review of these initiatives. For the latest position refer to the European Union website—*www.europa.eu.int*

[40] For example, Council Regulation (EC) No. 1347/2000 of 28 May 2000 on Jurisdiction and the Recognition and Enforcement of Judgments in Matrimonial Matters and in Matters of (Brussels II).

Contracting State are effectively respected in the other Contracting States'.[41] The means to achieve this are contained in Article 21:

> An application to make arrangements for organising or securing the effective exercise of rights of access may be presented to the Central Authorities of the Contracting States in the same way as an application for the return of a child.

> The Central Authorities are bound by the obligations of co-operation which are set forth in Article 7 to promote the peaceful enjoyment of access rights and the fulfillment of any conditions to which the exercise of those rights may be subject. The Central Authorities shall take steps to remove, as far as possible, all obstacles to the exercise of such rights. The Central Authorities either directly or through intermediaries, may initiate or assist in the institution of proceedings with a view to organising or protecting these rights and securing respect for the conditions to which the exercise of these rights may be subject.

It is often said that Article 21 has no real 'teeth' in so far as it provides for *assistance* from the Central Authority rather than the judicial *enforcement* of access orders. This is in stark contrast to the directly enforceable right to have an abducted child returned created by Article 12. In *Re G (A Minor) (Hague Convention: Access)*[42] the Court of Appeal held that Article 21 obliges contracting states to co-operate but does not create a separate or additional jurisdiction. Hence when considering an Article 21 application to secure an access order, the English court would require a separate application under section 8 CA. Moreover in *Re T and Others (Minors) (Hague Convention: Access)*[43] the court held that the Central Authority discharges its obligations under Article 21 simply by directing the applicant parent to a specialist lawyer in order to make the application for a contact order.

The non-resident parent living in England or Wales will of course be making an Article 21 application to another country. Nevertheless Lowe *et al*'s analysis of access applications under the Hague Convention revealed that many contracting states apply Article 21 in a similar manner to England and Wales: of the 33 judicially granted access applications in 1999, 12 were granted under the Convention and 21 under domestic law (Lowe, Armstrong and Mathias, 2001). Moreover all those applications considered by the courts in England/Wales and the USA, accounting for 43.1 per cent of all access applications, were decided under domestic law. One notable exception is Australia: Regulation 25(4) of the Family Law (Child Abduction Convention) Regulations 1986 permits the Australian court when considering an application to secure the effective exercise of access rights to make any order in relation to rights of access to a child that it considers appropriate to give effect to the Convention, provided the right of access is already established in another contracting state.

---

[41] Art 1(b).
[42] [1993] 1 FLR 669.
[43] [1993] 2 FLR 617.

In addition to the substantive deficiencies inherent in Article 21, there are significant procedural difficulties. Access applications take much longer than return applications: 60 per cent of access applications in 1999 took longer than 6 months before a judicial decision was obtained whereas the average length of time taken to reach a judicial decision in return applications was 97 days, and 42.5 per cent of voluntary access agreements took longer than 6 months to reach whereas the average number of days for a voluntary return was 78 days. Moreover, whilst 41.9 per cent of access applications resulted in the applicant securing access to the child (20.3 per cent by voluntary agreement and 21.6 per cent by court order), this is no indication of how many arrangements resulted in *actual* access to the child. Article 21 contains no enforcement provisions and so a non-resident parent must rely upon the enforcement mechanisms available in the country concerned.

Dissatisfaction with Article 21 is such that the Fourth Special Commission of the Hague Convention recommended that the Permanent Bureau carry out further consultation with contracting states to consider inter alia whether a protocol should be added to the Convention specifically dealing with access (Permanent Bureau of the Hague Conference on Private International Law, 2001).[44] The substantive and procedural defects of this Article are such that in cases of resident parental abductions, the non-resident parent is likely to have a more effective remedy by virtue of a return application under the Hague Convention than by an access application. This is cause for concern when the true intention of many non-resident parents might be to secure access to the child rather than to have the child returned and, moreover, might lead to the 'yo-yo' situation as previously discussed.

(ii) A European Convention Country[45]

The European Convention provides for the recognition and enforcement of court orders relating to the custody of children and access.[46] It is administered by the same Central Authorities as for the Hague Convention, and applications are transmitted from the requesting authority to the requested authority (where the child is now living) in the same way. Proceedings are then brought in the requested state under the legislation which implements this Convention (in England/Wales, the CACA). A decision made by one contracting state will be recognised and made enforceable in every contracting state under Article 5, unless one of the exceptions in Article 9 or 10 is established (procedural and substantive defences respectively). The requested state cannot review the substance of the decision but it can attach conditions for the enforcement of the right of access, for example as regards collecting or returning the child, or paying travel costs.

[44] See *www.hcch.net* for the latest position.

[45] A list of contracting states is contained in Child Abduction and Custody (Parties to Conventions) (Amendment) Order 2001 (SI 2001/3923).

[46] And/or the return of children if an order has been breached by their removal to or retention in another country. Note however that if both Hague and European Conventions are applicable, the Hague Convention will take precedence in cases where there has been a wrongful removal/retention of a child.

Although the European Convention contains stronger provisions relating to access than the Hague Convention, it seems to be little used. In an analysis of the applications dealt with by the Central Authority for England and Wales (the Child Abduction Unit of the Lord Chancellor's Department) during 1996, only 7 per cent were applications under the European Convention, as opposed to 93 per cent Hague Convention applications (Lowe and Perry, 1999). The research study found that this was indicative of the global picture rather than peculiar to England and Wales or the particular year analysed. The most likely explanation for this is that firstly, the European Convention is not in force in as many countries as the Hague Convention, and secondly the applicant must have a court order to enforce their custody/access rights under the European Convention, unlike the Hague Convention. Even when the European Convention is used, it is more often with the aim of enforcing custody orders: in the study of 1996 cases, only 25 per cent of incoming and 42 per cent of outgoing applications were for registration and enforcement of an access order.

(iii) A Non-Hague or European Convention Country

In cases where the child is now resident in a country which is not a signatory to either the Hague or European Conventions, the non-resident parent is likely to have significantly reduced prospects of securing and, if necessary, enforcing access. As discussed previously, it is likely to be more effective to obtain a mirror order of the English court order from the court of the foreign country *before* the resident parent and child move abroad. If this did not happen, the non-resident parent must usually bring proceedings in the foreign court since it is not bound to recognise or enforce a contact order of the English court. Bringing proceedings abroad will naturally entail practical, financial and legal difficulties as discussed previously in the context of abductions. The court that made the contact order must grant permission for the Foreign and Commonwealth Office (Consular Division) to send it to the Embassy in the country concerned for transmission to the relevant authorities. It is for the foreign court to decide what weight if any to attach to it.

If court action is not possible or successful, there might be alternative avenues for the non-resident parent, depending upon the country in which the child is now resident. Attempts to negotiate access might be assisted by the International Social Service if they have a correspondent in the country concerned; the Foreign and Commonwealth Office via its consul in that country; and/or a charity such as *Reunite* and its foreign counterparts or contacts. It will be seen that in cases where no formal arrangements are in place it is particularly true that the role of the law is limited: successful contact owes far more to the availability of a channel of communication and successful negotiation.

4. THE RESIDENT PARENT'S PERSPECTIVE

Contact between the child and non-resident parent provides an opportunity to abduct. In a US study (Chiancone, Girdner and Hoff, 2001), half of the abductions reported by the sample of left behind parents took place during court-ordered visitation between abductor parent and abducted child, and most of the left behind parents indicated that the abducting parent had connections with the country to which the child was abducted[47] and hence were returning home. Far less likely are dramatic snatch type abductions to an unknown country and life 'on the run' with the child.[48] Abductions might also be facilitated by contact taking place abroad between a child and a non-resident parent, where the non-resident parent fails to return the child at the end of the visit. In 2000, 10 per cent of the abductions that were reported to *Reunite* were classified as wrongful retentions (*Reunite*, 2001).

Making contact work in international cases from the resident parent's perspective must therefore involve putting safeguards in place to try to prevent a possible abduction by the non-resident parent. The options available to the resident parent will depend upon whether the contact is to take place in England/Wales or abroad. I now consider each of these types of contact in turn.

(a) **Contact Arrangements Taking Place in England/Wales**

Residence Orders

If they have not already done so, the resident parent might consider consolidating the legal position regarding the child's residence by making an application to the court for a residence order, defined in section 8 CA as: an order settling the arrangements to be made as to the person with whom a child is to live. The court will apply the principles contained in section 1 CA referred to above. If a residence order is made, its effect is simply to determine living arrangements: it does not deprive the other parent of their parental responsibility.

Some protection is afforded to a resident parent who has a residence order by the prohibition on the removal of the child from the United Kingdom without the written consent of every person with parental responsibility, or leave of the court, as discussed above. The parent with the residence order can also lodge an objection with the Passport Agency to request that it does not issue a passport for the child. However, if the child already has a valid passport or is included in the valid passport of a relative, the Agency is not able to compel the surrender of that passport to give effect to the objection. In those circumstances they note

---

[47] 83% spoke the language of that country, 76% had family there, 69% had lived there as a child.

[48] The extent of abduction planning was indicated by factors such as the abductor's actions, history of previous threats or attempts to abduct.

the name of the child for 12 months so that if during that time the passport comes into their possession or another application for passport facilities is made, the Agency could act on the objection (United Kingdom Passport Agency, 2000).[49]

Whether or not a residence order is in place, the removal of the child from the United Kingdom by the non-resident parent without the resident parent's permission constitutes abduction and might be a criminal offence under the CAA and/or a civil wrong according to the Hague Convention, as discussed above. Nevertheless the residence order would clarify 'rights of custody' for the purposes of the Hague Convention, in the event that the child is subsequently abducted to a contracting state.[50] Alternatively, if the child were subsequently abducted to a country which is not a signatory to the Hague Convention, the custody rights of the left behind parent with a residence order are more readily identifiable in any subsequent foreign court proceedings (although not necessarily enforceable, as we have seen).

Prohibited Steps or Specific Issue Orders

The resident parent might also consider making an application for a prohibited steps order defined in section 8 as:

> an order that no step which could be taken by a parent in meeting his parental responsibility for a child, and which is of a kind specified in the order, shall be taken by any person without the consent of the court.

The terms of the order would be such that the child is not to be removed from the jurisdiction without the permission of the court. This would also enable an objection to be lodged with the Passport Agency so that a passport cannot be issued for the child without the court's permission (United Kingdom Passport Agency, 2000). Equally a resident parent may make an application for a specific issue order to the same effect. However, whether the court would make such an order is unclear. Its power to do so is restricted by section 9(5)(a) which states that no court shall exercise its powers to make a specific issue order or prohibited steps order with a view to achieving a result which could be achieved by making a residence or contact order. It would seem to follow that the court could not make a specific issue or prohibited steps order restraining the removal of a child from the jurisdiction because this can be achieved with a residence order. However, in *Re B (Minors) (Residence Orders)*[51] the Court of Appeal overruled the decision of the judge to that effect and said that Parliament could not have intended to prevent the courts from exercising their powers to deal with child abduction.

---

[49] See further *www.ukpa.gov.uk*

[50] Although an order is not necessary to establish 'rights of custody' under Art 5 of the Hague Convention as previously discussed.

[51] [1992] Fam 162.

Wardship

The inherent jurisdiction of the High Court to make children wards of court might however be a measure with more teeth.[52] Indeed a third of all reported wardship cases since the Children Act 1989 came into force concern child abduction (Mitchell, 2001). Legal control of children who are made wards of court becomes vested in the High Court as soon as the originating summons is issued. This remains the position until such time as it discharges wardship, makes a care order or the child reaches the age of 18. Accordingly there is an automatic prohibition on removing the child from the jurisdiction without the court's consent. A person who does so is in contempt of court and might be penalised by a fine, removal of assets and/or a term of imprisonment. Again a wardship order enables an objection to be lodged with the Passport Agency so that a passport will not be issued for the child without the court's permission (United Kingdom Passport Agency, 2000).

If a ward is subsequently abducted to a Hague Convention country, the court has custody rights for the purposes of the Hague Convention, but since the parents retain parental responsibility despite wardship, they too will have rights of custody.[53] In cases of abduction to non-Hague Convention countries, the fact that a child is a ward of the High Court might prove more effective than a residence order in gaining the assistance of foreign authorities.

Contact Orders

Contact might also be safeguarded via the terms of the contact order itself, if one exists. As already discussed in the context of the non-resident parent's perspective, the court can include directions about how a section 8 order is to be effected, or indeed impose conditions. In the context of the resident parent's perspective, this provision might allow safeguards to be built into the contact order that lessen the risk of abduction in cases where the non-resident parent has connections with another country, for example the court could direct that the contact be supervised at a contact centre and/or the non-resident parent must lodge their passport(s) with their solicitor.

The court will apply the principles of section 1, as with other section 8 applications, but might be persuaded by considerations such as previous abductions, threats of abduction and opportunity, for example family and/or business in another country. In *Re A-K (Foreign Passport: Jurisdiction)*[54] a father appealed the order that the contact be supervised on the grounds that the judge had not balanced the risk of abduction against the benefits of less restricted contact and had given too much weight to the mother's fear of abduction. The Court of

[52] See *Re T (Staying Contact in Non Convention Country) (Note)* [1999] 1 FLR 262.
[53] See *Re J (A Minor) (Abduction: Ward of Court)* [1990] 1 FLR 276 and discussion in Lowe and Nicholls (1994).
[54] [1997] 2 FLR 569.

Appeal dismissed the appeal saying that it is a matter of discretion and it would only interfere if the judge had been unreasonable in exercising that discretion or had taken into account matters he should not have. That was not the case here: the judge had exercised his discretion reasonably as the father had previously abducted the child to Iran and there was little to keep him in the country.

It is important to note, however, that an order for supervised contact does not necessarily ensure that contact is safeguarded, or in some cases safe. Differing degrees of supervision will be available in different contact centres: some centres are staffed by volunteers, for example the ones run by the National Association of Contact Centres, and will only be able to offer *supported* contact whereas other specialist projects such as the Coram Family Project and the Accord might be able to provide fully *supervised* contact (see Maclean and Mueller, this volume, regarding contact facilities and services in the United Kingdom, USA and Europe). Of particular concern in this regard would be contact between violent non-resident parents and children, as discussed previously. If contact cannot be made safe for parents and children, then supervised contact is clearly no substitute for the court declining to order direct contact and perhaps limiting contact to indirect contact only (letters and e-mails).

Contact might also be safeguarded by the inclusion of a direction or condition in the contact order to the effect that the non-resident parent be compelled to surrender their passport (United Kingdom Passport Agency, 1999 and 2000). In *Re A-K (Foreign Passport: Jurisdiction)*[55] the Court of Appeal held that the order for the surrender of a passport as a condition of contact, not to be released without the permission of the court or the mother (or her solicitors), was within the judge's power in exercising the inherent jurisdiction of the court. The passport is usually lodged with a solicitor and the court informs the Passport Agency so that no further passport is issued.[56] Unfortunately this is not a cast iron safeguard for the resident parent because those non-resident parents who are dual nationals might obtain an additional passport for themselves and the child from their Embassy or Consulate. The resident parent or their solicitor might approach the Embassy or Consulate to request that no further passports are issued, on the basis of the court order requiring the surrender of passports, but naturally the Embassy or Consulate is not obliged to heed the request. Moreover, additional problems are created by the relaxation of embarkation controls for European Union countries meaning that abductors might not even need a passport to leave the United Kingdom and enter another country.[57]

The Criminal Law and All Ports Alerts

A non-resident parent who is minded to abduct will not always be deterred by the existence of a court order prohibiting them from leaving the country. In

---

[55] [1997] 2 FLR 569.

[56] Family Division Practice Direction 29 April 1983 [1983] All ER 253.

[57] For example, those travelling between the United Kingdom and the Republic of Ireland.

cases where court orders have failed to restrain the non-resident parent and the abduction of the child is imminent, the resident parent might need to resort to the criminal law and/or an all ports alert to prevent the non-resident parent and child leaving the country.

As previously discussed, international parental child abduction is a criminal offence under the CAA in addition to the civil wrong captured by the CACA. Since it is an offence to *attempt* to commit a crime under the Criminal Attempts Act 1981, the Police are empowered to apprehend a parent who has committed acts more than merely preparatory to the offence of child abduction.[58] If they think an offence might be committed they can arrest the parent without the need for a warrant and thereby prevent the child's removal from the country.[59]

In order to prevent the physical removal of the child from the country from airports and ferry ports, the Police may also instigate an all ports warning or alert.[60] They will invoke such an alert if they believe an offence is being or is about to be committed under the CAA and/or if a parent requests one and there is a real and imminent danger of the child being removed from the jurisdiction unlawfully. 'Real' means that the port alert is not being sought as insurance: rather that the potential abductor has the motive and ability to remove the child, for example connections with another country and taking the child's passport. 'Imminent' means that the child is likely to be removed within the next 48 hours. Hence there must be a specific and immediate threat, as opposed to a general fear of abduction. 'Unlawfully' means in breach of the other parent's rights. A court order proving this is not necessary, merely a statement to the Police giving evidence of the parent's rights in relation to the child—that their consent is necessary for the child's removal—and their objection to the removal. Accordingly if the other parent attempts to remove the child they have committed a criminal offence.

The all ports alert is circulated via the Police National Computer by the originating Police force to all ports in the United Kingdom. The 'child list' is a list of all those children currently deemed to be in real and imminent danger of abduction. Arrangements are made at each port for distribution of the list: in most cases it is passed to the private security firm responsible for security at the port[61] whose employees contact the Police if they become suspicious or come across anyone on the child list. It remains active for 28 days whereupon an application

---

[58] In *R v Griffin* [1993] Crim LR 515, the mother was found guilty of an offence under the Criminal Attempts Act 1981—her acts of buying single ferry tickets to the Republic of Ireland, making travel preparations and going to the school to ask for the children were held to be acts more than merely preparatory to the crime of child abduction, even though she had not yet embarked on her journey.

[59] Note that the Police can also act where no criminal complaint has been received but there are civil proceedings, for example where the child is the subject of a prohibited steps order or a ward of court. In addition, the Police are empowered under s 46 of the Children Act 1989 to take into protective custody any child they have reasonable cause to believe might otherwise suffer significant harm.

[60] See generally Practice Direction (1986) 1 All ER 983 and Home Office Circular No. 21/1986.

[61] Immigration embarkation controls were withdrawn from all UK ports on 14 April 1998.

for renewal must be made. The danger of unlawful removal must remain real and imminent for renewal.

The success of the criminal law and all ports alerts in terms of preventing abduction is dependant upon speedy action being taken. This in turn relies upon a parent knowing that their child is about to be abducted. If a non-resident parent has contact with the child for the whole day on Saturday, they may have left the country and be in another jurisdiction before the resident parent even realises they have been abducted. Even in cases where the parent realises there is a threat of imminent abduction, speed is of the essence in the Police activating an all ports alert. Moreover problems might still arise notwithstanding the existence of a port alert. If a child is on the non-resident parent's passport it is extremely difficult to trace them leaving the jurisdiction, whereas if the child has their own passport[62] it will be inspected when checking in at the airline desk and show up as being the subject of an all ports alert. Furthermore, the people checking departing passengers are privately employed and hence have no statutory powers. It is difficult to assess how successful all ports alerts are as the Police only record reported and resolved crimes but around 750 names per year are circulated on the child list and in 1998 the Police received reports of 390 offences, of which 104 resulted in prosecutions for child abduction being commenced (D'Alton and Caseley, 2001).

(b) Contact Arrangements Taking Place Abroad

As we have seen, a resident parent might be able to safeguard contact and prevent abduction by obtaining a court order to ensure permission is sought and granted *before* a child leaves the jurisdiction and/or taking measures to restrain the imminent removal of the child. However, none of the aforementioned measures can assist with the prevention of wrongful retention-type abductions where the non-resident parent fails to return the child after a lawful period of contact abroad. I now examine the measures a resident parent might take in order to safeguard contact taking place abroad.

Undertakings and Financial Safeguards

Contact taking place abroad might be safeguarded by means of undertakings from the non-resident parent, to return the child to the resident parent on a certain date for example, and/or the court exercising its powers to include directions or impose conditions on the contact order. In *Re K (Removal from Jurisdiction: Practice)*[63] a parent applied for leave to take their child on holiday to a non-Hague Convention country and the Court of Appeal said that the court

---

[62] Children are now required to have their own passports. See generally United Kingdom Passport Agency (1999).
[63] [1999] 2 FLR 1084.

was not simply to put trust in the parent or accept undertakings, rather it was up to the court to build in all practical safeguards. In order to do so the judge had to assess the magnitude of the consequences of any breach as well as the magnitude of the risk of breach. So for example in *Re A* (*Security for Return to Jurisdiction*)[64] permission was granted to the mother to take the child to Saudi Arabia conditional on her depositing her passport with her solicitors until she had provided a declaration in Arabic sworn on the Koran to return the child to England on a specified date and a declaration from her father.

Nevertheless it will be seen that undertakings are more a good faith gesture by the non-resident parent than an effective safeguard for the resident parent. If the non-resident parent fails to return the child at the end of the contact visit abroad, resort must be made to proceedings to remedy the abduction (Hague or non-Hague Convention) notwithstanding the existence or not of any undertakings since they are not enforceable per se. Accordingly the court may, in exceptional circumstances only and where there is a real danger that the child may not be returned, impose financial safeguards.[65] The parent taking the child abroad enters into a bond of an appropriate amount with the court and if they subsequently fail to return the child the bond is used to finance the legal costs of securing the child's return. The surety might be a sum of money or a charge on their property. So for example in *Re L* (*Removal from Jurisdiction: Holiday*)[66] permission was granted for the mother to take the child to United Arab Emirates on certain preconditions: mother to deposit a bond of £50,000 to the court, to be released once child returned to jurisdiction; mother to undertake to return the child by a certain date; mother, her father and her eldest brother to declare on the Koran to guarantee the safe return of the child; and mother to provide father with details of the journey, including copies of the tickets.

Nevertheless whilst the use of financial safeguards provides the resident parent with a means to finance abduction proceedings, as we have already seen the proceedings themselves might not necessarily result in the return of the child, particularly if the child has been retained in a non-Hague Convention country. Moreover, proceedings may not be brought if the child cannot be located.

Mirror Orders

A more effective means of safeguarding contact abroad might be to make it conditional upon the non-resident parent obtaining a 'mirror' contact order from the court in the jurisdiction to which the child will be travelling. If the contact order of the domestic court is recognised or 'mirrored' by an order of the court in the country the child is visiting, it should be readily enforced if the child is retained at the end of the contact period. The mirroring of contact orders has

---

[64] [1999] 2 FLR 1.
[65] Practice Note (1987) 17 Fam Law 263.
[66] [2001] 1 FLR 241.

been ordered by the court in non-Hague Convention cases, for example in *Re T (Staying Contact in Non-Convention Country) (Note)*[67] where the child was travelling to Egypt, and Hague Convention cases, for example in *Re HB (Child's Objections)*.[68] Indeed the English court has itself made mirror orders: in *Re P (A Child: Mirror Orders)*[69] the High Court was asked to issue a mirror order guaranteeing the return of the child to the USA at the end of the contact period.[70]

Nevertheless recognising or mirroring the domestic court's contact order is only one part of the story: if the order is breached, how will it be enforced? If enforcement proceedings are invoked, are there adequate enforcement mechanisms to ensure the court order is complied with? If not, the resident parent will need to resort to abduction proceedings, with all the attendant difficulties.

5. ANALYSIS: PROMOTING CONTACT WHILST PREVENTING INTERNATIONAL PARENTAL CHILD ABDUCTION

We have seen above that arrangements for contact can provide an opportunity, and even a trigger, for parental child abduction, both on the part of the non-resident and resident parent.

From a non-resident parent's perspective, making contact work can be extremely difficult. It goes without saying that failure to achieve this might cause the relationship between non-resident parent and child to flounder in all cases, domestic and international. However, in cases with an international dimension such a failure might also have adverse consequences for the risk of international parental child abduction in that it might be a causal factor in non-resident parental abductions, the motivation being that the abduction is a means to ensure a continuing and meaningful relationship with the child. In the study carried out by Greif and Hegar (1993), 18 per cent of the abductors were 'non violent visitors' (non-resident parents) whose motivation was a desire to be with the child and/or concern about contact. Agropian (1984) also found that one of the four reasons for abduction by parents was the desire to retain a full time parenting role. It follows that successful contact might negate the motivation to abduct where a non-resident parent simply wants to see more of the child. Nevertheless achieving contact would not prevent non-resident parental abductions that are motivated by other factors, for example the conflict between the parents. In the study carried out by Greif and Hegar (1993), 77 per cent of the abductions were motivated by the desire to hurt or punish the other parent.

---

[67] 1 FLR 262.

[68] [1998] 1 FLR 422.

[69] [2000] 1 FLR 435.

[70] The court had no jurisdiction to make a contact order under s 8 CA but Singer J relied upon s 2(3)(b) Family Law Act 1986: the court retains powers under the inherent jurisdiction if the child is present in England and Wales on the relevant date. See Beevers (2000) for discussion of why that decision might not apply in future cases.

Agropian (1984) also identified this as a motivation for abduction but more recent research carried out by Johnston *et al* (2001) found that anger and spite are not of themselves sufficient motivation for abduction and additional risk factors must be present.[71]

From a resident parent's perspective, making contact work can also be extremely problematic. In many cases the failure to safeguard contact will not necessarily cause or result in international parental child abduction. Equally, the existence of safeguards will not necessarily prevent international parental child abduction: in the research carried out by Chiancone *et al* (2001), 51 per cent of the left behind parents had taken measures to prevent the abduction, such as supervised visitation, custody orders prohibiting removal of the child from the jurisdiction, and passport restrictions. This is because there are of course other reasons why parents abduct their children, many of which are unaffected by the existence or not of safeguards.[72] Nevertheless in cases at risk for abduction, the failure to safeguard contact might precipitate resident parent abductions.

It must also be borne in mind that the very fact of achieving contact from a *non-resident* parent's perspective might be a causal factor in *resident* parental abductions. For a variety of reasons but particularly in violence cases, the resident parent might wish to sever all ties with the non-resident parent. Enforcing contact might then result in resident parental abductions borne of the desire to escape, particularly in cases where the resident parent has connections with another country and can seek refuge and/or obtain support there. Similarly the very fact of making contact work from a *resident* parent's perspective might be a trigger for *non-resident* parental abductions. Putting safeguards in place for the benefit of the resident parent might cause the non-resident parent to feel that their relationship with the child is threatened by constraints and that the way to preserve the relationship is to abduct the child. In the final analysis it may be that it is impossible to reconcile the conflicting needs of the resident and non-resident parents.

6. CONCLUSION

The foregoing discussion has established that making contact work in international cases means promoting contact whilst preventing international parental child abduction. From the non-resident parent's perspective this will entail securing and, if necessary, enforcing the contact arrangements, whilst

[71] They identified 6 profiles of parents at risk for abducting their children: when there has been a prior threat of or actual abduction; when a parent suspects or believes abuse has occurred and friends and family members support these concerns; when a parent is paranoid delusional; when a parent is severely sociopathic; when a parent who is a citizen of another country ends a mixed-culture marriage; when parents feel alienated from the legal system and have family/social support in another community.

[72] See previous discussion of abduction motivations in the context of the resident parent's perspective.

from the resident parent's perspective it will entail safeguarding contact. Failure to achieve this balance might have adverse implications for the risk of non-resident and/or resident parental child abductions.

Unfortunately, as we have seen, the law struggles to make contact work. Contact in international cases was not addressed in the government consultation on contact, culminating in the *Making Contact Work* report. This report acknowledges the importance of the issue of contact in international cases but said that there are a relatively small number of such cases and consideration of the complex legal issues involved would, 'detract from the main thrust of the report'. This is however no excuse for inactivity. Although the government consultation was not felt to be the most appropriate forum for discussion of the issues pertaining to contact in international cases, it is nonetheless extremely important to consider what 'Making Contact Work' might entail in such cases. This issue will become more pressing as the number of such cases is likely to rise, given the increasing mobility of the population and increasing numbers of dual-nationality relationships, and efforts must be made to find solutions. More research is needed into the relationship between contact and international parental child abduction. In the meantime if we truly desire to do more than pay mere lip service to the rights and welfare of all parents and children we must continue to strive to find ways to meet the new and additional challenges raised by international cases.

REFERENCES

AGOPIAN, MW., 'The Impact on Children of Abduction by Parents' (1984) 63 *Child Welfare* 511.

BANOTTI, M and HENNON, A, 'Problems in the Operation of the Hague Convention on International Child Abduction' (1999) *International Family Law* 3.

BEEVERS, K, '*Re P (A Child: Mirror Orders)*: Jurisdiction to Grant a Mirror Order' (2000) 12 *Child and Family Law Quarterly* 413.

BRUCH, C, 'How to Draft a Successful Family Law Convention: Lessons from the Child Abduction Conventions' in J Doek, H Van Loon, and P Vlaardingerbroek (eds), *Children on the Move: How to Implement Their Right to Family Life* (The Netherlands, Kluwer Law International, 1996).

CALDWELL, J, 'Child Welfare Defences in Child Abduction Cases—Some Recent Developments' (2001) *Child and Family Law Quarterly* 121.

CHIANCONE, J, GIRDNER, L and HOFF, P, 'Issues in Resolving Cases of International Child Abduction by Parents' (2001) *OJJDP Juvenile Justice Bulletin* 1.

D'ALTON, R and CASELEY, L, 'The Role of Law Enforcement Agencies in the UK in Child Abduction Cases'. *Paper presented at the Reunite International Child Abduction Centre International Family Law in a Commonwealth Context Conference* (Pretoria, South Africa, January 2001).

FINKELHOF, D, HOTALING, G and SEDLAK, A, 'Children Abducted by Family Members: A National Household Survey of Incidence and Episode Characteristics' (1991) 53 *Journal of Marriage and the Family* 805.

Foreign and Commonwealth Office, *International Child Abduction: Advice for Parents* (London, Foreign and Commonwealth Office, 2001).

FREEMAN, M, 'The Effects and Consequences of International Child Abduction' (1998) 32 *Family Law Quarterly* 603.

—— 'Primary Carers and the Hague Child Abduction Convention' (2001) *International Family Law* 140.

GREIF, GL and HEGAR, RL, *When Parents Kidnap: The Families Behind the Headlines* (New York, The Free Press, 1993).

HARRIS, D, 'Is the Strength of the Hague Convention on Child Abduction being diluted by the Courts?—The English Perspective' (1999) *International Family Law* 35.

HATCHER, C, BARTON, C and BROOKS, L, *Families of Missing Children* (Washington DC, US Department of Justice, 1992).

JOHNSTON, JR, SAGATUN-EDWARDS, I, BLOMQUIST, M-E and GIRDNER, LK, 'Early Identification of Risk Factors for Parental Abduction' (2001) *Office of Juvenile Justice and Delinquency Prevention Juvenile Justice Bulletin* 1.

KAYE, M, 'The Hague Convention and the Flight from Domestic Violence: How Women and Children are being Returned by Coach and Four' (1999) *International Journal of Law, Policy and the Family* 191.

Lord Chancellor's Department, The Advisory Board on Family Law: Children Act Sub-committee, *Contact Between Children and Violent Parents: The Question of Parental Contact in Cases Where There is Domestic Violence* (London, Lord Chancellor's Department, 1999).

—— *Making Contact Work: A Report to the Lord Chancellor on the Facilitation of Arrangements for Contact between Children and their Non-residential Parents and the Enforcement of Court Orders for Contact* (London, Lord Chancellor's Department, 2002).

LOWE, N, 'New International Conventions Affecting the Law Relating to Children—A Cause for Concern? (2001) *International Family Law* 171.

LOWE, N, ARMSTRONG, S and MATHIAS, A, *A Statistical Analysis of Applications made in 1999 under the Hague Convention of 25 October 1980 on the Civil Aspects of International Child Abduction* (The Hague, Hague Conference on Private International Law, 2001).

LOWE, N and NICHOLLS, M, 'Child Abduction: The Wardship Jurisdiction and the Hague Convention' (1994) *Family Law* 191.

LOWE, N and PERRY, A, 'International Child Abduction—The English Experience' (1999) 48 *International and Comparative Law Quarterly* 127.

MITCHELL, J, 'Whatever Happened to Wardship? Part II' (2001) *Family Law* 212.

Permanent Bureau of the Hague Conference on Private International Law, *Conclusions and Recommendations of the Fourth Meeting of the Special Commission to Review the Operation of the Hague Convention of 25 October 1980 on the Civil Aspects of International Child Abduction. 22–28 March 2001* (The Hague, Permanent Bureau, 2001).

REDDAWAY, J and KEATING, H, 'Child Abduction: Would Protecting Children Drive a Coach and Four through the Principles of the Hague Convention?' (1997) *The International Journal of Children's Rights* 77.

Reunite International Child Abduction Centre, *Annual Statistical Report 2000* (London, Reunite, 2001).

SAUNDERS, H, *Making Contact Worse? Report of a National Survey of Domestic Violence Refuge Services into the Enforcement of Contact Orders* (Bristol, Women's Aid Federation of England, 2001).

STURGE, C, 'Contact and Domestic Violence—the Expert's Court Report' (2000) *Family Law* 615.

TERR, L, 'Child Snatching: A New Epidemic of an Ancient Malady' (1983) 103 *The Journal of Paediatrics* 151.

United Kingdom Passport Agency, *Passports for Children and Young People* (London, Passport Agency, 1999).

——*Passport Facilities for Children* (London, Passport Agency, 2000).

WEBSTER, S, 'Analysis of Leave to Remove Authorities' (2000) *Family Law* 128.

18

Disputed Contact Cases in the Courts

ANN BUCHANAN and JOAN HUNT

The Act rests on the belief that children are generally best looked after within the family with both parents playing a full part and without resort to legal proceedings. (Department of Health, 1989, p 1)

War is not too strong a metaphor to apply to the experiences of some who divorce. (Clulow and Vincent, 1987, p 1)

1. INTRODUCTION

THE MAJORITY OF parents of the 150,000 or so children in England and Wales involved each year in parental divorces, as well as the unknown number of children of separated, never-married couples, make their own arrangements for their children without recourse to the courts. For the minority who cannot, the Children Act 1989 provides a range of orders (known as Section 8 Orders) to settle the issues, which are typically about contact and less frequently, residence. In determining the dispute the court will frequently seek the assistance of a welfare report, which since April 2001 will be provided by a Child and Family Reporter from the new Children and Family Courts Advisory and Support Service (CAFCASS) and was previously provided by a Family Court Welfare Officer (FCWO).

This chapter is based on a consumer study of families who were the subject of a welfare report because of disputes about residence and/or contact, prior to the creation of CAFCASS (Buchanan *et al*, 2001). The research consisted principally of face to face interviews with 100 parents (52 mothers, 48 fathers; 73 cases) shortly after the conclusion of the proceedings. A year later 81 parents were seen again and 30 children interviewed. Standardised tests of well-being were completed by parents on themselves and their children at both time-points and by the interviewed children at the second. Welfare reports were read and a postal survey of a selection of their authors conducted. The sample was drawn from a cohort of cases in which reports were filed over a six month period by three court welfare services, covering inner city, urban and rural areas. The sample was selected to reflect, as far as possible, the profile of the cohort and checked for representativeness through an analysis of reports on a further 143 cases.

Father Involvement and Child Contact

Although social norms are changing and are challenged in this volume (see Geldof), it remains the case that in most separated families the mother will be the resident parent while the father has varying degrees of contact, or in a still substantial proportion of cases, loses contact altogether (Maclean and Eekelaar, 1997; Dunn, this volume). In considering the issue of contact, therefore, the growing body of research showing the benefits of 'father involvement', albeit mainly carried out in intact families, is highly relevant. Amato, for instance (1994), showed that regardless of the quality of the mother-child relationship, the closer children were to their father, the happier, more satisfied and less distressed they were.

Flouri and Buchanan (2002a to e) have used data from the British National Child Development Study to explore the relationship between father involvement and outcomes for UK children. The findings are strong. Father involvement established before the age of seven is associated with good parent-child relationships in adolescence and also with later satisfactory partnerships in adult life; children with involved fathers are less likely to be in trouble with the police; father involvement is strongly related to children's later educational attainment.

What then, does research tell us about the relationship between contact and child well-being in separated families? While there is, unfortunately, not a great deal of UK research, what there is tends to be quite positive (Richards and Dyson, 1982; Walczak and Burns, 1984; Lund, 1987; Cockett and Tripp, 1994; Dunn, this volume) although Smith's study of contact in step-families (Smith *et al*, 2001) detected no difference. The considerable US literature is more ambiguous (Emery, 1999; Amato and Gilbreth, 1999; Pryor and Rodgers, 2001) although a recent meta-analysis of 63 quantitative studies (Amato and Gilbreth, 1999) suggests stronger associations in more recent research. On current evidence, however, it has to be said that, as Pryor and Rodgers (2001) have recently concluded: 'the assumption that contact per se is measurably good for children does not stand up to close scrutiny'.

This does not mean that research has shown that contact is unimportant. Frequency of contact, the measure used in many studies, may be less relevant than factors such as the nature, regularity and consistency of the arrangements, the child-parent relationship or the duration and quality of contact. Research has begun to test out these associations. Contact is likely to have different implications according to the temperament and developmental stage of the individual child (Healy *et al*, 1990), as is well demonstrated in qualitative research with children by Smart (Smart *et al*, 2001). This diversity of effect, it has been suggested, may help to explain the ambiguity of the research evidence, in which the positive and negative effects on individual children cancel each other out across the whole group (Simons *et al*, 1994). Although clearly much more work needs to be done to explore the ways in which contact may or may not be beneficial to children there are two areas in which research is beginning to sketch in the gaps in the picture. The first is the relationship between the child and the non-resident parent, the second the extent to which the child is caught up in adult conflict.

Amato and Gilbreth's meta-analysis (1999) found that feelings of closeness to, and authoritative parenting by, the non-resident parent were positively associated with children's academic success and negatively associated with externalising and internalising problems. This clearly has implications for patterns of contact since it is hard to see how active parenting and closeness can be maintained unless contact is relatively frequent and includes overnight stays (Hetherington and Kelly, 2002; Pryor and Rodgers, 2001). Indeed it could be used as an argument for shared residence as the arrangement which is most likely to facilitate high levels of involved and authoritative parenting.

In this context data on the impact of conflict is crucial, since many studies have found that this is associated with more long term problems (Rodgers and Pryor, 1998). Indeed it has even been suggested that conflict after divorce is worse for children than conflict within marriage (Hetherington and Stanley-Hagen, 1999). A degree of conflict, of course, is to be expected when relationships dissolve and, particularly in the immediate aftermath, may even be regarded as both normative and an integral part of the process of psychological uncoupling (Day Sclater and Piper, 1999). Conflict is considered to be particularly damaging, however, when it is frequent, intense, physical, unresolved and involves the child (Grych and Fincham, 1999). Buchanan *et al* (1991) suggest that the key factor is the extent to which the child feels 'caught' in the conflict, reporting that some parents in high conflict situations were able to refrain from behaviours which impacted on the child. McDonald (1990) found that where parents were able to agree about access arrangements, enabling children to have meaningful contact, other aspects of parental conflict did not seem to have the same impact. Recent qualitative research with UK children reports that:

> What was unacceptable for the children in our study was conflict which impacted on them. Such conflict, no less than poor parent-child relationships, can lead to significant unhappiness. At the least, children wanted their parents to contain their disputes so that they did not have to be involved, or used as emotional props, or turned into allies, spies or go-betweens in a parental war. (Smart *et al*, 2001)

Contact, then, is a double-edged sword. It provides the vital mechanism through which non-resident parents can remain (or indeed become) involved in the children's lives and thus potentially contribute positively to their well-being. Where involvement is more marginal there may be no observable effects on well-being but at least it may not be harmful, and there can be other, less readily measurable considerations to be taken into account. As Sturge and Glaser (2000) describe, contact can serve a variety of purposes, including knowledge and the reparation of distorted relationships and perceptions. One of the most important factors is likely to be the child's desire for, and enjoyment of, the company of their non-resident parent. Research with separated children tends to show that most see their fathers as important and value contact and that many want more contact than they have (Dunn, this volume; Funder, 1996; McDonald, 1990; Mitchell, 1985; Pryor and Rodgers, 2001; Walczak and Burns, 1984; Wallerstein and Kelly, 1980).

In families where there is significant conflict, however, contact may be positively damaging to children, either directly or through impairment of the parenting capacity of their primary carer. In such circumstances a careful assessment has to be made of the needs of the individual child and the balance of advantage and disadvantage. Such are the decisions with which the family courts are faced on a daily basis.

2. THE FAMILIES IN CONFLICT STUDY

The Parents and their Disputes

It is important to note that the study was not specifically focused on contact and the sample cases included those where disputes were primarily about residence. Since the data cannot readily be disaggregated, the findings reported here, unless otherwise indicated, should be understood to relate to all cases. Nonetheless most cases (81 per cent) did involve a contact application and as others have pointed out (Bailey-Harris *et al*, 1998), some residence disputes are also essentially about contact.

The disputed issues in *pure* contact cases spanned the spectrum. The commonest disputes were over the details of contact (34 per cent), although the second concerned the principle of contact (26 per cent), followed by those in which a child was refusing contact and where the issue was whether contact should be supervised (13 per cent each). There had been at least one set of previous proceedings in around half the sample and one case was back in court for the seventh time.

The Parental Relationship

One of the key factors associated with workable contact is the parental relationship (Ahrons and Miller, 1993; Koch and Lowery, 1984; Arditti and Bickley, 1996; Gibson, 1992; Funder, 1993; Smyth *et al*, 2001; Lund, 1987; Simpson *et al*, 1995; Bradshaw *et al*, 1999; Gorrell-Barnes *et al*, 1998; Dunn, this volume). It is relevant that the majority of parents interviewed described current relationships that were at best very poor and at worst highly conflicted, using words such as 'poisonous', 'vitriolic', and 'stormy'. Moreover with few exceptions, parents also described relationships which had been poor since the point of separation or had become even worse over time.

Domestic Violence

Domestic violence is increasingly recognized as a crucial factor to be taken into account in determining contact cases (Lord Chancellor's Department, 2002) but may be rendered invisible within the family justice system or subordinated to the presumed importance of contact (Hester and Radford, 1996; Kaye, 1996; Radford *et al*, 1999). This study therefore deliberately employed a broad definition, asking 'Was there ever a point in your relationship, before or after you split up, when you were frightened of your ex-partner, or s/he might have felt frightened of you?'

It was disturbing, nonetheless, to find that domestic violence was reported by at least one parent in 78 per cent of cases and physical violence in 56 per cent. (The estimated proportion in the general population is 1 in 4.) Moreover, an analysis of mothers' responses showed that they were rarely referring to occasional or minor incidents. Two-thirds described violence as a frequent or almost constant feature of their relationship and injuries ranging from severe bruising to broken bones and internal damage as well as sustained harassment, emotional abuse and intimidation. In almost two-thirds of the cases, violence or fear continued post-separation (and in 14 per cent of cases only started then). By the time of the sample proceedings, however, which in some cases was several years post separation, the proportion of cases in which violence/fear was continuing had reduced to one half, and only a quarter cited violence as an issue in the current case.

Child Welfare and Safety Concerns

Allegations of child abuse in private law proceedings have been described by Australian researchers as the 'core business' of the Family Court (Brown *et al*, 1998). Our sample (which slightly under-represents the most severe cases) does not reflect this extreme picture, child protection concerns being mentioned in only 11 per cent of welfare reports and only 4 per cent having current Social Services involvement because of such issues. Again, however, this is a much higher proportion than in the general population where only 3 per cent are even classified as 'in need'. Interviews with parents identified concerns about drug abuse (11 per cent of cases); alcohol abuse (21 per cent) and mental illness (26 per cent), with almost half expressing fears of some kind about a possible risk to the child's safety.

The most striking finding, however, was the high proportion of cases (86 per cent) where concerns were expressed about the parenting behaviour of the ex-partner. While some of these did not amount to fears for the safety of the children, they nevertheless weighed heavily as a reason for opposing the other parent's proposals. In the light of what was a very dominant theme in the research it is interesting that American research (Wolchik and Fenaughty, 1996) reports a significant association between contact difficulties and the resident parent's concerns about the parenting abilities of their ex-partner, which was evident not only in the immediate aftermath of separation but persisted three years later.

Mother Time, Father Time, Child Time

The priority to be given to a child's social activities was another, often bitter, source of conflict between parents. Some children would have needed a nine-day week to fit their extra-curricular activities in with the level of 'quality time' expected by the non-resident parent, as well as spending time with their resident parent. As children got older, more parents described the difficulty the children had in negotiating their commitments.

Parental Perspectives on the Process and Outcome of Litigation

The role of the courts in family disputes is acknowledged to be fairly limited (Davis, 1997; Bainham, this volume). Nonetheless for the parents in this study the process seemed to be delivering at least some of the goods, in that even among the unsuccessful applicants only a third were entirely dissatisfied and less than a quarter of all applicants thought they had achieved nothing.

There was, however, huge dissatisfaction with the process, six in 10 parents being entirely negative. Mothers and fathers, applicants and respondents, were equally dissatisfied. Delay was the principal complaint (identified by 7 in 10 parents), followed by the approach of the judge, the inappropriateness of the process, inadequate coverage/lack of understanding of the issues; judicial discontinuity, the stress of court hearings, lack of control by the court and inefficiency. The most dissatisfied were those whose disputes had gone to a full hearing, most of whom described the trauma of the occasion in terms strikingly reminiscent of the views of parents in public law proceedings (Freeman and Hunt, 1998). They too spoke of feeling '*belittled*', '*on the defensive*' and being upset and/or angry because they had not been listened to or able to get their point of view across. It raises again the question of whether family proceedings have to be like this or indeed, as over half the parents in this study believed, there needs to be an entirely different system.

Welfare Reporting

Opinion was more evenly divided about welfare reporting and only a fifth were entirely negative. Again there were no significant differences between mothers and fathers, applicants or respondents, although certain groups, notably mothers for whom domestic violence was a current issue in proceedings, were amongst the most dissatisfied. Views were also more closely (although not perfectly) tied to outcome, which was the only strong predictor of satisfaction. This inevitably raises questions about the extent to which changes in practice could significantly increase approval ratings. This does not, however, in our view, invalidate what parents were saying, nor relieve CAFCASS of the responsibility to strive to make improvements. The fact that criticism mainly emanated from those who were unsuccessful does not mean that what they were complaining about is unimportant.

Overwhelmingly what parents were unhappy about was the quality of the welfare enquiry. Two-thirds thought insufficient time had been spent for a thorough investigation. Over half felt more time should have been spent talking to the children and a third that FCWO's needed more training in talking to children. There was criticism of enquiries which did not include a home visit which three-quarters of parents felt should be routine. Many wanted the enquiry to include new partners and the extended family. Parents also rejected an exclusively future orientated approach, arguing that the past was relevant to the decisions being made. There were also calls for a more open and accessible system which involved parents in the process. Taking these points on board has huge implications for CAFCASS, not least in terms of the sufficiency and allocation of resources.

Gendered Systems?

Beyond changes in how welfare reports are prepared and court proceedings are conducted, some parents presented powerfully argued, gender-based critiques of the principles and assumptions underpinning the process which were held to result in systematic discrimination. Fathers challenged what they saw as a primary caretaker assumption which reduced them to the status of visiting parent, arguing instead for a presumption of shared care (see, Geldof, this volume). They also argued that contact was a right conferred by biological parenthood and were highly critical of the court's reluctance to enforce contact orders. Critical mothers, for their part, saw the system bending over backwards to preserve contact which they saw not as a right but something earned by the father's demonstration that he was a responsible and caring parent (see, Day Sclater and Kaganas, this volume). Many of these mothers believed that children who experienced such positive fathering did benefit and wished that their own children had been among them. These divergent approaches echo what Smart has described as an 'ethic of care' as compared to an 'ethic of rights' (Smart and Neale, 1999).

Outcomes and Perspectives One Year On

By the second interview, only two-fifths of families were still operating the same contact arrangements and under a quarter were doing so without intervening disruption or attempts at change. While in about a quarter, contact had 'progressed'—to more contact or less restricted/ more flexible contact, three in 10 arrangements had collapsed completely, contact having reduced/ceased or become more restricted. Only a quarter of interviewees were completely satisfied with the current arrangements although only 20 per cent were entirely dissatisfied.

One of the more positive findings of the research was that just over two-fifths of those interviewed reported some improvement in the relationship with their ex-partner, even though it was usually at best an uneasy rapprochement. However there were almost as many for whom relationships had either remained poor (19 per cent) or deteriorated further (15 per cent) with some parents despairing that the conflict would ever end. Around half the mothers (16) who had experienced domestic violence said that levels of conflict were either just as bad or worse. Five reported being frightened of the other parent; two that contact had placed them at risk; three cited specific incidents of perceived intimidation and one had been assaulted. There were also ongoing concerns about parenting behaviour. Although most centred on what might be termed lax parenting there were also allegations of sexual (2), emotional (3) and physical (4) abuse.

Children's Perspectives

The 30 children interviewed were asked their views about welfare reporting, which typically had been their only direct involvement in proceedings. Indeed, as found in other studies (Butler *et al*, 2002) most had little knowledge or understanding of the legal process. A few also had little recollection of the FCWO, but of the rest two-thirds said they knew why they were being seen and half had thought it would be useful, although others were nervous of being asked who they wanted to live with and the possible implications of this and seven had not wanted to be seen at all.

Despite being apprehensive most children were positive about the FCWO, with very few saying there was anything they did not like about him or her. Most felt listened to (23) and taken seriously (21). Far fewer, however (11), were confident that they had been understood and five said there were things they had been unable to say, sometimes because they were interviewed in the presence of a family member, including a parent, or siblings. Only 10 children wanted their parents told what they said and eight were anxious this might happen. It was clear that not all children were aware that what they said was not confidential. Similarly most children seemed unaware that the FCWO would be obtaining information from school.

Although only three children said the outcome of proceedings was definitely not what they wanted, only half (15) were entirely positive. Even fewer said they were happy about it, with ambivalence being the dominant reaction (12). As one poignantly put it:

I guess I was thinking that I should have felt happy for my mum and happy for me and sad for my dad and sad for me.

Children were also somewhat unsure as to whether proceedings had helped, although only two stated clearly that they had not, compared with eight saying that they had, even if this was largely expressed in terms of resignation—what else could be done?:

Helped? Not really, it is just the same.

Yes it helped because it stopped the arguments.

Well, they weren't going to sort it out any other way, so that was the final resort I think.

Despite the difficulties, one clear message was that while some children just wanted to stay out of it, many wanted to be involved in the decision-making process more than they currently are. As one put it succinctly *'because it's me the decisions are about'*. Not that they expected or wanted their views to be determinative, just to be heeded and their views taken into account:

Well I would like to make my point clear, and then let people say what they think about that so that they can tell me the good and bad points of what I have suggested.

So I have some sort of say, and I want to know what other people think as well.

Twelve children (mainly the older ones) were adamant that in principle children who wanted to should be allowed to go to court:

The most important thing is whether they want to go; the second is whether they are mature enough in their views.

Of all questions about the decision-making process, the one which prompted the most unequivocal response was whether there should be someone involved just for the children, with 20 of the 30 children giving an unconditional yes. Children were not asked whether they would have liked a professional advocate so this cannot be taken as direct support for separate representation. Indeed in general children seemed to be thinking in terms of a relative or family friend. Nonetheless it does again suggest that the children in this sample were not confident that the existing process enabled their voices to be heeded.

How Family Court Welfare Officers Can Help Children

The young people were asked what 'top tips' they would give to FCWOs. Most comments suggest that they could be *more skilful* at communicating with children and *more sophisticated* in assessing their wishes and feelings. Children saw the FCWO as a non-partisan person who could give them information and advise them what would be likely to happen. Some children also looked to the FCWO to try and ease the conflict and stop their parents *'being nasty'*.

Top tips for welfare officers

Don't pester

—If a child says 'don't know' you should accept it

—Less questions about how you are feeling etc., not too many 'feelings' questions

—Before questioning children, ask if they like drawing or prefer to answer questions

—Don't ask the same question again and again and again

—Don't pester children or they will feel uncomfortable

Listen and speak to us in a way we can understand

—If young children are going through a problem talk to them in a child's way; some children don't really understand what you are saying but they will not say so

—Listen to what children are saying and tell it to people who will help change things

Reassure

—Be trustworthy

—Answer questions as easily as you can

—You should realise that it is not easy for children—it might be hard for them to tell you what they are thinking

—Most children are more comfortable at home

—You should try and understand it from the children's point of view, explain things they do not understand

Advise/help/sort out the arguments

—Give more information

—Tell everyone what is going to happen

—Talk to the children and tell the parents what the children want

—When parents are being nasty, try and sort it out

Living with Conflict

Although the children's views about welfare reporting were informative, some of the most important findings from this study relate to their descriptions of living under the shadow of ongoing conflict.

Having a good relationship with at least one parent is considered to be an important protective factor against the adverse effects of parental separation (Pryor and Rodgers, 2001). The majority of the interviewed children might therefore be regarded as fortunate since almost all (27) felt very confident that both parents loved them and enjoyed their company and most considered themselves to have positive relationships with both parents. Contact was also usually described positively, 21 children saying they usually had a good time with their father and only six that they did not or that they resented contact because it interfered with their activities. Two children, however, said they were scared of their dad and a further two that this was 'sort of true'.

It cannot be established from the data whether the interviewed children were experiencing the authoritative parenting by the contact parent which, as described earlier, is held to be most beneficial for child well-being. However the majority reported that it was true (12) or sort of true (7) that whatever worries their father had himself, they could talk to him about theirs and only one said that Dad was not interested in how they were doing at school. Both these findings suggest that many of the fathers in this sample were 'involved' fathers.

Contact arrangements, however, were seen as a source of ongoing conflict. A year after the proceedings ended, a third of children reported that their parents often disagreed about the contact arrangements. Nearly half reported that one parent said critical things about the other and others that they were made to feel guilty about wanting to spend time with the non-resident parent. Only eight felt they were in control of the contact arrangements. Almost all had seen parental arguments, the majority involving shouting and in 11 cases 'pushing and shoving'.

This awareness of parental conflict may help to explain why, unlike many studies which report that children generally want to see more of their non-resident parent, only five children said this. Seven said they did not and many children were unable to answer; the underlying feeling appeared to be that it all depended on the hassle this might involve. Eight children said that if it would mean an end to the arguments they would rather not see the non-resident parent at all. However it is also true that 13 children said they did not take this view. It is not possible to say whether this was because the conflict was less severe or they were prepared to tolerate it for the sake of the contact.

Although, as reported earlier, most children felt they could talk to their parents about their worries in general, this did not necessarily apply to contact. Seven children agreed that they found it difficult to tell their parents what they really wanted and a further twelve that this was 'sort of true'. Some appeared to be constantly on guard about what they said. The stress also impinged on other parts of their lives. Twelve said that it was true/sort of true that worries about their family sometimes got in the way of schoolwork and seven that this sometimes kept them awake at night. On the more positive side, a high proportion of children said that they had lots of good friends they could talk to, which may have a protective effect (Douglas *et al*, in press).

The Well-being of Children and Parents

The emotional cost of these disputes to children and parents was a key theme in the research, amply demonstrated not only by the interview material but by the results of standardised tests (General Health Questionnaire for parents,

Goodman Strengths/Difficulties questionnaire for children). Eighty-six per cent of the parents interviewed post-proceedings had an abnormal GHQ score, indicating that they were extremely distressed and not functioning normally. As one mother put it:

> You just felt so useless in everything, you feel as if you're a zombie. You go along with doing your everyday things but you're not much use to anyone and you feel that no-one would notice if you had gone, sort of thing.

A year later just under half were still recording abnormal scores. Such high levels of stress would have made the day-to-day task of parenting very difficult, let alone coping with the needs of what were often very distressed children. The SDQ's completed by parents at first interview indicated that more than half the boys and just under half the girls had borderline or abnormal scores. At the second interview, while levels of distress in girls had dropped, levels in the boys remained high. There was a strong relationship between parental and child distress particularly at the second interview, with above threshold scores on the GHQ strongly associated with distress in children. Children between seven and nine recorded the highest scores at both parental interviews. Domestic violence was also strongly associated with maladjustment. Where this had been an issue in the proceedings, children were three times more likely than children in the general population to have borderline or abnormal scores.

For the researchers, though perhaps not for practitioners, one of the most telling findings of the research came in comparing the scores of the interviewed children approximately 15 months after these private law proceedings with those of children (using the same test) who had been made subject to care orders following public law proceedings some 21 months before (Harwin et al, forthcoming). The proportions of children with abnormal scores was the same, both groups having nearly double the levels of emotional and behavioural disturbance expected in the general population. Although there may be many reasons for this finding it is, prima facie, disturbing. Moreover, it should be emphasised that although our sample was towards the high conflict end of the spectrum of separated families in the sense that they were not only litigating but subject to a court welfare report, they did not consist entirely of the most difficult cases. Only 15 per cent, for instance, were what we have termed 'perennial' litigants. Studies by researchers focusing solely on the most intractable cases (Johnston and Strauss, 1998) have reported even more frightening levels of maladjustment.

How to Make Things Better: the Children's Views

> Parents think it is easier for children, but in fact it is harder.

Earlier in this chapter we noted some of children's 'top tips' for welfare officers. They also had some very telling suggestions for other children and most particularly, for parents, which painfully illustrated the stress that they were under.

Top tips for other children

How to cope
—Find something you like to do and the worries may go away
—Keep in touch with friends—don't go off in loneliness
—If you get annoyed don't lash out
—Don't start taking drugs and alcohol just because of your position
—Try helping a brother or sister to get through it—it might help you too

Don't get too involved
—Don't put yourself in the arguments, don't listen that much
—Don't let it take over your life.

Keep informed
—Try and find out everything that is going to happen beforehand
—Don't think your parents will be truthful about what you want
—If you are older ask to see the FCWO's papers [report]
—Concentrate on what they are asking—if you answer questions wrong, life might be miserable forever

Say what you think
—Say what you want to the FCWO as sometimes you can't say it to parents
—If there is something you really don't want stick up for yourself

Involve others
—Make your views heard. Talk to your family or anyone you feel comfortable with
—You can always speak to other people (not Mum and Dad)

Your parents will get over it
—Don't think that your parents will never talk to each other again. You will get over it even if it takes a long time. It won't change your school friends—you won't be different from other children

Young people's advice to parents was even more direct. They wanted them to be aware of the distress they were causing and not take out their unhappiness on the children, to be more prepared to listen to children's views and more willing to think about their feelings.

Top tips for parents

Tell your children what is going on
—Children want to know what happens—it affects them; they should know
—Explain in a nice, easy way. This should be in depth with older children. Younger children need an idea of where things are going

Argue somewhere else
—Parents shouldn't argue as much. Don't go to the other parent and start abusing them
—Try not to fight when the kids are around
—Keep calm when arguing

Don't pressurise
—Don't bribe your children
—If a child chooses the other parent then still love them and don't get mad with them or be mean or they will stop seeing you
—Don't push your children to do stuff or it will backfire
—Try not to be sad in front of the children
—Don't smack. Don't take out your frustration on the children

Remember we are distressed too
—Let them see as many friends as possible
—Remember your children
—Be happy when the children are around even if it's not true
—You are a parent so you should look after your kids

Our views matter
—Some children may want to spend more time with one parent than the other
—If a child wants to see their dad they should tell someone about it
—Be happy for your kids if that is the decision they have made

Think about us
—Think more about how it will affect your children than your own lives
—Parents need to know about bad things that may be happening to their children because of their problems. I know someone who is being badly bullied.

---

2. CONCLUSIONS

The cases in this study were positioned towards the high conflict end of the contact spectrum. Most families resolve questions of post-separation contact without invoking the court and those subject to a court welfare report are in even more of a minority. The findings presented here, therefore, paint only a small corner of the contact 'picture' and must be treated as such. Furthermore, although the overall sample was of a respectable size for a consumer study and was surprisingly representative, on most counts, of the cases coming to the three court welfare services studied, the number of children interviewed was small and since their participation depended on the consent of the resident parent, possibly skewed.

Nonetheless the research findings present major challenges to the family justice system, and more broadly to family policy, in relation to separated families. Most parents were highly dissatisfied with the court system and more than half with the court welfare service. Few children felt their voices had been heard. Mothers and fathers experienced high levels of distress which must have reduced their capacity to support children who were themselves very distressed. Moreover, while to some extent parents recovered their equilibrium once proceedings were over, some children, especially boys, did not. While it is impossible to determine how far these effects were related to the proceedings (rather than to persistent conflict), parents' reports suggest that for many it was a significant factor fuelling the flames and maintaining high stress levels over a prolonged period.

What Then Might be Done?

It could be argued that such consequences are unavoidable and certainly we are not so naïve as to believe that any system could be devised which satisfied all those involved or eliminated the adverse effects of these deeply personal conflicts. We do consider, nonetheless, there is scope for improvements, many of them suggested, as reported earlier, by the children and parents we interviewed.

Change, however, has to be more far-reaching than addressing deficiencies in the courts and related services. Vital as this is, it is very much 'shutting the stable door' after the 'horse' (in this case a positive continuing relationship between the child and the non-resident parent) has probably bolted. Rather the approach has to incorporate, as with many social or health problems, a comprehensive 'preventative' strategy. Indeed the levels of distress demonstrated in this study make the analogy of public health particularly apt, since these are not merely personal misfortunes which have no implications for the wider society. Many parents, for instance, spoke of adverse effects on their physical as well as emotional health and their reduced capacity to work effectively. The long-term effects on children involved in prolonged disputes over contact are not known but one would predict that they would be more likely to be among the minority of children who do not make a good long-term adjustment.

Prevention is generally held to have three tiers: primary, secondary and tertiary. Primary prevention is about providing services to all with the objective of reducing the overall prevalence of a particular health hazard. Education is normally a key element. In this context the focus would be a strategy aimed at shaping the culture about post-divorce parenting so that there is a public expectation that unless there are contraindications (such as domestic violence or child abuse) children will retain substantial meaningful contact with both parents. Although implicit in the Children Act concept of continuing parental responsibility it is not clear that this has percolated into the general population.

Such an expectation may need to be underpinned by the law, which, as Bainham points out (this volume) conveys powerful cultural messages. The Family Law Act 1996 made the importance of contact explicit, stating as a key principle the need to promote 'as good a continuing relationship between the parties and any children affected as is possible in the circumstances' (Section 1(c) and (d)). Since the relevant sections of the Act are no longer to be implemented an amendment to the Children Act may be necessary. Another point for consideration is whether the drafters of the Children Act were correct in replacing the concepts of custody, care and control with deliberately less symbolic orders aimed at settling disputes about the details of the child's life. Symbols may be important and there appears to be some evidence from other jurisdictions that orders for joint legal custody, even if this does not involve shared physical custody, are associated with reduced litigation (Gunnoe and Braver, 2001).

Many of the non-resident fathers in our study went further and argued, as others have done (Geldof, this volume) that conflicts over contact would be less likely to arise if the law started from the presumption that residence would be shared and time split equally between parents. Having listened to the painful stories of fathers struggling to retain a meaningful role in their children's lives, we have some sympathy for this argument. Clearly shared residence can work well for some children (Smart *et al*, 2001) and it would displace any outmoded notions of maternal preference. However apart from the fact that such an arrangement is unlikely to be feasible for the majority of parents, to our thinking there is a danger that such a presumption, which has uncomfortable resonances with Solomon's proposition to split the child in half, would come to be interpreted more in terms of parental rights than children's interests. Perhaps a more workable, and child-orientated, alternative, would be that the law should start from the explicit principle of maximising the time the child spends with each parent, subject, of course, to the stipulation that this is not detrimental to the child's welfare and safe for child and parents.

A more targeted form of primary prevention, focusing on separating families, would include the provision of information, advice and assistance. The parents in our study, almost all of whom saw this as necessary, wanted assistance in talking to their children about the separation, recognising and alleviating their children's distress and how to resolve conflict. Equally, children's need for information is a theme in several recent studies (Lyon *et al*, 1999; Butler *et al*, 2002; Smart and Neale, 1999). Although the information meetings which were to have been such a key part of the Family Law Act may not have proved the best way of meeting families' needs, those needs still need to be addressed. The creation of FAINS (Family Advice and Information Networks), announced by the LCD in 2001, could clearly be a cornerstone of a preventative strategy.

Secondary prevention would cover families where parents have begun to experience difficulties over contact and include a range of readily accessible therapeutic interventions for both parents and children, as well as mediation and legal advice. CAFCASS could clearly play an important part in developing and coordinating this strategy and perhaps even providing some services. One of the points made by a number of parents in our study, for example, was that they would have liked to have talked to someone like a FCWO *before* their difficulties had reached the point of court action.

The aim of *tertiary* prevention would be to provide more effective help to the very troubled families who reach the courts and prevent them returning to court again and again. The findings from this research suggest that many families subject to a welfare report need much more than a brief assessment resulting in a report to act as the basis for negotiation and in some cases, adjudication. Such brief 'interventions' no doubt assist the courts to dispose of the case and in the past may have served most families. This study indicates, however, that such a service is not likely to be adequate for the often very complex needs of the families now presenting themselves, in which there are high levels of conflict, concerns about domestic violence, substance abuse, mental illness and more generalised concerns about parenting capacity.

At the very least CAFCASS needs to have the resources to ensure that the welfare investigation is carried out thoroughly by well-trained and supported practitioners. Many parents are not confident that this is presently the case. More fundamentally, one has to question whether the role itself is now largely outdated. Where there is contact but a high level of conflict a satisfactory outcome for the child is likely to require both parents to change. This suggests that what is required is a more therapeutic, rather than forensic intervention.

Some welfare officers share this perception (Hunt and Lawson, 1999) and in the past may have been able to act on it, before a combination of workload targets and court expectations produced the currently dominant narrow interpretation of the role. It is time, we would suggest, to think again and to reconceptualise the role as primarily a social work service to disputing families, focused on helping them reach the least damaging solution for the child. Such a service, we would also argue, needs to be available to families once the court proceedings are over. One of the complaints of parents in the study was that the court made the order but then just left them to get on with it, not even checking that it was being complied with, let alone providing help to manage it.

The complex needs of some of the families in this study, plus the high levels of distress experienced by many of the children, suggest, indeed, that without the provision of services some may be at risk of significant harm and thus should be regarded as potentially 'children in need' as defined by the Children Act. Social Services departments, however, already overburdened, might be reluctant to widen their net in this way and it would seem unlikely that such children would get any sort of priority. The onus, therefore, may have to fall on the family justice system, and CAFCASS in particular, to ensure there is a range of more specialised services, drawing on what is already available in this country and the experience of other jurisdictions with more developed programmes. This should be regarded as one way of giving effect to the extra 'S' in CAFCASS, inserted late in the day, we understand, as the result of judicial representations.

Our research findings, therefore, chime with the general tenor of government policy to keep cases out of the courts where possible. They also support the concept of a more therapeutic, less forensic approach to contact disputes reflected in the arguments of Lord Justice Thorpe[1] (Thorpe, 2000) and much of the consultation paper *Making Contact Work* (Lord Chancellor's Department, 2002), which emphasises the facilitation (albeit sometimes compulsory facilitation) of contact, with enforcement as very much a last resort. We also subscribe to the principle, although the evidence is not conclusive, that in general, unless there are contraindications (a vital proviso) children are likely to benefit from extensive on-going contact with their non-resident parent and consider that the promotion of such contact is a legitimate objective of family policy. Indeed we would like to see more attention paid to the question of how to reduce the proportion of non-resident parents who 'drop-out' of their children's lives.

What is to be done, however, when facilitation does not work? The disturbing possibility is that the courts may become less reluctant to use punitive measures to enforce contact orders. Yet at the moment there is little evidence of the effectiveness of enforcement in ensuring compliance or the effects of this on children (Pruett and Pruett, 1998). Nor is there much research on why some resident parents and/or children resist contact, although research by Rhoades (2002) and Johnston (1993) suggests a more complex picture than *obstructive* mothers and *brainwashed* children. To proceed further down the punitive enforcement road, in our view, could potentially be very damaging to children, and in the absence of good evidence, very questionable, even in order to '*encourager les autres*'. Whereas children may be forced to go to school because there is considerable evidence that education is good for them , the evidence that contact in high conflict situations is good for children is much less certain.

Indeed, given the high levels of distress experienced by children there may be a case for arguing that the courts should be more willing to contemplate suspending direct contact, at least temporarily, to give the child, and their primary carer, some respite. It might even be argued that, at least in cases involving repeat applications, there should be no presumption of contact, each case being determined on its merits. Such an approach, however, would need to be buttressed by more substantial research evidence about the dynamics and outcomes of difficult contact cases than our study can claim to have produced. It would also be vital to ensure that the child's situation was very thoroughly investigated and their interests well-represented. Separate representation is no panacea—the difficult-

---

[1] *Re L (A Child) (Contact: Domestic Violence)* [2000] 2 FLR 334.

ies faced by the families in this study were not essentially legal ones nor readily susceptible to resolution by the courts and we are certainly not suggesting that separate representation should be routine. In many instances children's interests will be adequately served by the child and family reporter, particularly if the role becomes more than the fairly weak and marginal one available to the FCWOs at the time of our study, and more akin, in terms of focus, power and involvement in the process, to that of a children's guardian (Hunt and Lawson, 1999).

In some cases, however, particularly where there is the possibility of no contact, or of an order for enforcement, or the child is resisting contact, separate representation may be the only way to ensure that the voice of the individual child is heard strongly and their interests remain central in the decision-making process. In exploring the issue of separate representation in public and private law, Timmis has developed the concept of the 'Richter scale of family turmoil' (Timmis, 2000), using this to justify the presumption of separate representation of children in public law proceedings. While this conclusion may be warranted in most instances, in that children in private law proceedings are not facing the same catastrophic disruption to their family, the distress levels of the children in this study, which were, as reported earlier, comparable with those of children who had been subject to care proceedings, suggest that many of them were experiencing more than a few earth tremors. Separate representation for such children would, of course, have significant resource implications for CAFCASS but may, in the long-run, prove a cost-effective investment in the well-being of children.

REFERENCES

AHRONS, CR and MILLER, RB, 'The Effect of the Postdivorce Relationship on Paternal Involvement: a Longitudinal Analysis' (1993) 63 *American Journal of Orthopsychiatry* 441.

AMATO, PR, *Children in Australian Families: the Growth of Competence* (Sydney, Prentice-Hall of Australia, 1987).

——'Father-Child Relations, Mother-Child Relations, and Offspring Psychological Well-Being in Early Adulthood' (1994) 56 *Journal of Marriage and the Family*, 1031.

AMATO, PR and GILBRETH, JG, 'Non-Resident Fathers and Children's Well-Being: a Meta-Analysis' (1999) 61 *Journal of Marriage and the Family* 557.

ARDITTI, JA and BICKLEY, P, 'Father's Involvement and Mother's Parenting Stress Postdivorce' (1996) 26 *Journal of Divorce and Remarriage*, 1.

BAILEY-HARRIS, R, DAVID, G, BARRON, J and PEARCE, J, *Monitoring Private Law Applications under the Children Act: Research Report to the Nuffield Foundation* (Unpublished, Bristol, Department of Law, University of Bristol, 1998).

BRADSHAW, J, STIMSON, C, SKINNER, C and WILLIAMS, J, *Absent Fathers?* (London, Routledge, 1999).

BROWN, T, FREDERICO, M, HEWITT, L and SHEEHAN, R, *Violence in Families—Report Number One: The Management of Child Abuse Allegations in Custody and Access Disputes before the Family Court of Australia* (Clayton, Monash University, 1998).

Buchanan, A, Hunt, J, Bretherton, H and Bream, V, *Families in Conflict: Perspectives of Children and Parents on the Family Court Welfare Service* (Bristol, Policy Press, 2001).

Buchanan, CM, Maccoby, EE and Dornbusch, SM, 'Caught Between Parents: Adolescents' Experience in Divorced Homes' (1991) 62 *Child Development* 1008.

Buchanan, CM and Maccoby, EE, *Adolescents after Divorce* (Cambridge, MA, Harvard University Press, 1996).

Butler, I, Scanlan, L, Robinson, M, Douglas, G and Murch, M, 'Children's Involvement in their Parents' Divorce: Implications for Practice' (2002) 16 *Children and Society*, 89.

Clulow, C and Vincent, C, *In the Child's Best Interests: Divorce Court Welfare and the Search for a Settlement* (London, Tavistock Publications, 1987).

Cockett, LJ and Tripp, J, *The Exeter Family Study: Family breakdown and its Impact on Children* (Exeter, University of Exeter Press, 1994).

Davis, G, Inaugural Lecture, Faculty of Law, University of Bristol (Unpublished, 1997).

Day Sclater, S and Piper, C, *Undercurrents of Divorce* (Aldershot, Ashgate, 1999).

Department of Health, *An Introduction to the Children Act 1989* (London, HMSO, 1989).

——*Lost in Care* (London, Department of Health, 1999).

Douglas, G, Butler, I, Murch, M, Robinson, M and Scanlan, L, *Children's Perspectives and Experience of the Divorce Process* (Bristol, Family Law, in press).

Dunn, J and Deater-Deckard, K, *Children's Views of their Changing Families* (York, York Publishing Services, 2001).

Emery, RE, 'Postdivorce Family Life for Children: An Overview of Research and some Implications for Policy' in Ross A Thompson and PR Amato (eds), *The Post Divorce Family: Children, Parenting and Society* (Thousand Oaks, Calif, Sage, 1999).

Flouri, E and Buchanan, A, 'Childhood Predictors of Labour Force Participation in Adult Life' (2002a) 23 *Journal of Family and Economic Issues*, 101.

——'Father Involvement in Childhood and Trouble with the Police in Adolescence. Findings from the 1958 British Birth Cohort' (2002b) 17 *Journal of Interpersonal Violence* 689.

——'Life Satisfaction in Teenage Boys: the Moderating Role of Father Involvement and Bullying' (2002c) 28 *Aggressive Behavior* 126.

——'The Protective Role of Parental Involvement in Adolescent Suicide' (2002d) 23 *Crisis* 17.

——'What Predicts Good Relationships with Parents in Adolescence and Partners in Adult Life? Findings from the 1958 British Birth Cohort' (2002e) 16 *Journal of Family Psychology* 186.

Freeman, P and Hunt, J, *Parental Perspectives on Care Proceedings* (London, The Stationery Office, 1998).

Funder, K, 'Exploring the Access-Maintenance Nexus' in K Funder, M Harrison and R Weston (eds), *Pathways of Parents after Divorce* (Melbourne, Australian Institute for Family Studies, 1993).

——*Remaking Families: Adaptation of Parents and Children to Divorce* (Melbourne, Australia, Australian Institute of Family Studies, 1996).

Gibson, J, *Custodial Fathers and Access Patterns*. Family Court Research Report No 10 (Sydney, Family Court of Australia, Office of the Chief Executive, 1992).

Gorrell-BARNES, G, THOMPSON, P, DANILE, G and BURCHARDT, N, *Growing Up in Stepfamilies* (Oxford, Clarendon Press, 1998).

GRYCH, JH and FINCHAM, FD, 'The Adjustment of Children from Divorced Families: Implications of Empirical Research for Clinical Intervention' in RMRM Galatzer-Levy and L Kraus (eds), *The Scientific Basis of Child Custody Decisions* (New York, John Wiley and Sons,1999).

GUNNOE, ML and BRAVER, SL, 'The Effects of Joint Legal Custody on Mothers, Fathers and Children Controlling for Factors that Predispose a Sole Maternal versus Joint Legal Award' (2001) 25 *Law and Human Behaviour* 25.

HARWIN, J, OWEN, M, LOCKE, R and FORRESTER, D, *A Study to Investigate the Implementation of Care Orders Made Under the Children Act 1989* (London, The Stationery Office, forthcoming).

HEALEY, JM, MALLEY, JE and STEWART, AJ, 'Children and their Fathers after Parental Separation' (1990) 60 *American Journal of Orthopsychiatry* 531.

HESTER, M and RADFORD, L, *Domestic Violence and Child Contact Arrangements in England and Denmark* (Bristol, The Policy Press, 1996).

HETHERINGTON, EM and KELLY, J, *For Better or For Worse: Divorce Reconsidered*. New York, WW. Norton, 2002).

HETHERINGTON, EM and STANLEY-HAGEN, M, 'The Adjustment of Children with Divorced Parents: a Risk and Resiliency Perspective' (1999) 40 *Journal of Child Psychology and Psychiatry* 129.

HUNT, J and LAWSON, J, *Crossing the Boundaries: The Views of Practitioners with Experience of Family Court Welfare and Guardian ad litem Work on the Proposal to Create a Unified Court Welfare Service* (Bristol, National Council for Family Proceedings, 1999).

JOHNSTON, JR, 'Children of Divorce who Refuse Visitation'.in CE Depner and JH Bray (eds), *Non-Residential Parenting: New Vistas for Family Living* (New York, Sage, 1993).

JOHNSTON, JR and STRAUS, RB, *Traumatized Children in Supervised Visitation. What do they Need?* Paper presented at the First International conference on Child Access Services, Paris, 4–7 November 1998.

KAYE, M, 'Domestic Violence, Residence and Contact' (1996) 8 *Child and Family Law Quarterly* 285.

KOCH, MP and LOWERY, CR, 'Visitation and the Noncustodial Father'(1984) 8 *Journal of Divorce*, 47.

Lord Chancellor's Department, *Public Service Agreement* (London, Lord Chancellor's Department, 2002).

Lord Chancellor's Department, The Advisory Board on Family Law, Children Act Sub-committee, *Making Contact Work: A Report to the Lord Chancellor on the Facilitation of Arrangements for Contact between Children and their Non-Residential Parents and the Enforcement of Court Orders for Contact* (Lord Chancellor's Department, 2002).

LUND, M, 'The Non-Custodial Father: Common Challenges in Parenting after Divorce' In C Lewis and M O'Brien (eds), *Reassessing Fatherhood* (Thousand Oaks, CA, Sage, 1987).

LYON, C, SURREY, E and TIMMS, J, *Effective Support Services for Children and Young People when Parental Relationships Break Down* (Liverpool, National Youth Advocacy and the Calouste Gulbenkian Foundation, 1999).

McDonald, M, *Children's Perceptions of Access and their Adjustment in the Post-Separation Period. Research Report No 9, Family Court of Australia* (Sydney, Family Court of Australia, 1990).

Maclean, M and Eekelaar, J, *The Parental Obligation: A Study of Parenthood Across Households* (Oxford, Hart Publishing, 1997).

Maccoby, EE, Buchanan, CM, Mnookin, RH and Dornbusch, SM, 'Postdivorce Roles of Mothers and Fathers in the Lives of their Children' (1993) 7 *Journal of Family Psychology*, 24.

Mitchell, A, *Children in the Middle: Living through Divorce* (London, Tavistock Publications, 1985).

O'Brien, M and Jones, D, 'The Absence and Presence of Fathers. Accounts from Children's Diaries' in U Bjornberg and AK Kollind (eds), *Men's Family Relations* (Gothenburg, University of Göteberg Publications, 1996).

Pruett, MK and Pruett, KD, 'Fathers, Divorce and their Children' (1998) 7 *Child and Adolescent Psychiatric Clinics of North America*, 389.

Pryor, J and Rodgers, B, *Children in Changing Families: Life after Parental Separation* (Oxford, Blackwell Publishers Ltd, 2001).

Radford, L, Sayer, S and Amica, *Unreasonable Fears? Child Contact in the Context of Domestic Violence* (Bristol, WAFE, 1999).

Rhoades, H, 'The No Contact Mother' (2002) 16 *International Journal of Law, Policy and the Family*, 87.

Richards, M and Dyson, C, *Separation, Divorce and the Development of Children: A Review for the Department of Health and Social Security* (Cambridge, Cambridge University, 1982).

Rodgers, B and Pryor, J, *Divorce and Separation: The Outcomes for Children* (York, Joseph Rowntree Foundation, 1998).

Simons, RL, Whitbeck, LB, Beaman, J and Conger, RD, 'The Impact of Mother's Parenting, Involvement by Non-Resident Fathers and Parental Conflict on the Adjustment of Adolescent Children' (1994) 56 *Journal of Marriage and the Family*, 356.

Simpson, B, McCarthy, P and Walker, J, *Being There: Fathers after Divorce* (Newcastle, Relate Centre for Family Studies, 1995).

Smart, C and Neale, B, *Family Fragments?* (Cambridge, Polity Press, 1999).

Smart, C, Neale, B and Wade, A, *The Changing Experience of Childhood: Families and Divorce* (Cambridge, Polity Press 2001).

Smith, M, Robertson, J, Dixon, J, Quigley, M and Whitehead, Z, *A Study of Stepchildren and Step-Parenting* (London, Thomas Coram Research Unit, 2001).

Smyth, B, Sheehan, G and Fehlberg, B, 'Patterns of Parenting after Divorce: A Pre-Reform Act Benchmark Study' (2001): *Australian Journal of Family Law* 114.

Sturge, C and Glaser, D, 'Contact and Domestic Violence—the Experts Court Report' (2000) 30 *Family Law* 615.

Timmis, G, *The Child First and Foremost: Creating a Child-Centred Court Service* (Unpublished MA dissertation, University of Westminster, 2000).

Walczak, Y and Burns, S, *Divorce: the Child's Point of View* (London, Harper and Row, 1984).

Wallerstein, JS and Kelly, JB, *Surviving the Break-Up: How Children and Parents Cope with Divorce* (London, Grant McIntyre, 1980).

Wolchik, S and Fenaughty, A, 'Residential And Non-residential Parents' Perspectives On Visitation Problems' (1996) 45 *Family Relations*, 230.

19

Working and Not Working Contact After Divorce

LIZ TRINDER

1. INTRODUCTION

THE PUBLICATION OF *Making Contact Work* by the Advisory Board on Family Law Children Act Sub-Committee (Lord Chancellor's Department, 2002) begs the question of what 'work' means in the context of contact. What is 'working' contact, how does it differ from 'not working' contact, and what, if anything, can be done to help 'not working' contact work? The evidence from decades of research into the relationship between children's adjustment and contact gives a qualified answer that contact does work in terms of enhancing children's well-being, if the quality of the relationship between child and non-residential parent is reasonably good (Amato and Gilbreth, 1999). However, there is also ample evidence of instances where contact is not working, with seemingly intractable disputes over contact (eg Pearce *et al*, 1999; Brown and Day Sclater, 1999; Buchanan *et al*, 2001; Buchanan and Hunt, this volume), concerns about contact and domestic violence (eg Hester and Radford, 1996; Lord Chancellor's Department, 1999) and evidence of significant numbers of children who have lost contact with the non-resident parent (Maclean and Eekelaar, 1997). This second strand of research has led to some serious academic questioning of the presumption (or assumption) of contact (eg Smart and Neale, 1997; Bailey-Harris, 2001).

There clearly exist significant problems with the practice of contact in some families. The number of applications for section 8 orders, including contact orders, has risen steadily since the implementation of the Children Act in 1991, provoking Pearce *et al* (1999: 22) to comment:

Whilst judicial oversight of uncontested arrangements for children has indeed become more attenuated, parents appear to have compensated for this fact by positively forcing themselves upon the courts' attention through the presentation of an ever-increasing number of disputes.

Although the absolute numbers of applications for contact orders is rising, it is also true that the majority of parents still make their own arrangements for contact. In 2000, for example, there were 54,832 applications for contact orders, with 46,070 orders made (Lord Chancellor's Department, 2001). The size of the potential pool for contact orders of former married or cohabiting families is unknown. However, it is worth noting that 136,410 divorce decrees absolute were granted in 2000. Of course, applications for contact orders can arise at any time prior to, during or after divorce proceedings. The juxtaposition of the figures for contact order applications and the number of decrees absolute does give some indication that the pool of applicants for contact orders is significantly smaller than the pool of divorcing parents, and becomes relatively smaller with each annual cohort of divorcees. The proportion of contact order applicants is yet smaller if former cohabiting parents are included.

While the majority of parents do make their own arrangements for contact there has been surprisingly little attention given to these non-disputed cases, with just a few exceptions (eg Buchanan *et al*, 1996; Maclean and Eekelaar, 1997). Yet a comparison of 'working' and 'not working' contact could provide fruitful insights into the roots of contact disputes, as well as identification of the ingredients of what does make contact work. The focus of this chapter therefore is on how, and why, contact works or does not work, drawing on a recently completed qualitative study of contact arrangements in 61 families. The first part of the chapter outlines briefly the nature of working and not working arrangements and the factors that shape and distinguish them. The last part of the chapter considers the implications for policy and practice and whether the lessons of working contact can be generalised to address not working contact. My argument is that the components of working contact are reasonably clear although it is much less apparent that they underpin existing interventions or some of the proposals of *Making Contact Work*.

2. THE CONTACT PROJECT: RESEARCH DESIGN

The material on which this chapter is based is drawn from a two year qualitative interview study of contact funded by the Joseph Rowntree Foundation (Trinder *et al*, 2002). The aims of the study were to examine how adults and children negotiate contact, how contact is experienced and what factors or issues shape contact in the private law context. The study was based on a purposive sampling strategy seeking to build a sample roughly divided between disputed and non-disputed cases as a means to identify what gives rise to (or precludes) contact problems. We also sought to recruit 'family sets' of mothers, fathers and children from the same family to capture similar and divergent perceptions and evaluations of the same set of arrangements. Families were recruited from a wide range of sources, including a court service mailout to petitioners/respondents and snowballing.

The final sample consisted of 140 individuals: 48 resident parents, 35 contact parents[1] and 57 children/young people (mean age 10.8 years). The 140 individuals were from 61 families, including 19 full sets of both parents and at least one child, 19 families where both parents or one parent and at least one child were interviewed, and 23 families where only a single adult was interviewed. Consistent with our aims, the sample included a range of levels of involvement with the legal system, half of which had entirely privately ordered contact arrangements, with the remainder having varying degrees of involvement with lawyers and the courts to organise contact arrangements. The interview transcripts were analysed using grounded theory.

3. DEFINING WORKING AND NOT WORKING CONTACT

As might be expected from our sampling strategy the nature and experience of contact was widely divergent, with some arrangements clearly working well and others not working at all. The definition of working or not working contact developed from the study addressed issues of both the quantity and quality of contact. Our definition of 'working' or 'good enough' contact required the presence of all the following elements:

—Contact occurs without risk of physical or psychological harm to any party
—All parties (both adults and children) are committed to contact
—All parties are broadly satisfied with the current set of arrangements for contact and do not seek significant changes
—Contact is, on balance, a positive experience for all parties.

Conversely, we defined 'not working' or 'not good enough' contact as when at least one of the following applies:

—Contact poses an ongoing risk of physical or psychological harm to at least one party
—Not all parties are committed to contact
—At least one party seeks significant changes to the existing contact arrangements
—Contact is, on balance, not a positive experience for all parties.

The following sections briefly outline the characteristics of 'working' and then 'not working' contact arrangements.

---

[1] The terms 'resident' and 'non-resident' or 'contact' parent are used in this chapter. There clearly exist a wide-range of contact and residence arrangements, varying from shared (50/50) residence through to minimal amounts of indirect contact. The use of the term 'non-resident' or 'contact' parent is used here to refer to any parent spending less than 50% of time with a child.

4. WORKING CONTACT: CONSENSUAL COMMITTED CONTACT

There were three different types of 'consensual committed' arrangements where both parents and children were committed to regular contact and interparental conflict was low or suppressed. This type of arrangement was not problem-free, but with the difficulties relatively minor or manageable and outweighed by the perceived rewards of contact. In all three groupings parents subscribed to current child welfare principles of putting children first, enduring parental responsibility and parental amicability. Three of the 61 families were classified as 'Reconfigured Continuing Families'. In these families contact was regular and reliable and of near-daily frequency. There was a strong sense of the continuation of the family through contact and through friendly parental relationships. The rationale for contact was not based on a discourse of equal parental rights but on continuity of parent-child relationships to maintain the centrality and well-being of the enduring joint project (the children). Mothers remained in control although they were highly facilitative gatekeepers supporting contact and joint parental involvement in decision-making. Contact was not a battleground or major source of complaint and both adults and children were pleased with their arrangements. The involvement of professionals or friends/family in contact decision-making was actively avoided.

The pattern of contact for the two 'Distance Bridgers' families was much more ad hoc. Significant practical problems (money, time, distance) precluded high levels of regular contact. The logistical barriers resulted in a more irregular pattern of contact that was sustainable due to the level of interparental trust, sensitivity and flexibility that was also evident with the reconfigured continuing families. Similarly family members were pleased with contact arrangements and again external involvement in contact decision-making was actively avoided.

In 22 'Tensely Committed' families regular contact was sustained with both parents supportive of each other's relationship with the children despite a degree of parental tension. Much of the tension stemmed from the nature of the break-up, with third parties being involved in three-quarters of these families. In one case these difficulties precluded contact in the early months, but for all families in this grouping contact was ongoing at interview and parental relationships were reasonably friendly or workable, though with a degree of 'surface correctness' underlying the determination to 'do the right thing' for the children. Newer arrangements were typically alternate weekends plus weekday direct or indirect phone contact. The older established patterns, where children were now approaching their mid-late teens, were evolving into less frequent arrangements. All participants were broadly satisfied with contact although it was not without problems. For resident parents the necessary ongoing engagement with the other parent was difficult, and for contact parents the loss of daily interaction with children resulted in a sense of role insecurity. Older children especially found the somewhat artificial context of contact hindered their desire for a meaningful relationship with the non-resident parent. Nonetheless arrangements were privately ordered.

No fixed or regular pattern of contact had ever been established in eight faltering or '*Ambivalently Erratic*' families. Contact was intermittent and decreasing to the point in two families (both resident fathers) where no contact had occurred in the last year. Contact, when it occurred, tended to be day visits rather than staying contact. In this grouping both parents appeared ambivalent about the value of contact. Resident parents were frustrated at the lack of commitment of contact parents and had adopted, or were adopting, the belief that a clean break was more consistent with children's well-being than continuing sporadic contact. Contact parents were equally frustrated with attempts to organise a regular contact routine, and pointed to the emotional and logistical difficulties of contact. Children's response was variable, some expressing a profound sense of loss whilst others reflected back the contact parent's disinterest. In some cases the resident parent had consulted solicitors or attended mediation to establish a contact regime. All reported frustration at the capacity of the legal system to enforce contact.

There were five 'conflicted' groupings where there were significant disputes about the amount or form of contact, and/or where past or present violence or abuse was impacting on contact (see also Buchanan and Hunt, Day Sclater and Kaganas this volume). In five '*Competitively Enmeshed*' families, contact took the form of a private, rather than a legal, battle for increased time with the children and over the meaning of the resident and contact parent roles. Contact was based on a complicated pattern of daily or near daily frequency, with contact parents seeking to increase or sustain high levels of contact and resident parents seeking to establish a more restricted weekend contact regime. In two '*Conflicted Separate Worlds*' families, contact was continuing with children taking responsibility for organizing arrangements as parents had ceased all communication, ironically both following mediation.

Two groups took disputes to court hearings, in the two '*Rejected Retreaters*' families leading to the withdrawal of the contact parent with tentative attempts to re-establish contact via the resident parent being spurned. In seven '*Ongoing Battling*' families the parental conflict was prolonged and intensifying with an ongoing legal battle over the pattern, although not explicitly the principle, of contact. The timetable dispute was accompanied by allegations of emotional abuse and violent incidents accompanying contact. There were repeated cycles of solicitors' letters, directions and full hearings and ever more defined contact orders, but with little prospect of an end to the battle as the implementation of orders continued to give rise to disputes. In some cases weekend staying contact was continuing, in others contact had become indirect only.

In 10 '*Contingent Contact*' families, the primary issue from the point of separation was the attempt to continue contact whilst attempting to manage potential risk to a parent or child from domestic violence, physical, sexual or emotional abuse of the child, neglect or abduction. These were cases where the conflict related to managing risk, rather than disputes clearly about the relative involvement of each parent in the child's life. All the resident parents were facilitating contact to varying degrees, ranging from taking children to a contact centre, organising indirect contact, to organising 'informally supervised' contact through extended family members and neighbours. In each case contact orders were complied with. None of the resident parents were seeking to terminate contact although all were seeking continuing or further safeguards. Some of the contact parents acknowledged some element of risk, although they argued that the conditions placed were unreasonable or that their former partner was obstructing contact. In some of these families the perception of risk had diminished significantly and the arrangements had moved to resemble the tensely committed cases, in others the risk remained although with the exception of an indirect contact only case, the highest level of vigilance in these cases was a supported contact centre.

6. WHAT MAKES CONTACT WORK OR NOT WORK?

In the previous sections I described the very different processes of contact in different families. The critical question is why was it working in some families but not in others, that is, what determines contact? There are no straightforward explanations. There were no clear distinctions between groupings on socio-economic grounds, age of children or reason for the break-up. Instead there appear to be a wide range of interacting factors within a context or system of relationships. The model of contact we developed contains four layers:

1. *Direct Determinants*. These are overarching factors that directly determine the quality and quantity of contact, that is they are the three critical features that separate the three consensual committed, faltering and conflicted groupings.
2. *Challenges*. The challenges are contact-related issues or potential problem areas that families may or may not have to negotiate.
3. *Mediators*. The mediating factors are essentially filters that influence how challenges are responded to and in turn underpin, or contribute to, direct determinants.
4. *Time*. The challenges, mediators and direct determinants are interactive, but this interaction also develops over time.

These will be considered in turn (and see Box 1 for a summary).

Direct Determinants of Contact

What distinguished the three consensual committed, faltering and conflicted groupings, above all else, were commitment to contact, parental role clarity and quality of relationships (see Box 1). Working contact required the active commitment of all participants, resident and contact parent and children. Where the contact parent's commitment to contact was weak, in the ambivalently erratic and rejected retreaters groupings, contact was intermittent or had ceased. However the commitment to contact of the non-resident parent alone was insufficient to make contact work. What occurred in the consensual and also the contingent contact groupings, was that resident parents went well beyond a passive or rhetorical endorsement of contact, and adopted proactive facilitation strategies to ensure that contact did occur, that the non-residential parent remained engaged and that contact was a high quality and safe experience for children. Elements of this emotion work (Seery and Crowley, 2000) or facilitation of contact, included involving the contact parent in decision-making such as school report evenings, sharing travelling, providing a venue for contact, making suggestions for contact activities or routines, and peacekeeping or mediating between children and the contact parent. In some of the tensely committed cases this facilitation of contact appeared to keep some contact parents engaged who might otherwise find contact too difficult:[2]

> When I first met [new partner] he [father] backed off a bit and I rang him and said 'I'd hate to see him take your place, because he's not the dad.' It was like a shot up his backside and he just reverted back to how he'd always been and that's how it's gone on. (Resident mother, *tensely committed*)

In contrast, in the faltering and conflicted groupings (with the exception of the contingent contact grouping), residential parent facilitation was reactive, at best:

> I'll leave it to him to contact me. And that's partly because he's difficult to contact. I mean I've got an address, but I don't try, I leave it to him to contact. (Resident mother, *ambivalently erratic*)

Alongside commitment, clarity about the respective roles of parents was also critical. For the conflicted grouping the problem was not a lack of commitment, but a mismatch between the level of commitment between parents, where the non-resident parent was more committed to contact than the resident parent appeared to want them to be. In contrast, parents in the consensual committed groupings had struck an implicit role bargain where contact parents accepted their non-residential status (with no residence order bids or creeping encroachment through contact) and in turn the resident parents were secure enough in

---

[2] The chapters by Geldof and Simpson and Jessop, this volume, graphically illustrate some of the reasons why some non-resident fathers find it hard to sustain contact.

Box 1: Similarities and differences between the three umbrella groupings			
	Consensual committed	Faltering	Conflicted
Direct determinants			
Commitment to contact (parents and children)	Mid-high from both parents and children	Low-mid from both parents, low-high from children	High from contact parent, low-mid from resident parent, low-high from children
Role clarity	Parental role bargain: acceptance of non-residential status and proactive residential facilitation of contact and parenting involvement	No role bargain: acceptance of non-residential status but reactive residential facilitation	No role bargain: limited acceptance of non-residential status and no residential facilitation (except 'contingent contact')
Relationship quality: parent-parent	Limited or suppressed conflict, workable to friendly relationships	Mutual frustration but no overt hostility	Mutual hostility
Relationship quality: parent-children	Warm although problems of meaningful relationships	Mixed, strong sense of loss or disinterest	Mixed, reasonably warm to active rejection of contact parent
Mediators			
Beliefs and discourses	Current child welfare (children first, amicability, joint PR)	Alternative child welfare (clean break)	Current child welfare (self not other), parental welfare
Relationship skills/abilities	Empathy and insight into child and other parent's behaviour frustration	Limited insight into other parent's behaviour—mutual	Sense of mutual persecution, limited insight into impact of conflict

External agencies and networks	Nil or minimal role in organising contact	Solicitors consulted but nothing to offer	Extensive for most groupings, seen as unhelpful, risk management welcomed but inadequate
Challenges			
Nature of the break-up	Varied	Varied	Varied
New partners	Varied	Varied	Varied
Money	Agreed, resolved or unresolved with no linkage with contact	Unresolved, no or minimal child support	Agreed, resolved or unresolved, some linkage with contact
Logistics	Varied	Varied	Varied
Parenting styles/quality	Minimal or accepted differences with presumption of 'good intentions'	No obvious disagreements due to limited/nil non-residential involvement	Significant differences with presumption of 'bad intentions'
Risk/safety issues	Some historic only or low-level concern about adequate supervision/ accident	None impacting on contact	Significant in ongoing battling and contingent contact groupings
Time			
Trajectory	Virtuous circle	Vicious circle	Vicious circle

their role proactively to facilitate contact. Where resident parents considered their status under threat, as in the competitively enmeshed or ongoing battling groupings, there was very little facilitation of contact.[3] Ironically, providing that both elements of the role bargain were in place, and depending upon logistical factors, the formula could result in low conflict but extensive contact resembling shared care, albeit not interpreted as such by the participants.

Contact, above all else, is about relationships and the variable quality of relationships had a significant impact on how contact was organised and experienced

---

[3] Similar processes are evident in making contact work in open adoption, see the chapter by Elsbeth Neil.

by all parties. Our analysis, particularly of commitment and role clarity, suggests that the critical relationship for setting the framework for contact is that between resident and non-resident parents. It is not the only one that counts, however; relationships between children and both parents are also highly influential in shaping children's desire for, and experience of, contact. Other relationships in the network can also be important, particularly the relationships between children and parents' new partners and between siblings. Furthermore it is important to recognise that each set of relationships does influence the quality of other sets of relationships. The child-contact parent relationship, in particular, was acutely sensitive to the quality of the parent-parent relationship (and see Dunn and Deater-Deckard, 2001; Dunn, this volume).

The quality of the parental relationship varied significantly across the sample. In the consensual committed groupings, levels of parental conflict were significantly lower and parents were able to work together in organising contact and giving children emotional permission to retain relationships with both parents, even though for some parents 'doing the right thing' came at some emotional cost:

> I think, oh god, what does he have to ring [the children] every night for? In the early days that really, really got on my nerves, but now perhaps not so bad. I do resent the fact that he's going to have to be in my life for as long as the children are here with me. (Resident mother, tensely committed)

Children in these groupings were aware of the tensions between parents but were encouraged by both parents to maintain relationships with the other, even though this could be tinged at times with a degree of parental conflict:

> Even though mum would always say something nasty about dad or whatever, she'd then say, 'but he's your dad, you know', and 'I'm sorry' and she would say to me, you know, 'you always . . . love your dad, I want you to love [him]' . . . dad would always say, 'be good for your mum', even though they sort of hated each other they'd encourage us to be good and love the other one sort of thing. (16–18 age band, tensely committed)

Parental relationships in the faltering and conflicted groupings were barely or not workable, characterised by mutual frustration in the faltering groups, distrust or antipathy in the conflicted groupings:

> He just wants to make life as difficult as possible, so that, I am sure that he wants to make life as difficult as possible for me so that I will have a nervous breakdown and he will be able to take the kids. (Resident mother, ongoing battling)

The following extracts from parents and children in the ongoing battling grouping highlight the linkage between the quality of relationships and the quality of contact:

> I've gone up the school and they've said he's been in tears all day, because 'something about the judge', sobbing uncontrollably'. So I managed to actually speak to her [mother] and ask her 'What are you doing, why are you doing it?' . . . the last weekend I had him he said . . . 'The judge, Dad, I'm going to have a word with him', he said,

'It should be half each'. So, I don't know where he's getting it from. I've been taking all the Welfare Reports very seriously and, but he's been involved so much he knows exactly what's going on. (Contact father)

Interviewer: So before you see your dad, do you know how you feel?
Well the whole family usually gets well not upset but they all feel uptight with it. I feel that I have to make the most of mum before I leave the house, before I leave to go with dad. I shall feel a bit more sad than happy because every time I go with my dad then when I come back dad and mum always have an argument when mum comes to pick me up or something like that. (Child, 7–9)

She just came flying out and hit her [non-resident 'stepmother'] right in the face in front of the children. He [resident 'stepfather'] came out, pushed her across the lawn, the children were screaming . . . The poor kids are standing there and we just get in the car . . . , I said 'I'm sorry you had to witness that' and Annie just goes 'why can't you talk, why can't you talk?' and that's all she was. (Son) said nothing at all . . . That's him you see, he is very sensitive and he just doesn't show any emotion whatsoever. He just never cries. (Contact father)

Challenges and Mediators

The question then arises as to why some parents were able to establish or maintain workable relationships, establish a role bargain or commit to contact. Part of the reason was the presence or salience of challenges, such as risk, financial disputes, disagreement about parenting issues etc (see Box 1 above). All groupings, and all parents, experienced at least one challenge. The spousal relationship, and the nature of its ending, cast some form of a shadow over all contact arrangements, particularly through its impact on the quality of relationships between parents. But there was no clear linkage between the reason for the separation and type of arrangement. For example separations involving a sudden abandonment for a new relationship were highly traumatic for the parent who was left, and the children, but could result in working, as well as faltering or conflicted arrangements. Equally, financial disputes could be linked to or entirely disassociated from contact arrangements. Similarly, risk was present in both ongoing battling and contingent contact groupings but with different responses from resident parents to contact. We did not measure the severity of each challenge (which would vary anyway according to individual perceptions), but it also appeared that the way in which individuals perceived and responded to these challenges was related to another layer of mediating factors, that is, beliefs and discourses, relationship skills and external involvement.

The beliefs about contact expressed by parents were important, although not straightforward indicators of practice. One of the most striking aspects of the data was the extent to which current child welfare principles have become established as social norms, so widely held as to be recognised as clichés by some interviewees:

Well I really do think the cliché of not using your children as part of your armoury either in terms of money or access if you can possibly avoid it, whatever may have happened between the two of you, they don't deserve any of it and if you do have to split up it needs to be as good as you can make it for them. (Resident mother, tensely committed.)

The key idea was the principle of 'putting children first', based on ongoing contact with the non-resident parent as a means to meet child rather than adult needs. It also included the idea of separating child and adult issues, with an injunction, so far as possible, not to argue in front of the children, or denigrate the other parent and to continue to make joint parental decisions. With the exception of one (conflicted separate worlds) parent, all parents referenced these ideas. They do, clearly, mirror almost exactly the Children Act 1989 (and the Family Law Act 1996) and the drift of case law, although very few parents made that connection.

However, although it is apparent that current child welfare principles are the only ones that are socially sanctioned and acceptable,[4] the extent to which they guided practice (or how practice shaped the degree of investment in these principles) varied. Parents in the consensual committed (working contact) groupings made constant reference to these ideas, and only these ideas, as driving their approach to contact. These parents also considered that their former partner was also operating in line, or at least not contrary, to these principles. In contrast parents in the conflicted groupings disagreed in their interpretation of what the principles meant in practice or questioned whether the other parent was committed to child welfare (and see Blow and Daniel, 2002):

I was trying to think about what was best for [children]. I think [ex husband] was thinking for himself and quite often does still now. (Contact mother)

Alternatively, the package of beliefs expressed by some non-resident parents in the conflicted groupings would give equal prominence to parental needs (and rights) alongside children's welfare:

You cannot say the contact is important for the children, but should not have any importance to the absent parent, and the absent parent is just the person who should sign the cheque. You are fully entitled to see them, as much as the children are entitled to see the parent. (Contact father, ongoing battling)

Parents in the faltering group were fully aware of current interpretations of child welfare but felt that this approach was unrealistic or unworkable in their circumstances. Instead they adopted an older version of child welfare ideas, consistent with Goldstein *et al* (1979), based on the principle of letting go of the relationship with the contact parent and building children's relationship with the resident parent (and possibly his/her new parent):

---

[4] See Day Sclater and Kaganas, this volume, for how resident mothers in contact disputes feel required to frame their arguments according to current conceptions of child welfare.

I wish having left that I'd, you know, broken all contact and I also wish that I hadn't thought that the kids needed that link, because in fact since his contact has been very sporadic and erratic and in fact it's probably been more damaging than if they'd just never seen him. (Resident mother, ambivalently erratic)

I'm taking her out once a week, we're going out for an hour or two hours, on this part time basis, you know. And I thought well this is just fucking ridiculous you know, this is just not worth it, you know, and I thought you're just better off with your mum, (daughter), you know you really are. (Contact father, ambivalently erratic)

The second mediating factor to consider is relationship skills/abilities. Dealing with the aftermath of the break-up and the inevitable challenges of contact was emotionally taxing for all parents. A critical tool for dealing with challenges, and preventing escalation of problems, was empathy and insight and an ability to compromise. At least one of the adults, most typically the residential parent, in the consensual committed groupings, had these capacities. They were able, to some extent, to label and acknowledge their own feelings of loss, rejection or guilt about the break-up of the spousal relationship and could disaggregate these from their feelings about the parental relationship:

And he's still their dad and he's not changed in that respect. It's me he's fallen out with not them. (Resident mother, tensely committed)

It also involved attempts to recognise the other parent's and children's perspectives and an appraisal of the other parent that included their weaknesses and strengths:

He's harmless, it's not, you know, he's not horrible, he's good with Paul, but he's odd. (Resident mother, tensely committed)

Parents drew upon a number of ideas and strategies to do this, including child welfare principles and their children's wishes. Quite a few referenced their own childhood experience of father absence or conflicted divorce, or witnessing friends and families fighting over contact. Others used a process of behavioural rationalisation, attributing the behaviour of the other person to an external (and understandable) cause, rather than inherent and fixed characteristics:

He had a bad time with his dad when he was younger, you know he was in and out of homes and I suppose in a way he didn't really know how to be a dad properly because he hadn't had anybody to sort of show him the way. (Resident mother, tensely committed)

The other critical component of working contact was that one or both parents managed to compromise over issues and deal with conflict in a way that did not escalate a dispute. The presumption of 'good intentions' meant that differences in parenting style were accepted as legitimate or alternatively would be tackled without undermining the parental relationship, or contact:

He lets the [children] watch 18 videos. He lets them stay up very late ... I object to the late nights because I get them back on Sunday bad tempered, tired and whatever. So I have had arguments about that. But he is a good dad to them. (Resident mother, reconfigured continuing families)

Or alternatively issues that could fuel conflict were allowed to drop:

By this time I had completely given up any idea of maintenance at all. [New partner] and I had had long discussions about it. He said 'look there is just no point, you are not going to get anything, you don't want to go back to court, we're surviving quite happily, just leave it, just forget about it, stop it being an issue.' (Resident mother, tensely committed)

In contrast, in the erratic and conflicted groupings, the other parent was generally portrayed in black and white terms with few, if any, redeeming features. Nor could either parent understand the behaviour of the other. In the absence of any understanding of the conflict, each action of the other was interpreted as being uncaring, manipulative or punitive, setting up a negative spiral of interaction with each action/reaction fuelling the negative perception of the other:

It's just her, it's just her, she is punishing me because of the arguments I don't know what the reason is. (Contact father, contingent contact)

I always felt that he was playing a game, that I didn't know he was playing so that if I said anything there would always be an ulterior motive while he was listening and some reason for him and his perception of me is so different to how I feel I am that if I said anything it would drop into another universe almost and then I would be totally astonished by the response. (Resident mother, competitively enmeshed)

The final mediating factor to look at is the role of external agencies and supports to facilitate contact. In the working or consensual committed groupings this was a potential mediating factor that was barely utilised. As Table 1 indicates, in 23 of the 27 consensual committed families parents had either not consulted a solicitor or had only discussed the terms of the divorce with a solicitor. In the latter 'general divorce advice' cases, parents either could not recall any discussion of contact or reported that solicitors had encouraged parents to make their own arrangements if possible. None of these parents had anticipated being advised about contact or were surprised or disappointed by the private ordering message. The highest level of legal involvement in the consensual committed groupings were two families seeking specific legal advice regarding relocation issues with no further action taken and two further families where there was an early exchange of solicitors' letters but where contact settled down.

In a highly influential paper charting the trend towards private ordering in divorce Mnookin and Kornhauser (1979) argued that the law continued nonetheless to provide 'a framework within which divorcing couples can themselves determine their postdissolution rights and responsibilities'. According to their model, parents negotiate against a backdrop of knowing what courts would impose if no private agreement were to be reached, in other words parents bargain within the 'shadow of the law'. The model posits lawyers as a key source of informing parents what their 'bargaining endowments' are. The

Table 1. Highest Levels of Legal Involvement Per Family, By Umbrella Grouping

Umbrella grouping	No legal contact	General divorce advice	Specific contact advice	Solicitors letters re contact	In/out of court mediation or agreement	Court welfare report
Consensual committed	4	19	2	2	–	–
Erratic	1	3	1	1	1	1
Conflicted	1	2	2	1	8	12
Total	6	24	5	4	9	13

evidence from our study suggests, however, that the law is not casting its shadow at all for many privately ordering parents. If contact is not presented to solicitors as a problem then contact appears to be barely discussed, let alone information on bargaining endowments being sought or provided. Nor do family lawyers seem particularly keen to disturb or comment upon arrangements that appear to be working, as the study by Eekelaar *et al* (2000) suggests.[5]

There was more extensive involvement with the legal system in the erratic and conflicted groupings, although the capacity of the legal system to act as a positive or facilitative mediating factor was limited. There was little evidence that external involvement in establishing and regulating contact enhanced the quality of contact, and in some cases appeared positively unhelpful in helping families deal with challenges. In terms of the quantity of contact, resident parents in the ambivalently erratic grouping expressed considerable frustration with the inability of lawyers and the courts to encourage or force non-resident parents to establish a contact regime:

> The solicitor I last used said I could go to court and enforce contact. I was reluctant to do that because whenever I take legal action or any kind of threat, if [father] perceives himself being forced into something, he gets incredibly angry and I felt that if I took this legal action to enforce contact that would just make him even angrier so that put me off. (Resident mother, ambivalently erratic)

In the conflicted groupings, court involvement for the rejected retreaters was followed by no contact, and whilst a tightly defined contact schedule was laid down by the court in the ongoing battling group, it itself became a source of further conflict. Nor was there much more success in enhancing the *quality* of contact in the conflicted groupings, with court involvement followed by contact without parental communication in the conflicted separate worlds group or

---

[5] Two other empirical tests of Mnookin and Kornhauser's theoretical model suggest that the law casts a partial rather than universal shadow in private ordering, see the American study by Jacob (1992) and Dewar and Parker (1999). For a more extended discussion of the shadow of the law in contact decision-making see Trinder (forthcoming).

further entrenched positions in the ongoing battling group. The one positive aspect of court involvement was with the contingent contact group, at least for resident parents who found both lawyers and judges to be supportive of their concerns. However even here the lack of supervised contact was worrying, as are cases where the non-resident parent refused to use a contact centre or where the resident parent has had no legal advice.

Apart from solicitors and courts there was little use of other agencies. The exception was the ongoing battling grouping who typically had a wide range of agencies involved, including lawyers and CAFCASS, police, mediation, social services, psychiatrists and contact centres. A small number of parents from different groupings had sought support from a therapist or counsellor. Consistent with Davis (2001), there was a very low level of awareness or understanding of mediation, with many confusing mediation with marriage counselling or Relate. Only five families had attended out-of-court mediation. An agreement was reached in only two cases, neither of which endured or enabled parents to negotiate effectively themselves.

7. EVOLUTION OF ARRANGEMENTS OVER TIME

The families in our sample were at different stages in contact arrangements, ranging from a few months to 15 years post-separation. Nonetheless one of the most striking aspects of the data was the presence of two common trajectories of either a virtuous or a vicious circle over time, established early in the contact process. Where parents had a workable relationship in the beginning, the parental relationship continued to improve with the exercise of contact (and see Maclean and Eekelaar, 1997) and enabled families to ride out challenges such as the arrival of new partners. This was reflected in the amount of contact, with consensual committed arrangements stable over time, although tapering off for teenagers. Conversely, in the erratic and conflicted groupings, where contact was problematic to begin with, parental relationships did not improve, and in the ongoing battling cases continued to decline, as did the amount of contact. In the ambivalently erratic grouping both the parental relationship and amount of contact continued to decline from a low base. The operation of the virtuous/vicious circle meant that there was very little movement between groupings. The exceptions were some of the contingent contact cases where the threat of violence/abuse had diminished or disappeared and the parental relationship went on to resemble those in the tensely committed grouping.

8. GENERALISING THE INGREDIENTS OF WORKING CONTACT?

What can we learn from a comparison of working and not working contact? How might the lessons of what works with contact be transferred to not working contact, and with what prospect of success?

One of the obvious difficulties is that the working contact families were not recipients of an intervention that could be more widely replicated or more fully resourced. Instead of using sources of external advice to formulate contact arrangements, that is solicitors, courts, mediators or even books about divorce, what parents used to inform contact arrangements were their ideas about the 'proper thing to do' (Finch, 1989). They were informed by general social norms or discourses; their own personal experiences (as children, as witnesses of conflicted divorce); their personal circumstances (distance, employment patterns, second families etc); the quality of the relationships with the other parent and, to some extent, the preferences of their children. It is noteworthy that it was only parents within the not working contact grouping that made any reference to the Children Act 1989 or had any level of awareness of how courts typically handled contact cases. Quite simply parents where contact was working had formulated their own ideas about what was appropriate, and neither solicitors or the law informed this. That is not to say that the principles of working contact were inconsistent with the Children Act 1989 or, indeed section 1 of the ill-fated Family Law Act 1996.[6] If anything, what is remarkable is the degree of consistency between parental and legal principles. However it would be wrong to assume that legal principles had driven parental perceptions; instead what appears to be the case is that it is wider social norms that inform both parental and legal principles rather than the other way around.

The nature of the ingredients of working contact pose a second difficulty. What led to successful working contact were essentially relationship issues, of commitment to and facilitation of the contact relationship, the quality of relationships between adults and between adults and children, clarity about roles/relationships and the ability to manage relationships (empathy, insight, flexibility). However as Michael King (1987), amongst many others, has noted, the courts are inherently impotent when it comes to regulating and controlling, let alone repairing or facilitating human relationships. That is not to say that the law is redundant. Law can improve things, for example legal advice proved helpful in some cases concerning specific contact issues and there will be many instances of cases outside of our sample where the framework provided by court orders proves helpful. There is certainly a vital role for the law in cases involving risk to a parent or child. However it also apparent from our sample that we cannot expect the law or courts to do much to assist faltering contact cases where neither parent is especially committed to contact (even though the children might be). Equally it is clear that continued legal involvement in high conflict cases can be destructive as well as constructive, and expensive in emotional and financial terms for all the participants (and see Buchanan *et al*, 2001; Buchanan and Hunt, this volume).

---

[6] That when a marriage is being brought to an end regard should be had to the principle that it should be done so 'with questions dealt with in a manner designed to promote as good a continuing relationship between the parties and any children affected as is possible in the circumstances'.

Where does this leave the contact presumption in law (and as social norm)? Given that not all (albeit a minority) of parents will be able to make contact work without intervention, what are the implications? One possible approach is that the presumption of contact is wrong, that working contact is simply not realisable in all cases. There are indeed signs that, at least in cases involving domestic violence, the presumption of contact is being downgraded to a rebuttable assumption (Bailey-Harris, 2001). The Lord Chancellor's Report (1999) on Family Law on domestic violence seemed to endorse this approach. The other alternative to the problem of not working contact is to argue that the tools to tackle it require alteration and expansion, rather than to question the presumption of contact itself. In its second report on contact, *Making Contact Work* (2002), the Children Act Sub-Committee appears to have shifted its position to endorse this second alternative, particularly in its conclusions on enforcement.

Few would quarrel presumably with the argument that domestic violence can be a bar to contact. Equally the case for trying new and different interventions by *Making Contact Work* is well made and welcome. The emphasis on information for parents, on strategies for diverting parents from repeat court applications and a greater support rather than simply investigative role for CAFCASS could prove helpful in establishing more workable relationships and higher quality contact experiences for children. However, intertwined with the proposals on facilitation is the threat of compulsion. The report outlines a two stage enforcement process, a 'non-punitive' stage involving referral to a range of information-giving or therapeutic resources, and a second stage with orders incorporating penal sanctions (although the authors of the report shy away from explicitly labelling it the 'punitive' stage). Whether this approach will work is a moot point. The report makes a number of references to educational classes, notwithstanding the message from the information meeting pilots that emphasised the importance of greater personal tailoring of information to the needs of individuals (Walker, 2001). Equally, for many of the conflicted parents in our own study, the blockage was not lack of knowledge about child welfare principles but rather a belief that they could not be, or were not being, applied in their particular circumstances. Of perhaps more concern are the persistent references in *Making Contact Work* to the resident parent, in the chapter on enforcement and the presumption of a single 'culpable' person (eg para 14.53 p 98). Our analysis of both working and not working contact indicates that contact is a relational process, in which the attitudes, actions and interactions of *all* family members, that is resident and contact parents and children, combine to shape contact. In particular, in the entrenched (ongoing battling) cases the picture is more complex, with both parents needing help in working more effectively together and the concerns of both parents being explored and addressed, rather than one parent being forced into submission.

Regardless of the potential effectiveness of these interventions, a more significant source of concern is their potential impact on the participants and the quality of contact (and see Eekelaar 2002; James, this volume). *Making Contact*

Work does offer some new tools to facilitate parental relationships that are consistent with our analysis of the ingredients of working contact. Yet the thrust of the report, particularly on enforcement, is almost a position of contact at any cost. Resident parents (and children) can be forced into contact (although it is interesting that neither report addresses the question of forcing non-resident parents into contact). We must question though how this relates to child welfare or to the quality of contact. Ultimately the point of contact is about fostering enduring high quality relationships between children and their non-resident parent. There is scope for enabling this to happen, but it cannot be forced. For some families the level of parental conflict, or lack of commitment by both parties to contact will be too insurmountable to make contact a good enough experience for children. Making contact happen is not the same as making contact work.

REFERENCES

AMATO, P and GILBRETH, JG, 'Nonresident Fathers and Children's Well-Being: A Meta-Analysis' (1999) 61 *Journal of Marriage and the Family* 557.

BAILEY-HARRIS, R, 'Contact—Challenging Conventional Wisdom?' (2001) 13 *Child and Family Law Quarterly* 361.

BLOW, K and DANIEL, G, 'Frozen Narratives: Post-Divorce Processes and Contact Disputes' (2002) 24 *Journal of Family Therapy* 85.

BROWN, J and DAY SCLATER, S, 'Divorce: A Pschodynamic Perspective' in S Day Sclater and C Piper (eds), *Undercurrents of Divorce* (Aldershot, Avebury, 1999).

BUCHANAN, C, MACCOBY, E and DORNBUSCH, S, *Adolescents After Divorce* (Cambridge MA, Harvard University Press, 1996).

BUCHANAN, A, HUNT, J, BRETHERTON, H and BREAM, V, *Families in Conflict: The Family Court Welfare Service: The Perspectives of Children and Parents* (Bristol, The Policy Press, 2001).

DAVIS, G, *Monitoring Publicly Funded Family Mediation. Report to the Legal Services Commission* (London, Legal Services Commission, 2001).

DAVIS, G and PEARCE, J, 'Privatising the Family?' (1998) 28 *Family Law* 614.

DEWAR, J and PARKER, S, *Parenting, Planning and Partnership: The Impact of the New Part VII of the Family Law Act 1975 Family Law Research Unit Working Paper No 3* (Brisbane, Griffiths University, 1999).

DUNN, J and DEATER-DECKARD, K, *Children's Views of Their Changing Families* (York, Joseph Rowntree Foundation, 2001).

EEKELAAR, J, 'Contact—Over the Limit' (2002) 32 *Family Law* 271.

EEKELAAR, J, MACLEAN, M and BEINART, S, *Family Lawyers* (Oxford, Hart Publishing, 2000).

FINCH, J, *Family Obligations and Social Change* (Cambridge, Polity Press, 1989).

GOLDSTEIN, J, FREUD, A and SOLNIT, A, *Beyond the Best Interests of the Child* (New York, Free Press, 1979).

HESTER, M and RADFORD, L., *Domestic Violence and Child Contact Arrangements in England and Denmark* (Bristol, The Policy Press, 1996).

JACOB, H, 'The Elusive Shadow of the Law' (1992) 26 *Law and Society Review* 565.

KING, M, 'Playing the Symbols: Custody and the Law Commission' (1987) 17 *Family Law* 186.

Lord Chancellor's Department, Advisory Board on Family Law: Children Act Sub-committee, *Contact Between Children and Violent Parents* (London, Lord Chancellor's Department, 1999).

Lord Chancellor's Department, *Judicial Statistics 2000* (London, Lord Chancellor's Department, 2001).

Lord Chancellor's Department, *Making Contact Work*: A Report to the Lord Chancellor on the Facilitation of Arrangements for Contact Between Children and their Non-Residential Parents and the Enforcement of Court Orders for Contact (London, Lord Chancellor's Department, 2002).

MACLEAN, M and EEKELAAR, J, *The Parental Obligation* (Oxford, Hart, 1997).

MNOOKIN, RH and KORNHAUSER, L, 'Bargaining in the Shadow of the Law: The Case of Divorce' (1979) 88 *Yale Law Journal* 950–97.

PEARCE, J, DAVIS, G and BARRON, J, 'Love in a Cold Climate—Section 8 Applications under the Children Act 1989' (1999) 29 *Family Law* 22–28.

SEERY, B and CROWLEY, S, 'Women's Emotion Work in the Family' (2000) 21 *Journal of Family Issues* 100–128.

SMART, C and NEALE, B, 'Arguments Against Virtue—Must Contact Be Enforced?' (1997) 27 *Family Law* 332–334.

TRINDER, L, 'Contact after Divorce. What has the Law to Offer?' in G. Miller (ed.), *Frontiers of Family Law* (3rd edn, Chichester, Wiley, forthcoming).

TRINDER, L, BEEK, M and CONNOLLY, J, *Making Contact: How Parents And Children Negotiate And Experience Contact After Divorce* (York, Joseph Rowntree Foundation, 2002).

WALKER, J, *Information Meetings and Associated Provisions within the Family Law Act 1996: Summary of the Final Evaluation Report* (London, Lord Chancellor's Department, 2001).

Index

Printed in the United Kingdom
by Lightning Source UK Ltd.
132266UK00001B/35/A